Social Science Methodology

A Unified Framework

Second edition

John Gerring's exceptional textbook has been thoroughly revised in this second edition. It offers a one-volume introduction to social science methodology relevant to the disciplines of anthropology, economics, history, political science, psychology, and sociology. This new edition has been extensively developed with the introduction of new material and a thorough treatment of essential elements such as conceptualization, measurement, causality, and research design. It is written for students, long-time practitioners, and methodologists, and covers both qualitative and quantitative methods. It synthesizes the vast and diverse field of methodology in a way that is clear, concise, and comprehensive. While offering a handy overview of the subject, the book is also an argument about how we should conceptualize methodological problems. Thinking about methodology through this lens provides a new framework for understanding work in the social sciences.

John Gerring is Professor of Political Science at Boston University, where he teaches courses on methodology and comparative politics. He has published several books including *Case Study Research: Principles and Practices* (Cambridge University Press, 2007), and *A Centripetal Theory of Democratic Governance* (Cambridge University Press, 2008). He served as a fellow of the School of Social Science at the Institute for Advanced Study (Princeton, NJ), as a member of the National Academy of Sciences' Committee on the Evaluation of USAID Programs to Support the Development of Democracy, as President of the American Political Science Association's Organized Section on Qualitative and Multimethod Research, and was the recipient of a grant from the National Science Foundation to collect historical data related to colonialism and long-term development. He is currently a fellow at the Kellogg Institute for International Affairs, University of Notre Dame (2011–12).

Strategies for Social Inquiry

Social Science Methodology: A Unified Framework (second edition)

This new book series presents texts on a wide range of issues bearing upon the practice
of social inquiry. Strategies are construed broadly to embrace the full spectrum of
approaches to analysis, as well as relevant issues in philosophy of social science.

Forthcoming Titles
Michael Coppedge, *Approaching Democracy: Theory and Methods in Comparative
Politics*
Thad Dunning, *Natural Experiments in the Social Sciences*
Diana Kapiszewski, Lauren M. MacLean and Benjamin L. Read, *Field Research in
Political Science*
Jason Seawright, *Multi-Method Social Science: Combining Qualitative and
Quantitative Tools*
Carsten Q. Schneider and Claudius Wagemann, *Set-Theoretic Methods for the Social
Sciences: A Guide to Qualitative Comparative Analysis*

Social Science Methodology

A Unified Framework

Second edition

John Gerring

CAMBRIDGE
UNIVERSITY PRESS

CAMBRIDGE UNIVERSITY PRESS
Cambridge, New York, Melbourne, Madrid, Cape Town,
Singapore, São Paulo, Delhi, Mexico City

Cambridge University Press
The Edinburgh Building, Cambridge CB2 8RU, UK

Published in the United States of America by Cambridge University Press, New York

www.cambridge.org
Information on this title: www.cambridge.org/9780521132770

First published 2012
Reprinted 2012

Printed and bound by CPI Group (UK) Ltd, Croydon CR0 4YY

A catalogue record for this publication is available from the British Library

ISBN 978-0-521-11504-9 Hardback
ISBN 978-0-521-13277-0 Paperback

Additional resources for this publication at www.cambridge.org/gerring

There is no royal road to science, and only those who do not dread the fatiguing climb of its steep paths have a chance of gaining its luminous summits.

Karl Marx, "Preface to the French Edition," Capital (299),
quoted in Levi (1999: 171)

To have mastered "method" and "theory" is to have become a self-conscious thinker, a man at work and aware of the assumptions and the implications of whatever he is about. To be mastered by "method" or "theory" is simply to be kept from working, from trying, that is, to find out about something that is going on in the world. Without insight into the way the craft is carried on, the results of study are infirm; without a determination that study shall come to significant results, all method is meaningless pretense.

C. Wright Mills, The Sociological Imagination (1959: 120–121)

Surely, in a world which stands upon the threshold of the chemistry of the atom, which is only beginning to fathom the mystery of interstellar space, in this poor world of ours which, however justifiably proud of its science, has created so little happiness for itself, the tedious minutiae of historical erudition, easily capable of consuming a whole lifetime, would deserve condemnation as an absurd waste of energy, bordering on the criminal, were they to end merely by coating one of our diversions with a thin veneer of truth. Either all minds capable of better employment must be dissuaded from the practice of history, or history must prove its legitimacy as a form of knowledge. But here a new question arises. What is it, exactly, that constitutes the legitimacy of an intellectual endeavor?

Marc Bloch, The Historian's Craft ([1941] 1953: 9)

Contents

Part IV   Conclusions   359

Detailed table of contents

Figures

Tables

Preface

The natural sciences talk about their results. The social sciences talk about their methods.

Henri Poincaré[1]

In a very crucial sense there is no methodology without logos, without thinking about thinking. And if a firm distinction is drawn – as it should be – between methodology and technique, the latter is no substitute for the former. One may be a wonderful researcher and manipulator of data, and yet remain an unconscious thinker … the profession as a whole is grievously impaired by methodological unawareness. The more we advance technically, the more we leave a vast, uncharted territory behind our backs.

Giovanni Sartori[2]

The field of social science methodology has been hyperactive over the past several decades. Methods, models, and paradigms have multiplied and transformed with dizzying speed, fostering a burst of interest in a heretofore moribund topic. One sign of the growing status of this field is the scholarly vituperation it inspires. Terms such as interpretivism, rational choice, post-structuralism, constructivism, randomization, positivism, and naturalism are not just labels for what we do; they are also fighting words.

   Meanwhile, venerable debates over power, class, and status seem to have subsided. It is not that we no longer talk about these subjects, or care about them. Yet there appears to be greater consensus within the academy on normative political issues than there was, say, in the 1960s and 1970s. We are all social democrats now – for better, or for worse. Debates continue, especially over the role of race, gender, and identity. However, they do not seem to be accompanied by a great deal of rancor. Thus, over the past few decades methodological disagreements have largely displaced disagreements

---

[1] Attributed to Poincaré by Berelson and Steiner (1964: 14). See also Samuelson (1959: 189).
[2] Sartori (1970: 1033).

over substantive issues as points of conflict at conferences, at faculty meetings, and on editorial boards. Methodology, not ideology, seems to define the most important cleavages within the social sciences today.[3]

Readers disturbed by this development may feel that there is altogether too much methodology inhabiting the social sciences today – too much discussion about how to get there, and not enough about what's there. They may be partial to C. Wright Mills' admonition: "Methodologists, get to work!" This is consistent with the plea for a problem-centered social science, one directed toward solving problems of public concern rather than the application of particular methods.[4]

The question naturally arises, *how* is one to go to work? It is unlikely that this question is best answered in a purely inductive manner. V. O. Key points out, "Method without substance may be sterile, but substance without method is only fortuitously substantial."[5] Arguably, the best way to ensure that social science remains problem-oriented is to cultivate a deep knowledge of methodology and a large toolkit of methods. Only in this fashion can one be sure that substantive problems of theoretical concern and everyday relevance are driving our agendas, rather than a search for venues to apply the method *du jour*.

The stakes in our current *Methodenstreit* are indeed high. At issue is not merely who will make it into the first-tier journals and who will make tenure, but also the shape and focus of the social sciences in the twenty-first century. The winners of our current methodological wars will determine the sort of training that is offered to students, the sort of advice that is offered to policy-makers, and the sort of guidance that is offered to the lay public. Social science matters – perhaps not as much as we might like, but a good deal nonetheless. And because of its prominent place in shaping the course of social science, methodology matters.

The present volume

This book is a dramatically revised and expanded edition of a book that appeared a decade ago.[6] The overall argument remains intact. However,

---

[3] In 1958, V. O. Key admonished the members of the discipline of political science for having closed their minds "to problems of method and technique" (p. 967). The same could certainly not be said today.

[4] Mead (2010); Shapiro (2005); Smith (2003). See also discussion of *relevance* in Chapter 3.

[5] Key (1958: 967).

[6] Gerring (2001). This volume also draws on other manuscripts and publications written over the past decade, e.g., Gerring (1997, 1999, 2005, 2007, 2008, 2009, 2010); Gerring and Thomas (2011); Gerring and Yesnowitz (2006); Gerring and Barresi (2003).

I have reformulated the subtitle along with many of the lower-level arguments, added a great deal of new material, and re-written virtually every paragraph. All things considered, it probably deserves to be considered a new book. In any case, I hope that the reader of this book will find an improved rendition of *Social Science Methodology*.

Before entering the narrative, it may be worthwhile outlining a few general contrasts between this volume and others on the market.

First, I take social science as my primary unit of analysis. Social science, I believe, is not simply an offshoot of the natural sciences or the humanities. It is, rather, a distinctive realm of inquiry with a somewhat distinctive set of norms and practices. Thus, rather than focusing on a particular discipline, or on science at large, this book addresses all fields whose primary focus is on human action and social institutions. This includes anthropology, archaeology, business, communications, demography, economics, education, environmental design, geography, law, political science, psychology, public administration, public health, public policy, social work, sociology, and urban planning. From my perspective, the methodological issues faced by these fields are so remarkably similar that they deserve a unified treatment. Insofar as the book succeeds, it may help to restore a sense of common purpose to these often estranged fields.

Second, I attempt to speak across current methodological, epistemological, and ontological divides – interpretivist versus positivist versus realist, quantitative versus qualitative, and so forth. While recognizing the persistence of these cleavages I do not wish to reify them. Indeed, they are often difficult to define, and in this respect are uninformative.[7] For example, to say that a research design is "qualitative" or "quantitative" is to say very little, as most issues of methodological adequacy are not about sheer numbers of observations (Chapter 13). Here, as elsewhere, abstract, philosophical discussions often have the effect of obscuring methodological issues, which become clear only when framed in a highly specific, focused manner (and then do not always fit neatly within larger frameworks).

Third, the book approaches social science methodology through prose rather than through numbers. Although the topic pertains equally to qualitative and quantitative research, the *language* of the book is largely qualitative. A narrative approach has certain advantages insofar as one can cover a great

---

[7] The distinction between qualitative and quantitative methods is discussed in Brady and Collier (2004); Gerring and Thomas (2011); Glassner and Moreno (1989); Hammersley (1992); Mahoney and Goertz (2006); McLaughlin (1991); Shweder (1996); Snow ([1959] 1993); See also entry for "Qualitative" in the Glossary. Interpretivism is discussed in Gerring (2003).

deal of material in a relatively concise and comprehensible fashion. Moreover, many methodological issues are not mathematical in nature; they hinge on concepts, theories, research designs, and other matters that are best articulated with natural language. Even so, I make a point of referencing statistical procedures wherever relevant so as to facilitate the transit between the world of numbers and the world of prose. It is hoped that the book will be enjoyable and informative for those who are schooled in quantitative methods, as well as those more familiar with qualitative research.[8]

Fourth, the book aims to address the subject of social science methodology in ways that will be useful to practitioners. We should remind ourselves that there is little point in studying methodology if the discoveries of this field are shared only among methodologists. Rather than highlighting arguments with the literature I have sought to place these arguments in footnotes, in appendices, or have omitted them altogether. Chapters, sections, and tables are organized to facilitate easy access and reference. Specialized vocabulary is avoided wherever possible, and an extensive glossary is included to try to sort out the lexicon.

Finally, the book places the subject of social science methodology in a broad historical and intellectual context. It is helpful to remember that most of the questions we find ourselves grappling with today are iterations of classic methodological debates. Many were addressed as far back as 1843, when J. S. Mill published the first edition of his path-breaking, *System of Logic*. Some go back to Aristotle. Arguably, the introduction of new methods has had relatively little impact on the underlying logic of social science analysis. The same difficulties crop up in different circumstances. This may serve as cause for dismay or contentment, depending on one's orientation. From my perspective, it is another indication that there is something central to the social sciences that distinguishes our enterprise from others. We are defined, to a significant degree, by our methodological predicaments.

"God," note Charles Lave and James March, "has chosen to give the easy problems to the physicists."[9] What the authors mean by this provocative comment is not that it is easy to practice physics, but rather that it is fairly

---

[8] Although one hears a good deal of rhetoric nowadays about uniting qualitative and quantitative methodologies, this formidable task appears to be easier to recommend than to render. Hence, the general absence of texts that speak meaningfully to both audiences. But see Brady and Collier (2004); Firebaugh (2008); Goertz (2006); King, Keohane, and Verba (1994); Lieberson (1985); Ragin (1987, 2008); Shadish, Cook, and Campbell (2002). For further comments on the qualitative/quantitative divide see Chapter 13.

[9] Lave and March (1975: 2).

apparent when one has obtained a result in this field. The implications of this fact are far-reaching. The natural scientist can afford to cultivate a method, confident that his or her results, if significant, will be recognized. The social scientist, by contrast, must justify not only his or her findings but also his or her method.

Our blessing and our curse is to be implicated in the subjects that we study and to study subjects who are subjects, in the full Kantian sense. As a consequence, those working in the social sciences have harder problems, methodologically speaking. We disagree on more points, and on more basic points, and spend much more time debating these points than our cousins in the natural sciences. Indeed, methodology is central to the disciplines of the social sciences in a way that it is not to the natural sciences. (There is no field of "methodology" in physics or biology.) Clark Glymour observes, "Exactly in those fields where impressive and dominant results are difficult to obtain, methodological considerations are likely to be most explicit, and innovations in method are likely to occur most often."[10]

In recent years data have become available on a wider range of topics and quantitative techniques have become ever more sophisticated and more accessible to lay researchers (via user-friendly data packages). However, the gap between what we do and what we mean to do has not diminished. "Methods" and "ontology" still lie far apart.[11]

I believe that to do good work in the social sciences requires more than mastering a set of techniques. It requires understanding why these techniques work, why one approach might be more appropriate for a given task than another, and how a given approach might be adapted to diverse research situations. Good work in the social sciences is necessarily creative work, and creative work requires broad grounding.[12]

The goal of this book, therefore, is to explore the logic of inquiry that guides work in the social sciences, as well as the pragmatic rationale that, I claim, underpins these norms. Methods are inseparable from methodology; we can hardly claim to understand one without delving into the other. This work is concerned, therefore, with what social scientists do, what they say they do, and what they ought to be doing. These three issues, together, constitute social science methodology.

---

[10] Glymour (1980: 291).   [11] Hall (2003).

[12] "More than other scientists," notes Milton Friedman ([1953] 1984: 236), "social scientists need to be self-conscious about their methodology."

Acknowledgments

Comments and suggestions on various iterations of this manuscript were generously provided by Arnab Acharya, Paul Dragos Aligica, Julian Arevalo, Neil Beck, Stephen Bird, Taylor Boas, Bob Bullock, Tom Burke, Dave Campbell, Dino Christenson, David Collier, Michael Coppedge, Pearson Cross, Pierre-Marc Daigneault, Thad Dunning, Colin Elman, Tulia Falleti, Jon Farney, Marshall Ganz, Gary Goertz, Kristin Goss, Steve Hanson, Andy Harris, David Hart, Daniel Hidalgo, Peter Houtzager, Alan Jacobs, Michael Johnston, Elizabeth Kaknes, Orit Kedar, Markus Kreuzer, Doug Kriner, Dan Kryder, Marcus Kurtz, David Lyons, Jim Mahoney, Michael Martin, Amy Mazur, Patrick Mello, Rob Mickey, Doug Mock, Jairo Nicolau, Nathan Nunn, Betsy Paluck, Paul Pierson, Howard Reiter, Neal Richardson, Benoît Rihoux, Ingo Rohlfing, Kate Sanger, Carsten Schneider, Jay Seawright, Rudy Sil, Svend-Erik Skaaning, Theda Skocpol, Dawn Skorczewski, Laurel Smith-Doerr, Craig Thomas, John Williamson, and Joshua Yesnowitz. More informal – but no less useful – were conversations and email exchanges with Nik Blevins, Ben Campbell, Russ Faeges, Garrett Glasgow, Lincoln Greenhill, Cathy Harris, Samantha Luks, Jeff Miron, Jim Schmidt, Laura Stoker, Strom Thacker, Ned Wingreen, and Chris Winship.

I was also fortunate to have the input of participants at various talks at which portions of the manuscript were presented: at the University of Connecticut, Boston University, the University of California at Berkeley, University of Massachusetts Amherst, the University of Virginia, and the Institute for Qualitative and Multimethod Research (currently situated at the Maxwell School, Syracuse University). The book is vastly improved due to comments received from reviewers for Cambridge University Press and from several generations of students in my graduate methods course at Boston University.

I owe a special round of thanks to Bear Braumoeller, Patrick Johnston, Evan Lieberman, and David Waldner, who blessed the manuscript with extensive criticism and whose enthusiasm for methods and breadth of interests prompted many discussions and more than a few revisions. My debt to David Collier will be apparent to all.

Late in the day, Adam Glynn and I began to work together on alternative approaches to causal inference, understood through causal graphs. His contribution to topics addressed in Chapter 11 warrants special credit. For his creativity and his vast knowledge, I am grateful.

A final acknowledgment belongs to all the published work on methodology that I borrow from. Although it would be tedious to list authors by name, the lengthy bibliography and crowded footnotes serve as an expression of my gratitude.

1 A unified framework

Those sciences, created almost in our own days, the object of which is man himself, the direct goal of which is the happiness of man, will enjoy a progress no less sure than that of the physical sciences, and this idea so sweet, that our descendants will surpass us in wisdom as in enlightenment, is no longer an illusion. In meditating on the nature of the moral sciences, one cannot help seeing that, as they are based like physical sciences on the observation of fact, they must follow the same method, acquire a language equally exact and precise, attaining the same degree of certainty.

Nicolas de Condorcet[1]

There is ... progress in the social sciences, but it is much slower [than in the natural sciences], and not at all animated by the same information flow and optimistic spirit. Cooperation is sluggish at best; even genuine discoveries are often obscured by bitter ideological disputes. For the most part, anthropologists, economists, sociologists, and political scientists fail to understand and encourage one another ... Split into independent cadres, they stress precision in words within their specialty but seldom speak the same technical language from one specialty to the next. A great many even enjoy the resulting overall atmosphere of chaos, mistaking it for creative ferment.

Edward O. Wilson[2]

The subject of this book is the set of disciplines known as the *social sciences* (which in earlier times would have been referred to as the moral or human sciences). By this is meant a scientific study of human action focusing on elements of thought and behavior that are in some degree social (nonbiological). "The object of the social sciences," writes Hans Morgenthau, "is man, not as a product of nature but as both the creature and the creator of history in and through which his individuality and freedom of choice manifest themselves."[3] Wherever nurture matters more than nature, or where some significant decisional element is involved, we are on the turf of social science. (This does not mean that genetic dispositions are eliminated from consideration;

---

[1] Condorcet (writing in 1782), quoted in Scott (1998: 91).   [2] Wilson (1998: 198).
[3] Morgenthau (1955: 441). See also Almond and Genco ([1977] 1990).

indeed, they comprise an active research agenda in the social sciences today.[4] However, one presumes that any outcome of interest to the social sciences is not entirely biologically determined; there must be a significant component of choice.[5])

At the same time, and in marked contrast to the humanities, most research-ers in the social sciences take their moniker seriously. They aspire to science – which is to say, they intend to study human action in a systematic, rigorous, evidence-based, falsifiable, replicable, generalizable, nonsubjective, transparent, skeptical, rational, frequently causal, and cumulative fashion.[6] A fundamental premise of this book is that the social world can be studied in a scientific manner (understood through the foregoing list of attributes). This does not mean that the instruments of science provide the only method of insight into human behavior. The claim, rather, is that science offers *a* valid approach to explanation and understanding and that this approach is properly located within the academic disciplines known as the social sciences (Chapter 14).

Social science thus takes its cues from its component terms, *social* and *science*. While these terms often seem to be in tension with one another I want to propose that this tension can also be a productive one, generating insights into our subject that might not be apparent to a lay observer.

So defined, social science encompasses the disciplines of anthropology, archaeology, business, communications, demography, economics, education, environmental design, geography, law, political science, psychology, public administration, public health, public policy, social work, sociology, and urban

---

[4] Alford and Hibbing (2008); Carey (2002); Fowler and Schreiber (2008); Freese and Shostak (2009); Institute of Medicine (2006).

[5] This matters quite a lot to the conduct of scientific inquiry, justifying the focus of this book on social science, not science in general. In claiming a distinction between social science and natural science I am not, of course, asserting a clear dichotomy; indeed, many disciplines straddle the divide and there are many features of science that are shared by all scientific enterprises, whether focused on natural or social phenomena. However, the distinction is important because the nature of the phenomena are so different that they often require rather different approaches. A sign of this can be found in the definition of the key term "experiment." While in natural science the term is used loosely to refer to any manipulated treatment, in social science it has come to have a much more specific definition: a treatment that is randomized (and probably manipulated) across treatment and control groups. This is because control groups are generally necessary in order to overcome potential confounders in a social-science setting, while they are often unnecessary in natural-science settings (e.g., when two fluids are combined in a beaker and the result is immediately observable). See Cook *et al.* (2010: 109).

[6] I have purposefully strung together all the adjectives that are commonly applied to "science," forming an ideal-type definition (see Chapter 5). For a compendium of definitions from prominent writers see: www.gly.uga.edu/railsback/1122sciencedefns.html. For work addressing the meaning of science in a more nuanced and extended fashion see Laudan (1983) and Schaffer (1997). Evidently, there is disagreement over how to define science, and over the utility of the scientific ideal – however defined. For critical views, see Barnes and Bloor (1982); Feyerabend (1975); Harding (1986, 1987); Latour and Woolgar (1979); Woolgar (1988).

planning, along with various offshoots of these disciplines. Of course, the social science label does not encompass all practitioners of all the aforementioned disciplines, for some practitioners are engaged in studying aspects of human behavior that are largely biological (e.g., cognitive psychology), and others do not accept the goal of science, or have a different view of it than is presented here. (For example, they might question the possibility, or the pay-off, of generalizing about human behavior.[7])

I shall have something to say about objections to social science later on (see Chapter 14). For the moment, it should be stressed that my understanding of social science will not please everyone, and those unhappy with the point of departure are unlikely to be happy with the point of arrival. Some may regard my perspective on the social-scientific enterprise as unduly positivistic. Others may regard it as not positivistic enough. (Much depends on one's definition of that vexed term, positivism, discussed briefly in the Glossary.)

The problem of pluralism

Any book purporting to address the broad rubric of social science must come to terms with the many divisions that haunt these fields, and the repercussions of those divisions. As early as 1938, John Dewey complained: "One of the chief practical obstacles to the development of social inquiry is the existing division of social phenomena into a number of compartmentalized and supposedly independent non-interacting fields."[8] Arguably, social science is not a single endeavor, but rather many different endeavors, each with its own peculiarities, as averred by E. O. Wilson in the epigraph to this chapter.

The social sciences are divided, first of all, among the separate disciplines: anthropology, archeology, etc. Although scholars occasionally cross these borders, such crossings are arduous and often problematic. It is no surprise, then, that for the most part, anthropologists associate with other anthropologists, and economists with other economists. Whether sustained by methodological differences, organizational incentives, or simple inertia, academics tend to stick to their own tribe.

---

[7] This is true, for example, for those who embrace a poststructuralist or postmodernist perspective (Norris 1997; Rosenau 1992). A more difficult question of classification concerns cultural anthropology, history, and other fields or subfields with an interpretivist bent. They are clearly social and empirical, but they are also leery of science – especially the scientific quest to generalize about patterns of human behavior. In this respect, they may fall somewhat outside the framework described in this book. Examples of self-consciously scientific methodology applied to cultural anthropology can be found in Brim and Spain (1974) and Radcliffe-Brown ([1948] 1957, 1958), but are less frequent in contemporary work.

[8] Dewey (1938: 509). Contemporary work on this issue includes Easton and Schelling (1991).

The social sciences are divided, second, among *sub*disciplinary fields. The American Political Science Association currently recognizes forty-odd sections (e.g., federalism and intergovernmental relations, law and courts, legislative studies, etc.), the American Economics Association several hundred. Similar divisions may be found elsewhere. These cubbyholes define courses, jobs, conferences, journals, and scholarly activity generally. They comprise the *de facto* boundaries of most academic lives.[9]

The social sciences are divided, third, among specific substantive problems. Some study the welfare state, others study ethnic conflict, and others study market behavior. A problem-centered approach to social science presumes that, because there are many problems, each with its own specific methodological obstacles and opportunities, there are many ways of going about business.[10]

The social sciences are divided, fourth, among theoretical frameworks, each with its own implicit or explicit methodology. Behavioralism, conflict theory, ethnomethodology, exchange theory, institutionalism, interpretivism, ordinary language, rational choice, structural-functionalism, symbolic interactionism, systems theory (cybernetics), and the research schools associated with Freud, Marx, and Weber each offer their own research paradigm.[11]

The social sciences are divided, finally, and perhaps most importantly, by their methods. The methodological tool one employs, for example, experiments, time-series analysis, factor analysis, formal models, survey research, archival research, ethnography, qualitative comparative analysis, and so forth, helps to define one as a scholar and probably also affects how one views the social world.[12]

Beyond these fine divisions lies one over-arching cleavage between "quants" and "quals," that is, between those who are comfortable with statistical analysis and mathematical models and those who prefer the time-honored expedients of informal logic and natural language. This division, in evidence for well over a century, continues to provoke and offend. As the reader is no doubt aware, quantoids and qualtoids have developed different languages and different approaches to their topics. They are accustomed to arguing with each other or ignoring each other.[13]

---

[9] Almond (1990b).   [10] Shapiro (2005); Smith (2003).

[11] Collins (1985); Parsons (2007); Sil and Doherty (2000); Tang (2010).

[12] Moses and Knutsen (2007).

[13] An impression exists among some quantitativists that their colleagues writing prose (particularly those writing good prose) are compensating for a lack of rigor. "If you can't measure it," goes the unstated premise, "that ain't it." A corresponding impression exists among some qualitativists that to measure something – to "reduce it to a variable" – is to impoverish our understanding of a phenomenon. "If you can measure it," goes their credo, "that ain't it." Kaplan (1964: 206) attributes this dictum to members of

Divisions within the contemporary social sciences are therefore deep and complex, involving disciplinary, subdisciplinary, problem-based, theory-based, and method-based cleavages. From the obvious fragmentation of the social sciences today it is a small step to a pluralistic social science methodology. This accepts what is, by all appearances, an irrevocable fact on the ground. Richard Miller argues:

there is no framework of empirical principles determining what counts as an explanation in all social sciences. Rather, there are particular frameworks for particular fields. Each specific framework is, in turn, highly complex, with components serving many functions. Whether a true hypothesis explains, or whether a hypothesis should be accepted as explaining, in light of given data, is determined by facts specific, say, to the study of power structures or investment decisions.[14]

Methodological pluralism has an appealing air to it, suggesting tolerance for approaches employed by other scholars and pragmatism in selecting one's own approach to a topic. Be a good craftsman, C. Wright Mills advises us in a famous passage:

Avoid any rigid set of procedures. Above all seek to develop and to use the sociological imagination. Avoid the fetishism of method and technique. Urge the rehabilitation of the unpretentious intellectual craftsman and try to become such a craftsman yourself. Let every man be his own methodologist; let every man be his own theorist: let theory and method again become part of the practice of the craft.[15]

There are evidently many ways to do good social science. Methods may be statistical or nonstatistical, large-N or small-N, historical or nonhistorical, and so forth. Theories may be useful for one project, and useless for another. Much depends on the nature of the evidence available and the nature of the question

---

the University of Michigan faculty (satirizing the anti-quantoids). The same opposing sentiments can also be found in statements uttered long ago by Lord Kelvin ("When you cannot measure it, when you cannot express it in numbers, your knowledge is of a meagre and unsatisfactory kind") and Jacob Viner ("When you can measure it, when you can express it in numbers, your knowledge is still of a meagre and unsatisfactory kind"). Quoted in Berelson and Steiner (1964: 14). See also the words of Robert Fogel (on the quant side) and Carl Bridenbaugh and Arthur Schlesinger, Jr. (on the qual side), recorded in Landes and Tilly (1971: 12). Anti-quantificationist manifestos may be found in Winch (1958) and Wolin (1969). For other examples, including statements by Daniel Boorstin, Carl Bridenbaugh, Barrington Moore, Arthur Schlesinger, and E. P. Thompson, see Fischer (1970: 94–96). For historical background on the qual–quant distinction see Snow ([1959] 1993). Current statements on the subject include Brady and Collier (2004); Gerring and Thomas (2011); Glassner and Moreno (1989); Hammersley (1992); Mahoney and Goertz (2006); McLaughlin (1991); Shweder (1996); Snow ([1959] 1993). For further discussion see Chapter 13.

[14] Miller ([1983] 1991). See also Cartwright (2007); Hall (2003); Hitchcock (2007); Little (1991); Miller (1987); Reiss (2009); Roth (1987).

[15] Mills (1959: 224), quoted in Eldridge (1983: 37).

under investigation. It would be folly, therefore, to propose a uniform method or theoretical framework for all of social science, or even for a single discipline. In any case, specialization is necessary in order for social science to thrive. Perhaps, then, the current fragmentation of social science is the happy outcome of different scholars doing what they, individually, do best. Perhaps we ought to regard diversity as a mark of disciplinary maturity rather than as a mark of confusion and disarray.

In addressing this question, I shall invoke a distinction between *methods* and *methodology*.[16] The first refers to a specific procedure for gathering and/or analyzing data. The second refers to the tasks, strategies, and criteria governing scientific inquiry, including all facets of the research enterprise. While method refers to the particular choices made in a given study, methodology refers to the larger and more persistent features of the scientific enterprise.

Methods pluralism is easy to justify, and impossible to avoid. However, there are reasons to doubt the wisdom of methodological pluralism. Beneath the diversity of methods there is – or at least ought to be – a methodological consensus.[17]

Consider some of the practical questions that we face in the quotidian work of social science. How, for example, should we choose our methods and theoretical frameworks, and how, at the same time, might we judge the product of our choices? It is apparent that these questions are unclear to many social scientists, even to those working within the same subfield. Charles Lindblom relates the findings of a recent review of literature covering a small subfield of political science. Progress has been notable, the author reports. Yet, Lindblom discovers that

these claims were not posited by detailing findings but rather by alleging that political scientists had "illuminated," "were concerned with," "gave special emphasis to," "developed insights, hypotheses, and analytical categories," "codified," "stressed the importance of," "examined the significance of," "placed in the context of," "treated variables theoretically," "produced good work," "were fruitful," "applied concepts and models to," "vastly improved our understanding," "dealt with," and "increased the level of rigor."[18]

The reviewer's methodological difficulties are characteristic of the social sciences at large. Within many disciplines – and, *a fortiori*, across disciplines – we seem to have no clear way of charting progress.

[16] Sartori (1970).
[17] My perspective echoes that of a recent book edited by Henry Brady and David Collier (2004), subtitled *Diverse Tools, Shared Standards*.
[18] Lindblom (1997: 257).

Although some standards apply only to particular fields or topics there must also be standards applying to social science at large. Otherwise, we cannot make decisions among available methods and theoretical frameworks. On what basis does the method-pluralist choose his or her method? It does not make sense to argue that norms of truth should be field-specific or steeped in a particular tradition. For if standards of truth are understandable only within the context of specific fields or theoretical traditions there is no way to adjudicate among contending views. Where traditions are deemed to be incommensurable, whatever scholars in a subfield decide to believe becomes, by virtue of that fact, true (as long as scholars do not violate their own norms). This sort of epistemological relativism is not what Miller, Mills, and others intend, but it does seem to be a necessary conclusion if one is to accept the assertion that methodological norms are field-specific.

While it is reasonable to cultivate a diversity of tools, it is unreasonable to cultivate a diversity of methodological standards.[19] A discovery in sociology ought to be understandable, and appraisable, by those who are not sociologists; otherwise, it cannot claim the status of truth, as that term is generally understood. "The theoretical aim of a genuine discipline, scientific or humanistic, is the attainment of truth," writes E. D. Hirsch, "and its practical aim is agreement that truth has probably been achieved. Thus, the practical goal of every genuine discipline is consensus – the winning of firmly grounded agreement that one set of conclusions is more probable than others."[20]

Nor will it suffice to conclude that methodologies must be appropriate to "context."[21] Which contexts, and how many, will be privileged? And how might one justify one's choice of tools and arguments within a given context? It is all very well to say, as hard-nosed practitioners are wont to say, that the proof is in the pudding (i.e., that we can judge social science work only by its product, not its method). But if the proof is in the pudding, by what standards shall we judge the pudding?

No escape is possible from broader interdisciplinary standards if the enterprise of social science is to prove useful to humanity. Indeed, the rationale for a professional caste of scholars, financed at public expense, breaks down if we deny transdisciplinary standards. Naturally, scholarly consensus is not always possible. But surely there are certain things – craniology (phrenology), for example – that may safely be excluded from consideration. And if craniology is rejected, we must appeal to some transdisciplinary standards in doing so. Note that if knowledge across disciplines is truly incommensurable, we are

---

[19] Brady and Collier (2004).   [20] Hirsch (1967: viii–ix).   [21] See van Fraassen (1980).

compelled to leave the question of craniology to the craniologists. In this vision, social science is defined simply by what social scientists do; the fact of being a craniologist is self-justifying.

While one can ignore methodology, one cannot choose not to have a methodology. In teaching, in research, and in analyzing the work of colleagues, scholars must separate the good from the bad, the beautiful from the ugly. In so doing, broader criteria of the good, the true, and the beautiful necessarily come into play. Social science is a normative endeavor. Like members of any community social scientists create and enforce norms, rewarding good behavior and punishing – or simply ignoring – bad behavior. The gate-keeping functions of the academy cannot be abolished by a wistful appeal to diversity. For social science has a limited supply of goods, such as jobs, funding, journals, books, and public attention, which must be allocated according to some rationale, hopefully a rationale we can all agree upon.

Finally, as a matter of good scholarship, writers in the social sciences ought to be able to converse with one another.[22] Economists interested in political economy should be cognizant – and should seek to incorporate, wherever possible – work in political science. And vice versa.

While cross-disciplinary research is one of the most fertile areas of research in the social sciences today, it is not as common as it should be. The problem posed by academic parochialism stems from the fact that the world of human endeavor, which it is the business of social scientists to study, is remarkably interconnected. "The domain of truth," notes Abraham Kaplan, "has no fixed boundaries within it."[23] It is difficult, for example, to understand features of a political system without understanding something about the economic system. Yet if political scientists and economists conduct their work with different vocabularies and are guided by a narrow conception of method, they will not have the intellectual equipment to share insights. They may not read each other's work or understand it when they do, even when working on related topics.

Because the various methods and theories that populate the social sciences are not currently unified by a single methodology, cumulation of knowledge is impeded. It is obvious that knowledge cannot progress unless there is some shared ground on which such knowledge can rest.[24] Even arguments demand

---

[22] Hayek (1956: 462–463; quoted in Redman 1991: epigraph) once remarked, "The physicist who is only a physicist can still be a first-class physicist and a most valuable member of society. But nobody can be a great economist who is only an economist – and I am even tempted to add that the economist who is only an economist is likely to become a nuisance if not a positive danger." See also Wilson (1998).

[23] Kaplan (1964: 4).

[24] For discussion of what "progress" might mean in this context, see Laudan (1977). For discussion of the importance of shared standards see Brady and Collier (2004).

a common frame of reference; without such shared ground, they are merely statements of position. In the latter circumstance, science degenerates into a chorus of yeas and nays reminiscent of Monty Python's infamous "Argument Clinic" (excerpted in the epigraph to Chapter 3).

This book does not delve into the sociological aspects of social science. Even so, it is worth reflecting briefly on social science as a professional activity, with distinctive norms, habits, rewards, and sanctions. Donald Campbell's comments, synthesizing early work by Robert Merton, are worth quoting at length. Science, writes Campbell,

> requires a disputatious community of "truth seekers" ... The norms of science are explicitly anti-authoritarian, anti-traditional, anti-revelational, and pro-individualistic. Truth is yet to be discovered. Old beliefs are to be systematically doubted until they have been reconfirmed by the methods of the new science. Persuasion is to be limited to equalitarian means, potentially accessible to all: visual demonstrations and logical demonstrations. The community of scientists is to stay together in focused disputation, attending to each other's arguments and illustrations, mutually monitoring and "keeping each other honest," until some working consensus emerges (but mutual conformity in belief per se is rejected as an acceptable goal).[25]

Campbell notes that this is a difficult balancing act, requiring both individualism (everyone must think for him- or herself and refuse to engage in herd behavior) and collectivism (everyone in the community must focus on similar problems with the aim of finding consensus).

In order to get proponents of different methods and theories on talking terms we need to provide a common framework by which arguments and evidence can be evaluated and alternative methods understood. If each has something to contribute (as the phrase goes), then we ought to be able to explain what these contributions are. Whether, in point of fact, norms exist that might provide grounds for judgments of adequacy across the social sciences is the question taken up in the following chapters. For the moment it is sufficient to note that the normative argument for norms is strong. There is no profit in incommensurability.[26] To the extent that academics employ idiosyncratic or field-specific

---

[25] Campbell (1988: 290).

[26] Incommensurability is a term that entered the lexicon of philosophy of science with the work of Thomas Kuhn. It refers (broadly and ambiguously) to a condition where persons are unable to understand one another because of their different ideological, theoretical, or methodological commitments. It is a very old problem, of course. Bacon noticed that error was the likely result whenever "argument or inference passes from one world of experience to another" (quoted in Wilson 1998: 10), a condition we would now label incommensurability. It should be noted that pluralism and uniformity are matters of degree. All but the most rabid deconstructionists will admit that there are some general perspectives on truth and knowledge that tie the social sciences together. See Laudan (1983, 1996); Wallerstein et al. (1996: 92–93); and Wilson

theoretical frameworks, we become islands in a boatless archipelago. Knowledge will not cumulate. Progress – define it how you will – is impeded.

To be sure, the need for agreement varies by topic. Those subjects firmly embedded in the past – those, that is, with few contemporary ramifications – can perhaps afford a wider array of views. Yet, for all subjects, social scientists should always strive for agreement, and the greater agreement they achieve – *ceteris paribus* – the more useful that field of study is likely to be. Whether the issue is a declaration of war or a capital-gains tax, citizens and policymakers look for scholarly consensus. Profound scholarly disagreement over these matters hampers public action. How can we justify the expenditure of millions of dollars of public funds if the effectiveness of a policy is openly and repeatedly challenged by experts? Indeed, support for social welfare programs has been undermined by suggestions from prominent policy experts that these programs are not achieving their intended purposes.[27] Similarly, support for anti-missile defense systems has been weakened by expert testimony questioning the technological viability of these visionary weapons.[28] Citizens are rightfully loath to surrender their earnings in order to pay for programs that cannot demonstrate workability, a judgment we rely on experts to provide.

Under the circumstances, it is not very useful if the social science community generates fourteen different perspectives on vouchers or democracy (two key examples, introduced below, that will guide much of our discussion in this book). If this is the end result of academic endeavor, we have not advanced very far over sheer intuition. Perhaps we have increased our "understanding" of these matters by looking at them from such varied perspectives. However, if we have no way of adjudicating between conflicting visions – if dissensus reigns supreme among academics who study these matters – then we have little to offer policymakers or the general public.

Of course, scholarly dissensus may simply be a reflection of the uncertain nature of the phenomena. Consensus is useful only if it is warranted by the evidence. Even so, there is no advantage in cultivating diversity *per se*. One might applaud *différance* (a Derridean neologism) in the humanities, but not, I think, in the social sciences.[29] Scholars in anthropology, archaeology,

---

(1998) for further defenses of a unified ("objective") methodology. See Hollis and Lukes (1982) and Laudan (1983, 1996) for general discussions of relativism. For arguments in favor of unifying the "qualitative" and "quantitative" dimensions of social science methodology, see Lazarsfeld and Rosenberg (1955: 387–391) and King, Keohane, and Verba (1994). For doubts on this score, see McKeown (1999).

[27] Murray (1984).   [28] Lakoff and York (1989).

[29] The quest for consensus might also be referred to as a quest for objectivity. The trouble with this much abused term is that it fosters the illusion that such agreement will arise unproblematically from an empirical reality insofar as we view that reality neutrally (without prejudice). My argument for

business, communications, demography, economics, education, environmental design, geography, law, political science, psychology, public administration, public health, public policy, social work, sociology, and urban planning ought to strive for agreement.

A unified framework

If there are good reasons to seek methodological consensus across the fields, problems, and theories of social science, how might one craft such a consensus? What principles might provide grounds for agreement? More to the point, how can one construct a framework that is useful for practitioners who are learning their craft?

This book is a highly synthetic endeavor, building self-consciously on a prodigious literature spanning philosophy of science and methods texts over the past two centuries. Its purpose is to integrate extant methodological rules and norms into a unified framework that is concise, precise, and comprehensible. Insofar as I am successful, the narrative ought to appear as a compendium of common sense. Yet, I also stake some claims. Like all methodology texts, this book is both a reflection of, and an argument about, the subject matter.[30]

Inquiry of a scientific nature, I stipulated, aims to be cumulative, evidence-based (empirical), falsifiable, generalizing, nonsubjective, replicable, rigorous, skeptical, systematic, transparent, and grounded in rational argument. There are differences of opinion over whether, or to what extent, science lives up to these high ideals. Even so, these are the ideals to which natural and social scientists generally aspire, and they help to define the enterprise in a general way and to demarcate it from other realms.

Of course, these ideals are also rather vague. What, exactly, does it mean to be "rigorous," or "rational"? The challenge before us is to reformulate these abstract ideals in an operational fashion. This requires some disaggregation.

---

agreement is grounded in the pragmatic need for agreement, rather than in a particular theory of knowledge – empiricist, inductivist, verificationist, falsificationist, etc.

[30] It is worth pointing out that any work on methodology – except perhaps for the most assiduously historical – treads on normative ground. Why else would one write, or read, a treatise on this subject, if not to discover a should or a should not? Another way of stating this point is to say that the relevance of methodological study stems from its capacity to orient and direct research in the field. A purely descriptive study, assuming such a book could be written, is less interesting because it takes no positions on the methodological battles of the day. Moreover, as a practical matter, a book that traversed this territory while granting equal coverage to every method, practice, and premise would become too large and too heterogeneous to be of assistance to practitioners. Thus, I have self-consciously excluded or downplayed certain tendencies that seemed, to my way of thinking, idiosyncratic or unproductive.

Yet since the objective is to provide a unifying schema the disaggregation cannot go too far. The book is therefore pitched at a meso-level, in between the abstractions of philosophy of science and the specific rules that define various methods.

My approach centers on the identification of basic *tasks* of social science, *strategies* enlisted to achieve those tasks, and *criteria* associated with each task and strategy. These are laid out schematically in Table 1.1. (Tasks are in bold font; strategies and criteria are labeled as such.) Note that each strategy is also defined by a set of criteria, though these are generally not listed in Table 1.1 for reasons of space. Further explication is provided in later chapters and tables, as indicated in the final column of the table.

The goal of the book is to uncover the shared norms that govern activity – implicitly or explicitly – in the community of social scientists. What makes a work of social science true, useful, or convincing ("scientific")? Why do we prefer one treatment of a subject over another? What reasons do we give when we accept or reject a manuscript for publication? These are the sorts of ground-level judgments that define the activity of methodology. With these judgments, I hope to identify the threads that tie our methodological intuitions together into a relatively unified framework across the diverse disciplines of social science.[31]

Following the organization of Table 1.1, I shall now try to summarize the main arguments of the book in very broad strokes. (Readers should not be disturbed if the narrative is not crystal clear, as all of the concepts listed here will receive further explication.)

Part I: the first part of the book introduces elements of the social science enterprise that are general in purview.

Chapter 2 begins with a discussion of two criteria that inform every scientific investigation: (a) discovery and (b) appraisal. I then offer advice for research conducted in an exploratory mode, where the goal is to discover an important research question and hypothesis. (This is the only section of the book which, by reason of its rather unstructured subject matter, departs from the framework presented in Table 1.1.)

Chapter 3 lays out criteria that, I argue, pertain to all social science arguments: (a) truth; (b) precision; (c) generality; (d) boundedness; (e) parsimony; (f) coherence; (g) commensurability; and (h) relevance.

---

[31] Criteria are central to the present framework, which in an earlier rendition (Gerring 2001) was referred to as a "criterial" framework. Following Cavell (1979: 9), criteria are "specifications a given person or group sets up on the basis of which ... to judge ... whether something has a particular status or value."

Chapter 4 discusses criteria pertaining to the testing stage of research, that is, research design and data analysis. These fall into four general categories: (a) accuracy; (b) sampling; (c) cumulation; and (d) theoretical fit.

Part II: the second part of the book is focused on description, that is, on empirical propositions that answer *what, how, when, whom,* or *in what manner* questions.

Chapter 5 is focused on concepts, the linguistic containers by which we make sense of the world. I argue that empirical concepts in the social sciences strive to achieve (a) resonance; (b) domain; (c) fecundity; (d) differentiation; (e) causal utility; and (f) operationalization (a topic postponed until Chapter 7). In achieving these goals, a general strategy of conceptualization is introduced, beginning with a survey of plausible concepts, continuing with a classification of attributes for each chosen concept, and ending with one of three approaches to definition: minimal, maximal, or cumulative.

Chapter 6 outlines various strategies of descriptive generalization. I argue that these sorts of arguments may be usefully categorized as (a) indicators; (b) syntheses; (c) typologies; or (d) associations, each with various subtypes.

Chapter 7 is focused on the task of measurement. In this quest, multiple strategies may be employed. I argue that all strategies encounter the following choices and challenges: (a) levels of abstraction (high, medium, low); (b) concept/measurement structures (set-theoretic, additive, fuzzy sets); (c) aggregation techniques (Boolean logic, weightings); (d) scales (nominal, ordinal, interval, ratio); (e) objectives (grouping, discrimination); (f) approaches (deductive, inductive); (g) cross-referencing; (h) ethnography; (i) surveys and experiments; and (j) causal relations.

Part III: the third part of the book focuses on causation, that is, on empirical arguments that answer *why* questions. (*How* questions lie somewhere in between description and causation.) This sort of argument posits a generative relationship between a causal factor (X) and an outcome (Y).

Chapter 8 begins by introducing a definition of causality and reviewing the diversity of causal arguments. Diversity notwithstanding, I argue that all social science arguments strive for common criteria including (a) clarity, (b) manipulability, (c) separation, (d) independence, (e) impact, and (f) a mechanism.

Chapter 9 takes up the question of causal analysis. These issues may be divided into three categories – (a) the treatment, (b) the outcome, and (c) the sample – each with multiple criteria that apply to that task.

Chapters 10 and 11 explore various specific strategies of causal analysis. These are divided into three broad rubrics – (a) randomized designs,

(b) nonrandomized designs, and (c) methods that move beyond X and Y – each with multiple options. The first two are explored in Chapter 10 and the latter in Chapter 11.

Chapter 12, the concluding section of Part III, attempts to show how the framework laid out in preceding chapters integrates diverse approaches to causal inference.

Part IV: the fourth part of the book elaborates and defends the framework. Chapter 13 returns to the problem of unity and diversity, reviewing the qualitative–quantitative debate, the culturalist–rationalist debate, and the debate among contending causal paradigms.

Chapter 14 reconsiders several nagging concerns: how the framework handles conflicts among contending tasks, strategies, and criteria; how it sets reasonable standards for research; and how it might be justified. I argue that the tasks, strategies, and criteria summarized in Table 1.1 are those that (a) best fulfill the proclaimed goals of social science (understanding social action in a scientific manner) and (b) guide the work of social science in ways that are likely to be of use to policymakers and the lay public.

Clarifications

Several clarifications must be inserted before we continue.

First, there is the matter of length and detail. To some, Table 1.1 may seem an unduly long and complicated laundry list. To others, it doubtless appears short and reductivist. Indeed, entire books have been written about some of the subjects that I outline (rather cavalierly, it must seem) in a page or two. I do not claim to have ended discussion on these points. My claim is simply to have covered this territory as thoroughly as possible *at this level of analysis*. An intermediate level of analysis is chosen so as to afford us the benefits of breadth and parsimony, with some sacrifice of depth. Readers hungry for more discussion on various topics are encouraged to follow the trail of footnotes.

Second, there is the matter of how to understand each element of the taxonomy. Traditional methods texts have sought to identify categorical rules that define good research. By contrast, I regard each task and criterion as a *matter of degree*. Achieving discovery, for example, is not a binary issue (one either discovers something new or one does not). Rather, all research – if it is worthwhile at all – has some element of novelty: it is saying something new. The same might be said for all the other tasks and criteria listed in Table 1.1. (Strategies are more likely to be categorical in nature, though even here differences of degree are often encountered.)

Table 1.1 The framework summarized

I. GENERAL		*Table*
Overall		
Criteria	Discovery; Appraisal	*2.1*
Arguments		
Criteria	Truth; Precision; Generality; Boundedness; Parsimony; Coherence; Commensurability; Relevance	*3.1*
Analyses		
Criteria	Accuracy (validity, precision, uncertainty, internal/external validity); Sampling (representativeness, size, level of analysis); Cumulation (standardization, replication, transparency); Theoretical fit (construct validity, severity, partition)	*4.1*
II. DESCRIPTION		
Concepts		
Criteria	Resonance; Domain; Consistency; Fecundity; Differentiation; Causal utility; Operationalization	*5.1*
Strategies	Survey of concepts; Classification of attributes; Definition (minimal, maximal, cumulative)	*5.2*
Arguments		
Strategies	Indicators; Syntheses; Typologies (simple, temporal, matrix, taxonomic, configurational, sequential); Associations (trend, network, correlation)	*6.1*
Measurements		
Criteria	Reliability (precision); Validity	
Strategies	Levels of abstraction (high, medium, low); Structure (set-theoretic, additive, fuzzy sets); Aggregation (Boolean logic, weightings); Scales (nominal, ordinal, interval, ratio); Objective (discrimination, grouping); Approach (deductive, inductive); Ethnography; Surveys/experiments; Cross-referencing; Causal relations	*7.1*
III. CAUSATION		
Arguments		
Criteria	Clarity; Manipulability; Separation; Independence; Impact; Mechanism	*8.1*
Analyses		
Criteria	Treatment (exogeneity, variation, simplicity, discrete-ness, uniformity, even distribution, strength, proximity, scalability); Outcome (variation); Sample (independence, comparability)	*9.3*
Strategies	Randomized designs (pre-test/post-test, post-test only, multiple post-tests, roll-out, crossover, Solomon four-group, factorial); Nonrandomized designs (regression discontinuity, panel, cross-sectional, longitudinal); Beyond X & Y (conditioning on confounders, instrumental variables, mechanisms, alternate outcomes, causal heterogeneity, rival hypotheses, robustness tests, causal reasoning)	*10.1*

Third, there is the problem of conflicts across the tasks, strategies, and criteria. Achieving adequacy along one dimension may involve a sacrifice along another dimension: *tradeoffs* are ubiquitous. This means that every task, strategy, or criterion must be understood with a *ceteris paribus* caveat. Parsimony is desirable, all other things being equal. Coherence is desirable, all other things being equal. And so forth. This does not mean that "anything goes," but it does imply that several approaches to a given topic are often methodologically justifiable, and this, in turn, offers a strong *prima facie* argument for multimethod research. The job of the methodologist, in any case, is to arrive at a best-possible resolution of conflicting tasks, strategies, and criteria (Chapter 14).

To sum up, the purpose of the framework is to offer a relatively parsimonious and comprehensive review of issues that crop up in the process of designing and evaluating social science research so that methodological intuitions are sharpened, work is more reflective, and cumulation easier to achieve. Whatever methodological agreement is possible in social science must be provided by a foundation on which we can all (more or less) agree. Such a framework, I believe, is present already in our everyday judgments about good work, strong arguments, and solid evidence.

By contrast, consensus is not likely to arise through our conversion to a single theoretical paradigm or method, inaugurating that heavenly state known as "normal science." We are not likely to wake up one morning to find ourselves all doing game theory, or hermeneutics. Fortunately, agreement on theories, models, and methods is not necessary. Indeed, it would probably be foolhardy for social scientists to all pursue the same questions, or to pursue questions in the same way.

However, knowledge gathered with diverse tools will cumulate if we are able to put diverse evidence together in a common framework. Progress is a realistic goal as long as we understand that lasting progress is more likely to occur in small steps than in revolutionary ("paradigmatic") leaps. If a unified framework will not resolve all our strife it may at least point the way to a more productive style of debate: where arguments meet each other on common ground, where the advantages and disadvantages of different approaches to a problem can be specified and evaluated, and where cumulation can be assessed.

Exclusions

Although comprehensive relative to other approaches to the subject, the present framework does not encompass all aspects of social science. Let me note several omissions.

First, the tasks, strategies, and criteria encompassed in Table 1.1 do not pay explicit attention to *predictive* inference. Prediction may be understood either as forecasting into the future and/or as point predictions for particular cases (in the past, present, or future) derived from general causal models. Of course, insofar as either of these sorts of inference builds on general descriptive or causal models one might say that they are extensions of subjects discussed in this book. However, I shall have nothing explicit to say about how one reaches predictive inferences.

Second, the framework is only peripherally concerned with arguments focused narrowly on single events or outcomes (sometimes referred to as idiographic, purely descriptive, singular-causal, or token-causal). This stems from the initial definition of science, understood as a generalizing activity.[32] Of course, knowledge of specific events may assist in reaching conclusions about a larger population of cases. Just as a large sample of units reflects on a broader population so might a small sample consisting of a single unit, studied intensively. As such, *case study* research falls within the rubric of a generalizing science and thus within the rubric of this volume. That said, this volume does not delve deeply into case-based styles of descriptive and causal inference, a topic addressed elsewhere.[33]

Third, the framework does not extend to pragmatic, logistical, or ethical concerns. Quite often, one chooses a research design because it is more convenient for one to do so, or perhaps because it is impossible to do otherwise. For example, one may lack the language skills to study something else. Political or cultural barriers may prevent one from gathering additional information. Evidence itself may be scarce. Funding opportunities may be limited. And, of course, time is always limited.

Ethical considerations may also constrain one's ability to develop a solution to methodological difficulties. It is worth reminding ourselves that social research is subject to the same ethical norms that govern everyday life (vague though these may be). In addition, there are considerations that pertain specifically to research conducted on human subjects. Here, the immediate impact of a piece of research must be balanced against the anticipated long-term impact of that research on the general public and on the course of public policy. Sometimes,

---

[32] One might add that there is also relatively little one can say methodologically about the description or explanation of a particular event. To be sure, a high degree of expertise is necessary in order to reach a determination on a contested question of fact; such judgments do not come easy. But this expertise does not usually lend itself to general criteria of inference. It is based instead on highly contextual knowledge about particular times, places, and peoples. Lieberson (1985); Thompson (1978); Winks (1969).

[33] Gerring (2007). See also Bennett (2010); George and Bennett (2005).

long-term benefits outweigh short-term costs; sometimes, they do not. Unfortunately, these are not issues to which neat formulas apply; hence, the angst that accompanies the work of Institutional Review Boards (IRBs), assigned with the difficult task of approving research on human subjects in universities throughout the world.[34]

Practical considerations such as these are not methodological in the usual sense of the term. One could hardly argue, for example, that a given research design has a better grasp of the truth because it is cheaper, easier, or more ethical. This might have been the reason behind a study's success or failure, but it cannot be the grounds upon which we accept or reject a theory. If another researcher comes along with more time and money, better language skills, better access to key cases, or a solution to a persisting ethical obstacle, he or she will be able to construct a better research design. It is the latter – goodness in research design – that we are primarily concerned with in this text.

However, the fact that goodness in research design is conditioned by pecuniary, ethical, social, and political realities must enter ultimately into our judgment of a study's contribution to knowledge. If we took no cognizance of such matters we might find ourselves studying only those topics that are convenient, unethical, or data-rich. Thus, I do not want to downplay the importance of practical considerations in the conduct of social research. They are neglected in this text only because there is little that one can say about them in the general sense, and because these sorts of constraints are generally apparent to the researcher.[35] (For further thoughts on this issue see Chapter 14.)

Terminology

Distressingly, the vocabulary associated with the subject of methodology is ridden with ambiguity. Key terms such as "positivism," "qualitative," "mechanism," "experiment," "causality," "exogeneity," "heterogeneity," "validity," and "identification" mean different things in different research traditions and in different research contexts. Even within the same tradition and the same context they may mean different things to different people.[36]

---

[34] Kelman (1982) offers general reflections on research ethics in the social sciences. Mazur (2007) and Sales and Felkman (2000) discuss research on human subjects. Paluck (2009) and Wood (2006) investigate ethical dilemmas of field research, with special focus on areas of intense conflict.

[35] On practical constraints see Barrett and Cason (1997); Lieberman, Howard, and Lynch (2004); van Evera (1997).

[36] To aid in disambiguating, Judea Pearl recently called for a new "Wiki Glossary of Causal Terminology" (www.mii.ucla.edu/causality).

Moreover, because of the high degree of overlap in connotation across near-synonyms, there is almost always more than one way to express a single thought. An issue of *generality* might also be articulated as one of breadth, comprehensiveness, domain, extensivity, external validity, population, range, scale, or scope. A *variable* could also be referred to as a concept, condition, dimension, factor, indicator, measure, metric, or unidimensional description. And so forth. Each of these terms has a slightly different connotation – and in some contexts, a very different denotation.

A prime example of lexical abundance is provided by recent work on causal inference, which may be understood from the perspective of philosophy of science (e.g., by David Lewis, John Mackie, and Wesley Salmon), from the perspective of research design (e.g., by experimentalists such as Donald Campbell and collaborators), from the perspective of statistics (e.g., by Donald Rubin and collaborators), and from the perspective of causal graphs (e.g., by Judea Pearl and his collaborators). Each of these traditions has developed a highly specialized vocabulary. However, all are concerned with a similar set of issues; thus, one finds a rough equivalence of principles across these traditions (which I have tried to capture in as parsimonious a fashion as possible in the third part of the book).

Moving beyond issues of terminology, it should be pointed out that methodological issues are rarely separate and discrete. The incorrigible quality of our subject is its holism: everything is enmeshed in everything else. Thus, although a task, strategy, or criterion may be defined narrowly in the text it will quickly become clear to the reader that no issue is entirely self-contained. A proper understanding requires us to situate each element within the broad rubric of social science methodology. This, itself, is a strong argument for a comprehensive, book-length treatment, which affords the space to discuss interconnections across topics. However, it should also alert the reader to the fact that, like cookie dough, our subject can be subdivided in many different ways. That is, the tasks, strategies, and criteria set forth in Table 1.1 could be named and arranged differently.

Writers on methodological subjects are forced to make choices about which terms to highlight and which to ignore, and how to define the chosen terms. No lexicon is sacrosanct.[37] In making choices, I have given preference to terms and definitions that promise to travel widely across methodological and disciplinary cleavages and that divide up the subject in a manner consistent with the goals of the proposed framework. Sometimes, this involves the adoption of a term

---

[37] Indeed, the categories set forth in Table 1.1 are somewhat different from those employed in the previous edition of this book (Gerring 2001).

originally developed in a specialized realm. (Sometimes, I have been forced to coin new terms that do not have common currency.) In any case, I have done my best to make connections across varied lexicons. Wherever near-synonyms or rival definitions exist I have tried to clarify these similarities and differences. Important terms are italicized at the point in the text where they are defined. A Glossary provides definitions for all key terms, noting near-synonyms.

By way of conclusion, it should be stressed that the seeming arbitrariness of our methodological lexicon does not mean that issues of vocabulary are pointless. To the contrary, they are indispensable, for the alternative – a purely mathematical lexicon encompassing all methodological issues – does not exist, and probably would never be adequate to the task. I trust that quibbles over terminology or classification will not impugn the utility of the framework.

Examples

Because of the opacity of our methodological lexicon any discussion of methodological issues depends crucially upon a plentiful supply of specific examples. It is these examples – of work that has been conducted on a subject or might be conducted on that subject – that often serve to clarify a point.

In choosing examples I have tried to cross disciplinary boundaries so as to illustrate the pervasiveness of various methodological issues throughout the social sciences. Of course, space limitations preclude discussion of multiple examples for each argument, so readers will have to intuit how the argument links up with work in their own specialized field or subfield. Frequently, I have chosen older, "classic" studies that are likely to be familiar to readers, even if they have been superseded by more recent work. Discussion of a particular work does not imply an endorsement of its findings or methods. Examples are chosen to illustrate specific methodological points; that is all.

To maintain consistency, I often return to two central exemplars, *democracy* and *vouchers*. These subjects are relevant to many social science disciplines and have also aroused a good deal of scholarly controversy. The first exemplifies work where the unit of analysis is very large (e.g., nation-states) and the theoretical frame equally grand. The second exemplifies work on discrete policy inputs where individuals or small groups form the units of analysis and the theoretical frame is correspondingly small. Together, these two topics provide ample fodder for methodological illustration. Following is a very brief review of these complex issues (for further elucidation the reader is referred to the work cited below and to discussion throughout the text).

Democracy

Democracy is a familiar topic, though also a perplexing one. Scholars have difficulty defining this concept and, even once issues of definition are dispensed with, problems of measurement remain. Thus, descriptive questions remain somewhat unsettled: we feel confident in identifying countries that are very autocratic (e.g., North Korea) and those that are highly democratic (e.g., Sweden); but there is a good deal of dispute about how to conceptualize many of the countries that lie in between (e.g., Russia, Turkey, or Iran).[38] Under the circumstances, it is not surprising that scholars also wrestle with the causes of democracy (why do some countries democratize, and consolidate, while others remain autocratic or only intermittently democratic?)[39] and the causal effects of democracy (does regime type affect political outcomes and policy outcomes?).[40]

With respect to the causal effects of democracy, one theory known as the "democratic peace" will be discussed at various points in the text. This hypothesis, which harks back to Immanuel Kant's essay on "Perpetual Peace" (1795), proposes that democracies never fight wars with one another (the deterministic version) or are much less likely to fight wars with one another (the probabilistic version). Various reasons have been proposed for this apparent "law" of international relations. Not only the causal effect, but also the mechanisms that might be at work remain open to debate. And yet there is a strong empirical regularity and a number of plausible mechanisms that might account for it. Not surprisingly, the hypothesis has attracted a great deal of interest from academics and policymakers.[41]

Vouchers

The question of vouchers is a much more specific phenomenon than regime type. As such, it is easier to define and to measure, though less grand in theoretical sweep (a common tradeoff in the work of social science). Even so, descriptive questions remain. Diverse studies proclaiming to be about "vouchers" sometimes mask divergent policy interventions. And the question of policy impact is by no means resolved.[42]

---

[38] Coppedge and Gerring (2011); Munck and Verkuilen (2002).

[39] Berg-Schlosser (2007); Coppedge (forthcoming); Geddes (2007).

[40] Gerring and Thacker (2011); Mulligan, Gil, and Sala-i-Martin (2004).

[41] Brown, Lynn-Jones, and Miller (1996); Elman (1997).

[42] The literature on this controversial subject is vast. Recent work includes Chubb and Moe (1990); Fuller and Elmore (1996); Howell and Peterson (2002); Hoxby (2003); Krueger and Mhu (2004); Ladd (2002); Neal (2002); Smith (2005). See also Morgan and Winship (2007) for methodological commentary about vouchers as an issue in social science research. Although much of the current academic literature is centered on the US experience, the policy has been implemented on a much wider scale in other

Vouchers are most commonly discussed in the context of educational policy, though they are also applicable to other policy areas (e.g., housing, food, medical care). Voucher theories generally center on a marketplace model of service provision. Proponents of school vouchers beginning with Milton Friedman[43] believe that the best way to improve the quality of primary and secondary education is to introduce competition into school systems, which are usually dominated by a single government provider. In this fashion, education would be subjected to the rigors of the marketplace and parents (and their children) would be able to exercise choice among schools. It is argued, further, that an educational marketplace may be achieved without sacrificing the ideal of free, universal education through the medium of government-provided "vouchers" that students can redeem toward tuition at schools within a district – whether public or private (though generally with some conditions and qualifications). Advocates claim that this system, if properly instituted, will lead to improved school quality, improved student performance (as measured, e.g., by standardized tests), and perhaps additional benefits as well (e.g., parent and student satisfaction, narrowing test score gaps between black and white students, and so forth). Critics are dubious.

Advice to the reader

In approaching this rather large book the reader may wish to read selectively. This is advisable for those with extensive background knowledge, who may be familiar with some subjects and less familiar with others. Such readers may browse the detailed table of contents or the index in order to identify subjects of interest.

Selective reading is also appropriate for beginners in social science methodology, who may wish to familiarize themselves with essential elements first, leaving more complex issues – including arguments with the literature – for later. In this fashion, it is hoped that the book will be rendered accessible to all readers – beginners, intermediate, and advanced.

Of course, confusions may arise from selective perusals of the text. Within Part II and Part III topics are closely intertwined and therefore best approached as a set, not on a chapter-by-chapter basis. Moreover, the four parts of the book are cumulative, building upon each other. General criteria laid out in Part I apply to both descriptive and causal tasks. And since causal

---

countries, including Chile, Colombia, and Sweden. Vouchers are by no means an exclusively American preoccupation. Carnoy (1998); Chakrabarti and Peterson (2008); Gauri and Vawda (2004).
[43] Friedman (1955).

arguments build on descriptive arguments, the criteria laid out in Part II also apply to Part III.

Recall that social science is a holistic enterprise and the goal of this book is to encompass that activity in a reasonably comprehensive fashion. Bits and pieces of social science methodology may not make sense – and may even be misleading – if wrenched out of the larger context in which they are situated. This caveat must be borne in mind by those who choose to read selectively.

Additional resources for readers and instructors are located on-line at Cambridge University Press www.cambridge.org/gerring. This includes (a) tables and figures from the book (in separate files, for easy downloading and printing); (b) a powerpoint presentation (for use in lectures); (c) questions, exercises, assignments, and advice (for instructors incorporating the text into their methodology course); and (d) syllabi from instructors who have used this book in their courses.

Part I

General

2 Beginnings

During my career in science, now nearly a half century in duration, I have grown more and more aware that success in science, paralleling success in most careers, comes not so much to the most gifted, nor the most skillful, nor the most knowledgeable, nor the most affluent of scientists, but rather to the superior strategist and tactician. The individual who is able to maneuver with propriety through the world of science along a course that regularly puts him or her in a position of serendipity is often the one who excels.

Jack Oliver[1]

Broadly stated, the goal of science is to discover new things about the world and to appraise the truth-value of extant propositions about the world. Consider our exemplars, democracy and vouchers, introduced in Chapter 1. We want to uncover new things about the process of democratization and the impact of vouchers on school performance. At the same time, we want to test extant theories about these two subjects. Social science may, therefore, be understood as a twin quest for *discovery* and for *appraisal*, as summarized in Table 2.1.[2]

The chapter begins by introducing these goals, followed by a review of their implications for more specific methodological tasks. The next section approaches the goal of discovery through the concrete task of finding a research question. Since the remaining chapters of the book assume that a research question – perhaps even a specific hypothesis – has been identified, this chapter functions as a prologue to the rest of the book.

---

[1] Oliver (1991: ix).

[2] This contrast can be traced back to Reichenbach (1938), who distinguished between a "context of discovery" and a "context of justification." See also Hanson (1961); McLaughlin (1982); Nickles (1980); Popper (1965); Zahar (1983). Critics (e.g., Schiemann 2003) note that the distinction is not a dichotomy, i.e., the two goals are difficult to separate in practice. My claim, however, is not that they comprise a crisp typology. Rather, I claim that they are two fundamental goals of science that impose somewhat different methodological strategies and criteria upon the activity of science.

Table 2.1 General goals of social science

1. **Discovery** (conjecture, exploration, innovation, theory formation)
   Is it new?
2. **Appraisal** (assessment, demonstration, evaluation, justification, proof, testing, verification/falsification)
   Is it falsifiable?

Discovery

"An author is little to be valued," says Hume in his characteristically blunt fashion, "who tells us nothing but what we can learn from every coffee-house conversation."[3] We should like an argument, and corresponding empirical analysis, to contribute something novel to our understanding of a topic. A good piece of research is one that is innovative, one that makes a novel contribution – usually understood with respect to the key hypothesis or general theory.

Of course, some "discoveries" are not really new, or are not as innovative as they purport to be. Authors sometimes slight the accomplishments of others, formulate their argument against a ridiculous null hypothesis (a "straw man" argument), overstate the accomplishment of their own work, or adopt neologisms that repackage old wine in new bottles. Our contempt for various species of pseudo-innovation confirms the general point: good research should push the frontiers of knowledge forward.

In this quest, researchers are generally forced to adopt an exploratory approach to the world. New territory is entered, or established territories are interrogated for unexpected patterns (anomalies). New explanations are tested or invented out of whole cloth. Discovery requires an aggressive and critical engagement with the status quo.

This is characteristic of initial phases of research. But it is also the goal to which all top researchers aspire, for everyone wishes to situate themselves on the frontiers of knowledge. In the words of one scientist, "the only interesting fields of science are the ones where you still don't know what you're talking about."[4] In this sense, we are all – always – beginners.

Consider the question of democratization, introduced in Chapter 1. How and why do some states democratize, while others do not (or are unable to sustain those gains)? This is not an easy question to answer – some might

---

[3] Hume (1985: 254).   [4] I. I. Rabi, quoted in Root-Bernstein (1989: 407).

argue that it is not amenable to general theory – but it is undoubtedly an important one.[5]

Innovation at the descriptive level concerns ways in which the broad topic of democratization might be productively conceptualized and measured. Is there a critical moment of *transition* at which the process of democratization is achieved? Is there a point of *consolidation* beyond which reversals are unlikely? Are there distinctive *sequences* by which democratization occurs? How should democracy, and its various subtypes (illiberal democracy, electoral democracy, competitive authoritarianism), be defined? These are just a few of the descriptive questions that have occupied scholars in recent years.

At the causal level, scholars have focused on the possible preconditions for successful democratization. Are certain authoritarian regime types more likely to democratize than others? Does the existence of mineral wealth (e.g., oil or diamonds) in a country make democracy less likely? To what extent does a country's colonial experience color its propensity for achieving and maintaining a democratic form of rule? How much impact (if any) does economic development have on democratic/authoritarian outcomes?

In a more general vein, one can identify certain characteristic types of causal innovation. Sometimes, a new factor, X, is proposed as a contributing cause for a well-studied outcome, adding a new variable to existing models. That would describe most of the examples listed in the previous paragraph. Less common is the theoretical eclipse of existing theories about Y with a new causal framework. Thus, Daron Acemoglu and James Robinson have proposed that democratization can be understood as a distributional struggle between the haves and the have-nots.[6] A third type of causal reformulation consists in working back from an established causal factor, X, to some prior cause (X_1) that explains X, and thereby Y (reframing X as a causal mechanism). Thus, it might be argued that geographic circumstances (e.g., climate, soil quality, disease vectors, access to deep-water ports and navigable rivers) affected patterns of colonization and resource extraction, with lasting effects on the distribution of wealth and power, and, ultimately, on a country's propensity to democratize.[7] A fourth type of innovation focuses on the causal mechanisms lying within an established X/Y relationship. In this fashion, a good deal of work has been devoted to the causal links between resource wealth and authoritarian rule. Michael Ross summarizes:

---

[5] For recent reviews of the literature see Berg-Schlosser (2007); Coppedge (forthcoming); Geddes (2007).

[6] Acemoglu and Robinson (2005).

[7] This follows the line of argument initiated by Acemoglu, Johnson, and Robinson (2001); Sokoloff and Engerman (2000).

A "rentier effect" ... suggests that resources rich governments use low tax rates and patronage to relieve pressures for greater accountability; a "repression effect" ... argues that resources wealth retards democratization by enabling governments to boost their funding for internal security; and a "modernization effect" ... holds that growth based on the export of oil and minerals fails to bring about the social and cultural changes that tend to produce democratic government.[8]

A study focused on causal mechanisms typically culminates in a new explanation for why X causes Y (in this case, why there is a "resource curse"). If no plausible causal mechanism can be discovered, such a study might also serve to disconfirm the entire hypothesis. A fifth type of innovation focuses on the population of an inference (its breadth or scope). One might argue that the connection between resource wealth and authoritarianism is applicable only to the developing world, and not to advanced industrial countries (e.g., Norway). Or one might attempt to extend the ambit of the theory to apply to different time periods (e.g., Greek city-states) or different phenomena (corporate governance).

Evidently, there are many ways to innovate, which is to say, there are many types of discoveries. This is because there are many types of theories, and each theory has multiple parts – an issue we shall attempt to disentangle in the coming chapters.

Appraisal

The second over-arching goal of science is to ensure that the truth-value of propositions about the world can be tested rigorously. "The criterion of the scientific status of a theory is its *falsifiability*, or refutability, or testability," asserts Karl Popper.[9] This process, in contrast to the goal of discovery, must be hedged about with rules. Otherwise, we shall never be able to reach consensus on anything and the goal of truth (which presumes the possibility of reaching consensus) dissipates. Fortunately, the process of appraisal is more amenable to general principles than the process of discovery. And this, in turn, helps to explain why it has been an abiding preoccupation of methodologists. (It is virtually the sum total of the field of methodology, as traditionally conceived.)

With respect to the construction of arguments, it may be appropriate to begin by repeating an old story (perhaps apocryphal) about a physics doctoral

[8] Ross (2001: 327–328). See also Dunning (2008a).

[9] Popper (1965: 37). Arguably, Popper's ([1934] 1968) classic treatise, *The Logic of Scientific Discovery*, was mis-named. It offers not a logic of discovery, but rather a logic of testing. In any case, I prefer the term "appraisal" rather than "falsifiability," as the latter presumes a certain approach to testing that may not be entirely justified.

defense. At the conclusion of the proceedings, one of the examiners excoriates the hapless candidate with the following remark: "This is the worst thesis I have ever read. It is not even wrong."

The sign of a nonfalsifiable proposition, Popper points out, is that virtually "any conclusion we please can be derived from it."[10] It may be true by definition, but it is not true by any standards that one might subject to empirical test. Popper charged that a number of highly influential theories, including Marxism and Freudianism, suffered this fatal flaw. They could not be proven or disproven. They were neither right nor wrong.

As it happens, Marxism and Freudianism are still with us, along with Weberianism, realism (a theory of international relations), rational choice and a host of other difficult-to-appraise theoretical frameworks. In the natural sciences, as well, explanations such as string theory persist, despite their seeming nonfalsifiability. It would appear that broad and ambiguous frameworks are sometimes useful, even when they cannot be clearly appraised. Indeed, appraisal is by no means the only criterion of a good argument. That said, there is near universal recognition that falsifiability is *a* virtuous ideal – one to be striven for, even when conditions do not seem to be propitious.

Popper also recognized that falsifiability is not a dichotomous matter (either/or) but rather a matter of degrees. Some theories are more falsifiable than others. Indeed, none of the examples mentioned above are entirely resistant to empirical refutation. And even the most tractable theories put up some resistance.

Generally speaking, an argument is most falsifiable insofar as it is operational, parsimonious, general in purview (offering a large territory for empirical testing), well bounded (so that the population of an inference is clear, and defensible), coherent (internally consistent), clear with respect to counterfactuals and comparisons, and relying on as few assumptions as possible. Additional issues arise during the theory-testing phase of research. For example, one is more inclined to believe a result if a solid "partition" has been maintained between the construction of the argument and its subsequent testing; this ensures that there is minimal wiggle-room to adjust the argument to suit the results of a test or to adjust the test to suit the hypothesis. Good tests are "severe"; bad ones are permissive. With respect to causal analysis, the most stringent tests are usually experimental in nature. And so forth.

A great wealth of factors – many more than Popper explicitly considered – contribute to the rigor with which a hypothesis is appraised. These are explored

---

[10] Popper ([1934] 1968: 92).

in subsequent chapters. Some of these criteria are intrinsic to the formal structure of the argument; others relate to the procedures used to test that argument.

Tradeoffs

Arguably, all the tasks, strategies, and criteria introduced in the remaining chapters are ways of achieving or instantiating either discovery or appraisal. These primal goals inform every methodological endeavor.

Complicating matters, however, these methodological goals are often in tension with one another. On the one hand, researchers are encouraged to seek out the unknown. This requires an *exploratory* approach to the empirical world, for there is no systematic procedure for discovering new things. And the newer the thing (the more revolutionary), the less rule-bound is the procedure. Paul Feyerabend makes this point forcefully:

The idea of a method that contains firm, unchanging, and absolutely binding principles for conducting the business of science meets considerable difficulty when confronted with the results of historical research. We find then, that there is not a single rule, however plausible, and however firmly grounded in epistemology, that is not violated at some time or other. It becomes evident that such violations are not accidental events, they are not results of insufficient knowledge or of inattention which might have been avoided. On the contrary, we see that they are necessary for progress. Indeed, one of the most striking features of recent discussions in the history and philosophy of science is the realization that events and developments, such as the invention of atomism in antiquity, the Copernican Revolution, the rise of modern atomism (kinetic theory; dispersion theory; sterochemistry; quantum theory), the gradual emergence of the wave theory of light, occurred only because some thinkers either *decided* not to be bound by certain "obvious" methodological rules, or because they *unwittingly broke* them.[11]

The process of discovery is inherently anti-nomothetic – or, as Feyerabend would say, anarchic.[12] From this perspective, traditional scientific methodology is too respectful of existing theoretical constructs and methods. Scientists need to get outside the iron cage of normal science – to a place where the processes

---

[11] Feyerabend (1975: 23).

[12] Feyerabend (1963, 1975). Although Feyerabend took a radical stance against science (as traditionally understood), his work is digestible within the framework of traditional philosophy of science if approached as a corrective to a naive, Popperian ("positivistic") view of the scientific process. Much of what Feyerabend had to say applied with particular force to the context of discovery (though he rejected the utility of the discovery–appraisal distinction).

of exploration and testing are mutually intertwined and difficult to disentangle. Here, theories are not always neatly and cleanly falsifiable.

On the other hand, researchers are rightly encouraged to develop risky propositions and hard tests, so as to assist in the task of appraisal. This is the conservative moment of science, personified by Karl Popper. Here, there are plenty of rules (or at least general tasks, strategies, and criteria) to guide one's research.

The falsificationist considers the greatest sins of social science to be those of commission, rather than omission. The virtue of good science is to keep quiet when the truth is ambiguous – not to say more than one knows with a reasonable level of certainty. (Indeed, Popper counsels against the use of the term "truth" under *any* circumstances.) Only in this fashion will the products of science be distinguishable from conjectures, the stock-in-trade of politicians, journalists, and cocktail-party prognosticators. Only if the field is clear of nonsense will the long, slow process of scientific cumulation occur.

Many social scientists have embraced this austere, taciturn view of science (at least rhetorically). Here, the primary job of the methodologist is to vigilantly guard the gates of science, ensuring that no unauthorized entrants are admitted. Contra the orthodoxy, I will insist that at least half the battle of science lies in identifying interesting problems to solve. Indeed, finding the right question may be more important in the long run than finding the right answer for a less interesting hypothesis. From this perspective, good science is not just a matter of rigor but also of insight (or, if you prefer a more religiously tinged metaphor, of *inspiration*). Note that theoretical development could not occur, or would occur only very slowly and haltingly, if researchers kept their Popperian blinders on – limiting themselves to pre-formed hypotheses and yes/no empirical tests. A constructive methodology should enable researchers to think about problems in new ways; it should not focus narrowly and obsessively on testing.

To be sure, there is plenty of ammunition for protagonists in both camps. There are those who feel that there is altogether too much testing and not enough theory (or not enough good theory), and that our efforts should therefore be focused on the latter. And there are those who feel that there is too much theory (or too many theories) and not enough testing, and that our efforts should be focused on the latter. Which side of this debate one adopts depends upon how much confidence one has in either venture. If one is confident in one's ability to craft better theories and correspondingly skeptical of our ability to test them, one hews to the discovery camp. If, on the other hand, one is skeptical about obtaining lasting theoretical advances and relatively optimistic about devising new and better tests, one finds oneself in the appraisal camp. This is not a debate that we can settle; I simply note the issue for readers to consider.

The harder, and surely the more important, question is how innovative one ought to be in the choice of topic. Again, there are two positions, each of which has compelling points to make. Some bemoan the lack of theoretical ambition found among the current generation of scholars, presumably by reference to an earlier generation of "Big Thinkers." Adam Przeworski writes:

The entire structure of incentives of academia in the United States works against taking big intellectual and political risks. Graduate students and assistant professors learn to package their intellectual ambitions into articles publishable by a few journals and to shy away from anything that might look like a political stance. This professionalism does advance knowledge of narrowly formulated questions, but we do not have forums for spreading our knowledge outside academia.[13]

It is probably true that members of today's generation are more apt to accept the norms and extant theories of the discipline than the 1960s generation, which perhaps qualifies them as less theoretically ambitious. Probably, they are less politically engaged – though this is not necessarily connected to intellectual curiosity. Alternatively, one might argue that this generation has focused its energies in a more productive fashion than previous generations. Indeed, many of the "Big Theories" propounded in the social sciences – then and now – are difficult to digest. If a theory is not falsifiable, or does not cumulate well with other theories (either subsuming them or taking its place beside them), it is unlikely to move a field forward.

In sum, the question of how theoretically ambitious one should be is difficult to answer in the general sense. One should be exactly as ambitious as one can be, while retaining touch with the empirical reality under investigation. The goals of theoretical innovation must be balanced by the quest for theory appraisal.

Indeed, from Popper's perspective, the goals of discovery and appraisal are entirely compatible with one another. "Bold conjectures" can be combined with strenuous efforts at "refutation."[14] Sometimes this is possible, and to the extent that it is, it defines the *summum bonum* of science.

---

[13] Quoted in Snyder (2007: 20).   [14] Popper ([1934] 1968, 1965).

Even so, the tension between discovery and appraisal seems rather more intrinsic and irresolvable than Popper was willing to admit. Consider that if one's primary motivation is the discovery of new theories, then researchers must have latitude to propose broad and abstract theories without clearly testable hypotheses. Insofar as hypotheses are generated and tested, this testing process should be open-ended – involving numerous hypotheses and a continual process of adjustment between theory and evidence – before, during, and after the research is conducted. It is not surprising that research of the "soaking and poking" variety (whether qualitative or quantitative) is not very convincing – though it may be quite provocative, and may lead, down the line, to more convincing demonstrations of truth.

Insofar as one's primary motivation is to test the truth-value of an existing theory one's mode of procedure must be quite different. Here, a theory should be framed in as precise a manner as possible so that it issues specific, testable predictions. The process of theory discovery and appraisal should be segregated from one another as much as possible, so there is little room for subjective interventions in the testing process or *post hoc* alterations of the theory. In all respects, theory and research design should be "risky," allowing many opportunities for a theory to fail. The problem with this style of research is equally apparent. If taken seriously, Popper's injunctions would severely constrain the type of theories admissible to the canon of social science. In addition to Marxism and Freudianism, which Popper explicitly condemned, it would also raise doubts about Weberian theories, social capital theory, evolution-based models, theories of international relations (e.g., realism, liberalism, idealism/constructivism), rational-choice models, and many others as well. Within the natural sciences (Popper's home turf), the demand for falsifiability would presumably force one to reject string theory and other highly abstract and scarcely testable components of modern physics.

Popperians might respond that, whatever messiness might be involved in the process of discovery, *at some point* theories ought to be issued in falsifiable form. This merely begs the question: at what point should this be? Note that most of the theoretical frameworks mentioned previously have been extant for a century or more, and appear to be no closer to a definitive empirical test. Indeed, broad theories rarely fall when they fail empirical tests. These failures, contra Popper, can usually be explained away (perhaps by *ad hoc* adjustments of the theory), or treated as part of the error term.[15]

---

[15] Gorski (2004); Lakatos (1978).

To adopt a phrase from Douglas MacArthur: old theories never die, but they sometimes fade away. Specifically, they meet their demise when a more compelling theory is proposed, one which attracts researchers formerly committed to the long-established theory. Gradually, theory B eclipses theory A. The process is Lakatosian (involving grand theoretical frameworks) rather than Popperian (involving middle-range propositions). In this respect, progress at theoretical and empirical levels cannot be separated from one another. And in this respect, again, it may appear that our energies are better focused on the generative component of science than on the falsifiability–verifiability component. Marx, Freud, and Weber ought to be our avatars, not the thousands of assembly-line social scientists who spend their lives testing middle-range theories.

I shall conclude by returning to the central point: good science must embrace both the goal of discovery and the goal of appraisal. One without the other is not serviceable. Indeed, science advances through a dialectic of these two broad research goals.

In the language of statistical tests, the emphasis of exploratory analysis is on avoiding Type II errors (accepting a false null hypothesis), while the emphasis of falsification is on avoiding Type I errors (incorrectly rejecting a true null hypothesis).

In Kuhnian terms, the conflict between theory development and theory-testing may be understood as a contrast between "revolutionary" (paradigm-breaking) science and "normal" (paradigm-constrained) science. Although the terms are perhaps inappropriately apocalyptic, the contrast highlights a recurrent tension in the field of science, where some labor to invent new theories while others labor to test those theories.[16]

---

[16] One way of negotiating this dispute is to examine the specific circumstances of a piece of research to see which sort of approach is warranted. A falsificationist procedure is likely to be justifiable wherever research on a topic is abundant, the principal hypothesis is well defined, experimental methods can be applied, Type I errors are of greater concern than Type II errors, one has reason to be especially concerned about the personal biases and preconceptions of the researchers, a neutral oversight body is available to monitor research on a topic, and research funding is plentiful – in these cases, hypothesis-generation and hypothesis-testing are appropriately segregated, and rigid rules of procedure ought to be applied. Popper, not Feyerabend, should be our guide. And yet, these conditions are often absent – especially in the social sciences. Given this fact, there is little point in dressing up our research as if it fits the requirements of Popperian science. Note that social science journals frequently insist upon the presentation of *a priori* hypotheses ("suggested by the literature"), which will then (the writer characteristically moves into the future tense) be "tested against the data," even when the procedures actually followed in the course of the research are blithely exploratory. Nothing is gained – and a great deal may be lost – by presenting our findings in this misleading fashion. Recognizing this, the disciplines of social science need to do a better job of distinguishing work that is theory-testing from work that is – rightly, and justifiably – theory-generating. Both should be honored, insofar as circumstances (outlined above) warrant.

Finding a research question

Most of this book is devoted to problems of appraisal once a specific hypothesis has been identified. This follows standard practice among methodological texts. However, a few words on the problem of theory development are in order. How does one go about identifying a fruitful research question and, ultimately, a specific research hypothesis? This is the very early exploratory phase, when one quite literally does not know what one is looking for, or at. Arguably, it is the most crucial stage of all. Nothing of interest is likely to emanate from research on topics that are trivial, redundant, or theoretically bland – no matter how strong the research is from a falsificationist perspective.

Methodologists generally leave this task to the realm of metaphor – bells, brainstorms, dreams, flashes, impregnations, light bulbs, showers, sparks, and whatnot. The reason for this lack of attention is perhaps to be found in the fact that beginnings are inherently unformulaic. There are few rules or criteria for uncovering new questions or new hypotheses. Methodologists may feel that there is nothing – nothing scientific at any rate – that they can say about this process. Karl Popper states the matter forthrightly, as usual: "There is no such thing as a logical method of having new ideas," he writes. "Discovery contains 'an irrational element,' or a 'creative intuition.'"[17]

However, saying nothing at all may be worse than saying something unsystematic. The rest of this chapter therefore departs from the format adopted elsewhere. What I have to offer is more in the character of a homily than a framework. It reads like an advice column. I urge the reader to study the tradition, begin where you are, get off your home turf, play with ideas, practice dis-belief, observe empathically, theorize wildly, think ahead, and conduct exploratory analyses. As a result, the chapter is ridden with *shoulds* and *should nots*. I apologize in advance for the rather didactic tone.[18]

My advice is largely commonsensical and by no means comprehensive. It cannot help but reflect my own views and experiences, though I have drawn extensively on the writings of other scholars.[19] Nonetheless, it may help to

---

[17] Quoted in King, Keohane, and Verba (1994: 129).

[18] With regard to my own bona fides, let me note that in this particular area of research ("starting out") I can perhaps claim special authority. Over the past two decades, I have found myself continually starting afresh with new topics, some of which (perhaps inevitably) have turned out to be less enlightening than others.

[19] The literature relevant to this chapter emanates from research on the conjoined subjects of discovery, innovation, and exploration, as well as from advice columns in newsletters and introductory textbooks.

orient those who are setting out on their first journey, or who wish to begin again.

Study the tradition

The question of innovativeness necessarily hinges on the tradition of work that already exists on a subject. This is not a subjective prior; it is one established by a field of scholars working on a topic over many years, and it should be apparent in the published work that they have produced. (If not, the inquiry must be carried out through personal communication with established scholars in a field.)

Consider the state of the field on a topic. What are the frontiers of knowledge? What do we – collectively, as a discipline – know, and what don't we know? Consider also the probable location of this frontier a decade from now, extrapolating from current scholarly trends. What will the cutting-edge be then? Keep in mind that the most active research frontiers are usually moving frontiers; the tradition as it exists today may be quite different when you finish your research. So a better question (though a more difficult one) is, what will the cutting-edge be in a decade?

I doubt if anyone has happened upon a really interesting research topic simply by reading a review of the extant literature. However, this is an efficient method of determining where the state of a field lies and where it might be headed. Be aware that because of the length of time required by the publication process, the most recent work on a subject is usually to be found in conference papers or papers posted on personal web sites. Nowadays, these are easy to locate through search engines. Your first recourse might be Google rather than JSTOR.

In exposing oneself to the literature on a topic one must guard against two common responses. The first is to worship those that have gone before; the second is to summarily dismiss them. Respect the tradition – don't flagellate the forefathers. There is nothing so jejune as a reversal of hierarchies ("They're wrong and I'm right"). But don't be awed by the tradition either. Try stepping

---

Regrettably, this literature is focused mostly on the organizational context of discovery (e.g., by social psychologists and sociologists) and on discovery within the natural sciences, where the concept has its counterpart in the notion of a clear "finding." In the social sciences, where definitive findings are scarce and cumulation more dubious, the concept of discovery carries a more ambiguous meaning. With this caveat, the following works proved useful: Koestler (1964); Luker (2008); McGuire (1997); Mills (1959: 195–226); Oliver (1991); Root-Bernstein (1989); Snyder (2007). See also Abbott (2004); Fleck ([1935] 1979); Freedman (2008); Geddes (2003: 27–45); Hanson (1958); King, Keohane, and Verba (1994: 14–19); Kuhn ([1962] 1970); Langley *et al.* (1987); Most (1990); Root-Bernstein and Root-Bernstein (1999); Useem (1997); Watson (1969). On the creative act of constructing formal models, see Cartwright (1983); Hesse (1966); Lave and March (1975).

outside the categories that are conventionally used to describe and explain a subject. By this I mean not simply arguing against the common wisdom, but also thinking up new questions, new issues, that have not been well explored. Insofar as new theoretical paradigms are "revolutionary," this is what they consist of.

As you peruse the literature, be conscious of what excites you and what bothers you. Which issues are under-explored, or badly understood? Where do you suspect the authorities in a field are wrong? What questions have they left unanswered? What questions do you find yourself asking when you finish reading? Where does this line of research lead? Sometimes, typically in a conclusion or a review article, scholars will reflect self-consciously upon the future direction of research; this, too, can be useful.

In any case, you should not limit your eventual review of the literature to only the most recent publications. Of interest is not only the frontier but the history of a subject. Thus, a complementary strategy is to delve into the "classics" – the founding texts of a field or subfield.[20] This is useful (particularly if you have never done so) because it sometimes prompts one to think about familiar subjects in new ways, because classic works tend to be evocative (and thus raise questions), because a different vocabulary is often employed, and because it is a reminder that some things have, in fact, been done before. This last point is educational in two respects: it warns us that we may be about to reinvent the proverbial wheel and it informs us of ways that perceptions and conclusions about a familiar subject have changed within a discipline (and within society at large) over time. Every subject has an intellectual history and it is worthwhile familiarizing yourself with this history, not merely to find a pithy epigraph but also to inform your analysis of a problem.

As C. Wright Mills began his study of elites, he consulted the works of Lasswell, Marx, Michels, Mosca, Pareto, Schumpeter, Veblen, and Weber.[21] In commenting upon this experience, Mills reports:

I find that they offer three types of statement: (a) from some, you learn directly by restating systematically what the man says on given points or as a whole; (b) some you accept or refute, giving reasons and arguments; (c) others you use as a source of suggestions for your own elaborations and projects. This involves grasping a point and then asking: How can I put this into testable shape, and how can I test it? How can I use this as a center from which to elaborate – as a perspective from which descriptive details emerge as relevant?

---

[20] Snyder (2007).   [21] Mills (1959: 202).

Not every topic is blessed with such a rich heritage; but some are, and there it is worth pausing to read, and to think.

Begin where you are

With questions of method Charles Sanders Peirce points out, "There is only one place from which we ever can start . . . and that is from where we are."[22] The easiest and most intuitive way to undertake a new topic is to build upon what one knows and who one is. This includes one's skills (languages, technical skills), connections, life experiences, and interests.[23]

Hopefully, a chosen topic resonates with your life in some fashion. This is often a source of inspiration and insight, as well as the source from which sustained commitment may be nourished and replenished over the life of a project. C. Wright Mills writes:

You must learn to use your life experience in your intellectual work: continually to examine and interpret it. In this sense craftsmanship is the center of yourself and you are personally involved in every intellectual product upon which you may work. To say that you can "have experience," means, for one thing, that your past plays into and affects your present, and that it defines your capacity for future experience. As a social scientist, you have to control this rather elaborate interplay, to capture what you experience and sort it out; only in this way can you hope to use it to guide and test your reflection, and in the process shape yourself as an intellectual craftsman.[24]

Because the business of social science is to investigate the activities of people, any personal connections we might have to such people may serve as useful points of leverage. The hermeneutic act is eased if one can establish some personal connection – however distant or imaginative – with the group in question.[25]

Sometimes, our connection with a topic is motivated more by ideas than by personal connections. We are naturally drawn to subjects that are either horrifying or uplifting (or both). Indeed, many research projects begin with some notion – perhaps only dimly formulated – about what is wrong with the world. We all have bees in our bonnets and this normative motivation may be vital to our insight into that topic. What real-life problem, relevant to your discipline, bothers you?[26]

---

[22] Kaplan (1964: 86), paraphrasing Charles Sanders Peirce.
[23] Finlay and Gough (2003); Krieger (1991); Mills (1959); Snyder (2007).   [24] Mills (1959: 196).
[25] Gadamer (1975) refers to this as a fusion of horizons – us and theirs (the actors we are attempting to understand).
[26] Gerring and Yesnowitz (2006); Shapiro (2005); Smith (2003).

The desire to redress wrongs also helps to keep social science relevant to the concerns of lay citizens. We all begin, one might say, as citizens, with everyday ("lay") concerns. Over time, we come to attain a degree of distance from our subject, qua scholars. Thus, do the roles of citizen and scholar engage in dialogue with one another (Chapter 14).

Of course, at the end of a project one must have something to say about a topic that goes beyond assertions of right and excoriations of wrong. The topic must be made tractable for scientific inquiry; otherwise, there is no point in approaching it as a scientific endeavor. If one feels that the topic is too close to the heart to reflect upon it dispassionately, then it is probably not a good candidate for study. As a probe, ask yourself whether you would be prepared to publish the results of a study in which your main hypothesis is proven wrong. If you hesitate to answer this question because of normative pre-commitments you should probably settle on another subject.

As a general rule, it is important to undertake questions that one feels are important, but not projects in which one has especially strong moral or psychological predilections for accepting or rejecting the null hypothesis.[27] Thus, one might be motivated to study the role of school vouchers because one is concerned about the quality of education. But one probably should not undertake a study of vouchers in order to prove that they are a good/bad thing.

Get off your home turf

While the previous section emphasized the importance of building upon one's personal profile (skills, connections, druthers), it is also vital for scholars to stray from what is safe, comfortable, and familiar – their home turf.

Consider that the academy is not now, and likely never will be, a representative cross-section of humankind. At present, the denizens of social science are disproportionately white, Anglo-European, and (still, though decreasingly) male. They will probably always be disproportionately privileged in class background. Evidently, if members of these disciplines restrict themselves to topics drawn from their personal experience little attention will be paid to topics relevant to excluded groups, especially those that are less privileged.

The more important point is that advances in knowledge usually come from transgressing familiar contexts. After all, local knowledge is already familiar to those who live it. Whatever value might be added comes from transporting categories, theories, and ways of thinking across contexts, in the hope that new

---

[27] Firebaugh (2008: ch. 1).

perspectives on the familiar will become apparent. A good ethnography, it is sometimes said, renders the exotic familiar *or* the familiar exotic. The same might be said of social science at large. Try to think like a stranger when approaching a topic that seems obvious (from your "home turf" perspective). Likewise, do not be afraid to export categories from your home turf into foreign territory – not willfully, and disregarding all evidence to the contrary, but rather as an operating hypothesis. Sometimes, the foreign-made shoe fits.

Indeed, novel descriptive and causal inferences often arise when an extant concept or theory is transplanted from one area to another. For example, the concept of *corporatism* arose initially in the context of Catholic social theory as an alternative to state socialism. It was later adopted by fascist regimes as a way of legitimating their control over important economic and social actors. More recently, it has been seen as a key to explaining the divergent trajectories of welfare states across the OECD, and for explaining the persistence and resilience of authoritarian rule in the developing world.[28] There are endless ways of adapting old theories to new contexts. Sometimes these transplantations are fruitful; other times, they are not.

Most important, try to maintain a conversation with different perspectives on your subject. What would so-and-so say about *X*? If this does not drive you mad, it may serve as a helpful form of triangulation on your topic.

Another sort of boundary crossing is that which occurs across disciplines, theories, and methods. The trend of the contemporary era seems to be toward ever greater specialization, and to be sure, specialization has its uses. It is difficult to master more than one area of work, given the increasingly technical and specialized techniques and vocabulary developed within each subfield over the past several decades. Making a contribution to a field necessitates a deep familiarity with that field, and this requires a concentrated focus over many years.

Yet it is worth reflecting upon the fact that many of the works that we regard today as path-breaking have been the product of exotic encounters across fields and subfields. Indeed, all fields and subfields were the product of long-ago transgressions. Someone moved outside their comfort zone, and others followed. Note also that the social sciences are not divided up into discrete and well-defined fields. So, try reading inside, *and outside*, your area of training. Talk to people in distant fields. See how they respond when you describe your questions, and your projected research, to them. Beware of cultivating a narrow expertise, for this is apt to lead to work that is theoretically circumscribed or

---

[28] Collier (1995); Schmitter (1974).

mundane. If all academic work is theft of one sort or another, one is well advised to steal from distant sources. Another word for this sort of theft is creativity.

Play with ideas

The literature on invention and discovery – penned by science writers, philosophers of science, and by inventors themselves – is in consensus on one point. Original discoveries are usually not the product of superior brainpower (i.e., the ability to calculate or reason). Robert Root-Bernstein is emphatic:

> Famous scientists aren't any more intelligent than those who aren't famous. [Moreover,] I'm convinced that successful ones aren't right any more often than their colleagues, either. I believe that the architects of science are simply more curious, more iconoclastic, more persistent, readier to make detours, and more willing to tackle bigger and more fundamental problems. Most important, they possess intellectual courage, daring. They work at the edge of their competence; their reach exceeds their grasp . . . Thus, they not only succeed more often and out of all proportion; they also fail more often and on the same scale. Even their failures, however, better define the limits of science than the successes of more conventional and safe scientists, and thus the pioneers better serve science.[29]

The key question, as Root-Bernstein frames it, is "How can one best survive on the edge of ignorance?"[30]

One way of answering this question is suggested by Richard Hofstadter, who describes intellectual life as a counterpoint of *piety* and *playfulness*. The first refers to the somber and dogged search for truth. The second, which saves the enterprise from dogmatism and which may be less obvious, is the intellectual's capacity to play:

> Ideally, the pursuit of truth is said to be at the heart of the intellectual's business, but this credits his business too much and not quite enough. As with the pursuit of happiness, the pursuit of truth is itself gratifying, whereas the consummation often turns out to be elusive. Truth captured loses its glamor; truths long known and widely believed have a way of turning false with time; easy truths are a bore, and too many of them become half-truths. Whatever the intellectual is too certain of, if he is healthily playful, he begins to find unsatisfactory. The meaning of his intellectual life lies not in the possession of truth but in the quest for new uncertainties. Harold Rosenberg summed up this side of the life of the mind supremely well when he said that the intellectual is one who turns answers into questions.

---

[29] Root-Bernstein (1989: 408).   [30] Root-Bernstein (1989: 408).

Echoing Hofstadter's description, one might say that there are two distinct moments in any research project. The first is open-ended, playful; here, a wide variety of different ideas are generated and given a trial run. The second is filled with zeal and piety; here, one grips tightly to a single idea in the quest to develop it into a full-blown theory and test it against some empirical reality. This conforms to the distinction between discovery and appraisal introduced above. Whatever the shortcomings of this dichotomy, there is no question that the academic endeavor requires a crucial shift of attitude at some point in the enterprise. Since we are concerned here with the initial phase, we shall dwell on techniques of playfulness.

Although the art of discovery cannot be taught (at least not in the way that the technique of multiple regression can be taught), it may be helpful to think for a moment about thinking. The act of creation is mysterious; yet there seem to be a few persistent features. Arthur Koestler, synthesizing the work of many writers, emphasizes that discoveries are usually "already there," in the sense of being present in some body of work – though perhaps not the body of work with which it had heretofore been associated. To discover is, therefore, to connect things that had previously been considered separate. To discover is to think *analogically*:

This leads to the paradox that the more original a discovery the more obvious it seems afterwards. The creative act is not an act of creation in the sense of the Old Testament. It does not create something out of nothing; it uncovers, selects, re-shuffles, combines, synthesizes already existing facts, ideas, faculties, skills. The more familiar the parts, the more striking the new whole. Man's knowledge of the changes of the tides and the phases of the moon is as old as his observation that apples fall to earth in the ripeness of time. Yet the combination of these and other equally familiar data in Newton's theory of gravity changed mankind's outlook on the world.[31]

What frame of mind does this require? How does one think analogically? This trick seems to have something to do with the capacity to "relinquish conscious controls," to block out the academic superego that inhibits new thoughts by punishing transgressions against the tradition.[32] Above all, one must feel free to make mistakes:

Just as in the dream the codes of logical reasoning are suspended, so "thinking aside" is a temporary liberation from the tyranny of over-precise verbal concepts, of the axioms and prejudices engrained in the very texture of specialized ways of thought. It allows the mind to discard the strait-jacket of habit, to shrug off apparent contradictions, to

---

[31] Koestler (1964: 119–120).   [32] Koestler (1964: 169).

un-learn and forget – and to acquire, in exchange, a greater fluidity, versatility, and gullibility. This rebellion against constraints which are necessary to maintain the order and discipline of conventional thought, but an impediment to the creative leap, is symptomatic both of the genius and the crank; what distinguishes them is the intuitive guidance which only the former enjoys.[33]

It might be added that what also distinguishes the genius and the crank is that the former has mastered the tradition of work on a subject. The genius' liminal moments are creative because they take place on a foundation of knowledge. In order to forget, and thence recombine features of a problem, one must first know.

The analogy of discovery with a dream-like trance, although it borders on silliness, may not be far off. Koestler writes:

The dreamer constantly bisociates – innocently as it were – frames of reference which are regarded as incompatible in the waking state; he drifts effortlessly from matrix to matrix, without being aware of it; in his inner landscape, the bisociative techniques of humour and discovery are reflected upside down, like trees in a pond. The most fertile region seems to be the marshy shore, the borderland between sleep and full awakening – where the matrices of disciplined thought are already operating but have not yet sufficiently hardened to obstruct the dreamlike fluidity of imagination.[34]

It has often been suggested that the mind works semi-consciously on problems once they have been identified, and when sufficient motivation is present. At this stage, one becomes possessed by a question.

Practice dis-belief

One cannot think without words, but sometimes one cannot think well with them either. Sometimes, ordinary language serves to constrain thought-patterns, reifying phenomena that are scarcely there. When we define, Edmund Burke commented, "we seem in danger of circumscribing nature within the bounds of our own notions."[35] Language suggests, for example, that where a referential term exists a coherent class of entities also exists, and where two referential terms exist there are two empirically differentiable classes of entities. Sometimes this is true, and sometimes it is not. Just because we have a word for "social movement" does not mean that there are actually phenomena out there that are similar to each other and easily differentiated from other phenomena. Ditto for "social capital," "interest group," and virtually every other key concept in the

---

[33] Koestler (1964: 210).   [34] Koestler (1964: 210).   [35] Quoted in Robinson (1954: 6).

social science lexicon. Words do not always carve nature at its joints. Sometimes, they are highly arbitrary ("constructed"). *A fortiori*, just because we have a word for some phenomenon does not mean that cases of this phenomenon all stem from the same cause, or the same set of causes. It is not even clear that the same causal factors will be *relevant* for all members of the so-named set of phenomena.

The reader might respond that, surely, concepts are defined the way they are because they are useful for some purposes. Precisely. But it follows that these same concepts may not be useful for *other* purposes. And since one's objective at this stage of the research game is to think unconventionally, it is important to call into question conventional language. For heuristic purposes, try assuming a nominalist perspective: words are merely arbitrary lexical containers. As an exercise, put brackets around all your key terms ("social movement"). Try out different visions; see if any of them are persuasive. (This is a good example, incidentally, of the differing criteria applicable to the discovery and appraisal moments of science. A nominalist perspective on concepts is problematic when the writer turns to the task of formalizing his or her research. Here, the usual counsel is to *avoid* neologism, unless absolutely required [Chapter 6].) Another technique for thinking anew about a subject is to consider the terms that foreign lexicons or ancient lexicons impose upon a concept; often they will have different connotations or suggest different distinctions among phenomena.

A parallel skepticism must be extended to numbers, which also naturalize phenomena that may, or may not, go together in the suggested fashion. Here, the claim is more complicated. First, the use of a number is explicitly linked to a dimension – for example, temperature, GDP, number of auto accidents – that is thought to be relevant in some way. Moreover, the imposition of a numerical scale presupposes a particular type of relationship between phenomena with different scores on that variable – nominal, ordinal, interval, or ratio (Chapter 7). But is it *really*? More broadly, is this the dimension that matters (for understanding the topic in question)? Or are there other dimensions, perhaps less readily quantified, that provide more accurate or insightful information?

Another sort of conventional wisdom is contained in paradigm-cases. These are cases that, by virtue of their theoretical or everyday prominence, help to define a phenomenon: the way Italy defines fascism; the Holocaust defines genocide; the United States defines individualism; Sweden defines the welfare state; and the Soviet Union (for many years) defined socialism. Paradigm-cases exist in virtually every realm of social science inquiry. They often provide good points of entry into a topic because they are overloaded with attributes; they operate in this respect like ideal-types (Chapter 6). Yet because they anchor thinking on these topics, they are also thought-constraining. And because they are also apt to be somewhat unusual – for example, extreme – examples of the phenomenon in question, they may present misleading depictions of that phenomenon.

With respect to words, numbers, and paradigm-cases – not to mention full-blown theories – it is important to maintain a skeptical attitude. Perhaps they are true and useful, perhaps only partially so, or only for certain purposes. In order to test their utility, try adopting the Socratic guise of complete ignorance (perhaps better labeled as thoroughgoing skepticism). Once having assumed this pose, you are then free to pose naive questions of sources, of experts, and of informants. It is a canny strategy and can be extraordinarily revealing – particularly when "obvious" questions cannot be readily answered, or are answered in unexpected ways.

Observe empathically

One technique of discovery is empathic, or (to invoke the philosophical jargon) hermeneutic.[36] Here, one employs observational techniques to enter into the world of the actors who are engaged in some activity of interest – playing ball, drafting a bill, murdering opponents, casting a vote, and so forth – in order to understand their perspective on the phenomenon. Of course, this is easier when the actors are our contemporaries and can be studied directly (i.e., ethnographically). It is harder, and yet sometimes more revealing, if the actions took place long ago or are removed from direct observation and must be reconstructed. In any case, non-obvious perceptions require interpretation, and this interpretation should be grounded in an assessment of how actors may have viewed their own actions.

Consider that the process of understanding begins with an ability to re-create or re-imagine the experiences of those actors whose ideas and behavior we wish to make sense of. Somehow a link must be formed between our experiential horizons and the horizons of the group we wish to study. This may involve a form of role-playing (what would I do in situation X if I were person Y?). Some level of sympathy with one's subjects is probably essential for gaining insight into a phenomenon. This may be difficult to muster if the subject is grotesque. No one wants to empathize with Nazis. But the hermeneutic challenge remains; some way must be found to enter into the lives and perceptions of these

---

[36] Gadamer (1975).

important historical actors in order to explain their actions, however strange and repellant.

Although those who identify with the interpretivist label are not always theoretically inclined, we may grant that many of those who identify as "theorists" have at one time or another employed interpretive techniques (on the sly). In any case, this technique need not be monopolized by a few specialist practitioners ("interpretivists," "ethnographers," etc.). It is a game we can all play – indeed, must play, if we are to be successful social scientists.

Theorize wildly

Rather than working single-mindedly toward One Big Idea, you might consider the benefits of working simultaneously along several tracks. This way, you avoid becoming overly committed to a single topic too early. You can also compare different topics against one another, evaluating their strengths and weaknesses. "Just have lots of ideas and throw away the bad ones," advises Linus Pauling.[37]

At the same time, you should do your best to maintain a record of your ideas as you go along.[38] Take a look at this idea diary every so often and see which projects you find yourself coming back to, obsessing about, inquiring about. The objective should be to keep your mind as open as possible for as long as possible (given the practicalities of life and scholarly deadlines). "Let your mind become a moving prism catching light from as many angles as possible."[39]

Historians of natural science identify productive moments of science with the solving of anomalies – features of the world that do not comport comfortably with existing theories.[40] If these anomalies can be solved in a more than *ad hoc* manner, the frontiers of knowledge are pushed forward. Perhaps even a new "paradigm" of knowledge will be created.

One may question whether social science is ripe with theoretically tractable anomalies. Some would say that it exists entirely of anomalies; there are no unsolved interstices to fill, only a deep abyss of highly stochastic behavior that is resistant to theorizing of any sort. It seems clear that most social science fields are not – or not yet – in the realm of Kuhnian normal science. Still, we focus our energies, quite rightly, on areas that are thought to be less well explained. Whether these are understood as anomalies or as "areas of deeper-than-usual ignorance" hardly matters for present purposes.

[37] Quoted in Root-Bernstein (1989: 409).   [38] Mills (1959: 196).   [39] Mills (1959: 214).
[40] Kuhn ([1962] 1970); Lakatos (1978); Laudan (1977).

Another technique for theorizing wildly is to juxtapose things that do not seem to fit naturally together. Theorizing often consists of dis-associating and re-associating. One version of this is to examine a familiar terrain and think about what it resembles. What is "*X*" an example of? Charles Ragin refers to this as "casing" a subject.[41] Another tactic is to examine several diverse terrains in order to perceive similarities. (Can colonialism, federalism, and corporatism all be conceptualized as systems of "indirect rule"?[42]) A third version is to examine a familiar terrain with the aim of recognizing a new principle of organization. Linnaeus famously suggested that animals should be classified on the basis of their bone structures, a new principle of classification that turned out to be extraordinarily fecund.[43] In the realm of social science, scholars have provided organizational schemes for political parties, bureaucracies, welfare states, and other social phenomena – though few, it must be noted, have proven as fruitful or as enduring as the Linnaean. Of course, a reorganization of knowledge by way of classification need not be eternal or ubiquitous in order to prove useful for certain purposes. Each re-classification may have distinct uses.

A third technique for loosening the theoretical wheels is to push a conventional idea to its logical extreme. That is, consider an explanation that seems to work for a particular event or in a particular context. (It may be your idea, or someone else's.) Now push that idea outward to other settings. Does it still work? What sort of adjustments are necessary to make it work? Or consider the logical ramifications of a theory – if it were fully implemented. What would the theory seem to require?

Theories are tested when they are pushed to their limits, when they are tried out in very different contexts. Root-Bernstein observes that this strategy leads, at the very least, to an investigation of the boundaries of an idea, a useful thing to know. Alternatively, it may help us to reformulate a theory in ways that allow it to travel more successfully, that is, to increase its breadth. A third possibility, perhaps the most exciting, is that it may lead to a new theory that explains the new empirical realm.[44]

In theorizing wildly, it is important to keep a list of all possible explanations that one has run across in the literature, or intuited. As part of this canvas, one might consider some of the more general models of human behavior, for example, individual (aka rational) choice, exchange, adaptation (aka evolution), diffusion, and so forth.[45] Sometimes, these abstract models have applications to very specific problems that might not be immediately apparent. (How might the

---

[41] Ragin (1992).   [42] Gerring *et al.* (2011).   [43] Linsley and Usinger (1959).
[44] Root-Bernstein (1989: 413).   [45] Lave and March (1975).

topic of romance be understood as an exchange? As an adaptation? As a product of diffusion?)

Once achieved, this list of possible explanations for phenomenon Y can then be rearranged and decomposed (perhaps some propositions are subsets of others). Recall that theoretical work often involves recombining extant explanations in new ways. Your list of potential explanations also comprises the set of rival hypotheses that you will be obliged to refute, mitigate, and/or control for (empirically) in your work. So it is important that it be as comprehensive as possible.

In order to figure out how to correctly model complex interrelationships it is often helpful to draw pictures. (If one is sufficiently fluent in graphic design, this may be handled on a computer screen. For the rest of us, pencil and paper are probably the best expedients.) Laying out ideas with boxes and arrows, or perhaps with Venn diagrams or decision trees, allows one to illustrate potential relationships in a more free-flowing way than is possible with prose or math. One can "think" abstractly on paper without falling prey to the constraints of words and numbers. It is also a highly synoptic format, allowing one to fit an entire argument, in all (or most) of its complexity, onto a single sheet or wallboard.

Think ahead

All elements of the research process are intimately connected. This means that there is no such thing as a good topic if that topic is not joined to a good theory and a workable research design. So, the choice of a "topic" turns out to be more involved than it first appears. Of course, all the elements that make for a successful piece of research are unlikely to fall into place at once. And yet one is obliged to wrestle with them, even – one might say, especially – at the very outset.

Recalling the elements of your topic – containing, let us say, a theory, a set of phenomena, and a possible research design – it is vital to maintain a degree of fluidity among all these parts until such time as you can convince yourself that you have achieved the best possible fit. Beware of premature closure. At the same time, to avoid endless cycling it may be helpful to identify that element of your topic to which you feel most committed, that is, that which is likely to make the greatest contribution to scholarship. If this can be identified, it will provide an anchor in this process of continual readjustment.

Consider the initial decision of a topic as an investment in the future. As with any investment, the pay-off depends upon lots of things falling into place over subsequent years. One can never anticipate all the potential difficulties. But the more one can "game" this process, the better the chance of a pay-off when the research is completed. And the better the chance that the research will be completed at all. (Really bad ideas are often difficult to bring to fruition; the more they advance, the more obstacles they encounter.)

Although the prospect may seem daunting, one is obliged to think forward at the "getting started" stage of research. Try to map out how your idea might work: what sort of theory will eventuate, what sort of research design, and so forth. If everything works out as anticipated, what will the completed thesis/ book/article look like? (This brings us to the topics entertained in the rest of the book, that is, what *are* good concepts, descriptive inferences, causal inferences, and research designs?)

An obvious question to consider is what "results" a study is likely to generate. Regardless of the type of study undertaken there will presumably be some encounter with the empirical world, and hence some set of findings. Will the evidence necessary to test a theory, or generate a theory, be available? Will the main hypothesis be borne out?

Sometimes, the failure to reject a null hypothesis means that the researcher has very little to show for his or her research. Conventional wisdom has prevailed. Other times, the failure to prove a hypothesis can be quite enlightening.[46] Sometimes, a topic is so new, or a research design so much more compelling than others that came before, that *any* finding is informative. This is ideal from the perspective of the scholar's investment of time and energy, as it cannot fail to pay off.

In any case, it may be helpful to inquire of those who know a subject intimately (experts, key informants) what they think you will find if you pursue your projected line of research. What is their best hunch? And how would they respond to a failure to reject the null hypothesis? Would it be publishable? Would the *rejection* of your null hypothesis be publishable? This is an even more important question, and it is not always apparent to the novice researcher. That which seems novel to you may seem less novel to those who have labored in a field for many decades. And, by the same token, that which seems obvious to you may be surprising to others. Thus, you are well advised to market-test various findings. Consider how your anticipated findings might be situated within the literature on a topic. How will they be perceived? What will be their value-added? Will they be considered more compelling than other extant work

---

[46] This raises the question of how one ought to define a "null" hypothesis; but let us leave this matter in abeyance.

on the subject? Will they stand the test of current scholarship and the test of future scholarship (the "test of time")?

In test-driving your idea you should also keep a close eye on yourself. See if your oral presentation of the project changes as you explain it to friends and colleagues. At what point do you feel most confident, or most uncertain? When do you feel as if you are bull-shitting? These are important signals with respect to the strengths and weaknesses of your proposal. Indeed, the process of presenting – aside from any concrete feedback you receive – may force you to reconsider issues that were not initially apparent.

Conduct exploratory analyses

When the time is right, consider conducting an exploratory probe. This should be constructed so as to be as efficient as possible – requiring the least expenditure of time, energy, and money. You need to get a feel for your subject, and what the data might say; there is no pretense of drawing firm conclusions. Sometimes, the best way to think through a proposal is to implement the idea in a schematic fashion.

One time-honored approach is the exploratory case study, enabling one to gain more in-depth knowledge of one or a few cases that are thought to exemplify key features of a topic. Here, one finds a number of (more or less well-known) varieties.[47] A *typical* case is one that exhibits traits that are deemed to be highly representative of the phenomenon of interest. It may be useful as a clue to what is going on within other similar cases. An *extreme* case is one that exhibits an extreme (or rare) value on a relevant (X or Y) parameter. When understood against the backdrop of "normal" cases (lying nearer to the mean), an extreme case offers supreme variation on the parameter of interest; this may offer insights into what is going on across the larger population. A sample of *diverse* cases are those that exhibit a range of variation on one more or the relevant (X, Y, or X/Y) parameters. With only a small set of cases, this provides a way of exploring all the available variation that a larger population offers. A *deviant* case is one that exhibits an unexpected outcome, according to some set of background assumptions. This is commonly used to open up new avenues of inquiry, a way of identifying anomalies. A *most-similar* sample of cases have similar background characteristics, but exhibit

---

[47] Gerring (2007: ch. 5).

different outcomes along some parameter of theoretical interest. This allows the researcher to generate hypotheses about the possible causes of an outcome that varies across otherwise similar cases.[48]

Another exploratory approach allows one to probe a larger sample of cases in a more superficial fashion. The researcher might begin with an existing dataset (to which additional variables of interest can be added). Or the researcher may try to construct his or her own "truth-table," focusing upon a small number of cases and variables of interest. Suppose one is attempting to determine why some countries in sub-Saharan Africa have democratized while others have not in the decades since independence. One would begin by coding the dependent variable (autocracy/democracy), and proceed to add possibly relevant causal factors – economic growth, urbanization, landlocked status, colonial history, and so forth. Some of these factors might be binary, while others could be coded continuously or reduced to a binary format (e.g., high/low). Some of these factors are likely to be easy to code ("objective"), while others may involve considerable judgment on the part of the coder ("subjective"). In any case, this simple data-reduction technique allows one to incorporate a large number of hypotheses and to eye-ball their fit with the evidence across a small- or medium-sized sample.

The key point of these adventures in data exploration is to reveal new hypotheses and to expose one's hunches to preliminary tests, as quickly as possible. Do not be afraid to deal in stylized facts – rough guesstimates about the reality under consideration. More systematic testing procedures can wait for a later stage of the process. Data exploration should be understood as a series of plausibility probes.[49]

Of course, the point at which theory exploration segues into theory-testing is never entirely clear-cut. Any method of exploration is also, to some degree, a method of testing, and vice versa. The expectation, in any case, is that once a key hypothesis has been identified it will be subjected to more stringent tests than were employed in its discovery. The emphasis of research shifts subtly but importantly from avoiding Type II errors (failing to reject a false null hypothesis) to avoiding Type I errors (incorrectly rejecting a true null hypothesis), as discussed.

---

[48] These varied case-selection strategies can be implemented in qualitative (informal) or quantitative (formalized) ways. The latter requires a large sample of potential cases and relevant data on the parameters of interest. Statistical techniques for selecting one or a few cases from a large sample are explored in Gerring (2007: ch. 5).

[49] Eckstein (1975).

Concluding thoughts on beginnings

Published work in the social sciences presents a misleading appearance of order and predictability. The author begins by outlining a general topic or research question, then states a general theory, and from thence to the specific hypothesis that will be tested and his or her chosen research design. Finally, the evidence is presented and discussed, and concluding thoughts are offered.

This is nothing at all like the progress of most research, which is, by comparison, circuitous and unpredictable – hardly ever following a step-by-step walk down the ladder of abstraction. One reason for this is that knowledge in the social sciences is not neatly parceled into distinct research areas, each with specific and stable questions, theories, and methods. Instead, it is characterized by a high degree of open-endedness – in questions, theories, and methods.

Another factor is the circularity of the enterprise. Each element of social science – the research question, theory, hypothesis, key concepts, and research design – is interdependent. This is because each element is defined in terms of all the others. Thus, any adjustment in one element is likely to require an adjustment all around. As soon as I change my theory I may also have to change my research design, and vice versa. There is no Archimedean point.

This means that there are many points of entry. One might begin with a general topic, a research question, a key concept, a general theory, a specific hypothesis, a compelling anomaly, an event, a research venue (e.g., a site, archive, or dataset), a method of analysis, and so forth. Accordingly, some research is problem- or question-driven, some research is theory-driven, some research is method-driven, and other research is phenomenon-driven (motivated by the desire to understand a particular event or set of events). These are obviously quite different styles of research – even though, at the end of the day, each study must be held accountable to the same methodological criteria (summarized in Table 1.1).

Once begun, the correct procedure is difficult to diagram in a series of temporally discrete steps – unless one imagines hopping to-and-fro and back-and-forth in a rather frenetic fashion. Empirical investigation is necessarily contingent on pre-formed concepts and theories, as well as our general notions of the world; yet further investigation may alter these notions in unpredictable ways. In so doing, we revise our conception of what we are studying. In this respect, social science offers a good example of the so-called hermeneutic circle.[50]

---

[50] Hoy (1982).

To reiterate, there is no right or wrong place to start. All that matters is where you end up. And yet, where one ends up has a lot to do with where one starts out, so it is not incidental. Scholars are rightly wary of the consequences of choosing a bad topic – one that, let us say, promises few interesting surprises, has little theoretical or practical significance, or offers insufficient evidence to demonstrate a proposition about the world. No matter how well executed that research might be, little can be expected from it.

Moreover, changing topics midstream is costly. Once one has developed expertise in an area it is difficult to re-tool. Research, like many things in life, is heavily path-dependent. For this reason, one should anticipate living with one's choice of topic for a very long time. A dissertation will not only absorb your life over the course of its duration but also, in all likelihood, for decades to come – perhaps for the rest of your life. Indeed, many scholars continue to be defined, for better and for worse, by their first published work. So, the question of choosing a topic is by no means trivial. A great deal is at stake.

Because the selection of a good topic is difficult, careful deliberation is in order. Note that the difficulty of topic selection is a product of the fact that everyone is looking for the same thing: fruitful topics for research, the next breaking wave. This means that the low-hanging fruit is probably already picked. Accordingly, one should not expect a great and heretofore unexplored topic to fall into one's lap. Even if it so happens that one's first hunch is correct it will take some time before the promise of this topic is fully apparent. Many initial probes will have to be followed through and an extensive literature review must be undertaken in order to confirm that the topic is truly innovative.

In this arduous process, advice is welcome – from friends, family, advisors, experts in the field. Solicit all the feedback you can. But make sure that, at the end of the day, you are comfortable with the choice you make. It should represent your considered judgment.

This is likely to require some time. How much, it is difficult to say. Finding a topic is a process, not an event. It doesn't happen all of a sudden. It starts as soon as one takes up scholarship and transposes gradually into the research itself. There is no clear beginning or end-date. Although the writer may be required to compose a formal grant proposal or prospectus this usually turns out, in retrospect, to be an arbitrary marker within the ongoing life of a project.

Many scholars are not prepared for the agonizing and time-consuming task of head-scratching (aka chin-rubbing, forelock-tugging – choose your metaphor), which seems to run counter to the injunction to publish, publish, publish (quickly, quickly, quickly). Once upon a time, life in the academy was extolled as a *via contemplativa*. Nowadays, one is struck by the fact that there is a great deal of publishing but relatively little sustained cogitation. Most of our time is spent in the implementation of projects. We secure funding, oversee staff, construct surveys, design experiments, peruse evidence, write up results, all the while maintaining a frenetic email correspondence. Only in brief moments do we allow ourselves the luxury of thinking deeply about a subject. By this, I mean thinking in truly open-ended ways, ways that might lead to new insights.

At what point should one make a commitment to a research question and a specific hypothesis? How does one know when to reach for closure? Evidently, there are dangers associated with precipitous decisions and with decisions that are too long delayed.

Consider this familiar scenario, related by Kristin Luker. A student ("you") enters his or her advisor's office with a hazily framed idea of what he or she would like to work on. The advisor demands to know what the hypothesis is.

If you flounder around trying to answer this question, he or she may follow up by asking what your independent and dependent variables are. Even more basically, he or she will ask what your research question is. You just go blank, feeling like a rabbit trapped on the roadway with the headlights bearing down on you, as you try desperately to explain what's so interesting about, say, privatized water, or rising rates of imprisonment in America, or adolescent sexuality. When you and your advisor part at the end of the time allotted to you, more likely than not, you part in mutual frustration.[51]

In this setting, the student is probably not ready to identify a research question, much less a specific hypothesis. It is still a relevant question, and the advisor is obliged to raise it. However, in the haste to answer this question in a satisfactory way – and escape from the scene with self-esteem intact – the student may commit to a question that is not, in the long run, very fruitful. The same thing happens with arbitrary deadlines imposed by the academic calendar – a conference to which one has committed to present, a prospectus defense date, and so forth. This is the Scylla of premature closure.

On the other extreme, one encounters the danger of belated closure. Luker continues:

Suppose on the other hand that you have an easygoing advisor, and you are permitted to go off "into the field" ... without answering his or her questions. An even more dreaded fate may well await you, worse than being tortured into producing independent and dependent variables on demand for your advisor, namely ... the Damnation of the Ten Thousand Index Cards or the Ten Thousand Entries into your computer-assisted note-taking system. The Damnation of the Ten Thousand Whatevers happens

---

[51] Luker (2008: 18).

to unwitting graduate students who have spent many years ... gathering data without having stumbled upon exactly what it was that they were looking for when they first went out to that fabulous field site (... or library ...). There they sit, doomed and damned, in front of the computer screen, wondering how to make a story out of the ten thousand entries. Or, worse yet, they finally do stumble onto a story as they pore yet again over the ten thousand entries, but the single piece of information (or the body of data) which they need to really nail the point beyond quibbles is back in the field and they didn't know they needed it, or it's disappeared, or they can't afford to go back. Or they do find it, and realize that eighty percent of the data they have gathered is irrelevant ... An in-between outcome ... is that you may actually find the research question, come up with the data that you need to make the case, and have a compelling and ... well-written story to tell. The only problem is that you have eighteen boxes of data left over, and the entire enterprise took you at least four years longer than it should have.[52]

To describe this sort of disaster, Luker quotes a line from Pauline Bart: "Data, data everywhere and not a thought to think."[53]

In our own research – and regardless of whether we are just starting out as students of social science or have spent decades in the business – we must avoid the Scylla of premature closure as well as the Charybdis of belated closure. Neither will serve the cause of science, or our own careers. Push yourself to find a research question as quickly as possible, but don't settle on something that doesn't seem meaningful to you or to your intended audience.

[52] Luker (2008: 19).   [53] Luker (2008: 19).

3 Arguments

A: (*Knock*)

B: Come in.

A: Ah, Is this the right room for an argument?

B: I told you once.

A: No you haven't.

B: Yes I have.

A: When?

B: Just now.

A: No you didn't.

B: Yes I did.

A: You didn't

B: I did!

A: You didn't!

B: I'm telling you I did!

A: You did not!!

B: Oh, I'm sorry, just one moment. Is this a five minute argument or the full half hour?

Monty Python, "The Argument Clinic"

Argumentation in contemporary social science descends from the ancient art of rhetoric and the equally ancient science of logic. A complete argument consists of a set of key concepts, testable hypotheses (aka propositions), and perhaps a formal model or larger theoretical framework. A *causal* argument should also contain an explication of causal mechanisms (Chapter 8). An argument is what we speculate might be true about the world; it engages the realm of theorizing.

Sometimes, it is important to distinguish among arguments lying at different levels of abstraction. The most abstract may be referred to as *macro-level theories*, *theoretical frameworks*, or *paradigms*. Examples would include structural functionalism, modernization theory, exchange theory, symbolic interactionism, or conflict theory. At a slightly less abstract level one finds *meso-level theories* or *models*. And at the most specific level one speaks of *hypotheses*, *inferences*, *micro-level theories*, or *propositions*, which are assumed to be directly testable. (*Explanations* may apply to any level.) So, for example, work on the topic of school vouchers might include a general theory about why consumer choice enhances the educational process, a formal model incorporating various elements of that theory, and a specific hypothesis or set of hypotheses regarding the impact of a voucher-based intervention on educational attainment.

Granted, varying levels of abstraction are not always easy to discern. One person's abstraction is another person's specificity. Historical sociologists and demographers would understand abstraction quite differently. Moreover, the terms defined above are loosely applied. In the vouchers example sketched above, for instance, the general theory might be referred to as a model, the hypotheses might be accompanied by additional models (explaining the workings of each one), and virtually every element might be referred to as a theory.

Note that the word *theory* may imply a high level of abstraction or may simply indicate that there is a degree of speculation associated with an argument. In the latter sense, *theory* is synonymous with *proposition* or *hypothesis*. Theories are characteristically associated with causal inference – but not always.

Evidently, there is a great deal of terminological fluidity in this semantic field. Consequently, I shall not insist upon fine distinctions, and terms such as explanation, hypothesis, inference, model, proposition, theory will be employed interchangeably in the text. All are *arguments*, that is, assertions about the nature of some empirical reality.

Our interest in social science arguments lies not in their substance but rather in their methodological properties. What makes an argument useful for social science? What is a good argument? And what, by contrast, is a bad (unhelpful) argument? These questions are treated fleetingly in most methodology texts. Often, they are dismissed as a matter of philosophy.[1] And yet they turn out to play a critical role in social science inquiry.

I shall try to show here that all social science arguments strive for *truth, precision, generality, boundedness, parsimony, coherence, commensurability,* and *relevance*, as summarized in Table 3.1. Naturally, these desiderata mean slightly different things when applied in the context of descriptive and causal arguments. However, they are similar enough to be introduced together. In later sections of the book we explore the distinguishing characteristics of these two styles of argumentation (see Parts II and III).

---

[1] Brief lists of scientific desiderata appear occasionally in the literature on social science methodology (e.g., Laudan 1996: 132), but are rarely developed. Authors appear to place rather little weight on this approach to the subject.

Table 3.1 Arguments: general criteria

1. **Truth** (accuracy, validity, veracity)
   Is it true?
2. **Precision** (specificity)
   Is it precise?
3. **Generality** (breadth, domain, population, range, scope)
   How broad is the scope? How many phenomena does a theory describe/explain?
4. **Boundedness** (scope-conditions)
   How well bounded is it?
5. **Parsimony** (concision, economy, Occam's razor, reduction, simplicity)
   How parsimonious is it? How many assumptions are required?
6. **Coherence** (clarity, consistency; *antonym:* ambiguity)
   How coherent is it?
7. **Commensurability** (consilience, harmony, logical economy, theoretical utility; *antonym:* adhocery)
   How well does it cumulate with other inferences? Does it advance logical economy in a field?
8. **Relevance** (everyday importance, significance)
   How relevant is it to issues of concern to citizens and policymakers?

Truth

Arguments strive to be *true*. This is the first and foremost virtue of a social science proposition, for true arguments are generally more useful than false arguments. Granted, sometimes false inferences can achieve good things, but we do not think of social science as having any value except insofar as its inferences are by and large true. If science is untrue, there is little point to the enterprise.

Yet the issue of truth is not so straightforward as it may at first appear. First, one must bear in mind that the truth of an argument is usually understood by reference to the argument itself: that claim, or set of claims, that are made about the world. Scholars pick out specific issues to contest. They do not claim to represent the whole truth about any subject, much less about all subjects.

The scholar's chosen argument may be framed in a "positive" or "negative" way. The argument "Theory A is wrong" is a negative argument, which may be true or false. It is the author of the argument who decides the terms by which he or she will argue, that is, what the baseline or *null hypothesis* is, against which the argument will be framed.

There are also peripheral dimensions of an argument involving the boundaries of an inference (its scope or population), the mechanisms of a causal theory, and other issues associated with particular styles of descriptive and causal argumentation (as reviewed below and in subsequent chapters). Each may be judged true or false. It follows that an argument may be true in some respects and untrue in others.

Precision

A second question about any argument is its degree of *precision*. The more precise a claim, the more useful it is, in the sense of providing more information about a putative phenomenon. It also, not coincidentally, makes the argument more falsifiable.[2] If you are unconvinced by this, consider the obverse: a perfectly imprecise statement about the world, for example, "Municipal governments in Africa are democratic, autocratic, or somewhere in between." This sort of statement excludes no logical possibility, since all polities must be classifiable somewhere on this spectrum. At the limit, a statement of no precision whatsoever says absolutely nothing about the world, and therefore is completely unfalsifiable.

Of course, the imposition of greater precision may impose costs along other dimensions. In particular, precision generally varies inversely with the probable accuracy of an argument. The greater the precision, the less likely an argument is to be true. Thus, if we might modify our hypothetical example to read "65 percent of the municipal governments in Africa are democratic" we are less likely to be proven correct. There are many opportunities to fail.

The relative precision or imprecision of an argument may be expressed in a variety of ways. Qualifiers for precision (e.g., "exactly") or imprecision ("usually," "roughly," "sort of," "generally," "may," "approximately," "tends to") may be inserted in the formulation of an argument. Alternatively, a statement might be quantified ("65 percent"), and this number may be represented with a number of decimal places ("65.000 percent"), corresponding to the degree of precision associated with the estimate. Another technique is the confidence interval, the interval around an estimate that indicates the range of values that estimate is likely to take (at a given level of certainty, say 95 percent).

Generality

If the fundamental purpose of social science is to tell us about the world, then it stands to reason that an inference informing us about many phenomena is, by virtue of this fact, more useful than an inference pursuant to only a few phenomena. I will refer to this desideratum as *generality* (aka breadth, generalizability, or

---

[2] Indeed, precision and falsifiability are invoked as virtual synonyms by Popper ([1934] 1968).

scope). One wishes for a theory to encompass as many phenomena as possible. The more one can explain with a given argument (*ceteris paribus*) the more powerful that argument is. Theories of great breadth tell us more about the world by explaining larger portions of that world. Thus, a theory of democracy that satisfactorily describes or explains regime types across all nation-states is superior to one that applies to only a single region of the world or a single historical epoch. And a theory or theoretical framework describing or explaining different types of phenomena is more useful than one pertaining to only a single outcome.

Note that the power of Marxism derives from its application to a wide range of social behavior; it is not just a theory of revolution or a theory of economic behavior. The fact that members of every social science tribe find recourse to some version of Marxist theory testifies to the extraordinary breadth of this framework. By contrast, Malinowski notes in his anthropological classic, *Argonauts of the Western Pacific*:

> There is no value in isolated facts for science, however striking and novel they might seem. Genuine scientific research differs from mere curio-hunting in that the latter runs after the quaint, singular and freakish – the craving for the sensational and the mania of collecting providing its twofold stimulus. Science on the other hand has to analyse and classify facts in order to place them in an organic whole, to incorporate them in one of the systems in which it tries to group the various aspects of reality.[3]

While perhaps too strongly argued (surely, sometimes we are interested in particular outcomes), it may be agreed that breadth is superior, *ceteris paribus*, to narrowness.

Granted, researchers are differently enamored of generality as an analytic goal. Some work in the social sciences, usually with a historical theme, focuses on single events, for example, the decline of the English aristocracy, the French Revolution, the First World War, or the fall of the Soviet Union. Even so, this sort of work is not entirely heedless of generality. First, each of these events may have vast implications for the subsequent development of individual countries and/or for the world at large. In explaining *X*, one may also, by extension, be explaining other phenomena. Second, each of these events may be regarded as a case study of a more general phenomenon. Again, one is shedding light on a much larger population.[4] And finally, macrosocial events like revolutions may encompass hundreds, if not thousands, of micro events.

---

[3] Malinowski ([1922] 1984: 509). See also Easton (1953: 55); Kincaid (1990); Lakatos (1978: 33); Laudan (1977); Levey (1996); McIntyre (1996); Przeworski and Teune (1970: 4); Scriven (1962); Skyrms (1980), and the work of other naturalistically inclined scholars like Carl Hempel and Ernest Nagel.

[4] Gerring (2007).

Considerable reduction is required in order to reach any conclusion about a war, revolution, or a change in class structure. To generalize about the French Revolution is to generalize across a large chunk of reality. In these respects, even the most idiographic historian would probably not wish to absolve themselves of the demand for generality.

The most important point is that while generality is an acknowledged goal of science, parochialism is not. Indeed, what idiographically inclined writers cringe at in work of great breadth is usually not breadth *per se* but rather the sacrifice of other virtues, for example, truth or precision. Thus, my claim for generality, if couched in *ceteris paribus* terms (as all criteria are), may be viewed as a consensual norm within the social science disciplines (with the possible exception of anthropology, which has moved toward the humanities in recent decades).

However one views generality as a normative ideal, it will be seen that the criterion is always a matter of degree. No argument is unlimited in scope. (Boundary conditions are implicit in the terms contained in any hypothesis, descriptive or causal.) Likewise, few arguments in the social sciences pertain to only a single event (however that might be defined), as noted above.

Consider the following three research questions: (1) why did the French Revolution occur?; (2) what accounts for the revolutions that have occurred in the modern era (1789–2000)?; and (3) why do revolutions occur? The first way of framing the question is the most specific, the last is the most general. But even in the latter case we can identify boundaries to the population. For example, a revolution (as the term is usually understood) presumes the existence of a political entity more complex than a band or tribe, such as an empire or nation-state. This limits the scope of any argument that might be devised.

For purposes of this book, I am concerned primarily with arguments that speak to populations that are larger than whatever sample of observations is under study. Of course, external validity is contingent upon internal validity (terms that will be defined in Chapter 4). If one is studying the French Revolution in order to learn something about revolutions in general, then one must come to terms with the cause of the French Revolution. However, various features of the inferential process are different if one's ultimate goal is to explain revolutions rather than simply the French Revolution.

Note that even where populations are sampled exhaustively – that is, when all cases within a population are studied (as they often are in global studies of nation-states) – there is a difference between generalizing and particularizing inferences. A generalizing inference regards the chosen sample as a subset of some larger (perhaps difficult to define) population that extends backward and forward in time – beyond the chosen time-frame of the actual analysis. It may also regard the sample as one possible sample from a set of "alternate worlds" – a counterfactual thought-experiment.[5] By contrast, a particularizing inference is focused only on explaining what happened within the chosen cases during the time period of the study. With respect to causal inference, particularizing arguments are about "causes in fact" (aka actual causes) rather than causes in general.

Boundedness

With respect to the scope of an argument, bigger is better – but evidently only to a point. Indeed, as an argument is extended its veracity, precision, or coherence often declines. This is the point at which the criterion of generality begins to conflict with other scientific criteria (including those like fecundity and impact that are taken up in succeeding chapters in connection with descriptive and causal inference, respectively).

In framing an argument the researcher's objective is to identify those phenomena that properly belong within the scope of a theory, excluding those that do not. Inferences should be clearly and appropriately *bounded* – neither too big nor too small.

In empirical contexts, the population of an inference is usually understood as the population from which a studied sample is chosen. If a sample is drawn randomly from individuals living in the United States then the presumed population is the United States. Here, however, I am referring to the scope of an argument rather than the representativeness of a sample.

For causal inferences this has a particular meaning. The scope should extend to all cases for which the expected causal relationship is the same, given certain background factors. In formal notation, for all N, $E(Y|X)$. That is, for all prospective cases lying within the scope of an argument the expected value of an outcome, given a causal factor(s) of theoretical interest, should be the same.

Unfortunately, identifying this Goldilocks point is not always easy. Sometimes, the scope-conditions of a theory simply cannot be probed empirically. Sometimes, the empirical evidence is testable, but results are ambivalent: the argument fades out slowly as the scope of the inference expands, with no definitive cut-off points. And even where evidence is testable and registers apparently conclusive cut-off points, one can never solve the boundary

---

[5] Lebow (2007); Tetlock and Belkin (1996).

problem solely by appeal to evidence. The scope-conditions of an argument rest on underlying assumptions about the logical purview of a theory.

Consider the following example: voters care more about domestic policy than foreign policy. Our question is, what is the appropriate scope of this proposition? What are its boundary conditions? The empirical approach would be to test all voters, everywhere. But there are practical limits to this approach. And historical voters, prior to the initiation of survey research, cannot be polled. So, one is compelled to consider the logic of the argument. Under what circumstances would this proposition sensibly apply?

The specification of a clearly and properly bounded inference is essential to its falsifiability. Indeed, the entirely unbounded proposition cannot be tested, for it is not apparent where the theory applies. Failing to specify the boundaries of a theory is equivalent to saying, in effect, "The scope consists of those places where the theory is true, and the area outside the scope consists of those places where the theory is false." This is a research question, but not an argument. If the cases where a theory fails are excluded from the boundaries of an inference one has effectively defined out of consideration all cases that do not fit the theory. Studies in the rational choice genre have been accused of this sort of gerrymandering, which Don Green and Ian Shapiro refer to as an "arbitrary domain restriction."[6]

Whether rational-choicers are guilty of this sin is not important for present purposes. The point to remember is that the specification of scope is only the first step on the road to a meaningful argument. One must also ensure that the chosen boundaries make sense. An *arbitrarily* bounded inference, one that follows no apparent logic, is not convincing. The reader can surely think of examples of theories whose scope-conditions are too ambitious, not ambitious enough, or simply ambiguous (perhaps left implicit). Any inference may be stretched into nonsense by an arbitrarily large scope. By the same token, an inference may be rendered nonsensical by adopting an arbitrarily small scope.

What "making sense" means varies by context, and will be discussed in chapters to follow. Here, a few general remarks will suffice. Consider that some scope-conditions are patently absurd. For example, writers occasionally proclaim that their inference is intended to explain the past and the present, but not the future. While it may be granted that *at some point* in the future social realities will be so altered that the scope-conditions of current theories no longer obtain it seems unlikely that this moment will be reached on the day a book or article is published. Temporal boundaries are justifiable only if they can be connected to phenomena in the world that might impact the workings of a given

---

[6] See Green and Shapiro (1994: 45).

theory. The same applies to spatial boundaries, for example, "Latin America," "North Oswego," "schools with violent juveniles." To say that an argument is properly bounded is to say that clear boundaries have been specified, and – more importantly – that these boundaries make good theoretical sense.

Parsimony

A seventh general goal of science is reduction, that is, reducing the infinite plenitude of reality into a carefully framed argument from which unnecessary dross is removed. To the extent that an argument achieves this goal it is *parsimonious*. Like a lever, it lifts heavy weights with a moderate application of force. It is efficient, and its efficiency derives from its capacity to explain a lot with a minimal expenditure of energy. If, on the other hand, an inference is not summarizable in a compact form, its impact is diminished. (Readers will recognize that the goal of parsimony is implied by the goal of generality, and vice versa.[7])

The goal of parsimony is not necessarily at war with the total length of a study. Indeed, lengthy analyses may be required to provide evidence for a pithy argument. One might consider the work of Charles Darwin, Karl Marx, Adam Smith, Herbert Spencer, and Oswald Spengler in this regard. None of these men were known for their shortness of breath. All, however, are known for their parsimonious theories. Parsimony does not preclude length, though it does call for a summary statement of key propositions.[8]

Note that the criterion of parsimony, sometimes expressed as *Occam's razor*, applies in equal measure to arguments set forth in prose as well as those laid out in mathematical symbols. In the former, parsimony is equivalent to concision. In the latter, parsimony is reflected in the number of parameters contained within a model or the complexity and length of a proof.

Parsimony is valuable not because we assume that simplicity conforms to the natural order of things. This assumption may hold true for natural phenomena; but it is of doubtful application in the realm of human action and humanly created institutions, where the assumption of complexity usually claims greater face validity. It is for pragmatic, rather than ontological, reasons that one prefers a parsimonious inference over a prolix one. We need to bring knowledge

---

[7] For work on the interrelated questions of reduction, simplicity, and parsimony, see K. Friedman (1972); M. Friedman (1974); Glymour (1980); Hesse (1974); King, Keohane, and Verba (1994: 20); Kitcher (1989); Popper ([1934] 1968); Quine (1966); Simon (2001); Sober (1975, 1988).

[8] Contemporary examples of parsimony coexisting with length can be found in Collier and Collier (1991); Fischer (1989). Some long books, however, offer virtually no attempt at synopsis at all, e.g., Gay (1984–98); Kantorowicz (1957); Pocock (1975).

together in reasonably compact form in order for that knowledge to serve a useful purpose.[9]

Moreover, a parsimonious argument requires fewer assumptions about the world. Note that a scientific proposition is understandable only in light of an existing language (technical and ordinary) and body of knowledge. Inferences build upon what we know already – or think we know – about the world. Nothing starts entirely from scratch. A good argument requires fewer departures from common sense, fewer leaps of faith, fewer stipulations, fewer *a priori* assumptions. It rests, in these respects, upon more secure foundations. A poorly constructed theory, by contrast, asks the reader to accept a great deal about the world upon the authority of the author. This sort of inference does not build on solid foundations. It is stipulative.

Of course, all arguments rest upon assumptions, and it is advisable to render these assumptions as transparent as possible so that the argument can be easily evaluated. (This is one of the benefits of a well-constructed formal model.) That said, the fewer assumptions necessary for a proposition the more secure that proposition is, and the less empirical work is required in order to prove its veracity. One can think of each assumption in an argument as a link in a logical chain. One can evaluate the *prima facie* strength of the overall argument by the number of assumptions it requires and their relative certainty or uncertainty. The ideal argument has only one empirical question at issue – the main hypothesis – all else is regarded as firmly grounded, or already established.

The reasoning behind Occam's razor points to a larger truth about the conduct of science, namely, innovation cannot occur on all aspects of a problem at once. In Otto Neurath's much-cited analogy, scientific reconstruction occurs as it would for a ship while at sea. Each beam must be replaced immediately by another, drawn from the same vessel, but perhaps serving some different function such that the effect, over time, is to transform the original purpose of the vessel beyond recognition.[10] The point is that the removal of too many planks at once would cause the ship (by extension, the argument) to sink. We must work incrementally. Indeed, meaning breaks down entirely when language is stretched too far. Arguments no longer make sense. Thus, the fewer assumptions required by a theory the more falsifiable it is, and the more believable. It fits within what we take for granted about the world.

---

[9] King, Keohane, and Verba (1994: 20, 104) adopt the *reality-is-simple* interpretation of parsimony and reject the criterion on those grounds. If interpreted as a pragmatic norm, however, it might not be rejected by the authors. See, e.g., their discussion of the importance of leverage ("explaining as much as possible with as little as possible", p. 29).

[10] Neurath (1971: 47).

Coherence

In order to be meaningful an argument must demonstrate some degree of *coherence* (internal consistency). If there are many moving parts, as in a broad and abstract theory, they ought to hold together. A complex theory should revolve around a single core and the precepts should be logically linked. One facet should imply the others. Indeed, if the parts of an argument are inconsistent, the argument itself is virtually meaningless, and surely untestable. (For some writers, parsimony is equivalent to coherence. But since these terms have somewhat different implications, I list them separately.)

Commensurability

We have said that arguments assume meaning within a field of pre-existing concepts and theories; indeed, they are scarcely understandable purely on their own terms. (What terms would that be?) Like facts, theories do not stand alone. They relate to a broader set of theories, typically a field or subfield of study.

Does a theory fit comfortably within, above, or beside other theories? Does it advance logical economy in a field, perhaps by subsuming neighboring theories? If it does these things, then we may say that a theory aids in the cumulation of knowledge about a subject. It is *commensurable*. If it does not, if it sits by itself in a corner and does not relate productively to other theories. then, it is likely to be dismissed as "*ad hoc,*" or "idiosyncratic." It does not fit with present understandings of the world. It has little theoretical or conceptual utility.

Of course, deviant theories and neologisms (novel concepts) may be extremely useful in the long run. Indeed, the first sign of breakdown in a broad theory or paradigm is the existence of findings that cannot easily be made sense of. Yet until such time as a new theory or paradigm can be constructed (one that would gather the new findings together with the old in a single over-arching framework), the wayward proposition is *ad hoc*, idiosyncratic, and apt to be ignored.

Commensurability revisits the demand for parsimony at a broader scale. Rather than referring to the qualities of individual theories we are now concerned with parsimony in a field, a discipline, across the social sciences, and perhaps across the sciences at large. Ernst Mach saw the fundamental project of science in the effort to produce "the completest possible presentment of facts with the least possible expenditure of thought."[11] Einstein, several decades later, endorsed "the effort to reduce all concepts and correlations to as few as possible

---

[11] Mach ([1902] 1953: 450–451).

logically independent basic concepts and axioms."[12] More recently, Edward O. Wilson has argued that "there is only one class of explanation. It traverses the scales of space, time, and complexity to unite the disparate facts of the disciplines by consilience, the perception of a seamless web of cause and effect."[13] Arguments for the unity of science are many and various.[14]

Granted, we are likely to experience considerably less success in this endeavor in the social sciences than Mach, Einstein, and Wilson envisioned for the natural sciences. Commensurability is a matter of degrees. But this should not blind us to the need for logical economy, and the utility of such economy as we already enjoy. We are accustomed, for example, to categorizing works into various traditions – Durkheimian, Weberian, Marxist, Freudian, rational choice, behavioralist – and into smaller niches defined by particular subfields. This sort of grouping makes the academic enterprise manageable, to the extent that it is manageable at all. (Imagine if we had no such pigeon-holes.) Perhaps, over time, we shall do better. This is the ambition of rational choice and other broad theoretical frameworks.

Relevance

Social science is a species of practical knowledge. "Any problem of scientific inquiry that does not grow out of actual (or 'practical') social conditions is factitious," as Dewey writes:

All the techniques of observation employed in the advanced sciences may be conformed to, including the use of the best statistical methods to calculate probable errors, etc., and yet the material ascertained be scientifically "dead," i.e., irrelevant to a genuine issue, so that concern with it is hardly more than a form of intellectual busy work.[15]

If social scientists cannot tell us something useful about the world then they (we) are serving very little purpose at all (a point explored further in Chapter 14). One criterion of social utility – one might even regard it as a necessary condition – is *relevance*.[16]

---

[12] Einstein ([1940] 1953: 253).   [13] Wilson (1998: 291).

[14] See Hitchcock (2003); Homans (1967); King, Keohane, and Verba (1994: 15–17); Kitcher (1981); Mill ([1843] 1872: 143–144); Neurath, Carnap, and Morris (1971); Putnam and Oppenheim (1958). What I refer to as commensurability is also similar to "coherence" approaches to truth, as that term is employed in epistemology and philosophy of science (Kirkham 1992; Laudan 1996: 79).

[15] Dewey (1938: 499).

[16] Adcock (2009); Bloch ([1941] 1953); Bok (1982); Haan *et al.* (1983); Lerner and Lasswell (1951); Lindblom and Cohen (1979); McCall and Weber (1984); Mills (1959); Myrdal (1970: 258); Popper ([1936] 1957: 56); Rule (1997); Shapiro (2005); Simon (1982); Smith (2003); Wilensky (1997); Zald (1990).

By relevance, I mean significance to the lay citizens of the world. Unfortunately, in academic work one finds that writers sometimes confuse the notion of statistical significance with real-life significance. In a wide-ranging review of economics studies, McCloskey and Ziliak refer to this as the "standard error of regressions."[17] This is why I shall belabor what might seem to be an obvious point.

The relevance criterion does not imply a social science composed of zealous advocacy, where writers embrace particular policies or draw moral/ethical conclusions about historical actors and actions: where the past becomes, in Michael Oakeshott's apt phrase, "a field in which we exercise our moral and political opinions, like whippets in a meadow on Sunday afternoon."[18]

By the same token, it seems fruitless to insist that social science should entirely eschew opinionizing, for "normative" concerns are often difficult to avoid. Imagine writing about the Holocaust or slavery in a wholly dispassionate manner. What would an even-handed treatment of these subjects look like? Everyday language is not morally neutral, and social science must accept this affectively charged vocabulary as a condition of doing business.[19] Leaving aside such extreme examples, it is difficult to conceive of important statements about human actions and human institutions that do not carry some normative freight. At the very least, one's choice of subject is likely to be guided by some sense of what is right and wrong. "In theory," writes E. H. Carr,

> the distinction may ... be drawn between the role of the investigator who establishes the facts and the role of the practitioner who considers the right course of action. In practice, one role shades imperceptibly into the other. Purpose and analysis become part and parcel of a single process.[20]

I cannot fathom why anyone would choose to invest years (typically decades) researching a subject if it did not have some normative importance to him or her. Arguably, truth-claims are enhanced when a writer frankly proclaims his or her preferences at the outset of the work. This way, possible inaccuracies in evidence or presentation are easier to detect and to evaluate. Hidden prejudices probably do more harm than those that are openly avowed. Yet it must be stressed again that the value of a work of social science derives from its value-added, not its normative point of view. To say, "*Y* is good" or "We should do *Y*" is to say extraordinarily little. Few are likely to be persuaded by such a statement,

---

[17] McCloskey and Ziliak (1996); Ziliak and McCloskey (2008).   [18] Quoted in Fischer (1970: 78).
[19] Collier (1998); Freeden (1996); Gallie (1956); Hollis and Lukes (1982); MacIntyre (1971); Pitkin (1972); Searle (1969); Strauss ([1953] 1963); Taylor ([1967] 1994).
[20] Carr ([1939] 1964: 4).

unless it is simply by virtue of the authority of the writer. And what authority do members of the social science caste possess, aside from the authority of social science?

Typically, social science is most powerful when the normative angle of a work is handled delicately. The most compelling arguments for social welfare are those that demonstrate causal relationships, for example, that particular programs aid in alleviating conditions of poverty and do not have negative externalities. Such studies do not proclaim baldly "Poverty is bad," or "We should increase social welfare spending," although there is no question that these views undergird most research on poverty and social policy. As long as the author's research is sound, one is unconcerned with his or her normative position on the matter.

To put it otherwise: the persuasiveness of any normative argument is itself dependent on the persuasiveness of whatever descriptive and causal propositions comprise that argument. Descriptive and causal propositions serve as the meat of any prescriptive statement. Similarly, whether or not the researcher is motivated by some vision of a better society, or only by personal or material interests, is rightly immaterial to our judgment of the quality of his or her work. There are idiots and geniuses of every persuasion. One would prefer to read the geniuses and leave the idiots alone, leaving aside their personal views and ethical codes.

Finally, it seems appropriate to observe that the vast majority of social science analysis has little to do with what is good or bad. No one – or virtually no one – argues against the virtues of peace, prosperity, democracy, and self-fulfillment. What is relevant (in the larger sense of the word) is any knowledge that might help us to achieve these desiderata.[21] Here is where social science matters, or ought to matter.

I do not wish to give the impression that social science should be solely preoccupied with *policy* relevance. One would be hard-pressed, for example, to uncover a single policy prescription in work by David Brion Davis, Edmund Morgan, and Orlando Patterson on the institution of human slavery.[22] Yet, arguably, no one ignorant of these writers' work can fully comprehend any contemporary social policy debate in the United States. Similarly, although work on the American Revolution, the Constitution, the Civil War, and various other historical topics is undoubtedly important for understanding where we are today, it would be difficult to derive policy implications from each of these events. The same could be said for many subjects of study in the various fields of

---

[21] Friedman ([1953] 1984).   [22] Davis (1988); Morgan (1975); Patterson (1982).

the social sciences. The point, then, is not that every study should have a policy lesson, but that every study should reflect upon something that citizens and policymakers care about, or might care about.

The telos of relevance thus embraces work in history, anthropology, and other interpretive fields whose impact on public affairs is bound to be more diffuse. Indeed, one of the strongest arguments against a naturalist model for the social sciences is that such a model might prevent us from writing about things that matter. Too preoccupied with its status as a science, Barrington Moore thought,

> social science overlooks more important and pressing tasks. The main structural features of what society can be like in the next generation are already given by trends at work now. Humanity's freedom of maneuver lies within the framework created by its history. Social scientists and allied scholars could help to widen the area of choice by analyzing the historical trends that now limit it. They could show, impartially, honestly, and free from the special pleadings of governments and vested interests, the range of possible alternatives and the potentialities for effective action. Such has been, after all, the aim of inquiry into human affairs in free societies since the Greeks.[23]

No matter how virtuous a theory may be on other criteria, if it cannot pass the *so what?* test it is not worth very much. Inferences, large or small, have various levels of relevance. There are some things that, however much we may sympathize with the author, we cannot be bothered to argue about. Perceived relevance thus plays a vital role in identifying social science problems that are worthy of study.

In *causal* analysis, relevance also plays a role in identifying factors that are worthy of analysis. Consider the classic question of war, as elucidated by Patrick Gardiner:

> When the causes of war are being investigated, it may be decided that both economic factors and human psychology are relevant to its outbreak; yet since we deem it to be within our power to influence or alter the economic system of a society, whereas the control of human psychology seems, at least at present, to be beyond our capacity, we are likely to regard the economic rather than the psychological factors as the "cause" of war.[24]

Similarly, in discussions of social policy, causal arguments that rest upon deep-seated political-cultural factors are in some respects less interesting than arguments resting on policy design. The latter can be redesigned, while the former are presumably of long duration, and hence less relevant to contemporary

---

[23] Moore (1958: 159).   [24] Gardiner ([1952] 1961: 12).

policy discussions (except as boundary conditions). Relevant causes tend to be *manipulable*.[25]

By way of conclusion, it seems fair to judge the theories (or causal factors) that possess a strong claim to relevance as superior (*ceteris paribus*) to those that do not. And it seems fair to ask writers to justify the reader's potential expenditure of time, effort, and money with some sort of pay-off. This is traditionally handled in the preface of a book or article, where the author tries to find a hook (a point of general interest) on which to hang his or her argument, or in the conclusion, where the author reflects upon the ramifications of a study. Readers are not likely to be carried very far on the strength of a writer's method or prose if they do not feel that there is something important at stake in the investigation. They must care about the outcome.

---

[25] This follows Collingwood's (1940) analysis. We generally identify a causal factor that states "it is in our power to produce or prevent, and by producing or preventing which we can produce or prevent that whose cause it is said to be" (cited in Garfinkel 1981: 138). See also Gasking (1955); Harre and Madden (1975); Suppes (1970); von Wright (1971); Whitbeck (1977) – all cited in Cook and Campbell (1979: 25). Note that manipulability also enhances the testability of a causal argument, as discussed in Chapter 9.

4 Analyses

But is it true?

Aaron Wildavsky[1]

Having discussed the formal (super-empirical) criteria of a good argument, we turn now to the empirical portion of social science research, the hoped-for encounter with reality.[2] This stage may be referred to variously as analysis, assessment, corroboration, demonstration, empirics, evaluation, methods, proof, or testing. (While acknowledging the subtle differences among these terms, I shall treat them as part of the same overall enterprise.)

Of course, the distinction between theory formation and theory-testing is never clear and bright. As is the case everywhere in social science, tasks intermingle. One cannot form an argument without considering the empirical problem of how to appraise it, and vice versa. Moreover, the task of (dis)-confirming theories is intimately conjoined with the task of forming theories. As Paul Samuelson notes, "It takes a theory to kill a theory."[3]

Yet in coming to grips with the complex process of social science it is essential to distinguish between the formal properties of an argument and the methods by which that argument might be assessed. *What are you arguing?* and *Is it true?* are logically distinct questions, calling forth different criteria of adequacy.[4] Moreover, there are good methodological reasons to respect the separation between theory and analysis (see "Partition" below). We now proceed from the former to the latter.

Of course, not all hypotheses require explicit attention to methods of appraisal. Many hypotheses need not be formally tested at all, for they are already self-evident (e.g., "civil war is dislocating"), or are insufficiently important to justify the investment of time and energy that a formal analysis would require (e.g., "lifeguard training programs have positive effects on the probability of

---

[1] Wildavsky (1995).

[2] Scientific realists recognize an analogous distinction between the super-empirical and empirical elements of a theory (Hitchcock 2003: 217).

[3] Quoted in Rosenbaum (2010: 95).   [4] Bhaskar ([1975] 1978: 171); Bunge (1963: 45); Hoover (2001: 22).

marriage and child-bearing among program participants"). Our motivation here is centered on arguments that are important enough to submit to a formal testing procedure and complex enough, in terms of potential threats to validity, to worry about the niceties of research design. Methodology kicks in where common sense falls short.

Definitions

A standard empirical analysis involves a number of components, which must be clarified before we continue. Much of this vocabulary is borrowed from survey research; nonetheless, the concepts are helpful in all styles of research, quantitative or qualitative.

A *population* is the universe of phenomena that a hypothesis seeks to describe or explain. It remains unstudied, or is studied only in a very informal manner, for example, through the secondary literature. Sometimes, it is important to distinguish between a population from which a sample is drawn (and which it presumably represents) and a larger, more hypothetical population that the sample may or may not represent, but which nonetheless defines the scope-conditions of the argument.

The *sample* refers to the evidence that will be subjected to direct examination. It is composed of *units* or *cases*: bounded entities such as individuals (subjects), organizations, communities, or nation-states, which may be observed spatially and/or temporally (through time). (The terms *unit* and *case* are more or less equivalent. The only difference is that while a unit is bounded spatially, a case may also have implicit or explicit temporal boundaries.[5])

Typically, the sample is smaller than the population; hence, the notion of *sampling* from a population. (Note, however, that my use of the term sample does not necessarily mean that cases under study – the sample – have been randomly chosen from a known population.) Occasionally, one is able to include the entire population in a sample – a *census*.

The *observations* taken from units at particular points (or periods) in time compose the pieces of evidence presumed to be relevant to a descriptive or causal proposition. Collectively, the observations in a study comprise a study's sample. Each observation should record values for all relevant *variables* across each unit at a particular point (or period) in time. In causal analysis, this

---

[5] For further discussion see Gerring (2007).

includes X (the causal factor of theoretical interest) and Y (the outcome of interest), along with any other variables deemed essential for the analysis.

In matrix format, an observation is usually represented as a row and the total number of observations (rows) in a sample as "N." Confusingly, N also sometimes refers to the number of units or cases, which may be quite different from the number of observations. Varying usages are usually clear from the context.

A final concept, the data *cell*, is useful when one wishes to refer to the data pertaining to a particular unit at one point in time along only one dimension. Although the term is not commonly employed, it is sometimes essential. Consider that an observation consists of at least two cells in any causal analysis: the cell representing the value for X and the cell representing the value for Y. Sometimes, one needs to distinguish between them.

These interrelated concepts are illustrated in Figure 4.1, where we can see a fairly typical time-series cross-section research design in a rectangular dataset (matrix) format. Here, observations are represented as rows, variables as columns, and cells as their intersection. Note that cells are nested within observations, observations are nested within units (aka cases), units are nested within the sample, and the sample is nested within the population.

Hypothetically, let us imagine that the population of the inference includes all US schools and the sample consists of eight schools, observed annually for five years, yielding a sample of forty observations ($N=40$). The *units of analysis* (the type of phenomena treated as observations in an analysis) in this hypothetical example are school-years.

If the research design had been purely cross-sectional, only one observation would be taken from each unit, and the units of analysis would consist of schools rather than school-years, and the total number of observations would be eight ($N=8$). In this context, the number of units is equal to the number of observations and the distinction between unit and observation is lost.

If the research design is purely temporal the sample would be composed of one unit, observed through time. If the sample period is five years and observations are taken annually, the total number of observations is five ($N=5$). Here, the units of analysis are again school-years, as in the first example.

All these terms are slippery insofar as they depend for their meaning on a particular proposition and a corresponding research design. Any changes in that proposition may affect the sort of phenomena that are classified as observations and units, not to mention the composition of the sample and the population. Thus, an investigation of school vouchers might begin by identifying *schools* as the principal unit of analysis, but then shift to a lower level of analysis

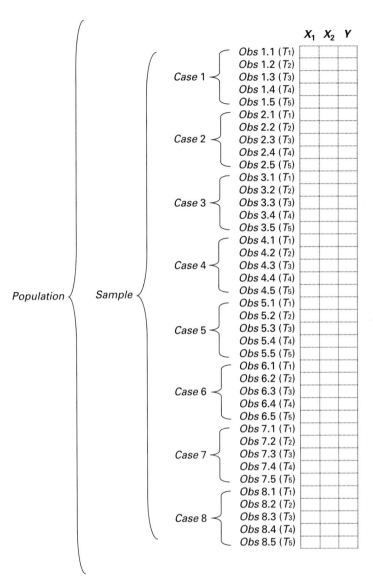

Population = indeterminate; Cases/units = 8; Sample/observations = 40;
Cells = 120; Time (*T*) = 1–5; Variables = 3.

Figure 4.1   Time-series cross-section dataset

(e.g., *students*), or a higher level of analysis (e.g., *school districts*) at different points in the study. Sometimes, different levels of analysis (e.g., students, schools, and school districts) are combined. This is common in *case study* work and is the defining feature of *hierarchical* (*multi-level*) statistical models.

Complicating matters further, the precise boundaries of a research design often remain ambiguous. This is because a subject is usually interrogated in a variety of ways during the course of a study. For example, key variables may change (perhaps to capture a different dimension or an alternative operationalization of a complex concept), the units of analysis may change (moving up or down in levels of analysis), the focus may change (from the main hypothesis to adjunct hypotheses or causal mechanisms), the sample may change, and different kinds of observations may be enlisted. These are just a few of the variations in method that typically co-habit in a single study. Each of these alterations may be considered as distinct research designs or as variations on a single research design. Likewise, they may be described as replications, robustness tests, or multimethod research (as discussed in later chapters). Thus, it becomes rather difficult to say what a given study's research design is, or how many there are, without making some rather arbitrary decisions about what lies in, and out of, the scope of this ambient concept. I shall leave this matter open because I do not think it can be easily settled. Perhaps it is not essential. The proviso is that writers must be clear about what they mean by "research design" in a given context.

Research design versus data analysis

Traditionally, one distinguishes between two stages of the testing process. *Research design* refers to the selection and arrangement of evidence.[6] *Data analysis* refers to the analysis of data once it is collected.

In an experiment, these stages are clearly separable: research design precedes data analysis. One is *ex ante*, the other *ex post*. (Of course, in successive cycles of research this line becomes blurred.) In observational research, the two stages are usually intermixed. Because much of this book is focused on observational techniques, the reader should be prepared for some slippage across these two concepts. Still, the distinction is consequential.

An older tradition of social science methodology focuses on reaching inferences about a phenomenon based on whatever data is at hand. The methodologist's job begins once the evidence is in. This is the "data analysis" approach to methodology that underlies most econometrics texts. Textbooks in this genre include discussions of statistical inference and of various classes of estimators

---

[6] An experimentally based understanding of design refers to "all contemplating, collecting, organizing, and analyzing of data that takes place prior to seeing any outcome data" (Rubin 2008: 810). This seems to narrow for present purposes, since in observational research the selection of a research site often depends on an initial consideration of "outcome" data. My understanding of design encompasses all factors that might (legitimately) impact the choice of observations to be studied.

employed for descriptive and causal inference (e.g., correlation, difference of means, regression, matching, randomization inference, Bayesian versus frequentist approaches), along with the assumptions each method invokes.[7]

Useful though such techniques are, it is important to remember that the contribution of advanced statistical protocols is focused largely on shortcomings of design. Econometrics is the *deus ex machina* hauled onto the stage to rectify problems of measurement error, ambiguous causal factors, insufficient variation along key parameters, insufficient observations, incomparabilities across comparison cases, biased samples, and other issues that we will shortly discuss. From this perspective, it seems appropriate to conclude that matters of design are primary, and matters of data analysis secondary – both sequentially and methodologically. "Design trumps analysis," in the words of Donald Rubin.[8] And from this perspective it follows that the methodologist's job begins at the front-end – the research design phase of a project.

Indeed, there is often not much one can do to rectify problems of design once the data is in. For those who are fond of medical analogies, the research design approach to methodology might be compared with the preventive approach to medicine, that is, how to avoid contracting illness, while the data analysis approach to methodology is akin to emergency care, that is, how to restore a patient who is already failing.

Sometimes, ingenious *ex post* statistical adjustments are successful. Yet there is increasing skepticism about our capacity to correct research design flaws at the post-research phase. The old adage, "garbage in, garbage out," is still true, despite many advances in the field of statistics. Richard Berk comments:

One cannot repair a weak research design with a strong data analysis. Almost inevitably what seems too good to be true is, and one is simply substituting untestable assumptions for the information one does not have.[9]

Indeed, the most worrying point of all is we usually cannot tell whether statistical corrections have achieved their intended purpose, for example, whether a two-stage approach to modeling selection bias has actually provided a correct and unbiased estimate of X's effect on Y. As Berk points out, this is because the assumptions required to conduct statistical protocols are often not directly testable; they hinge on *a priori* ("ontological") assumptions about the nature of the data-generating process. Reviewing the field of regression-based causal

---

[7] For example, Greene (2002).
[8] Rubin (2008). See also Angrist and Pischke (2010); Bowers and Panagopoulos (2009); King, Keohane, and Verba (1995); Rosenbaum (1999, 2010); Sekhon (2009); Shadish and Cook (1999: 294).
[9] Berk (1991: 316).

inference, David Freedman states baldly, "I see *no* cases in which regression equations, let alone the more complex methods, have succeeded as engines for discovering causal relationships."[10] While this conclusion seems a tad extreme, one is rightly cautioned to regard statistically based causal inferences with skepticism. Always, they rest on assumptions about the data-generation process, that is, on matters of research design.

Thus, although I do not wish to downplay the importance of data analysis, I do wish to stake a claim for the primacy of design – especially in causal analysis but also in descriptive analysis. The design components of research are general in purview; any attempt to disentangle empirical relationships must wrestle with them. Moreover, this perspective on methodology is often insightful. It clarifies the obstacles facing the social sciences and elucidates a range of possible solutions.

Finally, the design aspects of social science research are under-appreciated. Indeed, the only regions of social science where issues of design are granted primacy are those where experimental methods are employed. In light of this, it seems arguable that the way forward for social science is to be found in well-crafted research designs rather than in the development of new estimators. Borrowing from Paul Rosenbaum, our motto will be "choice as an alternative to [statistical] control."[11]

Accordingly, the following chapters include little discussion of statistics *except* as the latter bear upon matters of research design. This means that statistical methods closely associated with specific research designs, such as regression discontinuity and instrumental variables, will be discussed (Chapter 10), but not statistical methods that are general in employment, such as regression or matching.

Criteria

With these terms and perspectives clarified, we can now proceed to the main business at hand. What is it that qualifies a research design (and

---

[10] Freedman (1997: 114; emphasis added). On the problems of statistical inference based on observational data, and the corresponding importance of research design, see Berk (2004); Brady and Collier (2004); Clogg and Haritou (1997); Freedman (1991, 2008, 2010); Gerber, Green, and Kaplan (2004); Gigerenzer (2004); Heckman (2008: 3); Kittel (2006); Longford (2005); Pearl (2009b: 40, 332); Robins and Wasserman (1999); Rodrik (2005); Rosenbaum (1999, 2005); Seawright (2010); Summers (1991). Various studies comparing analyses of the same phenomenon with experimental and nonexperimental data show significant disparities in results, offering direct evidence that observational research is flawed (e.g., Benson and Hartz 2000; Friedlander and Robins 1995; Glazerman, Levy, and Myers 2003; LaLonde 1986). Cook, Shaddish, and Wong (2008) offer a more optimistic appraisal.

[11] Rosenbaum (1999).

Table 4.1 Analysis: general criteria

1. **Accuracy**
   Are the results (a) valid, (b) precise (reliable), and (c) accompanied by an estimate of uncertainty (confidence, probability) with respect to (d) the chosen sample (internal validity) and (e) the population of interest (external validity, aka generalizability)?

2. **Sampling**
   Are the chosen observations (a) representative of the intended population, (b) sufficiently large in number, and (c) at the principal level of analysis?

3. **Cumulation**
   (a) Is the research design standardized with other similar research on the topic? (b) Does it replicate extant findings and facilitate future replications by other scholars? (c) Are procedures transparent?

4. **Theoretical fit**
   (a) Does the research design provide an appropriate test for the inference (construct validity)? (b) Is the test easy or hard (severity)? (c) Is the test segregated from the argument under investigation (partition)?

corresponding data analysis) as satisfactory? What is a good empirical analysis?

I will argue that criteria applicable to social science analyses may be fruitfully divided into four fundamental areas: *accuracy* (validity, precision, and uncertainty); *sampling* (representativeness, sample size, level of analysis); *cumulation* (standardization, replication, transparency); and *theoretical fit* (partition, construct validity, difficulty).

These criteria, summarized in Table 4.1, are regarded as generic, which is to say they apply to all approaches. No method – whether descriptive or causal, qualitative or quantitative, experimental or observational – is exempt. To be sure, each study is apt to prioritize certain criteria over others. And occasionally, criteria may be legitimately ignored if they have been effectively established by other studies. In this respect, it is difficult to evaluate a given work in isolation from the field of studies in which it is situated. But the larger and more important claim remains: the criteria listed in Table 4.1 are broadly applicable wherever empirical questions of social science are in play.

Accuracy

The overall objective of empirical research is to accurately test an argument. Accuracy may be understood as having two dimensions: *validity* and *precision*, each with an associated level of *uncertainty*.

These notions are typically applied to the estimate that results from an empirical analysis (i.e., to the finding). However, they may also be applied to the research design and technique of data analysis by which that estimate is obtained. Indeed, the various phases of research are *all* subject to demands for validity and precision, and each is associated with a level of uncertainty. Thus, when speaking of these goals we shall speak of them applying across various tasks associated with the general task of theory appraisal.

Other criteria, discussed in succeeding sections of this chapter and in subsequent chapters, usually aim in one way or another to bolster the accuracy of an analysis, and in this respect may be viewed as ancillary to the fundamental goals of validity and precision.

Finally, a distinction will be introduced between the chosen sample and a larger population of theoretical interest. The former is understood as an issue of *internal validity* and the latter as an issue of *external validity*.

Validity, precision, uncertainty

Scholars often distinguish between the *validity* of a test and its *precision* (reliability). If an inference were to be tested repeatedly, the closeness of these results (on average) to the true value would capture the validity of the test. The closeness of these test results *to each other* would capture the precision of the test.

This contrast is best illuminated by illustration. Let us represent the object of interest (in its true, ontological reality) by a dark circle, and various attempts to measure that object by points. With this schema, three tests are compared in Figure 4.2. The first is reliable but not valid, as the points cluster closely together but are distant from the true center. The second is valid but not reliable, as the points are dispersed but are clustered around the true center. The third is both reliable and valid.

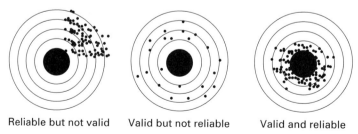

Reliable but not valid   Valid but not reliable   Valid and reliable

Figure 4.2   Reliability (precision) and validity

These concepts apply equally to the descriptive task of measurement (Chapter 7), as well as to the task of estimating causal effects (Chapters 9, 10, and 11). There is a slight alteration of vocabulary, insofar as the precision of a measurement is usually referred to as a question of *reliability* (rather than precision). But the basic ideas are the same across contexts.

Note that precision is also a criterion of an argument (Chapter 3). Here, however, we are concerned with the precision of a test, not the precision of the proposition that is being tested.

Now, let us explore these issues in greater detail.

A problem of validity may be expressed as a problem of *systematic error* or *bias*. Of course, it depends upon assumptions about the true reality, which may not be directly apprehensible. In some circumstances, it is possible to gauge the validity of a statistical model through *Monte Carlo* simulations.[12] But usually issues of validity are assessed in a more speculative manner. If there is recognizable bias, or potential bias, in some aspect of the research design we say that there is a problem of validity – even though we cannot know for sure.

Precision, we have said, refers to the consistency of a finding across repeated tests, and is thus a large-sample property. If iterated tests demonstrate the same result (more or less), the procedure is deemed to be precise. The *variance* across these results provides an empirical measure of the degree of precision thereby attained. If there is no opportunity to compare multiple iterations of a single research design (if the research is qualitative in nature), then the variance remains a theoretical property – though no less important for being so. Many factors may affect the relative precision of a test, including measurement error, the variability of the phenomena under study, and the size of a sample. Since precision is about variance, not validity, all such errors are regarded as stochastic (random), aka noise.

Implicit in the notion of validity is the concept of *uncertainty*. Any assertion about the world is associated with a level of confidence, or probability; for all empirical knowledge is to some extent uncertain. There is always a problem of inference, even if the degree of uncertainty is judged to be quite small. This uncertainty may stem from problems of concept formation (Chapter 5), measurement (Chapter 7), sampling (discussed below), and/or various issues associated with causal inference (Part III). It depends, obviously, on the argument in question.

It has been alleged that "perhaps the single most serious problem with qualitative research . . . is the pervasive failure to provide reasonable estimates

---

[12] Mooney (1997).

of the uncertainty of the investigator's inferences."[13] I have no doubt that there is some truth to this assertion, though qualitative scholars have worked hard to resolve it.

By contrast, quantitative methods generate estimates of uncertainty as a routine element of the analysis. Certain aspects of uncertainty can be captured in a statistic such as a confidence interval and associated p value, which measures the probability of a hypothesis relative to some null hypothesis. Here, the concepts of precision and uncertainty are merged in a single statistic. To be sure, these statistics are based on sampling variability and thus take no account of other threats to inference. Bayesian approaches are broader in reach, incorporating subjective knowledge about a subject. It is in this spirit that I propose an encompassing approach to the estimation of uncertainty, one that combines information drawn from large-sample methods of inference (wherever samples are large enough to permit this) with qualitative knowledge about additional threats to inference. Estimating the uncertainty of a particular finding is not easy. But it is essential.

Internal/external validity

Conventionally, one analyzes questions of validity, precision, and uncertainty at two levels. First, there is the question of whether a finding is true for the chosen sample – an issue of *internal* validity. Second, there is the question of how this finding might be generalized to a broader population of cases – an issue of *external* validity. Note that although this is phrased in terms of validity the same questions arise with respect to precision; I shall therefore assume that both are inferred when one utters the phrase "internal validity" or "external validity."

A study may be valid internally but not externally (beyond the chosen sample or research site). Likewise, the internal validity of a study may be questionable, while its claim to external validity – if true for the sample – is strong. Of course, the issue of external validity rests in some important sense on a study's internal validity. The greater our confidence about a finding in context A (the chosen research site), the greater our confidence about that finding in context B (somewhere in the larger population of interest). By the same token, if one is not confident about a result within a studied domain one is even less confident about extending that result to a larger domain.

---

[13] King, Keohane, and Verba (1994: 32).

The internal/validity distinction is crucial to virtually every methodological discussion, even though the dichotomy is not always crystal clear. As an example, consider a hypothetical study of a school district in the state of New York that rests on a sample of students drawn from that district, but purports to elucidate features of all schools within the state. This presents three potential levels of validity: (1) the sample of students; (2) the school district; and (3) schools throughout the state (across multiple districts). Internal validity may refer to (1) or (2), while external validity may refer to (2) or (3).

In this light, the issue of internal/external validity is perhaps more correctly articulated as *degrees of generalizability*. Just as arguments aim to generalize, so do research designs. Some do so more successfully, and more extensively (across a broader population) than others. In this vein, it is sometimes helpful to recognize concentric circles surrounding the sample that has been studied. Typically, the confidence with which one extrapolates results obtained from a given sample decreases as the size of the circle expands. Returning to the example above, let us consider six possible tiers of validity: (1) the sample of students; (2) the school district; (3) schools throughout the state (across multiple districts); (4) schools in other states; (5) schools in other countries in the OECD; and (6) schools elsewhere in the world. Each succeeding claim to validity seems less likely, but none is wholly implausible. And from this perspective there is no clear demarcation between internal and external. Or perhaps there is a fairly clear demarcation between internal and external, but there are multiple spheres of external validity.

For heuristic purposes, subsequent discussion will assume that there is one context for a study that is appropriately labeled "internal" and another that is appropriately labeled "external." But readers should bear in mind the attendant complexities.

In rare instances, the distinction between internal and external validity disappears because the entire population of an inference is directly studied. Here, the sample *is* the population. Even so, there is room for skepticism about exhaustive sampling procedures (a *census*). Since most social science theories are not limited to the past, the future provides a potential source for out-of-sample testing. This means that even if all available examples that fall into the domain of a subject are studied one may still be theoretically motivated to understand in a much larger – as yet unfathomable – population.

Conceptually, one may also recognize a distinction between cases that actually exist and those that could have existed (in the past). Thus, if I am studying the relationship between economic development and democracy among nation-states in the modern era I might consider even a comprehensive sample – including all nation-states since 1800 – to be a sample of all the nation-states that could have existed during that time period. From this perspective, there is always a larger population that cannot be directly studied.

Note that the distinction between internal and external validity is grounded in a distinction between what has been directly studied and what has not been directly studied. This means that the issue of external validity cannot be tested, by definition. It rests at the level of assumption. (Of course, it may be tested by some future study.) The question arises, on what (speculative) basis does one judge a study's external validity?

The most obvious criterion is the *representativeness* of the sample, as discussed below. A more subtle issue – relevant only to causal analysis – is the *scalability* of the treatment, as discussed in Chapter 9.

Sampling

The selection of units and observations for analysis is critical to any descriptive or causal analysis. Three objectives pertain broadly to this task: *representativeness*, *size*, and *level of analysis*. In constructing a sample one should aim to be representative of a broader population, to include sufficient observations to assure precision and leverage in the analysis, and to use cases that lie at the same level of analysis as the primary inference.

Representativeness

The most important ground for drawing conclusions about the external validity of a proposition is the *representativeness* of a chosen sample. Is the sample similar to the population with respect to the hypothesis that is being tested? If, for example, the hypothesis is causal, then the question is whether the relationship of X to Y is similar in the sample and in the population. Are we entitled to generalize from a given sample to a larger universe of cases?

In the case of voucher research, one must wonder whether the students, schools, and school districts (along with whatever additional features of the research site may be relevant to the inference) chosen for analysis are representative of a larger population of students, schools, and districts. And, if so, what is that larger population? Does it consist of all students and schools across the United States, or across the world? Does it consist of a smaller population of students who are willing to volunteer for such programs? These are critical questions. Unfortunately, they are often difficult to answer in a definitive fashion for the reasons already discussed.

The best way to obtain a representative sample is to sample randomly from a larger population. There are many techniques for doing so (much depends upon the character of that larger population, the methods at one's disposal for sampling from it, and the inference one wishes to estimate). But the basic idea is that each unit or observation within the population should have an equal chance of being chosen for the sample. An advantage of this approach is that one can estimate sampling variability (from sample to sample), thus providing estimates of precision to accompany whatever inferences one wishes to draw.[14]

Unfortunately, it is not possible to apply methods of random sampling to many research problems. Voucher studies, for example, depend upon the willingness of school districts to implement their protocols – a rare occurrence. As such, the sample of school districts studied by researchers is not likely to be drawn randomly from the general population.

Even where random sampling procedures are feasible, they are not always methodologically defensible. If the sample under study is very small – say, a single case or a handful of cases – it does not make sense to draw randomly from a large population. While the chosen sample will be representative of the population *on average*, any given sample (of one or several) is quite likely to lie far from the mean (along whatever dimensions are relevant to the question under study). Consequently, case-study research generally relies on purposive (non-probability) case-selection strategies, reviewed elsewhere.[15]

Wherever random sampling techniques are inapplicable, researchers must struggle to define the representativeness of a sample, and hence the plausible generalizability of results based on that sample. This is true regardless of whether the sample is very small (i.e., a case-study format) or very large.

Before concluding this section it is important to remind ourselves that the goal driving the selection of a set of cases is not simply to assure representativeness (and, hence, external validity). It is also, and perhaps more importantly, to achieve internal validity. Frequently, these two objectives conflict. For example, researchers often find themselves in situations where they can craft an experiment with a nonrandom sample *or* conduct a nonexperimental study with a random sample. Usually, they opt for the former approach, signifying that they place greater priority on internal validity than on external validity. But in some situations one can imagine making the opposite choice.

[14] Weisberg (2005).   [15] See Gerring (2007: ch. 5).

Size (*N*)

More observations are better than fewer; hence, a larger "*N*" (sample size) is superior to a smaller *N*, all other things being equal. (*N* may be understood as standardized "dataset" observations or as irregular "causal-process" observations, a distinction introduced in Chapter 11.) This is fairly commonsensical. All one is saying, in effect, is that the more evidence one can muster for a given proposition, the stronger the inference will be. Indeed, the same logic that compels us to provide empirical support for our beliefs also motivates us to accumulate multiple observations. The plural of "anecdote" is "data," as the old saw goes.

Suppose one is trying to figure out the effect of vouchers on school performance, but one has available information for only one student or one school. Under the circumstances, it will probably be difficult to reach any firm conclusions about the causal inference at issue. Of course, one observation is a lot better than none. Indeed, it is a quantum leap, since the absence of observations means that there is no empirical support whatsoever for a proposition. Yet empirical research with only one observation is also highly indeterminate, and apt to be consistent with a wide variety of competing hypotheses. Consider a scatter-plot graph of *X* and *Y* with only one data point. Through this point, Harry Eckstein observes, "an infinite number of curves or lines can be drawn."[16] In other words, one cannot know from this information alone what the true slope of the relationship between *X* and *Y* might be, and whether the relationship is in fact causal (a slope different from 0). The more observations one has, the less indeterminacy there is, and the more precision, with respect to *X*'s probable relationship to *Y*. Note that with a small sample, results are necessarily contingent upon the (perhaps peculiar) characteristics of the several chosen observations. Conclusions about a broader population are hazardous when one considers the many opportunities for error and the highly stochastic nature of most social phenomena.

A large sample of observations also helps with other tasks involved in causal assessment. It may assist in formulating a hypothesis – clarifying a positive and negative outcome, a set of cases which the proposition is intended to explain (the population), and operational definitions of the foregoing. All these issues become apparent in the process of coding observations, wherever there are multiple observations. But if there is only one observation, or multiple observations drawn from a single unit, these tasks often remain ambiguous. The

---

[16] Eckstein (1975: 113).

problem is that with a narrow empirical ambit the researcher is faced with an over-abundance of ways to operationalize a given hypothesis. School performance – the main outcome at issue in our vouchers example – could be measured by any observable feature in a given school. By contrast, where multiple schools are being observed the range of possible outcome measures is inevitably narrowed (by virtue of the paucity of data or costliness of tracking myriad indicators). Likewise, it will be necessary to stipulate in more certain terms how "success" will be defined – for the comparisons across schools must be explicit. The process of measurement across multiple observations forces one to come to terms with issues that might otherwise remain latent, and ambiguous.

One exception to the large-N criterion concerns an empirical study whose purpose is to disprove a causal or descriptive law (an invariant, "deterministic" proposition). As long as the observed pattern contradicts the hypothesis, a law may be disproven with a single observation.[17]

In all other settings, a larger sample is advisable – with the usual *ceteris paribus* caveat. Thus, if increasing the size of a sample decreases the representativeness of the sample one might decide that it is not worth the sacrifice: a smaller, more representative sample is superior. If one is limited by time or logistical constraints to study *either* a large sample of cross-case observations *or* a smaller sample of within-case observations one might decide that the latter offer stronger grounds for causal inference (for any of the reasons to be discussed in Part III). In short, there are many situations in which a smaller sample is preferred over a larger one. However, the reasons for this preference lie in other criteria. That is why it is still correct to view the size of a sample as a fundamental (*ceteris paribus*) criterion of social science.

Before concluding this section I must briefly mention the problem of *missing data*, as it intersects both sample representativeness and sample size. Usually, what is meant by missing data is that a sample lacks observations for some units that should (by some principle of selection, random or otherwise) be included. If the pattern of missing-ness is systematic, then the sample will be biased. If, on the other hand, it can be determined that the pattern of missing data is random, then the sample will be smaller than it should, but still perhaps representative (or at least as representative as it would have been without the missing data). A potential solution, if patterns of missing-ness are fairly predictable (using known data points) and the number of missing data points (relative to the total sample) is not too large, is to impute missing data.[18] In other situations, it may be feasible to generate a simple decision rule for establishing a "best guess" for

[17] Dion (1998).   [18] Allison (2002).

missing data points, without a formal statistical model. In any case, patterns of missing-ness must be reckoned with. A sample of 1,000 with missing data is not the same as a sample of 1,000 with no missing data. When one considers the problem of sample size one must wrestle with the completeness of the observations comprising the sample.

Level of analysis

Observations are most helpful in elucidating relationships when situated at the same level of analysis as the main hypothesis.[19] If the central hypothesis concerns the behavior of schools, then schools should, ideally, comprise the principal unit of analysis in the research design. If the hypothesis is centered on the behavior of individuals, then individuals should be the principal unit of analysis. And so forth.

One often faces difficulties if one attempts to explain the activity of a particular kind of unit by examining units at a higher, or lower, level of analysis. Suppose, for example, that one is interested in explaining the behavior of schools but has data only at the district level (an aggregation of schools). This is a common situation, but not an enviable one, for one must infer the behavior of schools from the behavior of school districts (raising a problem of estimation known as *ecological inference*).[20]

If, conversely, one has data at a lower level of analysis (for example, for students) then one faces a similar problem in the reverse direction: one must infer upward, as it were, from students to schools. This species of inference is also problematic. Sometimes, macro-level phenomena do not reflect observable phenomena at the micro-level, introducing a problem of *reductionism* (aka the *fallacy of nonequivalence*). Granted, knowing something about the response of students to a stimulus may be extremely helpful in understanding the response of schools. Indeed, it may be crucial to demonstrating the causal mechanism(s) at work. This is why case-study research, which typically invokes data lying at a lower level of analysis, is often employed. However, in proving the existence of a causal effect it is important also to muster evidence at the principal unit of analysis (as defined by the proposition). In this context, student-level data will be most useful if it can be aggregated across schools. And for purposes of estimating the *size* of a causal effect, along with some level of *precision/uncertainty*, observations drawn from the principal level of analysis are essential.

---

[19] Lieberson (1985: ch. 5).   [20] Achen and Shively (1995).

While the level-of-analysis problem is usually understood with reference to causal inference, it is equally problematic when the objective of the research is descriptive. For example, in addressing the question of global inequality the issue of theoretical and substantive import concerns individuals. Yet data for individuals prior to the 1980s is scarce throughout the developing world. Thus, analysts are in the position of trying to infer the income status of individuals from aggregate, national-level data (GDP) – the problem of ecological inference noted above.

Cumulation

Science is not a solitary venture; it is better conceptualized as a collaborative project among researchers working on a particular subject area. This means that a research design's utility is partly a product of its methodological fit with extant work. Three elements facilitate cumulation: the *standardization* of procedures across studies; the *replication* of results; and the *transparency* of procedures.

Standardization

One of the chief avenues to collaboration is the standardization of procedures across research designs. If there is a usual way of investigating a particular issue this should be slavishly imitated, at least as a point of departure, for the standardization of approaches provides a benchmark against which new findings can be judged.

This may sound like a recommendation for theoretically modest exercises that merely re-test old ideas. It is not. Recall that in this section we are discussing criteria relevant to theory appraisal, not theory construction. We assume that a theory (and a more specific hypothesis or set of hypotheses) is already at hand. Given this theory – be it bold and original, or tamely derivative – it is advisable to standardize the research design as much as possible, at least at the outset.

The standardization of research designs allows findings from diverse studies to cumulate. Consider that if each new piece of research on vouchers utilizes idiosyncratic input and output measures, background controls, and other research design features, our knowledge of this topic is unlikely to move forward. A thousand studies of the same subject – no matter how impeccable their internal validity – will make only a small contribution to the growth of knowledge about vouchers if they are designed in *ad hoc* (and hence incommensurable) ways.

Novelties must be distinguishable from original contributions, and the question is assessable only insofar as a study can be measured by the yardsticks provided by extant work on a subject.

The call for standardization is a call for a more organized approach to knowledge-gathering. Richard Berk notes the great potential gains that might be realized from "suites of studies carefully designed so that variants in the interventions [can] be tested with different mixes of subjects, in different settings, and with related outcomes, all selected to document useful generalization targets."[21] So constructed, the possibilities for meta-analysis are vastly enhanced, and with it the prospect of theoretical advance.

Unfortunately, in the current highly individualized world of social research it is virtually impossible to aggregate results emanating from separate studies of the same general subject, for each study tends to adopt an idiosyncratic set of procedures.[22] In contrast to the natural sciences, there appears to be very little premium on standardization in the social sciences. Yet the case for standardization seems strong. Just as theories should fit within a broader theoretical framework – the criterion of *commensurability*, discussed in Chapter 3 – research designs should fit within the broader framework within which a particular issue has been addressed.

Replication

Another way that scientific activity relates to a community of scholars is through the replication of results. This project of replication takes place at two stages: (a) at the beginning of a study, as a way to verify extant findings in a new venue; and (b) after a study has been completed, as a way of testing that study's internal and external validity. (If replication is conducted during a study it is likely to be referred to as robustness testing, discussed in Chapter 10.[23])

Research on a topic typically begins by replicating key findings related to that research. To be sure, not all subjects have "findings" in the natural-science sense. Yet most fields recognize a set of propositions that are widely believed to be true; we shall call them findings even if they are closer to common-sense beliefs. Whatever the terminology, it is helpful if new research on a topic

---

[21] Berk (2005: 16). See also Berk *et al.* (1992); Bloom, Hill, and Riccio (2002).
[22] Briggs (2005); Petitti (1993); Wachter (1988). One possible exception to this pessimistic conclusion may be found in the field of experimental studies that have been conducted over the past few decades on subjects such as voter turnout (see the GOTV web site maintained by Don Green at Yale: http://research.yale.edu/GOTV) or employment discrimination (Pager 2007).
[23] Firebaugh (2008: ch. 4).

begins by exploring these well-known hypotheses. Are they true *here* (in this setting)? This will help clarify the validity of the chosen research design, not to mention the validity of the previous finding. This is the initial replication.

Other replications occur after a study has been completed, either prior to or after publication. (This is the more usual employment of the term.[24]) In order to facilitate replication, a research design must be conducted in such a way that future scholars can reproduce its results. Consider that findings are likely to remain suspect until they can be replicated – perhaps multiple times. We are cognizant that any number of factors might have interfered with the validity of any particular study, including (among other things) measurement error and the willful mis-reporting of data. Verification involves repetition; claims to truth, therefore, involve assurances of replicability. If a finding is obtained under circumstances that are essentially un-repeatable, then we rightfully entertain doubts about its veracity. This conforms to the narrow understanding of replication – the ability of future researchers to replicate a study's findings by carefully following the methods of procedure and sources of data that were originally employed.

But replication does not refer only to the narrowly circumscribed reiteration of a study, in near-identical circumstances. It also refers to the *variations* that may be – and ought to be – introduced to the original study. Paul Rosenbaum comments:

> The mere reappearance of an association between treatment and response does not convince us that the association is causal – whatever produced the association before has produced it again. It is the tenacity of the association – its ability to resist determined challenges – that is ultimately convincing.[25]

A finding that persists in the face of dramatic alterations in setting (background conditions), measurement instruments, specification, and treatment strength is a finding that is strongly corroborated. It is much more likely to be true than a finding that has been replicated in only minor respects. In this vein, it is important to note that replications offer not only a way to check a study's internal validity but also a means of testing – and where necessary, re-evaluating – a study's external validity. What are the boundaries of a theory?

Granted, some styles of research are easier to replicate than others. Experiments and large-N observational studies are replicable to a degree that qualitative work is generally not. However, in the case of large-N observational studies the meaning of "replication" is usually understood in a fairly restrictive fashion, that is, taking

---

[24] Freese (2007); King (1995); King, Keohane, and Verba (1994: 23, 26, 51). [25] Rosenbaum (2010: 103).

the author's dataset (or a similar dataset) and replicating the author's results. This is a fairly mechanical procedure. For example, in replicating a cross-national statistical study of economic development and democracy a scholar might try to replicate extant findings and then proceed to make small alterations – adding countries (with imputed data), adding years, or using different measures of democracy.

By contrast, the replication of qualitative work is usually understood to involve the data-collection phase of research, which may be archival, ethnographic, or discursive. For example, a serious attempt to replicate James Mahoney's historical work on democratization in Central America would presumably involve a review of the author's extensive list of primary and secondary sources, and perhaps additional sources as well.[26] This represents months of research, and is not at all mechanical.[27]

The equivalent data-gathering replication in a large-N setting would be to re-code all the data for a key variable. In our previous example this might mean re-coding the democracy variable for all countries and all years. This is not what is usually intended by replication in a quantitative context. But there is no reason not to apply the concept of replication to this commendable cross-checking of findings.

Whatever the difficulties and ambiguities, replicability is an ideal for which all research ought to strive. Arguably, it is even more important for qualitative work than for quantitative work, given the degree of authorial intervention that is usually involved in the latter (and hence the greater possibility of investigator bias). Historical researchers should include scrupulous and detailed footnotes of their sources so that future scholars can re-trace their steps. Interview-based work should include notations about informants so that future researchers can locate these people. They may also put on file their set of notes, transcripts (or recordings) of interviews – whatever might be useful for purposes of replication (without compromising the identities of sources whose secrecy has been promised).[28]

Transparency

Evidently, standardization and replication are possible only insofar as procedures employed in empirical analyses are transparent to scholars. One cannot

---

[26] Mahoney (2002).

[27] An example of this sort of replication can be found in Lieshout, Segers, and van der Vleuten (2004), an attempt to replicate the archival work of Moravcsik (1998).

[28] See Hammersley (1997); Mauthner, Parry, and Backett-Milburn (1998), and the articles in Corti, Witzel, and Bishop (2005).

standardize or replicate what is ambiguous. Thus, implicit in the call for cumulation is the call for *transparency*. "The pathway between the data and the conclusions should be ... clear."[29] For, without transparency, no finding can be fully evaluated.

It is common in natural sciences for researchers to maintain a laboratory notebook in which a close record is kept of how an empirical analysis unfolds. While it may not be necessary to record every specification test, it should at least be possible for future scholars to see which tests were conducted, in what order, and with what implications for the theory. By contrast, if scholars see only the final product of a piece of research (which may have unfolded over many years) it is more difficult to render judgment on its truth-value. One fears, in particular, that the final data tables may contain the one set of tests that culminated in "positive" (i.e., theoretically significant) results, ignoring hundreds of prior tests in which the null hypothesis could not be rejected.

Granted, the achievement of full transparency imposes costs on researchers, mostly in the form of time and effort (since the posting of notebooks is essentially cost-less). And it does not entirely solve problems of accountability. Someone must read the protocols, an investment of time. Even then, we shall never know if all procedures and results were faithfully recorded. However, the institution of a transparency regime is a precondition of greater account-ability, and may in time enhance the validity and precision of empirical analysis in the social sciences.

Theoretical fit

Recall that the purpose of an empirical analysis is to shed light on an argument or theory. The relationship of the test to the argument is, therefore, a particu-larly sensitive issue. Three issues bear on the theoretical fit of a research design: *construct validity*, *severity*, and *partition*. All may be considered aspects of a general scientific ideal known as the *crucial* (or critical) *test*.[30]

Construct validity

Construct validity refers to the faithfulness of a research design to the theory that is under investigation.[31] This includes concept validity: the operationalization of

---

[29] Cox (2007: 2), quoted in Rosenbaum (2010: 147).
[30] Eckstein (1975); Forsyth (1976); Popper (1965: 112). Platt (1964) suggests that the notion may be traced back to Francis Bacon.
[31] Shadish, Cook, and Campbell (2002).

a key concept with a set of indicators. But it also includes basic assumptions or interpretations of the theory. Consider that if a research design deviates significantly from the theory – involving, let us say, questionable assumptions about the theory or building on peripheral elements of the theory – then the theory can scarcely be proven or disproven, for the research design does not bear centrally upon it. By the same token, if a researcher chooses a hypothesis that lies at the core of a theory, the research design has greater relevance.

In this context, one might contemplate the vast range of work on education policy that bears in some way or another on vouchers.[32] A good deal of this research lies at the periphery of the core hypothesis about school vouchers and school performance; it is somewhat relevant, but not primary. For example, if a study shows that vouchers have no effect on racial harmony in schools this finding, while interesting, is not likely to be considered central to the theory. As such, the theory is relatively unaffected by the finding. If, by contrast, a study shows that vouchers have no effect on educational performance this is devastating to the theory, precisely because the research design and the theory are so closely aligned.

Granted, many grand theories do not rest on a single central hypothesis (such as vouchers and educational performance). Consider the larger theory of free market competition that informs the voucher idea. This theory, as framed by Milton Friedman, Friedrich von Hayek, or Adam Smith, is not amenable to any knock-down tests of which I am aware. Capitalism, like socialism, resists falsification. Evidently, the more abstract the theory, the harder it is to translate that theory into a viable empirical test.[33] Even so, researchers must work hard to ensure that empirical tests are not theoretically trivial. A high level of internal and external validity will not rescue a theoretically irrelevant study, for which we reserve the epithet "straw-man."

Severity

Some empirical tests are easy, requiring little of a theory to clear the hurdle (which may or may not be formalized in a statistical test such as a t-test). Other empirical tests are hard, requiring a great deal of a theory. *Ceteris paribus*, we are more likely to believe that a theory is true when it has passed a severe empirical test (as long as the test has some degree of construct validity). "Confirmations should count," insists Popper,

---

[32] Daniels (2005).   [33] Gorski (2004); Green and Shapiro (1994); Lieberson (1992).

only if they are the result of *risky predictions*; that is, if, unenlightened by the theory in question, we should have expected an event which was incompatible with the theory – an event which would have refuted the theory.[34]

The same factors work in reverse if one is attempting to disprove (falsify) a theory. If the theory fails a very hard test, one may not be inclined to conclude that it is wrong. If, on the other hand, it fails an easy test – one that, according to the premises of the theory it ought to have passed – then one's attitude toward the theory is apt to be more skeptical.

An analogy drawn from track-and-field may help to illustrate the point. Suppose, for example, we wish to test the relative ability of various athletes in the high jump, an event that traces its lineage to ancient Greece. In the first test, we set the bar at 10 ft (3 m) – a ridiculous goal, given that the highest recorded free jump is just over 8 ft (2.5 m). Predictably, all the athletes fail to clear this most-difficult test. In the second test, we approach the matter differently, setting the bar at 3 ft (1 m). Predictably, all the athletes clear this least-difficult test. Evidently, we have learned nothing whatsoever of the relative abilities of this group of athletes at the end of these two tests. To be sure, had any of these athletes passed the hard test (or failed the easy test) we would have learned, beyond a shadow of a doubt, that that particular athlete was an extraordinarily good (bad) high jumper. This is the irony of the criterion of *severity*: it depends on the outcome of the test. Otherwise stated, one wishes to set the bar just high enough that it can be cleared by some people (but no higher), or just low enough that it cannot be cleared by some people (but no lower).

One apparent resolution of this problem is to avoid setting arbitrary thresholds. Instead, ask athletes to jump as high as they can and simply measure their relative performance – a *continuous* metric. Or, if circumstances demand (e.g., if it is necessary to establish a bar in order to measure the height of a jump), set up numerous tests with varying thresholds. These two approaches amount to the same thing, except that the latter requires multiple iterations and is in this sense less efficient.

A flexible approach to testing is justified in many contexts. However, the sacrifice one makes in adopting a flexible standard should be clear. Wherever the criteria for success and failure are not spelled out clearly in advance the resulting research is less falsifiable, that is, more liable to varying interpretations of success and failure.

---

[34] Popper (1965: 36). See also Popper ([1934] 1968); Howson and Urbach (1989: 86); Mayo (1996: ch. 6); Mayo and Spanos (2006).

Moreover, even if one eliminates an *a priori* threshold for success/failure, many factors are likely to remain that serve to structure the degree of difficulty of a test. Returning to our track-and-field example, it will be seen that athletes' performance is affected by a great many "contextual" factors – altitude, whether the event is held indoors or outdoors, the quality of the surface, the audience in attendance, and so forth. Relative performance varies with all of these factors (and perhaps many more). In social science settings, the list of contextual factors is also quite large. Here one might consider various research design factors that "load the dice" for, or against, a school vouchers study. Suppose, for example, that a study of vouchers is conducted in a community where teachers and administrators, as well as many of the participants in the program, are skeptical about – and even downright hostile to – the reform. Or suppose that teachers working in vouchers schools (schools attended by children with vouchers) are less experienced or less educated than teachers working in public schools. Suppose, finally, that the monetary value of the voucher that students received was minimal – less than prior work and theory suggests would be necessary to achieve significant changes in student achievement. These are all factors that would seem to load the dice against a positive finding. If, under the circumstances, that study finds that vouchers induce a positive (and statistically significant) effect on student performance, we are likely to be especially impressed by the finding. On the other hand, if the foregoing factors are reversed, and the bias of a study appears to *favor* the vouchers hypothesis, a positive finding will have little credibility. Indeed, it is quite likely spurious.

Assumptions about the direction of probable bias may play an important role in evaluating the empirical findings of a study (*ex post*), as well as in designing a study (*ex ante*). Rosenbaum notes that a

sometimes compelling study design exploits a claim to know that the most plausible bias runs counter to the claimed effects of the treatment. In this design, two groups are compared that are known to be incomparable, but incomparable in a direction that would tend to mask an actual effect rather than create a spurious one. The logic behind this design is valid: if the bias runs counter to the anticipated effect, and the bias is ignored, inferences about the effect will be conservative, so the bias will not lead to spurious rejection of no effect in favor of the anticipated effect.[35]

In short, the degree of difficulty imposed by a research design with respect to a particular hypothesis is an intrinsic part of any study. Whether the purpose of

---

[35] Rosenbaum (2010: 123).

the research is positive (to prove a causal proposition) or negative (to disprove a causal proposition), the value of a research design derives partly from its relative "crucial-ness." The following question thus arises with respect to any study: how likely is it that theory A is true (false), given the evidence? The harder (easier) the test, the more inclined we are to accept the conclusion – *if* the test is passed (failed).

Even if one dispenses with arbitrary thresholds for judging success and failure, it will still be the case that background factors built into a research design qualify that test as "easy" or "difficult" with respect to a particular hypothesis. These factors, which move well beyond the narrow issues addressed by quantitative measures of statistical significance or statistical power, must be taken into account if we are to arrive at a judgment of the overall truth-value of a finding. Such issues beg consideration *ex ante*, during the design of a study, and *ex post*, as researchers assess a study's contribution.

Whether one opts for a research design that leans toward greater or lesser difficulty depends upon many factors. Easy tests are often appropriate at early phases of hypothesis testing, when a project is still largely exploratory and when few extant studies of a subject exist. Hard tests become appropriate as a hypothesis becomes well established and as the number of extant studies multiplies.

Of course, hard tests are better if they can be devised in a way that is fair to the theory under investigation – if they maintain *construct validity*, in other words. A good deal of research in the natural sciences seems to follow this model. Consider this list of risky predictions that served to confirm or refute important theories in physics:

Newton's prediction of elliptical orbits of the planets from the inverse square law of gravitation; various experiments confirming the wave theory of light; Maxwell's prediction of electromagnetic waves from a mathematical model; the Michelson–Morley experiment that disproved the existence of the ether and confirmed the constant velocity of light; Kelvin's prediction of absolute zero temperature; derivations from Poisson's and Fourier's mathematical theory of heat; inferences based on the kinetic theory of gases and statistical mechanics; the prediction of various subatomic particles; Gamow's prediction that the Big Bang had left its mark in radiation at the edge of the universe; and, most famously, Einstein's predictions that led to the confirmation of his special and general theories of relativity, such as the "bending" of a star's light by gravitational attraction.[36]

---

[36] Coleman (2007: 129–130).

The author of this compendium, Stephen Coleman, also helpfully identifies several features of these theoretical predictions that proved useful in establishing a crucial test. These include:

• Prediction of a constant or invariant (like the speed of light or a freezing point) • Prediction of a specific number • Prediction of a symmetry, often derived from a mathematical model • Prediction of a topological fixed point • Prediction of a limit or constant, or dynamic limit cycle • Prediction of a specific or unusual dynamic behavior pattern • Prediction of a specific spatial (geographic) pattern • Prediction of a statistical distribution, possibly an unusual distribution • Prediction that data will have a "signature" – a unique mathematical shape (as used for detecting heart arrhythmias, nuclear tests, tsunamis, or submarines).[37]

These are useful exemplars and suggestions. It is especially important to appreciate that there are a multitude of ways to construct a test for a given hypothesis, only one of which takes the form of a classic linear and additive model. A common approach is to specify (or examine for clues, *ex post*) a dose–response relationship, that is, the way in which Y responds to a change in X.[38] Many of these alternatives offer a higher degree of falsifiability because they offer highly specific predictions, drawn directly from the theory – predictions that are unlikely to be true unless the theory is true – as opposed to the run-of-the-mill social science prediction that "an increase in X will lead to an increase in Y."

Of course, one may be skeptical about the practicality of this advice.[39] How many social phenomena are amenable to precise *a priori* predictions? How many are amenable to mathematical models of the sort that would yield precise, *a priori* predictions? The present state of formal modeling in most social science disciplines, while aiming to achieve the crucial tests of physics, is still a long way from that goal.

We do not need to resolve this question. For present purposes, it is sufficient to observe that the precision of a theory is essential to the severity of a test. Both are a matter of degrees, and both are a key component of that theory's falsifiability.

Partition

Falsifiability is also enhanced insofar as an argument can be effectively isolated, or *partitioned*, from the empirical analysis. This reduces the possibility that a theory might be adjusted, *post hoc*, so as to accommodate negative

---

[37] Coleman (2007: 130). See also Taagepera (2008).   [38] Rosenbaum (2010: 124–125).
[39] Grofman (2007).

findings. It also reduces the temptation to construct arguments closely modeled on a particular empirical setting ("curve-fitting"), or research designs
whose purpose is to prove (rather than test) a given argument. Ideally – at least
for purposes of appraisal – the construction of an argument should be
considered a separate step from the testing of that same argument.[40]

Another sort of partition can sometimes be erected between the research
design phase of a study and the data analysis phase of a study. This distinction –
between prospective design and retrospective analysis – is a hallmark of the
experimental method, and one of the reasons why experiments are rightly
regarded as enhancing the falsifiability of a study.[41] There is less opportunity
for *ex post facto* adjustments of design to rectify inconvenient empirical results.

Granted, the goal of partitioning is always a matter of degree. It is not clear
how the advance of knowledge could occur if partitions were to be complete
and final. (What does "final" mean?) Note that any failed test (not to mention
successful tests) must be followed up with further tests, and these further tests
must take the failures (and successes) of the past into account. In this sense, all
research is an iterative process, moving back and forth between theory and
evidence.

The criterion of partition may be understood, first, as referring to the length
of time that ensues between initial testing and subsequent reformulation and
re-testing. If the duration is minute – for example, statistical specification tests
conducted at intervals of several seconds through an automated routine – then
we are apt to label the procedure curve-fitting. One is not really testing a model;
one is finding the best fit between a set of variables (representing a set of very
loose hypotheses) and a sample of data. If, on the other hand, the duration is
lengthy – say, a year or more – then we would be more inclined to feel that the
goal of partition has been achieved. Theory formation has been segregated from
theory-testing.

Second, partition refers to data employed for testing. Ideally, arguments
should be tested with a sample of observations different from those employed
to generate the theory. This provides *out-of-sample* tests. To be sure, if samples
are large and representative this should not make much difference; the same
results should obtain. And if samples are small and/or non-representative,

---

[40] King, Keohane, and Verba (1994) advise: "Ad hoc adjustments in a theory that does not fit existing data
    must be used rarely" (p. 21). "Always . . . avoid using the same data to evaluate the theory [you] used to
    develop it" (p. 46). Original data can be reused "as long as the implication does not 'come out of' the data
    but is a hypothesis independently suggested by the theory or a different data set" (p. 30). See also Eckstein
    (1992: 266); Friedman ([1953] 1984: 213); Goldthorpe (1997: 15).
[41] Rubin (2008: 816).

a strong argument can be made for combining all available data into a single sample – thereby maximizing sample size and representativeness. So, one may be skeptical of how practical the out-of-sample test is in practice. Nonetheless, where practicable, it is certainly desirable.

Finally, and most importantly I think, partition refers to a state of mind. Insofar as theorizing and testing are separable, the most important feature of this separation is not the length of time that one is segregated from the other or the difference in samples, but rather the attitude of the researcher.

Mental partition requires multiple personalities. At the stage of theory-generation, the researcher must be nurturing – a booster of the theory that is being created. All efforts are focused single-mindedly on the creation and sustenance of that new and still fragile idea. *A priori* speculations about the world are *de rigueur*, for one must posit a great deal in order to establish the foundation for a theory. Arguments are argumentative.

At the stage of theory-testing, by contrast, a second personality must be adopted. This personality is non-partisan, or perhaps even openly skeptical with respect to the main hypothesis under examination. The baby has been born, it has suckled, it is now strong enough to face the rigors of the world (i.e., empirical testing). To continue the metaphor, good research requires killing one's own children from time to time.

This is the sort of mental partition that research requires. Arguably, it is only fully achievable when the two stages of research – theory-formation and theory-testing – are carried out by different persons, that is, where the tester has no incentive to disprove the null hypothesis. But in the real world of research, especially social science research (where funding and personnel are limited relative to the number of research questions under consideration), this is rarely possible. So, we must appeal to the researcher's good sense and to his or her capacity to transition from the mentality of theorizing and nurturing to the mentality of analysis and severe tests, that is, from discovery to appraisal (Chapter 2).

It is vital that the audience for a piece of research feel confident in the impartiality of the researcher throughout the testing phase. There are many ways in which researcher bias can creep in, and there is no way for audiences to monitor the situation if researchers are in charge of testing their own hypotheses. Principal–agency complications are too great. This means that trust is required, and the researcher must work hard to earn the audience's trust.

One technique is to declare one's biases at the outset, so that it is clear to the reader of a report where the researcher's point of departure is (and so that the distinction between theorizing and testing is preserved, at least rhetorically). If it happens that a research finding runs *counter* to the original hypothesis, audiences may be more inclined to believe that result, on the assumption that it has cleared an especially high hurdle (or, at the very least, that investigator bias has not infected the result). In situations of poor oversight, the mind-set of the researcher is highly relevant to an *ex post* analysis of findings.

Part II

Description

5   Concepts

The history of the social sciences is and remains a continuous process passing from the attempt to order reality analytically through the construction of concepts – the dissolution of the analytical constructs so constructed through the expansion and shift of the scientific horizon – and the reformulation anew of concepts on the foundations thus transformed ... The greatest advances in the sphere of the social sciences are substantively tied up with the shift in practical cultural problems and take the guise of a critique of concept-construction.

Max Weber[1]

As we are ... prisoners of the words we pick, we had better pick them well.

Giovanni Sartori[2]

Description will be understood in this book as any empirical argument (hypothesis, theory, etc.) about the world that claims to answer a *what* question (e.g., *how*, *when*, *whom*, or *in what manner*). By contrast, wherever there is an implicit or explicit claim that a factor generates variation in an outcome the argument will be regarded as causal. The distinction between these two key concepts thus hinges on the nature of the truth-claim – not on the quality of the evidence at hand, which may be strong or weak.[3] Description

---

[1] Weber ([1905] 1949: 105–106).   [2] Sartori (1984: 60).

[3] This is somewhat at variance with current linguistic practices, where these terms are frequently employed as a signal of the quality of the evidence at hand: with "causal" reserved for experimental or quasi-experimental evidence and "descriptive" reserved for evidence that is (for whatever reason) weak. Andrew Gelman advises: "When describing comparisons and regressions, try to avoid 'effect' and other causal terms (except in clearly causal scenarios) and instead write or speak in descriptive terms": www.stat.columbia.edu/~cook/movabletype/archives/2009/03/describing_desc.html. In this vein, some researchers prefer to regard *all* evidence as descriptive, so as to emphasize the interpretive leap that causal inference requires (Achen 1982: 77–78). The evident problem with this definitional move is that it deprives us of a way of distinguishing between arguments that embrace different goals. Note that any attempt to appraise the truth-value of an empirical proposition must begin by resolving what the goals of that proposition are, i.e., descriptive, causal, or some other. If the truth-claim is unclear then it is impossible to falsify. From this perspective, preserving the traditional distinction between *what* questions and *why* questions ought to be a high priority for the discipline.

is the topic of Part II, while causation is the topic of Part III. Description rightly comes first; one must describe in order to explain (causally). However, the reader will find many comparisons and contrasts across the two topics interwoven throughout the book.

Because this book is focused on generalizing statements about the world (Chapter 1), I am not concerned with descriptions that reflect only on individual cases or events (without any attempt to exemplify larger patterns).[4] Consequently, in this book description is always an *inferential* act. To generalize is to infer from what we know (or think we know) to what we do not know.[5] One sort of inferential leap is from observations within a sample that are deemed secure to those that are uncertain or missing (problems of "measurement error" or "missing data") and to dimensions that are inherently unobservable ("latent characteristics"). Another sort of inferential leap is from a studied case or sample to a larger (unstudied) population. In both respects, descriptive models offer a "theory" about the world,[6] "a 'formula' through which the data can be reproduced."[7]

In recent years, the quest for scientific understanding has come to be equated with the quest for a causal understanding of the world across the social sciences. By contrast, the task of description is identified with idiographic storytelling – impressionistic narratives relating details about particular times and places – or with issues of measurement. The term itself has come to be employed as a euphemism for a failed, or not yet proven, causal inference. Studies that do not engage causal or predictive questions are judged "merely" descriptive.[8] Likewise, evidence for a causal proposition that is judged especially weak is likely to be characterized as "descriptive." More generally, the view of description that obtains in the social sciences (and especially in economics and political science) is of a mundane task – necessary, to be sure, but of little intrinsic scientific value.

The subordination of description to causation is problematic from a number of perspectives. First and foremost, a large class of descriptive topics is

---

[4] To reiterate: this does not preclude the discussion of particular events and outcomes, but it does mean that the goal of these cases is to reflect upon the characteristics of a larger population.

[5] On some fundamental level, all empirical knowledge may be considered inferential. However, it is helpful to distinguish between readily apprehensible facts about the world ("observables") and those which must be speculated upon ("unobservables"). I reserve the concept of inference for the latter.

[6] Jacoby (1999).   [7] Berk (2004: 207).

[8] It is not clear when, precisely, this pejorative connotation arose. It was invoked, or commented on, in the social science literature at various points in the mid- to late twentieth century (e.g., Klimm 1959; Sen 1980; Singer 1961). However, it probably stretches back further in time within the tradition of Anglo-American economics and political science (e.g., Clark and Banks 1793: 157).

intrinsically important. Into this class fall subjects like democracy, human rights, war, revolution, standards of living, mortality, ethnic conflict, happiness/ utility, and inequality. These topics (and many others) deserve to be explored descriptively. We need to know how much democracy there is in the world, how this quantity – or bundle of attributes – varies from country to country, region to region, and through time. This is important regardless of what causes democracy or what causal effects democracy has.[9]

The concern is that if conceptualization and measurement of democracy occurs only in the quest for causal inference we may not achieve the same level of accuracy, precision, and comprehensiveness with respect to the topic. A research agenda motivated solely by a causal hypothesis is apt to take short-cuts when it comes to describing the left- and right-hand variables. Moreover, that which one chooses to describe may be influenced by the general X/Y relationship one expects to find, and this may introduce biases into how we describe the phenomenon. To be sure, there is nothing wrong with causally oriented description. But it may pose a problem if this is the principal means of approaching a topic within a field over many years.[10]

A second reason for liberating description from specific causal hypotheses is practical in nature. Often, it is more efficient to collect evidence when the objective of the investigation is descriptive rather than causal. Consider that

---

[9] For examples of natural science research that is descriptive rather than causal see Bunge (1979).

[10] Naturally, if the social sciences were grounded in a single causal-theoretical framework on the order of evolution within the biological sciences then we would possess a causal model around which a coherent description of the world might be reliably constructed. However, we lack such a unifying paradigm, and in its absence it is difficult to say how a causally ordered description of the political world might be organized or what it would look like (in concrete terms). One might counter that in a multiparadigmatic universe one should look to smaller-scale causal hypotheses to organize the work of the discipline, along the "behavioralist" model. But here one stumbles upon another problem of indeterminacy. Because causal attribution is difficult to establish for most nontrivial questions in social science it is problematic to assert that X matters as a subject of investigation only insofar as it causes Y (or Y matters only insofar as it is caused by X). Ambiguity about whether X *really* causes Y means that it may be safer to approach X and Y first as descriptive phenomena – important in their own right – rather than as potential independent and dependent variables. As an example, let us reconsider the question of "democracy." Presumably, this feature has many causal properties. However, we do not know for sure what these are; and certainly, we do not know *precisely* what they are. Consequently, the subject is perhaps better approached, at least initially, as a descriptive issue. Of course, I do not mean to suggest that descriptive inference be carried out in ignorance of all causal potentialities. I mean, rather, that in circumstances where causal frameworks are open-ended – presumably the vast majority of cases in social science – descriptive inference ought to be carried out independent of any *particular* causal hypothesis. This helps to avoid a highly prejudiced (i.e., particularistic, idiosyncratic) definition of a subject matter. All plausible causal hypotheses are relevant – those in which a subject serves as an independent variable, those in which it serves as a dependent variable, and those in which it serves as a causal pathway in some larger subject. When considered in this open-ended fashion the subject of interest (e.g., democracy) is rightly approached descriptively rather than simply as an adjunct to subsequent causal analysis.

data is collected from persons, governments, archives, and other organizations. Collecting evidence from these sources in a systematic fashion requires considerable energy and resources, sustained over many years. When a data-collection effort is constructed around a single causal hypothesis or theory the scholar's purview is naturally quite limited; only those factors having direct bearing on the hypothesis will be collected. This may be efficient in the short run, but it is not likely to be efficient in the long run. Narrowly focused data expeditions entail scaling high cliffs and returning to base camp with only a small sample of what one finds at the peak. Later expeditions, focused on different hypotheses, will require re-scaling the same peak, a time-consuming and wasteful enterprise. By contrast, if an evidence-gathering mission is conceptualized as descriptive rather than causal (which is to say, no *single* causal theory guides the research), it is more likely to produce a broad range of evidence that will be applicable to a broad range of questions, both descriptive and causal.[11]

In sum, there are good reasons to approach description as a distinctive – and essential – task of social science. This is the motivation of Part II of the book. This chapter focuses on social science concepts, the linguistic containers we use to carve up the empirical world. Chapter 6 offers a typology of descriptive arguments, and Chapter 7 focuses on the task of measurement, the "analysis" of descriptive propositions.

The quandary of description

Conventional wisdom presumes that causal inference is harder, methodologically speaking. "*What* questions are generally easier to answer than *why* questions" states Glenn Firebaugh.[12] "Empirical data can tell us what is happening far more readily than they can tell us why it is happening," affirms Stanley Lieberson.[13] Reading the methodological literature, one might infer that description is a relatively simple and intuitive act of apperception.

And yet, many descriptive questions circulating through the disciplines of social science are recalcitrant. Consider the following:

(1) Do voters conceptualize politics ideologically[14] or nonideologically?[15]
(2) Is global inequality increasing[16] or remaining about the same?[17]

---

[11] Schedler (forthcoming).   [12] Firebaugh (2008: 3).
[13] Lieberson (1985: 219). See also Gelman (2010).   [14] Nie, Verba, and Petrocik (1976).
[15] Converse (1964).   [16] Milanovic (2005).
[17] Bourguignon and Morrisson (2002); Dollar (2005); Firebaugh (2003).

(3) Is American political culture liberal/egalitarian,[18] republican,[19] or a mixture of both, along with various ascriptive identities?[20]

These are all essentially descriptive questions about the social world (though, to be sure, they contain causal implications). They have also proven to be hotly contested. And they are not unusual in this regard. A random sample of (nontrivial) descriptive arguments would likely reveal a high level of uncertainty. Indeed, there is great consternation over the poor quality and measly quantity of evidence by which we attempt to make sense of the social world.[21] Descriptive accounts of mid-level phenomena like corruption, campaign finance, civil service protection, judicial independence, and party strength are often highly problematic, or are restricted in purview to very specific contexts (and hence resist generalization). And the big concepts of social science – such as democracy and governance – have no standard and precise meaning or measurement.[22] Meanwhile, whole tracts of social and political activity remain virtually *terra incognita*.[23] As a result, empirical phenomena on the left and right sides of the typical causal model are highly uncertain. To paraphrase Giovanni Sartori, the more we advance in causal modeling, the more we leave a vast, uncharted territory at our backs.[24]

To get a glimpse of the methodological problems we face in reaching descriptive inferences let us contrast the following two questions:

(1) What is democracy, and how might it be operationalized?
(2) Does democracy enhance the prospect of peaceful coexistence?

Note that the causal question (2) presumes an answer to the descriptive question (1). In order to estimate democracy's causal effect one must first establish the definition and measurement of this vexing concept. Logic suggests that if Proposition 2 builds on Proposition 1 it must be at least as difficult to prove as Proposition 1. And yet, by all appearances, there is greater scholarly consensus on the answer to question (2) than on the answer to question (1). Scholars of

---

[18] Hartz (1955); Tocqueville (1945).   [19] Pocock (1975).   [20] Smith (1993).

[21] Heath and Martin (1997); Herrera and Kapur (2007); Kurtz and Schrank (2007); Munck (2009); Rokkan *et al.* (1970: 169–180).

[22] On democracy, see Bowman, Lehoucq, and Mahoney (2005); Coppedge (forthcoming); Hadenius and Teorell (2005); Munck (2009); Munck and Verkuilen (2002). On governance, see Kurtz and Schrank (2007); March and Olson (1995); Pagden (1998); Pierre (2000). A wide-ranging compendium of indicators for democracy and governance can be found in USAID (1998).

[23] As one example one might consider local government in the developing world, a topic that has elicited little systematic empirical attention, despite its evident importance. For a recent review of this neglected field of study see UN Habitat (2004).

[24] Sartori (1970: 1033).

international relations generally agree that regime status has a causal effect on peace and war such that democracies are less likely to fight wars with one another, all other things being equal. Whether or not democracy is a *sufficient* condition for peace may never be determined, and scholars continue to debate the causal mechanisms at work in this relationship. However, there is still a large measure of agreement on the democratic peace as – at the very least – a probabilistic causal regularity.[25] All things being equal, two democratic countries are less likely to go to war with one another than two countries, one or both of which are nondemocratic. By contrast, no such consensus exists on how to conceptualize and measure democracy. The causal proposition is fairly certain, while the descriptive proposition that underlies it is highly uncertain.

This is the paradoxical pattern for many descriptive inferences. Despite the fact that causal inferences build on descriptive inferences the former are often more certain and more falsifiable. The reasons for this are partly intrinsic to the enterprise. For example, descriptions often center on matters of definition, and therefore are not as amenable to appeals to evidence. Descriptions are also often exploratory in nature, and therefore constructed in close contact with the evidence (a problem of insufficient *partition* [Chapter 4]).

That said, some of the methodological problems encountered by descriptive inference are remediable. Arguably, they are a product of the general lack of methodological self-consciousness that permeates this enterprise. My hope is that by clarifying the common criteria pertaining to descriptive arguments, and by classifying the immense variety of descriptive arguments, we may improve the quality of descriptive inference – and, perhaps, over time, enhance its standing in the social sciences.

Concepts

Concept formation lies at the heart of all social science endeavors.[26] It is impossible to conduct work without using concepts. It is impossible even to conceptualize a topic, as the term suggests, without putting a label on it. Concepts are integral to every argument for they address the most basic question of social science research: what are we talking about?

If concepts allow us to conceptualize, it follows that creative work on a subject involves some *re*conceptualizing of that subject. A study of democracy, if persuasive, is likely to alter our understanding of "democracy," at least to some

[25] Brown, Lynn-Jones, and Miller (1996); Elman (1997).   [26] Sartori (1970: 1038).

degree.[27] No use of language is semantically neutral. Authors make lexical and semantic choices as they write and thus participate, wittingly or unwittingly, in an ongoing interpretive battle. This is so because language is the toolkit with which we conduct our work, as well as the substance on which we work. Progress in the social sciences occurs through changing terms and definitions. This is how we map the changing terrain (or our changing perceptions of the terrain).

Unfortunately, all is not well in the land of concepts. It has become a standard complaint that the terminology of social science lacks the clarity and constancy of natural science lexicons. Concepts are variously employed in different fields and subfields, within different intellectual traditions, among different writers, and sometimes – most alarmingly – within a single work. Concepts are routinely stretched to cover instances that lie well outside their normal range of use.[28] Or they are scrunched to cover only a few instances – ignoring others that might profitably be housed under the same rubric. Older concepts are redefined, leaving etymological trails that confuse the unwitting reader. New words are created to refer to things that were perhaps poorly articulated through existing concepts, creating a highly complex lexical terrain (given that the old concepts continue to circulate). Words with similar meanings crowd around each other, vying for attention and stealing each other's attributes. Thus, we play musical chairs with words, in Giovanni Sartori's memorable phrase.[29]

A result of these pathologies is that studies of the same subject appear to be talking about different things, and studies of different subjects appear to be talking about the same thing. Cumulation is impeded and methodological fragmentation encouraged. Concepts seem to get in the way of clear understanding.

One solution to our seemingly endless conceptual muddle is to bypass conceptual disputes altogether, focusing on the phenomena themselves rather than the labels and definitions we attach to them. If, as Galileo observed, all definitions are arbitrary, then we might as well begin by recognizing this fact.[30] It is commonly said, for example, that one can prove practically anything simply by defining terms in a convenient way. This is what prompts some commentators to say that we ought to pay less attention to the terms we use, and more to the things out there that we are talking about. "Never let yourself be goaded into taking seriously problems about words and their meanings," Karl Popper warns. "What must be taken seriously are questions

---

[27] Discussion of the concept of democracy in this chapter and the next draws on Coppedge (forthcoming); Coppedge and Gerring (2011); Munck (2009).
[28] Collier and Mahon (1993); Sartori (1970).   [29] Sartori (1975: 9; see also 1984: 38, 52–53).
[30] Robinson (1954: 63).

of fact, and assertions about facts, theories, and hypotheses; the problems they solve; and the problems they raise."[31]

The empiricist perspective seems reasonable on the face of things. And yet we are unable to talk about questions of fact without getting caught up in the language that we use to describe these facts. To be sure, things exist in the world separate from the language that we use to describe them. However, we cannot talk about them unless and until we introduce linguistic symbols. Any cumulation of knowledge depends upon reaching an understanding about what to call a thing and how to define it. This militates against a blithe nominalism ("call it whatever you want").

A second approach to resolving conceptual difficulty in the social sciences suggests that concept formation is irreducibly a matter of context. There is little one can say in general about concept formation because different concepts will be appropriate for different research tasks and research venues. This hoary bit of wisdom is absolutely true – but also highly ambiguous. What does context mean, and how might it help to guide the process of concept formation? I suspect that every author has their own preferred context, which means that conceptual disputes are simply displaced from "concept" to "context." Of course, I am not arguing that the choice of terms and definitions should be insensitive to research contexts. I am, rather, raising the question of precisely *how* contexts would or should guide concept formation.

A third approach to conceptual dis-ambiguation advises us to avoid high-order concepts in preference for less abstract (more "concrete") concepts. Because most of the conceptual ambiguities of social science involve large conceptual containers, such as culture, democracy, ideology, legitimacy, power, public goods, rationality, and the state, perhaps we ought to pare down our conceptual ambitions in favor of manageable units such as deaths, votes, and purchasing power. This also seems reasonable. However, there are important tradeoffs to such a strategy (known to philosophers as *physicalism*). Most obviously, we would be limited in what we could talk about. We could discuss votes but not democracy. And although this concretized lexicon might lead to greater agreement among social scientists one would have to wonder about the overall utility of a social science reconstructed along such lines. Does the act of voting matter outside a framework of democracy? Is it meaningful at all? Arguably, a social science limited to directly observable entities would have very little of importance to say. Moreover, it would have no way of putting these small-order ideas together into a coherent whole. Large-order concepts comprise

---

[31] Popper (1976: 19; quoted in Collier 1998).

the scaffolding on which we hang observables. Without general concepts, science cannot generalize, and without the ability to generalize science cannot theorize.[32] A social science composed purely of concrete concepts would be a series of disconnected facts and micromechanisms.

A final approach to concept dis-ambiguation seeks a taxonomic reconstruction of scientific concepts, an approach sometimes designated as "Classical" after the work of Aristotle and latter-day logicians in the Aristotelian tradition.[33] This is an attractive ideal, as the taxonomy possesses many desirable qualities (reviewed in the previous chapter). Yet while it may be practicable in some areas of natural science such as biology, the taxonomic approach does not seem to apply across the board in social science. Taxonomies have their uses, but these uses tend to be restricted to specialized settings: individual studies or very specific terrains. It is a specialized tool, not a general-purpose tool.

The general employment of social science concepts cannot be successfully contained within a set of taxonomies – much less, within a single all-embracing taxonomy. Meanings overflow the neat and tidy borders of social science taxonomies; rarely are concepts reducible to necessary and sufficient attributes. And even if social scientists were to accept such a reconstruction, one might wonder about the utility of a rigidly taxonomic lexicon. Note that the world of decisional behavior that the social sciences seek to describe and explain is characterized by a great deal of messiness and in-discreteness. Phenomena of this nature do not readily group together in bundles with clear borders and hierarchical interrelationships. Thus, while it is true that a simplified taxonomic language would reduce semantic confusion it might also reduce our capacity to correctly understand the social world. We could agree on a lot (if we all agreed to use symbols in the same way), but we could not say very much.

In this chapter I offer a somewhat new approach to the task of conceptualization. The chapter begins with a discussion of several key criteria pertaining

---

[32] By "theorize," I mean the search for descriptive or causal inferences that are general in scope – not the development of a theory about a single event or context. For further discussion, see Chapter 4.

[33] The classical approach to concept formation is usually traced back to Aristotle and the scholastic philosophers of the Middle Ages. Nineteenth-century exponents include Mill ([1843] 1872: 73) and Jevons (see discussion in Kaplan 1964: 68). In the twentieth century, see Chapin (1939); Cohen and Nagel (1934); DiRenzo (1966); Dumont and Wilson (1967); Hempel (1952, 1963, 1965, 1966); Landau (1972); Lasswell and Kaplan (1950); Lazarsfeld (1966); Meehan (1971); Stinchcombe (1968, 1978); Zannoni (1978); and, most importantly, Sartori (1970, 1984). For a somewhat different reconstructive approach based on the analytic philosophic tradition see Oppenheim (1961, 1975, 1981). For further discussion of the classical concept and its limitations see Adcock (2005); Collier and Levitsky (1997); Collier and Gerring (2009); Collier and Mahon (1993); Goertz (2006); Kaplan (1964: 68); Lakoff (1987); Taylor (1995).

to all empirical concepts. It continues by offering a set of strategies that may help to structure the task of concept formation in social science settings.

Criteria of conceptualization

Four elements of an empirical concept are conventionally distinguished: (a) the *term* (a linguistic label comprising one or a few words); (b) *attributes* that define those phenomena (the definition, intension, connotation, or properties of a concept); (c) *indicators* that help to locate the concept in empirical space (the measurement or operationalization of a concept); and (d) *phenomena* to be defined (the referents, extension, or denotation of a concept).

As an example, let us consider the concept of democracy. The term is "democracy." A commonly cited attribute is "contested elections." An indicator might be "a country that has recently held a contested election." And the phenomena of interest are, of course, the entities out there in the world that correspond to the concept, so defined.

When a concept is formulated (or reformulated) it means that one or all of the features is adjusted. Note that they are so interwoven that it would be difficult to change one feature without changing another. The process of concept formation is therefore one of mutual adjustment. To achieve a higher degree of conceptual adequacy one may (a) choose a different term, (b) alter the defining attributes contained in the intension, (c) adjust the indicators by which the concept is operationalized, or (d) redraw the phenomenal boundaries of the extension.

It follows that a change in any one aspect of a concept is likely to affect the other three.[34] And for this reason, our topic must be viewed holistically. It is difficult to separate out tasks that pertain only to the phenomenal realm from those that pertain to the linguistic/semantic or theoretical realms. Social science, from this perspective, is an attempt to mediate between the world of language (the term and its attributes) and the world of things (beyond language). Neither is temporally or causally prior; both are already present in a concept.

With this understanding of our task, seven criteria may be deemed critical to the formation of empirical concepts in the social sciences: (1) *resonance*, (2) *domain*, (3) *consistency*, (4) *fecundity*, (5) *differentiation*, (6) *causal utility*, and (7) *operationalization* (i.e., measurement). The last criterion forms the topic of Chapter 7, so this chapter will cover only the first six criteria. For convenience, all seven desiderata are summarized in Table 5.1.

---

[34] Hoy (1982).

Table 5.1 Criteria of conceptualization

1. **Resonance** (familiarity, normal usage; *antonyms:* idiosyncrasy, neologism, stipulation)
   How faithful is the concept to extant definitions and established usage?
2. **Domain** (scope)
   How clear and logical is (a) the language community(ies) and (b) the empirical terrain that a concept embraces?
3. **Consistency** (*antonym:* slippage)
   Is the meaning of a concept consistent throughout a work?
4. **Fecundity** (coherence, depth, essence, fruitfulness, natural kinds, power, real, richness, thickness)
   How many attributes do referents of a concept share?
5. **Differentiation** (context, contrast-space, perspective, reference point, semantic field)
   How differentiated is a concept from neighboring concepts? What is the contrast-space against which a concept defines itself?
6. **Causal utility** (empirical utility, theoretical utility)
   What utility does a concept have within a causal theory and research design?
7. **Operationalization** (measurement)
   How do we know it (the concept) when we see it? Can a concept be measured easily and unproblematically, i.e., without bias? (Chapter 7)

Resonance

The degree to which a term or definition makes sense, or is intuitively clear, depends crucially on the degree to which it conforms or clashes with established usage. A term defined in a highly idiosyncratic way is unlikely to be understood. At the limit – that is, with nonsense words – it is not understood at all. The achievement of communication therefore involves a search for *resonance* with established usage.[35]

Anyone inclined to discount the importance of resonance in concept formation might contemplate the following definition of democracy: *a furry animal with four legs.* This is nonsense, of course. The important point, for present purposes, is that the non-sense of this definition lies in its utter lack of resonance. It violates norms of usage to define "democracy" with the attributes commonly associated with "dog." This is the problem encountered by definitions that are purely stipulative (on the authority of the author). Concepts

---

[35] Resonance is the criterial embodiment of ordinary-language philosophy. The meaning of a word, declares Wittgenstein (1953: 43), "is its use in the language." Pitkin (1972: 173) expatiates: "The meaning of a word . . . is what one finds in a good dictionary – a word or phrase that can be substituted for it. The meaning of 'justice' has to do with what people intend to convey in saying it, not with the features of the phenomena they say it about." See also Austin (1961); Caton (1963); Chappell (1964); Ryle (1949); Ziff (1960), as well as the various writings of G. E. M. Anscombe, Stanley Cavell, Jerry Fodor, Jerrold Katz, Norman Malcolm, and John Wisdom.

seem arbitrary if they do not fit with established understandings of a term or a phenomenon.

Resonance in the *definition* of a given term is achieved by incorporating standard meanings and avoiding non-standard ones. Resonance in the choice of a *term* is achieved by finding that word within the existing lexicon that (as currently understood) most accurately describes the phenomenon of interest. Where several existing terms capture the phenomenon in question with equal facility – as, for example, the near-synonyms "worldview" and "Weltanschauung" – achieving resonance becomes a matter of finding the term with the greatest common currency. Simple, everyday English terms are more familiar than terms drawn from languages that are dead, foreign, or highly specialized.

Where *no* term within the existing lexicon adequately describes the phenomena in question the writer is evidently forced to invent a new term. Sometimes, neologism is unavoidable, and therefore desirable. Indeed, all words were once neologisms, so we cannot complain too loudly about the forces of innovation. Tradition must occasionally be overturned. That said, one must carefully justify every neologism, every departure from ordinary usage. "The supreme rule of stipulation," writes Richard Robinson, "is surely to stipulate as little as possible. Do not change received definitions when you have nothing to complain of in them."[36]

An example of rather pointless neologism may be drawn from Robert Dahl's work on (as I would say) democracy. Noting the semantic difficulties of this term, and wishing to avoid its "large freight of ambiguity and surplus meaning," Dahl proposed a distinction between democracy, understood as an unattainable ideal, and "polyarchy" (derived from the Greek: *rule of many*), which was to be understood as existing states that exhibit some of the qualities of democracy and are commonly referred to as democracies. This, Dahl thought, would resolve the recurrent tension between "is" and "ought" that embroils the term democracy in scholarly and popular discourse.[37] Dahl's motives are laudable, but one cannot say that the attempted neologism has been successful, despite his prominence in the field. The problem is that the meanings of the two terms are so close that we have trouble hearing polyarchy without thinking of democracy. One might also observe that the attempt to wean social-scientific words from their normative freight is apt to be unavailing, for social science is

---

[36] Robinson (1954: 80). See also Linnaeus, Aphorisms 243–244 (reproduced in Linsley and Usinger 1959: 40); Connolly ([1974] 1983); Durkheim ([1895] 1964: 37); Mahon (1998); Mill ([1843] 1872: 24); Oppenheim (1975); Pitkin (1972).

[37] Dahl (1971: 9).

generally concerned with things that people have strong feelings about, and these feelings are embedded in ordinary language. Moreover, even if this descriptive–normative division were ultimately successful it would have the unfortunate effect of depriving academic work of popular relevance (Chapter 3). In any case, the key point is that any striking departure from normal usage imposes a cost on the reader of a text. More often than not, this cost is too high and the term is discarded.

Likewise, even the invention of new terms is never entirely removed from the extant lexicon. Neologisms, while rejecting ordinary usage, strive to re-enter the universe of intelligibility. They are rarely nonsense words; they are, instead, new combinations of existing words (e.g., bureaucratic-authoritarianism) or roots (e.g., polyarchy, heresthetic), or terms borrowed from other time periods (e.g., corporatism), other language regions (e.g., equilibrium), or other languages (e.g., laissez faire).[38] By far the most fertile grounds for neologism have been Classical (e.g., Id, communitas, polis, hermeneutics) and eponymous (e.g., Marxism, Reaganism). In all these cases words, or word roots, are imported from their normal contexts to a different context where they take on new meaning or additional senses. However severe the semantic stretch, some original properties remain intact.[39]

To sum up: terms and definitions chosen for use in the social sciences ought to resonate as much as possible with established usage. Inconsistencies with ordinary usage usually introduce ambiguity into a work or a field, despite an author's best intentions. Those concepts that resonate least with ordinary usage may be referred to as neologisms or stipulative definitions; they are excusable only if a more resonant concept is unavailable.

Domain

Granted, all of this depends upon the linguistic terrain within which a concept is expected to resonate. A concept, like an argument, can be evaluated only insofar as its domain of usage is understood. Greater breadth of comprehension and usage is always desirable, all other things being equal. Even so, no social science concept can hope to be truly universal. "Democracy" is understood

---

[38] On polyarchy, see Dahl (1971); on heresthetic, see Riker (1986); on corporatism, see Collier (1995) and Schmitter (1974).

[39] Robinson (1954: 55) notes: "Men will always be finding themselves with a new thing to express and no word for it, and usually they will meet the problem by applying whichever old word seems nearest, and thus the old word will acquire another meaning or a stretched meaning. Very rarely will they do what A. E. Housman bade them do, invent a new noise to mean the new thing." For a survey of contemporary neologisms, see Algeo (1991).

somewhat differently in different parts of the world.[40] Other terms, such as "vouchers," may have little or no resonance for lay citizens anywhere. Even within the social sciences there are important terminological differences across fields and subfields, and through time. Economists speak a somewhat different language than anthropologists. Consequently, we must be concerned not only with how resonant a concept is, but also with how many language communities it will embrace. There will always be someone, somewhere, who understands a term differently, for whom a proposed definition does not resonate.

Thus, it is important that authors specify – whenever the matter is ambiguous – which language regions a given concept is expected to encompass. Of foremost concern is the distinction between lay and academic audiences. As has been said, it is desirable for social scientists to avoid specialized terms ("jargon") in favor of natural language so that a broader audience can be cultivated for their work. And yet, it must be acknowledged that social science, like all language regions (e.g., medicine, law, street gangs, baseball), requires a specialized vocabulary.[41] Social science cannot accept words simply as they present themselves in ordinary speech. Some fiddling with words and definitions is incumbent on the researcher, if only because ordinary usage is unsettled. Social science concepts, Durkheim points out,

> do not always, or even generally, tally with that of the layman. It is not our aim simply to discover a method for identifying with sufficient accuracy the facts to which the words of ordinary language refer and the ideas they convey. We need, rather, to formulate entirely new concepts, appropriate to the requirements of science and expressed in an appropriate terminology.[42]

The limits of ordinary language as a foundation for social science definition are apparent in the fact that most complex terms – for example, democracy, justice, public goods – carry multiple meanings. Insofar as social scientists need to craft specialized concepts with greater coherence and operationalizability, they are compelled to depart from ordinary usage.

Establishing the domain of a concept depends upon the goals of a piece of research. Sometimes, a general definition – one that travels widely across academic and nonacademic venues – is required. If one is attempting to appeal to policymakers and/or the general public then one must pay close attention to how a given concept will resonate with ordinary usage. If one is attempting to reach beyond a particular culture or language, then usages in other cultures and languages must also be considered. On other occasions, it may not be necessary

---

[40] Schaffer (1998).   [41] Robinson (1954: 73); Sartori (1984).   [42] Durkheim ([1895] 1964: 36–37).

to travel widely or to garner universal consensus. This goes for many social science settings, where concepts are crafted for use in a specific project. Here, a more specialized approach to concept formation is warranted – also known as a *stipulative definition, definition-in-use, contextual definition,* or *systematized concept.*[43]

To illustrate the notion of a conceptual *domain* let us consider the concept of democracy. The domain of this concept may be said to range from a single subfield (e.g., the democratization subfield of political science), to an entire discipline (e.g., political science), to a set of disciplines (e.g., social science), to natural language (e.g., English), or to all natural languages. Each requires a broadening of language communities, and hence (probably) a broader range of definitions and usages that must be encompassed. In order for the concept to function adequately within its domain it must be understood (i.e., resonate) within that domain. This is true regardless of how large, or small, the domain might be.

Just as every concept has a linguistic domain (i.e., the language region where it is intended to resonate) it also has an *empirical* (phenomenal) domain. Consider four contexts in which the concept of democracy is currently employed: (1) local communities; (2) nation-states; (3) trans-national advocacy coalitions; and (4) modes of dress and comportment. Evidently, some attributes are more valid in some of these contexts than in others. For example, "contestation" seems to apply most clearly to (2), and not at all to (4).

In this light, the many definitions of democracy that have been propounded in recent years are not wrong, but rather partial. They explore the meaning of democracy in some contexts while ignoring or downplaying other contexts. They are, in this sense, stipulative, arbitrary – but only if understood as all-purpose definitions. If, instead, we look upon these definitions as limited in domain it becomes possible to restore a modicum of clarity to the vexed enterprise of concept formation.

Consistency

The criterion of *domain* implies the associated criterion of *consistency*. A concept ought to carry the same meaning (more or less) in each empirical context to which it is applied. The range of contexts lying within a concept's population should not elicit different connotations.[44]

---

[43] Adcock and Collier (2001); Bierwisch (1981); Bierwisch and Schreuder (1992); Robinson (1954); Taylor (1995: ch. 14).

[44] Goertz (2008: 109) calls this "homogeneity."

A violation of consistency – where a term means something different in different contexts – creates a problem of conceptual "stretching."[45] Thus, if corporatism is defined as an institution of peak bargaining among relatively autonomous units within civil society it might be considered a conceptual stretch to extend this concept to include Latin American cases, where unions and other actors in civil society were (and in some cases still are) often manipulated by the state. Of course, if corporatism is defined more broadly – as, say, including any formal bargaining among organized sectors of civil society (with or without state control) – then it does not compromise the concept's integrity to apply it to the Latin American context.

The usual way to adjust the scope of a concept is to add to or subtract from its defining attributes. Usually, one finds an inverse correlation between the intension and extension of a concept. Specifically, when attributes are understood as necessary, necessary-and-sufficient, or additive-and-continuous, adding attributes to a definition diminishes the number of phenomena that satisfy the definition. More focused definitions encompass fewer phenomena. In this manner, an inverse relationship exists between intension and extension, illustrated by the solid line in Figure 5.1.[46]

As an example, let us suppose that we start out with a definition of democracy that includes only the criterion "free and fair elections." Now suppose that we decide to add a second attribute, "civil liberties." If these attributes are understood as necessary or necessary-and-sufficient the addition of each defining trait is likely to narrow the number of polities that qualify as democratic, limiting the extension of the concept. If these qualities are understood as additive and matters of degree (elections are more or less free, civil liberties are more or less respected), the addition of attributes will attenuate the empirical fit between the intension and its extension, in this manner narrowing the empirical boundaries of the concept. (The same set of entities will be viewed as less democratic.) In either situation, the addition of attributes cannot *increase* the extension of a concept, for one is adding definitional requirements.

---

[45] Collier and Mahon (1993); Sartori (1970).

[46] This relationship is sometimes referred to as a "ladder of abstraction." However, this way of viewing things is somewhat misleading. If democracy is defined by three attributes rather than four it is not more abstract; it simply has a narrower scope (with the caveat noted in the text). In any case, the tradeoff between intension and extension has a long lineage in the literature on logic and concepts. Over a century ago, Stanley Jevons ([1877] 1958: 26) pointed out that when the definitional attributes of a word are expanded – e.g., when "war" becomes "foreign war" – its empirical breadth is narrowed. Weber (quoted in Burger 1976: 72) also noticed that "concepts with ever wider scope [have] ever smaller content." In recent years, this idea has come to be associated with the work of Giovanni Sartori (1970: 1041, 1984; Collier and Gerring 2009). See also Angeles (1981: 141); Cohen and Nagel (1934: 33); Collier and Mahon (1993); Frege (quoted in Passmore [1961] 1967: 184).

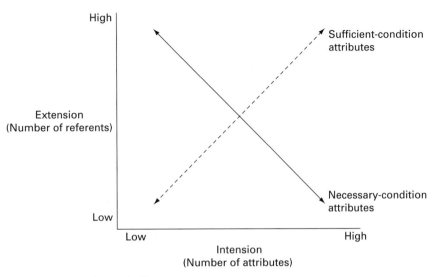

Figure 5.1   Intension and extension: tradeoffs

The utility of this schema is that it allows the conceptualizer to adjust the scope of a concept to fit the needs of an analysis so that violations of consistency are avoided. A concept should be defined so as to "travel" as far as needed, but no further. If one wishes to form a concept of democracy that applies to both Ancient Athens and to the contemporary era, one will need a broader concept than if one is seeking to describe only one or the other. Broadening the concept means choosing a definition that has fewer attributes, and therefore a wider ambit of applicability.

Of course, this tradeoff works differently when defining attributes are understood as sufficient conditions. Here, any addition of attributes *increases* the potential entity space, for each attribute is substitutable for any other attribute.[47] If "contestation" is individually sufficient for a polity to qualify as democratic, then the addition of a second sufficient condition (e.g., "participation") can only increase the population of democracies.[48] Here, we find a direct correlation between intension and extension, illustrated by the dotted line in Figure 5.1.

---

[47] Goertz (2006).
[48] If the reader feels that this example is forced, one might consider the following. Democracy may be defined generally as rule by the people, with specific dimensions of the concept including: (a) direct popular rule (through referenda and mass assemblies); (b) indirect popular rule (through elected representatives); and (c) deliberative popular rule (through consultative bodies). Arguably, each of the foregoing elements serves as a functional substitute for the others. As such, they may be regarded as sufficient-condition attributes.

It should be recognized, however, that conceptual attributes are rarely understood as sufficient. More typically, they are regarded as necessary-and-sufficient, necessary, or continuous (matters of degree). This means that the tradeoff exemplified by the solid line is more commonly encountered in the work of social science than the tradeoff exemplified by the dotted line. (Further discussion of concept structure is postponed until Chapter 6.)

Fecundity

Social scientists generally associate explanation with causal arguments and understanding with descriptive arguments. However, there is a sense in which descriptive concepts also explain. They do so by reducing the infinite complexity of reality into parsimonious concepts that capture something important – something "real" – about that reality. I shall call this criterion *fecundity*, though it might also be referred to as coherence, depth, fruitfulness, illumination, informative-ness, insight, natural kinds, power, productivity, richness, or thickness. Whatever the terminology, it seems clear that a bid for concepts is a bid to tell us as much as possible about some portion of the empirical world.

Concepts developed by researchers working within the interpretivist tradition often give priority to fecundity. Interpretivists insist that social science cannot evade the call for rich, evocative analysis. Thick description offers advantages over thin description, and thick theories over thin theories: they tell us more about a set of cases. One must appreciate, however, that narrative analysis in and of itself does not ensure fecundity, just as statistical work does not lead inexorably to thin, or reductive, analysis. One can think of many prose artists whose forte is the sweeping generalization, which is neither informative nor evocative. One can think of an equal number of statistical studies that describe or explain a great deal about their subject.[49]

Indeed, qualitative and quantitative methods of concept formation seek the same goal, though by different means. Thus, when systems of biological classification shifted to computer-generated models in the 1960s, resulting classifications were strikingly similar to the existing categories (largely inherited from Linnaeus).[50] Likewise, quantitative explorations of political culture have tended to follow the outline of arguments laid down decades before by Tocqueville, Hartz, and others writing at a time when quantitative analysis was not routinely applied to social questions.[51] Note that the purpose of all descriptive statistical routines

---

[49] For example, Campbell *et al.* (1960); Verba, Schlozman, and Brady (1995).   [50] Yoon (2009: 202).
[51] Almond and Verba ([1963] 1969).

(e.g., Pearson's r, factor analysis, principal component analysis, cluster analysis, and Q-sort analysis) is to elucidate similarities and differences among entities, with the usual aim of sorting them into most-similar and most-different piles. (The same objective applies whether the sorting focuses on cases or on traits.)

Above the level of measurement, the overall goal of a concept might be specified as follows: to focus our attention on some aspect of reality – to pluck it out from the ubiquity of extant data. What makes the concept convincing or unconvincing is the degree to which it "carves nature at the joints" (to use the Platonic metaphor) or identifies "natural kinds" (in Aristotelian language). Concepts strive to identify those things that are alike, grouping them together, and contrasting them to things that are different. Apples with apples, and oranges with oranges.

To be sure, all concepts are on some elemental level conventional. (People are born with the capacity for language, but they are not born with knowledge of a specific language.) However, good concepts move beyond what is merely conventional. They reveal a structure within the realities they attempt to describe. To the extent that a concept manages to identify real similarities and differences it has succeeded in identifying natural kinds. It is ontologically true.

Consider three conceptualizations of regime type. One differentiates between democracies and autocracies;[52] another distinguishes pure democracies, competitive authoritarian states, and pure autocracies;[53] and a third establishes a twenty-one-point index that is intended to function as an interval scale.[54] Which of these is most satisfactory? Evidently, each may be satisfactory for different causal purposes (see below). However, for descriptive purposes the utility of a schema hinges largely upon its fecundity. In the present instance, this means: which schema best describes the subject matter? More specifically, which schema most successfully bundles regime characteristics together, differentiating them from other bundles? Is the natural break-point among regimes to be found between autocracies and democracies (a two-part classification); among pure democracies, competitive autocracies, and pure autocracies; or is there instead a continuum of characteristics with no clear "bundles," justifying a continuous dimensional space? Naturally, many other options might also be considered. Some might argue that regime types are multidimensional, and therefore inappropriate for an ordinal or interval scale.[55] But all such arguments appeal to the ideal of fecundity.[56]

---

[52] Alvarez *et al.* (1996).   [53] Levitsky and Way (2002).   [54] Marshall and Jaggers (2007).
[55] Coppedge and Gerring (2011).
[56] A recent quantitative attempt, employing factor analysis, can be found in Coppedge, Alvarez, and Maldonado (2008).

Because of its centrality to concept formation – and to descriptive inference more generally – it is important that we pursue the notion of fecundity in more detail.

Concepts do not make sense unless the attributes that define the concept belong to one another in some logical or functional manner. They must be *coherent*. Within the United States, for example, the concept of "the West" is vulnerable to the charge that western states do not share many features in common (aside from contiguity). Thus, although one can stipulate a precise set of borders (e.g., the seven western-most states) one cannot help but feel that these borders are a trifle artificial. This does not make the concept wrong, but it certainly makes it less meaningful – less fecund – and hence presumably less useful in many contexts. The deeper or richer a concept the more convincing is its claim to define a class of entities deserving of being called by a single name. A coherent term carries more of a punch: it is, descriptively speaking, more powerful, allowing us to infer many things (the common characteristics of the concept) with one thing (the concept's label). The concept of "the South," following the opinion of most historians, would be considered more coherent than "the West," since a much longer list of accompanying attributes could be constructed and differences vis-à-vis other regions are more apparent.

The most coherent definitions are those that identify a core, or "essential," meaning.[57] Robert Dahl, in his influential work on power, sets out to discover "the central intuitively understood meaning of the word," "the primitive notion [of power] that seems to lie behind all [previous] concepts."[58] This essentializing approach to definition is common (and, indeed, often justified). The essential meaning of democracy, for example, is often thought to be rule by the people. This may be viewed as the single principle behind all other definitional characteristics, associated characteristics, and usages of the term. When one says democracy, what one is really talking about is rule by the people. To the extent that this reductionist effort is successful – to the extent, that is, that a single principle is able to subsume various uses and instances of the concept – the highest level of coherence has been achieved in that concept. (Note that essentializing definitions often take the form of minimal definitions, discussed below.)

---

[57] An "essential," "real," or "ontological" definition is defined as: "Giving the essence of a thing. From among the characteristics possessed by a thing, one is unique and hierarchically superior in that it states (a) the most important characteristic of the thing, and/or (b) that characteristic upon which the others depend for their existence" (Angeles 1981: 57). See also Mill ([1843] 1872: 71); Goertz (2006).

[58] Dahl ([1957] 1969: 79–80).

Differentiation

A concept cannot be internally coherent unless it is distinguishable from other concepts. External differentiation is thus implied by the notion of fecundity. Fecundity refers to how similar a set of phenomena are to each other, while differentiation refers to how different they are from surrounding phenomena. They are flip sides of the same coin. If apples are indistinguishable from oranges, the coherence of "apple" is called into question.[59]

The importance of differentiation is embedded in the words *definition* and *term*. Definition is "the act or product of marking out, or delimiting, the outlines or characteristics of any conception or thing."[60] Term has similar connotations, John Dewey points out. It is "derived from the Latin *terminus* meaning both boundary and terminal limit."[61] Hanna Pitkin explains, "the meaning of an expression is delimited by what might have been said instead, but wasn't. Green leaves off where yellow and blue begin, so the meaning of 'green' is delimited by the meanings of 'yellow' and 'blue.'"[62] A good concept is, therefore, one with clearly demarcated boundaries.

How, then, does a concept establish clearly demarcated borders? A key element is to specify carefully how a concept fits within a larger semantic field composed of neighboring concepts and referents. We shall refer to this as the background context or *contrast-space* of a concept.

We have noted that concepts are defined in terms of other concepts – boys in terms of girls, nation-states in terms of empires, parties in terms of interest groups. These neighboring terms (synonyms, near-synonyms, antonyms, and superordinate–subordinate concepts) give meaning to a concept. Precisely because of the interconnectedness of language, the redefinition of a term

---

[59] The twin desiderata of coherence and differentiation correspond to "lumping and splitting" operations in social classification (Zerubavel 1996) and to "similarity and difference" judgments in cognitive linguistics (Tversky and Gati 1978). The twin desiderata may also be recognized in Rosch's work on basic-level categories, which "(a) maximize the number of attributes shared by members of the category; and (b) minimize the number of attributes shared with members of other categories" (Rosch, quoted in Taylor 1995: 50–51).

[60] Reprinted in Chapin (1939: 153). Angeles (1981: 56) traces the Latin origins of the term in the verb "definire," which is translated as "to limit," "to end," "to be concerned with the boundaries of something."

[61] Dewey (1938: 349).

[62] Pitkin (1972: 11). "We call a substance silver," writes Norman Campbell ([1919] 1957: 49), "so long as it is distinguished from other substances and we call all substances silver which are indistinguishable from each other. The test whether a property is a defining or a non-defining property rests simply on the distinction between those properties which serve to distinguish the substance from others and those which it possesses in common with others. Any set of properties which serve to distinguish silver from all other substances will serve to define it."

necessarily involves some resettling of its semantic field. It is impossible to redefine one term without also, at least by implication, redefining others. Any redefinition of corporatism changes our understanding of pluralism, just as a redefinition of democracy changes our understanding of authoritarianism.

It follows – if the meaning of a language is to be sustained – that a new concept should unsettle the semantic field as little as possible, leaving other concepts as they were (more or less).[63] Indeed, a new term or redefinition that poaches attributes from neighboring concepts is laying the ground for future conceptual anarchy. It may resonate on first reading, but is likely to foster confusion in that field or subfield over the longer term. "Crowded" semantic fields are an example of this. Consider the many terms that have been developed over the past several decades to refer to citizen-based groups, including civic association, voluntary association, civil society organization (CSO), citizen sector organization, non-governmental organization (NGO), interest group, and grassroots organization. While subtle differences may be established among these terms it is difficult to accept the endless propagation of terms as productive for the field. Often, neologisms are a sign of conceptual disarray rather than of theoretical fecundity.

In any case, it is incumbent upon writers to clarify how their chosen concept(s) differ from neighboring concepts sharing the same semantic and phenomenal space. This requires establishing clear contrasts with what lies *outside* the boundaries of a concept.

Consider rival concepts seeking to explain American political culture, which may be summarized as *liberalism* (Louis Hartz, Alexis de Tocqueville),[64] *republicanism* (J. G. A. Pocock, Gordon Wood),[65] and a combination of *liberalism*, *republicanism*, and *ascriptive* identities (Rogers Smith).[66] What is of interest here is that these divergent perspectives are often informed by different temporal and/or spatial contrasts. Partisans of the liberal thesis invoke an implicit comparison between the United States and Europe. Partisans of the republican thesis invoke comparisons between the eighteenth and nineteenth centuries – the former being more republican and the latter more liberal. Partisans of the ascriptive thesis invoke comparisons with contemporary ideals and practices – deemed more egalitarian. Each school of thought is probably correct. However, they are correct with respect to different comparisons. American political culture looks different when different temporal and spatial contrasts are invoked.

---

[63] Sartori (1984).   [64] Hartz (1955).   [65] Pocock (1975); Wood (1969). See also Shalhope (1972).
[66] Smith (1993).

The same problem of competing contrast-spaces can be observed in many other conceptual debates. For example, writers argue vehemently over the basis of political conflict in contemporary American politics, with some emphasizing the pre-eminence of status, race, and morality[67] and others emphasizing the pre-eminence of social class.[68] (At present, these arguments will be regarded as primarily descriptive rather than causal.) Again, there are many fine points to this debate. That said, it appears that some portion of the disagreement can be explained by contending frames of comparison. Those who hold to the status/values argument may plausibly enlist (a) a spatial comparison with Europe (as did the partisans of the liberal thesis), (b) a temporal comparison with the New Deal era, and (c) a focus on elite-level behavior. Those who hold to the socioeconomic interpretation generally have in mind (a) a temporal comparison that embraces the past half-century (but not Europe or a longer chunk of historical time), (b) mass-level political behavior, and (c) contemporaneous comparisons between the relative strength of status/values issues and class issues in structuring the vote. Again, both schools have plenty of ground to stand on. But it is not the same ground.

Things are similar with respect to recent arguments about global inequality. Those who emphasize the widening gap in global distribution of income tend to base their arguments on evidence drawn from the past several decades, a period when individual-level data is available.[69] Those who emphasize the relative constancy of inequality generally encompass a longer time period – extending back to the mid-twentieth century, and perhaps further.[70] Again, one's conclusions depend critically upon the historical context one chooses to invoke.

Of course, causal arguments also unfold against a contrast-space and this too may create problems, as discussed in Chapter 8.[71] However, it is less likely to engender confusion because the counterfactual is usually more explicit. To say that "X causes Y" is to say, implicitly, that when X changes value, so will Y (at least probabilistically). This is fairly well understood, and is formalized in the null hypothesis. But to say that "Y is X" (i.e., X, an adjective, describes Y), is to invoke a much more ambiguous contrast-space. "Not Y" can refer to *any* temporal or spatial contrast or to the (nonempirical) meaning of the term "X" (as in Rogers Smith's argument about American political culture). We are at

---

[67] Frank (2004); Ladd and Hanley (1975); Morone (2004); Rogin (1987).
[68] Bartels (2006); Fiorina (2005); McCarty, Poole, and Rosenthal (2008).   [69] Milanovic (2005).
[70] Bourguignon and Morrisson (2002); Dollar (2005); Firebaugh (2003).
[71] Achinstein (1983); Garfinkel (1981); Hitchcock (1996); van Fraassen (1980). All work in the "counterfactual" tradition emphasizes this point.

sea, for the null hypothesis – against which the hypothesis might be judged – is not apparent.

Nonetheless, the problem of context becomes tractable insofar as writers are able to address a variety of competing reference points, explicitly and empirically. Of these, there are three possible dimensions: *spatial*, *temporal*, and *conceptual*. The latter, of course, refer to the defining attributes of a concept, and of neighboring concepts. By bringing these comparisons to the fore, virulent arguments, even over highly abstract matters such as political culture and equality, may be joined, and perhaps over time resolved. This is the virtue of explicit comparison, which plays an even more vital role in descriptive inference than in causal inference.

Causal utility

Concepts function causally, as well as descriptively. That is, they serve as components of a larger causal argument. In this latter capacity, they face desiderata that sometimes shape the way they are formed.

For example, suppose one is examining the role of electoral systems in structuring political conflict. Here, one would probably want to limit the ambit of study to polities that are reasonably, or at least minimally, democratic. Consequently, one needs a concept of democracy that achieves this objective. An ideal-type definition (see below) will not suffice; clear borders between democratic and nondemocratic regimes are required. Hence, causal concerns rightly drive concept formation.

In the foregoing example, concepts of democracy demarcate the boundaries of a causal inference. Likewise, concepts also identify causal factors (independent variables) or outcomes (dependent variables). A variable in a causal argument must also function as a concept; there is no such thing as a concept-less variable (if there was, it would lack meaning).

Typically, concepts designed for use as dependent variables group together many attributes. Here, an ideal-type definition may be fruitful. By contrast, concepts designed for use as independent variables are generally smaller, more parsimonious. This fits with the goal of causal argumentation: to explain a lot with a little. It also fits with the goal of causal argumentation to have a clearly defined, discrete "treatment," one that is specific enough to be manipulated (at least in principle) and that can be clearly differentiated from background factors (potential confounders). Additionally, concept formation in the context of causal models must be careful to employ concepts that differentiate a cause from its effect, so that circularity in the argument is avoided.

Of course, concepts defined for use in a specific causal analysis are specialized concepts, not ones that are intended to cover all circumstances and all settings. They are not general in purview. Sometimes, this sort of specialized definition breaks with established usage and thus incurs a cost in the resonance of a concept. This cost must be reckoned with. Causal models are confusing, and impossible to generalize from, if key concepts are defined in idiosyncratic ways.

In sum, causality is only one factor, among many, that rightly affects the formation of concepts (see Table 5.1). Even where the needs of a causal model are pre-eminent, a concept never entirely loses its descriptive purpose. If it did, the causal argument within which it is embedded would lose connection with reality. This is, of course, the very thing of which highly abstract causal models are often accused.[72]

Strategies of conceptualization

Having surveyed general criteria pertaining to concept formation, we turn now to strategies that may help to achieve these goals. Concept formation generally begins with a formal or informal survey of potential concepts. It proceeds by classifying the attributes of each concept so that an overview of each (relevant) concept can be attained. From thence, three general strategies of definition are recommended: *minimal*, *maximal*, and *cumulative*. These sequential strategies are summarized in Table 5.2. The chapter concludes with a brief discussion of the potential utility of this approach for bringing greater order and clarity to the social science lexicon.

Table 5.2 Strategies of conceptualization

1. **Survey of plausible concepts**
2. **Classification of attributes**
3. **Definition**
    (a) **Minimal**   Necessary (and perhaps sufficient) conditions of membership, understood as establishing a minimal threshold of membership.
    (b) **Maximal**   All (nonidiosyncratic) characteristics that define a concept in its purest, most "ideal" form.
    (c) **Cumulative**   A series of binary attributes (0/1) arranged in an ordinal fashion.

---

[72] Bewley (1999); Hausman (1994); Hedstrom (2005: 3); Maki (2002); Piore (1979); Spiegler and Milberg (2009).

Survey of plausible concepts

Many investigations begin in a frankly inductive mode. There is an empirical terrain of interest – perhaps a community, an institution, or a policy – that becomes the subject of investigation, but without a clear research question or hypothesis. Here, the researcher arrives slowly at a concept, or a set of concepts, to encompass the subject. This is conceptualization in its broadest sense. In this situation, the researcher must canvas widely before settling on a key term(s). Premature closure may cut short the deliberative process by which a subject is processed and understood. Granted, preliminary concepts will always be required; without them, one cannot deliberate at all. However, the canvassing of potential terms – each one treated gingerly, as a hypothesis – is what allows a researcher to test alternative ways of thinking about a topic. What stories are contained in the research site (the archive, the dataset, the ethnographic setting)? Which is the most interesting of these stories? Every story suggests a different label for the project. This is the exploratory process discussed in Chapter 2.

Once the researcher has settled on a preliminary concept he or she ought to briefly review the possible alternatives – that is, the family of near-synonyms that most closely fits the circumstance – resorting to neologism only where absolutely necessary (as discussed above). Since each extant term brings with it a certain amount of semantic luggage, the choice among terms – as well as the choice of how to define the chosen term – rightly involves a canvassing of potential attributes. This step finds precedent in virtually all traditions of conceptual analysis. It is the conceptual equivalent of a "literature review."

Of course, some topics are simple enough to preclude an extensive canvas. Here, recourse to a natural language dictionary or a specialized technical dictionary is sufficient. Alternatively, the author may be able to rely on articles or books that provide a more expanded discussion of a term's meaning and usage patterns, and perhaps its etymology. However, where these short-cuts are unavailing the author will be forced to undertake his or her own conceptual research.

A conscientious semantic canvassing begins with a representative sample of formal definitions and usage patterns for a chosen term, as drawn from relevant scientific fields, from natural language, and from history (etymology). Note that usage patterns may bring to light meanings that are not contained in formal definitions (perhaps because they are so obvious), and may help to clarify meaning when formal definitions are vague. Usage also entails a consideration of the referents of a concept (the phenomena out there to which the concept refers – its extension).

In situations where the different senses of a word are radically disparate – for example, "pen" (writing instrument) and "pen" (enclosure) – one must narrow the conceptual analysis to only one meaning of a term. Of course, homonymy (of which the two radically different meanings of "pen" are an example) and polysemy (where a word invokes a number of closely related meanings) is often a matter of degrees. In borderline cases, the analyst will have to judge which sense should be hived off (to be considered as an independent concept), and which should be retained, so as to create a relatively coherent concept.

Representativeness in the sampling process is achieved by searching for whatever variation in usage and formal definition might exist within a language region and keeping track of the approximate frequency of these various usages and definitions. In future, we may be able to rely on digitized libraries that can be sampled randomly, enabling one to attain a more precise estimate of the frequency of usage and definitional variations. Even so, mechanized sampling will probably not alter our understanding of key terms significantly, for usage patterns within a language region tend to exhibit great regularity. Moreover, our intent is to discard only very idiosyncratic usages and definitions. Thus, as long as the sample is sufficiently broad one is likely to pick up all common (nonidiosyncratic) usages. The principle of redundancy may serve as an indicator of sufficiency: when one reaches a point where definitional attributes and usages begin to repeat, one may justifiably terminate the expedition. One has sampled enough.

The issue of linguistic domain – how many language regions to survey – is also crucial. A sampling is better if it covers more language regions. Yet if this broad search reveals significant differences in meaning then the analyst may restrict the scope of the investigation in order to preserve consistency and coherence. Any sampling is likely to have a home turf – perhaps a particular field of social science – that is extensively canvassed, and other areas that are surveyed more superficially. In any case, the domain of the survey will help to establish the domain of the resulting definition.

Classification of attributes

The next task is to reduce the plenitude of meanings implied by a term into a single table. The construction of such a table rests on the assumption that, although definitions for a given term are, in principle, infinite (since even a small number of attributes can be combined in many ways, and since there are always multiple ways to convey a similar meaning), most definitions and usages juggle the same basic set of attributes. By combining near-synonyms and by organizing them along different dimensions one ought to be able to reduce the definitional profusion of even the most complex concept into a relatively parsimonious table of attributes. We regard this table as the lexical definition of a term because it reports the many meanings of that term extant across a given linguistic domain.

As an example, let us explore the definitional attributes of "democracy." Our survey of definitions and usages rests on a number of recent studies that attempt to delineate the meaning of this key term, focusing primarily on the Western tradition (historical and contemporary).[73] This is therefore regarded as the principal domain of the concept. Empirically, I choose to focus on applications of this concept within political contexts, and especially in large polities such as the nation-state (rather than within small, local bodies). This will be the empirical domain of the concept. From this compendium of definitions and usages, one may distill a list of common attributes, depicted in Table 5.3. Obviously, this list rests at a fairly abstract level; one could extend it to include much more specific features of the political landscape. But this would require a much larger table and is unnecessary for present purposes.

With a complex subject like democracy it is helpful if the attributes can be arranged in a taxonomic fashion (Chapter 6). Of course, this is not always possible, and one can glimpse more than a few violations of taxonomic principles (e.g., components that traverse several categories). Still, this exercise in semantic reduction is useful wherever practicable.

Definition: concept types

With the caveats noted above, it seems fair to regard Table 5.3 as a fairly encompassing lexical definition, including most of the attributes commonly associated with the term in the Western tradition. Even so, because of the number and diversity of these attributes, Table 5.3 does not take us very far toward a final definition. In order to create a more tractable empirical concept, one must go further. This next step – from lexical definition to specialized definition – is crucial. To achieve it, three approaches will be reviewed: *minimal, maximal,* and *cumulative.*

---

[73] Beetham (1994, 1999); Collier and Levitsky (1997); Held (2006); Lively (1975); Sartori (1962); Saward (2003); Weale (2007).

Table 5.3 A classification of fundamental attributes: "Democracy"

Core principle: rule by the people	
I Electoral	**II Liberal**
(aka elite, minimal, realist, Schumpeterian)	(aka consensus, pluralist)
Principles: contestation, competition.	*Principles*: limited government, multiple veto points, horizontal accountability, individual rights, civil liberties, transparency.
Question: are government offices filled by free and fair multiparty elections?	*Question*: is political power decentralized and constrained?
Institutions: elections, political parties, competitiveness, and turnover.	*Institutions*: multiple, independent, and decentralized, with special focus on the role of the media, interest groups, the judiciary, and a written constitution with explicit guarantees.
III Majoritarian	**IV Participatory**
(aka responsible party government)	*Principle*: government by the people.
Principles: majority rule, centralization, vertical accountability.	*Question*: do ordinary citizens participate in politics?
Question: does the majority (or plurality) rule?	*Institutions*: election law, civil society, local government, direct democracy.
Institutions: consolidated and centralized, with special focus on the role of political parties.	
V Deliberative	**VI Egalitarian**
Principle: government by reason.	*Principle*: political equality.
Question: are political decisions the product of public deliberation?	*Question*: are all citizens equally empowered?
Institutions: media, hearings, panels, other deliberative bodies.	*Institutions*: designed to ensure equal participation, representation, protection, and politically relevant resources.

Institutions: both governmental and nongovernmental (e.g., interest groups, parties, civic associations).
Source: Coppedge and Gerring (2011).

Minimal

One long-standing definitional strategy seeks to identify the bare essentials of a concept, sufficient to differentiate it extensionally without excluding any of the phenomena generally understood as part of the extension. The resulting definition should be capable of substituting for all (nonidiosyncratic) uses of the term without too much loss of meaning. This means, of course, that it should not conflict with any (nonidiosyncratic) usages. Each attribute that defines a concept minimally is regarded as a necessary condition: all entities must possess this attribute in order to be considered a member of the set. Collectively, these attributes are jointly sufficient to bound the concept extensionally. Minimal definitions thus aim for crisp borders, allowing for the classification of entities as "in" or "out." Of course, they may not always achieve this goal, but this is their aim.[74]

Sometimes, minimal concepts are crafted around an abstract core principle such as "rule by the people." In this instance, the core meaning satisfies the criterion of resonance, for all invocations of democracy revolve in some way around this idea. However, such an abstract definition does not achieve crisp borders for the concept; indeed, it scarcely identifies borders. In this respect, it is problematic.

A more common approach is to identify a specific component of the term that everyone (or nearly everyone) agrees upon. If we are limiting ourselves to representative polities (excluding direct democracies) one might argue that free and fair elections constitutes a necessary condition of democracy. This attribute suffices as a minimal definition, for it is sufficient to bound the entity empirically. That is, having free and fair elections makes a polity a democracy; no other attributes are necessary. At least, so it might be argued.

The caveat, of course, is that we are defining democracy in a very minimal fashion, leaving other attributes often associated with the concept in abeyance. This imposes some costs in resonance. The stripped down meaning of the term sounds strange to those attuned to democracy's many nuances.

Maximal

Maximal definitions, in contrast to minimal definitions, aim for the inclusion of all (nonidiosyncratic) attributes, thereby defining a concept in its purest, most "ideal" form. This would, of course, include the attribute(s) that defines the concept minimally: its necessary condition(s). As Weber describes it, "an ideal-type is formed . . . by the synthesis of a great many diffuse, discrete, more or less present and occasionally absent *concrete individual* phenomena, which are arranged according to those one-sidedly emphasized viewpoints into a unified *analytical* construct."[75]

Following this recipe, one might create an ideal-type definition of democracy that includes most, or all, of the dimensions listed in Table 5.3. Of course,

---

[74] Definitional strategies similar to the "minimal" strategy have been employed by various writers, although not usually by this name. See, e.g., Debnam (1984) on "power"; Freeden (1994: 146) on "ineliminable" attributes; Hamilton (1987) on "ideology"; Pitkin (1967: 10–11) on "basic meaning"; Murphey (1994: 23–24). Sartori endorses minimal definition in early work (1975: 34–35, 1976: 61), but drops the matter in his classic work on concept formation (1984). It should be noted that minimal definition is similar, though not identical, to a "procedural minimum" definition (Collier and Levitsky, 1997). In the latter, the search is for an operationalization that satisfies all definitional requirements of a concept.

[75] Weber ([1905] 1949: 90). See also Burger (1976). In citing Weber, I do not claim to be using the concept of an ideal-type in precisely the way that Weber envisioned.

some might be excluded if it could be argued that they detract significantly from the coherence of the overall concept. Blatantly contradictory elements should be avoided.

Ideal-types, as the term suggests, need not have a specific real-life empirical referent. Perhaps no extant polity achieves perfect democracy. However, in order to be of service an ideal-type must approximate real, existing entities, which are then scored according to how closely they resemble the attributes of the ideal-type. Ideal-types are always matters of degree, and hence generally operationalized by interval scales (discussed in Chapter 6).

Cumulative

A third strategy of concept formation is an attempt to reconcile minimal and maximal approaches by ranking the (binary) attributes commonly associated with a concept in a cumulative fashion, that is, as more or less essential to a concept.[76] This results in an ordinal scale (discussed in Chapter 6).

Following these principles, one can envision a cumulative scale indicator of democracy that begins with free and fair elections – the minimal definition – and proceeds through eight additional criteria, listed in order of centrality to the concept of interest, as depicted in Table 5.4. If this ordering of attributes is accepted – if, that is, it is agreed that 1 is more essential than 2 and 2 is more essential than 3 – then it may be possible to arrive at an acceptable definition of democracy that incorporates many of the attributes commonly associated with the term, while also recognizing the relative importance of each of these attributes. It has the additional advantage of allowing us to order all extant polities empirically according to their degree of democracy: the more attributes a polity possesses, the more democratic it is.[77] (This solves the aggregation problem, an issue of measurement discussed in Chapter 6.)

Of course, we will not be able to determine *how much* more democratic one polity is than another, for we cannot presume that each level is equidistant from the next (the distinction between an ordinal and interval scale). A second shortcoming of this particular cumulative definition is that the ordinal scale of attributes may not be fully comprehensive; some attributes may be difficult to rank in terms of their centrality to the concept. Indeed, one can see that not all of democracy's lexical attributes (see Table 5.3) are contained in the cumulative concept in Table 5.4.

---

[76] This is very similar in spirit to the construction of a Guttman scale, except that we are dealing with attributes rather than indicators, and with the theoretical (rather than empirical) properties of these attributes.

[77] For another example of the ordinal technique see Coppedge and Reinicke (1990).

Table 5.4 Cumulative definition: "Democracy"

	Ordinal scale								
Attributes	**1**	**2**	**3**	**4**	**5**	**6**	**7**	**8**	**9**
(a) Free and fair elections	x	x	x	x	x	x	x	x	x
(b) Self-government (domestic)		x	x	x	x	x	x	x	x
(c) Self-government (complete)			x	x	x	x	x	x	x
(d) Executive elected and paramount				x	x	x	x	x	x
(e) Universal male suffrage					x	x	x	x	x
(f) Universal suffrage						x	x	x	x
(g) Executive constitutionality							x	x	x
(h) Executive constraints								x	x
(i) Civil liberty									x

(a) Free and fair elections: national elections are regularly held, are open to all major parties and candidates (including all opposition parties and figures who might pose a significant challenge to the ruling group), and appear on balance to reflect the will of the electorate (whatever irregularities might exist).
(b) Self-government (domestic): sovereignty over domestic policy.
(c) Self-government (complete): sovereignty over domestic and foreign policy.
(d) Executive elected and paramount: executive is elected and is paramount (i.e., superior, *de facto*, to other leaders and institutions).
(e) Universal male suffrage: all adult male citizens are allowed to vote and no group of citizens is selectively discouraged from voting. Presumption: citizenship includes a majority of permanent residents in a territory.
(f) Universal suffrage: all adult citizens are allowed to vote and no group of citizens is selectively discouraged from voting. Presumption: citizenship includes a majority of permanent residents in a territory.
(g) Executive constitutionality: executive acts in a constitutional manner, and does not change the constitution to suit its political needs (though it may try).
(h) Executive constraints: executive, although paramount, is effectively constrained by other political institutions, acting in their constitutional role (e.g., judiciary, legislature, monarch, independent agencies).
(i) Civil liberty: citizens enjoy freedom of speech and freedom from politically motivated persecution by government.

Discussion

Having outlined three strategies of concept definition – minimal, maximal, and cumulative – the reader may wonder whether this exhausts the field. Naturally, it does not. Concepts serve many theoretical and empirical functions, and these functions rightly condition how they are formed within the purview of a given work. However, *general* definitions of a concept – those intended to travel widely – tend to adopt minimal or maximal approaches to definition. (Occasionally, they may employ a cumulative approach.) This is because these approaches tend to be most successful in establishing resonance, consistency, and coherence across a broad domain. (Issues of measurement are generally secondary when a concept must travel widely.) In other words, minimal and maximal definitions offer a better resolution of the criterial demands that all concepts face (see Table 5.1).

To be sure, some concepts resist this effort at semantic reduction. It is alleged that some concepts embody "family-resemblance" attributes, where different usages share no single characteristic in common and therefore have no core meaning. An oft-discussed example is "mother," which may be defined as (a) a biological fact, (b) the person who plays a principal role in nurturing a child, or (c) according to rules and norms within specialized domains (e.g., Mother Superior within the Catholic hierarchy). These definitions share no single element in common. They are disparate.[78]

In social science context, however, we are less likely to witness family-resemblance concepts. Democracy is an essentially contested concept. Even so, all commentators seem to agree that, as applied to political contexts, this concept revolves around a single core attribute – rule by the people. "Justice," another bone of contention, also has a core meaning: to each his or her due. (As it happens, both of these core meanings can be traced back to Ancient Greece.)

More to the point, even in situations where family resemblances might be said to exist there is little profit in trumpeting the disparate nature of a term's definitions. Thus, while "corporatism" has been regarded as a family-resemblance concept[79] it could also be subjected to a minimal or maximal definition. I would argue that we are better served by the latter than by the former precisely because minimal and maximal definitions create more coherent concepts, and ones that are easier to locate in empirical space (i.e., to measure), albeit with some loss of resonance. Better a minimal, maximal, or cumulative definition that is flawed – as in some sense, all social science definitions are – than a family-resemblance definition that results in an incoherent concept.

Before concluding it is worth taking note of the fact that we have focused thus far on "hard" cases – democracy, justice, and the like. Other concepts in the social science lexicon are rarely as troublesome. From this perspective, the problem of conceptualization is perhaps somewhat less severe than it may seem from a cursory reading of this chapter.

By way of contrast, let us quickly examine an easier, more concrete concept. "Political party" may be defined minimally as an organization that nominates individuals for office. This definition imposes crisp borders and is substitutable for all extant usages of which I am aware. A maximal definition would,

---

[78] Wittgenstein (1953). See also Collier and Mahon (1993); Goertz (2006); Taylor (1995: ch. 3).
[79] Collier and Mahon (1993: 847).

of course, encompass other attributes commonly associated with the work of political parties, such as a shared ideology, an organizational apparatus, well-defined membership, and endurance over time. These attributes describe parties in their strongest, most ideal sense, and are matters of degree. A cumulative definition would arrange these same attributes (or some subset of them) according to their centrality to the concept.[80] Whichever strategy one chooses to employ, defining "political party" is considerably easier than defining "democracy." And so it may be for other concepts that lie closer to the empirical bone.

Even with the most complex concepts, carefully crafted definitions in the minimal, maximal, or cumulative mold should provide a common scaffolding upon which the work of social science can rest in a reasonably stable and consistent manner. To be sure, meanings change over time; but such change occurs slowly. New terms, or new meanings for old terms, appear idiosyncratic at first. Over time, if neologisms gain adherents, they become established. However, *at any given point in time* reasonably authoritative definitions should be feasible – with the caveat that multiple approaches to the same concept (minimal, maximal, and cumulative) can often be justified.[81] Thus, it is incumbent upon authors to clarify what style of definition they are adopting.

Note also that the construction of minimal and maximal definitions establishes semantic *boundaries* around a concept. It specifies the minimal and maximal attributes, and the corresponding minimal and maximal extensions. This sort of exercise – equivalent to an "extreme bounds" analysis – is especially useful when dealing with far-flung concepts such as democracy.

---

[80] For further discussion of this concept see Gunther and Diamond (2003: 172).
[81] For further discussion and additional examples, see Gerring (1997); Gerring and Barresi (2003).

6 Descriptive arguments

Obviously there is no classification of the Universe not being arbitrary and full of conjectures. The reason is quite simple: we do not know what the universe is.

Jorge Luis Borges[1]

What the devil is going on around here?

Abraham Kaplan[2]

How do social scientists describe a social reality? What arguments do we employ in our attempts to bring order to the great blooming, buzzing confusion of the world?[3] One might suppose that the shape of a descriptive inference is limited only by the social phenomenon that we seek to describe, the models (cognitive, linguistic, mathematical, and visual) that we have at our disposal, and our imagination. In practice, however, descriptive inferences draw from a standard itinerary of tropes.

I shall argue that most descriptive claims can be classified as *indicators*, *syntheses*, *typologies*, or *associations*, along with their various subtypes as illustrated in Table 6.1. This is how social scientists carve up nature at the descriptive level. These are the patterns that we look for when attempting to describe classes of events in the social world.

Each of these ways of describing the world has a long history. Indeed, they are almost second-nature. Yet they rarely receive the attention that they deserve. Their very familiarity seems to have fostered a degree of nonchalance. In rendering a formal treatment of these informal subjects my goal is to bring greater self-consciousness to the act of description and, at the same time, to establish a valued place for descriptive analysis in the social science disciplines.

Naturally, these genres of description may also be enlisted in causal inference. Indeed, it is often the case that the same pattern of data can be interpreted as either descriptive or causal. This depends upon the researcher's

---

[1] Borges ([1942] 1999: 231).   [2] Kaplan (1964: 85).   [3] James (1981: 462).

Table 6.1 Descriptive arguments

Indicators	• Unidimensional (aka attributes, dimensions, factors, measures, parameters, properties, scales, variables).
Syntheses	• A single multidimensional category in which diverse attributes revolve around a central theme.
Typologies	• Multidimensional categories that are mutually exclusive, exhaustive, and defined by uniform principles.
Simple	• (No additional criteria.)
Temporal	• Categories correspond to discrete time periods.
Matrix	• Categories derived from the intersection of several factors.
Taxonomic	• Categories arranged in a *genus et differentium* hierarchy.
Configurational	• Categories defined by subtracting attributes from a core concept.
Sequential	• Categories arranged in a temporal sequence, with consequences for each category.
Associations	• Multidimensional with a strong probabilistic component.
Trend	• Correlation between a phenomenon and time.
Network	• Interrelations among units – spatial, temporal, or functional.
Correlational	• Correlation among indicators and/or sets.

understanding of the data-generation process; it is an inference not a self-evident fact about the world.[4]

Indicators

An *indicator* aims to describe one feature of a population, and may also be referred to as an *attribute, dimension, factor, measure, parameter, property, variable,* or *unidimensional description*. It may be directly observable (e.g., test scores) or may be observable only through proxies (e.g., intelligence). It may be composed of a single phenomenon (e.g., the answer to a particular question on a survey) or of multiple phenomena (e.g., the answer to several questions on a survey). However, if multiple components contribute to an indicator they must be reducible, without too much loss of information, to a single dimension, that is, an *index*. This is what qualifies it as a species of indicator. (Whether or not this reduction of property space is successful is an empirical matter. For the moment, our focus is on the *a priori* quality of the argument.) Likewise, indicators may be calibrated according to any type of scale except a nominal scale with more than two categories, which would, of course, be multidimensional (Chapter 7).

[4] Achen (1982: 77–78).

Some indicators lie close to the empirical bone, requiring little or no interpretation. A measure of infant mortality based on the number of deaths prior to age one per 1,000 live births is fairly self-evident. Here, the indicator is the infant mortality rate (IMR). If, on the other hand, this variable is employed as an indicator of some more abstract concept such as human welfare it becomes more controversial: questions of conceptual validity come into play, as discussed in Chapter 7. For present purposes, the realm of indicators is understood in an inclusive fashion, including both self-evident "facts" and larger claims.

Note, for an indicator to have meaning it must be associated with a (linguistic) concept. Well-known indicators are famous by virtue of the conceptual freight they are asked to pull. These include indicators of democracy (e.g., Polity IV[5] and Freedom House[6]), interstate conflict (e.g., Correlates of War[7]), good governance (e.g., the World Bank Governance indicators[8]), electoral malapportionment,[9] and party ideology.[10]

Likewise, any empirical study draws on at least one indicator. There are no "nonindicator" studies, because indicators are the primitive empirical propositions underlying all other propositions, descriptive or causal. That is to say, more complex, multidimensional arguments are composed of indicators.

Of course, not all indicators are explicitly measured across a large number of cases. Qualitative research often rests on unmeasured factors or factors that are measured for only a few cases. Yet this does not dispel their importance, or their difficulty. If a case study of Angola asserts that this country has a "high" mortality rate, this is a qualitative judgment that rests on a broader set of comparative reference points (presumably other countries in the region and the world). For our purposes, this is also an indicator, despite the fact that it is not associated with precise measurement.

Syntheses

A synthesis is a multidimensional category in which diverse attributes are said to revolve around a central theme. The theme, usually expressed in a single concept, unifies the attributes, thus lending coherence to an otherwise disparate set of phenomena. A synthetic argument thereby offers an explanation

[5] Marshall and Jaggers (2007).   [6] See Freedom House at: www.freedomhouse.org.
[7] Singer and Diehl (1990).   [8] Kaufmann, Kraay, and Mastruzzi (2007).
[9] Samuels and Snyder (2001).
[10] For example, Budge, Robertson, and Hearl (1987); Laver, Benoit, and Garry (2003); Poole and Rosenthal (1985).

for the phenomena, though not of a causal nature. There is no explicit attempt to distinguish a cause and an effect. Instead, the synthesis embraces everything (or at least many things) within its domain. The synthesis is therefore a holistic endeavor, emphasizing similarities rather than differences among the chosen sample of cases. Typically, this conceptual umbrella is abstract enough to require extensive efforts at definition and operationalization.

A few examples will suffice to illustrate the genre. Consider, first, the variety of competing arguments about American political culture, introduced above: egalitarian-liberal-individualist;[11] republican;[12] or a combination of multiple traditions, including that which Smith describes as ascriptive.[13] Consider, second, the role of the American President, which Richard Neustadt likened to the office of "clerk," since his power resides largely in persuasion rather than command.[14] Consider, third, the topic of nationalism, which according to Benedict Anderson draws on imagined communities.[15] Consider, fourth, the idea (credited to James Scott) that peasants in resource-threatened environments are imbued with a moral, rather than strictly instrumental, view of market behavior.[16] Consider, finally, Orlando Patterson's argument that slavery is a form of social death.[17]

These are all descriptive syntheses. They are synthetic insofar as they aim to summarize many attributes and many phenomena in a single concept or phrase. Of course, the attempt to synthesize is also, at the same time, an attempt to differentiate. For example, the liberalism of American culture (according to Tocqueville and Hartz) is contrasted to the nonliberal cultures of Europe. Insofar as these distinctions are explicit and insofar as they provide the grist for extensive empirical analysis a synthesis begins to look more like a typology – our next topic. (Indeed, in a later study Hartz applies his "fragment" thesis to settler societies in the United States, Canada, Australia, and South Africa.[18] Here, the comparisons across cases are explicit, and the resulting study is rightly classified as typological.)

Typologies

Typologies resolve cases into discrete categories that are mutually exclusive and exhaustive on the basis of a uniform categorization principle(s).[19] These

---

[11] Hartz (1955); Tocqueville (1945).   [12] Pocock (1975); Shalhope (1972); Wood (1969).
[13] Smith (1993).   [14] Neustadt (1960).   [15] Anderson (1991); Gellner (1983).   [16] Scott (1976).
[17] Patterson (1982).   [18] Hartz (1964).
[19] Confusingly, three words are often used semi-synonymously: typology, classification, and taxonomy. In my adopted usage, "taxonomy" refers to a specific kind of typology. For work on these interrelated

come in several common varieties: (a) simple, (b) temporal (periodization), (c) matrix, (d) taxonomy, (e) configurational, and (f) sequential.

Simple typology

A simple typology follows only the general rules for a typology, as explained above. Let us explore a few examples. Polities may be classified in Aristotelian fashion as monarchies (rule of one), oligarchies (rule of a few), and democracies (rule of many). Historical polities, argues Samuel Finer, may be classified according to their rulers as palace, church, nobility, or forum.[20] Albert Hirschman argues that the influence of constituents on organizations may be felt through exit and/or voice.[21] Max Weber argues that political authority draws upon three forms of legitimacy: traditional, charismatic, and rational-legal.[22] Gosta Esping-Andersen divides the world of welfare regimes into three sorts: liberal, corporatist, or social democratic.[23] Theodore Lowi finds that the politics of public policy follows one of four logics: distributive, constituent, regulative, or redistributive.[24]

Note that while most typologies assume the form of a nominal scale, some reveal an implicit or explicit ranking among categories, qualifying the typology as an ordinal scale (Chapter 7). For example, Aristotle's classification of polities might be viewed as establishing an ordinal scale of greater or lesser popular involvement in politics.

Temporal typology

Temporal typologies (aka *periodizations*) are simple typologies that are temporally ordered. For example, it is argued that several waves of democratization have broken over the world in the course of the past two centuries, each with distinctive features.[25] An even broader attempt at historical periodization is Tocqueville's proclamation of a democratic age, beginning sometime in the late eighteenth century, which may be compared with the previous feudal or aristocratic ages. Along these lines, Marx proposed to typologize recorded human history into feudal, capitalist, and communist stages.

Other periodization schemes focus on a single country. For example, many students of American political history are convinced that fundamental

subjects see Bailey (1972); Capecchi (1968); Collier, LaPorte, and Seawright (2008); Elman (2005); George and Bennett (2005: ch. 11); Lange and Meadwell (1991); Lenski (1994); Lijphart (1968); McKinney (1950, 1957, 1969); Nowotny (1971); Smith (2002); Whittaker, Caulkins, and Kamp (1998); Wiseman (1966).
[20] Finer (1997).　[21] Hirschman (1970).　[22] Weber ([1918] 1958).　[23] Esping-Andersen (1990).
[24] Lowi (1972).　[25] Doorenspleet (2000); Huntington (1991).

political changes have occurred only episodically, during "realignment" periods.[26] Others defend an older tradition, dividing American political history into "eras" (Revolutionary, Jacksonian, Civil War, Reconstruction, etc.). Still others argue that the topic is best approached through an even more differentiated periodization defined by presidencies.[27]

Each attempt to establish a temporal typology appeals to the same general desiderata, that is, to identify key points of change within a historical topic such that the resulting periods are mutually exclusive and exhaustive (along whatever dimensions are of interest to the study).

Matrix typology

Matrix typologies are subject to similar criteria, but are formed in a more complicated fashion. Here, the categories of a typology are the product of an intersection of several categorical variables. Suppose, for example, one begins with two components of democracy, contestation and participation, which we assume vary independently and can be coded dichotomously without too much loss of information. The intersection of these two factors produces four types, which Robert Dahl has labeled (a) closed hegemony, (b) inclusive hegemony, (c) competitive oligarchy, and (d) polyarchy, as illustrated in Table 6.2.[28]

Note that matrix typologies, like simple typologies, often produce ordered categories, and thus are ordinal scales. In this example, polyarchy is the most democratic and closed hegemony the least democratic. However, the matrix, by itself, does not reveal an ordering among the other two cells.[29]

Table 6.2 A matrix typology: regime types

		Participation	
		Low	*High*
Contestation	*Low*	Closed hegemony	Inclusive hegemony
	High	Competitive oligarchy	Polyarchy

---

[26] Sundquist (1983).   [27] For discussion, see Cochran (1948), Zelizer (2002).

[28] Dahl (1971: 7). Another example of a matrix typology is Aristotle's ancient typology of regime types (Lehnert 2007: 65). Here, the number of rulers (one, a few, or many) is cross-tabulated with the rulers' goals (self-interest or the greater good) to produce six categories: tyranny, oligarchy, democracy, monarchy, aristocracy, and polity. Additional examples of matrix typologies related to the concept of democracy can be found in Almond and Verba ([1963] 1989: 16); Weyland (1995).

[29] Collier, LaPorte, and Seawright (2008: 157).

Note also that matrix typologies may contain any number of factors, resulting in any number of compound types (cells). However, the two-by-two matrix is still the most common – presumably because adding a third (or fourth) dimension does not usually create discrete and recognizable types.

Taxonomy

Taxonomies are typologies that stretch in a hierarchical fashion across several levels of analysis. Accordingly, one might stipulate that there are two basic polity types: autocracy and democracy. Among democracies, some are direct and others representative. Among representative democracies, one finds electoral, liberal, majoritarian, participatory, and egalitarian varieties. The nested quality of this family of terms may be illustrated in tabular format (see Table 6.3) or in a tree diagram (see Figure 6.1).[30]

Note that each subordinate level of the taxonomy possesses all the attributes of the superordinate category, plus one (or several). Each concept within a taxonomy may therefore be defined by specifying its superordinate category plus its differentiating attribute or attributes – its *genus et differentium*. (Concepts so defined are sometimes described as "classical" in reference to their Aristotelian lineage and their venerable place within the field of logic.)

Configurational typology

Configurational typologies, like taxonomies, form subtypes out of a single superordinate category. However, subtypes are created from a superordinate category by subtracting, rather than adding, attributes. This generates diminished subtypes – sometimes called *radial* categories – rather than augmented subtypes (as in the taxonomy). These subtypes radiate outward from the superordinate category, which takes the form of an ideal-type (Chapter 5).[31]

In this fashion, it is sometimes argued that democracy is best understood as a set of relatively distinct models – electoral, liberal, majoritarian, participatory, deliberative, and egalitarian (or social) – each emphasizing a different aspect of the key term.[32] As an ideal-type, the superordinate category contains all the attributes of the subtypes. The subtypes, however, possess only one (or some) of the attributes of the ideal-type, as illustrated in Table 6.4.

---

[30] As a second example, one might consider Reynolds' and Reilly's (2005: 28) taxonomy of electoral systems. The still classic example of a taxonomy is the Linnaean system of biological classification (Linsley and Usinger 1959).

[31] Collier and Mahon (1993); Lakoff (1987).   [32] Coppedge and Gerring (2011). See also Held (2006).

Table 6.3 A taxonomy in tabular format

ATTRIBUTES

CONCEPTS	Form of government	Rule by few	Rule by the people	Direct	Indirect	Elections	Rule of law	Majority rule	Popular participation	Consultative bodies	Equality	Total
(I) Polity	X											1
(A) Autocracy	X	X										2
(B) Democracy	X		X									2
(1) Direct	X		X	X								3
(2) Representative	X		X		X							3
(i) Electoral	X		X		X	X						4
(ii) Liberal	X		X		X		X					4
(iii) Majoritarian	X		X		X			X				4
(iv) Participatory	X		X		X				X			4
(v) Deliberative	X		X		X					X		4
(vi) Egalitarian	X		X		X						X	4

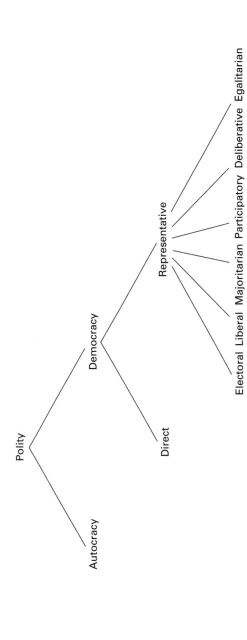

Figure 6.1 A taxonomy in tree-diagram format

Table 6.4 A configurational typology: ideal-type and radial categories

CONCEPTS	ATTRIBUTES						
	Competitive elections	*Rule of law*	*Majority rule*	*Popular participation*	*Consultative bodies*	*Equality*	*Total*
Democracy	X	X	X	X	X	X	6
Electoral	X						1
Liberal		X					1
Majoritarian			X				1
Participatory				X			1
Deliberative					X		1
Egalitarian						X	1

Sequential typology

Sequential (aka *processual*[33]) typologies, like simple periodizations (temporal typologies), are organized along a temporal axis: time matters. However, while the periodization simply asserts that time periods are different (in ways defined by the typology), a sequential typology asserts that the *sequence* of events matters for subsequent events.

Like taxonomies, the sequential typology may be diagramed in a tree fashion. But here, the branches represent temporal sequences (which may or may not embody taxonomic features). The classic example is the "cladistics" method of biological classification, which supposes that each branch ("clade") in the tree of life is distinctive such that species sharing the same point of origin also share significant biological characteristics (a claim that has subsequently been disputed).[34]

In the social sciences, claims associated with sequential typologies are generally more modest and the typologies less elaborate. Still, many writers assert that the sequence of events matters, and that these sequence effects can be theorized in a general fashion.[35] For example, T. H. Marshall argues that democratic development is characterized by three phases: civil, political, and social.[36] W. W. Rostow conceives of modernization as a five-stage process: "the traditional society, the preconditions for take-off, the take-off, the drive to maturity, and the age of high mass-consumption."[37] Here, the authors' methods are qualitative. Where large samples are available, sequential typological

---

[33] Nowotny (1971: 24–29).   [34] Gould (1983: ch. 28).
[35] Falleti (2010: chs. 1–2); Pierson (2004); Rueschemeyer, Huber, and Stephens (1992); Shefter (1994).
[36] Marshall (1964).   [37] Rostow (1960: 4).

features may be discerned with various statistical techniques, as developed by Andrew Abbott and others.[38]

Associations

Associational descriptions are *probabilistic* multidimensional comparisons across indicators or units. There is, in other words, no attempt to achieve the crisp features of a typology. Three major subtypes may be distinguished.

Trend

A trend is an association between a phenomenon and time. If the dimension of interest is correlated in some manner with time (e.g., linearly or non-linearly, monotonically or nonmonotonically, cyclically or noncyclically), we say that the data is trended. Reaching a determination on these matters may be assisted by a wide variety of time-series modeling techniques as well as by visual graphs.[39]

Leaving aside their obvious utility to causal inference, trends provide insight into the nature of processes and sometimes allow us to extrapolate into the future. It is not surprising that a good deal of investigatory research has been devoted to the discovery of trends in the social sciences. We have already noted the debate over global inequality.[40] Some see signs of a secular decline in social capital within the United States,[41] while others view this apparent trend as an artifact of measurement error and/or an unusual point of initial comparison.[42] Some argue that policy-making trends align with a model of punctuated equilibrium, with long periods of stasis or incremental change followed by short bursts of comparatively "revolutionary" change.[43] Others view policy-making as incremental[44] or stochastic, and therefore not characterized by any clear and persistent trends.[45]

Network

A network signifies an association in which the interrelationship among multiple units forms the topic of interest. This may be understood in spatial, temporal, or functional ways. A network analysis might focus on the distance between various units (understood as mean distance, total distance, shortest

---

[38] Abbott (1995, 2004); Abbott and Forrest (1986); Abbott and Tsay (2000); Everitt, Landau, and Leese (2001: ch. 4).
[39] Hamilton (1994).   [40] Contrast Milanovic (2005) and Dollar (2005).   [41] Putnam (2001).
[42] Paxton (1999).   [43] Baumgartner and Jones (1993).   [44] Lindblom (1979).
[45] Cohen, March, and Olsen (1972); Kingdon (1984).

distance, and so forth). It might try to estimate the time elapsed between separate events (understood as mean, total, shortest, longest, and so forth). Or it might focus on functional interrelationships, for example, trade, diffusion of ideas and practices, conflict, and so forth.

A more differentiated typology is provided by David Knoke and Song Yang, who categorize network relationships as *transactions* ("actors exchange control over physical or symbolic media, for example, in gift giving or economic sales and purchases"); *communications* ("linkages between actors are channels through which messages may be transmitted"); *boundary penetration* ("ties consist of membership in two or more social formations, for example, corporation boards of directors with overlapping members"); *instrumental* ("actors contact one another in efforts to secure valuable goods, services, or information, such as a job, abortion, political advice, or recruitment to a social movement"); *sentimental* ("actors express their feelings of affection, admiration, deference, loathing, or hostility toward one another"); or *kinship* ("bonds of blood and marriage").[46]

One prominent type of network is geographic in nature, focused on the spatial relationships among units. Historians often find it useful to map changes through time, providing a spatial representation of history.[47] Social scientists are keen to map spatial inequalities in income, wealth, innovation, technology, and health across countries and regions.[48] Especially close attention is paid to trade networks.[49] Political scientists and sociologists are often interested in spatial patterns of global hegemony.[50] Sociologists have examined the spread of religion through time and space.[51] Spatially ordered processes of change are often described as *diffusion* (a mechanism that sits astride the descriptive–causal divide).[52] The diffusion of democracy has inspired a good deal of work.[53]

Where precise locations are important, the empirical component of a spatial network may be plotted in a Geographic Information System (GIS) format. This provides a standardized method for recording the location of units and events, and is increasingly prominent in the work of social scientists.[54]

Networks, like other empirical patterns, may be probed qualitatively or quantitatively. Statistical models are advisable wherever data is sufficiently

---

[46] Knoke and Yang (2008: 12). See also Wasserman and Faust (1994).   [47] Knowles (2008).
[48] Clark, Gertler, and Feldman (2000); Goesling and Firebaugh (2000); Kanbur and Venables (2005).
[49] Kim and Shin (2002).   [50] Wallerstein (1974).   [51] Montgomery (1996).
[52] Henisz, Melner, and Guillén (2005).   [53] Brinks and Coppedge (2006); Gleditsch and Ward (2006).
[54] Gregory and Ell (2007).

numerous and sufficiently complex that patterns of interaction surpass that which can be analyzed through informal methods.[55] As an example, let us consider the question of policy networks. We know that a great many people are consulted in the course of policy deliberations, especially in mass democracies. Yet we know very little about the precise nature and shape of these networks (despite a good deal of theorizing). A study by Heinz *et al.* attempts to shed light on this important question. On the basis of a relatively comprehensive network analysis of four issue areas in the contemporary United States the authors conclude that policy networks have no consistent center. Rather, they are highly dispersed and much more random than writers on the subject had previously surmised: a "hollow core" rather than an "iron triangle."[56]

Correlation

A correlational style of argument refers to any multidimensional association that is not founded on trends or networks. Admittedly, this is a large residual category. However, it correctly describes a good deal of the descriptive work in the social sciences, and there seems no better way to describe it.

A correlational argument might, for example, focus on the question of whether democracies are less likely to persecute minorities than autocracies. Or it might focus on features of an individual polity. Is support for democracy correlated with income? Is the structure of organized interests tilted – in membership, staffing, and mission – toward the middle and upper classes? In other words, does political position co-vary with social class?[57] Are elites more "ideological" in their view of politics than rank-and-file voters?[58] These are all correlational arguments insofar as the effort is to demonstrate a multidimensional associational pattern without causal assumptions. That is, the association may be the product of some underlying causal factor(s), but the author is not staking any claims of this sort because the correlation is interesting and important in its own right (and the causal forces at work may be difficult to uncover).

Conclusions

There are an infinite number of ways to describe a given reality. However, if the writer's purpose is to generalize across a population, a description is likely

[55] Knoke and Yang (2008); Wasserman and Faust (1994).   [56] Heinz *et al.* (1993).
[57] Schattschneider (1960); Verba, Schlozman, and Brady (1995).
[58] McClosky, Hoffmann, and O'Hara (1960).

to take the form of an *indicator*, a *synthesis*, a *typology*, or an *association* – each presupposing a different set of criteria.

Description is thus unified by several common criteria (captured in Table 6.1) and differentiated by criteria pertaining to each descriptive strategy (as summarized in Table 6.1). Additional criteria pertain to each element of a descriptive argument – the *concepts* employed (Chapter 5) and the *measurement* strategies enlisted (Chapter 7).

7 Measurements

Grown-ups love figures. When you tell them that you have made a new friend, they never ask you any questions about essential matters. They never say to you, "What does his voice sound like? What games does he love best? Does he collect butterflies?" Instead, they demand: "How old is he? How many brothers has he? How much does he weigh? How much money does his father make?" Only from these figures do they think they have learned anything about him.

If you were to say to the grown-ups: "I saw a beautiful house made of rosy brick, with geraniums in the windows and doves on the roof," they would not be able to get any idea of that house at all. You would have to say to them: "I saw a house that cost $20,000." Then they would exclaim: "Oh, what a pretty house that is!"

Just so, you might say to them: "The proof that the little prince existed is that he was charming, that he laughed, and that he was looking for a sheep. If anybody wants a sheep, that is a proof that he exists." And what good would it do to tell them that? They would shrug their shoulders, and treat you like a child. But if you said to them: "The planet he came from is Asteroid B-612," then they would be convinced, and leave you in peace from their questions.

They are like that. One must not hold it against them. Children should always show great forbearance toward grown-up people.

But certainly, for us who understand life, figures are a matter of indifference. I should have liked to begin this story in the fashion of the fairy-tales. I should have liked to say: "Once upon a time there was a little prince who lived on a planet that was scarcely any bigger than himself, and who had need of a sheep . . ."

To those who understand life, that would have given a much greater air of truth to my story.

Antoine de Saint-Exupéry[1]

The Little Prince articulates the invidious, de-humanizing element inherent in any attempt to measure, and thereby compare, human beings. "Treating them like statistics," as the phrase goes. Abhorrent though it may seem (and surely, the measurement of intimate material and emotional states is an act of extreme

---

[1] de Saint-Exupéry ([1943] 1971: 16–17). I was led to this passage by Freedman *et al.* (1991: 29).

hubris), there may also be good reasons for measuring, say, the incomes of families in a community.

Measurement might be regarded as the *analysis* phase of description. It is here where the researcher makes contact with empirical reality (one hopes). It is here that concepts (Chapter 5), and the larger descriptive arguments they sit within (Chapter 6) are operationalized.

Of course, arguing, conceptualizing, and measuring blend into one another, and this means that there is considerable overlap among topics discussed in Part II of the book. This chapter should, therefore, be understood as a continuation of topics broached in previous chapters. Chapters 5 and 6 have a more deductive flavor, while this chapter has a more inductive flavor. But the more important point is that none of these topics can be neatly separated from the others. Investigations always contain a mix of deductive and inductive components – usually, there is a continual back and forth. It is impossible to define a concept without some sense of the empirical terrain, and it is impossible to operationalize a concept without some sense of how the concept is defined. Concepts and percepts are inseparable; one can hardly be considered without the other.

The task of measurement may be defined narrowly as "the assignment of numbers to objects or events according to rules"[2] or, more broadly, as "the process of linking abstract concepts to empirical indicants."[3] For our purposes, a broader definition is appropriate. Indeed, it is not clear what assigning numbers to objects would mean, unless connected to identifiable concepts (numbers of *what*?). The critical question, in any case, is how we recognize a concept when we see it. Can democracy be distinguished from autocracy? Can power be distinguished from powerlessness? What do these concepts mean *empirically*?

Intimately related to the topic of measurement is the adjoining topic of *data collection*. When one is collecting data in a systematic fashion – that is, data organized around selected concepts of theoretical interest – one faces the challenge of measurement. Measurement and systematic data collection are therefore virtually synonymous. (They are, of course, quite different from an *ad hoc* collection of data.)

So defined, the topic of measurement is vast and unbounded, extending into all terrains of social science. Each field and subfield offers its own challenges,

---

[2] Stevens (1951: 22).

[3] Carmines and Meller (1979: 10). In this vein, see Seawright and Collier (2004: 295). Additional work on measurement in the social sciences includes Adcock and Collier (2001); Bartholomew (2007); Blalock (1982); Boumans (2007); Duncan (1984); Goertz (2006); Jackman (2008); Kempf-Leonard (2004); Krantz *et al.* (1971, 1989, 1990); Reiss (2007).

and each has generated its own literature. Arguably, this is the most context-specific of all the social science tasks discussed in this book.

That said, there are some common challenges. The problem of measurement stems from the fact that most (and perhaps all) important social science concepts are not directly observable. They are *latent*. All abstract concepts fall into this category. We cannot "see" justice, democracy, governance, or power. With respect to the latter, Robert Dahl writes, "The gap between the concept and operational definition is generally very great, so great, indeed, that it is not always possible to see what relation there is between the operations and the abstract definition."[4] Even something as concrete as a vouchers program cannot be directly observed. Many terms in the social science lexicon suffer from this problem. Alienation, anomie, charisma, civil society, collective conscience, crisis, culture, democracy, dogmatism, equality, false consciousness, hegemony, ideology, legitimacy, mass society, national character, pattern variable, petty bourgeois, rationalization, sovereignty, state, and status anxiety are all "fuzzy" concepts. We may be able to define them in a general way, but we have immense difficulty locating their referents in empirical space.[5] These are the sorts of measurement problems that social science is at pains to resolve.[6]

The difficulty of measurement in the social sciences also stems from the recalcitrant nature of our subject matter. Recall that we have defined social science as the study of human action: behavior that is in some degree decisional (Chapter 1). Human action is therefore infused with actor-defined meanings and motivations, and this raises a set of measurement challenges that are distinctive to the social sciences. In specific terms, what we are dealing with is a set of phenomena that are sensitive and/or difficult to interpret. The twin effect is to obscure a good deal of the ideas and actions of interest to social science from the prying eyes, and abstract classificatory categories, of

---

[4] Dahl (1968: 414), quoted in Debnam (1984: 2).

[5] Geddes (1996: 5) notes that "state autonomy" is generally "inferred from its effects rather than directly observed. No one, it seems, is quite sure what "it" actually consists of. State autonomy seems at times to refer to the independence of the state itself, the regime, a particular government, some segments or agencies of the government, or even specific leaders. It seems the phrase can refer to any independent force based in the central government.

[6] Recall that all social science concepts aspire to capture something real in the world around us. The referent may be highly attenuated, but it is nonetheless always present. The more easily these referents can be located and differentiated from other similar referents the more useful that concept will be, *ceteris paribus*. A concept of democracy that cannot tell us which phenomena are democratic and which are not is less useful on that account. Concepts of justice, capitalism, socialism, ideology, or anything else in the social science universe are subject to the same demand. "Concepts without percepts are empty; percepts without concepts are blind," notes Kant (quoted in Hollis 1994: 71).

researchers. I shall refer to this measurement challenge as *hermeneutic* or *interpretive*.[7]

For example, in investigating the topic of corruption we face the problem that those who engage in corrupt activities try hard to conceal these actions and, perhaps equally important, are often informed by different definitions of corruption. The latter issue is important because it bears centrally on how we might interpret "corrupt" behavior. It is quite different if an act of patronage is seen as a moral obligation (e.g., to help kith or kin) rather than an act of self-advancement. Because questions of meaning and intentionality are often central to our understanding of a phenomenon they are also central to the problem of measurement.[8] (I do not mean to imply that the understandings of actors are *always* critical to problems of measurement. Sometimes, it is sufficient to know whether or not an action has taken place without worrying about the meanings ascribed to it.)

The same difficulties are encountered with many other social science subjects, for example, clientelism, crime, democracy, discrimination, economic output, happiness, human rights, identity, ideology, intelligence, nationalism, prejudice, public opinion, utility, and wellbeing.[9] We have trouble measuring these things because actors have strong incentives to mis-represent themselves *and* because these actors often have differing understandings of their own actions or experiences. Adding to our perplexity, issues of duplicity and perspective are often difficult to disentangle. It is hard to tell when someone is (a) lying or (b) telling the truth from a different angle.

I begin by reviewing general criteria that all measurements seek to achieve. Next, I discuss various strategies of measurement. Finally, I offer a brief review of *ex post* validity tests (ways of judging the validity of indicators once they are arrived at).

Criteria

In pursuing the task of measurement, two overall goals are ubiquitous and paramount: *reliability* (aka *precision*) and *validity*. These criteria were introduced

---

[7] The difficulties of obtaining sensitive information are addressed in Lee (1993). The hermeneutic task is addressed from philosophical and empirical angles by Gadamer (1975); Geertz (1973); Rabinow and Sullivan (1979); Taylor (1985); von Wright (1971); Winch (1958); Yanow and Schwartz-Shea (2006).

[8] Issues of intentionality are, of course, central to the interpretivist tradition. However, they are by no means incidental to the positivist tradition. Indeed, they are central to the practice of survey research (Chong 1993; Kritzer 1996; Schwartz 1984; Stoker 2003).

[9] Detailed expositions of problems of measurement connected to particular concepts are worth consulting, e.g., on *wellbeing* (Gough and McGregor 2007), *identity* (Abdelal, Herrera, and Johnston 2009), *happiness* (Bertrand and Mullainathan 2001), and *corruption* (reviewed in the final section of this chapter).

initially in Chapter 4. Here, we are concerned solely with their application to problems of measurement.

Precision – usually understood as *reliability* in measurement contexts – refers to level of stochastic (random) error, or noise, encountered in the attempt to operationalize a concept. This is often assessable through *reliability tests*. If multiple applications of a measurement instrument reveal a high level of consistency one may regard the chosen measure as reliable (precise). Levels of reliability are typically calculated as the inverse of the *variance* (i.e., dispersion around the mean) across measurements. Greater variance means less reliability.

Tests depend, of course, on the specific instrument though which the measurement is obtained. If, for example, the instrument involves coding then trials may consist of inter-coder reliability tests conducted on the same material. Surprisingly, such tests are not commonly administered among those who develop and use cross-national indicators of democracy, despite the fact that these indices rest to a considerable extent upon coding decisions.[10]

If the opportunity to test multiple iterations of an indicator is not present then the issue of reliability remains at the level of an assumption. But it is nonetheless crucial. A high probability of random error may doom even the simplest generalization about the world. Moreover, if the concept forms the basis for subsequent causal analysis then errors associated with a causal factor (X) are prone to introduce bias into the resulting analysis, generally attenuating the true causal effect of X on Y.[11]

Validity refers to *systematic* measurement error, error that – by definition – introduces bias into the resulting concept (and presumably into any causal analysis that builds on that concept). One often finds, for example, that the level of accuracy with which an indicator is measured varies directly with some factor of theoretical interest. For example, it could be that better quality schools are also more conscientious at record-keeping, meaning that we will have more data, and more reliable data, from certain schools and this characteristic of the data will be correlated with the outcome of interest (school performance). It could also be that bad measurement tools offer opportunities for mis-reporting that bias results for schools across the sample, such that bad schools (with sloppy accounting procedures) report inflated school

---

[10] Freedom House does not conduct such tests, or at least does not make them public. Polity does so, but it appears to require a good deal of hands-on training before coders reach an acceptable level of coding accuracy.

[11] For a full discussion see Coppedge (forthcoming).

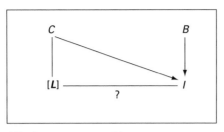

[L] = Latent concept of interest
 I = Indicator
 B = Covariate (source of noise, i.e., unreliability)
 C = Confounder (source of bias, i.e., invalidity)

General features
→ Causal relationship
── Covariation (possibly causal)

Figure 7.1   A measurement diagram

performance. This is the sort of systematic measurement error that researchers must be on guard against, and for which there is usually no easy fix.

In clarifying these ideas it may be helpful to consider the problem of measurement in diagrammatic form. Figure 7.1 represents the underlying concept of interest as *L* (i.e., the term, its defining attributes, and the phenomena it is intended to describe), which is bracketed to indicate its latent status. The observable trace of *L* is *I*, the chosen indicator(s). Sources of background noise *not* correlated with *L* are represented by *B*, an orthogonal covariate (i.e., random measurement error). Potential confounders, that is, factors that are correlated with *L* and with *I*, therefore introducing systematic bias into measurement, are represented by *C*. In this simplified schema, the task of a measurement instrument is to identify an indicator (*I*) that is correlated with *L*, but not with confounders (*C*), and minimizes noise (*B*).

Note that the potential threats to inference are virtually limitless – extending, as they do, to anything that might have a causal effect on *I* that is also correlated with *L* (the unobservable concept of interest). This includes investigator bias, a failure in instrumentation (the technical part of a measurement), and all manner of contextual features, including similar phenomena that are difficult to distinguish from *L*. Because the factor of theoretical interest, *L*, is (by definition) not measurable it cannot be directly verified. This is why it is so hard to write a general treatise on measurement; so much rests on matters of assumption. But let us briefly consider some of the obstacles.

Measurement is an inherently comparative venture. It presumes a scale: that is, a standard metric by which heterogeneous things can be systematically and precisely compared. Hence, all attempts at measurement face a problem of equivalence or consistency across contexts. A chosen measure must mean the same thing, and must adequately represent the concept of theoretical interest, across all contexts to which it is being applied. The challenge is therefore to find a way to compare things across diverse contexts without too much loss of meaning or distortion.

Consider the concept of corruption. This abstract concept is easier to operationalize if one focuses in on particular types of corruption, for example, bribes given by businessmen to government officials for the purpose of obtaining a business license. Even so, there are considerable difficulties if one wishes to compare this indicator across countries on a global scale. First, reports of corrupt actions are probably not going to be directly observable, and will therefore rely on surveys of businessmen. This, in turn, introduces multiple potential sources of bias (systematic error). Businessmen in one country may be more likely to answer questions about bribes in a more forthright fashion than businessmen in another country, even if the actual level of bribe-giving is identical. (For example, greater frankness may be manifested in democratic countries than in authoritarian countries.) Second, the meaning and purpose of these bribes may be quite different across contexts, as has already been alluded to. For example, in one country a bribe may signal a more or less voluntary gift, a sign of respect in gift-giving cultures. In another country, a bribe may be coerced by the official. These are evidently quite different events, even if the monetary transaction is identical. Finally, it may be problematic to generalize from one specific indicator of corruption to the larger concept of theoretical interest. That is, bribes on the occasion of obtaining a business license may not be indicative of the overall scale of corruption in a country: corruption may be rife in different sectors. (Later, we shall explore some possible solutions to these problems.)

Note that the question of validity in measurement refers to the correspondence between a concept's definition (its attributes) and the chosen indicators (represented by I). As such, it is never a purely empirical problem. Consider that any concept can be operationalized by the simple act of stipulating a measurable indicator. We proclaim, "L shall be operationalized by I." As long as I is measurable, one can claim that L has been operationalized. And if multiple measures of L are consistent, the measure can claim high reliability. However, it is another matter to prove that I is a valid measure *of L*. Perhaps I captures only one dimension of L (a multifaceted concept), excluding others. Perhaps I measures something else entirely (some concept other than L). In these circumstances, there is a problem of conceptual validity.

Issues of conceptual validity bedevil most large social science concepts. Let us consider our usual exemplar, democracy. An influential team of researchers led by Adam Przeworski (including Michael Alvarez, Jose Antonio Cheibub, Jennifer Gandhi, and Fernando Limongi) adopts a minimal definition of democracy centered on the existence of competitive elections.[12] To operationalize this definition three necessary conditions are posited: (1) the chief executive and legislature must be elected; (2) there must be more than a single party competing in these elections; and (3) at least one alternation in power under identical electoral rules must take place.[13] Note that this set of decision rules makes it easy to measure. We anticipate little disagreement over the coding of cases. Thus, the measure can claim high reliability.

However, two problems of conceptual validity can be raised. The first concerns the fit between the operationalization and the chosen definition. In particular, this set of coding rules cannot distinguish between (a) a polity where a single party wins election after election under free and fair electoral rules and would be prepared to cede power to a competitor (if it lost) and (b) a polity where a single party wins election after election under free and fair electoral rules and would *not* be prepared to cede power. This has come to be known as the "Botswana" problem.[14] The reason this poses a problem of validity is that democracy is generally understood to rest upon free and fair elections (an understanding to which Przeworski *et al.* also subscribe), which means that the party winning the election should be allowed to assume office. But we do not have empirical information about this, and the coding rules treat situations (a) and (b) as identical, even when it seems fairly obvious that they are not. (There are some countries where the continual victory of a party is a signal of authoritarian rule and others in which it probably is not.)

A second problem of conceptual validity concerns the way in which the chosen indicator fits within the overall concept of democracy. Many understandings of democracy extend beyond the electoral features of a polity, or have a broader view of what electoral democracy is than that adopted by Przeworski and colleagues, as discussed in the previous chapter. In this respect, the problem of validity is largely conceptual in nature. It hinges upon how we choose to define a key term. Thus, one might object that although Przeworski and colleagues have effectively operationalized one aspect of democracy they have neglected others, and therefore have adopted an invalid, or only partially valid, measure. Przeworski *et al.* might defend themselves by claiming to represent

---

[12] More specifically, the Przeworski *et al.* definition entails: "(1) *Ex ante* uncertainty: the outcome of the election is not known before it takes place, (2) *Ex post* irreversibility: the winner of the electoral contest actually takes office, and (3) Repeatability: elections that meet the first two criteria occur at regular and known intervals" (Cheibub and Gandhi 2004).
[13] Cheibub and Gandhi (2004: 3).   [14] Cheibub and Gandhi (2004).

only one facet of democracy, captured in the radial concept of *electoral* democracy. Or they might claim to adopt a minimal definition of the subject. In any case, debates over measurement validity often hinge upon how to label and define the concept of interest (L); they are conceptual rather than purely empirical.

Here, we encounter what might be called the fundamental problem of measurement: issues of conceptual validity (unlike issues of reliability) cannot usually be tested empirically, at least not for most key concepts of social science, which are latent rather than directly observable. Indeed, if validity could be measured there would be no problem of measurement, for we would know what it is that we want to know. The problem of measurement lies in the fact that the correlation between L and I in Figure 7.1 remains – and must remain – to some extent hypothetical.

Strategies

We have said that the problem of measurement in social science stems from the fact that most concepts of theoretical interest are not directly observable. Concepts like clientelism, crime, democracy, discrimination, economic output, and happiness cannot be counted like bicycles. Of course, there are observable features that we presume to be connected to these concepts; otherwise, they would not be amenable to empirical inquiry of any sort. It is from these observable features that we construct indicators.

In this section, we review various strategies for doing so, along with the challenges that each strategy entails. These strategies involve: (a) levels of abstraction; (b) structure; (c) aggregation techniques; (d) scales; (e) basic objectives; (f) deduction versus induction; (g) ethnography; (h) surveys and experiments; (i) cross-referencing; and (j) causal relations, as summarized in Table 7.1.

The reader should bear in mind that these are vast subjects and my treatment here will be focused on the implications of these strategies for the task of measurement. The reader should also bear in mind that because measurement is a highly contextual art, strategies for operationalizing concepts differ from field to field and topic to topic. This chapter rests at a fairly general level (despite the fact that we entertain quite a number of concrete examples), and leaves aside specific statistical techniques of measurement, of which there are quite a few (e.g., content analysis, cluster analysis, discriminant analysis, and so forth).

Table 7.1 Measurement strategies

Levels of abstraction	High; Medium; Low
Structure	Set-theoretic (necessary, sufficient, necessary-and-sufficient); Additive; Fuzzy sets
Aggregation	Boolean logic; Weightings
Scales	Categorical (nominal, ordinal); Numeric (interval, ratio)
Objectives	Discrimination; Grouping
Approaches	Deductive; Inductive
Ethnography	Participant-observation
Surveys/experiments	Standardized surveys and randomized treatments
Cross-referencing	Establishing equivalence across diverse contexts
Causal relations	Causes and effects of the phenomenon of interest

Levels of abstraction

In grappling with the problem of measurement it is helpful to acknowledge that all empirical concepts of interest to social science encompass multiple levels of abstraction. At the very least, one generally distinguishes between the attributes that define a concept and the indicators that operationalize it, generating two tiers: (1) conceptualization and (2) measurement. This is probably sufficient for a small-order concept like vouchers.

For more abstract concepts like democracy multiple tiers may be required in order to adequately represent all the levels of analysis implicit in the concept, and in order to fully operationalize it – to bring it down to earth, so to speak. Consider the following hierarchy:

> *Democracy* (the latent concept of theoretical interest)
> *Electoral* (a conception of democracy)
> *Free and fair elections* (a key component of electoral democracy)
> *Validation of an election by international election observers* (an indicator of free and fair elections)

Here, four tiers of a concept are illustrated. Of course, one might add further levels, for example, a more specific and operational definition of how the freeness and fairness of elections should be validated. Evidently, one faces a potentially infinite regress. As originally devised (in a 1927 physics textbook by P. W. Bridgman), operationalization referred to the actual physical operations a person would employ to locate a phenomenon. In constructing a reasonable standard one must fall back on what is necessary in order to achieve a high degree of reliability (precision). Once this has been achieved, there is no further need for specification. In any case, the lowest level of abstraction is usually referred to as an indicator, regardless of how precise the latter is.

Problems of reliability (precision) can often be resolved, or at least mitigated, by moving *down* this ladder. In the case of democracy, conceptions are easier to measure than the core meaning, components are easier to measure than conceptions, and indicators are the easiest of all. Small, concrete things are usually easier to measure than large, abstract things.

Naturally, at a certain point micro-level phenomena become less observable, and more difficult to measure. This is the situation faced in fields like biology and physics, where cells, molecules, and subatomic particles are the frontiers of measurement. In the social sciences, however, the individual (i.e., the whole human being) is usually regarded as the most disaggregated unit of analysis. Here, problems of measurement are generally the product of abstraction, not specificity.

It should also be remembered that the problem of measurement involves both reliability and conceptual validity. As one scopes down from "democracy" to low-level indicators one may find that the connection between the concept of interest and the phenomena being measured becomes highly attenuated. A chosen indicator may be highly precise, but of questionable validity with respect to a high-order concept of theoretical interest. This is the tradeoff encountered when moving along a ladder of abstraction: precision is usually enhanced as one moves down, while conceptual validity is enhanced as one moves up.

Structure

Concepts and their indicators are differently structured. This is because membership in the concept is determined not just by the choice of attributes and indicators, but also by the role defined for each attribute or indicator. While we cannot afford a lengthy disquisition on this subject, it is important that we review some of the choices that determine how concepts and indicators are structured.[15]

Attributes and indicators may be understood as *set-theoretic* (necessary/sufficient) or *additive*. Consider the "free and fair elections" component of democracy.

If understood as a *necessary-and-sufficient* condition of democracy, this is the only characteristic that matters. A polity with free and fair elections is a

---

[15] Goertz (2006) discusses these issues in great detail, though his terminology is somewhat different to mine.

democracy; one without is an autocracy. Note that a necessary-and-sufficient condition may be the product of several necessary conditions, deemed jointly sufficient (e.g., free and fair elections, civil liberties, and turnover of power). It need not be limited to a single factor.

If free and fair elections is understood as a *necessary* condition then a polity must embody this attribute, though there may be other membership conditions as well. Minimal definitions – those that define a concept by its bare essentials – rely on necessary-condition attributes (Chapter 5).

If free and fair elections is understood as a *sufficient* condition then it is sufficient by itself to qualify a polity as democratic, though there may be other conditions that would also qualify a polity as democratic. Each is substitutable for the other. This is, to be sure, an unusual way to define a key concept, though it is more common at the indicator level.[16]

If, on the other hand, free and fair elections is understood in an *additive* fashion then a polity is considered more democratic insofar as it possesses this attribute. This is how attributes are handled in maximal definitions (Chapter 5).

The choice between set-theoretic and additive structures is thus highly consequential. Indeed, the same set of attributes or indicators will yield very different concepts when different choices are made with respect to concept structure.

Another approach to the role of an attribute or indicator is through *fuzzy sets*, which may be regarded as a midway position between set-theoretic and additive structures.[17] Note that in the real world phenomena often cluster in categories, but their membership in these categories is not perfect. Fuzzy sets allow the conceptualizer to assign a score to each entity that reflects its partial (or complete) membership, based on whatever membership conditions are defined. The boundaries are 0 (entirely absent) and 1 (fully present). Of course, the use of fuzzy sets may complicate the interpretation and use of a categorization scheme since it no longer carries its usual "crisp" or "continuous" meanings. Yet for some purposes it may be useful to know which entities are 30 percent or 40 percent members of a given set. Indeed, for some purposes, it may be important to be able to define category boundaries in nonexclusive terms (e.g., as 51 percent membership rather than as 100 percent membership). For other purposes, the integration of such complexities would serve only to distract and confuse. Like many things, choices in conceptualization and measurement rest upon the purpose that a concept is expected to serve.

---

[16] Goertz (2006).

[17] Ragin (2000, 2008); Smithson (1987); Smithson and Verkuilen (2006). The application of fuzzy sets to democracy is explored by Bowman, Lehoucq, and Mahoney (2005) and Schneider (2011).

Aggregation

The researcher must also consider how to *aggregate* (put together) all the attributes and indicators attached to a concept.

Set-theoretic conditions are easy. They aggregate in an explicit and clear-cut fashion, following the dictates of Boolean logic. Any number of necessary or sufficient conditions can be accommodated in a single definition, and any number of conditions may be regarded as collectively necessary and sufficient.[18]

However, many social science concepts regard attributes and indicators in an additive fashion. This means that the task of aggregation is not self-evident, and therefore an explicit aggregation principle(s) must be adopted. For example, attributes (or indicators) may be equally weighted (the approach taken by many democracy indices). Alternatively, a differential weighting scheme may be applied according to *a priori* assumptions about the importance of different components to the overall concept. If one believes that some dimensions of democracy (say, electoral and participatory) are more important than others (say, deliberation or equality), then the former might be granted greater weight in the aggregated concept. Weightings may also be arrived at inductively, as described below.

Whatever solution to structure and aggregation is chosen, it should be *clear*, *explicit*, and *replicable*. That is, it should be possible for another researcher to follow the choices made by the original researcher and to make different choices with the same underlying data, that is, to reconstruct the concept. This allows for sensitivity tests (how robust is an analysis in the face of different aggregation choices?) as well as for disaggregation, which may serve useful purposes in different contexts.

Unfortunately, although most extant indicators of democracy have fairly explicit aggregation rules they are sometimes difficult to comprehend and consequently to apply (e.g., Polity). They may also include "wild card" elements, allowing the coder free rein to assign a final score in accordance with his or her overall impression of a country (e.g., Freedom House). This violates the ideal of a systematic approach to aggregation.

Scales

In order to operationalize a concept one must choose a scale, or set of scales (if the concept is multidimensional), to employ.[19] Some scales are *categorical*

---

[18] Goertz (2006); Ragin (1987).   [19] Stevens (1946).

Table 7.2 Typology of scales

		Different categories	Ranked categories	Distance between categories measured	True zero
Categorical	Nominal	x			
	Ordinal	x	x		
Numeric	Interval	x	x	x	
	Ratio	x	x	x	x

(aka "qualitative"), by virtue of the fact that the distance between categories is undefined. Other scales are *numeric* (aka "quantitative") by virtue of the fact that the distance between categories is defined and measured along a numeric scale. Within this two-part classification other subtypes fall, as indicated in Table 7.2. Note that this classification has ramifications for the sort of statistical analysis that can be performed on the resulting indicator. In principle, parametric tests should be used only for data that is properly numerical (though exceptions may be tolerated in certain instances).[20]

Among categorical scales, those that are *nominal* define members of the same class (they are examples of something) but are un-ranked. For example, apples, oranges, and grapes are not more or less of anything relative to each other, though they are all fruit.

Ordinal scales are members of the same class and also ranked: very sweet is sweeter than sweet. But one does not know the true distance separating each level in the scale. It is unclear, for example, how much sweeter "very sweet" is relative to "sweet."

Among numeric scales, those that are *interval* are characterized by a consistent measure of distance between categories. For example, the distance between 3 and 4 on a temperature scale (Celsius or Fahrenheit) is the same as the distance between 25 and 26, and is defined by a formal rule, consistently applied across the scale.

Ratio scales are interval scales with a true zero, indicating the absence of whatever quantity is being measured (a null set). In the case of money, 0 signals no money. In the case of temperature on the Kelvin scale, 0 indicates the absence of all thermal energy.

Frequently, interval and ratio scales fulfill the requirements of a numeric scale only within certain bounds. For example, life span is bounded on the lower

---

[20] Stevens (1946, 1951).

end at 0 (arguably, it is also bounded at the upper end, though this boundary is more difficult to define). A more complicated situation occurs when a numeric scale possesses the characteristic of "equidistance" only within certain boundaries: that is, distances between adjacent points on a scale are equidistant, but only above a certain threshold and/or below a certain threshold. An example of this is discussed below with respect to the concept of democracy, where scales seem to break down at the extremes.

Because scales are defined for specific purposes the same phenomena may be differently classified according to the researcher's purpose. For some purposes, it may be sensible to consider varieties of fruit as nominal categories. For other purposes, it may be sensible to consider them as part of a nominal scale (more or less acidic) or a ratio scale (using a ratio measure of acidity).

For many topics, it is correct to regard higher-level scales as more informative. Thus, we would ordinarily interpret an ordinal scale for temperature ("hot," "medium," "cold") as less precise (and therefore less informative) than an interval or ratio scale. However, this is true only with reference to that particular phenomenon. It would not be true for sex, for example, since this dimension admits of only two categories. Here, an interval scale reduces to a nominal scale.

Note also that while more precise indicators promise more, they also demand more. Specifically, they require a greater number of assumptions about the nature of the underlying data. If any of these assumptions are false, or only partially true, any inference building upon that indicator will be cast into doubt.

An additional consideration rests on the utility of each sort of scale for subsequent analysis. In bivariate and multivariate analyses, where one is interested in the relationship between two or more factors, it may be important to change the scale by which some factor or factors are measured. Often, ordinal scales are treated as is if they were interval. At other times, an interval or scale variable is re-coded as nominal or ordinal. The point to keep in mind is that such re-scaling efforts, while analytically convenient, often involve either a loss of information and/or the introduction of bias in the variable of interest. There are no "natural" scales; however, some interpretations of reality are more plausible than others.

For many purposes, it is essential to distinguish polities in a binary fashion, as democratic or authoritarian (autocratic).[21] This produces a nominal scale with two categories, or perhaps more accurately, an ordinal scale with two categories (since they are ordered). Whatever disagreements may exist over how to operationalize this concept, most binary approaches to democracy

---

[21] Przeworski *et al.* (2000).

Table 7.3 A single scale with multiple interpretations: "Electoral contestation"

0 **Authoritarianism**: No elections or elections with only one party or candidate.

1 **Semi-authoritarianism**: Elections in which more than one party or candidate runs, but not all parties and candidates face the possibility of losing.

2 **Semi-democracy**: Elections in which more than one party or candidate runs and all parties and candidates face the possibility of losing, but not all parties or candidates are allowed to participate.

3 **Democracy**: Elections in which only anti-system extremist groups are banned and all parties and candidates face the possibility of losing.

Source: drawn from Munck (2009: 45).

feature the key component, free and fair elections, which we have already discussed in the context of the minimal definition (Chapter 5). Because of the tendency for minimal definitions to impose crisp (operational) borders on a concept there is a natural affinity between this strategy of definition and the two-category nominal (or ordinal) scale.

For other purposes, one may require a more finely graded indicator of democracy. A cumulative concept is constructed of categories that can be ordered in a unidimensional fashion, for example, as degrees of centrality to the concept of democracy. Limiting himself to the concept of electoral contestation (a dimension of the larger concept of democracy), Gerardo Munck defines a four-part nominal scale including categories for authoritarianism, semi-authoritarianism, semi-democracy, and democracy.[22] Here, each category is distinguishable and clearly ranked relative to the concept of theoretical interest. Defining attributes for each category are elaborated in Table 7.3.

The advantage of this approach is that it allows one to incorporate a wider array of attributes and one is not constrained to separate each attribute into a different category. The unconstrained nominal-scale indicator is also more likely to approximate the virtues of an interval scale, where neighboring categories are equidistant from each other.

Indeed, as the number of categories increases scholars may be inclined to treat nominal scales as interval scales. The Freedom House index of Political Rights, as well as the Polity index, are both commonly treated as interval scales, even though it seems unlikely that the criterion of equidistance between categories is fully satisfied. Consider the Polity scale of democracy, which runs from −10 to +10 in integer intervals, thus creating a twenty-one-point index.[23] Although commonly

---

[22] Munck (2009: 45).   [23] Marshall and Jaggers (2007).

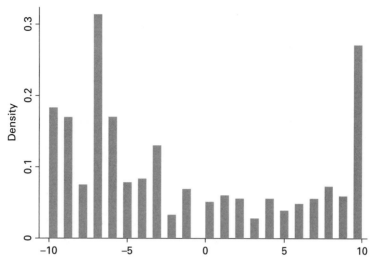

Figure 7.2   Histogram of "Polity" scale of democracy

treated as an interval scale, the empirical properties of the data belie this interpretation. Figure 7.2 displays a histogram of Polity scores across all countries and
all years (1800–2006). It will be observed that the data "bunches" at two points,
at –7 and +10. This could be an empirical property of the world. However, it
seems more likely to be an artifact of the scale itself. A look at Polity's complex
codebook suggests that there are multiple ways a country may achieve a –7 score.
And the fact that +10 defines an end-point of the scale (perfect democracy)
suggests that the members of this large category may be relatively heterogeneous
(some may be more democratic than others, despite having the same score).[24]
Constrained scales (where there is an imposed maximum or minimum) often
encounter this problem. For these reasons it may be more appropriate to view the
Polity scale as ordinal rather than interval. But again, it depends upon one's
purposes. Sometimes, it is imperative to reduce the dimensions of a concept in
order to achieve empirical tractability.

A final option for the four-point scale in Table 7.3 may also be envisioned.
Insofar as the first category comprises a true zero – no contestation whatsoever – the key dimension of electoral contestation may be redefined as a ratio
scale (an option that Munck endorses).

This example nicely illustrates the fact that the same set of categories may be
differently interpreted, according to different assumptions about the underlying

---

[24] This interpretation is borne out by several re-aggregations of the underlying data using Bayesian
techniques (Pemstein, Meserve, and Melton 2010; Treier and Jackman 2008).

empirical phenomena and different uses for which the same indicator may be enlisted.

Objectives

The construction of an indicator may aim to achieve maximum *discrimination* among entities or optimal *grouping* among entities. (The first will utilize numeric scales and the second will utilize categorical scales, as discussed above.) One or the other of these fundamental objectives seems to govern all measurement instruments. Needless to say, a single instrument is unlikely to serve both goals at once.

Discrimination refers to the ability of an instrument to reveal finely graded differences of degree – usually unidimensional but occasionally multidimensional – in some latent trait possessed by a sample of people, objects, or events. This is the traditional goal of measurement in psychometrics, and especially in item-response theory (IRT).[25] Accordingly, a test of educational achievement should provide the basis for maximally sensitive scale (measuring differences in knowledge or ability in a subject among test-takers) with a minimal number of standardized questions. This requires that each question on the test be independent of all others and that each reflect different levels of the latent trait of interest (knowledge/ability in some subject area), thus adding to the information provided by the other questions. If two individuals with different levels of knowledge/ability give the same answer to the same question that question is not helping to discriminate between them; it is redundant. Likewise, if two questions are interdependent – such that an answer to question 2 depends (in some logical fashion) upon the answer given to question 1 – then no new information is learned from question 2. The result of a well-crafted measurement tool (constructed for the purpose of maximum discrimination) is a finely graded scale with no bunching, that is, scores are evenly distributed across the sample of respondents.

Grouping, on the other hand, refers to the ability of an instrument to sort items into discrete categories on the basis of similarities and differences in some latent trait(s). Common techniques include factor analysis, principal component analysis, cluster analysis, and Q-sort analysis. Note that the goal of crisp categories may not always be fully achievable. Nonetheless, it is the guiding objective. The success of a technique is its ability to sort items into discrete categories, apples with apples, oranges with oranges. If phenomena are not

---

[25] Hambleton, Swaminathan, and Rogers (1991).

grouped naturally into categories ("apples," "oranges," etc.), then the job of the measurement instrument is to discern break-points in numeric scales. This may be accomplished in an inductive or deductive manner – which brings us to our next topic.

Approaches: deductive and inductive

Broadly speaking, there are two ways of gaining purchase on a concept that is not directly observable (and hence measurable).

Deductive approaches to measurement construct indicators according to *a priori* decision rules. These may be fairly simple, as in the set of necessary conditions adopted by Adam Przeworski and collaborators (see above). Or they may be highly complex, as in the multiple probabilistic components that comprise the Polity and Freedom House indices. In either case, a deductive approach to measurement derives indicators from the defining attributes of a concept (Chapter 5) or a larger descriptive argument (Chapter 6). The task of measurement is to test how some aspect of the empirical world fits the concept, so defined.[26]

An *inductive* approach begins with a set of empirical measures that are thought to capture elements of a concept (this part of the process is deductive), and then arrives at an ultimate indicator (or indicators) by looking at observed patterns in the data. Researchers generally wish to discover whether multiple measures of a concept correlate with one another, and if so whether these correlations are one-dimensional or multidimensional. Having resolved this question, they will want to know whether the revealed patterns are interpretable, that is, whether they conform to recognizable components of the concept. Techniques for interrogating empirical patterns in a sample of data – and restructuring to form new indicators – include factor analysis, principal components analysis, structural equation models, regression, maximum likelihood models, and IRT.[27]

---

[26] Here, one might contrast the Rasch model of measurement (which implements an *a priori* model of the trait to be measured) with the IRT approach to measurement (which constructs a measurement tool in dialogue with the phenomena being measured).

[27] Choices among these options depend largely upon the envisaged sources of error and the scale of the variables one is dealing with. Jackman (2008) offers an overview. Bollen (1989); Bollen and Lennox (1991) address structural equation modeling. Hambleton, Swaminathan, and Rogers (1991) is a textbook on item-response theory. Examples of some of these techniques applied to political science questions can be found in *Political Analysis* 17(3), Summer 2009.

In this fashion, Michael Coppedge, Angel Alvarez, and Claudia Maldonado explore empirical patterns across fifteen measures of democracy, including the well-known Freedom House and Polity indices.[28] They discover that about 75 percent of the variance in these measures is reducible to two relatively distinct components: *contestation* (competitive elections and associated institutions) and *inclusiveness* (e.g., broad suffrage and high turnout). Since these components have strong grounding in democratic theory (especially in the work of Robert Dahl),[29] there are good reasons to regard them as more than empirical artifacts. They satisfy the inductive as well as the deductive logics of concept measurement.

Of course, it is important to bear in mind that an inductive approach to measurement is not immune to errors contained in the data employed for the construction of the indicator. While random errors in measurement will be reduced when multiple measures are combined into a smaller number of indicators, systematic errors will be reproduced. Thus, if proxy measures capture only certain components of an underlying concept it is these components that will be reflected in the new indicator. As it happens, extant measures of democracy (such as Freedom House and Polity) probably emphasize the electoral and participatory dimensions of this phenomenon, excluding other dimensions such as deliberation, responsiveness, accountability, and social equality. Accordingly, inductive approaches to the measurement of democracy (including Coppedge, Alvarez, and Maldonado) reflect this bias.[30]

The problematic aspect of an inductive measure of anything is usually not the technical issue of which statistical method to employ to analyze the chosen proxies. It is, rather, the identification of suitable proxy variables, as well as the question of what interpretation to grant the resulting dimension(s). One may, for example, resolve problems of conceptual validity by redefining a concept so that it aligns properly with its indicators – in this instance, by calling the resulting indicator *electoral* democracy rather than democracy. But this does not resolve the problem at issue if our objective is to measure *democracy* (*tout court*). Inductive techniques cannot perform alchemy.

More generally, it is worth reiterating a central theme: all deductive approaches to measurement contain an inductive component, and all inductive approaches to measurement contain a deductive component. Concepts and percepts are

---

[28] While Coppedge, Alvarez, and Maldonado (2008) employ principal components analysis, other recent studies have enlisted Bayesian techniques (Pemstein, Meserve, and Melton 2010; Treier and Jackman 2008).

[29] Dahl (1971).

[30] Coppedge, Alvarez, and Maldonado (2008: 645) acknowledge this as a limitation of their approach.

inseparable. Nonetheless, it is sometimes helpful to distinguish approaches to measurement that lean to one or the other side of the spectrum: they are either predominantly deductive or predominantly inductive, as specified above.

Ethnography

Problems of measurement are sometimes best approached in an ethnographic fashion, especially where an element of mystery is involved (i.e., when problems of duplicity and ambiguity are suspected). If you wish to know what is going on, observe the people closest to the action. To understand crime talk to the police, to criminals, to the families of perpetrators, and to the members of the affected community.[31] (I do not mean to imply that ethnography is equivalent to measurement; evidently, there are many other important uses for this technique, some of them related to causal inference, as discussed in Part III.)

Naturally, informants are often cagey. And getting the truth out of them – or anything at all – may require a good deal of soaking and poking. It may also require a degree of trust and familiarity. Informants with much at stake in an issue are not likely to divulge secrets to an outsider. Moreover, an outsider may misunderstand the subtle signals of an informant, thereby introducing measurement error.

The practice of ethnography is focused on gaining local knowledge and this knowledge may require "going local." Sometimes, investigators are born into the sphere that they study, or are already members of that sphere when they begin their research. Some of our best insights into social action are provided by natives of that culture or class.[32] Likewise, some of our best insights into the behavior of the media come from current and former correspondents,[33] and some of our best insights into politics come from current or former public servants.[34]

Alternatively, researchers may assume positions within a culture or an organization as a temporary participant: for example, joining a club or engaging in some activity of interest. Martin Sanchez Jankowski was obliged to participate in

---

[31] On open-ended interviewing see Chong (1993); Dexter (2008); Hammer and Wildavsky (1989); Kritzer (1996); Leech *et al.* (2002); Peabody *et al.* (1990); Rubin and Rubin (1995). The contributions of ethnographic approaches to social science are discussed in Adler and Adler (2003); Bayard de Volo and Schatz (2004); Lieberman, Howard, and Lynch (2004); Schatz (2009); Vidich (1955); Yanow and Schwartz-Shea (2006). Examples of work in this vein (in addition to studies cited above) include Allina-Pisano (2004); Burawoy, Gamson, and Burton (1991); Edin and Lein (1997); Francis (1991); Laitin (1986); Liebow (1967); Luker (1984); Scott (1985).

[32] Ortner (2005).   [33] Crouse (2003); Epstein (2000); McGinniss (1988).

[34] Crossman (1976); Reedy (1970).

initiation rites when researching gangs in Los Angeles, Chicago, and New York in order to gain access to informants.[35] Arguably, the best way to understand an activity, and the ideas and incentives that motivate it, is for the researcher to engage in it him- or herself.

Of course, this is not always possible, or advisable. Even so, one may gain insight into an activity by close observation, intensive open-ended interviews, and long acquaintanceship. In order to understand the meaning ascribed to infant death in a poor community Nancy Scheper-Hughes spent several years in a shantytown community in northeastern Brazil. What she uncovered during the course of her residence (first as a Peace Corps volunteer and then as a professional anthropologist) is rather surprising – and probably would not have occurred to distant observers poring over spreadsheets or secondary accounts.[36]

When studying the behavior of members of Congress, Richard Fenno (one of the most influential interpreters of this storied but secretive institution) got as close to the action as possible – riding along with members as they held constituency meetings, addressed public functions, officiated at fundraisers, and made deals.[37] There is a long tradition of American political scientists who apprentice themselves as congressional aides or staffers on the Hill prior to entering the academy. Likewise, academics from many fields often find that their personal background and connections serve as an entrée into the activity they are studying.

All forms of local knowledge are welcome, including those that are entirely fortuitous. Scott Palmer happened to be stationed as a Peace Corps volunteer in the Peruvian Ayacucho community that spawned the Shining Path (*Sendero Luminoso*) in the 1960s. Indeed, he knew Abimael Guzmán, the founder of *Sendero*, personally. Later, having joined the academy, Palmer was able to bring his personal acquaintance with the culture and the personalities of *Sendero* to bear, providing rare insight into a reclusive and violent political movement.[38] Sometimes, serendipity is the best research strategy.

Very sensitive subjects can sometimes be broached if a researcher is able to enter into a community as a trusted observer. Indeed, research subjects are sometimes delighted to unburden themselves, and may become quite chatty when questioned by an interested and seemingly sympathetic observer, once they are assured of anonymity. When Kathryn Kirschenman and Joleen Neckerman interviewed white employers in the Chicago area about their

---

[35] Sanchez Jankowski (1991). A similar approach is taken by Bill Buford in his study of soccer hooliganism (Buford 1991).
[36] Scheper-Hughes (1992).   [37] Fenno (1978, 1986, 1990). See also Glaser (1996).   [38] Palmer (1992).

hiring practices they were surprised at the forthright discussion that ensued. Employers spoke openly about why they preferred members of one racial group over another, giving examples of their own decisions and experiences. They also freely discussed their understandings of racism and discrimination, the two concepts of theoretical interest.[39] Gaining a rich, contextual "feel" of an activity will assist the researcher in judging the sagacity and forthrightness of his or her informants.

While ethnographic approaches are common to many fields, they are not extensively practiced in economics. And yet it seems likely that they hold great promise, even in this "dismal" science. One recent study of the relationship between recession and wages relies centrally upon open-ended interviews with those who most directly affect wage policy: personnel managers, union representatives, labor lawyers, and job service counselors. Truman Bewley's method is qualitative, but his results are highly informative – and, insofar as one may judge, as accurate as traditional, large-N approaches to measurement.[40] (My hunch is that economists are more influenced by their personal experiences in the private and public sector than they are in the habit of revealing.)

In any case, there is clearly much to be said for the value of ethnographic methods. Granted, such approaches do not always get to the bottom of things, that is, render an authoritative interpretation of an activity. They are prone to problems of unrepresentativeness and observer bias, and are often difficult to replicate. Moreover, subjects may withhold information. However, it is difficult to imagine a nontrivial topic that would not benefit from close observation. Wherever measurement error in some realm of human action is suspected, ethnography is well advised.

Surveys and experiments

In the context of survey research – where there is ordinarily no opportunity to gain the trust of respondents or to judge their responses in a contextual fashion – there are nonetheless ways of accessing sensitive subjects.[41]

In order to preserve anonymity, one may omit the individual's name from the survey. One can also adopt an anonymous setting for the survey, which may be administered by mail or on-line. Another approach is to construct a survey instrument in which sensitive subjects are couched as questions about

---

[39] Kirschenman and Neckerman (1991).   [40] Bewley (1999). See also Helper (2000).

[41] These issues are addressed in Dryzek (1988); Fowler (2008); King *et al.* (2004); Lee (1993); Schaeffer and Presser (2003); Schwartz (1984); Stoker (2003); Tourangeau and Smith (1996); Weisberg (2005); Zaller and Feldman (1992).

other people, for example, "Do you think that other employers use race as a criterion for making hiring decisions?" The assumption here is that those engaged in activities that are denigrated by society (e.g., discrimination or corruption) will be inclined to see these activities as widespread, as this may assuage feelings of guilt or shame. (Of course, it could also be that those who refrain from such activities see others as especially active, by way of explaining their lack of success or popularity.)

One may also enlist an experimental survey design in order to mask individual identities.[42] The *list experiment* begins by sorting respondents randomly into two groups, each of which is given a small set of questions to ponder. The questionnaires are identical except that the treatment group is given one additional question of a sensitive nature (e.g., pertaining to racism or corruption). Respondents are then asked to report the total number of questions that they agree (or disagree) with, but not their answers to any specific question. Since the treatment and control groups are assumed to be comparable in all respects except the one additional question asked of the treatment group, any differences in responses (i.e., in percentage of "agree" answers) may be attributed to this question. The innovation of the method is to allow for accurate aggregate-level results, while avoiding any possibility of linking an individual with a specific answer.[43]

Another experimental survey research technique varies the questions on a questionnaire in small ways so as to gauge the effect of a carefully chosen treatment. For example, in order to probe hidden racism Paul Sniderman and colleagues construct surveys that inquire about respondent views of government's responsibility to assist those in need. In one version of the *split-sample survey* the scenario involves an unemployed black worker, while in another version it involves an unemployed white worker. The scenarios (i.e., the questions) are identical, with the exception of the race of the worker, and so are the two groups (which have been randomly chosen). Thus, any differences in response across the two groups may be interpreted as a product of the treatment.[44]

One may also adopt a field experiment in order to determine values and beliefs on sensitive subjects. For example, in order to gauge the extent of racism among employers one might design experiments in which job applicants – identical in all respects except for race – apply to the same position. The rate of

---

[42] Peeters, Lensvelt-Mulders, and Lashuizen (2010); Warner (1965). Experiments employed to measure the concept of trust are reviewed in Nannestad (2008).

[43] Kane, Craig, and Wald (2004); Sniderman and Carmines (1997).   [44] Sniderman *et al.* (1991).

success across the matched applicants may then be interpreted as a gauge of racism among employers.[45]

Of course, in shifting from articulations to actions we may lose sight of the motivations of the participants. We know from an experiment such as that described above which employers choose the white applicant and which choose the black applicant, but it may be difficult to infer from this why they made those choices. For this reason, experiments whose purpose is to gauge issues of meaning and motivation are often accompanied by ethnographic investigation. Alternatively, the set-up of the experiment may be altered in subtle ways, for example, to adjust for the social background of the applicants, their education, their place of residence, and their mannerisms. If any of these alterations affects the variable of theoretical interest – race – then we may be able to reach tentative conclusions about the motivations behind the actions of employers. In short, experiments can shed light on motivations, but it generally requires multiple iterations.

It may seem strange to employ an experimental framework in order to solve problems of measurement, for the experiment seems to presuppose a causal question (embodied in the treatment). However, the experimental technique has many uses, and the uses to which it is put depend largely on the purpose of the investigation. If one's investigation is causal, one is interested in gauging the causal impact of a treatment like race on employer decisions. If one's investigation is descriptive the same set-up may be employed to shed light on measurement questions, for example, the pervasiveness of racism among employers. Here, the treatment is merely a stimulus that affords an occasion to observe responses. In the terms of our measurement diagram (Figure 7.1), it is a way to control confounders (C) so that the latent concept of interest (L) can be precisely and accurately observed.

Cross-referencing

When faced with recalcitrant problems of measurement, sometimes it is possible to gain traction by looking at an adjacent context in which the concept of theoretical interest is measured in a convincing fashion. I shall refer to this as a *cross-referencing* strategy.

The problem of "media bias" is a case in point. There is a general sense that media outlets offer differing ideologically informed perspectives on the news.

---

[45] For example, Kenney and Wissoker (1994); Neumark, with Bank and Van Nort (1996). For an overview of this genre of field experiment see Pager (2007).

Some are acknowledged to be more liberal or conservative than others. But we do not seem to be able to measure this bias with any degree of precision, and it occasions enormous controversy (most media outlets resist the idea that their reporting is anything but "fair and unbiased", and untainted by partisanship).

Tim Groseclose and Jeffrey Milyo address this question by referencing across three contexts. As a baseline, they adopt ADA (Americans for Democratic Action, a liberal policy group) scores for members of Congress as measure of liberalism/conservativism. Second, they count the frequency with which different members of Congress cite various think tanks in their speeches from the floor of the House and Senate. This allows for a coding of all think tanks along a single liberal/conservative spectrum. Third, they count the frequency with which various media outlets cite these same think tanks. This allows for a judgment of where each outlet stands on the ideological spectrum. By this accounting, most American media outlets are judged to be to the left of the congressional mean. In the authors' words:

> Our results show a strong liberal bias: all of the news outlets we examine, except for Fox News' Special Report and the *Washington Times*, received scores to the left of the average member of Congress. Consistent with claims made by conservative critics, *CBS Evening News* and the *New York Times* received scores far to the left of center. The most centrist media outlets were *PBS NewsHour*, *CNN's Newsnight*, and ABC's *Good Morning America*; among print outlets, *USA Today* was closest to the center.[46]

The findings are controversial, and not beyond reproach. It could be, for example, that think tanks on the liberal end of the spectrum offer more comprehensive and scholarly analysis of policy problems than those on the right end of the spectrum. If so, then the predominance of liberal think tanks in the press might be a reflection of their superior information rather than a sign of ideological bias in the news media: that is, members of Congress as well as reporters for the *New York Times* might be more inclined to cite the Brookings Institution (on the center-left) than the Liberty Fund (on the right) because the former offers more detailed and reliable analysis of a problem of current interest. If so, the proposed measurement instrument is flawed. (Other objections might be found with the study.[47])

The point remains that Groseclose and Milyo have offered an intriguing solution to an intransigent measurement problem, and one with important theoretical and practical repercussions. Moreover, it is a good example of a

---

[46] Groseclose and Milyo (2005: 1191).

[47] Brendan Nyhan's blog posting (accessed: August 2009) addresses several of the critiques and defenses, available at: www.brendan-nyhan.com/blog/2005/12/the_problems_wi.html.

technique that can be applied in many realms. Anywhere a baseline measure of a quantity of interest can be located in one realm and transported to another – via some measure of equivalence – initial problems of measurement may be overcome, as long as potential confounders (such as those discussed above) are not too severe.

Causal relations

A final angle on the problem of unobservables is to consider causal relationships implicit in the concept of interest. What causes L (the concept of interest), and what does L cause?

Occasionally, factors that are presumed to have a causal effect on a phenomenon are easier to measure than the phenomenon itself. If, for example, one can measure the degree of education received by an individual with greater facility than that individual's level of actual intelligence, and if we can assume that education is the principal causal factor behind intelligence, then it may make sense to operationalize intelligence (L) with an input indicator composed of educational attributes (I). Here, the presumed causal arrow runs from I to L.

Alternatively, one might consider the causal effects of an unobservable concept. Suppose, for example, that we are studying an organizational sphere where intelligence is the principal criterion of advancement. In this meritocratic setting it may be plausible to regard an individual's position within that hierarchy as an outcome indicator (I) of his or her intelligence (L), under the assumption that his or her level of intelligence caused him or her to reach that position. Here, the presumed causal arrow runs from L to I.

In most realms of social science, outcome-based strategies of measurement are more promising than input-based strategies. Indeed, many of the foregoing examples discussed in this chapter might be regarded as output-based.

As an additional example, let us consider the problem of ideology. Specifically, what is the true (sincere, authentic) "ideal-point" of a citizen, legislator, or party? The question has agonized political scientists for a century or more. It is a classic hermeneutic problem, for subjects – especially those holding elite positions – often have strong reasons to camouflage their true policy preferences. Moreover, the question itself may be difficult to articulate and, hence, be open to multiple interpretations. Under the circumstances, it is not surprising that scholars have resorted to behavioral measures such as voting. When attempting to analyze the ideal-points of members of the US Congress, for example, researchers examine patterns of correspondence among voting records, under the assumption that those who vote together share the same ideology. This is the basis for the widely used "NOMINATE" score developed by Keith Poole and Howard Rosenthal.[48]

Not only is this outcome measure objective, but it is also consequential – and therefore arguably a better measure of an individual's true preferences, all things considered. Outcome measures follow the old adage about politicians: "Watch their feet, not their mouth." Of course, the researcher must still interpret the meaning of these actions, which are not always self-evident. "Objective" measures may require "subjective" judgments in order to be useful. This is the case, for example, when attempting to determine the meaning of different dimensions in the voting data provided by the NOMINATE project. More fundamentally, one might wonder about the presence of confounders – factors other than personal ideology that influence a legislator's voting record. Presumably, legislators are also affected by pressures from constituents, lobbyists, and party leaders. These pressures strain the interpretation of a legislator's NOMINATE score as an expression of personal ideology.

Closely related is the question of how to measure the quality of governance in countries around the world. We have little information about the inputs of governance that might allow us to judge the performance of governments around the world. Of course, we know how much governments tax and spend, and we know something about the categories of expenditure (how much is spent on different programs). But we can infer little about the quality of governance from how much governments are spending and where they are putting their money. Big government may not be better or worse than small government.

An outcome-based approach to governance might begin with outcomes such as growth, inflation, unemployment, health, mortality, education, or infrastructure. We assume that these outcomes are influenced by government actions – even if they are also influenced by many other factors, which may be classified as random (B) or nonrandom (C). Thus, if levels of infant mortality are higher in Country 1 than in Country 2 we might infer that Country 2 enjoys better governance than Country 1, all other things being equal.[49] The sticking point is the *ceteris paribus* (other things equal) clause.

Sometimes, it may be possible to adjust an outcome-based indicator by controlling for potential confounders and potential sources of noise so that the resulting index captures more accurately what it is intended to capture: that is, the quality of governance in a particular policy area. Thus, if we wish to measure the quality of governance in public health with the infant mortality rate we might wish to control for the impact of economic factors by including

---

[48] Poole and Rosenthal (1991).   [49] Gerring and Thacker (2008: ch. 6); Gerring *et al.* (2008).

a measure of economic development (e.g., GDP per capita) and we might wish to control for the impact of geographic factors by including a series of climate and geographic controls that are thought to affect the health of populations. Wherever the outcome of concern and potential confounders are measurable, a model-based approach to operationalization is informative.[50]

A simpler approach is to identify suitable baseline comparisons. Thus, in attempting to measure the number of women whose deaths are a consequence of gender discrimination (as opposed to poverty and other factors), Amartya Sen identifies sub-Saharan Africa (SSA) as a baseline. Countries below the Sahara constitute the poorest portion of the world, but it is also an area of the developing world where the female/male ratio is relatively favorable – roughly 1.05 in the 1980s. Sen reasons that ratios below that level in countries that are at an equal or higher level of economic development must be a product of discriminatory policies and practices. By this accounting, he reckons that there were more than 100 million "missing women" in the world (a number that has probably grown substantially in subsequent decades).[51] Again, the approach is causal, even though there is no explicit causal model.

From a certain perspective, it might be argued that *all* measurement techniques (except where the phenomenon of interest can be directly observed) are causal. We know that something latent exists insofar as it causes something else, or insofar as it can be presumed to be caused by something else. Thus, given that corruption is an abstraction (and therefore inherently unobservable), all indicators of the concept might be regarded as either causes or effects. This is the perspective adopted by many statistical techniques (e.g., regression-based or structural-equation models), which distinguish between "independent" and "dependent" variables.

In other respects, causal models employed for purposes of measurement do not meet the desiderata of causal analysis. Those that are outcome-based posit causal interventions (L) that cannot be observed, much less manipulated. Those that are input-based posit causal connections (from I to L) that cannot be tested. This is not very satisfactory if one wishes to establish causal relationships, for reasons discussed at length in Part III. Indeed, the inability to directly measure L, the concept of interest, means that any potential causal relationships involving L must remain notional. Empirical evidence is useful – at the very least, for discarding false theories about L. But such evidence is never conclusive, except insofar as we can devise ways to observe L in a more direct fashion.

---

[50] Gerring *et al.* (2008).   [51] Sen (1990).

Consider the matter of emotion, an important element of any theory that does not rest solely on rational motivations. Emotions like hatred, love, and grief presumably motivate a good deal of human behavior, and may have vast ramifications for outcomes of interest to social science.[52] We can measure the "outputs" of emotions, for example, violence, tears, self-reports of emotional status (*I*), and regard them as evidence of the inner lives of our subjects (*L*). Of course, we don't really know whether our hunch is correct, that is, whether some inner emotional drive is causing subjects to manifest particular behavioral patterns, or to testify that they are angry, in love, or sad. However, if we can measure chemical processes that are associated with emotions (as revealed by self-testimony), then we are arguably closer to a direct measurement of the phenomenon of interest. Thus, when psychologists measure emotions they commonly employ physiological indicators such as blood pressure, galvanic skin response (GSR), heart rate, pupillary dilation, and eye blink (startle) response in addition to self-reports.[53]

These measurement strategies may be regarded as causal only if the chemical processes actually help to generate the lived experience that we know as hatred, love, or grief, or are a by-product of that experience. They are correlative insofar as they are symptomatic of these emotions. However, for purposes of measurement the distinction is immaterial. We do not care whether *I* causes *L*, is a cause of *L*, or is merely a trace of *L*. All that counts is the *alignment* (i.e., correlation) between concept and indicator. This is what occupies our attention when the purpose of an analysis is to validate a measurement instrument.[54]

Corruption: a detailed example

Threats to measurement reliability and validity may be described in a general way, as we have attempted to do. However, many of the problems and solutions can be explored only by example, for they are heavily contextual. There is no general solution to problems of measurement on the order of the experimental research design for causal questions. There are only particular solutions.

Thus, we close this chapter with discussion of a topic of central importance to the social sciences, and one that also poses recalcitrant problems of

---

[52] Petersen (2002).

[53] Rose McDermott (personal communication, November 2009). See also Oxley *et al.* (2008).

[54] Of course, I recognize that if our assumptions about alignment are informed by assumptions of causality then we must wrestle with the latter. Even so, the purpose of this approach to measurement is to deal with situations in which the concept itself appears to be impossible to measure in a direct fashion. This implies that it will also be impossible to test the causal assumptions underlying the (causal) measurement technique.

measurement: *political corruption*, understood as the use of public office for private gain.[55] How do we know when corrupt activities are occurring, and how extensive they are? And how might we compare these occurrences systematically over time and across polities so that the measurement instrument can be generalized?

In recent years, cross-national survey-based indicators of corruption have gained prominence, both among academics and among lay publics. Principal among these are the Corruption Perceptions Index (CPI) developed by Transparency International (TI) and the Corruption Control Index developed by Daniel Kaufmann and collaborators at the World Bank (WB).[56] For each index, a variety of questions are compiled that seek to gauge an informant's sense of how common corrupt practices are in a country, with special focus on corrupt practices like bribes that directly impact investors. Data is now available for most countries in the world, allowing for comparisons across countries with very high (e.g., Nigeria) and very low (e.g., Norway) levels of corruption. The chief advantage of a survey-based measure, based on general questions about perceived corruption, is that one can craft a generalized measure of this ambient concept.

However, numerous criticisms have been leveled at these measures.[57] The TI and WB indicators aggregate surveys taken by many outfits, most of which are commercial consultancies with a wide range of objectives. Usually, that purpose is tailored to the needs of investors. Arguably, the TI and WB indexes are better understood as indexes of bribe-paying rather than of corruption at large. Combining multiple surveys into a single index provides multiple measurements, which should increase precision and allows for an estimate of a confidence interval. However, it also creates ambiguity with respect to interpretation, since each question, and each survey, is different. Moreover, it is unclear to what extent responses to multiple surveys are actually independent of one another, since they may simply reflect common assumptions about how corrupt or clean a country is. Questions usually probe *perceptions* of corruption, or of bribes, and so may incorrectly reflect realities on the ground.[58] Respondents may not answer truthfully; worse, the degree of frankness may vary by country or region, impeding systematic comparisons. Because samples vary from year to year, and are normalized to zero each year,

---

[55] There are, of course, many ways of defining this key concept (Johnston and Heidenheimer 2002; Sampford *et al.* 2006). I leave these issues aside so as to focus on the empirical aspects of the measurement problem. I want to acknowledge Michael Johnston's input to the following section.

[56] Kaufmann, Kraay, and Mastruzzi (2007); Lambsdorff (2003).

[57] Knack (2006); Sampford *et al.* (2006).   [58] Abramo (2007); Kenny (2006); Seligson (2006).

comparisons are not possible through time; it is difficult to say, for example, whether a country's governance is improving or deteriorating. Respondents are generally concentrated among urban dwellers and business people, often not native to the country, raising questions of representativeness. Some questions ask respondents to compare a country to a selected list of others; some ask for a global comparison. Some invite the conclusion that where economic problems are severe, corruption must be extensive.

Despite these flaws, these indices continue to be employed in a wide array of settings, suggesting that they are performing an important function. Some of the flaws are inherent to the measurement instrument (mass surveys); others might easily be rectified. Certainly, it is possible to construct more representative samples, to standardize survey questions and formats, to carefully distinguish between different types of respondents (e.g., in-country and out-of-country, elite and mass, business and nonbusiness, urban and rural), to distinguish different types of corruption (e.g., bribes, fraud, vote-buying, etc.), to employ polling techniques that provide some guarantee of anonymity to the respondent (as discussed above), and to focus on actual experiences of corruption rather than simply on general perceptions.

The principal obstacle to these sorts of improvements is not methodological but rather organizational. One must bear in mind that the consultancies who commission most of the polls comprising the TI and WB indexes have specific and limited goals focused on their business clienteles. Moreover, these outfits are not in a position to pool their resources so as to construct regular, standardized surveys of corruption throughout the world. This sort of public good is unlikely to be created by market forces. Thus, citizens, policymakers, and academics who yearn for a more precise and systematic survey instrument are unlikely to get it by continuing to free-ride off the private sector. Doing so will require international organization and commensurate funding – something on the order of the World Values Survey (though with better execution and an annual or semi-annual survey). Good measurement of difficult subjects often involves considerable expense.

In recent years, one can perceive a turn away from "macro" surveys such as those incorporated in the TI and WB indexes, which attempt to measure the overall quality of governance in a country. Instead, researchers are developing "micro" surveys, which focus on (a) a narrow and carefully identified set of respondents who are in a situation to know about a particular form of corruption; (b) a particular industry, sector, or region; and (c) highly specific questions, mostly about objective events or facts that the respondent can evaluate from personal experience.[59] For example, the World Business Environment Survey, financed jointly by several international financial institutions, asks respondents about the experiences of "firms like yours" with bribes to government officials.[60]

Occasionally, it is possible to measure the extent of corruption in a more or less direct and "objective" fashion (i.e., without the use of subjective interpretations on the part of respondents). In a study of corruption in Indonesia Ben Olken manages to measure the inputs and outputs of a roads project built under public contract. Olken explains:

I assembled a team of engineers and surveyors who, after the roads built by the project were completed, dug core samples in each road to estimate the quantity of materials used, surveyed local suppliers to estimate prices, and interviewed villagers to determine the wages paid on the project. From these data, I construct an independent estimate of the amount each road actually cost to build, and then compare this estimate to what the village reported it spent on the project on a line-item by line-item basis. The difference between what the village claimed the road cost to build and what the engineers estimated it actually cost to build forms my objective measure of corruption, which I label "missing expenditures."[61]

This measurement strategy follows the outlines of a normal government audit procedure (with some extra bells and whistles).[62] For example, public expenditure tracking surveys (PETS) follow the paper trail of government projects in order to determine whether the record provided by agencies and subcontractors matches the moneys spent.[63] Wherever government expenditures culminate in a discrete service or product, this element may be directly observed (is the trash picked up regularly?). Truancy among workers is also fairly easy to observe. If classrooms are empty during official school hours, or doctors are not present at medical facilities, this is a sign that something is amiss.[64]

Naturally, it is difficult to differentiate between intentional corruption and unintentional inefficiencies. (For some purposes this distinction may be consequential; for others, it may not be.) Moreover, extensive oversight procedures are sometimes quite expensive – an indirect cost that may rival the cost of the corruption it is intended to deter. Finally, one must reckon with the possibility that highly specific measurement strategies might lead to more sophisticated strategies of corruption (many measurement instruments can be

---

[59] Reinikka and Svensson (2006).   [60] Galtung (2006: 103).   [61] Olken (2009: 950).

[62] In another study in Indonesia, Olken (2006) examines the efficiency of an anti-poverty program that distributes rice to the poor. Corruption is estimated by comparing "administrative data on the amount of rice distributed with survey data on the amount actually received by households" (Olken 2006: 853). See also Golden and Picci (2005).

[63] Duncan (2006: 149–150); Reinikka and Svensson (2006).   [64] Chaudhury and Hammer (2003).

gamed), thereby invalidating the measurement instrument. For example, in response to Olken's measurement of outputs from a road project, village leaders might in future report inflated figures of what they spent on road construction. Highly targeted measurement instruments are difficult to generalize for the simple reason that actors have strong incentives to evade the monitoring regime. By contrast, general survey questions about the extent of corruption in a sector are more robust for changing practices of corruption and are in this sense amenable to cross-temporal and cross-contextual comparisons (though they suffer from problems of ambiguity, as discussed above).

Fraud may also be inferred (though not directly observed) from unusual patterns of activity. Such a technique has been developed by Malcolm Sparrow to estimate fraud in the US government-provided medical program known as Medicaid. Sparrow focuses on networks among providers. Typical networks are fairly broad, and by virtue of that fact are less prone to corruption since more providers must be complicit. Smaller networks, by contrast, are easier to game. By looking at the structure of medical networks, while controlling for a host of potential confounders, Sparrow is able to provide an estimate of the total fraud in the Medicaid system, as well as a clue as to its precise location.[65]

Another inferential approach to corruption examines the relationship between politically connected firms and share prices. It is widely suspected that firms in corrupt countries receive preferential treatment by virtue of their political connections. Yet, as with many corrupt practices, crony capitalism is difficult to prove – much less to measure with any precision. Raymond Fisman applies a quasi-experimental design to this persistent issue of measurement. Specifically, he compares changes in share prices of firms that are politically connected with those that are not when rumors of a leader's ill-health are circulating. The assumption is that the value of a political connection is threatened when the key political player is in jeopardy, and this insecurity should be registered in stock market behavior. Fisman applies this measurement technique to Indonesia (connections to Suharto)[66] and to the United States (connections to Vice President Dick Cheney),[67] finding that connections mattered a good deal to the share price of certain politically connected firms in the former case but not in the latter.[68]

Of course, there are limitations to a measurement instrument of this sort. First, it rests on the subjective perceptions of investors. If they believe that

---

[65] Duncan (2006: 139); Sparrow (2000).   [66] Fisman (2001).   [67] Fisman *et al.* (2006).
[68] The Opacity Index, developed by the Milken Institute, incorporates a similar measurement strategy, available at: www.milkeninstitute.org/publications/publications.taf?function=detail&ID=38801146&cat=ResRep.

connections matter, a "connected" firm will respond to changes in their patron's health status or political status, regardless of whether or not the firm actually receives preferential treatment from the government. Second, it supposes that connections to a particular individual, rather than to a group or institution, are what affects the fortunes of a firm. Finally, it is difficult to construct a temporally and cross-nationally comparable measurement instrument from this technique since every health rumor is different (some being more serious than others, some occurring in a more dramatic and unexpected fashion than others), and since the set of companies to which an influential politician is attached are diverse (introducing a set of potential confounders).

Another quasi-experimental setting is exploited by Raymond Fisman and Ted Miguel to measure national propensities to engage in corrupt behavior. The occasion is provided by New York City's extreme scarcity of parking spaces, the location of the United Nations headquarters in that crowded city, and the diplomatic immunity that allowed mission personnel and their families to avoid paying parking fines (prior to 2002). Note that these circumstances place diplomats from all countries of the world in a situation where they enjoy identical incentives to break the law, that is, to park illegally. It follows that variation in parking tickets may provide an indicator of norms against corrupt practices around the world. Independent verification of the validity of this measure is provided by survey-based cross-national indexes such as those constructed by TI and WB, which are highly correlated with Fisman and Miguel's measurement instrument. Of course, one might challenge the generalizability of these findings: do diplomats behave similarly in New York as in their home countries? Are diplomats representative of the political class? Even so, the measurement instrument is highly suggestive, for it holds constant many of the confounders and the sources of noise that usually obscure our estimates of this latent concept.[69]

The topic of corruption has also been approached within an experimental framework. Cameron, Chaudhuri, Erkal, and Gangadharan recently conducted a set of parallel laboratory experiments in Australia, India, Indonesia, and Singapore in order to determine if the incidence of corruption and anti-corruption practices is similar or dis-similar across these diverse cultures. The set-up builds on public goods experiments, except that here the various actions are explicitly labeled with charged words such as "bribing." Participants (students

---

[69] It should be noted that Fisman's and Miguel's (2007) primary purpose in this study is to assess a causal question – whether norms or sanctions are more important in influencing corrupt behavior. However, the strength of that causal assessment rests largely on the strength of the measurement instrument.

at universities) are assigned to one of three roles: as a member of a firm, a government official, or a citizen. The firm is first given an opportunity to offer a bribe to the government official, who may accept or reject. Both will benefit if the bribe is offered and accepted. The citizen is then given an opportunity to sanction the firm and the government, but choosing to do so involves a sacrifice (for the citizen) equal to the cost of the bribe (monetary incentives are adjusted for purchasing power parity in the four countries). The researchers find that there is greater cross-national variation in willingness to punish than in willingness to participate in bribing.[70]

While the main purpose of the research is to assess the effect of culture on corrupt practices, we shall leave aside the question of causal attribution so as to focus on the viability of the measurement instrument. Is this a good way to measure corrupt practices across diverse settings? Because an important part of the treatment is verbal one must worry about the translatability of these key-words (e.g., "bribe"). If subjects in the experiment are responding to specific verbal cues rather than to common situations the results may not be general-izable. One must also worry about generalizing from the behavior of students – a particular concern in poor societies where few attain a college education. Even if these concerns are assuaged, it is not clear that behavior registered in these experiments would necessarily translate into differences of behavior in the real world – or they may map onto real-world behavior in different ways across these four settings. That said, there is much we can learn by examining corruption in carefully controlled settings.

A final approach to the measurement of corruption is ethnographic in nature, relying on close observation and intimate acquaintance with a par-ticular setting. A classic example is Robert Wade's study of irrigation systems in several dozen south Indian villages in the late 1970s.[71] Wade reports:

Only gradually, from conversations with dozens of engineers, government officials from other departments and farmers did it become apparent that a "system" was a work, which probably had an important impact on how canals are operated and maintained. In particular, once some degree of trust was established, farmers often volunteered information about how much they had to pay the Irrigation Department; and while one would discount their figures in one, two or three instances, the regularity in farmers' statements across many villages did suggest that something more than wild exaggeration or generalisation was involved ... This led to cautious, always informal enquiries of officers in other departments and of irrigation staff themselves, as part of wider con-versations about the sorts of difficulties they saw themselves facing in doing their jobs

---

[70] Cameron *et al.* (2009).   [71] Wade (1982). See also Smith (2007).

well. These conversations, it should be noted, were with irrigation staff from outside the area of detailed fieldwork as well as with many serving within it, and covered the way "the department" and "the government" worked in the state as a whole, as well as in the specific district. Some of the engineers were thoroughly disgruntled at the situation they were caught in, and since disgruntled people tend to exaggerate the reasons for their discontent, one had to be cautious about accepting details from any one person at face value. Again, as with farmers, it is the regularities in the individual comments and incidents, and the consistency in the orders of magnitude (as between, for example, what a district Collector told me a Superintending Engineer had told him he had had to pay to get a one-year extension, and what an Assistant Engineer in one Division – in another district from the first case – said in strictest confidence his Executive Engineer had had to pay to get the transfer) that gives confidence in the correctness of the broad picture.

Wade's detailed research narrative provides a clear description of this approach to measuring corruption, its promises and its pitfalls. Evidently, ethnographic investigations are possible only when informants can be assured of anonymity, as is possible (sometimes) with work of an academic nature. If the investigating body is governmental, mouths are likely to be shut. And if any repercussions follow from a report, no further access to the research site is likely to be forthcoming. More importantly, this sort of intensive soaking and poking does not provide fodder for systematic comparisons across time and space, or across sectors. Though the measurements may be quite precise – Wade offers estimates of how large the typical bribe is in a variety of specific settings connected to irrigation in the studied villages – one cannot derive a *generalizable* measurement instrument.

Even so, one can learn a lot from iterated conversations once one has gained the trust of informants and a certain amount of savvy about the subject under investigation. Moreover, the meanings embedded in the actions under study are more likely to be interpretable when gained through an ethnographic style of inquiry than when garnered from the other approaches we have reviewed.

Ex post validity tests

Having discussed various strategies of measurement, we conclude this chapter with a brief discussion of *ex post* tests that may help to shed light on the validity of a chosen indicator.

Face validity is not really a test at all. It refers to an obvious or intuitive appeal – an indicator that seems related to a concept in a way that obviates systematic empirical testing. Elections, one might argue, are an indicator (though not necessarily *the* indicator) of democracy with high face validity.

Convergent strategies attempt to validate an indicator, *I*, by comparing it with other measures that are deemed to be valid measures of the same concept, I_2. A high correlation demonstrates convergent validity. Convergent validity studies have shown that the leading indicators such as Freedom House and Polity are highly intercorrelated, rendering a Pearson's *r* correlation of 0.88 across all countries in recent decades, and this has been interpreted as evidence that all such indicators are valid.[72] Of course, the operating assumption is that additional indicators of a concept are themselves valid. If the measures that compose a convergent validity test are subject to bias the technique holds little promise.

Discriminant strategies attempt to distinguish the entities belonging to the concept of interest, as measured by *I*, from those presumed to belong to neighboring concepts, *C*. A low correlation between *I* and *C* demonstrates divergent validity. This strategy is less common, at least with respect to democracy (perhaps because the borders of this ambient concept are so hard to identify).

Causal strategies attempt to validate a measure by looking at its (presumably causal) relationship to an input or output to which it is presumed to be strongly related. A strong relationship (in the predicted relationship) may be regarded as providing confirmation for a measure. Writers have attempted to gauge the validity of cross-national democracy indicators by examining whether they are responsive to factors presumed to be unrelated to democracy, such as shifts in US foreign policy (functioning here as a confounder). If US foreign policy appears to predict coding changes on Freedom House's Political Rights Index one might presume that the index is measuring something other than what it purports to measure.

Case-based strategies examine key cases to see if the coding for these cases corresponds to the expected pattern.[73] For example, scholars of Central America have shown that scores for these cases are often patently erroneous, and cannot be accounted for by chance error. This sort of investigation rests on a scouring of primary and secondary sources for the countries in question, including local newspapers, government documents, and US diplomatic correspondence, as

[72] However, on closer examination, it appears that consensus across the two dominant indices is largely the product of countries lying at the democratic extreme – Sweden, Canada, the United States, etc. When countries with the highest democracy scores are excluded from the sample the intercorrelation between these two indices drops to 0.78. And when countries with the top two scores on the Freedom House scale (1–2 out of 7) are eliminated, Pearson's *r* drops again – to 0.63. This is not an impressive level of agreement, especially when one considers that scholars and policymakers are usually interested in precisely those countries lying in the middle and bottom of the distribution – countries that are undemocratic or imperfectly democratic. Coppedge and Gerring (2011). See also Goertz (2008); Hadenius and Teorell (2005).
[73] Bowman, Lehoucq, and Mahoney (2005).

well as interviews with local informants – a far more extensive review than is common in most cross-national coding operations.[74]

Of course, the *ex ante* construction of a measure and the *ex post* testing of that variable are not rigidly segregated from one another. Most methods of validation can also be employed as measures of variable construction. Indeed, validation tests of the concept of democracy are often performed as a prelude to the construction of a new index. This brings us full circle.

[74] Bowman, Lehoucq, and Mahoney (2005).

Part III

Causation

8 | Causal arguments

Surely, if there be any relation among objects which it imports to us to know perfectly, it is that of cause and effect. On this are founded all our reasonings concerning matter of fact or existence. By means of it alone we attain any assurance concerning objects which are removed from the present testimony of our memory and senses. The only immediate utility of all sciences is to teach us how to control and regulate future events by their causes. Our thoughts and enquiries are, therefore, every moment, employed about this relation: Yet so imperfect are the ideas which we form concerning it, that it is impossible to give any just definition of cause.

David Hume[1]

I argued in Part II for a resuscitation of descriptive inference within the social sciences, both as a topic of methodology and as a topic of substantive research. However, I do not suppose that description will displace causation as the reigning motif of social science. We wish to know not only what happened but also, perhaps more critically, why these things happened.

Causation is the central explanatory trope by which relationships among persons and things are established – the cement of the universe, in Hume's much quoted words.[2] Without some understanding of who is doing what to whom we cannot make sense of the world that we live in, we cannot hold people and institutions accountable for their actions, and we cannot act efficaciously in the world. Without a causal understanding of the world it is unlikely that we could navigate even the most mundane details of our lives, much less matters of long-term policy. This is obvious in the policy world, where causal understanding undergirds any rational intervention. And it is obvious in other areas of politics, for example, in social movements, lobbying, voting, and revolutionary change. Anyone who engages in these activities must be conscious of oneself as a causal actor in the world, and accordingly, must make assumptions (implicit or explicit) about what one's actions might achieve – whether one supports the status quo or wishes to undermine it.

---

[1] Hume (1960: 220).   [2] Hume (1888).

Lenin, like Metternich, was vitally concerned with the causes of revolution. Even where causal understanding does not lead to social change (for not all causal analysis is directly relevant to public policy, and more to the point, not all policy proposals are implemented), we are likely to be reassured when we can order events around us into cause-and-effect relationships. "When we have such understanding," notes Judea Pearl, "we feel 'in control' even if we have no practical way of controlling things."[3]

One important purpose of causal inference is to offer insight into what may happen in the future. Although there is an unfortunate tendency to dichotomize causal and predictive knowledge, the distinction is rarely hard and fast. Consider that few causal arguments are entirely restricted to the past tense. To say that X causes Y is to imply (usually) that it will continue to do so – perhaps not indefinitely, but at least tomorrow and next year. Thus, although prediction is by no means identical to causation, forecasting (one type of prediction) is *implied* by most causal arguments in the social sciences, which tend to focus on contemporary phenomena, or phenomena in the past that have contemporary relevance. Note that every policy intervention – every rate change by a central bank, every social program, and every reform of the tax code – implies a prediction about the causal effects of that intervention. Many of these forecasts turn out to be substantially correct. All are based primarily on causal models, formal or informal. In any case, those who complain about the inability of social science models to offer reliable forecasts of the future are not usually arguing for the abandonment of causal models. There is, as far as I can see, no viable alternative.

Problems of causality will be divided into four areas. This chapter defines causality and lays out criteria pertaining to all causal arguments. Chapter 9 discusses general criteria of causal inference (i.e., analysis). Chapters 10 and 11 explore a variety of approaches to causal analysis. Chapter 12 serves as a coda to Part III of the book, incorporating several approaches to causality that appear to lie outside the present framework.

Definitions

Causal theories involve at least two elements: a causal factor and an outcome. Sometimes, several factors and/or outcomes are combined in an abstract

---

[3] Pearl (2000: 345). See also Bunge (1959); Homans (1961); MacIver ([1942] 1964: 5–11); Mackie (1974); Sloman (2005); Woodward (2005).

theory. However, that theory must be translatable into specific hypotheses involving individual causal factors and an outcome. In formalizing these elements a general theory is transformed into a causal model.

Confusing matters, there are various synonyms for these terms. A *cause* may be referred to as a causal factor, condition, covariate, exogenous variable, explanatory variable, explanans, independent variable, input, intervention, parent, predictor, right-side variable, treatment, or simply "*X*." An *outcome* may be referred to as a dependent variable, descendant, effect, endogenous variable, explanandum, left-side variable, output, response, or "*Y*." (Of course, there are subtle distinctions among these terms. However, for present purposes the similarities are more important than the differences.)

Whatever the terminology, to say that a factor, *X*, is a cause of an outcome, *Y*, is to say that a change in *X* generates a change in *Y* relative to what *Y* would otherwise be (the counterfactual condition), given certain background conditions (*ceteris paribus* assumptions) and scope-conditions (the population of the inference). This will serve as a minimal definition of causality.

Given the importance of *variation* in *X* and *Y*, it may be helpful to think of *X* as ΔX ("delta *X*") and *Y* as ΔY ("delta *Y*"). If the relationship between *X* and *Y* is causal, a change in *X* generates some change in *Y*: $\Delta X \rightarrow \Delta Y$ (at least probabilistically).

When an outcome is continuous, ΔX affects the value of *Y* along some scale, which may be unbounded or bounded. When an outcome is binary (*Y*=0, *Y*=1) or multichotomous (e.g., *Y*=1, 2, 3, 4, or 5), ΔX affects the probability (*P*) of *Y* achieving one of these outcomes.

Whatever the nature of *X* and *Y* there is always an implied *counterfactual*: if *X* varies, *Y* should also vary in some manner (at least probabilistically). A causal theory must explain why one thing happened (happens) and some other thing did (does) not.

Another way of framing this issue is to say that a cause raises the *prior probability* of an outcome occurring. Let us assume two factors, *X* and *Y*, each of which assumes one of two possible values, 0 and 1. We shall denote *X*=1 as *X* and *X*=0 as *x*, *Y*=1 as *Y* and *Y*=0 as *y*. In the notation of probability theory, *X* causes *Y* if, and only if, $P(Y|X) > P(Y|x)$,[4] with a set of understood background conditions.[5]

While this definition of a causal effect may seem prejudicial to probabilistic causes, it can be seen that set-theoretic causes also fit within the rubric. If *X* is

---

[4] The probability of *Y* given *X* is greater than the probability of *Y* given *not-X*.
[5] Cartwright (1983); Dupre (1984: 170); Guala (2005: 82).

a *necessary* condition for Y, then $P(Y|x)=0$ while $P(Y|X) > 0$. That is, the change from x to X raises the probability of Y from 0 to some undefined probability greater than 0, as long as X is a nontrivial necessary condition. If X is a *sufficient* condition for Y, then $P(Y|x) < 1$ while $P(Y|X)=1$. That is, the change from x to X raises the probability of Y from something less than 1 to 1, as long as X is a nontrivial sufficient condition. Further discussion of set-theoretic causes is postponed until Chapter 12.

Importantly, when one asserts that X causes Y one is asserting that the actual (ontological) probability of an event is increased by X, not simply a theory's predictive capacity. This is what distinguishes a causal argument from a description or prediction. To be causal, the factor in question must *generate*, *create*, or *produce* an effect. Of course, it is not always possible to specify precisely why X generates Y. Yet in identifying X as a cause of Y one is presuming the existence of some causal *mechanism* – understood here as the pathway or process or chain of intermediary variables by which X affects Y, illustrated as M in Figure 8.1.

Causal relationships occur against a background of other factors. These are the conditions that make any causal relationship possible. Note that even an experiment conducted in a perfect vacuum presumes a background that provides the conditions for the experiment – in this case, the vacuum. Background factors include all factors other than X (the factor of theoretical interest) that may influence the outcome, directly or indirectly.

One sort of background factor, labeled A in Figure 8.1, lies *antecedent* to the causal factor of interest. It affects Y indirectly, through X.

Unless otherwise specified, background conditions are presumed to hold constant: they do not vary. This is known as the *ceteris paribus* (all else equal) assumption, and is implicit in all causal arguments. For example, when constructing an argument about the causal impact of economic development in democratization one must assume that other factors affecting democratization, such as natural resource wealth, religion, political culture, and international influences, are constant. This is not simply a problem of empirical

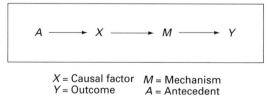

X = Causal factor M = Mechanism
Y = Outcome A = Antecedent

Figure 8.1   A simple causal graph

testing; it is inherent in the very act of making a causal argument. Without *ceteris paribus* conditions (implicit or explicit), causal arguments are impossible. Of course, one can change the *ceteris paribus* conditions of a causal argument by specifying how background factors interact with X, or by altering the scope-conditions of the argument. We shall have more to say about this in later chapters.

Causal factors are also often classified according to their relative distance to the outcome of interest. Factors close to Y are referred to as *proximate*. Factors distant from Y are *distal* (aka *remote, structural*). In Figure 8.1, M is most proximate and A is most distal. Of course, causal regress is potentially infinite. We can imagine causes of A, causes of the causes of A, and so forth. Likewise, we could insert causal mechanisms in between M and Y, which would then be regarded as most proximate relative to Y. The notion of a distal or proximate cause is always relative to some other set of posited causal factors. Generally, distal causes are those in which several mediating factors separate X (the variable of theoretical interest) from Y and in which X and Y are separated by a stretch of time.

Relatedly, it is often important to distinguish between factors that are *independent* or *exogenous* (causal in nature), and factors that are *dependent* or *endogenous* (outcomes). In Figure 8.1, A is exogenous to X, M, and Y; X is exogenous to M and Y; M is exogenous to Y. Likewise, Y is endogenous to A, X, and M; M is endogenous to A and X; X is endogenous to A. Endogeneity/exogeneity is also a relative matter.

All factors in Figure 8.1 may be treated as *variables*. By this, we mean that they are assumed to vary – even if only hypothetically (as in a counterfactual thought-experiment).[6] In the simplest scenario, X assumes two possible values (X/x) and Y assumes two possible values (Y/y). Variation along X and Y may also be multi-categorical (e.g., Catholic/Protestant/Jewish/Muslim), ordinal (e.g., a Likert scale), or numeric (an interval or ratio scale). In short, X and Y, along with other variables listed in Figure 8.1, may embody any of the scales laid out previously in Chapter 7. They may represent events (dynamic, swift, and discrete) or processes (dynamic and slow). They may also take the form of static conditions, though they must be changeable in principle. Thus, in saying that a geographic factor such as altitude or distance from the equator exerts a causal force on some outcome one is implicitly acknowledging the possibility that it could have been different in the past or could be different in the future.

---

[6] Tetlock and Belkin (1996).

It is true that some factors are difficult to measure and difficult to conceptualize counterfactually, and therefore don't conform to our traditional sense of a "variable." Still, it must be possible to conceptualize a process as something that varies; otherwise, it can do no causal work. If something cannot be other than it is then it cannot serve as a cause. In treating factors in Figure 8.1 as variables we are saying that they vary, at least potentially. We are not implying that they are easily conceptualized and measured, or that they can be directly manipulated.

Adding to the complexity of Figure 8.1, each factor may be understood as an individual variable or as a *vector* (set) of variables. Indeed, we are often interested in combinations of causal factors, combinations of causal pathways, combinations of antecedent causes. Occasionally, we may be interested in multiple outcomes.[7] Most of our examples will concern individual factors, but these examples can usually be generalized by treating the variable as a vector.

Finally, it should be clarified that in employing the terminology of "variables" we are not supposing that all causal models are statistical in nature. Nothing in the foregoing passages necessitates a large sample or a probabilistic model. I find the language of variables to be a convenient means of simplifying and unifying our understanding of causation. It is not meant to enforce a uniform method of causal analysis (a subject addressed in succeeding chapters). Nor is it intended to eliminate the use of other near-synonyms (e.g., causes, conditions, factors, influences), which will be employed sporadically in the following chapters.

Causal criteria

Having defined causation minimally, we turn to the ideal-type. What is a good causal argument? Recall from Chapter 3 that all arguments strive for *truth, precision, generality, boundedness, parsimony, coherence, commensurability,* and *relevance.* I will argue here that causal explanations in social science also strive for *clarity, manipulability, differentiation, genesis, impact,* and a *mechanism.* For convenience, all fourteen criteria applicable to causal theories

---

[7] Note that since we are primarily concerned in this book with classes of events rather than singular events (Chapter 1), a number of difficult philosophical and practical problems of inference are minimized. One thinks, e.g., of "pre-emption" and various additional issues that arise when attempting to determine the cause of a singular event. See Brady (2008); Lewis (1973). That said, it should be pointed out that insofar as our knowledge of causal relations among a class of events builds upon our knowledge of causal relations of specific events, the sorts of practical and philosophical problems posed by singular causation are *not* resolved.

Table 8.1 Causal arguments: criteria

ARGUMENTS

(Chapter 3)

1. **Truth** (accuracy, validity, veracity)
   Is it true?
2. **Precision** (specificity)
   Is it precise?
3. **Generality** (breadth, domain, population, range, scope)
   How broad is the scope?
4. **Boundedness** (population, scope-conditions)
   How well bounded is it?
5. **Parsimony** (concision, economy, Occam's razor, reduction, simplicity)
   How parsimonious is it? How many assumptions are required?
6. **Coherence** (clarity, consistency; *antonym*: ambiguity)
   How coherent is it?
7. **Commensurability** (consilience, harmony, logical economy, theoretical utility; *antonym*: adhocery)
   How well does it cumulate with other inferences? Does it advance logical economy in a field?
8. **Relevance** (everyday importance, significance)
   How relevant is it to issues of concern to citizens and policymakers?

CAUSAL ARGUMENTS

(this chapter)

9. **Clarity** (*antonym*: ambiguity)
   What is the envisioned variation on X and Y, the background conditions, and the scope-conditions of the
   argument? Can X and Y be operationalized?
10. **Manipulability**
    Is the causal factor manipulable (at least potentially)?
11. **Separation** (differentiation; *antonym*: tautology)
    How separable is X relative to Y?
12. **Independence** (foundational, original, prime, prior, structural, unmoved mover)
    Is X independent of other causes of Y?
13. **Impact** (effect size, magnitude, power, significance, strength)
    How much of the variation in Y can X explain? Is the causal effect significant (in theoretical or policy terms)?
14. **Mechanism** (intermediary, mediator, pathway, process)
    How does X generate Y? What are the causal mechanisms (M)?

are reproduced in Table 8.1. However, our focus in this chapter is on factors that distinguish causal propositions from descriptive propositions (Nos. 9–14).[8]

---

[8] Other attempts to specify the desiderata of causal argument, upon which this effort builds, can be found in Eckstein (1975: 88); Hempel (1991: 81); King, Keohane, and Verba (1994: ch. 3); Kuhn (1977: 322); Lakatos (1978); Laudan (1977: 68, 1996: 18, 131–132); Levey (1996: 54); Marini and Singer (1988); Przeworski and Teune (1970: 20–23); Simowitz and Price (1990); Stinchcombe (1968: 31); van Evera (1997: 17–21); Wilson (1998: 216).

Clarity

We have defined causality as a situation in which a change in X (the causal factor of theoretical interest) generates a change in Y (the outcome of interest) relative to what Y would otherwise be, given certain background conditions and scope-conditions. It follows that a good causal argument should provide clarity along each of these dimensions. Clarifying (aka specifying, operationalizing) causal theories makes them more useful, as well as easier to test. Indeed, a theory that is highly ambiguous is impossible to verify or falsify; it is neither true nor false.

One must wrestle at the outset with terminological ambiguities, for there are a great many ways to articulate a causal claim. Writers may state that a causal factor, X, *leads to* an outcome, Y, *is related to Y*, *is associated with Y*, *influences Y*, *results in Y*, and so forth. Of these, only the last two are clearly causal in the sense in which we have defined the term. But all *may* be causal, depending upon the context. A simple suggestion for writers is to clarify whether an argument is intended to be causal or not. Intuition on the part of the reader should not be required.

A second issue is the specification of Y. To evaluate an argument we need to know the variation in Y that is understood as the outcome of interest. Usually, this is apparent; but sometimes it remains ambiguous. The humorous (and presumably apocryphal) tale is told of a priest who queried the notorious bank robber, Willie Sutton, about why he robbed banks. To this, the miscreant patiently explained that this is where the money is. Evidently, the priest and the bank robber have different ideas about variation in Y. For the priest, it is robbing ($Y=1$) versus not robbing ($Y=0$). For Sutton, it is robbing banks ($Y=1$) versus robbing other establishments ($Y=0$).

An analogous confusion arises in some historical arguments over specific outcomes, for example, a revolution, a war, or the passage of a bill. For some writers, the outcome of interest may be understood in a dichotomous fashion (revolution/no revolution) and over a period of many years. Why, for example, did France experience a revolution while Sweden did not? For other writers, the outcome of interest may be understood in much more specific terms. Why, for example, did the French Revolution occur in 1789 and in precisely the manner in which it did? It is easy to see how two studies of what is nominally the same phenomenon (the French Revolution) may end up constructing very different arguments. As we are dealing in this book with classes of events, rather than singular events, this genre of problem is somewhat less prevalent. Even so, a class of outcomes may be variously interpreted, and unless this matter is clarified there will be no clarity about the overall set of claims.

A third issue is the specification of X, that is, the change in X that is envisioned as a causal factor or *treatment*. This is the causal counterfactual, and it must be specified, even if it cannot be directly observed or manipulated (an issue discussed in the next section).

An analogous problem is raised by causal inputs or outputs that are difficult to operationalize (i.e., to measure). In this situation, it may be conceptually clear what is meant by a change in X or Y, but empirically ambiguous. A concept that cannot be measured cannot be tested – at least not very precisely. Likewise, if a concept can be operationalized with a variety of (poorly inter-correlated) indicators, then this ambiguity impairs its falsifiability. It is somewhat problematic, for example, that democracy can be measured dichotomously or continuously, and that each choice of measurement offers a number of (not so highly correlated) indicators, as discussed in Chapter 7. School vouchers, although seemingly more specific, can be constructed in any number of ways (e.g., by varying the monetary value of vouchers or the regulations associated with a voucher program). Vouchers may be applied to choices among "charter" schools (public schools whose enrolments are not constrained to a particular neighborhood) or to private and public schools. Each of these decisions about X has different implications for Y. The simple point is that in order to achieve clarity in a causal argument it must be possible to locate X and Y empirically. Operationalization is essential.[9]

A fourth issue concerns the *background conditions* of an argument. Under normal circumstances, it is not necessary to specify what these are. Thus, if one is arguing that countries are more likely to democratize when more economically developed, one is assuming that all other factors impacting X and/or Y are held constant. This would include conditions such as mineral wealth, which many commentators regard as an impediment to democracy.[10] If unmentioned, these factors should be regarded as *ceteris paribus* conditions: that is, economic development fosters democratization for countries with similar natural resource endowments. Sometimes, however, the background conditions of an argument are important enough, and ambiguous enough, that they really ought to be mentioned explicitly. This will further clarify the

---

[9] Note that this is different from the problem of manipulation. A manipulable cause may nonetheless remain ambiguous (as, e.g., when an argument about vouchers does not specify how a vouchers regime will be operationalized). Likewise, an operational causal factor may be nonmanipulable (as, e.g., inequality, which can be precisely measured but is difficult to manipulate).

[10] Dunning (2008a); Ross (2001).

nature of the argument, and indicates to the reader that the author has considered a potentially confounding factor.

A fifth (and closely related) issue concerns the *scope-conditions*, or *population*, of the inference. As we have said, all causal arguments have scope-conditions, even when these remain implicit. Typically, scope-conditions are contained within the key concepts that articulate a causal argument. So, any argument about economic development and democracy presumes certain things about the units of analysis – that they are large political units, for example. Suppose someone objects that when *families* become wealthier they do not necessarily become more democratic. While this may be true, it is not really a counterargument because the topic lies outside the presumed scope of the original proposition.

The distinction between a background condition and a scope-condition is not always clear, and therefore bears some discussion. Suppose, for example, that economic development has different effects on democracy when development is spurred by natural resource wealth as opposed to some other economic foundation. This issue may be treated as a background condition, in which case it is understood as a *ceteris paribus* assumption: in countries with similar levels of natural resource wealth, economic development will have similar effects on democratization. Or it may be treated as a scope-condition, in which case the author may state that the posited relationship between economic development and democracy holds only for countries with low levels of natural resource wealth: resource-rich countries lie outside the scope (population) of the argument. (A third option is to explicitly theorize the relationship between resource wealth, economic development, and democratization. However, this changes the causal argument – broadening it to include three factors rather than two – and so is not about background conditions or scope-conditions.)

Readers can readily see the tradeoff implied in this choice – to maintain a large scope while accepting a good deal of background noise or to reduce noise by narrowing the scope. Specifically, the tradeoff is between generality, on the one hand, and precision and impact, on the other.

To be sure, there is often a degree of ambiguity surrounding the scope-condition of a causal argument in social science. For example, theories of democratization are usually understood to apply to sovereign nation-states. However, the argument might also apply to subnational units (regional and municipal governments), to semi-sovereign colonies and protectorates, and even to other types of organizations (e.g., social movements, interest groups, and so forth). The bounds of this argument, like many others, are not entirely apparent. Typically, there is a home turf where the argument really must apply: the best possible scenario for X to affect Y. In this instance, it is probably the sovereign nation-state. Beyond this home turf, one may encounter a series of concentric circles where the logic of the argument seems more and more tenuous – though still plausible.

Likewise, the temporal scope of an argument demands consideration. Typically, authors apply the development/democratization thesis to the contemporary (twentieth-/twenty-first-century) era. But it might also be applied to earlier periods, even as far back as ancient Greece. Nor is it clear how far into the future this relationship might hold. Will development enhance democracy into the twenty-second century? As a rule, the temporal bounds of social science arguments are less clear than their spatial boundaries, precisely because of the ambiguity of futurity and the continuous nature of time (which stretches backward along an infinite arc, with no clear cut-off points). Further discussion of appropriate scope-conditions is found in Chapter 3 (see "Boundedness").

Manipulability

Ideally, the treatment of primary theoretical interest should be amenable to *manipulation*, that is, deliberate change by the researcher (or someone). If it is not, then the argument will be very difficult to evaluate (not to mention, to test). Manipulation is to causal arguments what operationalization is to conceptual arguments (see Table 5.1). It clarifies what it is we are talking about. This idea is implicit in the common understanding of a cause as something that changes. By asking the question of manipulability we are asking, in effect, for a clarification of what aspect of the world changes and what stays constant (the background conditions of an argument).

As an example, let us return to our perennial exemplars. Vouchers are manipulable in principle and in fact. As such, any argument about vouchers is clear enough with respect to X; one has only to specify what the vouchers regime consists of ($X=1$) and what the non-vouchers regime consists of ($X=0$). This defines the treatment and control, and hence clarifies the argument.

With democracy, however, considerable ambiguity persists about the treatment, and this in turn is a product of the fact that democracy is difficult to imagine as a manipulable treatment. What about democracy would be manipulated (changed)? Note that some elements of the concept are directly changeable, such as electoral law. One can re-write provisions of statute and constitutional law. Other elements, such as competitive elections, are not directly manipulable. One can create the conditions for party competition, but achieving competition depends on many factors that are outside anyone's ability to directly control. If people continue to support the dominant party (of their own free will) there is not much that an experimenter can do to alter this fact. In any case, the things that one could directly alter – such as electoral law – are the things that are easy to conceptualize as causes. One can imagine X as a cause if one can imagine changing X, while leaving everything else as it is (the *ceteris paribus* conditions of the causal argument). If it is necessary to change other things in order to (possibly) get X to change, then one is dealing with an ambiguous causal argument.

Impediments to manipulability stem partly from the free will of social actors. Recall that social science is distinguished from other sciences by its focus on decisional behavior, that is, actions in which there is a choice element. This poses a dilemma to explanation: namely, that something important lies in between things that we can manipulate and outcomes we want to explain. This something is actors' emotional and cognitive states of mind, which we cannot directly manipulate precisely because they are subject to free will. We can do things to *facilitate* feelings of anger, love, or desire, but we cannot manipulate these psychological states directly. Likewise, we can do things to facilitate or impair the development of intelligence, but we cannot directly manipulate intelligence. As a consequence, there is an ineffable quality to explanations that rest on mental states or conditions. Additional examples include trust, legitimacy, cognitive dissonance, adaptive preferences, or (that old standby) rationality.

Another category of explanation rests on the volitional behavior of groups of people. Concepts such as competition, equilibrium, self-fulfilling prophecies, diffusion, threshold-based behavior, or reference groups fall into this category. The problem, again, is that individual states of mind are not amenable to manipulation. Likewise, group behavior – because it rests on individual states of mind – is not amenable to direct manipulation.[11]

Additional impediments to manipulability stem from causal factors that are processual in nature. Demographers assert the causal importance of the demographic transition, a phenomenon with several phases. In the pretransition phase, births and deaths are in equilibrium; the population regenerates itself without growing because of Malthusian constraints (land, food,

---

[11] Likewise, since all social science explanations must ultimately make sense of the actions of individuals (even though the explanation may rest at a high level of abstraction and may pertain to organizations), one might say that all social science is subject to a degree of indeterminacy. We cannot directly manipulate the mechanisms by which X causes Y.

health care, and so forth). In the second phase, mortality rates drop while fertility rates remain constant, resulting in population growth. In the final phase, fertility rates drop bringing population back to equilibrium at a new level. Many phenomena are said to follow from a demographic transition – including (according to Tim Dyson) urbanization, expansion of government and systems of administration, division of labor, the growth of civil society, increased independence of women and reduced gender differences, and wider distribution of political power.[12] The problem, from the point of view of explanatory tractability, is that the process of transition is continuous; one cannot intervene directly so as to observe the counterfactual. Naturally, one can manipulate some of the factors that are supposed to produce the demographic transition, for example, supplies of food and medical care, sanitation, and so forth. This mirrors the situation of mental states: one can manipulate factors that are thought to produce mental states, but one cannot directly manipulate the mental state itself.

A third impediment to manipulability arises in situations where manipulation is possible, but doing so introduces problems of interpretation or external validity. Consider the example of democracy. What would it mean to change a basic feature of a country's constitution? This is a very big and necessarily contentious sort of change and probably not replicable in a laboratory. So one must think about how this sort of intervention would happen in a real society. It might be imposed from without, as the United States-led force has attempted to do in Iraq. Yet invasion by a foreign power introduces all sorts of confounders that problematize any causal argument about democracy. Who is the occupying power and under what circumstances did it invade? Was the conquest lengthy or short? Was the conquering power successful in vanquishing opponents and establishing order? Was it viewed as a liberator or as an oppressor? Answers to all of these questions (and many others) will complicate any attempt to conceptualize the impact of X on Y.

Alternatively, let us presume a home-grown transition to democracy (or something like it) such as occurred in Russia in 1991. This seems easier, and, yet, it is more difficult in other respects. Consider that a society that is ready to change the most basic features of its polity is also presumably undergoing fundamental change on many levels. Indeed, the transition from autocracy to democracy in Russia was accompanied by an equally transformative change from communism to capitalism. How is one to separate one from the other such that one can make an argument about democratization

---

[12] Dyson (2001).

while maintaining *ceteris paribus* conditions? If one cannot state clearly what the *ceteris paribus* conditions of a causal argument are one cannot state clearly what the argument is. And in situations where a treatment cannot be manipulated without disturbing *ceteris paribus* conditions it is unclear what one is talking about.

Let me give a few more examples to illustrate the ubiquity of this sort of ambiguity in social science. Consider a causal factor such as inequality. Unequal societies are thought to be prone to civil conflict, autocracy, and underdevelopment (relative to societies that feature a more egalitarian distribution of wealth). One can, of course, directly manipulate wealth, at least in principle. One could confiscate the wealth of rich people and give it to the poor. Or one could take everyone's wealth, leaving all citizens of a society at a very low level. Likewise, one could intervene to distribute wealth *un*equally. Lots of manipulated interventions can be imagined. However, each one of these interventions would be associated with enormous turmoil. As such, it is difficult to imagine how *ceteris paribus* conditions could be maintained.

Alternatively, one could imagine a situation in which rich members of a society voluntarily give away their money to the poor, bringing themselves down to the median wage. Here is a mechanism of transfer that does not rely on coercion. However, it asks us to imagine a very different type of person, that is, an altruist who cares more about equality than about personal possessions. This dramatic alteration of *ceteris paribus* circumstances changes the scope-conditions of the argument, which is no longer about the world in which we live, but rather about some other, imagined society – perhaps somewhere off in the future.

In short, one cannot ask: what would the United States be like if wealth were distributed more equally without asking a prior question: how would wealth be redistributed, and how would this mechanism affect the *ceteris paribus* conditions of the causal argument? When dealing with nonmanipulable causes one is necessarily dealing with the causes of those causes, that is, the various things that bring about (in)equality or democracy.

A fourth sort of obstacle is posed by nonmanipulable causal factors that serve a proxy role. Consider the role of race in educational attainment in the United States. We know that there is a persistent gap in test scores between white and black students,[13] and one is inclined to say that race has a strong causal impact on educational attainment. Few would dispute this claim. However, it is an ambiguous claim, and the reason for its ambiguity is that

---

[13] Jencks and Phillips (1998).

one does not know (without further clarification) what the manipulable feature of the causal argument might be.

It could be race itself, which it is possible to imagine manipulating through genetics, either at the point of conception or at some later point in development. (For heuristic purposes, I shall leave aside discussion of ethical considerations.) This sort of manipulation envisions the following counterfactual: a black (or white) child is born to white (or black) parents. That child has all the genetic endowments of his or her parents except the color of their skin. And those parents are similar to all other white (or black) parents in all respects except the treatment, that is, the race of their child (they are not more "progressive" than other parents).

Another sort of manipulation focuses on a feature that is presumed to follow from minority status: namely, discrimination. A counterfactual in this setting would be that a black child is moved from a community in which he or she faces a great deal of (racially based) hostility to one that is similar in all respects, but is not hostile to persons of a different complexion. This is a very different species of argument than the previous one.

Many additional manipulations can be imagined: for example, those based on socioeconomics, the educational background of parents, family structure, and so forth. The point is that the concept of "race" – because it is open to many possible manipulations – is highly ambiguous. It is not clear what one means when one says that race causes some outcome. Not only is the counterfactual condition ambiguous, but so also is the mechanism. (If we don't know what a real-life change in X entails, we certainly don't know much about the processes by which X might affect Y.)

Some methodologists view manipulability as a necessary condition of any causal argument.[14] By this interpretation, arguments about the effect of democracy, inequality, race, and other abstract factors are not really causal in nature. This seems a little extreme. Instead, I will treat manipulability as a desirable trait, among others, and one that is best approached as a matter of degrees. As we have seen, causal factors that seem nonmanipulable can sometimes be manipulated, though it takes some ingenuity to do so and the manipulation may not be ethically or practically feasible or generalizable to real-world situations. One may also manipulate the antecedent causes of a theoretical factor of interest. Although these manipulations may be impossible to implement in the real world they nonetheless help to clarify the nature of a

---

[14] Holland (1986); Rubin (1975, 2008: 812).

causal claim. One knows what "X causes Y" means if one can describe the manipulation of X that would achieve the envisioned change in Y. This is why manipulability is understood here as a formal element of a causal argument rather than simply as a matter of research design.[15]

Separation

A cause must be separable from the effect it purports to explain; otherwise the argument is tautological. This seems obvious. Yet, on closer reflection, it will be seen that separation is a matter of degrees. To begin with, Xs and Ys are always somewhat differentiated from one another. A perfect tautology (e.g., "The Civil War was caused by the Civil War") is simply nonsense, and never actually encountered. One occasionally hears the following sort of argument: "The Civil War was caused by the attack of the South against Fort Sumter." This is more satisfactory. Even so, it is not likely to strike readers as a particularly acute explanation. Indeed, there is very little explanation occurring here, because the X is barely differentiated from the Y (the attack against Fort Sumter was, of course, part of the Civil War). Equally problematic is an argument that links the Civil War to a warlike relationship between North and South, one that persisted from the 1850s to the outbreak of the conflict in 1861. Again, one is at pains to distinguish between cause and effect.

Consider a second example, this one classical in origin. To say that this man (X) is father to this child (Y) is to infer that the father caused the child to exist; he is a necessary (though not, of course, sufficient) cause of the child. (One might speculate that present-day notions of causation are rooted in the primordial question of legitimacy.) We are less impressed, however, by the argument that a fetus is the cause of a child, or a child the cause of an adult. There is something wrong with these formulations, even though X is clearly necessary for Y (and prior to Y). What is wrong is that there is little separation between X and Y; they are the same object, observed at different points in time. In short, we have treated a "continuous self-maintaining process" as a causal factor, and this violates the precept of separation.[16] By contrast, we might accept the argument that an adult is the product of his or her childhood, precisely because the notion of a childhood is separable from adulthood. (Even so, the argument lacks clarity.)

---

[15] Angrist and Pischke (2009).   [16] Marini and Singer (1988: 364).

Independence

In addition to separation, a good causal factor is characterized by *independence* relative to other causes of an outcome. If one proposed cause of an outcome is explained by something else, the latter has better claim to the status of "cause." Typically, we describe the independent cause as structural, and the intervening factor as superstructural, endogenous, or epiphenomenal. A satisfactory cause embodies Aristotle's quest for an "Unmoved Mover," a factor that affects other things but is not explained, or only partially explained, by any single cause.

Of course, every general causal factor is affected by something. There are no unmoved movers. Yet some factors are entirely (or almost entirely) explained by something else. Here, we are dubious about calling the superstructural factor a cause. It does not fulfill our expectations of a good cause because it lacks independence. It is entirely endogenous to something else. By contrast, the factor labeled a cause is apt to be a factor that has no single explanation. Many things affect it, some of which may be purely stochastic. Although it is not an unmoved mover, it is an unexplained (or difficult to explain) mover.

Consider Figure 8.1. If X is largely explained by A (if most of the variation in X is due to variation in A), and both are causes of Y, then A is probably more correctly regarded as "the" cause of Y. X is subsumed by A. Once one knows the status of A one can predict the status of X, M, and Y. X and M add no further information about the causal effect. (Of course, they do provide information about causal mechanisms, as discussed below.)

If, on the other hand, A explains only a small portion of X – which is a product of many factors, some of which may be purely stochastic – then X may properly be regarded as the cause of Y. It is not subsumed by A.

Generally speaking (and with the usual *ceteris paribus* caveat), the more foundational a factor is, the greater its standing among the various causes of some outcome. Indeed, debates about causal questions often rest on which causal factor is properly judged most foundational. Which X explains all the other Xs? Consider the various factors that have been proposed as explanations of long-term economic development, that is, for explaining why some nations are rich and others poor. A short list of such causal factors would include geography, colonialism, domestic political institutions, technology, human capital, culture, population, and demographic transitions.[17] Note that arguments among partisans of these different schools are not simply about

---

[17] Work on these various subjects includes: geography (Diamond 1992), colonialism (Grier), domestic political institutions (Acemoglu, Johnson, and Robinson 2005), technology (Mokyr 1992), human capital (Clark 2008), culture (Landes 1999), population (Kremer 1993), and demographic transitions (Dyson 2001).

whether a single factor – say, demography – has a large impact on long-term economic development. They are also, perhaps more importantly, about relationships among the various causal factors, namely, which are independent and which are dependent. In this argument, geography has an important advantage: it is not easily explained. Indeed, geography approximates Aristotle's unmoved mover. Of course, there are geological explanations for why land masses were formed in certain ways, why rivers appear, why some are navigable and others are not, and so forth. However, these explanations would be quite complex and would involve a considerable amount of contingency. Geographic explanations would be difficult to explain away. By contrast, cultural explanations seem quite vulnerable, as they are often endogenous to other factors. Those who wish to restore the status of cultural explanation must show that a set of values and practices that impacted economic development is not superstructural, that it has causal independence in the long sweep of history.

The relevance of these considerations may escape researchers accustomed to experimental settings. Where the treatment of interest is manipulated it is by definition independent relative to everything else. However, our topic here is the formal properties of causal argumentation not research design. The point is that when constructing causal arguments we must be attentive to the way things work in the world (as opposed to the laboratory). There is little point in designing an experiment for a causal factor that is, in the real world, controlled by some prior factor. This would serve to elucidate causal mechanisms, but little else. Of course, if the causal factor of interest can be manipulated by experimenters, then it can probably also be manipulated by policymakers, which means it may have some relevance to the real world. Under this circumstance, it can claim causal independence; it is not simply the product of something else.

Impact

Causal arguments strive to explain variation in an outcome. The more variation the causal factor explains – the greater the *impact* of X on Y – the more significant that argument is likely to be. This may also be articulated as a question of effect size, magnitude, power, or strength.

Necessary-and-sufficient causal arguments (discussed in Chapter 12) are compelling because they explain *all* the variation in Y, while remaining admirably concise. It is no wonder that they continue to serve in common parlance as the ideal-type causal argument. By contrast, wherever there are exceptions to a causal argument, or where some factor other than X accounts for variation in Y, we can see that the argument is weakened: it no longer suffices to account for Y.[18]

There are a number of ways in which the question of relative impact can be gauged. In a regression format, where the relationship between X and Y is assumed to be probabilistic, impact is measured by the coefficient (slope) for X or by a model-fit statistic such as R^2 for X, a vector of independent variables.

Of course, estimates of causal impact from an empirical model depend upon the specifics of that sample and model, and may or may not correspond to real-world impact. If the model is not realistic in this respect, then a separate evaluation of impact – perhaps in a more speculative mode – may be required. It is often helpful to consider the impact of X on Y in practical terms, for example, as a matter of public policy. Could a significant change in Y be achieved by manipulating X? At what cost and with what opportunity costs?

The impact of X on Y may also be gauged by comparing its impact to other factors. If the impact of these other factors is well understood, this may provide a useful metric of significance (i.e., relative impact).

Whatever the metric of evaluation, the impact of X on Y is a key measure of success. One of the criteria of a good causal argument is that it explains a lot about the phenomenon of interest. It should not be trivial.

Mechanism

We have said that causes generate – alter, change, condition, create, effect – outcomes. It follows that there must be a causal mechanism, or mechanisms, at work. The mechanism is "the agency or means by which an effect is produced or a purpose is accomplished."[19] In model-based terminology it may be understood as the causal pathway, process, mediator, or intermediate variable by which a causal factor of theoretical interest is thought to affect an outcome – illustrated by M in Figure 8.1. (By contrast, a *moderator* is an intervening variable that alters the nature of an X/Y relationship.[20])

To clarify, my use of the term mechanism in this book encompasses *any* factor that is considered part of the generative process by which X affects Y,

---

[18] A vector of factors may also account, cumulatively, for all the variation in Y (this is the goal of a *causes-of-effects* theory, discussed in Chapter 12), but at the cost of parsimony.
[19] *Webster's Unabridged Dictionary* (New York: Random House, 2006).   [20] Wu and Mumbo (2008).

whether it consists of a series of discrete steps (e.g., dominoes falling into one another on a table) or a continuous process (e.g., a billiard ball rolling across a table and hitting another ball).

All that is required is that the mechanism be free to vary in some fashion – even if the variation is only hypothetical. Thus, in the dominoes example, if one domino is missing the chain may be broken and the usual result – running from the first domino to the last – will not occur. Similarly, if the effect of a vouchers treatment on educational attainment runs through a causal mechanism centered on teacher quality, and the latter factor is minimized, we expect the X/Y relationship to be altered (vouchers will have less impact on educational attainment, or will have no impact at all). This is what justifies our understanding of causal mechanisms as *variables*. Like X and Y, they vary.

Sometimes, the working of a causal mechanism is obvious and can be intuited from what we know about the world. This is likely to be the case when the X/Y relationship is proximate in nature. Suppose that an experiment alters the monetary incentives of teachers and finds that this has a significant impact on teacher performance (by various metrics). It may not be necessary to provide a long-winded explanation of M since it seems a safe assumption that the mechanism at work is the monetary incentive. Enough said.

Alternatively, M may be obscure. This is likely to be the case when the X/Y relationship is distal and/or when the causal pathways connecting X and Y are complex: involving long causal chains, diverse routes traveling from X to Y (equifinality), or the combined but simultaneous effect of multiple factors. Here, the causal mechanisms of a theory require extensive discussion, albeit in a speculative manner (as processes that *may plausibly* connect X with Y). The impact of economic development on democratization, or of democracy on peace, are two examples of this sort.

Although this chapter is focused on the formal properties of a causal argument, it is important that we say a few words about the empirical properties of a causal mechanism. Sometimes, the causal mechanism in a theory is directly measurable and hence amenable to empirical testing. Sometimes, it is not – or is so only through proxies. Sometimes, empirical tests may be conducted in a quantitative manner (across a large sample). Sometimes, qualitative modes are sufficient, or are all that can be managed given data limitations. These issues are discussed at some length in later chapters. I mention them now only to help clarify our working definition of a mechanism, which is not intended to tilt toward qualitative or quantitative styles of analysis or toward assumptions of testability or nontestability. All I mean by a mechanism is a pathway that runs from X to Y.

It should also be pointed out that some causal theories are centered on a core X/Y relationship, while others are centered on a causal mechanism (M). Duverger's theory about the role of electoral systems in party conflict is driven by an X/Y hypothesis: that district size influences party system size. Marxism, by contrast, is driven by a causal mechanism: class struggle. Note that each type of theory generates its own species of confusion. A theory centered on a core X/Y prediction may not specify a determinate set of causal mechanisms (indeed, a good deal of work on Duverger's theory in subsequent decades has concerned the possible pathways by which electoral system rules affect the behavior of voters and elites).[21] A theory centered on a causal mechanism may not generate a set of specific and testable predictions about how X varies with Y. In the case of Marxism, predictions flow from the central causal mechanism of class struggle in all directions, and no single prediction is critical to the theory – leading some critics to accuse the theory of unfalsifiability.

For our purposes, what bears emphasis is that all three elements – X, Y, and M – are important for causal argumentation. An X/Y hypothesis without a clear causal mechanism is an argument in search of an explanation. It may be true, but it will be not be very meaningful, will be difficult to generalize upon, and may also be difficult to prove in a convincing fashion. Thus, it is incumbent upon the writer to clarify the causal mechanism(s) at work in a causal argument, if it cannot be intuited from context.[22] This may be accomplished in prose, in diagrams, and/or in mathematical models, and is implicit in the very act of *theorizing*.[23]

---

[21] Riker (1982).

[22] The importance of mechanisms in generalizing (i.e., extrapolating) a finding is discussed in Steel (2008).

[23] For further discussion of causal mechanisms, and alternate ways of understanding this key term, see Gerring (2008, 2010).

9 Causal analyses

When we look about us towards external objects, and consider the operation of causes, we are never able, in a single instance, to discover any power or necessary connexion; any quality, which binds the effect to the cause, and renders the one an infallible consequence of the other. We only find, that the one does actually, in fact, follow the other. The impulse of one billiard-ball is attended with motion in the second. This is the whole that appears to the *outward* senses. The mind feels no sentiment or *inward* impression from this succession of objects: Consequently, there is not, in any single, particular instance of cause and effect, any thing which can suggest the idea of power or necessary connexion.

David Hume[1]

Since Hume, writers have been aware that the assessment of causal relationships is rather ethereal. One can never know with absolute certainty whether some factor caused an outcome to occur, because one cannot go back in time to re-play events exactly as they happened, changing only the factor of interest and observing the outcome under this altered condition. The causal counterfactual can never be directly observed for there are no time-machines. This is sometimes referred to as the fundamental problem of causal inference.[2]

In recent years, social scientists have become acutely conscious of the insubstantial nature of the evidence that typically undergirds causal propositions in anthropology, economics, political science, sociology, and various offshoots of these disciplines. Methodologists have little confidence in inferences drawn from observational data, and no statistical machinery seems likely to provide secure foundations. There is, some have insinuated, a "crisis of causality."[3]

---

[1] Hume (2007: 59).   [2] Holland (1986).

[3] McKim and Turner (1997). On the problems of statistical inference based on observational data, and the corresponding importance of research design, see Berk (2004); Brady and Collier (2004); Clogg and Haritou (1997); Freedman (1991, 1997, 2008, 2010); Gerber, Green, and Kaplan (2004); Gigerenzer (2004); Heckman (2008: 3); Kittel (2006); Longford (2005); McKim and Turner (1997); Pearl (2009b: 40, 332); Robins and Wasserman (1999); Rodrik (2005); Rosenbaum (1999, 2005); Seawright (2010);

While causality may be in crisis, it is certainly not dead. Indeed, social science is more fixated on causal questions today than at any point in the past. Fortunately, although causal attribution is always a gamble, there are ways to maximize validity and precision, given evidentiary constraints.[4] It is in this spirit – of doing the best we can – that the book is written.

Before jumping into the argument it is important that we define the problem of causal analysis more precisely. I begin by discussing the notion of a causal effect. I then lay out a causal graph showing essential research design components as they pertain to questions of internal validity. Next, I proceed to the main business of the chapter: a discussion of methodological criteria that apply broadly to research designs whose purpose is to test a causal proposition.

Causal effects

In Chapter 8, I proposed a general definition of causality. A key part of that definition is the causal (aka treatment) effect: the effect of some change in a causal factor (X) on an outcome (Y), relative to what that outcome otherwise would be. This has come to define causality in the social sciences and is central to the "potential outcomes" model of causation (discussed in Chapter 12). (It is not, of course, the only way in which causation can be understood. For some purposes, for example, in legal settings, it is important to define causality with reference to the cause-in-fact, as discussed below.)

Let us say that X is a school voucher and Y is school performance, as measured by an achievement test. Here, the causal effect is the impact (on school performance) of having a voucher ($X=1$) relative to not having a voucher ($X=0$). Note that a causal effect is understood counterfactually: what effect would a change in X have on Y? The causal or treatment effect is therefore the change in Y corresponding to a given change in X.

We begin by introducing a variety of different treatment effects. In the next section we proceed to discuss various relationships that might obtain between X and Y: varieties of causal relationships. In the third section, I introduce an elaborated causal diagram, building on Figure 8.1.

Summers (1991). Various studies comparing analyses of the same phenomenon with experimental and nonexperimental data show significant disparities in results, offering direct evidence that observational research is flawed (e.g., Benson and Hartz 2000; Friedlander and Robins 1995; Glazerman, Levy, and Myers 2003; LaLonde 1986). Cook, Shaddish, and Wong (2008) offer a more optimistic appraisal.

[4] For a general formulation see Guala (2005: 136).

Varieties of treatment effects

Treatment (causal) effects can be understood in different ways, and the differences sometimes matter quite a lot when interpreting results from a study.[5] Thus, a short digression may be warranted (those who wish to skip ahead may return later to this rather technical discussion). Note that while the following terms are often defined by their application to experimental research designs their most important applications are often in settings where researchers cannot randomize the treatment of interest. Here, as elsewhere, experiments serve a heuristic role.

An *individual treatment effect* (ITE) is the impact of a treatment condition (X=1) on a single unit relative to the control condition (X=0). In our vouchers example, a single unit might be a single student. Thus, ITE for that student is his or her performance in the treatment condition (having a voucher) versus his or her performance under the control condition (without a school voucher). Strictly speaking, any estimation of ITE must take the form of a counterfactual thought-experiment, for we cannot directly observe the treatment and control conditions for a single unit. This is the fundamental problem of causal inference, referred to at the outset of the chapter. However, we can observe a single individual pre- and post-treatment (without and with a voucher), and make inferences accordingly. Alternatively, we can infer ITE from the properties of a larger sample, as discussed below. In any case, ITE is usually not the most interesting property of a causal analysis, especially if our goal is to elucidate properties of a larger population.

An *average treatment effect* (ATE) is the mean impact of a change in X on Y across a population, that is, the average ITE. The intuition is that individual treatment effects are likely to be different from unit to unit. Indeed, causal heterogeneity abounds in social science phenomena. It seems probable, for example, that some students will respond to a vouchers stimulus more positively than others. Some may not respond at all, or may respond negatively. ATE represents the average value of these heterogeneous effects. It is the usual goal of large-sample analysis. In an experiment, ATE is estimated by comparing a group of units randomly assigned to receive the treatment (the treatment group) with a group that is randomly assigned to the control condition (no vouchers). Unfortunately, the correct estimation of ATE is not always possible; hence, the development of a set of alternative treatment effects, as follows.

---

[5] For further discussion see Heckman (2000); Manski (1995); Morgan and Winship (2007: ch. 2); Rosenbaum (2002).

Sometimes, average treatment effect refers only to relationships found within a chosen sample, not to a larger population. This is referred to as a *sample average treatment effect* (SATE).

An *intent-to-treat effect* (ITT) is a way of framing ATE in situations where it is suspected that some units assigned to the treatment group are not actually exposed to the treatment: a problem of *noncompliance* (discussed later in this chapter). It may be read as "ATE with probable noncompliance," that is, including units in the treatment group that are not actually treated. Let us imagine an experiment in which some students are granted vouchers, but not all of them take advantage of the opportunity; they continue to attend their local (non-voucher) school. One can still compare school performance for students who receive the vouchers (the treatment group, including noncompliers) and students who do not (the control group), but the comparison has a different interpretation. It measures the ITT. Note that for some purposes ITT may be more policy-relevant than ATE, for there is often some degree of noncompliance associated with a policy initiative. In any case, these two sample-based causal effects suggest different interpretations about X's effect on Y. Where inferences to a larger population are improbable, one may refer to a *sample intent-to-treat effect* (SITT).

An *average treatment effect on the treated* (ATT) also focuses on the problem of nonrandom assignment and/or noncompliance. ATT designates the effect of X on Y for all units that are actually treated – as opposed to all those that are assigned, or might be assigned, to the treatment group. So, if students are allowed to self-select into a vouchers program it is probably safe to assume that they have different background characteristics than students who do not self-select into treatment. They may be more ambitious, more intelligent, with better-educated parents, and so forth. These features will likely affect their performance on whatever outcome measure of school achievement is employed as a post-test. Under the circumstances, there are several bases for making a judgment about the ATT. We might compare the scores of these students with others who did not receive the treatment but who seem similar on background characteristics. We might compare the scores of students before and after they receive the treatment. In each of these analyses, the causal effect of interest is properly regarded as ATT, rather than ATE, because we are dealing with a special subset of the population of interest – those who are treated (perhaps because they elect to be treated).

Although ATT is usually correctly regarded as a corruption of the ATE ideal, in some circumstances it may be more relevant than ATE. Consider the question of whether college professors socialize their students to particular points of view: for example, do liberal faculty cause students to become more liberal?[6] In this situation, let us suppose that there are a range of universities available to most students – some liberal in orientation and some conservative. Students can therefore choose what sort of ideological climate they wish to inhabit while attending college. Let us further suppose that no government program or regulation is likely to inhibit this freedom of choice. Here, we may be more interested in the effect of the treatment (attending classes with liberal/conservative faculty) on the treated (ATT) than the average effect of the treatment across the population (ATE), were they to be randomly assigned to liberal or conservative institutions. For the latter is unlikely ever to happen. The ATE may still be of theoretical interest, but it is not of great practical import. Where ATT refers only to a sample rather than a larger population, it is helpful to designate a *sample average treatment effect on the treated* (SATT).

A *local average treatment effect* (LATE) is a more specialized term used in the context of *instrumental-variable* analysis (explained in Chapter 10). Specifically, it refers to the effect of X on Y for those units whose treatment status (treated/untreated) is affected by the chosen instrument. It explicitly excludes those units which would receive the treatment condition regardless of the instrument (always-takers) and those who would be in the control condition regardless of the instrument (never-takers). To reiterate, LATE defines the treatment effect as referring only to those units within the population whose assignment to treatment is a product of the identified instrument. A better label for this would be *complier average treatment effect* (CATE); however, this term is rarely encountered in the literature, so we will stick with LATE. Although not often acknowledged, one can appreciate the occasional utility of another sort of treatment effect that is local and also limited to the studied sample, rather than a larger population, that is, a *sample local average treatment effect* (SLATE).[7]

The alphabet soup of acronyms is confusing, to be sure. Readers new to this literature are well advised to stay focused on the concepts, rather than the terminology. However, since the terminology is becoming ubiquitous, and the concepts they represent are surely important, some familiarity with ATE and its variants is recommended. Fortunately, the distinctions among these terms may be summarized in a taxonomic form, as illustrated in Table 9.1.

To be sure, no taxonomy of this sort can claim comprehensiveness. Indeed, there is no limit to the sort of thing that could be designated as a treatment effect as long as it respects the definitional criterion of describing a difference

---

[6] Mariani and Hewitt (2008).
[7] I am indebted to Adam Glynn for pointing this out to me (personal communication, 2010).

Table 9.1 Treatment effects: a noncomprehensive taxonomy

	Average		Average among units intended to be treated		Average among the treated		Average among compliers		Unit
	Population	sample	Population	sample	Population	sample	Population	sample	
ATE (average treatment effect)	X								
SATE (sample average treatment effect)		X							
ITT (intention to treat effect)			X						
SITT (sample intention to treat effect)				X					
ATT (average treatment effect on the treated)					X				
SATT (sample average treatment effect on the treated)						X			
LATE (local average treatment effect)							X		
SLATE (sample local average treatment effect)								X	
ITE (individual treatment effect)									X

in Y when X varies. Following a Bayesian approach to causal inference, one can imagine a full distribution treatment effect (DTE) describing the difference in Y across its entire distribution (by means of a density function) – as opposed to a point estimate representing mean values of Y. In this same spirit, one can imagine a quartile treatment effect (QTE), a double frontier treatment effect (DFTE),[8] a variance treatment effect (VTE),[9] and so forth – each with sample- and population-based variants. I have not included these in Table 9.1 because they have not yet gained common currency.

Another sort of causal effect is one that eschews precise estimates of X's impact on Y in favor of a judgment about the general direction of causal impact (positive or negative). This is a plausible reading of many qualitative and quantitative studies where there is potential measurement error, where the intervention of interest is not randomized, and where the research design bears scant resemblance to a natural experiment.

This brings us to a final point. For practical and theoretical purposes, the ATE is usually the most desirable way of structuring the outcome. This does not mean that it can always be achieved. However, other sorts of treatment effects may be regarded as deviations from ATE insofar as ATE is what one would prefer to estimate in the best of all possible research designs. This is why ATE is listed first in Table 9.1. Wherever the terms treatment effect and causal effect are encountered without embellishment, the reader can usually infer that the writer is interested in average treatment effects.

Varieties of causal relationships

A causal (treatment) effect may take many different forms, as discussed. Likewise, there is an immense variety of different relationships that qualify as causal (i.e., in which a change in X generates a change in Y). Although some of the following terms are rather arcane it will be helpful to review them briefly, for they illustrate ontological possibilities (what may be going on "out there" in the world) and common modeling strategies.

Conjunctural causality refers to a situation where a particular combination of causes act together to produce an effect. *Causal equifinality* is where several causes act independently of each other to produce a particular effect. *Monotonic causality* is where an increase (decrease) in the value of X causes an increase (decrease) or no change in Y. In other words, the relationship between X and Y

---

[8] Fried, Lovell, and Schmidt (2008), described in Russo (2009: 98–101).
[9] Braumoeller (2006); Heckman (2005: 21–22).

is either always positive or null *or* always negative or null. *Nonlinear causality* is where the impact of X on Y varies with the value of X (but may still be monotonic). *Irreversible causes* (e.g., ratchet effects) are those whose impact on Y cannot be reversed. *Constant causes* operate continually upon an outcome rather than through discrete interventions. *Proximal causes* operate immediately upon an outcome. *Distal causes*, by contrast, have long-term effects on an outcome. *Sequential causes* have different effects on Y depending upon the sequence in which they are applied. A *causal chain* describes a situation in which many intermediate causes lie between X and Y. *Path-dependency* refers to a situation in which a single causal intervention has enduring, and perhaps increasing, effects over time on an outcome. *Causal laws* usually refer to perfect (exception-less) relationships between X and Y, observable across a large population. *Probabilistic causes* are not perfectly related to Y (there are exceptions, which may be represented with an error term) even though X is a cause of Y. *Set-theoretic ("deterministic") causes* are necessary and/or sufficient to produce an outcome. This class of causes encompasses the technique known as qualitative comparative analysis (QCA), which focuses on conjunctures of factors that, together, constitute a sufficient cause of an outcome (Chapter 12).

Evidently, there are many ways to think about causation. The unitary concept of causation introduced in Chapter 8 shelters a plurality of potential causal relationships. Indeed, once one heads down this analytic road it is not clear where one ought to stop. There is potentially always some new way in which two factors may co-vary or some new set of causal mechanisms that might explain their covariation. The terms introduced above, summarized in Table 9.2, are a small portion of the infinite variety of causal relationships that may exist in the universe. (Note: Table 9.2 is a list rather than a typology, as it identifies neither exhaustive nor mutually exclusive categories.) Nonetheless, this menu is useful as a quick-and-dirty canvass of the field. The vast majority of causal arguments bandied about in contemporary social science embody one of these relationships.

Departures from the treatment effect

Having explored variations in treatment effect, and variations in causal relationships, it is time to discuss some departures. These will be briefly mentioned.

Sometimes, investigations of causality are focused on causal *mechanisms*, as discussed in Chapter 8 and again in Chapter 11. Note that mechanismic investigations may be oriented toward estimating causal effects, in which case

Table 9.2 Causal relationships: a partial list

Conjunctures (aka compound cause, configurative cause, combinatorial cause, conjunctive plurality of causes): Where a particular combination of causes act together to produce an effect.

Equifinality (aka multiple causes, multiple causal paths, a disjunctive plurality of causes, redundancy): Where several causes act independently of each other to produce, each on its own, a particular effect.

Monotonicity: Where an increase (decrease) in X always causes an increase (decrease) or no change in Y.

Linearity/Nonlinearity: If the impact of X on Y changes across different values of X the relationship is nonlinear.

Irreversibility: X affects Y as X increases but not as it decreases, or vice versa.

Constancy/Delimited: A constant cause operates continually upon an outcome; a delimited cause operates only briefly (though it may have enduring effects).

Proximal/Distal: A proximal cause operates immediately on an outcome; a distal cause has long-term effects.

Sequence: The effect of X_{1-3} on Y depends upon the sequence in which X_1, X_2, and X_3 are applied.

Causal chain: Multiple mechanisms (M) form a chain from X and Y.

Path-dependency (aka critical juncture): A single causal intervention has enduring, and perhaps increasing, effects over time.

Causal laws: Exception-less relationships between X and Y.

Probabilistic causes: With errors, i.e., exceptions.

Set-theoretic causes: Where X is necessary and/or sufficient for Y.

they are not departures from the traditional goal of ATE. But they also comprise a separate research agenda. We want to know why X causes Y, not simply the treatment effect of X on Y.

Sometimes, the investigation of causality is focused on ascertaining the *boundaries* of an inference. The question is not what causal effect does X have on Y, but rather where (across what sort of units) does it have this effect? What is the true population of the inference?

Sometimes, researchers are interested in calculating the *probability* of an outcome based on a causal model. That is, given that a unit has a particular value for X, what is the probability of Y? This may be referred to as prediction (if one is interested in out-of-sample cases) or description (if one is interested only in features of the sample). It is central to set-theoretic causal relationships: where X is necessary, sufficient, or necessary-and-sufficient for Y (Chapter 12).

Another sort of causal argument focuses on establishing the *cause-in-fact*, aka *actual* cause, *singular* cause, *single-event* cause, or *token-level* cause.[10] This point is often illustrated with a stylized narrative about a man wandering in the desert with a small canteen of water. It so happens that the canteen has a

---

[10] Hart and Honore (1959); Hitchcock (1995); Pearl (2009b: ch. 10).

hole in it and water leaks out, after which he dies. Upon investigation it is discovered that the water is poisoned. Now, the ITE of (a) the hole in the canteen and (b) the poisoned water is the same if both are assumed to be fatal. Estimating this ITE depends upon assumptions about the man's condition with and without the treatments and whether the treatments are administered simultaneously or independently. For present purposes, what is significant is that if both of these causal factors are fatal, and if background conditions are the same, their ITEs are the same. However, there is only one cause-in-fact. This might be the hole in the canteen (if the man actually died of thirst) or it might be the poisoned water (if the man actually died of poisoning). It might even be both, if it is determined that these factors interacted to cause his death. The key point is that this sort of causality is not defined by a counterfactual and so does not conform to the traditional understanding of a causal effect.

Of course, the cause-in-fact *might* be crafted in a counterfactual manner if the counterfactual is understood in an extremely narrow fashion (i.e., whether the man dies in a particular way or at a particular time) or if the various elements of the causal story can be represented in a causal diagram (as claimed by Pearl).[11] However, the point of the cause-in-fact is usually to assign moral and legal responsibility, not to shed light on a class of events. Insofar as one is interested in generalizable arguments – a key point of departure for most scientific investigations, as argued in Chapter 3 – the cause-in-fact is likely to play a small role. If we are seeking to generalize from the case described here – that is, to other desert wanderers – we are probably more concerned with the conclusion that both leaks in canteens and poison increase the probability of death. It is of less significance what caused this particular man to die in a particular way and at a particular point in time.

In sum, an investigation into causal relationships need not be restricted to questions about causal effects. Some interesting and important features of causality are left out of ATE and its variants.[12] This does not mean that they are in contradiction with the potential-outcomes model (Chapter 12), but it does testify to the diverse meanings and purposes of the concept of causation. In any case, the treatment effect retains a central position in causal investigations within the social sciences. Consequently, most of our discussion in this chapter and the next focuses on this traditional objective.

---

[11] As Pearl (2009b: 311) notes, "the more episode-specific evidence we gather, the closer we come to the ideals of token claims and actual causes." See also Pearl (2009b: ch. 10).

[12] One may quibble about whether these alternative forms of causal inference are focused on "causal effects." Evidently, this depends on how narrowly one wishes to define the notion of a causal (treatment) effect.

An elaborated causal graph

Causal analysis is not a mechanical procedure, for the data never speaks for itself. It must be interpreted, and many assumptions are required. In order to clarify what these assumptions are it is often helpful to construct a visual representation of what we think is going on in the world. A causal graph should replicate the *data-generating process* (DGP), that is, the actual process by which the data one is examining was created.[13] Of course, we cannot really know what the true DGP is, so a causal diagram is correctly regarded as a presentation of the author's assumptions, some of which may be testable while others may not be. A causal diagram is the author's best guess about the nature of some reality.

Drawing graphs is helpful regardless of whether the sample is small or large, whether the data was generated experimentally or observationally, and whether data analysis is quantitative or qualitative. All of these situations can be quite complex; all require assumptions; and all are subject to similar threats to inference.

Our first causal graph, Figure 8.1, included the cause of theoretical interest (X), the outcome (Y), the mechanism (M), and an antecedent factor (A). Figure 9.1 reiterates these features with two additions.

Each letter in Figure 9.1 (and in other diagrams throughout the book) represents a single variable or a vector of variables. (Thus, X might refer to a single cause or a set of causes.) A variable (aka condition, factor, etc.) refers to any feature that has the potential to vary – whether measurable or un-measurable, qualitative or quantitative, continuous or categorical. Variables are understood as *causally* related if there is a directed arrow pointing from one to another. They are understood as *correlative* (associational) if a line without arrows connects them. A correlative relationship between A and B might mean that A causes B, that B causes A, that a third factor, C, causes both A and B, or that there is no discernable causal relationship between A and B (they are accidentally correlated).

Now, let us expand upon the elements in this causal graph.

A causal *mechanism* was defined in Chapter 8 as the path(s) connecting X with Y, labeled M in Figure 9.1.[14] A mechanism mediates, and in this sense

---

[13] Readers will note that this causal diagram borrows certain features from the tradition of causal graphs (e.g., Pearl 2009b), but is not equivalent to a "directed acyclic graph" (DAG). It is simpler in some respects (though further elaboration is offered in Chapter 10), and more general in some respects. For example, while DAGs express all relevant relationships as causal, and focus primarily on the assignment problem (the formal research design, if you will), the framework offered in Figure 9.1 should also be applicable to confounders that creep into a research design after the assignment of treatment, e.g., noncompliance, mortality, and the like. Each of these threats to inference introduces a species of confounder (something correlated with X, or with the change of X over time), though they are often difficult to conceptualize in a causal fashion.

[14] For further discussion see Gerring (2008, 2010).

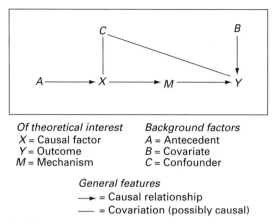

Of theoretical interest
X = Causal factor
Y = Outcome
M = Mechanism

Background factors
A = Antecedent
B = Covariate
C = Confounder

General features
⟶ = Causal relationship
— = Covariation (possibly causal)

Figure 9.1   An elaborated causal graph

explains, X's relationship to Y. Let us suppose that vouchers have a positive impact on school performance; thus, students receiving vouchers score better on some measure of performance than those who do not receive the treatment (all other things being equal). Mechanisms for this causal effect might include (a) higher-quality instruction, (b) smaller classes, or (c) greater motivation on the part of teachers and/or students.

Recall that all causal arguments take place against a background, presumed to be held constant so that the true effect of X on Y can be observed. This is the contextual "noise" against which the "signal" (X's effect on Y) must be assessed. Three genres of background factors are worth distinguishing.

The first is the *antecedent* cause of X, labeled A in Figure 9.1. Generally speaking, an antecedent cause is any factor lying prior (causally) to some other factor. M is antecedent to Y, X is antecedent to M, and A is antecedent to X in Figure 9.1. In this usage, antecedent is synonymous with "prior," "parent of," or "exogenous to." In Figure 9.1, the factor labeled antecedent, A, has a direct effect on X, and an indirect effect on M and Y.[15] In the context of vouchers research, antecedent causes would include factors that influence which students receive vouchers and which do not. Because the antecedent cause (A), as illustrated in Figure 9.1, has no direct effect on the outcome except through the designated cause of theoretical interest (X), the adoption of a voucher program may impact school performance, but only through the working of the voucher program.

[15] If, by contrast, a cause antecedent to X has an independent effect on an outcome other than through X, or if it is correlated with some other factor that has an independent effect on that outcome, it is properly classified as a confounder, C.

A second background factor takes the form of an orthogonal *covariate* (B). This species of causal factor has an effect on Y but is independent of X. This means that B is orthogonal to (stochastic, random, uncorrelated with) the treatment, even when conditioning on other factors in the model (an issue whose importance will become apparent in Chapter 10). In an experimental study of vouchers (where the treatment, vouchers, is randomized across a treatment and control group), covariates might include individual-level factors related to student test performance such as age, race, sex, social background, and years of schooling. They might also include truly random factors that we can neither identify nor measure.

A final background factor, and by far the most important, is the *confounder* (C). Generically, a confounder is any factor that might compromise a true (unbiased) estimate of X's effect on Y and thus pose a threat to causal inference. A confounder therefore co-varies with X, a fact that distinguishes it from an orthogonal covariate (B). (For further discussion see Chapter 11.[16])

The simplest and most common strategy of causal inference rests on the covariation of X and Y. If the problem of confounders can be solved, or at least mitigated, the pattern of covariation between X and Y should provide the basis for a valid (unbiased) estimate of the causal effect. If, in addition, the noise emanating from covariates (B) is limited, controlled by conditioning on these factors, or outweighed by the sheer number of observations in a sample, then the estimate of causal impact will be relatively precise (stable, reliable). All issues associated with estimation are thereby partitioned into two categories: *validity* (the absence of confounders) and *precision* (noise from covariates), represented by C and B in Figure 9.1.

This is, of course, a very brief discussion, omitting a great deal of importance to causal inference. It should also be recognized that the graphs represent a highly simplified depiction of what may be an extremely complex reality. Not all causal factors necessarily fit neatly into one of these categories (A, B, C, X, Y, or M). A factor may exhibit elements of M and C, for example; that is, it may be partly endogenous to X (a causal mechanism, M) but also exert an independent causal effect on Y (a common-cause confounder, C). However, the schematic features of Figure 9.1 are useful for heuristic purposes. Additional problems of causal inference require more complex causal graphs, as explored in Chapter 11.

---

[16] They include: the *common cause* (or classic confounder), which has a causal effect on both X and Y; the *incidental confounder*, which affects Y and is correlated with X (but not by reason of any identifiable causal relationship); the *compound treatment confounder*, which fails to distinguish between a causal factor of theoretical interest and a confounder; the *endogenous confounder*, in which a conditioned factor (other than Y) is endogenous to X; the *feedback* confounder, in which Y affects X; the *antecedent confounder*, in which a conditioned factor affects Y only through X; and the *collider*, in which a conditioned factor is affected by both X and Y.

Criteria

Having clarified the problem of causal assessment and the nature of potential threats to inference (with reference primarily to questions of internal validity), we turn now to general criteria of causal analysis. What desiderata do research designs and associated data analyses strive to achieve when testing causal arguments?

In Chapter 4, I argued that a good research design addresses four generic criteria: *accuracy, sample selection, cumulation,* and *theoretical fit,* each with various components. At this point, I will introduce dimensions of inference that pertain uniquely to causality. I divide this subject into three broad categories: the *treatment,* the *outcome,* and the *sample,* each with associated criteria. These will form the basis for our discussion. For convenience, all seven dimensions pertaining to research design in causal analysis are listed in Table 9.3.[17]

It is vital to bear in mind that here, as elsewhere in this volume, every criterion presupposes a *ceteris paribus* caveat. Each is good, all other things being equal. Where other things are not equal, the researcher must strive for the best possible adjustment of criteria so that the net effect maximizes utility along these many desiderata.

Before beginning, I must alert the reader to a stylistic division of labor in upcoming sections of the book. This chapter approaches the topic of research design from an ideal-type (maximal) perspective. It asks, what are the features of the archetypal, canonical research design? If one could wave a magic methodological wand at one's chosen problem of causal inference, what research design features would one wish into existence? In later chapters, I acknowledge the reality that there are no magic wands or methodological fairies; the canonical research design is therefore rarely attainable in practice – at least, not without sacrificing important features of a researcher's theoretical agenda. It is hoped that these chapters will be read together. Researchers need to know what to strive for, but they also need to know how and when to make compromises. Idealism is important, but so is pragmatism. We commence in a utopian mode.

---

[17] Insofar as causal research employs descriptive inferences such as *indicators* (which all do) or *typologies* (which some do) they are liable to criteria specific to these inferences, as discussed in Chapter 5. I shall leave these criteria implicit.

Table 9.3 Causal analysis: criteria

ANALYSIS

(Chapter 4)

1. **Accuracy**
   Are the results (a) valid, (b) precise (reliable), and (c) accompanied by an estimate of uncertainty with respect to (d) the chosen sample (internal validity) and (e) the population of interest (external validity, aka generalizability)?

2. **Sample selection**
   Are the chosen observations (a) representative of the intended population, (b) sufficiently large in number, and (c) at the principal level of analysis?

3. **Cumulation**
   (a) Is the research design standardized with other similar research on the topic? (b) Does it begin by replicating extant findings and end by facilitating future replications by other scholars? (c) Are research procedures transparent?

4. **Theoretical fit**
   (a) Does the research design provide an appropriate test for the inference (construct validity)? (b) Is the test easy or hard (severity)? (c) Is it segregated from the argument under investigation (partition)? (d) Are alternative explanations ruled out (elimination)?

CAUSAL ANALYSIS

(this chapter)

5. **Treatment**
   Is X (a) exogenous (to Y), (b) varying, (c) simple, (d) discrete, (e) uniform, (f) evenly distributed, (g) strong, (h) proximate (to Y), and (i) scaleable?

6. **Outcome**
   Is Y (a) varying, or at least free to vary?

7. **Sample**
   Are the chosen observations (a) independent (of one another) and (b) causally comparable?

Treatment

The counterfactual associated with any causal question is, what would happen to an outcome (Y) if the treatment (X) were to change? For purposes of testing, a good treatment should be: (a) exogenous (to Y); (b) varying; (c) simple; (d) discrete; (e) uniform; (f) evenly distributed; (g) strong; and (h) proximate (to Y).

Exogeneity

A good treatment is *exogenous* relative to the outcome under investigation. X should not be affected by Y. This is implicit in the nomenclature of "independent" (X) and "dependent" (Y) variables. (Sometimes, exogeneity has a broader meaning, signifying that the treatment is randomly, or as-if randomly, assigned, which is to say X is not correlated with potential confounders. I employ the term in a narrower manner, referring only to the relationship between X and Y.)

Of course, we know that many causal relationships in the real world are probably reciprocal. Presumably, economic development affects population health, and population health affects economic development. Presumably, social class affects education, and education affects social class. However, in formulating a causal hypothesis we generally identify one factor as X and the other as Y. Thus, a researcher imposes a specific conjecture upon the manifold complexities of the world. All else being equal, we ask what effect (if any) a change in X might have on Y.[18]

In order to test this hypothesis, it is essential that X be independent (exogenous) relative to Y – or that any remaining endogeneities be correctible by statistical legerdemain (corrections that are usually open to question). Another way of phrasing this problem is in terms of endogeneity between Y and X, as discussed in Chapter 11.

One empirical test of exogeneity is temporal precedence.[19] However, it is by no means a sufficient test of exogeneity; indeed, it is often misleading. Simply measuring X at some time period before Y does not provide a foolproof method of "exogenizing" X, and tests of causality resting only on temporal priority (e.g., Granger causality), while informative, are by no means definitive. For this reason, I view temporality as a secondary issue – one of many possible clues about exogeneity.

Variation

Empirical evidence of causal relationships is largely covariational in nature. In observing two billiard balls collide we observe that X and Y are associated: where X hits Y, Y responds by moving. Prior to X's arrival, Y was stationary and after X's departure Y becomes stationary once again. This indicates (though it does not by itself prove) that X is a cause of Y, and it also says something about the nature of the relationship.

Covariation can take many forms, including all those listed in Table 9.2. And there are numerous near-synonyms for this basic idea, for example,

---

[18] Very occasionally, one might try to measure both causal effects at the same time. However, this is much more difficult to do and, in any case, may be approached as two separate unidirectional causal hypotheses: (a) does X affect Y?; and (b) does Y affect X?

[19] Reichenbach (1956); Suppes (1970).

association, correlation, constant conjunction (Hume), *concomitant variation* (Mill), and *congruity*. Sometimes, the covariation follows a perfect (exceptionless, invariant, "deterministic") pattern, that is, X is necessary and/or sufficient for Y. Sometimes, it is probabilistic in nature.[20]

Whatever the nature of the relationship, X and Y must display some covariational pattern – at least hypothetically. Without it, causation cannot be at work. Empirical covariation is thus appropriately regarded as a necessary (though by no means sufficient) condition of a causal relationship.

Variation in X – the explanatory variable of interest – is especially crucial. An experimental study ensures variation in X by manipulating the treatment. An observational study looks for cases that exhibit natural variation in X. For example, a study of vouchers might incorporate variation on this key parameter by comparing schools with vouchers to schools without, or by comparing students with vouchers and students without (switching the unit of analysis from schools to individuals). Or it might take the form of a temporal comparison between schools (or students) prior to, and after, the institution of vouchers. If we have no such variation, our analysis must take the form of a counterfactual thought-experiment in which such variation is imagined – a much weaker research design.[21]

Simplicity

Simple treatments are easier to test than complex treatments. This is commonsensical. However, the costs imposed by more complex treatments deserve attention. Even if it is not in the power of the researcher to simplify the treatment (perhaps the theory demands a more complex treatment), he or she will still have to reckon with these costs.

The simplest treatment involves only two conditions: a treatment condition ($X=1$) and a control condition ($X=0$). Normally, it is easy to identify which is which, that is, which condition exemplifies the status quo or "null" hypothesis and which condition exemplifies the treatment. Occasionally, however, two treatment conditions are compared with one another without a pure control.

---

[20] Bennett (1999); Hume (1960: 219); Marini and Singer (1988); Mill ([1843] 1972: 263); Neuman (1997: 50). Bowley (quoted in Morgan (1997: 62), an early pioneer of statistical modeling, put it this way: "It is never easy to establish the existence of a causal connection between two phenomena or series of phenomena; but a great deal of light can often be thrown by the application of algebraic probability . . . When two quantities are so related that . . . an increase or decrease of one is found in connection with an increase or decrease (or inversely) of the other, and the greater the magnitude of the changes in the one, the greater the magnitude of the changes in the other, the quantities are said to be *correlated*." See also Frendreis (1983); Russo (2009).

[21] Fearon (1991); Lebow (2007); Tetlock and Belkin (1996).

For example, an investigation of electoral systems must compare different electoral systems; there is no "absence-of-treatment" condition (pure control). In any case, these distinctions are largely semantic. The methodological issues involved when comparing $X=0$ with $X=1$ are identical to those involved when comparing $X=1$ with $X=2$. Both are simple treatments.

Complexity may mean many things. It might mean multiple treatment groups arranged in an ordinal scale $(0, 1, 2, 3, 4, \ldots)$. It may involve categorical distinctions that are nominal rather than ordinal (e.g., Catholic, Protestant, Jewish, Muslim). It may also involve interactions among several categorical variables (e.g., Catholic+Male, Catholic+Female, Protestant+Male, Protestant +Female). Here, the number of treatments is equal to the number of combinations.

Another kind of complexity involves continuous treatments, where X varies across some interval. Here, the treatments are essentially infinite in number since an infinite number of points lie within any interval. Generally, continuous treatments are modeled mathematically so as to reduce their complexity. Thus, a continuous treatment might be modeled as a linear function ($Y=X+\varepsilon$) or as some nonlinear function (e.g., $Y=X+X^2+\varepsilon$). To be sure, there are, in principle, an infinite number of nonlinear functions (an infinite number of nonlinear ways for X to be related to Y), so continuous treatments are inherently complex, even if the math is parsimonious.

The general point is this: complexity entails a greater number of treatments. This means that the researcher will have to either incorporate a larger sample in order to test these multiple hypotheses or reduce the number of hypotheses through some mathematical expression. The cost of the latter approach is that one must introduce assumptions about the true shape of the underlying relationship, assumptions that cannot always be fully tested – especially if the composition of X in the sample is not evenly distributed (as discussed below).

Discrete-ness

The discrete-ness of a treatment partly determines the ease with which causal relations will be observable. A discrete treatment is abrupt, that is, short in duration. It can be described as a *dose*. As a result, it is easier to compare units pre- and post-treatment, or across treatment and control groups, without a lot of potential confounders entering into the picture.[22] If the treatment of a study consists of a voucher, one has only to mark the time at which this treatment

---

[22] Rosenbaum (2002: 354–357).

was administered and the targets who receive the voucher (we presume that there are no important anticipatory effects).

If, however, the treatment is nondiscrete, there may be no baseline against which the effect of the treatment can be compared. Consider a vouchers program that hands out money to students at monthly intervals, with different disbursements at different times, and no clear point of commencement or termination. Here, the analysis would have to depend upon some simplification of the data, for example, a linear relationship between money disbursed (to a student or school) and results achieved.

While this example may seem rather artificial, it does exemplify a common trait of many observational settings. Because the experimenter is not in control of the treatment, a natural treatment is likely to be introduced in a haphazard fashion. What is "messy" about observational data is not simply the non-randomized assignment of the treatment (as discussed below), but also the nature of the treatment itself.

Uniformity

In order to test the impact of a causal factor it is essential that the intervention be relatively uniform across the chosen units. If the treatment is binary (0/1) or multichotomous (0/1/2/...), then achieving uniformity is a simple matter of making sure that the doses are correct. If the treatment is continuous, the requirements of an interval scale must be upheld.

In some respects, the issue of uniformity is an issue of measurement, that is, the construction of indicators (Chapter 7). Since causal arguments build on concepts and indicators, all criteria pertaining to concepts and indicators necessarily pertain to causal analysis. In this respect, our discussion is redundant.

However, the problem of nonuniform treatments is worth mentioning again because insofar as a treatment is heterogeneous in nature – or heterogeneously administered – its causal effect will be difficult, if not impossible, to interpret. Consider what happens if we regard a binary measure of democracy (e.g., as provided by Przeworski and colleagues) as a causal factor in explaining some outcome (e.g., economic growth). In coding all countries as 0=autocratic or 1=democratic we are assuming that all countries coded as 1 receive the same treatment, and all countries coded as 0 experience the same "control" status. Because the treatment is observational, and because it is difficult to imagine what manipulation of reality would achieve this treatment, this is a difficult matter to evaluate. Suffice to say, there is a strong likelihood that all countries coded 1 are not the same on the dimension of theoretical interest (democracy) and countries coded 0 are not the same on the corresponding dimension of interest (autocracy).

In this respect, interval measures of democracy may seem preferable. Yet here we must also worry about uniformity of treatment. Consider that a composite indicator, such as polity, which is constructed through a complex aggregation rule from a variety of components, may not be truly unidimensional. Specifically, a coding of "3" may mean something different in different cases: that is, the various ways of achieving a "3" may not be truly interchangeable in terms of their causal effects. If so, the impact of this treatment is fundamentally ambiguous.[23] Again, the importance of a uniform treatment is paramount to interpreting a causal effect.

Even distribution

In addition to variation, simplicity, and uniformity, it is also desirable for the factor of theoretical interest to embody an even *distribution* across whatever values are deemed theoretically significant. This issue may be also expressed as a problem of "missing values."[24]

Suppose we are examining the effect of vouchers on school performance and we have a highly skewed distribution of values for X. Let us say that only two students have been granted vouchers ($X=1$), while the remaining 10,000 students in our sample receive the control condition ($X=0$). This is not an ideal setting for resolving questions of causality, for any results drawn from the analysis rest on the disposition of the two positive cases. The N of the study is large, but it is not very informative and has little claim to generality.

Similarly, with a continuous treatment one would like to see dose levels at all levels of X – high, medium, and low, for example. If, however, the theoretical aspirations of the theory surpass the actual variation in X one is in the position of intuiting values for Y when there is no corresponding value for X – a counterfactual thought-experiment. If X ranges only from 0 to 5, one must be wary of predictions about Y for values of X that surpass 5.[25] Likewise, if values of X include only the top and bottom of a presumed distribution (e.g., $X=0$ or $X=10$), one must be wary of making predictions about Y when $0<X<10$.

All these problems concern the distribution of values for the theoretical variable of interest. Simply stated, if there are no observations for a given value of X then we do not really know – at least not from any direct empirical

---

[23] Goertz (2006).   [24] Rosenbaum (1984).   [25] King and Zheng (2006).

knowledge – what value Y would have if X were, counterfactually, to be assigned that missing value.

Strength

A strong signal is easier to detect than a weak signal. Thus, it is helpful if the treatment chosen for empirical testing has a (putatively) strong effect on Y. Miniscule causal effects are likely to result in a failure to reject the null hypothesis, even if (some form of) the hypothesis is true.

Consider if we set out to test the effect of vouchers on school performance with a voucher system consisting of only US$500 per student per year (which could be allocated toward tuition at a private school). This measly stipend will not cover more than a small fraction of the tuition at most private academies in the United States. As such, its aggregate effect on the treated group is likely to be small, perhaps to the vanishing point. Little is served by a research design of this nature – unless, of course, the researcher has some reason to suppose that the signal will be strong enough to detect. (Perhaps he or she imagines that a small sum of extra cash will make a difference to a sizeable category of lower-middle class students.) We do not know, *a priori*, the true causal effect of a given change in X on Y; this is the goal of the research. However, testing a hypothesis requires that we make assumptions about the likely strength of this relationship. Thus, when we refer to a strong signal we mean a *putatively* strong signal – strong enough so that it may be expected to register in the research design at hand, if the hypothesis is correct.[26]

Granted, a weak signal can sometimes be compensated by other research design virtues, for example, sensitive instrumentation (leading to high precision and low measurement error), few confounders, and a large sample of observations. But, *ceteris paribus*, one would prefer a strong signal.

Proximity

In order to observe X's effect on Y it is helpful if the treatment lies fairly close (in causal and temporal distance) to the chosen outcome. In this fashion,

---

[26] Causal strength is a key component of statistical power (Cohen 1988). Note that increasing causal strength can often be achieved by increasing variation in X (e.g., by increasing the size of the voucher). However, these two criteria are not identical. Causal strength refers to the expected relationship between a particular treatment and a particular outcome. Thus, increasing causal strength may involve increasing the range of variation found in X, changing the outcome variable to one that is more sensitive to X, or changing the X factor (from one proxy of a key concept to another).

limits are placed on the number of possible confounders and on the temporal scope of the investigation. Note that a lengthy waiting period between the initiation of treatment and the outcome of interest means that, unless the units under investigation can be isolated for long periods, they will be subject to all manner of post-treatment threats to inference, as discussed below. Moreover, a close proximity between X and Y means that the causal mechanism(s) running from X to Y is likely to be easier to observe and to identify.

Consider the case of vouchers. Short-term effects, for example, on educational achievement, are fairly easy to test. Long-term effects, for example, on lifetime earnings or occupational status, are harder. The logistics of a research design generally become more complicated the longer the duration of the test. Tracking individuals over a forty-year period is harder than doing so over a two-year period. Non-response (perhaps due to mortality or mobility) will be a serious problem. Moreover, many potential confounders are likely to creep in during this extended period; after all, many things affect a person's earnings over a lifetime that would not affect educational performance over a two-year period. Controlling these factors, even if they are random, will necessitate a much larger sample. For the same reasons, any attempt to identify causal mechanisms will be much more difficult.

Of course, one is often interested in distal causes for theoretical or substantive reasons. Indeed, one might argue that the short-term effects of vouchers – along with many other policy treatments – are trivial. If all a vouchers program achieves is a two-year increase in educational performance it is certainly not worth the bother. This illustrates a recurring tension between the formal desiderata of a good theory and the desiderata of a good research design. Distal causes are often more interesting and important, but they are also usually harder to test.

Sometimes, a resolution of this dilemma can be found in a proximal measure that serves as a proxy for the distal outcomes of theoretical interest. For example, in the case of vouchers we might attempt to measure levels of motivation or self-identity – things that might translate into long-term changes in performance. Do students in voucher programs develop higher aspirations, stronger self-esteem, or better work-habits than students in the control group? However, short-term proxies for long-term outcomes are always suspect. There is no reason to presume that gains in motivation and self-identity will persist over many decades.

Scaleability

Some interventions are more generalizable than others. Suppose that the number of treated subjects in an experiment is limited – a common occurrence in experimental work, where it is often not possible to expand a treatment to include the full population of interest.

The problem that arises from a limited test is that it may not be possible to generalize a causal effect from the sample to the intended population. Will a vouchers program with 1,000 recipients work as well if there are 100,000 recipients? Will a tax credit scheme provide the same incentives when its value is increased from US$1,000 to US$10,000?

The danger of extrapolating causal effects from a limited test are evident. What is perhaps not evident is the frequency with which scaling up affects the nature of the causal relationship.[27] Consider that when a voucher program is scaled up from a limited test to a whole school district it is likely to bring with it compound effects that are not easy to anticipate. Teachers from that district may enter, or leave, the system, thus changing the composition of its educational staff. Large movements of students into, or out of, the system may also occur. Competition effects, introduced by vouchers, presumably will be compounded. These are the sort of issues that one would like to identify – and, if possible, overcome – when constructing or identifying a treatment. *Scaleable* treatments are preferable to treatments whose impact cannot be generalized at a different (usually higher) scale.

Outcome

Variation

With respect to the outcome of a hypothesis, the dependent variable, there are few requirements except that Y be free to vary. Of course, one might say that this is precisely the point of testing a hypothesis, and therefore scarcely bears mentioning.

The trouble is that even with carefully constructed experimental designs one must always be wary of hidden moderators that suppress the effect of X on Y, or constrict Y's movement entirely. If these factors lie outside the theoretical parameters of a theory they are impeding the process of testing. One must also be wary of problems of instrumentation and measurement. For these reasons, one will probably feel more comfortable with a research design that reveals some variation – perhaps small, and perhaps due to stochastic factors – in the outcome. Consider an experimental test of vouchers, at the conclusion

---

[27] Duflo (2004).

of which it is discovered that there is no variation over time or across students in educational achievement: all students achieve the same score on the post-test. This is an absurd example, but it illustrates a potential problem. One suspects that there is some constraint on Y other than X, in which case the test is invalid: by virtue of some background condition, Y could not respond to X under any circumstances.

That said, the problem of "variation in Y" is much more relevant to observational settings than to experimental settings. In observational contexts, what one usually means by Y-variation is maximum *range* of variation (minimum to maximum) in an outcome as well as maximum *dispersion* around the mean. These twin concepts are captured in the statistical concept of *variance*.

In observational work, it is highly desirable to identify settings in which Y actually does vary (rather than is simply free to vary, from some hypothetical perspective). Here, we cannot manipulate X and we may have much less assurance about Y's capacity to respond to a given change in X. Confounding factors are legion, and a stable outcome could therefore be credited to many things. We are reassured if we observe some variation in Y, whether or not it was caused by X. This does not mean that we learn nothing from a situation in which X changes but Y does not. It means that we learn more – much more – from a setting in which there is variation on both X and Y. Thus, if one were conducting an observational study focused on a cause (or multiple causes) of democracy one would not want to choose a sample of countries in which there was little variation in the outcome (autocracy/democracy).

The problem of Y-variation is most apparent when it is largely absent, as it is with some outcomes such as war, revolution, or school shootings that happen very rarely. Rare events pose a problem for causal analysis precisely because any assessment of their causes rests on the few instances in which variation in Y is observable. And if no variation at all on Y is present in the sample it will be difficult to say anything about X, aside from the elimination of sufficient causes. The first goal of a rare events research design must be to capture as many of those rare cases as is possible within the sample, despite the fact that this is likely to bias the representativeness of that sample. Fortunately, methods have been developed to provide unbiased estimates from samples that have an estimable bias (known variously as case-control sampling, response-based sampling, or choice-based sampling).[28] Also, it should be noted that the

---

[28] Breslow (1996); Manski (1995: ch. 4); Schlesselman (1982).

supposed sin of "selecting on the dependent variable" is often mis-labeled when applied to case-control or case-study designs.[29]

One point that should be mentioned before leaving this subject is that Y-variation matters more for exploratory studies of Y (where there is no specific hypothesis being tested) than for studies focused explicitly on a specific cause of Y. In the former instance, one wishes to explain variation in Y, regardless of its causes, so it makes sense to identify a sample that maximizes variation (variance) in Y. In the latter instance, it is justifiable to sample on X as long as there is *some* variation in Y. (For further discussion of the distinction between *effects-of-causes* and *causes-of-effects* investigations see Chapter 12.)

Sample

In Chapter 4 we discussed the problem of sample selection as it applies generically to all social science analysis. Here, we focus on elements that are specific to causal analysis.

These issues may be summarized by two general criteria: *independence* and *comparability*. Units and observations (drawn from those units) should be independent of one another and comparable with one another in ways that are relevant to the X/Y hypothesis.

Note that sometimes it is appropriate to consider the sample in terms of the characteristics of *units*, while at other times it is more appropriate to consider the characteristics of *observations*. The distinction is not critical for present purposes.

When assumptions of independence or comparability within the sample are violated this introduces a problem of noise (orthogonal covariates) or of bias (confounders), as illustrated in Figure 9.1. Since bias is a much more significant problem, the following discussion is focused primarily on the latter. As previously, we are primarily concerned here with issues of internal validity rather than of external validity.

Independence

In order to provide evidence about a causal proposition, treatment and control conditions should be independent of one another. This refers to the separateness of observations such that each observation can be regarded as providing

---

[29] Collier and Mahoney (1996); Gerring (2007).

new evidence of a causal proposition. Alternately phrased, variation in Y should be the product of the treatment, not of interactions among units or among treatment and control conditions.

Typically, the issue of independence is played out across units, as when a treatment group is compared with a control group, or various members of a treatment group are compared with each other. However, problems of independence may also arise *within* a given unit, as in a longitudinal design, where a single unit is compared at T_1 and T_2 (Chapter 10), or an alternate-outcomes design (Chapter 11).

An example of independence across trials is the flipping of a coin. In a typical coin-tossing exercise the result of one toss does not affect the result of any toss. They are independent. Knowing whether the coin came up heads or tails in one trial does not help one predict the outcome in the next trial. And this means that we learn about the outcome of interest – the probability of a heads or tails – from each toss.

An example of *non*independence across trials would be an educational test in which students' knowledge of a subject is tested sequentially with the same exam, each person taking the same exam, one by one. In between exam sittings, they are allowed to communicate with one another. Evidently, the results of one test may not be independent of the results of the previous test. Students will probably share information about questions and answers.

Violations of independence, that is, dependence, may be introduced by *serial* (temporal) *autocorrelation*, where one observation of a given unit depends upon a previous observation of that unit, or by *spatial correlation*, where the observations obtained from one unit depend upon observations taken from another unit.

Violations of independence may be generated pre-treatment or post-treatment. Prior to treatment, commonalities among units may create a *clustering* of attributes (aka *correlated groups*) that violate the independence of each unit. After treatment is administered one often faces a problem of *interference*, where units "contaminate" each other.[30] (Both violate the important statistical assumption of independent and identically distributed (i.i.d.) errors.)

Consider a social science example. If one is testing the relationship between economic development and democratization one may decide to enlist a global sample of countries, observed over some period of time. Unfortunately, these countries cannot be considered entirely independent of one another with respect to this hypothesis. What happens in Belgium is not independent of

---

[30] Rosenbaum (2007).

what happens in France, for example – especially after the formation of the Common Market/European Union. Even prior to this continental confederation, European states learned from one another's experiences. Arguably, democratization was a continent-wide phenomenon rather than a country-level phenomenon. In this respect, any analysis that counts each country equally is counting observations that are not truly independent of one another – an example of spatial dependence, or clustering.

Often, violations of independence are caused when a treatment has spillover effects, that is, from treated units to nontreated units (interference or contamination). Suppose, for example, that economic development promotes democratization in the country undergoing development, but also has ramifications for democratization in neighboring countries (in ways unrelated to economic development). Suppose, in a vouchers experiment, that a voucher program has spillover effects to students, families, or schools not participating in the program (the control group). These will introduce problems into the analysis by virtue of the fact that units interact with one another, and are therefore no longer independent with respect to the causal hypothesis. (They also introduce problems of causal comparability, as discussed below.)

If one is observing units over time, problems of temporal independence must be considered. Suppose that a study of development and democracy counts every year as an independent observation, a typical approach in cross-national panel analysis. Arguably, one is overstating the degree of causal independence through time, for a country's regime type in one year is presumably contingent upon its regime type in the previous year. If one doubts this, consider the absurdity of observing regime-type outcomes at daily or hourly intervals. At some point, the exercise becomes futile. One is not learning anything (or hardly anything) from a panel of countries observed hourly that one would not learn from the same panel observed daily or monthly.

Of course, this depends upon what one is measuring. For some purposes, an hourly panel might be extremely useful. Whether it is useful or not depends upon the nature of the X/Y interaction. Changes in the inputs and outputs should be proportional to the chosen time unit. Changes that are rapid may be productively measured in milliseconds. Changes that are slow ought to be measured in larger temporal units.

To clarify, violations of independence are rarely complete and total. If it were so, then one would learn precisely nothing from observing Belgium once one had observed France, or nothing from observing France at T_2 once one had observed France at T_1. This is clearly not the case. But it is apparent that one learns more from some observations than from others. Venezuela is probably more independent of France than is Belgium. In this respect, once we know about France we learn more about the hypothesis by observing Venezuela than we do by observing Belgium. Likewise, France at T_{20} is probably more independent of France at T_1 than is France at T_2. Issues of independence are generally matters of degree; observations are rarely *entirely* dependent upon each other.

Violations of independence may have two distorting effects on an empirical analysis. They may lend a false sense of precision to the results by virtue of artificially inflating the number of observations (which are not fully independent of each other). More troubling, they are likely to introduce bias into the analysis insofar as observations are *differently* independent/dependent of one another, and in ways that are likely to be correlated with the treatment. Here is where problems of independence and comparability (discussed in the next section) merge.

Violations of independence can sometimes be corrected by sampling or modeling procedures. Suppose, in our previous example, that one could sample continents rather than countries, tracking the evolution of regime types across these larger – and presumably more causally independent – bodies. Moving up to higher-order units usually involves a sacrifice in the number of observations; in this instance, it may be prohibitive. However, it does assuage concerns about nonindependence and in some settings it may be practical to do so. If a study of vouchers experiences problems of nonindependence among students or classrooms the researcher may elect to observe schools or school districts. A problem of clustering is overcome by regarding clusters of individuals, rather than individuals, as the appropriate unit of analysis. Thus, moving to a higher unit of analysis often assuages concerns about nonindependence.

Another approach is to try to model violations of independence so these violations can be controlled, *ex post*, in the empirical analysis. Suppose, for example, a country's regime type is positively influenced by other countries in its neighborhood: if they are democratic, it is more likely to become democratic, and so forth. If this is the case then we may be able to model the diffusion process with a single variable that measures all countries' regime types and their relative distance to each country (distance being a proxy for exposure to the diffusion process). The modeling procedure is simple. It is, of course, another question to determine whether this model has correctly and fully accounted for all violations of independence. Models of diffusion are notoriously difficult to prove.

Naturally, the meaning of independence/dependence is contingent upon what one is studying. Sometimes, the causal hypothesis focuses explicitly on a process of cross-case dependence. Thus, one might like to know how the diffusion process works and how strong its effects on regime type are. In this setting, the control variable described above becomes the variable of theoretical interest. However, there are still issues of independence to worry about. Specifically, one must worry about any interference that is not captured in one's key variable, and one must worry about clustered cases and temporal autocorrelation, as described above. The problem of independence never vanishes from a research design; it merely assumes a different form.

Unfortunately, the independence of observations in a sample is not always testable. Of course, one can measure degrees of association (correlation) across observations, and this often provides important clues into potential autocorrelation. However, the fact that there is an association among a group of observations does not mean that the independence criterion has been violated, and the fact that there is no association does not mean that it has been satisfied. Just because countries in the same region of the world tend to share similar regime characteristics does not mean that they are nonindependent cases, though it surely raises questions.

Comparability

Intermingling with the criterion of independence is the issue of causal *comparability*. By this we mean that the expected value of Y for a given value of X should be the same across the studied observations and throughout the period of analysis. If they are, we can say that a group of observations is causally comparable (equivalent) with respect to a given hypothesis.[31] If, for example, a set of students is causally comparable with respect to vouchers then we would expect them to experience roughly the same change in educational outcomes when subjected to the same vouchers treatment.

Naturally, causal comparability differs with the treatment that is envisioned. Two groups of students may be causally comparable with respect to vouchers (X_1) and educational outcomes (Y_1), but not with respect to truancy programs (X_2) and criminal behavior (Y_2). People are alike in some ways and different in others. So, evaluating causal comparability in a sample depends upon the argument of theoretical interest.

A minimal understanding of causal comparability requires only that units be comparable to one another *on average*, which is to say that a large error rate across units is satisfactory as long as its distribution is centered on the true mean (i.e., as long as the error is random). A maximal understanding of causal comparability (sometimes expressed as *unit homogeneity*) is that units should

---

[31] Strictly speaking, a single observation cannot be causally comparable with another because a single observation does not register variation between X and Y. Causal comparability is the attribute of a set of observations, sometimes understood as a case or unit.

evidence *identical* responses of Y to a given value of X across units. The latter ideal is rarely, if ever, realized in the world of social science, and perhaps not even in the world of natural science. However, the minimal definition seems too minimal. After all, noncomparabilities are always somewhat problematic – at the very least, they introduce problems of noise (random error). They also may hide heterogeneous causal effects within the chosen sample (where different units respond differently to the same treatment). Thus, we will regard this desideratum as a matter of degrees. All things being equal, greater causal comparability in a sample is desirable.[32]

To clarify, randomly distributed incomparabilities across units introduce noise (stochastic error) into the analysis. They are not correlated with the treatment; they are therefore orthogonal covariates, represented by vector B in Figure 9.1. These are not troublesome as long as there are sufficient observations in the sample to overcome the threat to inference posed by stochastic events. A second sort of noncomparability is correlated with the treatment and is therefore regarded as a source of systematic error or bias, represented as a confounder, C, in Figure 9.1. This is the sort of problem that is primarily of concern when one considers issues of causal comparability.

A straightforward way to clarify the problem of causal comparability is by envisioning the simplest possible research designs, illustrated in Figure 9.2. Let us say that one group of units receives a treatment ($X=1$) and another group does not ($X=0$), and a post-test is administered to gauge the impact of the treatment, as illustrated in panel (a). Now, let us assume there is some background factor distributed across the sample that is likely to affect each unit's response to the treatment. If these heterogeneities are random – that is, distributed randomly across the treatment and control groups – then the error introduced by causal incomparabilities is random. It is not likely to be correlated with the treatment; the treatment and control groups are therefore balanced with respect to potential confounders. If, on the other hand, the heterogeneous elements of the sample are unequally distributed then the treatment and control group are not causally comparable, and systematic error in the analysis is likely to result.

The same logic holds if the causal analysis is temporal (longitudinal) rather than spatial, illustrated in panel (b) of Figure 9.2. Suppose a treatment is administered to all units in a sample. In order to gauge causal impact pre- and post-tests of the

---

[32] Rosenbaum (2010: ch. 15). Granted, if the purpose of a study is exploratory one might wish to interrogate a heterogeneous sample, as discussed in Chapter 2. However, our focus in Part III of the book is on testing specific hypotheses, and for this purpose causal comparability is important.

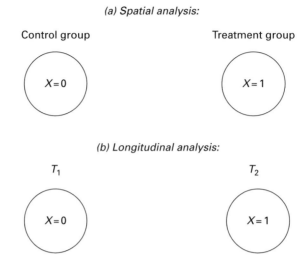

(a) Spatial analysis:

Control group   Treatment group

$X = 0$ $X = 1$

(b) Longitudinal analysis:

T_1 T_2

$X = 0$ $X = 1$

Comparability: $E(Y|X)$ is the same for treatment and control groups (spatial analysis)
or for the treatment group at T_1 and T_2 (longitudinal analysis)

Figure 9.2   Causal comparability: two simple illustrations

outcome are administered. This means that the pre-test functions as the "control" group and the post-test as the "treatment" group. Again, one is less concerned with heterogeneities that are randomly distributed across the sample period. But one must be extremely concerned with causal incomparability prior to, and after, the initiation of the treatment. The sample must remain the same from T_1 to T_2 in all respects that might affect the outcome – except, of course, the treatment itself.

These are, of course, very simple research designs. The problem of comparability also applies in more complex situations, for example, where there is no clear demarcation between treatment and control groups or no clearly demarcated "pre" and "post" periods. Another situation is faced when the treatment and control conditions are experienced by the same units at the same time, an "alternate outcomes" research design (Chapter 11). For present purposes, we shall simplify the discussion by assuming that most problems of comparability apply across units or through time, as illustrated in Figure 9.2.

Causal comparability may be achieved at the beginning of an analysis by *random assignment*, that is, by randomly assigning a treatment across a sample of cases. This generates treatment and control groups that are similar (on average) in all respects except for the causal factor of interest (the treatment), ensuring that X is orthogonal to all covariates. In the diagram of Figure 9.1, potential confounders (C) become orthogonal covariates (B), and are thereby "controlled."

Another way of stating this issue is to say that when a treatment is randomized the assignment to treatment is independent of (random with respect to) the outcomes under study. Knowing whether a unit has been assigned to the treatment or control group tells us nothing about whether the unit will exhibit an outcome (except what might be intuited from the treatment itself). Assignment is *ignorable* (we do not need to worry about it); *conditional independence* has been achieved.[33] A weaker version of this claim is that the assignment of a treatment is independent of the outcomes *conditional on background factors* – hopefully, those which can be adequately measured and controlled through some statistical protocol (e.g., matching or regression). Here, it may be claimed that "selection is on the observables." This weaker version of ignorability is a necessary assumption of most nonexperimental analyses, where the treatment has not been randomized. It is, of course, easier to assert than to prove, as discussed in Chapter 11.

Wherever treatments are *not* randomized, assumptions of causal comparability are less likely to hold and confounders are likely to be present. This is sometimes referred to as *selection bias* (aka selection effects), that is, bias in the assignment of X across the sample. Note, however, that selection bias can also mean something quite different: biases in a sample introduced by a biased case-selection procedure, discussed under the rubric of sample representativeness (Chapter 4). Another term for this genre of confounder is *pre-treatment* bias, since it occurs prior to (or coincident with) assignment of treatment. But this, by itself, seems rather vague. For myself, I prefer the term *assignment problem* or *assignment bias*, which lays the emphasis squarely on the problem of how the treatment is assigned. In any case, readers should be aware of the multiplicity of terms used to characterize this important concept.

One sort of assignment problem arises when subjects are allowed to *self-select* into the treatment condition. Consider what might happen if vouchers were made available to all applicants in a school district. One can imagine that those families most motivated by a desire to improve their children's education would be most likely to take advantage of the program. If so, the treatment and control groups are not comparable. A post-treatment comparison of the treatment and control groups will reflect not only the impact of the treatment, but also the impact of the confounding factor of family motivation. Without further adjustments, the causal question of voucher impact on educational performance is impossible to answer because we have no way of distinguishing the effect X on Y from the effect of C (the confounders) on Y. Indeed,

---

[33] Sometimes, a causal factor with these characteristics is described as being *exogenous*; however, exogeneity can also mean many other things (see above).

the most common source of assignment bias is the self-selection of units to a treatment condition. It is a problem in most social science contexts because the subjects of interest have decisional capacities, because they generally have a personal interest in the same outcomes that social scientists are trying to study (e.g., educational quality), and because we are often unable or unwilling to restrict the liberty of our subjects to exercise their volition.

Another form of assignment bias arises from *endogeneity* (aka *feedback, circularity, bi-directionality, dependence,* or *symmetry*) between X and Y.[34] Suppose, for example, that high-performing students are more likely to be chosen (by school administrators) for a vouchers program. Here Y affects the value of X, and the true effect of X on Y will be difficult to assess.[35]

The key point is that wherever the assignment of a treatment is not random the assumption of causal comparability is likely to be violated, which is to say that the expected value of Y given X is not likely to be the same across treatment and control groups. By contrast, wherever a treatment has been randomized causal comparability has been achieved – at least *initially*.

In the simplest analysis, where outcome measures are taken immediately after a treatment is administered, no further issues of comparability arise. However, most causal factors in social science must be observed over a period of time in order to render a precise and accurate verdict on their possible causal effects. Sometimes, the treatment itself is administered continuously over a period of time. In these circumstances we must consider additional confounders, that is, potential violations of comparability, up to the final post-test. In a study of vouchers, for example, students (or schools) receiving vouchers must remain comparable to students (or schools) without vouchers up to the point when they receive grades or test results that determine their level

---

[34] King, Keohane, and Verba (1994: 94, 108, 185) offers a mathematical treatment of this problem. Mackie (1974: ch. 7) provides a philosophical treatment.

[35] To clarify, most of the causal relationships that social scientists are interested in examining exhibit a degree of endogeneity in natural settings (i.e., in the real world). They are "mutually constitutive." For example, it seems quite possible that economic development fosters democracy and that democracy fosters economic development. Yet for some purposes – both theoretical and practical – we would like to know what the independent impact of one particular factor on another might be, or has been. That is, what impact did economic development have on democracy, *net* (holding constant) any effect that democracy might have had on economic development? Or, what impact did democracy have on economic development? Answering this question requires that we "exogenize" one (or more) chosen causal factor. Indeed, in labeling something a cause we are presuming that it can, in principle (if not in fact), be approached as an exogenous treatment. Thus, to make a causal argument about X's effect on Y is not necessarily to say that this is the way the world actually works. It is to say, rather, that this is the way the world *would* work if the conditions of a hypothetical experiment were repeated in some natural setting where X was truly exogenous.

Table 9.4 Violations of causal comparability: a partial list of confounders

Pre-treatment (aka assignment) bias

Self-selection: where assignment to treatment is governed by the subjects under study.

Post-treatment bias

Attrition: the loss of subjects during the course of a study (e.g., by mortality).

Noncompliance: when subjects do not comply with instructions, i.e., when members assigned to the treatment group remain untreated or members of the control group receive treatment.

Contamination (aka *spillover* or *interference*): where treatment and control groups are not effectively isolated from one another, creating the possibility that members of one group might affect members of the other group in ways relevant to the studied outcome.

Reputation effects: where the reputation of the treatment in the minds of subjects, rather than the treatment condition itself (as defined by the researcher), affects an outcome.

Researcher (aka *experimenter*, *Hawthorne*) *effects*: where the condition of being tested or studied, rather than the treatment of theoretical interest, affects an outcome.

Testing effects: where responses to a test are influenced by a previous test, or by expectations from previous testing experiences, rather than the treatment itself.

Pre/post-treatment bias in longitudinal studies

History (aka *trends*): where the treatment is correlated with some other factor that affects the outcome of interest, which is to say, where the variation over time under observation is driven by some factor other than the treatment.

Regression to the mean: where some change observed over time is a product of stochastic variation rather than the treatment of interest.

Instrumentation effects: a change in the measurement of an outcome (or, occasionally, a stimulus) over the course of a study in ways that might alter the estimate of X's effect on Y.

---

of achievement (the post-test). This means that random (or as-if random) assignment is a necessary *but not sufficient* condition for valid causal inference.

Violations of post-treatment comparability may be introduced by a variety of threats, for which a specialized vocabulary has evolved (Table 9.4).[36] Note that while most of these terms were originally developed for use in experimental contexts they often have analogs in nonexperimental designs. Thus, we consider them as part of a general class of confounders that threaten equivalence across units.

Attrition refers to the loss of subjects during the course of a study. Suppose that a significant number of families leave a school system – perhaps because of the closing of a large factory in that district – during the period in which a study of school vouchers is being conducted. Or suppose that subjects initially chosen for a study cannot be located for follow-up surveys (e.g., the post-test). This will affect the composition of the treatment and control groups, and thus the

---

[36] Shadish, Cook, and Campbell (2002: 55, *inter alia*).

interpretation of results. *Mortality* (of subjects in a study) is a specific cause of attrition – generally more problematic in medical studies than in social science studies.

Noncompliance refers to the threat to inference that occurs when subjects do not comply with their instructions: they either refuse to be treated (despite being placed in the treatment group) or insist upon receiving treatment (despite being placed in the control group). This issue was discussed above in the context of school vouchers.

Contamination (aka *spillover* or *interference*), which we have already addressed in the context of *independence*, refers to a situation in which treatment and control groups are not effectively isolated from one another, thus creating the possibility that members of one group might affect members of the other group in ways relevant to the studied outcome. Suppose that siblings are randomized to voucher and nonvoucher schools in an experimental study. This sort of matched-comparison maximizes pre-treatment equivalence but at the expense of post-treatment contamination, for siblings are apt to share experiences and help one another with their homework, thus confounding the conditions that define treatment and control. Another sort of contamination may occur as a result of communication among teachers and principals working for voucher and nonvoucher schools. If this communication results in behavioral changes that affect student performance, then one may have cause to worry that comparisons across treatment and control groups are not the product of the voucher system itself, but rather of communication channels that lie outside the parameters of the theory.

Reputation effects refer in this context to reputational factors – unconnected with the theory being tested – that serve to introduce a confounder into the analysis. Suppose, for example, that voucher schools gain a reputation for superior education relative to traditional (nonvoucher) schools, and that this reputation prompts an exodus of good teachers from traditional schools to alternative schools (eligible for vouchers). And suppose, further, that the initial reputation for superior educational performance in voucher schools is *false*. Yet, over time, after the transfer of good teachers from traditional to voucher schools, it becomes true. Under these conditions, any differences in student achievement that appear over time between voucher and nonvoucher schools are likely to be the product of changing conditions in these schools rather than of the voucher system *per se*. The net effect of vouchers on the school system is nil, even though demonstrable differences in school performance appear after the initiation of treatment.

Researcher (aka *experimenter*) *effects* are a confounding effect arising from unintended effects of the treatment. A famous example occurred in a series of studies focused on workers at a General Electric plant in Hawthorne, Illinois. Here, it appeared that workers in the treatment group applied themselves with greater diligence than those in the control group, regardless of what the treatment consisted of. It was eventually determined (rightly or wrongly) that workers were responding not to the intended treatment, but rather to the position of being intensively monitored.[37] Experimenter effects due to the condition of being studied have been known ever since as "Hawthorne effects." It is easy to imagine Hawthorne effects at work in voucher experiments, since teachers in voucher schools may feel that their performance is being more closely monitored than teachers in nonvoucher schools (who may not be aware of their status as part of an experiment). Another form of experimenter effect occurs whenever subjects are influenced by the demographic or personality characteristics of an interviewer in ways that affect the outcome of an experiment or an observational study. For example, white respondents often react differently when interviewed by white and black researchers, thus introducing an important confounding factor into any study in which racial attitudes constitute the outcome of interest. (Note: the researcher effect is not a confounder in the classic sense since it does not affect both X and Y, as discussed in Chapter 11.)

Testing effects arise whenever responses are influenced by the previous test, or by expectations from previous testing experiences, rather than the treatment itself. One sort of testing effect is *fatigue*, in which subjects' responses change over time simply because they tire. Suppose that standardized tests are administered to students in a study of vouchers every month over the course of several years. Here, we can anticipate several sorts of testing effects (perhaps in combination): an acceleration of performance, due to increased practice, and overall fatigue with the process itself. Under the circumstances, results may be difficult to interpret.

These sorts of confounders normally appear in comparisons across groups, that is, in spatial comparisons, as illustrated in panel (a) of Figure 9.2. Now let us consider the problem of comparability as it occurs in a *within-group* (*longitudinal*) comparison, illustrated in panel (b) of Figure 9.2. Returning to our perennial example, let us suppose that the main evidence available for the effectiveness of vouchers on educational performance is not across treatment and control units, but rather through time; that is, we are comparing student grades and/or test results prior to the institution of a voucher program with those obtained afterwards. In this setting we must be concerned with virtually all of the foregoing confounders, as these are likely to be correlated with the timing of the intervention, thus rendering our pre- and post-comparison spurious.

---

[37] Gillespie (1991).

In addition, one must be concerned with threats from *history*. One may suspect, for example, that a fairly radical policy deviation such as vouchers would be accompanied by other educational reforms – higher spending, lower class sizes, a new curriculum, and so forth. If so, then the condition of these schools is no longer equivalent (in ways that might affect the outcome of interest) pre- and post-treatment. Comparability is compromised. Indeed, it is quite common in naturalistic settings to find that the treatment of interest correlates with possible confounders. Change often takes the form of punctuated equilibrium. As a result, the initiation of human interventions is often correlated with other factors that might also have an effect on the outcome of interest, creating confounders.

Another important obstacle concerns the timing of interventions, which often coincide with unusual performance in a particular arena. Typically, new programs are initiated to address some pressing need, and the need is registered by abysmally poor performance in that area. Thus, a new vouchers program might coincide with unusually poor student test results in the previous year. In this setting, any apparent improvement in student performance may have nothing to do with the treatment itself, but rather with the return of a phenomenon to its equilibrium position, a phenomenon known as *regression to the mean*.

A third threat to temporal comparability involves underlying trends – unrelated to the treatment – that a unit may exhibit. In the simplest situation, a unit is stable; there is no change over time in the outcome of interest and thus no trend to account for. If we are studying the effect of vouchers on educational performance a simple post-test should be sufficient to judge whether the intervention has a causal effect. A slightly more complicated situation is posed by a constant trend: for example, test scores that are increasing or decreasing over time at a constant rate. Here, several measurements of the outcome, prior to the intervention, will be necessary to judge the slope of this trend. Having measured the slope, any change in slope that sets in after the intervention may be credited to the voucher program. Of course, trends are often much more complicated. They may combine a constant trend, regular cycles, one or more changes in trend, as well as random variation (noise). To sort all this out (if indeed it can be sorted out at all), one will need multiple pre-tests and post-tests. The intricacies of time-series analysis remain elusive.[38]

A fourth threat to temporal comparability arises from the nature of the measurement tool itself. Suppose that the pre- and post-tests employed for a study of vouchers consist of standardized achievement tests taken annually over the course of a decade. And suppose, further, that these tests become easier over

---

[38] Campbell ([1968] 1988); Hamilton (1994).

time. Under the circumstances, true causal effects will be impossible to calibrate. A special term – *instrumentation effects* – refers to any change in the measurement of an outcome (or, occasionally, a stimulus) over the course of a study in ways that might alter the estimate of X's effect on Y.

Generally, whenever the evidence of interest concerns changes over time within a group, one must be very concerned with any possible variation over time that affects within-unit comparability over time. While a long time-series (lots of pre- and post-tests) will assist in constructing a plausible counterfactual, all such constructions involve assumptions about the true shape of the data and are not, in principle, testable. The difficulty, tersely stated, is that "the evolution of Y prior to the treatment may not be a sufficiently good predictor of how Y would evolve in the absence of treatment."[39] This is the unobservable counterfactual that challenges the assumption of comparability in causal analyses focused on before-and-after comparisons.

In summary, there are many potential sources of spatial and temporal incomparability. Consumers of social science research should be wary of problems of attribution lurking beneath the surface of neat regression tables and/or polished narratives. This is not a "qualitative" or "quantitative" problem; it is redolent in all styles of nonexperimental research, and in many experimental studies as well.[40]

---

[39] Morgan and Winship (2007: 244).

[40] Not every incomparability poses a threat to causal inference. The exception arises where we can make assumptions about the probable direction of the bias contained in a research design (and corresponding causal model) and where this bias leans *against* the hypothesis of interest. If the hypothesis withstands this bias (it is still corroborated by the evidence), one can reach conclusions about the general direction of the causal effect (e.g., negative or positive). One can say, for example, that a one-unit change in X is likely to result in *at least* a two-unit change in Y if the testing procedure is biased against the achievement of a positive causal effect. This is not a precise estimate, and for the purpose of precise estimate it is therefore clearly inferior to the research design that manages to achieve causal comparability. However, one may regard such a research design as a "severe" (most-difficult) test of a proposition (Chapter 4). From this perspective, comparability is a problem insofar as incomparabilities are judged to run with the hypothesis under investigation. Of course, this presupposes that the researcher (and subsequent reviewers) will be able to adequately assess the direction of bias contained in a given research design. For those predisposed to perfectly controlled experiments, this may seem like another avenue to bias and subjectivity. However, if we are willing to acknowledge that all work requires some background knowledge, as well as considerable deliberation over the fit between the evidence and the analysis (Chapter 10), then the idea of judging the direction of bias introduced by incomparabilities in a sample seems matter-of-course. If we can reject a hypothesis because we judge (on the basis of our background knowledge and intuition about the data generation process) that it is biased *for* a proposition, then we ought to be able to muster such judgments when they *support* a proposition.

Causal strategies: *X* and *Y*

There is perhaps no more controversial practice in social and biomedical research than drawing causal inferences from observational data. When interventions are assigned to subjects by processes not under the researcher's control, there is always the real possibility that the treatment groups are not comparable in the first place. Then, any inferences about the role of the interventions are suspect; what one takes to be the causal effects of the interventions perhaps derive from "preexisting" differences among the treatment groups. Despite such problems, observational data are widely available in many scientific fields and are routinely used to draw inferences about the causal impact of interventions. The key issue, therefore, is not whether such studies should be done, but how they may be done well.

Richard Berk[1]

Chapter 9 set forth general criteria applying to research designs whose purpose is to assess causal relationships. In this chapter and Chapter 11 I lay out specific *strategies* of causal inference. To be sure, there is a high degree of overlap between these topics. Indeed, each strategy can be analyzed according to the criteria that it fulfills (or does not fulfill). Yet the shift from criteria to strategies is an important one. While Chapter 9 is about principles, Chapters 10 and 11 come closer to a "how-to" guide, complete with detailed discussions of specific studies.[2]

Strategies of causal inference will be divided into three categories: (1) randomized designs; (2) nonrandomized designs; and (3) strategies that move beyond *X* and *Y*, as summarized in Table 10.1.[3] Because this covers a

---

[1] Berk (1999: 95).

[2] Unfortunately, I cannot afford the time that would be necessary to explore these examples with great subtlety and detail. My attention is targeted on the main design elements, not on their findings, ancillary research designs, theoretical arguments, methods of data analysis, or contributions to the literature.

[3] A fourth approach that perhaps deserves mention involves reformulating the causal effect of a study. In Chapter 9 we noted that the usual interpretation of a causal effect is the average treatment effect (ATE) across a population. But one might also describe the results of a study as measuring intention to treat (ITT) or local average treatment effects (LATE). Shifts from ATE to ITT or LATE often involve a retreat

Table 10.1 Strategies of causal inference

1. **Randomized designs** (aka experimental)
   (a) pre-test/post-test, (b) post-test only, (c) multiple post-tests, (d) roll-out, (e) crossover, (f) Solomon four-group, (g) factorial.
2. **Nonrandomized designs** (aka nonexperimental, observational)
   (a) regression discontinuity, (b) panel, (c) cross-sectional, (d) longitudinal.
3. **Beyond *X* and *Y*** (factors other than the covariation of *X* and *Y*) (Chapter 11)
   (a) conditioning confounders, (b) instrumental variables, (c) mechanisms, (d) alternate outcomes, (e) causal heterogeneity, (f) rival hypotheses, (g) robustness tests, (h) causal reasoning.

lot of ground the material is divided into two chapters, with this chapter focused on the first two topics and Chapter 11 on the third.

Note that some of these strategies are practicable only where the sample is large; others are practicable in qualitative and quantitative settings; and a few are generally qualitative in nature. (Further discussion of the qualitative–quantitative divide is postponed until Chapter 13.)

The general argument of the two chapters will not be surprising to most readers. Strategies of causal inference are satisfactory (with respect to internal validity) insofar as they approach the experimental ideal. In this respect, there is a clear hierarchy of methods.

In other respects, the notion of a single hierarchy of methods must be hedged with caveats. Note that the utility of a chosen method rests on its fit to the question and data at hand. While it is easy to identify methodological hierarchies in the abstract what really matters is not whether one has chosen to employ a superior method, but whether the method is the right one for the job. A good observational study may trump a bad experiment, for example, one which is fraught with noncompliance or contamination, which has little external validity, or which does not shed light on a substantive issue of theoretical or policy relevance. This means that one cannot reach conclusions about the validity of a study merely by describing its method. One must look closely at the presumed data-generating process to see how it maps onto the chosen method – not to mention, the overall theoretical goals of the research.

The most important point is that the various strategies of causal inference laid out in this chapter and Chapter 11 are not mutually exclusive. Indeed,

from what is substantively and theoretically most important. However, it may in some circumstances prove to be a necessary expedient, and has entered periodically into the discussion. (For purposes of evaluating the practical effects of a public policy, ITT is sometimes more relevant than ATE, since compliance is never perfect in the real world.)

they are frequently used in tandem. What matters, ultimately, is whether the *constellation* of methods employed in a study provides strong grounds for causal inference. Thus, rather than seeing these strategies as rivals we might better view them as complementary. For heuristic purposes we introduce these strategies one at a time. But researchers who face tradeoffs among these methods are well advised to consider ways in which they can be productively combined. (For further thoughts on multimethod research see Chapter 14.)

Randomized designs

The surest expedient for solving the assignment problem is to randomize the treatment across units, creating multiple groups – at the very least, a "treatment" group (where $X=1$) and a "control" group (where $X=0$). This is one way of defining an *experimental* design. However, the latter can be defined in a variety of ways (see Glossary entry), leading to confusion. Consequently, the more precise term for what we are talking about is *randomization*.

The utility of randomized designs was established by Ronald Fisher's path-breaking work nearly a century ago, and is widely acknowledged today.[4] Of course, there are many ways to randomize. In order to illustrate this immense variety, seven common protocols are arrayed in Table 10.2. Here, X refers to the treatment condition, while x refers to the control condition. Observations (pre- and post-tests) are signaled by O. Groups are represented by Roman numerals (I, II, . . .).

The number of units assigned to each group is undefined. However, the randomization procedure is premised on the existence of a sufficient number of observations to overcome stochastic threats to inference. The greater the number of units, the greater our assurance that results obtained from a randomized design are not simply the product of chance. Thus, the virtues credited to the technique of randomization become likely only as the number of units increases. And this, in turn, means that the experimental method is implicitly a large-N method of analysis.

The number of groups incorporated into a single randomized design is also undefined. This means that a single experiment can test multiple hypotheses, instantiated in multiple treatment groups (I, II, III, IV, . . .). For expository reasons, the following examples include only the simplest version of each

---

[4] Fisher (1935).

Table 10.2 A typology of randomized designs

1.	*Pre-test/post-test*	*I*	O_1	*X*	O_2			
		II	O_1	*x*	O_2			
2.	*Post-test only*	*I*	*X*	O_1				
		II	*x*	O_1				
3.	*Multiple post-tests*	*I*	O_1	*X*	O_2	O_3	O_4	...
		II	O_1	*x*	O_2	O_3	O_4	...
4.	*Roll-out*	*I*	O_1	*X*	O_2	*x*	O_3	
		II	O_1	*x*	O_2	*X*	O_3	
5.	*Crossover*	*I*	O_1	$X_1 x_2$	O_2	$x_1 X_2$	O_3	
		II	O_1	$x_1 X_2$	O_2	$X_1 x_2$	O_3	
6.	*Solomon*	*I*	O_1	*X*	O_2			
	four-group	*II*	O_1	*x*	O_2			
		III		*X*	O_2			
		IV		*x*	O_2			
7.	*Factorial*	*I*	O_1	$x_1 x_2$	O_2			
		II	O_1	$x_1 X_2$	O_2			
		III	O_1	$X_1 x_2$	O_2			
		IV	O_1	$X_1 X_2$	O_2			

I–IV = Groups. O_{1-n} = Observations.   *x* = Control condition.
X = Treatment condition. X_{1-n} = Treatment variables.

experimental design, with one or two causal factors and only a few "doses" for each causal factor.

I shall assume that an appropriate statistical test for evaluating the impact of an intervention will be adopted. This might be as simple as a *t*-test measuring the difference of means between two groups. It might involve a multivariate model incorporating additional factors to reduce background noise. Or it might be more complicated.[5] Typically, more complex models are required whenever the desiderata of a good research design (as outlined in Chapter 9) are violated. In any case, our focus remains on research designs rather than on statistical models.

The most common type of experiment involves a single treatment that is randomly assigned across the sample, creating two groups: the treatment group (receiving the treatment) and the control group (not receiving the

[5] Rubin (1991) reviews four approaches.

treatment).[6] If properly administered, only one feature – the presence or absence of treatment – differentiates the two groups. All relevant background features should be similar, on average, across the groups. Typically, observations are taken before and after the intervention, providing *pre- and post-tests* (No. 1 in Table 10.2). The potential effect of the treatment is calculated by comparing difference scores, that is, differences on the measured outcome between the first set of observations (the pre-test) and the second set of observations (the post-test) for each group. If the change in scores on the outcome across this time period for group I is different, on average, from the change in scores for group II, if this difference surpasses conventional thresholds of statistical significance, and if other assumptions hold (as discussed in Chapter 9), it may be assumed that a causal relationship is at work.

Variations on this archetypal design are legion.

Sometimes, it is impossible or unnecessary to measure the outcome of interest prior to the intervention. Here, a *post-test only* design (No. 2 in Table 10.2) is employed. This is sufficient if the signal-to-noise ratio is high (i.e., there are few unit effects and the effect of X on Y is quite strong) and/or a great many units are available to overcome background noise (stochastic threats to inference).

Sometimes, it is suspected that the effect of a treatment may vary over time (after the initiation of the treatment), requiring *multiple post-tests* (No. 3 in Table 10.2) in order to track these variations. Indeed, wherever long-term causal effects are of interest multiple post-tests staged at regular intervals are advisable so that the endurance or attenuation of a treatment effect can be gauged.

Sometimes, it is desirable to stage an intervention across several sequences so that the same treatment is administered to all groups at different times. In varying the timing of an intervention, a *roll-out* design (No. 4 in Table 10.2) overcomes potential confounders that are coincident with the first intervention. Moreover, one is able to offer the treatment to all groups, which may be important for political or ethical reasons.

A *crossover* design (No. 5 in Table 10.2) may be employed if one is interested in testing sequencing effects. Does it matter whether X_1 is introduced before X_2, or vice versa? Sometimes, it does, and a crossover design allows one to test the possibility by constructing groups that are subjected to different sequences of treatments.

---

[6] The notion of a "control" makes sense if there is an obvious absence-of-treatment condition. Sometimes, it is more accurate to say that two treatments are being compared with one another. For present purposes it is helpful to label one of these treatments as the control.

A *Solomon four-group* design (No. 6 in Table 10.2) is intended to test for possible experimenter effects (Chapter 9). In certain circumstances, the pretest – by itself (i.e., without any explicit treatment conditions) – may shape the behavior of subjects and thus confound the results of an experiment. This possibility can be tested by distinguishing groups that are subjected to the pretest (I, II) with groups that are not (III, IV). If outcomes for group I are different from outcomes for group III, or if outcomes for group II are different from outcomes for group IV, then "testing" effects are present. The Solomon four-group design allows one to identify these confounders, and to estimate their causal effects.

A *factorial* design tests the interactive effects of several categorical treatment variables (No. 7 in Table 10.2). In the simplest version, two binary causal factors are combined into four possible treatments. If, for example, treatments consist of X_1=vouchers (–/+) and X_2=increase in teacher salaries (–/+), these can be combined into four groups by randomizing across two dimensions: I (x_1x_2), II (X_1x_2), III (x_1X_2), and IV (X_1X_2). (*X* indicates one condition and *x* indicates a second condition.)

This concludes our itinerary of randomized research designs. Note that well-established names exist for only a few of these protocols. For others, a variety of names (usually rather long and cumbersome) may be employed, for example, a "two-group design with pre- and post-tests" (No. 1 in Table 10.2). Despite the non-standard terminology, the construction of these designs is remarkably consistent across diverse research settings. Indeed, most randomized designs may be understood as variants of the classics.

If spillover (contamination) across groups is anticipated, an experiment may be re-designed so that each group is more thoroughly isolated from each other. This might mean spreading the experiment across multiple communities so as to avoid contact among the participants in treatment and control groups.

Randomized designs may be carried out in a wide variety of settings. If the setting is constructed and controlled by the researcher it may be referred to as a *laboratory* experiment. If the setting is natural (i.e., more realistic) it may be referred to as a *field* experiment. And yet there is no hard and fast distinction between these two types of settings, which are, after all, matters of degree (what is a "laboratory"?).

As for the randomization procedure, this may be carried out across the entire sample or within pre-selected strata. In the latter case, known as *blocking* (or sometimes as *matching*), units chosen for analysis are first stratified according to some background feature(s) relevant to the outcome of interest. Thus, in an experiment on vouchers one might stratify a sample of students by race, sex, age, and parental educational attainment. Within each stratum, the treatment (e.g., the voucher) is then randomized. If the strata consist of only two units each (e.g., two students), then one is working with blocked-pairs (i.e., blocks of two). This is a common technique to limit background noise wherever the heterogeneity of units is high and sample size is moderate-to-low.

Examples

It remains to be seen how applicable the randomization approach might be to the research agenda of the social sciences. Indeed, the hard methodological question is not whether experiments work (there is little doubt that they do), but what they work for. As an entrée into this issue, we review five examples of randomized studies drawn from diverse fields: (1) employment discrimination; (2) corruption control; (3) historic election campaigns; (4) gender and leadership; and (5) democracy promotion. Each will be briefly discussed to give a flavor of the sorts of subjects that experimenters have tackled in recent years, as well as potential methodological difficulties.

Example 1: employment discrimination

Employment discrimination is a policy question of obvious and enduring importance. Of course, few employers will admit to racially based hiring practices.[7] This must be inferred. For example, one might compare the racial complexion of a sector with the racial complexion of a pool of eligible workers in that sector. Or one might use a representative sample of the adult population to test (through regression analysis) the relationship between income and race, holding other factors constant. Many caveats must be attached to either approach. Have the sector and the pool been adequately defined? Has the regression analysis been properly specified? Can employers themselves be blamed for any remaining differences between white and black earnings (or between the actual set of employees in a sector and the eligible labor pool)?[8]

One genre of experiment involves sending white and black (or male and female) applicants – matched in all respects and coached to answer questions in a similar fashion – into the same job interviews.[9] If white candidates

---

[7] But see Kirschenman and Neckerman (1991).   [8] Darity and Mason (1998).

[9] For example, Kenny and Wissoker (1994); Neumark with Bank and Van Nort (1996). For an overview of this genre of field experiment see Pager (2007).

experience higher success rates, this fact may be accorded to race-based discrimination. However, this procedure – known generically as an audit study – is subject to experimenter bias. In particular, those conducting the experiments may respond to questions in a way that affects the employer's decision, but has nothing to do with race *per se*.[10]

In order to alleviate this potential bias, Bertrand and Mullainathan removed the experimenters entirely from the conduct of the experiment. Instead, they mailed out hundreds of résumés in response to jobs advertised in the Boston and Chicago areas.[11] These applications differed in one key respect: some of the names on the résumés were distinctively African-American and the others identifiably white. (There were other differences, such as the neighborhood of the applicant, but these are ancillary to the main finding.) The researchers found that applications with "white" names, such as Emily and Greg, were more likely to be contacted by employers for a follow-up interview than applications with recognizably black names, such as Lakisha and Jamal. This provides some of the strongest evidence to date of employment discrimination.

Example 2: corruption control

The causes of corruption are a central preoccupation among citizens and among scholars across the world. Yet the question remains agonizingly diffuse. Studies generally build on cross-sectional analyses of countries (or states within a country), whose varying levels of corruption are measured through surveys of the public or country experts (e.g., the Transparency International and World Bank indices of corruption). If an institution is found to correlate with a higher level of corruption (taking all other relevant and measurable factors into account), then it may be interpreted as a causal relationship.[12] This genre of work is evidently open to the same, familiar objection: perhaps it is a merely correlational relationship, accountable to some unmeasured common cause.

In order to bring experimental evidence to bear on the question of corruption, Ben Olken observed levels of corruption in road projects spread across over 600 Indonesian villages. Corruption is measured by a variety of direct methods – most interestingly, by sampling the cores of selected roads in order to determine whether materials used were standard or substandard

---

[10] For other criticisms of the audit technique see Heckman and Siegelman (1993) and discussion in Pager (2007).
[11] Bertrand and Mullainathan (2005).   [12] For example, Gerring and Thacker (2004).

(Chapter 5).[13] Two theories were tested. The first concerned the effect of an impending government audit, a top-down approach to corruption control. The second concerned grassroots participation in monitoring the road project, a down-up approach to corruption control. Each of these treatments was randomized across the 600 villages. Olken finds that the threat of an audit had a much greater effect in reducing corruption than the institution of village-level monitoring (though both had some effect).

Example 3: historic election campaigns

Traditionally, the use of experimental methods has been understood as a prospective, rather than retrospective, exercise. Because the research is designed by the experimenter, it may help us to shed light on general phenomena that pertain to the past, but it cannot shed light on particular events in the past. While generally true, there are exceptions to this rule.

The role of the infamous "Willie Horton" advert in the 1988 US presidential campaign has exercised scholars and pundits since the day it was aired.[14] In the political advertisement, sponsored by a group loyal to George Bush's campaign, a black man, Willie Horton, is shown along with a voice-over explaining that Horton was released from prison on furlough by Massachusetts Governor George Dukakis, after which he proceeded to rape a woman and viciously beat her fiancé. Was this a "race-baiting" advert, or was it really more about crime? What sort of effect might it have had on the general public? And what, more generally, is the effect of attack adverts that seek to capitalize on fear?

Tali Mendelberg's ingenious approach to these questions is to expose a sample of white college students to a laboratory experiment in which the treatment is exposure to the Horton advert, which is embedded within a news story.[15] (Students chosen for the experiment had little or no knowledge of the advert, and are thus unaware of its notoriety.) The control consists of a similar news story, without the Horton excerpt. Mendelberg finds that the advert enhanced the salience of race, rather than crime, and interacted with

---

[13] Olken (2007: 203) explains: "I assembled a team of engineers and surveyors who, after the projects were completed, dug core samples in each road to estimate the quantity of materials used, surveyed local suppliers to estimate prices, and interviewed villagers to determine the wages paid on the project. From these data, I construct an independent estimate of the amount each project actually cost to build and then compare this estimate with what the village reported it spent on the project on a line-item by line-item basis. The difference between what the village claimed the road cost to build and what the engineers estimated it actually cost to build is the key measure of messing expenditures": i.e., the measure of corruption.

[14] Jamieson (1996).   [15] Mendelberg (1997). See also Mendelberg (2001).

existing prejudices so as to affect subjects' views on a range of issues in a more conservative direction.

Of course, this study is unable to determine (or even estimate) how long this effect lasted, how many voters it reached, and how many votes (if any) it changed. These very specific historical outcomes are beyond the scope of experimental methods to explore. (Additional issues pertaining to internal and external validity are discussed in a subsequent study by Gregory Huber and John Lapinski.[16]) Even so, Mendelberg's influential study prompts us to consider ways in which experimental protocols might be enlisted to shed light on past events – a relatively new purview for the venerable experiment.

Example 4: gender and leadership

Does the sex of a politician affect his or her policy decisions? The question has been much studied and much debated.[17] However, there is little strong evidence to show whether gender has effects on the quality of political decisions, primarily because observational data is replete with potential confounders. If we simply compare the behavior of male and female legislators we run the risk of confusing gender effects with other factors that happen to co-vary with the gender of a legislator, for example, party identification, the character of the election, or the character of the district. And if the empirical comparisons are cross-country, the number of potential confounders is even greater. A recent study by Dollar, Fisman, and Gatti reports a negative correlation between representation of women in parliaments and corruption.[18] The causal question, raised pointedly by Chattapadhyay and Duflo, is whether this means that women are less corrupt (as Dollar *et al.* claim), or that "countries that are less corrupt are also more likely to elect women to parliament."[19] This gets to the heart of our topic.

To shed light on this issue, Chattapadhyay and Duflo take advantage of a federal law passed in India in 1993 requiring that one-third of all village council heads (an elective position) be reserved for women. Because the assignment of women to positions of authority is randomized (though not by the researchers), it is possible to interpret policy choices made by village councils under male and female leadership as an indication of the causal effect of gender. Prior to this, of course, it is necessary to determine what the varying

---

[16] Huber and Lapinski (2006). See also the colloquy between Huber and Lapinski (2008) and Mendelberg (2008a, 2008b) and Hutchings and Jardina (2009).

[17] Beckwith and Cowell-Meyers (2007); Mansbridge (1999); Paxton and Hughes (2007: ch. 7); Reingold (2008).

[18] Dollar, Fisman, and Gatti (2001).   [19] Chattapadhyay and Duflo (2004: 1410).

preferences of men and women in West Bengal and Rajasthan, the two states under study, might consist of. This is accomplished by examining the types of formal requests brought to the village council by male and female citizens:

In West Bengal, women complain more often than men about drinking water and roads, and there are more investments in drinking water and roads in [village councils] reserved for women. In Rajasthan, women complain more often than men about drinking water but less often about roads, and there are more investments in water and less investment in roads in [village councils] reserved for women.[20]

The authors find that these preferences are indeed reflected in the sort of public goods provided by governments in villages where a female council head is in charge – understood relative to villages in the control group, which are generally governed by men. In short, the sex of political leaders counts. Goods valued more highly by women are more likely to be distributed in villages where women hold important leadership positions.

The design features of this natural randomization are close to ideal. There are many units to study, the process of randomization seems to have been strictly adhered to, and there are viable outcome indicators by which one might judge the impact of the treatment. In short, the set-up in this experiment appears to be about as sound as one might have achieved even with an experiment that was controlled by the researcher.

Of course, the precise causal mechanisms at work in this setting are somewhat open to interpretation. Is the difference in policy outcomes between quota and non-quota villages a product of female leaders' desire to represent the interests of women in their constituencies or a product of the personal attributes and life-histories of the chosen female leaders? (Would well-off and politically empowered female leaders behave differently?) The authors try to address this question by running statistical analyses that control for various characteristics of female leaders, finding no effect. Even so, one may suspect that there is insufficient variation in these properties to provide a proper test. The general point is that once one moves from questions about the main causal effect (which is randomized) to questions of causal mechanisms (which, in this case and most others, are not randomized) the precision and confidence of the analysis suffers accordingly. (This also provides a good example of a study in which experimental and nonexperimental styles of analysis coincide.)

---

[20] Chattapadhyay and Duflo (2004: 1411).

A final point of clarification is in order. Chattapadhyay and Duflo are careful to present their research as a test of gender quotas, not a test of gender *per se*. Note that it is the gender quota that is being randomized not the gender of specific political leaders or the gender of constituents within the studied communities (of course). What one may reasonably conclude from this experiment is that gender quotas influence public policy outcomes wherever gender preferences diverge (men and women in a community want different things) and one group is politically disadvantaged. We do not learn what features of gender are driving divergent preferences, either on the part of elites or of masses. What is it about "gender" that affects public policy?

Example 5: democracy promotion

In recent decades, democracy promotion has become a major focus of foreign aid. However, there is considerable debate over how much of a difference all of this assistance is bringing to the developing world. Specifically, are aid-assisted countries more likely to hold democratic elections? One approach to this question is to examine the global correlation between democracy (as measured, e.g., by Freedom House) and the amount of foreign aid a country receives, with appropriate control variables.[21] This approach, however, faces the usual difficulty associated with the problem of assignment. Specifically, it seems likely that the allocation of foreign assistance might be related to a country's democratization prospects: donors do not want to waste their scarce resources on "hopeless" cases. If so, any estimates that one might arrive at that purport to measure the independent causal effect of foreign assistance on democratization are subject to a fatal flaw.

However, if one scopes down to smaller, more proximate outcomes related to democratization the methodological challenges become somewhat more tractable. Susan Hyde focuses on the effect of foreign assistance on the conduct of elections. In particular, she inquired as to whether election observers reduce the incidence of electoral fraud in countries where fraud constitutes a principal obstacle to electoral competition. The 2003 presidential election in Armenia offered an ideal subject of analysis, for in this election international election observers were allocated in a fashion that, she argues, was equivalent to a true randomized experiment. Hyde explains:

In this particular election, delegation leaders [from various international monitoring groups] gave each team of short-term observers a preassigned list of polling stations to

[21] For example, Finkel, Pérez-Liñán, and Seligson (2007).

visit during election day. These lists were made with two objectives in mind: (1) to distribute the observers throughout the entire country … and (2) to give each observer team a list of polling stations that did not overlap with that of other teams.[22]

These objectives were pragmatic in nature, and unlikely to be correlated with any confounders; that is to say, the polling stations visited by international monitors were similar, in all important respects, to polling stations that were left un-monitored.

In order to measure the impact of these observers on the incidence of fraud, Hyde compared the incumbent vote in districts with observers to those districts without observers. The assumption is that the incumbent party is the principal instigator of vote-buying and intimidation. On the basis of this analysis, which follows a post-test only design (No. 2 in Table 10.2), Hyde concluded that the deterrent effect of international observers was significant in both rounds of that election.

Let us return for a moment to the method of assignment. Although random-number generators were not used, Hyde argues that the choice of sites was orthogonal to any possible confounders. Under the circumstances, it seems fair to regard this as a natural randomization with the desirable characteristics of a classic experiment. One element of doubt remains: because the experimenter did not control the assignment process she may never know for sure whether it was truly random, or just *apparently* random. Of course, this is also true of a purposefully manipulated treatment; sometimes, reality escapes our grasp, even when we have our fingers on the treatment. But the closer the researcher's involvement in the assignment of treatment, and the more control he or she has over this process, the surer this judgment is likely to be. Although we regard natural randomizations as experiments in this chapter, it is important to keep in mind that they typically involve a degree of ambiguity about the true assignment principle, which must be reconstructed after the fact.

Obstacles

Our discussion would be remiss if we did not also dwell on some of the limitations of randomized designs. Some of these limitations pertain to internal validity and others to external validity (a distinction introduced in Chapter 4).[23]

---

[22] Hyde (2007: 48).

[23] The limitations of experimental methods are explored in Acharya, Greco, and Masset (2010); Deaton (2010); Harrington (2000); Heckman (2010); Humphreys and Weinstein (2009); Leamer (2010); Lieberson and Horwich (2008); Scriven (2008).

Internal validity

We have defined the experiment as a study with a randomized treatment. This means that, given sufficient units, the treatment and control groups should be causally comparable with one another (no confounders). The assignment problem is solved. However, there are still important threats to inference.

The first point to note is that assumptions of unit independence and causal comparability are not always fully satisfied in social science field experiments – or, to put the point somewhat differently, the number of true (independent and comparable) observations is sometimes less than it appears, leaving these studies open to stochastic error. Consider that most field experiments cannot effectively randomize a treatment at the individual level. In Olken's experiment, which explores methods of controlling corruption, both treatments of interest are community-wide: the suggestion of an impending government audit and grassroots participation in monitoring the road project. Consequently, randomization occurs across villages rather than across individuals. Likewise, Chattapadhyay and Duflo's field experiment on the role of gender in leadership occurs at the village level, and Hyde's field experiment on the effect of election monitoring occurs at the district level. This is not a problem if there are sufficient community-level units to sustain the analysis, as there are in these carefully chosen examples.

However, not all field experiments are blessed with hundreds of community-wide units across which treatments can be randomized. Sometimes, there are only several. Granted, the outcome of the experiment may be measured at the individual level (through surveys), and this may produce a sample of hundreds, or thousands. However, the point to remember is that if the treatment has been randomized across communities (rather than individuals) the individuals within a community are likely to share many characteristics in common – a problem of *clustering* (aka *nonindependence*). Some of these shared characteristics may affect they way they respond to the treatment. Moreover, individuals within a given community are likely to be in close contact with one another, posing a threat of post-treatment *contamination*. If either of these circumstances obtains, the number of individuals in a study becomes a misleading measure of the true sample size, which is probably better understood as the number of communities.

Problems of noncompliance are ubiquitous in field experiments. This is because, although exposure to treatment can be manipulated, many experiments require the active participation of subjects. They must use their assigned education voucher, take their assigned pill, or follow some other sort of regimen. If they refuse to do so (or forget, skip town, whatever), the treatment and control groups are no longer causally comparable.

Extreme heterogeneity within a chosen sample may also compromise results, especially if the sample size is modest or characterized by extensive clustering. Consider that some treatments may have differing effects, depending upon the characteristics of the units being treated. For example, a vouchers program may enhance the educational performance of motivated students while diminishing the performance of un-motivated students. If both sorts of students are contained within the same sample, the measured causal effect will be true in the sense of giving an unbiased estimate of the impact of X on Y across the chosen sample. However, it will give a misleading impression of the true causal effect of the treatment at the unit level. The results of such an experiment may indicate no effect across the sample, when the causal impact at the unit level is actually quite profound (though in different directions for different kinds of participants).

Finally, experiments involving human beings are subject to a variety of experimenter effects, as discussed in Chapter 9. Many social experiments are not truly blind (where subjects do not know whether they are in the treatment or control group), much less double-blind (where neither subjects nor researchers know who is in the treatment and control groups). And even when subjects are ignorant of their status they may respond to aspects of the treatment that are not of theoretical interest, thus introducing confounders into the analysis. Consequently, experimenter effects are difficult to avoid, and – worse – are not always apparent when they appear.

Thus, the magic of randomization by no means resolves all threats to inference. It does not reduce background noise, for example.[24] Likewise, it does not solve threats to inference that arise after the treatment has been assigned (e.g., noncompliance, contamination, attrition, testing effects, and the like). One must bear in mind that unit independence and causal comparability must be sustained throughout the life of the experiment. It is in the interval between the first pre-test and the last post-test that many threats to internal validity appear.

Eliminating these confounders is, first and foremost, a matter of careful attention to the details of the research design and vigilant observation of the

---

[24] Heterogeneity within a sample may be handled by (a) selecting different samples that are more homogeneous, (b) randomizing after matching on covariates ("blocking"), or (c) controlling relevant covariates (including unit effects) in an *ex post* statistical model.

research as it progresses in real time. In this respect, constructing a sound experiment involves an ethnographic set of skills and resources. One must know one's subjects and one must anticipate a good deal about what the reaction to a treatment will be in order to devise an adequate test of that treatment. Experiments cannot be constructed by rote adherence to an experimental handbook. Local knowledge, including qualitative evidence, is usually essential.[25]

In the event, some pre- or post-treatment threats to inference may be unavoidable. This does not mean that all is lost. Often, adequate corrections can be applied, *ex post* (Chapter 11). However, these work-arounds usually involve the introduction of causal assumptions (e.g., about the nature of noncompliers) that are difficult to test empirically, and which therefore compromise the confidence with which we may regard an experimental finding. Insofar as an experiment depends upon "statistical" corrections, it begins to look more like observational research, with all its ambiguities.

External validity

Randomized studies are commonly criticized for their lack of external validity, that is, generalizability. One often-cited reason is that experimental studies take place in artificial settings constructed by the researcher and not at all reminiscent of real-life settings that are of ultimate theoretical interest. This is the "laboratory" vision of the experiment, and it is true as far as it goes. However, not all laboratory experiments are artificial in this sense, since laboratory conditions are sometimes able to replicate *relevant dimensions* of reality. Recall that the purpose of any empirical analysis of causal relations is not to reproduce all the features of a real-world setting, but rather to focus on those features that are necessary to reach conclusions about *X*'s effect on *Y*. Laboratory experiments are sometimes able to achieve this trick. The trouble is, we do not always know when this simulation of reality has succeeded.

In any case, a good many experimental studies now take place in naturalistic settings, as denoted by the increasing popularity of experiments undertaken "in the field." While the stereotypical image of experimental research remains that of the lab-coated scientist, the technique of randomization is by no means limited to artificially controlled venues. In this respect, the experiment's Achilles' heel may be less vulnerable than once thought.

Unfortunately, a second structural constraint regarding external validity persists. This concerns the selection of the units to be studied. Random

---

[25] Cook *et al.* (2010); Dunning (2008c); Paluck (2010); Rosenbaum (2010: 323–324).

sampling procedures are *very* rarely employed. As such, experimental samples are generally not representative samples, at least not in the strict sense of the term. This is not coincidental. Because experimental work involves an intentional manipulation – subjects are "treated" – it is necessary to obtain consent. As such, many prospective participants are likely to demur, leaving the researcher with a less than random sample (even if random sampling procedures are employed to identify potential participants). Moreover, because *ceteris paribus* conditions must be maintained in order to observe the effect of the treatment, it is often necessary to draw subjects who are similar to one another in relevant respects. This chosen sample of homogeneous subjects is unlikely to be representative of the larger population of interest. Finally, many experiments involve a treatment that is parochial in the sense of being rooted in a particular time and place. If one is altering an institutional feature of the landscape, such as an electoral system rule, it goes without saying that the subjects under study will all have to be living within the confines of one polity. This, too, limits the generalizability of experiments, even those conducted in naturalistic settings.

An exception may be made for experiments embedded in survey instruments. Here, a specially designed "split-sample" survey is constructed so as to be identical for all respondents except in one respect – constituting the treatment.[26] This difference across surveys might involve the re-wording of a question, the re-ordering of questions, or a different framing device. In this setting, random sampling from a larger population is easy (or, at any rate, as easy as it is for traditional survey research). However, the split-sample survey is a rather limited tool since the intervention is unsuited to many theoretical questions of interest.

In summary, the feature that defines experimental research designs also tends to limit the generalizability of experiments. This means that the typical experiment is perhaps best approached as a "case study" of some larger subject. They are case studies with high internal validity (noting the caveats above and below), but questionable external validity.

This does not doom the experimental method to triviality. Because of their generally high internal validity, experimental case studies have the potential to cumulate – *if* the protocols employed in these studies are standardized, and hence replicable across diverse settings (Chapter 4). Multiple experiments on the same subject in different settings may help, ultimately, to bring a larger picture into focus if the key features of those individual experiments are commensurable with one another. In this fashion, we have learned from repeated field experiments what effects a variety of different treatments have

---

[26] Glaser (2003); Sniderman and Grob (1996).

on voter turnout (at least, in the United States).[27] The same replication may, over time, contribute to the cumulation of knowledge on other subjects of interest to social science. Of course, this will not happen quickly, or cheaply, and will require significant adjustment of scholarly incentives (which do not generally reward replication). It will also involve a cost in foregone knowledge about other subjects (since time and money is limited), calling forth a common tradeoff between discovery and appraisal (Chapter 2).

Conclusions

Perhaps the most surprising feature of recent experimental work by economists, political scientists, and sociologists is the diversity of topics that have been explored through randomized treatments.[28] A *prima facie* case can be made that experiments are – contrary to common expectations – a highly flexible form of analysis, adaptable to a wide range of topics.

How far the randomization protocol might be extended remains a matter of speculation. With respect to many questions of public policy, where the treatment is, by definition, manipulated (all policy interventions being attempts to manipulate some feature of social reality), there would appear to be substantial opportunity for randomized trials. But this depends, in turn, upon a change of attitude among politicians, policy experts, and the mass public – who must, after all, approve of such experimentation. If we are to become an experimenting society, as Donald Campbell recommended many years ago, it will require a public commitment to a method that has, until now, been viewed with suspicion from many quarters.[29]

Nonrandomized designs

Wherever a treatment cannot be randomized across units (by reason of practical or ethical constraints) or when doing so would involve a significant

---

[27] For a compilation of experimental studies on turnout see the "Get Out The Vote" (GOTV) web site maintained by Yale University's Institute for Social and Policy Studies, available at: http://research.yale.edu/GOTV.

[28] For additional examples of interesting experimental work, see Bjorkman and Svensson (2009); Finan and Ferraz (2005); Humphreys, Masters, and Sandbu (2006); Simon and Sulkin (2002); Wantchekon (2003). For literature reviews in economics see Carpenter, Harrison, and List (2005); Duflo, Glennerster, and Kremer (2008); Falk and Heckman (2009); Kagel and Roth (1997). For literature reviews in political science see Green and Gerber (2001, 2003); Kinder and Palfrey (1993); McDermott (2002). For work in various areas of public policy see Banerjee (2007); Bloom (2005); Moffitt (2004); Nathan and Hollister (2008), and the web site maintained by the Poverty Action Lab, available at: www.povertyactionlab.com.

[29] Campbell (1988: ch. 11).

loss of external validity, the next-best solution is to find (or devise) circumstances in the natural world that approximate the features of an experiment. Insofar as data generated through natural processes is "as-if" randomized (as good as, or nearly as good as, a study in which the treatment is explicitly randomized), the resulting study may be described as a *quasi-experiment* or *natural experiment*.[30]

Of course, this is a matter of degree. All nonexperimental studies strive for quasi-experimental status and the extent to which this goal is achieved is a matter of judgment (and no little dispute). Consequently, rather than attempt to distinguish between those that qualify as quasi-experimental and those that do not we shall lump all nonexperimental studies in the same general category – *nonrandomized*.

Nonrandomized designs generally involve the *ex post* evaluation of data generated "naturally," that is, without manipulation or control of the researcher. This is why nonrandomized designs are often classified as *observational*, in contrast to experimental designs. However, there are circumstances in which a nonrandomized treatment may be manipulated by the researcher. Suppose, for example, that one is able to design a study in which certain aspects of a treatment are controlled – say, the construction of the treatment and its timing – but the treatment is not randomized (perhaps because there is no way to establish a suitable control group). This would constitute an *ex ante* design – and, in some lexicons, an "experiment" (though I shall adhere to our original definition of an experiment as a randomized design). In any case, the reader should be aware that "nonrandomized" usually, though not always, implies "observational." Consequently, these two concepts are often used interchangeably in the following discussion.

Regrettably, there is no neat and parsimonious typology for nonrandomized research designs. Once one dispenses with randomized treatments the sort of data relevant to causal inference is infinitely varied. Nonetheless, most studies can be usefully classified as (1) regression discontinuity (RD) designs,

---

[30] For examples, see Angrist (1989, 1990); Ansolabehere, Snyder, and Stewart (2000); Brady and McNulty (2004); Card and Krueger (1994); Cox, Rosenbluth, and Thies (2000); Doherty, Gerber, and Green (2006); Glazer and Robbins (1985); Grofman, Brunell, and Koetzle (1998); Krasno and Green (2008); Luy (2003); Miguel (2004); Mondak (1995); Stasavage (2003), articles published in *Political Analysis* 17:4 (Autumn), as well as examples discussed below in the text. For general discussion, see Angrist and Kruger (2001); Angrist, Imbens, and Rubin (1996); Lee (1989); Meyer (1995); Robinson, McNulty, and Krasno (2009); Rosenzweig and Wolpin (2000). My discussion draws, in particular, on Dunning (2008b). How close nonexperimental results are to experimental results is the subject of a series of studies that directly compare these results, e.g., Agodini and Dynarski (2004). The general conclusion seems to be: not very close.

(2) panel designs, (3) cross-sectional designs, or (4) longitudinal (single-group) designs.

These archetypes encompass most nonexperimental research. For example, *case-control* studies may be viewed as a type of cross-sectional analysis. *Difference-in-difference* (DD) and *fixed-effect* models adopt a panel design. *Hierarchical* (multi-level) models combine analyses conducted at different levels into the same research design. *Case-study analyses* can be understood as a small-*N* version of panel, cross-sectional, or longitudinal designs, as discussed in Chapter 12.[31] And so forth.

Regression-discontinuity (RD) designs

The regression-discontinuity (RD) design may be diagramed as a pre- and post-test or post-test only experiment (options 1 and 2 in Table 10.2). There are two groups, one of which is subjected to a treatment (*X*=1), the other serving as a control (*X*=0). There may or may not be a pre-test, measuring the outcome prior to treatment. However, in this setting the treatment has not been randomized and therefore the assignment problem remains.[32]

Unique to the RD design are several additional characteristics that serve to mitigate worries about the assignment problem. First, the assignment principle is known. Second, it is measurable, prior to treatment, for all units in the sample. Third, it consists of an interval variable in which a cut-off, or discontinuity, defines the assignment of subjects, producing a binary treatment variable. (It may consist of multiple assignment variables, though this is more rare and complicates the analysis.) Fourth, many units fall on either side of this cut-off – ideally, situated at the middle of the distribution. And, finally, this assignment principle is maintained (no exceptions). If units fall above

[31] Of course, in case-study research the sample of studied units is very small, by definition. This means that inferences are subject to threats from stochastic variation, and will not be able to employ statistical techniques of control, as adumbrated in this chapter. However, the same logic of causal inference holds even if each group contains only a single case (Gerring and McDermott 2007).

[32] My exposition follows Shadish, Cook, and Campbell (2002: ch. 7). For further discussion, with particular focus on estimation issues associated with the RD design, see Battistin and Rettore (2002a, 2002b); Hahn, Todd, and van der Klaauw (2002); Imbens and Lemieux (2007); Judd and Kenny (1981); Lee and Lemieuxa (2010); Porter (2003); Rubin (1977); Stanley (1991); Trochim (1984). Comparisons between RDD and experimental (properly randomized) designs are the subject of Cook and Wong (2005). The technique itself can be traced back to Thistlewaite and Campbell (1960), though it appears to have been independently discovered in several fields (Shadish, Cook, and Campbell 2002: 207–208). For examples of this design see Angrist and Lavy (1999); Berk and de Leeuw (1999); Berk and Rauma (1983; discussed in the text); Butler (2006); Butler and Butler (2006); DiNardo and Lee (2004); Lee (2008); Lee, Moretti, and Butler (2004); Ludwig and Miller (2007); van der Klaauw (2002); Zuckerman *et al.* (2006).

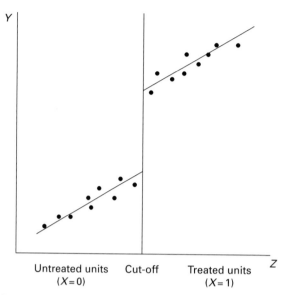

Figure 10.1   Illustration: the regression-discontinuity design

(below) the cut-off they are treated; if they fall below (above) the cut-off they are not eligible for treatment.

The RD design thus applies to a very specific, and very demanding, set of circumstances. However, if all the foregoing requirements are met, the assignment problem can be solved even though the treatment is not randomized and the treatment and control groups are obviously quite heterogeneous (in ways that presumably affect the outcome of interest).

(Minor deviations from this demanding set of criteria can sometimes be handled by further analysis. For example, if the assignment principle is not rigidly followed – if some subjects falling above (below) the cut-off are treated (not treated) – this may be corrected by the use of instruments in a two-stage analysis.[33] For heuristic purposes, we stick to the simplest case where all requirements are fully met.)

Consider the model $Y=X+Z$, where X is a dichotomous variable indicating treatment ($X=1$) or control ($X=0$), and Z is the (continuous) assignment variable. An illustration of sample data in which X has a strong effect on the outcome is provided in Figure 10.1. Here, it can be seen that with the inclusion of the assignment variable Z, the treatment variable (X) will correctly model

---

[33] Imbens and Lemieux (2007).

the discontinuous shape of the regression surface. Hence, the origin of the term, "regression discontinuity."

Regression discontinuity is referred to as a "design" because it may be implemented prospectively as well as retrospectively. Indeed, wherever the randomization of a treatment is considered unethical or unpalatable, but where some restriction of treatment (perhaps needs-based) is acceptable, a RD design may provide a good alternative to a randomized design.

As an example, let us consider Richard Berk's and David Rauma's study of the California penal system. In 1978, California extended unemployment insurance to recently released prisoners, in the hopes of easing their transition to civilian life and reducing rates of recidivism. Former inmates were eligible only if they had worked a requisite number of hours while in prison, thus setting up a cut-off point that provided the basis for an RD design. Subjects became part of the sample if they actually applied for benefits, which means that the analysis compared those who applied and were eligible for benefits with those who applied but were ineligible (presumably because they were unaware of their ineligibility). The data model assumes the following simple form:

Y: failure (re-incarceration) $=$
   X: benefits (the binary treatment variable) $+$
   Z: hours worked (the assignment criterion) $+$
   C: control variables (background characteristics that might affect
      recidivism)   (10.1)

On the basis of this procedure, Berk and Rauma conclude that members of the treatment group experienced 13 percent lower re-incarceration rates than those in the control group (i.e., those ineligible for the program), suggesting that providing post-prison assistance reduces recidivism by an appreciable degree.

A second example of the RD design is drawn from a recent study of labor unions. It is sometimes alleged that the formation of labor unions causes businesses to fail by imposing extra costs that cannot be recouped through enhanced sales, increased productivity, or changes in a firm's pricing structure. In order to test this proposition, John DiNardo and David Lee examine the fate of over 27,000 American firms over the course of fifteen years. Noting that unionization occurs as a partial product of a secret ballot election (the results of which are publicly available), the authors use this cut-off to conduct an RD design in which firms where a union vote narrowly wins are compared with firms where a union vote narrowly loses. They find that a successful union election scarcely affects the subsequent survival rate of those firms; moreover, little evidence of a causal effect on employment levels, output, and productivity is discovered. (They also consider the possibility that the threat of a successful union drive may alter the wage structure, and hence a firm's chances of survival, prior to the vote for recognition.)

Readers should be aware that a variety of statistical methods may be employed to calculate causal effects from a regression-discontinuity design. Our first example presumes a simple ordinary least-squares cross-sectional format. Berk and Rauma employ logit regression, since their outcome is dichotomous. DiNardo and Lee combine the usual assignment feature – in this case, percentage of the vote for unionization – with temporal data on firm failure to see if the timing of the unionization vote is associated with a higher failure rate. This combines evidence about vote-share with an event-history analysis. The trend among recent studies is to weight those observations lying closest to the cut-off more heavily, for which various techniques have been devised.[34]

Where an assignment rule is more complicated, researchers may decide to treat it as an instrument in a two-stage analysis, a technique described in Chapter 11. This is the approach taken by Angrist and Lavy in their study of the effect of classroom size on educational achievement. Here, government-set limits on class size (derived from Hebraic tradition) provide a discontinuity in treatment that serves as an instrument for the theoretical variable of interest: class size.[35]

Methodologists have been fond of the regression-discontinuity designs since their discovery half a century ago. Until fairly recently, however, there had been few practical applications. It is thus with some surprise that we note the efflorescence of this research design over the past several years (see sources cited above). Time will tell whether this recent enthusiasm is warranted, but for now the signs are propitious.

To be sure, there are some potential difficulties with the analysis of data from an RD design. Comparisons are easiest on either side of the cut-off; observations lying very far from the cut-off point are, arguably, quite dissimilar on background characteristics and hence inappropriate for this nonrandomized research design. Thus, decisions must be made about the size of the "bandwidth" around the discontinuity, or what weighting principle should be applied to observations that fall further away from the cut-off.[36]

---

[34] Butler (2006); Lee, Moretti, and Butler (2004); van der Klaauw (2002).
[35] Angrist and Lavy (1999).   [36] Green *et al.* (2009).

Some uncertainty necessarily remains about the randomness of the above cut-off/below cut-off comparison, as the treatment is not truly randomized. In particular, one must be wary of circumstances where participants in a sample are aware of the consequences of a threshold, and able to self-select. For example, in the RD design conducted by DiNardo and Lee, where the effect of unionization on firm survival, employment, output, productivity, and wages is tested, we must count the possibility that the failure/success of unionization drives are not random with respect to the outcomes of interest. Consider that workers in a union representation election may be conscious of the potential effect of their vote on the financial health of the firm. Management often argues that a union will put the firm at a competitive disadvantage and lead, ultimately, to a loss of jobs. Under the circumstances, workers may be more inclined to support unionization if they are convinced of a firm's strength, and less inclined if they feel that the firm is in a vulnerable position. If enough workers vote strategically on this basis, and if their hunches have some basis in fact (presumably they are familiar with their firm's market position), then the results of this RD design speak only to local average treatment effects (LATE). That is, we may be willing to believe that firms that were/are unionized are no more likely to go bankrupt than firms that remain un-unionized, but we should not infer from this that unionization – if assigned randomly across the universe of firms – would have no causal effect on the probability of firm failure. (DiNardo and Lee are careful not to over-generalize from the limited data at hand.)

Indeed, it is often the case that nonrandomized treatments have a narrower purview (a narrower breadth of generalizability) than randomized treatments because the out-of-sample counterfactual (what would have happened to firm performance if more union drives had been successful) cannot be simulated. On the other hand, one might argue that the more important question, for policy purposes, is the effect that unionization drives actually have, rather than the effect that they might have under very different, and possibly unrealistic, counterfactual conditions.

Panel designs

A *panel* design will be understood here as any nonrandomized research design in which several observations are taken from each unit and there is some variation in *X* through time and across units. As such, it might take the form of any of the experimental designs illustrated in Table 10.2, except the post-test only design (option 2). Of course, the absence of a manipulable treatment means that the more complex of these designs are very unlikely to appear naturally (by sheer happenstance). Indeed, most panel designs are impossible to diagram in a neat and tidy fashion. That is to say, X does not vary in a regular way (it may be continuous rather than binary), or observations are not taken at regular intervals. Sometimes, the weight of the analysis rests on variation through time (as is the case for example with fixed-effect designs). Other times, the weight of the analysis rests on variation across units (moving it closer to the cross-sectional designs discussed below). In short, there is a great deal of variability within the compass of a "panel" design.

In order to focus our discussion we shall dwell on one very simple variety of panel design known as the *difference-in-difference* (DD) design. This replicates the classic setting of an experiment with pre- and post-tests (No. 1 in Table 10.2). One group receives the treatment; another does not. Outcomes are measured prior to and after the intervention.

We must remind ourselves that, unlike the true experiment, the treatment has not been randomized across groups. Nor do the features of the assignment process fulfill the requirements of an RD design. Therefore, the assignment problem is quite bothersome: there may be confounders (C in Figure 9.1).

A standard econometric approach – the difference-in-difference estimator – has arisen to handle this sort of data. This estimator compares the difference in some outcome within the treatment group before and after the intervention of theoretical interest (Y at T_2 minus Y at T_1 for group I) with the difference in that same outcome within the control group over the same period (Y at T_2 minus Y at T_1 for group II). If the change from T_1 to T_2 is greater for group I than for group II (and is statistically significant), then there may be grounds for causal attribution. This estimation technique thus calculates a "difference-of-differences" or difference-in-difference.

For those interested in the corresponding regression model, the usual DD estimator takes the following form:

$$Y = B + T + X + T^*X \tag{10.2}$$

where Y is the outcome, B is a series of control variables (optional), T is a time dummy ($T=0$ for the pre-test, $T=1$ for the post-test), X is the treatment ($X=0$ for the control group, $X=1$ for the treatment group), and the product of T^*X is the DD, the quantity of interest.[37]

---

[37] An intercept and error term are assumed. For further discussion, see Abadie (2005); Bertrand, Duflo, and Mullainathan (2004); Meyer (1995). For further examples, see Ansolabehere, Snyder, and Stewart

This particular estimator is not appropriate for all DD estimations. When analyzing binary outcomes (e.g., mortality), for example, one must enlist a nonlinear estimator (e.g., logistic regression).[38] Moreover, when analyzing very small samples it is evidently implausible to apply probabilistic logic resting on the behavior of large samples. Statistical analysis is therefore impossible. This would be true, for example, with small-*N* "most-similar" analyses.[39] For the moment, we shall suppose that all the requirements of a DD estimator are present.

An example may help to fix ideas. The economic effect of setting minimum wages by government fiat has been a primary topic in labor economics for decades. And yet, despite multiple studies and a great deal of model-building, the empirical issue remains elusive. As with other social science questions, a key methodological obstacle is the endogeneity of the treatment in most extant studies. States (or countries) that set high minimum wages are also likely to be different in other respects from states (or countries) that set low (or no) minimum wages. These heterogeneous factors, relating to other labor market regulations, fiscal policy, or the character of societies and labor organization, serve as potential confounders. The institution of labor market reforms may also be a response to features of macroeconomic performance, introducing potential feedback effects.

In a widely cited paper, David Card and Alan Krueger approach this problem by focusing on an episode of policy change: the rise in minimum wages in New Jersey in 1992. Their data-collection strategy focuses on a single sector – fast-food restaurants – that is likely to be sensitive to changes in the minimum wage. Several hundred restaurants in New Jersey, and a neighboring state, Pennsylvania, were surveyed to determine whether levels of employment, wages, and prices underwent any change before and after this statutory change came into effect. Pennsylvania restaurants thus serve as the spatial control group. (Comparisons are also drawn between stores in New Jersey which paid more than, and less than, the newly instituted minimum wage. Since the former were unaffected by the rise in minimum wages, this group forms a second control group.)

Card's and Krueger's empirical approach fits the mold of the pre-test/post-test design (No. 1 in Table 10.2), since measurements are taken before and

---

(2000); Brady and McNulty (2004), as well as examples discussed in Abadie (2005); Bertrand, Duflo, and Mullainathan (2004); Dunning (2008b); Meyer (1995).

[38] For example, Lauderdale (2006).

[39] A most-similar analysis taking the form of option No. 2 in Table 10.2 may be referred to as a "dynamic" analysis (Gerring 2007: ch. 6).

after the intervention in both treatment and control groups. This is analyzed in a DD model, allowing for the inclusion of numerous control variables, in order to determine whether statistically significant effects can be found. It is determined that no differences in employment levels followed New Jersey's increase in minimum wages.

It is an impressive study, though – like all studies – not without potential difficulties. Questions might be raised, for example, about the representativeness of the chosen sector (is the total economy-wide effect of a minimum wage law reflected in the behavior of a single industry?). One also wonders about the tightness of the timeline (would the economic effects of an increase in minimum wages become manifest in the short space of eight months – the time elapsed between pre- and post-tests?). One wonders whether economic conditions in the two states were sufficiently similar to constitute paired comparisons, and whether the remaining differences were adequately modeled in the statistical analysis. It may also be questioned whether the research design incorporates enough power to constitute a fair test of the null hypothesis. Has the positive hypothesis – that minimum wages affect labor market behavior – been given a fair chance to succeed? At least one commentator has questioned whether the rise in minimum wages actually represents the factor of theoretical interest, or whether it should be regarded as an instrument for that underlying (un-measured) factor – wages actually paid to workers.[40] It should be noted, finally, that Card's and Krueger's causal argument is negative (an increase in minimum wage does *not* increase unemployment). Frequently, negative arguments are more difficult to prove in a definitive fashion than positive arguments as they are more ambiguous and wide-ranging: showing that a positive hypothesis that fails in one setting may be insufficient to prove that it would fail in other plausible settings.[41]

Some of these issues might have been overcome by slight alterations in the research design; others are inherent by virtue of the fact that the treatment cannot be directly manipulated, and others inhere in the problem of negative arguments.[42] The problem of nonrandom assignment haunts all DD designs (just as it haunts all other nonexperimental designs). One can never be entirely

---

[40] Reiss (2007: 138).

[41] Positive arguments usually take the following form: "In this setting (that which the researcher has tested), and others that are at least as favorable to the hypothesis, X affects Y." By contrast, negative arguments usually take the following form: "In no (reasonable) setting does X affect Y." The latter is more difficult to prove than the former. The reason, I think, is that it is usually easier to judge the generalizability of a positive result than the generalizability of a negative result.

[42] For further discussion of the Card and Krueger (1994) study, see Neumark and Wascher (2000); Reiss (2007: 138–140).

sure, for example, that businesses in Pennsylvania (the control group) would have responded to a rise in minimum wages in the same manner as New Jersey. If not, then the generalizability of the finding is cast in doubt. One's doubts about causality are amplified wherever the treatment is nonrandomly assigned, because one worries that there might be something about the assignment of the treatment – some unmeasured factor – that differentiates the treatment group from the control group, and accounts for their responses. More specifically, one worries that the rate of change in the outcome might differ across the treatment and control groups. If this is the case, then the chosen comparison-case (in this case, Pennsylvania) is not doing the job of a true control (or it is doing it poorly, leading to biased estimates).

Cross-sectional designs

The cross-sectional design is similar to the post-test only experimental design (No. 2 in Table 10.2); except, of course, that the treatment has not been randomized and is thus open to the sort of confounders common to non-experimental research designs. Cross-sectional designs may be applied to large samples (analyzed with quantitative models) or small samples (analyzed qualitatively). A small-sample cross-sectional design might take the form of a "most-similar" case comparison, across two or several cases. Wherever a large sample can be enlisted, a variety of estimators may be employed to analyze differences between the treatment and control groups, or across multiple treatment groups. As always, the choice of an appropriate estimator rests on the nature of the data and the presumed data-generation process.

As an entrée to this class of research designs, we shall follow Daniel Posner's study of the politicization of ethnicity.[43] Ethnic groups are everywhere, but only in some instances do they become fodder for politics, that is, lines of cleavage between party groupings. Here lies a classic question regarding the construction of political identities. Posner surmises that the political salience of ethnic boundaries has a lot to do with the size of the ethnic groups relative to the size of the polity. Specifically, "If [a] cultural cleavage defines groups that are large enough to constitute viable coalitions in the competition for political power, then politicians will mobilize these groups and the cleavage that divides them will become politically salient."[44]

---

[43] For further examples, see Doherty, Green, and Gerber (2006); Miguel (2004); Mondak (1995); Stratmann and Baur (2002).
[44] Posner (2004: 529–530).

In order to pursue this hypothesis, Posner takes advantage of the arbitrary nature of political borders in Africa, where national boundaries are largely the product of intra-European colonial struggles rather than indigenous nation-building.[45] This means that, unlike political boundaries in Europe, borders in Africa may be regarded as random elements of the political universe. The assignment problem is presumably (or at least plausibly) solved. In particular, Posner focuses on the border between Zambia and Malawi, which has separated members of two tribes, the Chewa and Tumbuka, since 1891, when these territories were held by the British (as Northeastern and Northwestern Rhodesia). As a product of this line-drawing exercise (conducted purely for administrative purposes, Posner says), Chewas and Tumbukas became very small minorities within the Zambian polity (7 percent and 4 percent, respectively, of the national population) and large minorities within the – much smaller – Malawian polity (28 percent and 12 percent, respectively, of the national population). Posner argues that this difference in relative size explains the construction of ethnic group relations in the two countries. In Zambia, Chewas and Tumbukas are allies, while in Malawi they are adversaries. This is borne out by surveys that Posner administered to villagers within each ethnic group on both sides of the border, and is also the received wisdom among scholars and experts.

Of course, a good deal of time elapses between the treatment (whose causal effect presumably begins with the initial partition of the territory in 1891, and accelerates after the independence of the two countries in 1964) and the post-test (in the early twenty-first century). Typically, institutional factors exert a small but steady causal influence over many years, so this is a reasonable way to test the theory of theoretical interest. And yet whenever a great deal of time elapses between a treatment and an outcome of interest it is difficult to reach firm conclusions about causality. And when pre-tests are lacking, as they are (by definition) in all cross-sectional designs, inferential difficulties are compounded. In these respects, cross-sectional (post-test only) designs are a lot weaker than panel designs.

In Posner's study, even if the assignment problem is solved, there are still a large number of potential confounders that threaten to creep into the research design after (or coincident with) the establishment of national borders. Specifically, any factor correlated with the treatment – "country" – is a potential confounder. It might well be, for example, that ethnicity is treated

---

[45] Posner's study falls into a grand tradition of natural randomizations in which the arbitrary assignment of borders provides the quasi-experimental treatment (e.g., Miles 1994).

differently in Zambia and Malawi for reasons other than the sheer size of the ethnic groups. Posner looks closely at several of these alternative accounts including the actions of the colonial power, missionaries, ethnic entrepreneurs, and diverse national trajectories. This portion of the study draws on ancillary evidence composed of causal-process observations (Chapter 12).

Posner does a good job of addressing the historical evidence. Even so, such confounders are difficult to dispense with, and stochastic threats to inference (factors that cannot be readily identified or theorized) are equally problematic. Under the circumstances, it might help to compare the politicization of ethnicity across small and large groups within each country, to study an ethnic group that is found in a large number of countries (e.g., Han Chinese), or to observe changes in the politicization of ethnicity as an immigrant community grows in size over time within a single country (a longitudinal design). There are many ways to skin this cat. In any case, Posner offers an ingenious solution to a difficult question.

Longitudinal designs

Although the spatial component of a research design – the variation across treatment and control groups – is important, it is not always possible to find appropriate comparison cases, that is, units that are similar to the treatment unit(s) in all or most respects except the treatment itself. Needless to say, bad controls do not control. In these circumstances, it may be preferable to re-situate the analysis from cross-group comparisons to within-group comparisons over time, that is, from a latitudinal to a longitudinal (within-group) research design. Instead of comparing the treatment and control groups one now observes a treatment group through time as a clue to causal relations. (Another way of conceptualizing the longitudinal research design is to say that the prior, un-treated state of the unit provides the control condition, as suggested in Figure 9.2.) Because longitudinal research designs consist of a single group, the terms "longitudinal," "single-group," and "within-group" are used synonymously.[46] (Readers should be aware that longitudinal also carries

---

[46] In principle, causal propositions tested in a longitudinal design could be randomized. That is, a researcher could randomly assign the *timing* of a treatment within the chosen group. This is why single-group analyses are sometimes referred to as experiments, particularly within the natural sciences and within the field of psychology (e.g., Franklin, Allison, and Gorman 1997; Hersen and Barlow 1976). However, in the social sciences the concept of an experiment has become associated with the existence of multiple groups, across which the treatment is randomized. As we have shown, there are strong reasons for this development, given the numerous confounders that threaten causal inference in social science settings – most of which can be dealt with adequately only by enlisting cross-group comparisons.

Table 10.3 A typology of longitudinal research designs

1. *One group pre-/post-test*	I		O_1	X	O_2							
2. *Interrupted time-series*	I	...	O_1	O_2	O_3	O_4	X	O_5	O_6	O_7	...	
3. *Repeated observations*	I	...	O_1	X	O_2	X	O_3	X	O_4	X	...	

I = A group. $O_{1\text{-}N}$ = Observations. X = Treatment condition.

a more general meaning: any design where more than one observation through time is available for the studied units.)

Recall that a single group may comprise any number of units. And each unit may exhibit any number of observations. This means that longitudinal designs may be analyzed quantitatively (with a large sample of units and/or a very long time-series for one or several units) or qualitatively (when neither of these conditions holds).

Table 10.3 distinguishes three archetypal sorts of longitudinal research design. The simplest involves a single treatment with pre- and post-tests. A second species of within-group design involves a single treatment accompanied by multiple pre- and post-tests. This is commonly referred to as an *interrupted time-series*. A final variety of single-group design involves the multiple iteration of a single treatment. This is known as a *repeated observations* (or *repeated measures*) design. Because these settings are similar, we treat them as variants of the same family of research design.

Note that the illustration provided in Table 10.3 gives the impression that interventions occur at precisely the same time in all cases within the (treatment) group; each case has identical temporal features. This may or may not be true. Sometimes, interventions occur serially, or repeatedly within one case and episodically (or not at all) in another. All these circumstances fall within the longitudinal framework (as I use the term here) as long as the variation of empirical interest lies within each case rather than across cases (by reason of sample heterogeneity or some other threat to inference). Another way to think

Moreover, as a practical matter, it is rare that an investigator finds him- or herself in a position to affect the character and timing of a treatment within one group (the treatment group) but not another (which might serve as the control). This accounts for the fact that there are not many examples of manipulated treatments without controls outside the natural sciences (where controls are sometimes extraneous because causal effects can be observed immediately and/or there are no conceivable confounders). Thus, as a matter of practice, it makes sense to associate the experimental method with randomized treatments across groups, and to assume that longitudinal designs will usually be constructed with observational data.

of this is to say that each case constitutes a "group" and there is no cross-group comparison; one is simply iterating the analysis for each group.

A key criterion for longitudinal designs is that the treatment be unassociated with potential confounders. Unfortunately, since there is no spatial control it is often difficult to tell whether the criterion is satisfied. Suppose that the treatment of interest is a voucher system and a suspected confounder is a threat of pay cuts and firings for teachers with poor performance. If these features are instituted at the same time, one cannot distinguish empirically between the theoretical variable of interest and the confounder: they coincide.

In addition, one must contend with a variety of other possible confounders – especially pre-existing trends that affect all observed units in common. Suppose, for example, that 100 schools implement voucher programs at the same time, and pre- and post-tests are performed on various measures of student achievement. In all (or most) schools, these tests reveal that performance has improved after the initiation of the voucher programs. While this offers somewhat stronger evidence than a study focused on a single school (purely stochastic variation can be ruled out), it is nowhere near as strong as a study that incorporates a strong control (a school that is similar in relevant respects but does not implement a voucher program). This is because the longitudinal study of 100 schools may simply be reflecting society-wide trends (e.g., improving school performance, easier achievement tests, or a changing population base of students) that have nothing to do with the treatment.

By contrast, the incorporation of a spatial control allows the researcher to test the null hypothesis directly – what student performance would look like in the absence of a voucher program. To reiterate, it is not always possible to find pure controls – in this case, schools that are similar in all relevant respects to the schools that implement the voucher program. Under the circumstances, a longitudinal study may provide the best available option.

If so, there is some hope of handling the problem of pre-existing trends (but not omitted variables coterminous with the treatment). This can be accomplished with a careful examination of the trend-line, followed by corrective action. Of course, any correcting of the temporal qualities of a time-series requires a good deal of temporal data. A simple pre- and post-test is insufficient. Where the data is rich, an extensive set of operations has been developed for "de-trending" time-series data so that the counterfactual – X's true effect on Y – can be estimated correctly. It should be recognized that each of these operations involves significant, and difficult to test, assumptions about the data-generating process.[47] Time-series econometrics, even in the most sophisticated hands, is plagued with ambiguity. If the trend is complicated – involving, let us say, a long-term nonlinear trend, a short-term cyclical trend, and lots of stochastic variation – one will be at pains to estimate the true causal effect of X on Y.

At first glance, the repeated measures approach to longitudinal analysis appears to solve these problems. To be sure, if the unit returns to equilibrium after each intervention, then each intervention may be understood as an independent test of a given proposition. A single case observed longitudinally thus serves the function of a number of treatment and control cases, observed latitudinally. In effect, one tests and re-tests a single unit.

In some instances, these assumptions may be satisfied. For example, Milton Friedman and Anna Schwartz explore the interrelationship of monetary policy and economic fluctuations by looking at monetary policy through US history.[48] The empirical heft of the study rests on four historical occasions in which the stock of money changed due to policy choices largely unrelated to the behavior of the economy (and hence exogenous to the research question). These four interventions consisted of "the increase in the discount rate in the first half of 1920, the increase in the discount rate in October 1931, the increase in reserve requirements in 1936–1937, and the failure of the Federal Reserve to stem the tide of falling money in 1929–1931."[49] Each was followed by a substantial change in the behavior of the stock of money, thus validating a central pillar of monetarist theory.

In many other situations common to social science there are enduring testing effects. Typically, the effect of an intervention is to change the unit experiencing the intervention. If so, the *tabula* is no longer *rasa*. Even if the unit remains the same, other contextual elements may vary from T_1 to T_2, rendering the second test nonequivalent to the first. This is why repeated-measures designs usually offer a poor substitute for a spatial control group.

I do not want to give the impression that longitudinal designs are inherently problematic. Indeed, they are sometimes quite strong, especially if the factor of theoretical interest is subjected to multiple independent tests. An example of this procedure can be found in recent study of employment discrimination conducted by Claudia Goldin and Cecilia Rouse.[50] We have already shown the potential of randomized experiments for analyzing the effects of employment discrimination in low-skill jobs. High-skill jobs offer a special obstacle to

---

[47] Hamilton (1994).   [48] Friedman and Schwartz (1963). See also discussion in Miron (1994).
[49] Miron (1994: 19).   [50] Goldin and Rouse (2000).

causal assessment because there are fewer positions, they are less standardized (and hence less comparable with one another), and the selection process is based on skills that are difficult to manipulate artificially (for example, through audit or résumé experiments). And yet, suspicion persists that a "glass ceiling" prevents the movement of women and minorities to the top of highly skilled occupations.[51]

An opportunity for testing this hypothesis arose recently when a number of orchestras instituted blind audition procedures. Before entering into the specifics of the study it is worth considering that a classical orchestra is perhaps the ideal prototype of a skill-based occupation. All that matters, or should matter, is how one plays an instrument. Moreover, there are shared standards about what constitutes good playing in the field of classical music. (It is conceivable that aesthetics are race- or gender-based, but this is not the general impression.) Thus, from a certain perspective, the producers of "classical" music fall into a sector of high-skill occupations that are *least* likely to exhibit discriminatory practices.

Goldin and Rouse exploit the change from non-blind to blind auditions in order to determine whether this shift in hiring practices has any effect on the propensity of women to attain positions in professional orchestras – where they were, and are, grossly under-represented relative to their presence in the general populace. The study gains leverage on the problem by looking closely at variation before and after the initiation of treatment, a point in time that varies from orchestra to orchestra. Specifically, they compare the probability of a female orchestral candidate passing various stages in the interview process (from the first audition to the final audition and job offer) prior to institution of blind auditing procedures and after the institution of blind auditing procedures. Data are collected for several decades prior to, and after, the change in hiring protocol. Thus, the comparison groups consist of (a) years prior to the change (the "control") and (b) years after the change (the "treatment"). Since the experiences of multiple orchestras are analyzed separately, this study may be understood in our terms as an interrupted time-series design, iterated for each orchestra under study.

The authors find that the existence of a screen separating the artist from the orchestral decision-makers (and thus concealing the gender of the player) increased the probability that a woman would be hired severalfold. This seems to prove the thesis that women face obstacles to upward mobility that are due to their gender only, not to job-relevant characteristics. Indeed, it is difficult to

---

[51] England *et al.* (1988).

identify any possible confounder in this research design. Of course, the analysis does not illuminate precisely why this form of gender discrimination persists. But it does show the power of longitudinal designs for estimating causal effects, at least in some circumstances.

To be sure, longitudinal designs are generally weaker than the corresponding across-group design – *if* a viable control group is available. However, as stressed, the identification of a suitable control group is not always possible. In these settings, a longitudinal design often offers the best available alternative. Certainly, it is more viable than a badly matched control.

11   Causal strategies: beyond *X* and *Y*

One of the mistakes commonly made in contemporary social research is assuming the existence of standards or procedures that are applicable in a mechanical way to evaluate data (as, say, variance explained, predictive power, tests of significance, and the like). Social science methodology should not be viewed as developing a foolproof system in which data are plugged in at one end and the best answer is generated at the other. As is the case in all areas where evidence is gathered to evaluate a theory, success is often marked by imaginative and creative efforts. This is at least partly what might be called an "art."

Stanley Lieberson and Joel Horwich[1]

We have now reviewed randomized and nonrandomized approaches to the assignment problem, and to causal analysis more generally. Our discussion has focused on the ways in which these strategies attempt to isolate the *covariational* pattern between a causal factor, *X*, and an outcome, *Y*. This pattern may be of many sorts: positive or negative, proximal or distal, and so forth. There are many types of causal relationships (as summarized in Table 9.2), and each presupposes a somewhat different covariational pattern. The key point is that *X/Y* covariation is a necessary condition of causality. If *Y* does not vary with *X*, at least some of the time and in some real or imagined sample, then *X* cannot be a cause of *Y*. Accordingly, the discovery of *X/Y* covariation may provide strong evidence of causality, if various assumptions hold.

However, the problem of confounders is ubiquitous when one is dealing with nonexperimental data. (Additionally, background factors lying orthogonal to the factor of theoretical interest may present an obstacle to causal inference if the signal is overwhelmed by stochastic noise.) Consequently, one is often obliged to move beyond an exclusive focus on *X* and *Y*. Other factors will need to be measured, and conditioned, if the covariation between *X* and *Y* is to be interpreted as evidence of a causal relationship.

---

[1] Lieberson and Horwich (2008: 19).

As prelude to this venture, we review the meaning of "conditioning" and various rules of conditioning. We do so with the visual tools of causal graphs – a key tool of causal inference, recently synthesized by Judea Pearl.[2] Using these diagrams, we then elucidate a typology of confounders that may inflict themselves on causal inference. With this under our belt, we proceed to the main business of the chapter: elucidating strategies that might be enlisted to overcome problems of confounding.

Conditioning and confounding: a primer

In the simplest setting, testing an empirical relationship between two factors, X and Y, involves *conditioning* (aka decomposition, stratification, subclassification, subgroup analysis) on only X and Y, as illustrated in panel (a) of Figure 11.1. Where both factors are binary (0/1), we look to see if $X=0$ is associated with $Y=0$ or $Y=1$ and if $X=1$ is associated with $Y=0$ or $Y=1$. If X is associated with (co-varies with) Y, we might have some basis for calling the relationship causal and some guess as to the causal impact of X on Y.

When conditioning on more than two factors at a time the nature of conditioning becomes more complex, as illustrated in the remaining diagrams in Figure 11.1.

If two factors, X and Y, are related to one another through Z (only), conditioning on Z breaks the connection between X and Y – rendering them independent of one another. Consider panel (b) in Figure 11.1. Let us say that X is an educational voucher (no/yes), Z is teacher quality (high/low), and Y is student achievement (high/low). Here, Z serves as a causal pathway between X and Y. Let us further assume that Z is the only factor by which X affects Y. In this situation, conditioning on Z allows one to analyze the X/Y relationship separately for those students with high-quality and low-quality teachers. Within the strata of students receiving high- (low-)quality instruction, one expects to find no association between X and Y – if, that is, Z is the only factor causing an association between X and Y. (If there are other factors, these will also have to be conditioned in order to render X independent of Y.) In this manner, a previous association has been blocked by conditioning.

Likewise, if both X and Y are caused by Z, conditioning on Z breaks that particular connection between X and Y. Consider panel (c) of Figure 11.1. Let us say that Z is an educational voucher (no/yes), X is teacher quality (high/low), and

---

[2] Pearl (2009b).

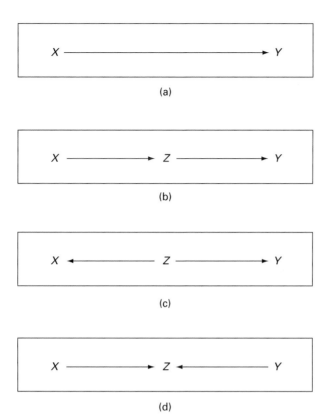

Figure 11.1   Basic principles of conditioning illustrated

Y is student achievement (high/low). Here, *Z* is a common cause, affecting both *X* and *Y*. Conditioning on *Z* allows one to analyze the *X*/*Y* relationship separately for those students with vouchers and without. Within the strata of students receiving vouchers, one expects to find no association between *X* and *Y* – if, that is, *Z* is the only factor causing an association between *X* and *Y*. (If there are other factors, these will also have to be conditioned in order to render *X* independent of *Y*.) In this manner, a previous association has been blocked by conditioning.

The exception is a situation in which an intermediary variable functions as a *collider*. In panel (d) of Figure 11.1, *X* and *Y* are both causes of *Z*. Let us stipulate that *X* is an educational voucher, *Z* is student achievement, and *Y* is teacher quality. Let us further suppose that *X* and *Y* have no association with one another (they are independent), prior to conditioning on *Z*. The probability that one receives a voucher is stochastic with respect to the probability that one receives high-quality instruction. However, both of these factors affect student performance. So, if one conditions on the latter one will induce a relationship between vouchers and educational vouchers. That is, within the strata of students who perform well (*Z*=high student achievement) one will find an association between *X* and *Y*. In this manner, an association has been created by conditioning.

Confounders

With this under our belt, we can proceed to a discussion of confounders. A *confounder*, as understood here, is any factor that might interfere with an attribution of causality from covariational evidence, that is, anything that produces a spurious or biased association between *X* and *Y*.

Readers should note that this is a capacious definition of the term. In some methodological circles the notion of a confounder is limited to specific problems of causal inference (e.g., the common cause). However, in the present context, because we are attempting to encompass a wide range of inferential problems, it makes sense to adopt a broader meaning.

With this broad rubric, seven types of confounders may be differentiated: (1) *common cause*; (2) *incidental*; (3) *compound treatment*; (4) *mechanism*; (5) *collider*; (6) *antecedent*; and (7) *endogenous*. Several of these will be familiar to the reader from Chapters 9 and 10. Each is illustrated by a causal graph in Figure 11.2. Here, it is important to distinguish factors that are measured and conditioned from those that are not, indicated by square brackets [ ]. Confounding may arise from conditioning a factor that should not be conditioned *or* from failing to condition on a factor that should be conditioned.

Note that most of these confounders take the form of "back-door" routes (causally ordered sequences) from *X* to *Y*. In the presence of back doors, variation in *Y* cannot be attributed to *X* alone; other factors are at work.[3] All confounders are associated with *X*; this is what distinguishes a confounder (*C*) from background noise (*B*), in the familiar terms of Figure 9.1.

The first type of confounder is the *common cause* (or classic) confounder, which has a causal effect on both *X* and *Y* – represented in panel (a) of Figure 11.2. For example, any vouchers study must reckon with the strong impact of students' family background (parental income and education) on their school performance. If this factor conditions who receives the treatment (vouchers) then it constitutes a common cause, for it also affects the outcome of interest.[4]

[3] Pearl (2009b), which updates earlier work.
[4] An early philosophical treatment of the problem of the common cause appears in Reichenbach (1956).

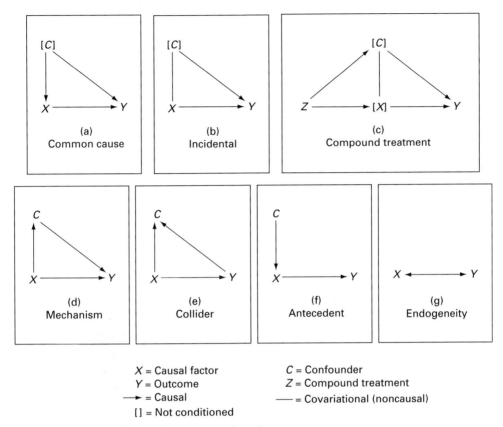

X = Causal factor C = Confounder
Y = Outcome Z = Compound treatment
——▶ = Causal   —— = Covariational (noncausal)
[] = Not conditioned

Figure 11.2   A typology of confounders using causal graphs

Although all confounders are equally troublesome in principle, the common cause often turns out to be the most troublesome in practice: that is, the most ubiquitous and the most difficult to neutralize by various conditioning strategies, as discussed below. For this reason, our discussion here and in the previous chapter privileges the common cause over other confounders.

A second type of confounder is *incidental*. It is correlated with *X* but not by reason of any identifiable causal link, as illustrated in panel (b) of Figure 11.2. This is a confusing issue since normally we associate a random assignment to treatment – that is, an experiment – with the absence of confounders. However, it is important to remember that with small samples (or with large samples characterized by clustering) the chance of stochastic error is very real. Where experiments are conducted in a small-*N* environment, unanticipated confounders may appear even if the randomization process is carefully controlled (e.g., through blocking).

In nonrandomized settings, coincidental confounders are endemic. Consider a study of vouchers in which contamination occurs across students and across schools, necessitating an approach to analysis focused on school districts within a state. This, in turn, limits the number of units in the sample. The assignment of voucher systems to school districts is not governed by any factor that would appear to affect the outcome, so there is no common-cause confounder. However, because of the way the voucher opportunity is advertised across the state, vouchers are more common in school districts in the north than in the south. As it happens, the north contains better-performing school districts, so there is imbalance between treatment and control groups on a factor that might affect the outcome of interest (school performance).[5]

Let us consider one other example, this one from the democratization literature. Suppose one is interested in examining the effect of British colonialism on democratization. It so happens that most of the places that Britain chose to colonize lacked easily exploitable mineral resources (e.g., oil) that gained value in the twentieth century. Consequently, former British colonies do not suffer from a "resource curse" to the same extent as former Dutch, French, Spanish, and Portuguese colonies. Let us assume that the resource curse is a hindrance to democratization. In this setting, as well, the confounder is incidental. The presence of oil had no impact on the decision to colonize, and yet it has a large impact on the outcome of interest.

Granted, sometimes confounders that appear to be coincidental actually have a prior cause, and are therefore proxies for an unmeasured common cause. This is, one might say, a philosophical issue, for it has no empirical resolution. However, for purposes of causal inference, it hardly matters whether C is a proxy for some other confounder or a confounder in its own right.

A third type of confounder is generated by a *compound treatment*. Here, an intervention (Z) contains multiple components, one of which is of theoretical interest (X), others being extraneous (C), as illustrated in panel (c) of Figure 11.2. Note that although the intervention, Z, is measurable one cannot distinguish X from C, as neither is directly measurable. Consequently, there is a serious problem of confounding. Change in Y might be the product of X, C, or some combination of the two.

In experimental contexts this sort of confounder is encountered wherever there are experimenter effects, that is, where a treatment of theoretical interest is accompanied by an (undesired) additional causal impetus stimulated by subjects' knowledge that they are being tested. Thus, an experimental study of

---

[5] For extended discussion see Sober (2001).

vouchers may have trouble distinguishing between the effects of vouchers and the effects of being part of the treatment group (insofar as students are aware of this). Later, we will discuss the problem of compound treatments in nonexperimental research, where it is much more common.

A fourth type of confounder arises from the inclusion of a *mechanism*, that is, a factor that is endogenous to X and exogenous to Y, as illustrated in panel (d) of Figure 11.2. In the vouchers setting, a mechanism might be the quality of classroom instruction – which, let us say, is superior in vouchers schools relative to nonvouchers schools and is a product of the voucher system. Of course, evidence about mechanisms provides important information about a causal relationship, as explored later in this chapter. However, when a mechanism is conditioned in a simple, one-stage covariational analysis it serves as a confounder.

Note that if all conditioned factors are measured prior to treatment, this sort of problem does not arise. However, it is not always possible to identify which factors are pre-treatment and which are post-treatment, especially when causal factors appear to be partly exogenous and partly endogenous relative to the factor of theoretical interest. This is what gives rise to the problem of mechanismic confounders.

A fifth type of confounder is the *collider*, as discussed in the previous section and illustrated in panel (e) of Figure 11.2. In the vouchers context, a potential collider would be a measure of occupational attainment, a factor that is presumably affected by both the vouchers experience (X) and the level of educational performance achieved by an individual (Y). (This, too, might be articulated as a problem of conditioning on post-treatment variables.)

A sixth type of confounder is *antecedent* to X, having no effect on Y except through X, as illustrated in panel (f) of Figure 11.2. The reader will recall that antecedent causes are labeled A in Figure 9.1. Here, we adopt the label C because of its threat to inference. As an example, one might consider the possibility that location influences a family's decision to join a vouchers program. Specifically, if they live near a school that is eligible for vouchers they might be more inclined to sign up for vouchers, and thus become part of the treatment group. Now, let us further suppose that "distance from a vouchers school" is not a proxy for other factors that might impact educational attainment, the outcome of theoretical interest; it is solely a factor that affects assignment into treatment. Another way of putting this is to say that "distance" affects Y only through X. Here, an antecedent factor may serve as a confounder if conditioned in a simple covariational analysis with a limited sample size.

To be sure, in infinite samples the problem of conditioning on an antecedent factor no longer confounds the analysis. In effect, one records the effect of X on Y for each value of C, estimates that can then be combined to arrive at an accurate overall estimate of X's impact on Y. By this accounting, and by Pearl's back-door definition of confounding, factor C in panel (f) of Figure 11.2 would not be understood as a confounder. However, real-world research is carried out with limited samples. Here, issues of *collinearity* must be attended to, and avoided wherever possible. It is in this practical sense that we refer to conditioning on antecedent causes as presenting a problem of confounding.

A final type of confounding arises from *endogeneity* between Y and X, also known as circularity, feedback, symmetry, or tautology. As panel (g) of Figure 11.2 makes clear, this sort of confounding is different from the previous types insofar as there is no identifiable node, C, that confounds the relationship between X and Y. The outcome, Y, *is* the confounder. If Y affects X (causally) then it will confound any attempt to estimate X's causal impact on Y.

Consider the following classic problem. Suppose, as many scholars believe, that regime type (X) affects growth performance (Y) while growth performance (Y) affects regime type (X). Under these circumstances it will be very hard to arrive at a valid estimate of X's effect on Y, or indeed of Y's effect on X.[6]

Having presented a fairly comprehensive typology of confounders using the machinery of causal graphs, let us return for a moment to the virtues of randomization. When a treatment is randomly assigned most of these confounders are avoidable, at least at the outset. (Often, confounders creep into an experiment after the initiation of treatment.) X will be independent of C and Y. Naturally, confounders could be introduced into the analysis if C is endogenous to X or C is an antecedent cause and the researcher makes the mistake of conditioning on C; but this sort of error is usually easy to identify and to avoid. The compound treatment confounder, by contrast, is not resolved by experimental methods unless the researcher figures out a way to measure C independent of X, or X independent of C, as diagramed in panel (c) of Figure 11.2. In any case, most of the discussion in this chapter is premised on the failure of experimental methods – contexts where, for whatever reason, X cannot be randomized.

Before quitting this subject, it is important to acknowledge its complexity – especially for those unfamiliar with causal graphs. However, we must also

---

[6] To be sure, there are potential solutions (several of which are discussed below), e.g., instrumental variables, dynamic models, Grainger causality tests, and causal reasoning about the direction of bias. But none of these solutions is easy or unproblematic, and the difficulties are often more severe than is presented by other species of confounders – if, that is, the degree of suspected endogeneity is considerable. (A small degree of endogeneity may not be so troubling.)

remind ourselves that the complexity of the causal graphs is a reflection of the complexity of causal inference. The role of the diagrams is to clarify, as much as is possible, what is *already* an extraordinarily messy situation, not to further complicate the situation. If a DGP cannot be diagrammed it certainly cannot be modeled successfully in a statistical format. Of course, one may be entitled to ignore factors having only a very slight impact on *X* or *Y*. But ignoring significant confounders will do violence to the analysis. Of this, one may be certain.

Strategies of causal inference that reach beyond *X* and *Y*

With the assistance of causal graphs we have set forth basic principles of conditioning (summarized in Figure 11.1) and arrived at a typology of confounders (summarized in Figure 11.2). We turn now to specific strategies that might be enlisted to overcome these obstacles to causal inference. They are eight in number: (1) conditioning on confounders; (2) instrumental variables; (3) mechanisms; (4) alternate outcomes; (5) causal heterogeneity; (6) rival hypotheses; (7) robustness tests; and (8) causal reasoning (see Table 10.1).[7]

Conditioning on confounders

The typology of confounders illustrated in Figure 11.2 suggests a simple strategy for causal inference: eliminate back-door paths from *Y* to *X* and avoid conditioning on antecedent causes. In other words, condition on [*C*] and *un*condition on *C*. This will eliminate all confounders except those caused by compound treatments or *X/Y* endogeneity.

Let us review how this works in the case of the common cause (panel (a) of Figure 11.2). By conditioning on *C*, we decompose *C* into its component parts, allowing us to observe the *X/Y* relationship within each stratum separately. For example, if the confounding variable in an analysis of vouchers is family educational background, conditioning on this factor would involve decomposing the latter into components: for example, low, medium, and high levels of family education. The covariation of vouchers and school performance

---

[7] Some of these strategies are also helpful in overcoming problems of measurement; however, since we discussed this topic in Chapter 7 it is left in abeyance.

would then be observed for students falling within each of these strata, thereby "controlling" for the confounding effect. This restores the principle of causal comparability (Chapter 9). Controlling for C, the expected value of Y is now the same for all values of X.

Of course, one must presume that the relationship between X and Y (vouchers and achievement) is similar within each designated stratum of educational achievement; if these categories are large and heterogeneous, further stratification may be necessary. The reader will note that stratification is easier to accomplish when confounders can be decomposed into simple, "natural" categories – as opposed to artificial categories such as high/medium/low that may hide a good deal of causal heterogeneity. Confounders that are continuous in nature, such as income, may be represented by a single continuous variable; however, this presupposes what is perhaps an even more problematic assumption: that the causal effect of C on Y is correctly modeled with a continuous function (linear, log-linear, or whatever). Note that the principle of *simplicity* applies to conditioning on confounders just as it does to the construction of a treatment (Chapter 9).

Conditioning directly on a confounder can be accomplished in many ways. In a simple bivariate framework, one records the association between X and Y separately for each value of C, perhaps with a difference-of-means test (comparing values of Y for $X=0$ and $X=1$ while holding C constant). In a regression framework, one regresses Y against X along with C. In a matching framework, one uses information about observable confounders to establish appropriate matches between "treated" and "untreated" cases ($X=1$, $X=0$), which are then compared with one another to reveal a treatment effect (either directly via exact matching, or indirectly via propensity scores).[8] The logic, in any case, is to hold factors C_{1-N} constant so that the true (unbiased) effect of X on Y can be observed.

A second approach to the common-cause confounder focuses on blocking the connection between X and C, rather than conditioning directly on C. This is a plausible solution whenever it is impossible to measure (and thus condition) on C or on C's parents. In the setting laid out in Figure 11.3, one may condition on the parents of X: namely, D and A. Having done so, X is now independent of E (and its offspring, C), so its covariation with Y may be regarded as providing a valid (unbiased) estimate of the causal effect (leaving aside potential problems of collinearity, as discussed in the previous section).

---

[8] Morgan and Winship (2007: 136–142).

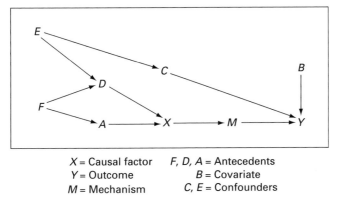

X = Causal factor   F, D, A = Antecedents
Y = Outcome   B = Covariate
M = Mechanism   C, E = Confounders

Figure 11.3   A complex DGP illustrated

The reader may wonder why conditioning on *D* and *A* – but not *D* alone – is necessary. Recall from our earlier discussion that conditioning along a causal path breaks the relationship between two factors on either side of the conditioned factor *unless* the conditioned factor is a collider. In Figure 11.3, *D* is a collider, since both *F* and *E* are causes of *D*. This means that by conditioning on *D* we open up a back-door path from *X* to *Y* through *A*–*F*–*D*–*E*–*C*–*Y*. And this back door will serve as a confounder in any attempt to measure *X*'s impact on *Y* unless we also condition on *A*, which blocks the path.

How effective is the strategy of conditioning on confounders (aka conditional-covariation, or avoiding back-door paths)? In principle, statistical adjustments can solve the problem of causal attribution, neutralizing confounders by blocking back-door paths from *X* to *Y*. Under these circumstances, the observed covariation of *X* and *Y* should offer a valid and perhaps even relatively precise estimate of the causal effect. However, there are many reasons to doubt.

Note that causal graphs represent assumptions about the world, assumptions that may or may not represent the true DGP accurately. This is the key problem. One does not know what is really going on, and in the absence of this information one cannot devise a correct modeling strategy (more precisely, one cannot know when one has found it).

Recall that in a properly designed and implemented experiment there are no confounders, for all potential confounders have been distributed evenly across the treatment and control groups. They are balanced, and therefore are represented as *B* (orthogonal covariates) rather than *C* (confounders) in Figure 9.1. This is somewhat deceptive, given that experimental data analysis often includes covariates (*B*). The critical point is that these covariates are included in the model for the purpose of improving model fit, that is, enhancing precision, rather than for the purpose of achieving validity (alleviating bias). This is a relatively modest role. In principle, the inclusion or exclusion of covariates in an analysis of experimental data should have no impact on the measured causal effect of X on Y – precisely because these covariates are independent of (uncorrelated with) X. This, in turn, means that specification issues are of minor importance in experimental studies. The burden carried by statistical analysis is comparatively light and relatively straightforward whenever the treatment has been randomized (assuming, as always, that no additional confounders have crept into the analysis post-treatment).

By contrast, with a *non*randomized treatment, control variables are expected to play a much more important – some would say heroic – role: purging the analysis from otherwise confounding influences. As we have stressed repeatedly, there is a world of difference between covariates that lie orthogonal to X (B) and those that are correlated with X (C). Outside the framework of a well-conducted experiment one has no way to verify that one has correctly identified, measured, and modeled (conditioned) all confounders. The specification problem is extreme.

Of course, one need not actually measure each confounder; it is sufficient to have conditioned on proxies or on intermediate variables that lie on a given path to Y. For example, in Figure 11.3 one may condition on either E or C. Alternatively, one could condition on proxies for these factors – as long as the association between the proxy and the unobserved variable is fairly strong.

Still, one has no way to ensure that one has correctly conditioned on all confounders or their proxies. Note that any factor that cannot be measured, such as parental involvement, cannot be conditioned, and therefore remains at the level of an assumption. Motivational factors are perhaps the most obdurate confounders precisely because they resist measurement and are often critical to both the assignment of X and the outcome of concern, Y.

Even for factors that can be measured there is no way to prove that they are, in fact, confounders. Of course, one can measure their correlation with X. But proving their causal impact on Y is a problem of causal attribution in and of itself, involving all the usual problems of causal assessment. Under the circumstances, one has no recourse except to make assumptions about how the world works.

One might suppose that in the business of neutralizing potential confounders, more is merrier. That is, the more factors one can condition on in a statistical model the more likely it is that one will successfully neutralize (block) confounders, thereby arriving at a valid estimate of X's impact on Y. However, there is little safety in numbers (i.e., in "packed" models).[9]

---

[9] Clarke (2005).

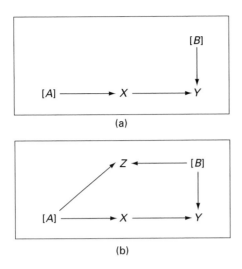

X = Causal factor A = Antecedent cause
Y = Outcome B = Orthogonal covariate
Z = Collider   [] = Not conditioned

Figure 11.4   The intractable problem of colliders

Consider the situation depicted in panel (a) of Figure 11.4, where we find an antecedent cause, A, and an orthogonal covariate, B. Neither of these is measurable (perhaps because they are not clearly identified). However, their absence from the model does not cause a problem for valid inference because no back-door routes exist from X to Y. However, let us suppose that the wary researcher suspects that back-door paths may be present – perhaps from A to Y (in which case A is a common-cause confounder, C, rather than an antecedent cause). In order to alleviate this perceived problem, the researcher introduces another control variable, Z, that is intended to block the path of the unmeasured confounder. However, as it happens, Z functions as a collider – it is affected by both A and B – and therefore introduces a back-door path from X to Y, as illustrated in panel (b) of Figure 11.4. In this fashion, a back door is created where none may have existed in the data-generating process.[10]

Note that the problem persists even if the researcher's hunch is correct: that A is a confounder (C) rather than an orthogonal covariate. In this scenario, one problem is solved by the introduction of Z (C's back-door path to Y), but another is created (the back-door path from B to Y). A common setting in which this issue arises is when lagged dependent variables are introduced as

---

[10] Pearl (2009b) refers to this as an M-structure, which it is if the diagram is drawn with A sitting on top of X rather than to the left of X.

a way of modeling temporal autocorrelation. If Y lagged is affected by both C and B, a back door is introduced.[11]

Instrumental variables

In many situations it is impossible to neutralize confounders simply by blocking back-door paths from Y to X. Suspected common-cause confounders may be difficult to identify or to measure (which amounts to much the same thing). This leads to a wide-ranging discussion of alternative strategies of causal inference, ones that stretch beyond X, Y, and C. Although these alternative approaches are by no means unproblematic, sometimes they offer the best available route to causal inference.

A common-cause confounder can be overcome if a suitable proxy, or *instrument*, for X can be identified. In Figure 11.5, the antecedent causal factor, A, may be regarded as an instrument for X if: (a) A is strongly correlated with X (either because it is a direct cause of X or is associated with some unmeasured cause of X); (b) A (and whatever unmeasured cause it is associated with) has no causal impact on Y except through X (the *exclusion restriction*); and (c) there are no unconditioned confounders associated with the relationship between A and Y.[12] In brief, a good instrument is one in which the A/Y relationship compensates for defects exhibited in the X/Y relationship.

How does this work in practice? Let us consider a simple example based on ordinary least-squares – specifically, *two-stage least-squares* – analysis. In the

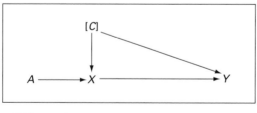

X = Causal factor A = Antecedent (instrument)
Y = Outcome C = Confounder
[ ] = Not conditioned

Figure 11.5   Instrumental variable strategy

[11] For further discussion and a more detailed example, see Morgan and Winship (2007: 179–181).

[12] For discussions of the IV estimator, see Angrist and Krueger (2001); Angrist, Imbens, and Rubin (1996); Bartels (1991); Dunning (2008b). For examples of this technique in action, see Angrist (1989, 1990); Angrist and Krueger (1991); Edin, Fredrickson, and Åslund (2003); Miguel, Satyanath, and Sergenti (2004); Neal (1997), and Acemoglu, Johnson, and Robinson (2001), discussed in the text.

first stage, X is regressed against the instrument, A, along with any relevant covariates (additional predictors of X). Recall that A may represent a single variable or a vector of variables. In the second stage, Y is regressed against the fitted values from this model, assumed to represent X purged of bias, along with the covariates. Problems caused by confounders (C) are thereby obviated, at least in principle. Note that because this procedure assigns units imperfectly into treatment – there is some noncompliance, perhaps quite a lot – the causal effect is best understood as a local average treatment effect (LATE) rather than an average treatment effect (ATE). (These technical terms were introduced at the outset of Chapter 9.) It allows one to estimate the causal effect for units which are introduced to the treatment via the chosen instrument.

A recent influential application of instrumental variables (IV) addresses the classic question of long-term economic development. Why are some countries so much richer today than others? Acemoglu, Johnson, and Robinson (hereafter AJR) suggest that a principal factor affecting secular-historical growth rates is the quality of institutions, that is, the strength of property rights.[13] The methodological obstacle is that we have at our disposal no measure of institutional quality that is assigned in a fashion that is random with respect to economic development. Wealth and good institutions tend to go together. In order to surmount this difficulty, AJR constructed the following causal story. Over the past several centuries, European colonial powers established strong property rights protection in some parts of the world (e.g., North America) and not in others (e.g., most of Africa and Latin America). Schematically, they protected property rights in areas where large numbers of Europeans decided to settle and instituted "extractive" regimes in areas where Europeans were outnumbered by indigenous populations. This, in turn, was a factor of geographic circumstances, such as the prevalence of tropical disease, which determined the likelihood of European survival in Africa, Asia, and the New World. Europeans settled, and thrived, where they had high survival rates. Estimates of varying mortality rates for European settlers in the course of the nineteenth century thus provide a suitable instrument for patterns of colonial settlement and, ultimately, for the quality of institutions that AJR presume the colonists are responsible for. This allows for a two-stage analysis, which may be simplified as follows:

$$X = A + B + U_1 \tag{11.1}$$

$$Y = \overline{X} + B + U_2 \tag{11.2}$$

---

[13] Acemoglu, Johnson, and Robinson (2001).

where X=property rights measured in the late twentieth century (expropria-
tion risk), A=the instrument (European settler mortality), B=covariates (other
causes of Y), Y=per capita GDP, $\overline{X}$=the fitted values from Equation (1), and
U=error terms for the two equations. (Intercepts are omitted.)

As with other corrections for nonrandomized treatments, the IV technique
is not without its difficulties. Indeed, the three assumptions outlined above
seem rarely to be fully satisfied in empirical work.[14] The chosen instrument,
A, may be weakly correlated with the theoretical variable of interest, X; A
may have an effect on the outcome, Y, *other than* through X; or there may be a
common cause operating on both A and Y (an unconditioned confounder). As
with most modeling assumptions, these potential violations are difficult to
test,[15] and perhaps best viewed as theoretical priors. For example, in the study
explored above, critics have suggested that a common cause – geography –
affects both settler mortality and current levels of economic development in
ways not mediated by property rights.[16] If this story about the data-generating
process is true then the chosen instrument is not valid. Even so, the two-stage
analysis is probably more convincing than any conceivable one-stage analysis
for this particular problem; in this respect, and to this extent, the IV approach
is useful.

Mechanisms

The role of mechanisms in causal theorizing was discussed in Chapter 8. Here,
we focus on the role of mechanisms (M) in causal analysis, variously referred
to as process tracing, process analysis, causal narrative, colligation, congruence, contiguity, discerning, intermediate processes, or microfoundations.[17]

---

[14] Dunning (2008b); Reiss (2007: ch. 7); Rosenzweig and Wolpin (2000).   [15] Murray (2006).
[16] McArthur and Sachs (2001).
[17] Terms and associated works are as follows: "process-tracing" (George and McKeown 1985: 34ff);
"discerning" (Komarovsky 1940: 135–146); "process analysis" (Barton and Lazarsfeld 1969); "pattern-
matching" (Campbell 1975); "microfoundations" (Little 1998); "causal narrative" (Abbott 1990, 1992;
Abrams 1982; Aminzade 1992; Bates *et al.* 1998; Griffin 1992, 1993; Katznelson 1997; Kiser 1996; Mink
1987; Quadagno and Knapp 1992; Roth 1994; Rueschemeyer and Stephens 1997; Sewell 1992, 1996;
Somers 1992; Stone 1979; Stryker 1996; Watkins 1994); "congruence" (George and Bennett 2005);
"colligation" (Roberts 1996); "intermediate processes" (Mill [1943] 1872). For general discussion see
Bennett (1999); Brown (1984: 228); Collier and Mahoney (1996: 70); Goldstone (1997). For
philosophical discussion in the "realist" tradition, see Bhaskar ([1975] 1978); Harre (1972); McMullin
(1984); Salmon (1984). The idea of process-tracing is also similar to judgments about context, which
often play an important role in causal inference (Fenno 1986; Goodin and Tilly 2006). Note that when
invoking "context" one is invoking an idea of how X influences Y – or not – within a particular setting.
Thus, I treat the broad category of contextual evidence as a species of process tracing.

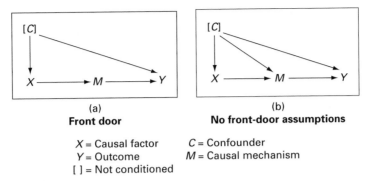

(a)   (b)
Front door   **No front-door assumptions**

X = Causal factor   *C* = Confounder
Y = Outcome   *M* = Causal mechanism
[ ] = Not conditioned

Figure 11.6 Mechanismic strategies

Because the latter terms have additional connotations, which may or may not be appropriate in the present context, I avoid them here.

In some scenarios, *M* may allow for an unbiased estimate of causal effects (at least in the limited sense of LATE) when a treatment of theoretical interest is plagued by potential confounders. Judea Pearl calls this the *front-door* approach to estimation, as illustrated in panel (a) of Figure 11.6. This strategy is practicable if (a) vector *M* serves as the exclusive and exhaustive pathway(s) between *X* and *Y*; (b) the components of *M* (if any) are isolated from one another (they do not have any reciprocal causal impact) and independently measurable; and (c) any confounders (*C*) affecting *X* do not directly affect *M*.[18]

As an example, let us imagine that we wish to determine whether smoking causes cancer – until recently, a much-debated proposition.[19] While the correlation between these two factors is high, there are, of course, many possible confounders. Perhaps people who smoke are also prone to other risky actions that expose them to a greater risk of cancer. Or perhaps the same genetic predisposition that leads them into addiction also causes them to contract cancer at a later age. As such, the question is unproven, and perhaps unprovable, since we are at present unable to measure these genetic predispositions, or the health-averse behavior patterns that might serve to enhance the risk of cancer (independent of smoking). And, for obvious reasons, we are unable to randomize the treatment (smoking). Yet, if it is the case that smoking always causes a build-up

[18] This account is based largely on Morgan and Winship (2007: 182–184, 224–230), which, in turn, builds on Pearl (2000).
[19] Pearl (2000: 83–84).

of tar in the lungs, there are no other causes of tar, and tar is a proximate cause of cancer, we may be able to estimate the enhanced risk of cancer that comes with smoking by targeting this causal mechanism. This would involve a simple two-stage analysis, allowing us to disregard any confounding effects (from genetics and/or behavior patterns): (1) smoking → tar and (2) tar → cancer.

Unfortunately, good front-door set-ups are relatively rare. This is especially true for the social sciences, where one suspects that violations of these demanding criteria ((a)–(c), as enumerated above) are the rule rather than the exception. Suppose that the suspected confounder affects X and Y, and also M, as diagramed in panel (b) of Figure 11.6. Here, we are faced with a more difficult empirical scenario. Yet even here mechanismic evidence may serve as a complement (though not a substitute) for covariational evidence about X and Y.

This is the general approach suggested by Adam Glynn and Kevin Quinn.[20] As an example, they explore the following question: what impact (if any) does the availability of same-day registration (the option of registering to vote on any day prior to, or including, election day) have on voting turnout rates among African-Americans? In recent years, some American states have instituted same-day registration, while others continue to require registration in advance (usually a month or two) of an election. The intention of the election law reform is to enhance turnout. And yet there is considerable debate about whether, or to what extent, these reforms are effective.[21]

The standard approach to this problem utilizes information about registration laws (either same-day or delayed) and turnout (voted or did not vote), along with any potential confounders that can be readily measured. In this fashion, a relationship between X (registration laws) and Y (turnout) can be inferred. While there is nothing necessarily wrong with the conditioning-on-confounders approach, it neglects information about the causal process at work. Note that in order to vote an individual must have registered to vote. Registration thus serves as a necessary condition of voting. In order for $Y=1$ (vote), M must be equal to 1 (registered). And yet registration is not a sufficient condition of voting. Some registered voters do not turn out to vote, despite having the statutory right to do so. These nonvoters are evidently not deterred by registration laws. In the standard conditioning-on-confounders model this information is ignored; one examines only the treatment (whether one lives in an early-registration state or a same-day registration state) and the outcome (vote/not vote). Glynn and Quinn

---

[20] Glynn and Quinn (2011). See also Imai, Keele, and Tingley (2010); Imai, Keele, Tingley, and Yamamoto (2010).
[21] Highton (2004).

propose a Bayesian potential-outcomes framework in which information about this intermediate variable can be incorporated into the analysis, bolstering the usual evidence about *X* and *Y*.

Information about causal mechanisms is often integrated in a less formal manner – perhaps because *M* is not easily measured, or can be measured only for a small and perhaps unrepresentative subsample of the population of interest. Even so, this sort of information is not incidental. To the extent that we are given a peek into the black box of causation – what goes on *in between* *X* and *Y* – we are more likely to be convinced that *X* actually does (or does not) cause *Y*. Consider the question of vouchers in a situation where traditional covariational methods are unavailing (even with statistical adjustments). Let us suppose that there is no causal mechanism like "tar" that exhibits the necessary conditions for precise estimation of causal effects. And yet let us also suppose that there are several observable implications of the theory that ought to be true if the theory is true, and are unlikely to be the product of common causes. For example, we might find that recipients of vouchers show higher class attendance, do more homework, and have higher self-reported levels of ambition and enthusiasm. We might also find that teachers who have work experience at both voucher and nonvoucher institutions report that the former are better teaching vehicles. Insofar as these findings cannot be attributed to some other factor (e.g., self-selection of students and teachers), we are likely to regard them as providing strong evidence for the proposition that vouchers improve the quality of education. Likewise, insofar as such mechanismic evidence is absent (we find no difference in these factors across students and teachers in voucher and nonvoucher institutions), we are less likely to accept the proposition.

Equally important, information about mechanisms helps to build theory. Indeed, insight into causal mechanisms is virtually inseparable from causal explanation, as discussed in Chapter 8. Consider again the question of vouchers. Let us suppose that a bevy of well-constructed studies (e.g., randomized field trials) have shown a positive relationship between school vouchers and student achievement, and opinion within the field of scholars has shifted: vouchers work. Even so, it matters *why* vouchers have improved student performance on achievement tests, not merely that they have done so. Identifying the causal mechanism is critical to advancing our understanding of educational achievement, as well as to future policy innovations in this area. Policymakers need to know, in this instance, what *about* vouchers has improved the quality of schools in these experimental tests in order to devise the most effective school reforms. The operative ingredient of a vouchers program might be (a) the introduction of competition into the school system, (b) the greater flexibility afforded to teachers in nontraditional schools, (c) the enhanced responsibility that parents feel toward their child's schooling, or (d) any number of additional factors. Each suggests a differently crafted vouchers policy, or perhaps even a reform *not* centered on vouchers. A finding that is not explainable is less likely to advance the field or to improve the quality of public policy. It has less generalizability. Moreover, skeptics of the voucher scheme are likely to remain doubtful about the finding itself – both its internal and external validity – until it can be adequately explained.[22]

Investigations into causal mechanisms thus serve multiple functions. They may help to identify a causal effect and they most assuredly help to identify the reason for that causal effect, the generative force that is causality at work.

Alternate outcomes

A quite different approach to the common-cause confounder involves an alteration of the chosen comparison – from variation across units or through time to variation across *alternate outcomes*. (This may also be referred to as a *within-unit* or *nonequivalent dependent variables* design.[23]) There are three variants, illustrated in the panels of Figure 11.7.

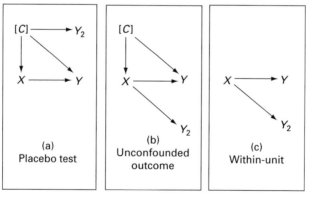

X = Causal factor
Y = Outcome of theoretical interest
[ ] = Not conditioned

C = Confounder
Y_2 = Secondary outcome

Figure 11.7 Alternate outcomes

[22] Obstacles to mechanism-centered causal analysis are explored in Gerring (2008, 2010).
[23] See Cook and Campbell (1979); Green *et al.* (2009); Marquart (1989); McSweeny (1978); Minton (1975); Reynolds and West (1987); Ross, Campbell, and Glass (1970); Shadish, Cook, and Campbell (2002: 152, 184); Trochim (1985, 1989).

Suppose one is interested in studying the impact of a new foreign language enrichment program that focuses on a specific language, say Russian, as measured through standardized language competency tests. The program is run parallel to whatever normal classroom curriculum exists, which means that the students in the program are studying Russian in a normal school setting as well as in the enrichment program. The conventional research design compares the treatment group (those attending the enrichment program and regular classes in Russian) with the control group (those attending only the regular language instruction in Russian). This "covariational" research is, of course, subject to common-cause confounders. Students who select-in to the treatment are likely to be more motivated and/or more intelligent than those students left in the control group, as illustrated in panel (a) of Figure 11.7 (ignoring Y_2).

In order to gauge the presence of the confounder, and to estimate its possible impact, let us shift our focus to an alternate outcome that is also presumably affected by C. In the context of our example such an outcome might be another language program, for example, Hungarian, administered through the regular curriculum. Students attending both the enrichment program in Russian, the regular class in Russian, and the regular class in Hungarian are subject to the same confounders (e.g., native intelligence and/or motivation). Consequently, any differences found in the rate of improvement across both languages would be attributable only to the enrichment program itself, rather than to the confounder. If these differences match the differences found in the conventional comparison between the treatment and control group then one may conclude that the enrichment program has had its desired effect, understood as an ATE. If, on the other hand, there is no difference between the rate of improvement for students in the treatment group across the two languages, then presumably any differences discovered between the treatment and control group are spurious – the product of confounders rather than the treatment itself. This strategy is sometimes referred to as a *placebo test*, and is illustrated in panel (a) of Figure 11.7.

An example in practice comes from a recent public health study of highly active antiretroviral therapy (HAART). As explained by the authors, "HAART stops HIV replication on a sustained basis and, as a result, plasma HIV-1 RNA concentrations (... viral load) typically become undetectable. This change allows for immune reconstitution to take place, leading to long-term disease remission and aversion of the otherwise fatal course."[24] This particular study has as its aim the measurement of HAART's impact on AIDS transmission

---

[24] Montaner *et al.* (2010: 1).

across the population of British Columbia. Representative surveys of the province indicate that between 1996 and 2009, the number of individuals receiving HAART increased from 837 to 5,413, while the number of new HIV diagnoses fell from 702 to 338 (annually). This strong X/Y correlation is nonetheless subject to a variety of confounders, including the very real possibility that the marked decrease in new HIV cases is attributable to behavioral changes – a possible secondary effect of the HAART campaign – rather than to HAART's physiological impact on the rate of transmission. In discussing this threat to causal inference the authors note that "rates of sexually transmitted infections *increased* during the last 15 years of our study, which implies that our findings cannot be accounted for by decreasing sexual HIV risk behavior."[25] Here, sexually transmitted infections perform the function of a placebo test, a secondary outcome (Y_2) that allows us to check on the probability of confounding in the X/Y relationship of theoretical interest.

A second variant of the alternate outcomes design attempts to identify an alternate outcome, Y_2, that is assumed to correlate with Y_1, but is free of confounding. Imagine an educational program in the United States that teaches English as a second language (ESL). In order to evaluate the impact of the program the researcher adopts a longitudinal design, for it is difficult to identify a suitable control group. Thus, participants in the program are tested for English proficiency at the beginning of the course and again at the end of the course, a simple pre- and post-test design. A potential confounder is the presence of other channels by which students might learn to speak English. They are, after all, living in an English-speaking country and are exposed to the language in other venues, for example, television, radio, work, and any relationships they might have with Anglophones. If the pre-/post-test design reveals a treatment effect this might be the product of the course and/or of various confounders (from which subjects cannot be isolated). Now, let us say that we know something about the mechanism of language attainment, namely, that a person learns to speak with an accent that mimics the accent to which he or she is most commonly exposed. And let us suppose that the accents displayed by English instructors in this course are different from those in evidence in the society at large. Specifically, let us suppose that instructors are from England, and therefore speak with a British accent, while all other sources of English (television, radio, casual conversation) are accompanied by an American inflection. Under these circumstances, the accents with which students speak English demarcate true treatment effects from confounder effects. If they learn to speak with a British

25 Montaner *et al.* (2010: 7) (emphasis added).

accent they are presumably learning from the course; if they learn to speak with an American accent they are presumably learning from other sources. Accent serves as the unconfounded alternate outcome, Y_2, in panel (b) of Figure 11.7.

A third variant of the alternate outcomes strategy leaves aside the control group entirely, focusing simply on alternate outcomes for the subjects in the treatment group. To illustrate this, we return to our earlier example focused on Russian-language acquisition. In this scenario, we might choose to measure change in performance over time for students across two outcomes, one understood as the treatment condition (Russian) and the other understood as the control condition (Hungarian), as illustrated in panel (c) of Figure 11.7. Note that these are *conditions*, not *groups*, as in a standard research design. Note also that the resulting causal effect now pertains only to students who select-in to treatment, not to the population at large: ATT rather than ATE.

A perfect setting for the latter strategy would be one in which subjects are in the same year of instruction for both languages – Russian and Hungarian – and one compares rates of improvement in these two languages over time. Here, a difference-in-difference (DD) estimator (introduced in Chapter 10) may be appropriate to measure the impact of the program on performance. However, if students are at different stages of instruction in each language, or if it is feared that these languages are not causally comparable (one might respond more strongly to outside-the-classroom instruction than the other), then one may enlist average classroom performance (for students *not* in the enrichment program) as a baseline by which to measure the student's change in performance between pre- and post-tests. This sort of estimator may be referred to as DD for treated units relative to DD for untreated units, or difference-in-difference-in-differences (DDD).[26]

The key point is that if ΔY (performance on Russian-language tests) is different from ΔY_2 (performance on Hungarian-language tests) this difference is unlikely to be the product of a common-cause confounder, since most such confounders affect units at large (persons) and would not be expected to have a differential impact on different outcomes experienced by the same person at the same time, that is, Y and Y_2.

To reiterate, the within-unit approach to research design utilizes a single unit to embody both treatment and control conditions. However, unlike the longitudinal designs discussed in Chapter 10, treatment and control conditions are administered simultaneously, obviating threats from history (factors correlated with X in time that might also affect Y).

[26] Wooldridge (2007).

A key assumption is that X affects Y but not Y_2. If, in the previous example, participation in a Russian-language program improved students' motivation or study habits, with spillover effects on educational attainment in other areas (e.g., Hungarian), then the analysis breaks down. The effect of X on Y must be partitioned from Y_2, as diagramed in panel (c) of Figure 11.7.

Judith Huber Minton utilizes this approach to test the impact of *Sesame Street*, the famed production of the Children's Television Workshop, on literacy. Specifically, for kindergarteners under study, she compares improvements in understanding the alphabet for letters taught on *Sesame Street* (Y) with improvements for letters not taught extensively on *Sesame Street* (Y_2). It is discovered that improvement in the taught letters is significantly greater than improvement for non-taught letters. This effectively eliminates a large set of potential confounders, for example, those associated with parents, siblings, pre-school programs, and the individual characteristics of children (all of which would presumably give equal weight to all letters).[27]

One must assume, of course, that the letters chosen as the treatment (those which *Sesame Street* highlights) are causally comparable with the letters that constitute the control. Learning the letter A may not be equal to learning the letter Q. This suggests the possibility of randomizing the treatment and control conditions, that is, selecting letters at random so as to establish equivalence across groups. In this instance, because of the modest number of treatment conditions afforded by the English language, some form of pre-treatment blocking (based on a judgment of difficulty) prior to randomization is advisable. In any case, randomization is a desirable strategy wherever practicable. Likewise, more complex randomization designs, such as those diagramed in Table 10.2, might also be applied – though one wonders about their practicability in alternate outcome designs. The important point to note is that this is not randomization in the standard sense of the term for one is manipulating the assignment of conditions for the same units rather than manipulating the assignment of units into treatment and control conditions.

---

[27] Note, however, that the control condition is not well defined; in order to interpret the results as ATE we must assume that students would not have learned about the taught letters through some other venue if they had not been watching television. For further discussion see Shadish, Cook, and Campbell (2002: 152–153).

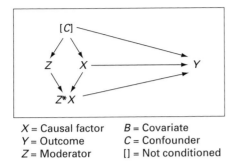

X = Causal factor   B = Covariate
Y = Outcome   C = Confounder
Z = Moderator   [] = Not conditioned

Figure 11.8   Causal heterogeneity strategy

Causal heterogeneity

Causal heterogeneity, that is, the varying impact of a causal factor, *X*, on units within a sample, is usually regarded as noise (*B*).[28] However, in certain situations it may also provide clues to inference. This is so in situations where causal heterogeneity is not stochastic (random), in which the relevant moderators (*Z*) can be measured, and in which the interaction effect of X^*Z on *Y* is not subject to confounding. Figure 11.8 presents the causal diagram consistent with this strategy. What one learns from this sort of analysis may (a) enhance (or decrease) one's confidence in the measured causal effect and/or (b) shed light on the causal mechanisms at work in a causal effect.

Consider an after-school vouchers program with students from many linguistic backgrounds that is geared to students whose native language is Spanish. All students in the course receive the same treatment. However, by virtue of fixed characteristics (Hispanic/non-Hispanic), subjects can be expected to respond differently. In particular, one expects faster progress for Hispanic students relative to non-Hispanic students if the vouchers program is working as intended.

Naturally, one could test the aforegoing proposition in an experimental fashion by randomizing the treatments of interest (1=vouchers program geared to Hispanics, 0=vouchers program with no special linguistic tilt). However, one is not always in a situation where randomization is possible. Moreover, randomization is unlikely to extend to the moderator, a fixed characteristic (Hispanic/non-Hispanic), and in this sense is incomplete, forcing the researcher to infer causality from certain fixed characteristics of subjects. Whatever the research design, one always encounters some degree of causal heterogeneity.

---

[28] Heckman (2001); Heckman and Vytlacil (2007a, 2007b); Rhodes (2010).

Insofar as various assumptions are satisfied (as listed above), one may be in a position to learn from heterogeneous causal effects.

To see how anticipated heterogeneity can help us to deal with confounding in this case, consider the following two scenarios. First, suppose we believe that any unmeasured confounding will affect both the Hispanic and non-Hispanic students equally. If we find that the estimated effects of the vouchers program are the same for Hispanic and non-Hispanic students, then we will conclude that the estimated effect is due to a confounder and not to the program.

As a second example, suppose we further believe that the program will have zero effect on non-Hispanic students (perhaps the course is taught in Spanish). If we find an effect for the non-Hispanic students then it must be the result of confounding. If we also assume that this confounding will be similar among the Hispanic students then we can subtract the bias due to confounding from the estimate for the effect among the Hispanic students. This is functionally equivalent to a difference-in-difference design, as described in Chapter 10.[29]

Rival hypotheses

Information about rival hypotheses is a persistent feature of causal inference, even if not always explicitly acknowledged. Note that any experiment (even a laboratory experiment) requires a consideration of potential confounders. These factors are, in effect, rival hypotheses about the outcome (how else can variation in Y be explained?). Likewise, even the most well-constructed experiments often leave considerable room for interpretation about the mechanisms at work. Here, the logic of inference often relies heavily on an evaluation of rival hypotheses (which may or may not be empirically testable).

The logic of "elimination" is also solidly grounded in the philosophy of science. It is the basis for J. S. Mill's "Method of Agreement" (aka the most-different case method); a central feature of the Peircian tradition of causal inference known as "abduction" or "inference to the best explanation"; and

---

[29] Even when the additional assumptions of this fictional example do not hold strictly, we still may be in a position to learn something about the effect of X on Y. Suppose we are willing to assume that the confounding is the same for the Hispanic and non-Hispanic students, but we are only willing to assume that the effect of the vouchers program cannot exceed a certain value for the non-Hispanic students. If the estimated effect for the non-Hispanic students exceeds this value, then the difference between the estimate and the upper bound on the effect for the non-Hispanic students represents a lower bound on the bias for our estimate of the effects of the vouchers program on the Hispanic students.

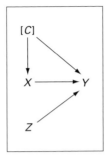

X = Causal factor
Y = Outcome
Z = Rival hypothesis(es)

Figure 11.9   Rival hypotheses strategy

frequently cited in other influential studies.[30] It has even received some recognition among methodologists.[31]

How, then, does one integrate knowledge about other causes of *Y* into an analysis of *X*'s relationship to *Y*?[32]

Let us suppose that problems of measurement, confounding, sample representativeness, or some other feature of research design prevent a strong causal inference about *X*'s relationship to *Y*. There is, for whatever reason, a degree of uncertainty about the matter. The distinctive feature of the rival hypotheses strategy is that the relationship of *X* with *Y* is probed by examining causal factors other than *X* – denoted as *Z* in Figure 11.9. The causal factor of theoretical interest is not involved in the analysis, even by way of proxy. Naturally, the investigation of rival hypotheses could be (and usually is) conducted in tandem with an investigation focused on *X*, as discussed in previous sections. However, the rival hypotheses strategy does not hinge on *X* in any empirical sense. All it requires is a hypothesis that *X* is a cause of some outcome, *Y*, which must be measurable (or measurable by proxy).

As an example, consider Philip Keefer's argument that young democracies are more corrupt and provide fewer public goods than old democracies, because of "the inability of political competitors in young democracies to make credible,

---

[30] The method of elimination was first articulated as a "method of residues" by J. S. Mill ([1843] 1872). For other work emphasizing the importance of theory comparison see Campbell (1966); Day and Kincaid (1994); Gruenbaum (1976); Hanson (1958); Harman (1965); Kuhn ([1962] 1970); Lakatos (1981: 114–115); Laudan (1977); Miller (1987); Popper (1965: 112); Rindskopf (2000); Yin (2000).
[31] Reiss (2007: 7–8); Rosenbaum (1999: 267–269, 2002: 347–350, 2010: ch. 4); Scriven (2008).
[32] Note that this strategy of causal inference in effect merges the effects-of-causes approach with the causes-of-effects approach, as outlined in Chapter 12.

pre-electoral promises to voters." Keefer acknowledges that a direct test of the proposition is not possible (because the mechanism of interest is virtually impossible to measure). However, he invokes the logic of rival hypotheses – "whether alternative, noncredibility explanations can account for the performance of young democracies" – in order to verify his argument.[33]

In probing Z's relationship to Y any of the strategies reviewed in this and the previous chapter may be employed. However conducted, the viability of a rival hypotheses strategy depends upon five factors.

First, one must assume that the outcome of interest, Y, is not entirely stochastic. There is a systematic component of Y that can be explained. We are primed to expect this of phenomena that are widespread (they occur repeatedly) and receive a label (drawn from ordinary language or some technical language). However, it deserves to be stated explicitly because – unlike the other strategies laid out in this and the previous chapter – the null hypothesis of a purely stochastic phenomenon is assumed away from the start.

Second, the viability of the rival hypotheses strategy depends upon assumptions about *how many* causal factors influence Y. In certain settings, it may be reasonable to assume that there is only one cause of Y. This is often the case for very specific medical symptoms. The rival hypotheses strategy is easy to apply in this setting: if Z is found to be a cause of Y, X cannot be a cause of Y. It is eliminated. In other settings, it is apparent that there are likely to be many causes of Y (extreme equifinality). This would be the case if Y is defined in a broad manner – say, death. Still, as long as the causes of Y are finite the strategy may be applied to reduce uncertainty about the hypothesis of interest, X/Y. Knowing whether Z causes (caused) Y affects our belief about whether X causes (caused) Y – even if only minutely.[34]

Third, the viability of the strategy is affected by assumptions of how many *plausible hypotheses* there are about Z. Even if there is thought to be only one cause of Y there may be many plausible hypotheses about what that cause consists of. If there are only two viable hypotheses about what causes Y – X and Z – then one learns a lot about X/Y by examining Z/Y.

Fourth, our conclusions about X/Y from Z/Y are influenced by the success of Z in explaining Y. If Z seems to explain a great deal of the variation in Y we may be less inclined to think that X matters. If, on the other hand, Z shows

---

[33] Keefer (2006: 805).

[34] Naturally, there is some ambiguity about how to divide up the universe of causes: is falling off a horse the same as falling off a short ledge (both instances of falling), or are they separable causes?

only a slight relationship to Y (Y's relationship remains stochastic, i.e., unexplained) then we are more optimistic about X's potential role.

Finally, any knowledge we gain about X/Y from Z/Y is contingent upon the strength of the inferences one draws about Z/Y. The latter is quite naturally subject to all the usual problems of causal inference, as outlined previously. Sometimes, Z/Y inferences are solid – either because the empirical evidence is very strong and/or because our background assumptions about the world allow for reaching strong conclusions. In these cases, prior opinions about X/Y may be fundamentally altered. Sometimes, conclusions about alternative hypotheses rest upon flimsy evidence or flimsy assumptions about the world and therefore scarcely affect our priors about X/Y.

The examination of rival hypotheses is not a formal strategy in quite the same way as others discussed above. However, this strategy is fairly ubiquitous if considered as an informal adjunct to formal research designs. It is especially prominent in studies based on nonexperimental data, or in experimental studies where the researcher wishes to comment on the external validity of a finding drawn from a nonrandom (and quite possibly unrepresentative) sample.

Robustness tests

With nonrandomized designs, and with experiments that involve some post-treatment confounders (e.g., noncompliance), there are often many ways to model the data, *ex post*. There may be a number of plausible estimators, a number of plausible specifications for each statistical model, and so forth. In addition, one faces issues of conceptualization and measurement, of sampling, and of design that are separate from the assignment problem.

Each of these choices is likely to have some impact on estimates of the causal effect. Some choices may affect only the magnitude of the coefficient. Others may affect the direction (positive/negative) of the apparent effect or the acceptance/rejection of the null hypothesis.

Unfortunately, appeals to "theory" are unlikely to resolve these issues. Note that if the theory is strong there is little point in testing; we already know what is out there. If the theory is weak, we are not really strengthening our faith in assumptions by appealing to it.

There is, however, one potentially saving grace. This is the opportunity to test the *robustness* (sensitivity) of a result while altering various elements of the analysis – thus, providing a crude test of various assumptions. To be clear, the purpose of robustness testing is not to arrive at a precise estimate of causal effects. Indeed, the technique of robustness tests more or less presumes that a precise estimate of X's impact on Y is impossible. Instead, the purpose is to test *how* precise a given estimate (drawn from the researcher's best-guess or benchmark model) is in the face of different assumptions. Alternatively, one might say that the purpose is to test whether a posited relationship – conceptualized vaguely as "positive" or "negative" – is true or not. By running a series of robustness tests – for example, alternative operationalizations for key variables, alternative samples or sampling (case-selection) strategies, alternative strategies for measuring a causal effect, alternative estimators, and alternative specifications – one can discover which (if any) assumptions matter and how much the estimated causal effect varies across tests.[35]

Robustness tests help the researcher to arrive at a level of overall uncertainty that is appropriate in light of the evidence, moving us beyond the rather superficial and model-dependent tests normally reported in statistical analyses. If all plausible robustness tests have little impact on a finding then a high level of certainty may be justified. If, on the other hand, the finding is sensitive to small changes in the model, this is quite another story. In either case, multiple tests are more revelatory than one wherever that single best test is difficult to identify, as it generally is with nonrandomized studies (or in experimental studies where some slippage between design and implementation is suspected).

To a large extent, robustness tests are what social scientists facing intractable identification problems do – albeit unsystematically, with great embarrassment, and little transparency. This approach to modeling has the unfortunate feel of *ex post* curve-fitting (adjusting a model until it appears to fit the data). And so it is *if* the process is haphazard and flies below the radar. In recent years, however, a number of procedures have been proposed to standardize this model-testing process, to allow for full reporting, and to distinguish among the variable strength of different results – thereby allowing for a better estimate of X's true effect on Y, given different (plausible) modeling assumptions. The common thread is the move toward a broader conception of probability than is usual in frequentist

---

[35] Robustness/sensitivity tests are discussed in most statistics texts as well as in more specialized monographs, e.g., Bartels (1997); Blalock (1984: 184–185); Imbens (2003); Leamer (1983); Levine and Renelt (1992); Montgomery and Nyhan (2010); Rosenbaum (2002); Rosenbaum and Rubin (1983); Sala-I-Martin (1997); Sims (1988); Western (1995); Young (2009). Note that my understanding of a "robustness" test incorporates both alternative specifications (the usual focus of extreme bounds analysis and sensitivity testing) and alternative estimators (as discussed in most econometrics texts), as well as various operationalizations for key variables (X, Y, C). *Any* important assumption underlying an empirical model that can be tested by altering some element of that model ought to be included in a set of robustness tests.

statistics, incorporating the likelihood of correct modeling strategies in the estimate of *X*'s probable effect on *Y*.

Suppose, for example, that a wide range of plausible operationalizations (for *X* and *Y*), estimators, and specifications for a particular causal hypothesis can be tested. And suppose further that a particular causal factor, *X*, retains directionality (positive or negative) and statistical significance in all of these tests. In this circumstance one is entitled to some optimism. Although one would certainly not invest much importance in any particular point estimate, it may be reasonable to conclude that *X* has some effect on *Y*. Likewise, if repeated attempts to prove *X*'s relationship to *Y* find that virtually no plausible specifications of the model exhibit a significant relationship between the two variables, one can conclude with some confidence that the null hypothesis is true. *X* does not impact *Y*.

This may not seem terribly scientific, at least not according to the experimental model of science. But it does represent a reasonable approach to causal inference where the treatment is not randomized and where correct causal modeling strategies are unclear. As long as the researcher is honest in reporting the procedures used to reach his or her conclusions the problem of curve-fitting is at least rendered transparent and an appropriate level of uncertainty is assigned.

Causal reasoning

Evidence does not speak for itself. Causality is an inference, and does not follow apodictically from a research design and a subsequent data analysis. This is true of qualitative studies and of quantitative studies, of studies based on nonexperimental data and studies based on randomized treatments.

To be sure, assumptions required for reaching causal inference in experimental work are fewer, and generally less problematic. But they are essential nonetheless. Note that setting up a randomized design requires many *a priori* assumptions about what sort of confounders might threaten the result and therefore what sort of precautions might be necessary to preserve the validity of the research design. Is contamination across treatment and control groups a possibility? Will the independence of units be preserved? Might units in the treatment group be subject to experimenter effects? (And so forth.) Likewise, after the experiment is complete the same questions must be asked by reviewers in order to determine its validity (*ex post*). Additionally, both the researcher and the reviewers will need to speculate about the mechanism(s) that might be at work if *X* is shown to have a causal relationship to *Y*. Mechanisms in social science are rarely self-evident, and often resist empirical testing.

Clearly, something other than explicit rules and methods are at issue in causal inference. This is true, *a fortiori*, in nonexperimental studies. In the words of Donald Rubin:

Causal inference is impossible without making assumptions, and they are the strands that link statistics to science. It is the scientific quality of those assumptions, not their existence, that is critical. There is always a trade-off between assumptions and data – both bring information. With better data, fewer assumptions are needed. But in the causal inference setting, assumptions are always needed, and it is imperative that they be explicated and justified. One reason for providing this detail is so that readers can understand the basis of conclusions. A related reason is that such understanding should lead to scrutiny of the assumptions, investigation of them, and, ideally, improvements. Sadly, this stating of assumptions is typically absent in many analyses purporting to be causal and replaced by a statement of what computer programs were run.[36]

What is it, then, that constitutes the "scientific quality" of an assumption? This brings us to the subject of *causal reasoning*.

Bear in mind that, strictly speaking, all we know is the pattern of data that we have observed and the fact that there is, somewhere (though rarely directly observable), a data-generating process (DGP) that accounts for that data. Our causal theory is only one possible explanation for the data, and perhaps not the best. Thinking carefully about the theory and its relationship to the DGP serves to focus our attention in productive ways.

It also serves to unwind our usual way of thinking about causation. Rather than beginning with a theory, the notion of a DGP forces us to begin with the data, working backward to the explanation. Just as a detective investigates a crime, we must reconstruct the process that generated the data, inquiring into all possible causes.

Causal reasoning often takes the form of a *counterfactual thought-experiment*, in which the researcher considers an outcome of interest under different hypothetical (what if?) scenarios. If the results stand to reason, then the finding may be granted greater weight.[37]

In this investigation, all manner of evidence is considered, whether or not it was included in the formal research design. Purely stochastic outcomes are also considered. It could be that there is no (generalizable) explanation for Y.

---

[36] Rubin (2005: 324). See also Day and Kincaid (1994); Freedman (2008); Garfinkel (1981); Heckman (2008: 3); Robins and Wasserman (1999); Rosenbaum (1999, 2005).
[37] Fearon (1991); Lebow (2007); Tetlock and Belkin (1996).

It could be that *Y* is not a coherent outcome, but rather a congeries of different things lumped together by a composite concept. Causal reasoning should open up space for a more wide-ranging perusal of causality than is typical when formulaic research designs are followed.

Causal reasoning should also focus attention on the relative "fit" between theory and data, as discussed in Chapter 4. Sometimes, a theory presents highly specific predictions about the pattern of expected data. This might relate to the distribution of the outcome (precisely how *Y* varies with *X*), the mechanism, or other outcomes that are not of theoretical interest (nonequivalent dependent variables). While these strategies have already been introduced in a general way, here I want to highlight the role of theory and of causal reasoning in making use of these strategies. If, for example, a theory presumes that certain causal mechanisms, *M*, will be in evidence and it can be ascertained that these causal mechanisms are present, one has offered an important sort of evidence for the theory. The degree of weight one might be inclined to rest on this information depends upon how likely it is that *M* would be present if *X* did *not* cause *Y*. In short, it rests on theoretical suppositions about the theory, and about the nature of the reality under investigation. This method of analysis is sometimes referred to as *pattern matching* or *theory-driven* since it matches a pattern of data onto a set of theoretical predictions.[38]

The point, then, is not to deny the role of assumptions, or to shy away from causal inference (or to play around with words that imply causality but do not actually invoke the root word). Rather, I propose a six-part strategy. First, try to limit the number and the fragility of the assumptions necessary for a causal inference. The best research designs require the fewest, and least problematic, assumptions about the world. (This recalls the *parsimony* criterion, introduced in Chapter 3.) Second, make all such assumptions manifest for the reader, perhaps with the assistance of a formal model and/or causal graph. Third, subject those assumptions to robustness tests wherever possible. Fourth, enlist adjunct evidence to demonstrate the viability of assumptions wherever possible. Fifth, consult experts in the topic, that is, those with knowledge of the theoretical problem you are attempting to solve and the data-generating process you are attempting to interpret. We must recognize the importance of experience and wisdom in crafting and in vetting social science studies. Sometimes, the experts know best and their views should always be consulted. Finally, wherever feasible (and sensible), consult the subjects you are studying. See if your analysis makes

---

[38] Bickman and Peterson (1990); Chen and Rossi (1983); Donaldson (2003); Trochim (1985, 1989).

sense to them. If it does not, see what sort of objections they raise. You may be surprised.

Ultimately, we cannot escape the role of causal reasoning in scientific research. As Karl Polanyi pointed out many years ago, "there is a residue of personal judgment required in deciding – as the scientist eventually must – what weight to attach to any particular set of evidence in regard to the validity of a particular proposition."[39]

The assignment problem revisited

In methodological circles today the assignment problem lies front-and-center.[40] The first question we tend to ask of a research design is whether a hypothesis can be tested in an experimental fashion, that is, with a randomized treatment. The second question we ask is whether a nonrandomized setting can be identified in which the treatment (usually assigned naturally, i.e., without intervention by the researcher) is random with respect to the outcome of concern. This experiment-by-serendipity has come to be known as a *quasi-experiment* or *natural experiment*. Because of the ambiguity of the designation, I employ the term *nonrandomized*. But it is nonetheless the case that all research designs aim to replicate the virtues of a true experiment. To the extent that the data-generating process departs from a randomized treatment one is forced to make *ex post facto* adjustments, that is, to move "beyond X and Y," as explored in this chapter.

The punch-line is simple. The one reliable method of solving the assignment problem is a treatment that is randomized across multiple units, allowing comparison across treatment and control groups. The other approaches, while occasionally adequate to the task, are almost never as assured or as precise.

Of course, there is no question that all of the nonrandomized methods reviewed in this and the previous chapter *can* work, that is, provide a valid and precise estimate of X's impact on Y. The trouble is that one never knows for sure whether the circumstances of the case justify the chosen method, for

[39] Polanyi ([1946] 1964: 30–31), quoted in Rosenbaum (2002: 335). See also Robinson, McNulty, and Krasno (2009: 348).

[40] Following Fisher (1935), contemporary work by Donald Campbell, David Freedman, James Heckman, James Robins, Paul Rosenbaum, and Donald Rubin is critically concerned with the assignment problem. For recent reviews see Angrist and Pischke (2009); Imbens and Wooldridge (2009); Morgan and Winship (2007); Rubin (1991). For additional citations, see entries for the aforelisted writers in the References.

example, whether nonrandomized data replicates the features of a true experiment or whether one has conditioned on all confounders (and not introduced other confounders). Recall that the features in any causal graph other than X and Y (which we shall suppose for present purposes are correctly measured) are speculative. They are the researcher's best-guess about the data-generating process with which he or she is faced. If these guesses are true then a chosen strategy of analysis may be justified. But if they are not, all bets are off. And the guesses are generally not subject to empirical verification.

By contrast, an experiment generally requires fewer assumptions about the world. X is controlled by the researcher, Y is observed. As long as confounders do not creep into the analysis after initiation of the treatment and prior to the final post-test (e.g., noncompliance or contamination across groups), the result may be regarded as solid. Additionally, the method of data *analysis* following an experiment may be quite simple, for example, a comparison of means across groups, obviating complex statistical models that require additional – possibly problematic – assumptions.

This suggests that one never really knows the truth of a nonexperimental result until one has conducted an experiment on the same question – a rather damning conclusion for those of us who wallow in the mire of observational data. It follows that nonexperimental methods are methodologically justifiable only when, for practical or ethical reasons, a randomization procedure cannot be devised or when a nonexperimental method promises greater construct validity or external validity. It also follows that research involving a nonrandom assignment ought to be complemented by additional evidence in order to compensate for shortcomings in the research design. While a modest-sized sample and a single post-test measuring only one feature of the sample (the outcome of interest) may be sufficient to determine the causal effect of a randomized intervention (option No. 2 in Table 10.2), if the intervention is not randomized one would hope for a larger sample, multiple pre- and post-tests (a time-series), a good deal of information on the units under observation (so as to model the selection process and measure potential confounders), and the utilization of a number of noncovariational (beyond X and Y) techniques, including contextual information about the research setting, which may be necessary in order to provide a plausible interpretation of the causal effect. In this way, multiplying the number of observable features of a causal phenomenon may help to compensate for problems inherent in a nonexperimental research design.

To be sure, the foregoing factors may also prove helpful in the purest experimental setting. The point is that they become even more essential when violations to the randomization ideal are present. Methodological tools and assumptions must expand in number and sophistication when the main research design is problematic.

Beyond randomization

While celebrating the achievements of the experimental method we do not want to lose sight of its limitations. Randomization ensures that there is variation in *X*, that the treatment is discrete (or can be made discrete), that it is distributed evenly across the sample, that the treatment is exogenous to the outcome, and that there is causal comparability across treatment and control groups at the point at which treatment is assigned. It implies that there is also a large sample, vitiating threats to inference arising from stochastic factors.

However, other threats to inference, reviewed in Chapter 9, are not assured. In particular, experiments are often subject to confounders that creep into the analysis *after* the assignment of treatment, including experimenter effects, attrition, and contamination. For a variety of reasons causal comparability is often difficult to maintain throughout the life of the experiment. And randomization addresses only issues of internal validity, not external validity. Whether or not the results of a randomized study can be generalized to a larger population is another question entirely. Nor, finally, is it always the case that strong experiments can be constructed to test issues of pressing theoretical or policy significance (Chapter 3). An experiment may be internally and externally valid, but also trivial.

It remains to be seen whether experimental methods can be adapted to satisfactorily address all issues of concern to the social sciences.[41] In all likelihood, nonexperimental techniques will remain the workhorse of these disciplines in the foreseeable future. This means that the assignment problem will remain an obstacle.

This should not cause the researcher to throw up his or her hands and assume all is lost. In any given research situation, some expedients are usually demonstrably better than others. A careful consideration of the available options, as provided by the menu in Table 10.1, should help in choosing the best method – or combination of methods – available. (For further thoughts on *best-possible* methods, see Chapter 14.)

---

[41] Note that among the many questions that have not been subjected to experimental testing is the impact of experimental methods. This is rather ironic, given the vehemence with which experimentalists champion the use of experimental methods.

12 Varying approaches to causal inference

Behind many ostensibly theoretical disputes in political science lurk disagreements about the nature of valid explanations. Confrontations among advocates of realist, constructivist, and institutionalist approaches to international relations, for example, concern explanatory strategies more than directly competing propositions about how nations interact. Similarly, rampant debates about nationalism more often hinge on specifying what analysts must explain, and how, than on the relative validity of competing theories. Recent debates about democratization concern not only the choice of explanatory variables but also the very logic of explanation.

Charles Tilly[1]

My approach to the subject of causality has been self-consciously syncretic, drawing from many currents of scholarship. Yet readers may wonder if I have covered this ground in a truly comprehensive fashion. Indeed, several topics of current interest are treated schematically, or not at all, in the foregoing chapters.

In this chapter, which functions as a coda to the third part of the book, I briefly review approaches to causal inference that seem, at least on the face of things, anomalous. This includes *causal-process observations*, *causes-of-effects*, *necessary/sufficient arguments*, and *qualitative comparative analysis* (QCA). As many of these topics overlap, each of the following sections builds on the previous.

I will try to show that these approaches can be accommodated – with some fairly minor modifications – within the framework presented in previous chapters. Despite the expansion in ways of thinking about causality in recent years, attested by Charles Tilly (above), there is a core area of consensus that can be discerned at the level of tasks, strategies, and criteria.

[1] Tilly (2001: 22).

Causal-process observations

The most elemental unit of evidence is an *observation*. In keeping with standard practice I have treated observations as potential members of a larger sample. Each piece of evidence is presumed to be causally comparable with other members of that sample. This is implicit in the matrix format of a dataset (illustrated in Figure 4.1). To be sure, just because observations can be arrayed in a matrix does not mean that they are fully comparable (Chapter 9). But this, at any rate, is the expectation.

A somewhat different form of evidence takes the form of a *causal-process observation*.[2] What defines this species of evidence, in my view, is that each datum is not causally comparable with other data employed in the study. As an example, one might consider a recent effort by a team of geologists to demonstrate the meteorite theory of dinosaur extinction. King, Keohane, and Verba explain:

One hypothesis to account for dinosaur extinction, developed by Luis Alvarez and collaborators at Berkeley in the late 1970s, posits a cosmic collision: a meteorite crashed into the earth at about 72,000 kilometers an hour, creating a blast greater than that from a full-scale nuclear war. If this hypothesis is correct, it would have the observable implication that iridium (an element common in meteorites but rare on earth) should be found in the particular layer of the earth's crust that corresponds to sediment laid down sixty-five million years ago; indeed, the discovery of iridium at predicted layers in the earth has been taken as partial confirming evidence for the theory. Although this is an unambiguously unique event, there are many other observable implications. For one example, it should be possible to find the meteorite's crater somewhere on Earth.[3]

Alvarez and colleagues identify two potential types of evidence: (1) iridium (present in a particular layer of the earth's crust) and (2) a meteorite crater. These observations are noncomparable insofar as they shed light on different aspects (subhypotheses) of the theory. They are both relevant, but they are "apples and oranges," as the saying goes. Indeed, they are drawn from different populations. And because they are noncomparable they cannot be handled in a standard matrix format. They are properly regarded as two $N=1$

---

[2] Brady (2004); Brady and Collier (2004); Brady, Collier, and Seawright (2006); Collier, Brady, and Seawright (2010); Freedman (2008); Rosenbaum (2010: 323).
[3] King, Keohane, and Verba (1994: 11–12), summarizing Alvarez and Asaro (1990).

pieces of evidence. Causal-process observations are therefore *qualitative* by nature.[4]

This sort of evidence is especially valuable when attempting to reach causal inferences about single (and perhaps highly singular) events, such as the extinction of the dinosaurs. The congeries of disparate evidence requires noncomparable observations, all of which may shed light on that single event (though the ramifications of the answer may be generalizable). Why did a school district adopt vouchers? Why did a school change its curriculum after the adoption of vouchers? Why did a student sign up for the voucher program, and how were the student's work habits affected by this choice? These are just a few examples of the sort of questions that a study of vouchers might address with causal-process observations, perhaps drawn from interviews or participant-observation.

Note that because each observation bearing on these questions is qualitatively different from the next the total number of causal-process observations in a study – though it may be quite large – is indeterminate. Noncomparable observations are, by definition, difficult to count. In an effort to count one may resort to lists of discrete pieces of evidence. Thus, one might say that two causal-process observations were generated by way of confirming the meteorite theory of dinosaur extinction. This approximates the numbering systems employed in legal briefs (e.g., "there are fifteen reasons indicating that Smith killed Jones"). But lists can be composed in multiple ways, and each individual causal-process observation (and associated argument) is likely to carry a different weight in the researcher's overall assessment. So the total number of observations remains an open question. One is uncomfortable with the notion that Alvarez *et al.* have an "*N*" of two. Causal-process observations are not quantitative by nature. We do not know, and cannot know, precisely how many causal-process observations are present in well-known qualitative studies such as Jeffrey Pressman's and Aaron Wildavsky's *Implementation*, Theda Skocpol's *States and Social Revolutions*, Richard Fenno's *Home Style*, Herbert Kaufman's *The Forest Ranger*, or Clifford Geertz's *Negara*.[5]

To reiterate: noncomparable observations are not different examples of the same thing (as dataset observations are). They are *different things*. Consequently, it is not clear where one observation ends and another begins. They flow seamlessly together. We cannot re-read the foregoing studies with the aid of a

---

[4] Another way of thinking about this is to say that these causal-process observations constitute *variables* rather than observations. In this rendering, one has a research design with low-*N* and high-*K* where the variables serve to provide clues to causal inference, rather than potential confounders (Adam Glynn, personal communication, 2011).

[5] Fenno (1978); Geertz (1980); Kaufman (1960); Pressman and Wildavsky (1973); Skocpol (1979).

counter and hope to discover the total number of observations; nor would we gain any analytic leverage by doing so.

Quantitative researchers may be inclined to assume that if observations cannot be counted they must not be there, or that they should not be assigned very much weight. Qualitative researchers may insist that they have many "rich" observations at their disposal. But they are unable to say, precisely, how many observations they have, or how many observations are needed for what is sometimes referred to as *thick description*, *contextual analysis*, or *process tracing*. Indeed, the observations remain somewhat undefined.

Although causal-process observations are especially useful when reaching inferences about single events, they also commonly serve an adjunct capacity in the context of large-N research designs. Often, quantitative studies will note parenthetically that the account is consistent with "anecdotal" or "narrative" evidence, that is, with evidence that falls outside the formal (large-N) research design. It makes sense of the statements made by the actors, of their plausible motives, and so forth. This is often extremely important supporting evidence and deserves a more respectful and informative label than "anecdotal" or "narrative" (what is the evidentiary status of a narrative?). To say that a method is nonstandardized or informal is not to say that the evidence drawn from that method is weak or peripheral. It is only to say that the information cannot be subjected to sample-based methods of analysis.

A good example of noncomparable observations as an adjunct mode of causal analysis appears in a recent paper examining the behavior of the US Federal Reserve during the Great Depression. The central question of theoretical interest is whether the Fed was constrained to adopt tight monetary policies because any deviation from this standard would have led to a loss of confidence in the nation's commitment to the Gold Standard (i.e., an expectation of a general devaluation), and hence to a general panic.[6] (The proposition promises insights into monetary theory, so it also provides a good example of how case-based analysis can bolster general theory.) To test this proposition, Chang-Tai Hsieh and Christina Romer examine an incident in monetary policy during the spring of 1932, when the Federal Reserve embarked on a brief program of rapid monetary expansion. "In just fourteen weeks," the authors note, "the Federal Reserve purchased $936 million worth of US government securities, more than doubling its holdings of government debt."[7] To determine whether the Fed's actions fostered investor insecurity Hsieh and Romer track the forward dollar exchange rate during the spring of 1932, which is then

---

[6] Eichengreen (1992).   [7] Hsieh and Romer (2001: 2).

compared with the spot rate, using "a measure of expected dollar devaluation relative to the currencies of four countries widely thought to have been firmly attached to gold during this period."[8] Finding no such devaluation, they conclude that the reigning theory is false – investor confidence could not have constrained the Fed's actions during the Great Depression.

This conclusion would be questionable were it not bolstered by additional evidence bearing on the likely motivations of Federal Reserve officials at the time. To shed light on this matter, the authors survey the *Commercial and Financial Chronicle* (a widely read professional journal, presumably representative of the banking community) and other documentary sources. They find that "the leaders of the Federal Reserve . . . expressed little concern about a loss of credibility. Indeed, they took gold outflows to be a sign that expansionary open market operations were needed, not as a sign of trouble."[9] Thus, adjunct evidence provided by noncomparable observations is instrumental in helping the authors dis-confirm a theory. Moreover, this evidence also sheds light on a new theory about Fed behavior during this critical era:

Our reading of the Federal Reserve records suggests that a misguided model of the economy, together with infighting among the twelve Federal Reserve banks, accounts for the end of concerted action. The Federal Reserve stopped largely because it thought it had accomplished its goal and because it was difficult to achieve consensus among the twelve Federal Reserve banks.[10]

This interpretation would not be possible (or at least would be highly suspect) without the adjunct evidence provided by causal-process observations.

This brings us to a final characteristic of causal-process observations: they lean heavily on general assumptions about the world, which I have characterized as causal reasoning (Chapter 11). Precisely because of the paucity of evidence provided by a noncomparable observation, the researcher must assume a great deal about how the world works. The noncomparable observation works to the extent that it fits snugly within a comprehensible universe of causal relations. I do not wish to imply that noncomparable evidence is shaky; indeed, much of it is quite matter-of-fact and close to the ground. My point is simply that these facts are comprehensible only when they can be ordered, categorized, "narrativized," and this, in turn, rests upon a set of assumptions about the world. Insofar as these assumptions provide priors against which subsequent pieces of evidence can be evaluated, the analysis of noncomparable observations takes on a

---

[8] Hsieh and Romer (2001: 4).   [9] Hsieh and Romer (2001: 2).   [10] Hsieh and Romer (2001: 3).

Bayesian flavor.[11] To be sure, background knowledge of this nature informs *all* causal analysis. Even so, it is usually more prominently on display where some portion of the evidence derives from noncomparable observations, for each observation must be separately evaluated.

Having emphasized the distinction between dataset and causal-process observations I now want to underline their essential similarity. The key point is this: there is nothing about a causal-process observation that prevents its reconstruction into a dataset observation. In the previous example, the authors might have conducted a content analysis of *Commercial and Financial Chronicle* and/or of Federal Reserve records. This would have required coding sentences (or some other linguistic unit) according to whether they registered anxiety about a loss of credibility. Here, the sentence becomes the unit of analysis and the number of sentences comprises the total N (the number of comparable observations) in a large-N research design. A qualitative research design is thereby expanded into a quantitative research design.

In principle, it is possible to convert any noncomparable observation into multiple comparable ("dataset") observations by including more observations drawn from the same population. However, it is not always possible to do so *in practice*. Moreover, there may be little advantage in doing so. In the previous example, it is not clear that anything would be gained from this sort of expansion of observations. If there is, as the authors claim, no evidence whatsoever of credibility anxieties in the documentary evidence then the reader is not likely to be more convinced by an elaborate counting exercise (coded as 0, 0, 0, 0, 0, ...). More useful, one imagines, are specific examples of what leaders of the Fed actually said, as provided by the authors of the study.

Sometimes standardized data is useful, and sometimes not. If an argument is obvious from one observation it is redundant to collect further observations. If multiple noncomparable observations can be integrated into a single summary statement – for example, "the leaders of the Federal Reserve ... expressed little concern about a loss of credibility" – without a formal analysis, there is no point in the latter. Larger samples of comparable observations are extraneous if noncomparable observations will do the job.

To conclude, sometimes causal-process observations are employed in an adjunct capacity to help demonstrate a causal inference for which a formal research design exists (within the same study). These sorts of causal-process observations are sometimes more appropriately labeled as descriptive rather than causal. They seek to establish some aspect of X, M, or Y, rather than the

---

[11] George and Bennett (2005); Gill, Sabin, and Schmid (2005).

relationship between X and Y. Alternatively, they may seek to establish a causal relationship that is ancillary to the main argument, but which supports the main X/Y argument. Thus, causal-process observations might be enlisted to demonstrate that a chosen instrument is indeed a cause of X but not of Y, and thus a useful tool for instrumental-variable analysis. Occasionally, causal-process observations carry the burden of the main causal inference.

In one capacity or another, causal-process observations play a ubiquitous role in causal inference. Arguably, they are more valuable than dataset observations because they pertain to *different aspects* of a causal relationship, providing a form of triangulation. They are not simply more of the same thing; they are different things – all of which are presumed to bear in some fashion on the causal inference of theoretical interest.

Yet I do not regard these sorts of observations as constituting a separate genre of research design or of causal inference. This relates back to a previous point: all causal-process observations can, in principle, be expanded into dataset observations. It follows that all causal-process observations could be formalized as a standard research design following one of the strategies laid out in previous chapters (summarized in Table 10.1). This is why the topic appears in Chapter 12 rather than in Chapters 10 or 11.

Causes of effects

Commonly, arguments focus on a single X/Y hypothesis or a small set of related X/Y hypotheses. This is sometimes referred to as an *effects-of-causes* approach, and is for the most part assumed in the foregoing chapters.

Sometimes, however, causal arguments are more wide-ranging, encompassing all the systematic (i.e., nonstochastic) causal factors presumed to contribute to a particular outcome (Y) – a *causes-of-effects* approach.[12] Here, X refers to a vector of causes rather than to a single causal factor. Thus, instead of attempting to estimate the effect of vouchers on educational performance one might attempt to evaluate all the causes (and combinations of causes) of educational performance: socioeconomic, family, neighborhood, peer group, curriculum, classroom size, teacher, gender, age, personality, along with vouchers.

---

[12] Dawid (2007); Heckman (2005); Holland (1986); Mahoney (2008); Mahoney and Goertz (2006). Mahoney and Terrie (2008: 741) report that 55 percent of studies published in top comparative politics journals in political science take a causes-of-effects approach. Of course, this is but one subfield of one discipline.

This style of analysis is typical of single-outcome case studies,[13] comparative-historical analysis (CHA)[14], and qualitative comparative analysis (QCA – discussed below). It is sometimes embraced by regression-based studies, where attention is focused on total model-fit rather than a single factor of theoretical interest.[15] It is implicit in many formal models, especially equilibrium models of the economy, where researchers attempt to represent all significant inputs to economic performance. And it is *de rigueur* wherever researchers wish to predict an outcome based on a model that is at least partly causal. In this setting there is a premium on identifying and testing all (nontrivial) causes.

Of course, the analytic difficulties involved in assessing multiple causal factors are considerable. First, the search for causes of effects presumes that the evidence at hand is observational (*ex post*) rather than manipulated (*ex ante*). One is explaining an outcome that occurs naturally, and in order to come to terms with this pattern of data one must observe a natural setting. Of course, a group of experiments might, collectively, identify the causal impact of multiple factors on a single outcome. But in identifying what these causes are in the first place one would have to rely on observational evidence. Any setting that is largely restricted to observational evidence is apt to resist strong causal inferences.

Second, each causal factor within the vector, X, must be separately assessed. Let us say that there are ten plausible causes of Y. Here, a causes-of-effects analysis of X/Y is equivalent to ten effects-of-causes (X/Y) analyses. From this perspective, the causes-of-effects study of Y is ten times as difficult as the effects-of-causes study of Y – and an order of magnitude more difficult if each potential interaction effect (across the ten factors) is taken into account.

Third, choices must be made about what level(s) of causal proximity to explore. Consider that an outcome like educational performance is likely to be affected by proximate causes (e.g., the number of persons in the room during the time of the test) as well as distal causes (e.g., the degree to which different religious and ethnic traditions value educational achievement). Since the causal regress is potentially infinite, a causes-of-effects study must limit the analysis to some point in the causal chain. This lends the analysis a degree of arbitrariness insofar as others approaching the same question might begin the causal funnel at a different point. Two causes-of-effects studies of the same outcome may arrive at quite different (though not contradictory) conclusions, based on the authors' choices about where to cut into the causal stream.

---

[13] Gerring (2007: epilogue).   [14] Mahoney and Terrie (2008); Mahoney and Rueschemeyer (2003).
[15] For example, McGuire (2010).

Finally, no such endeavor is likely to be truly comprehensive, especially with an outcome such as educational performance. Since any alteration in a student's personality or environment may plausibly affect his or her performance there is no limit, in principle, to the potential causes of Y. This is true, I suspect, for most outcomes of theoretical interest in the social sciences.

In sum, causes-of-effects studies are much more ambitious than effects-of-causes studies. They purport to tell us *all* about Y, rather than just one thing about Y. So it is no surprise that they are more difficult to achieve, and probably impossible to achieve with the level of certainty that we associate with well-constructed effects-of-causes studies. This does not mean that this form of causal inference should be eschewed. Sometimes, we want to know as much as possible about Y, as the long list of genres that utilize this form of analysis (above) attests.

In any case, comprehensive causal evaluations of Y do not change the basic problem of causal assessment. For each individual causal factor, X, the same problems of assessment are encountered, as reviewed in previous chapters. From this perspective, the causes-of-effects approach to causality may be viewed as an extension of the effects-of-causes approach.[16]

Necessary/sufficient causal arguments

Sometimes, causes are understood as necessary and/or sufficient to achieve an outcome.[17] This way of conceptualizing causal relations is *set-theoretic* insofar as it arranges phenomena in sets and subsets, as described below. It also derives from the ancient tradition of logic, involving relations that can be described with logical operators (AND, OR).[18]

Typically, the conditions and the outcome are binary (0/1) in nature, although this assumption can be relaxed (by fuzzy-sets).

Sometimes, necessary/sufficient arguments are referred to as "deterministic" since the relationships they envision are, in the extreme, perfect (no exceptions). However, I shall view perfection as a limiting condition, allowing for a probabilistic interpretation of necessity and sufficiency.

By whatever name, these sorts of causal relationships appear to pose a challenge to the definition of causality (Chapter 8) and causal effects (Chapter 9)

---

[16] Halpern and Pearl (2005). For a contrary view, see Mahoney (2008).
[17] See Braumoeller and Goertz (2000); Goertz (2006); Goertz and Starr (2003); Seawright (2002).
[18] Braumoeller and Goertz (2000); Cohen and Nagel (1934); Dul *et al.* (2010); Goertz (2006); Mahoney, Kimball, and Koivu (2009).

adopted in this volume. I want to argue, however, that the challenge is not as severe as some have claimed, that is, that necessary/sufficient arguments also presume causal effects in the traditional sense, but, at the same time, that they call attention to aspects of a causal relationship left in abeyance by ATE (and its variants), and are therefore a useful addition to our vocabulary about causality.

Let us quickly review the concepts of necessity/sufficiency. For convenience, in the following section wherever X or $Y = 0$, I will use lower-case letters (x,y). Wherever X or $Y = 1$, I will use upper-case letters (X,Y). This means that x will be understood as the control condition and X as the treatment condition.

The reader should be reminded that here, as elsewhere, I employ terms such as condition, factor, and variable as near-synonyms. Specifically, a causal condition is a binary independent variable (X,x).

A cause is *necessary-and-sufficient* if its presence is both necessary and sufficient for an outcome: X always causes Y and is furthermore the only cause of Y. This means that X and Y go together invariably, as do x and y. In set-theoretic terms, the set of units containing X is coterminous with the set containing Y.

This sort of argument encapsulates an *ideal-type* vision of causal argumentation – a cause that explains everything about an outcome (and therefore falls into the causes-of-effects category of explanation) and does so perfectly (no exceptions). It is, arguably, what every causal theory strives for. Likewise, within the purview of set-theoretic causes: necessary causes become more important (less trivial) as they approach sufficiency and sufficient causes become more important (less trivial) as they approach necessity.[19]

Nonetheless, because necessary-and-sufficient theories are so rare in the real world of social science (or are restricted to single events), the following discussion focuses primarily on arguments cast in terms of necessity *or* sufficiency. These will be treated as generalizing statements about the world – laws/generalizations/regularities – not as explanations for specific events.[20]

A cause is *necessary* if its presence is required for an outcome to occur: X is necessary for Y, but X does not always cause Y (at least not by itself). This means that one may find X without Y, but one does not find Y without X. In set-theoretic terms, the set of units containing Y is a subset of the set of units containing X.[21] Necessary-condition arguments of a generalizing sort include

---

[19] Braumoeller and Goertz (2000); Goertz (2006); Mahoney, Kimball, and Koivu (2009).

[20] For a discussion of set-theoretic "laws" in social science see Goertz (2010).

[21] Causal conjunctures necessary to cause an outcome may also be referred to as SUIN causes insofar as each component of a conjuncture is regarded as a sufficient but unnecessary part of a factor that is insufficient but necessary for an outcome (Mahoney, Kimball, and Koivu 2009).

the democratic peace hypothesis (introduced in Chapter 1), where it is argued that the presence of at least one nondemocracy is a necessary condition for war between two states.

A cause is *sufficient* if its presence guarantees the occurrence of an outcome: X always causes Y, though Y also has other causes. This means that one may find Y without X, but one never finds X without Y. In set-theoretic terms, the set of units containing X is a subset of the set of units containing Y. Sufficient causes are the stock-in-trade of qualitative comparative analysis (QCA), discussed in the next section.[22]

Note that where only a single causal factor is identified necessity and sufficiency are mirror images of each other. One can re-cast any necessity argument in terms of sufficiency simply by shifting the terminology (and vice versa). Thus, instead of saying that nondemocracy (autocracy) is a necessary condition for war between two states (the usual formulation), one might say that democracy is a sufficient cause of peace. The choice between these terms is dictated by the researcher's conceptualization of the outcome: does one wish to explain war or peace? Where, on the other hand, *multiple* paths are found to the same outcome (as in QCA), the language of sufficiency is preferred.

Discussion

My contention is that necessary/sufficient causal arguments are consistent with the general definition of causality adopted in Chapter 8: causal factors (in order to be considered truly causal) must raise the prior probability of an outcome. In probability notation, $P(Y|X) > P(Y|x)$. By this we mean that X raises the real probability of Y occurring – through some generative mechanism – not simply our enhanced ability to predict Y. It is causal not simply correlative.

Likewise, for any necessary/sufficient argument one ought to be able to calculate a causal effect, understood as ATE or some variation thereof (Chapter 9). Thus, if a cause is necessary or sufficient we would expect to find a difference in outcomes across treatment (X) and control (x) groups. More specifically, if X is a *necessary* condition for Y, then $P(Y|x)=0$ while $P(Y|X) > 0$. That is, the change from x to X raises the probability of Y from 0 to some undefined probability greater than 0. If X is a *sufficient* condition for Y,

---

[22] Causal conjunctures sufficient to cause an outcome may also be referred to as INUS causes insofar as each component of a conjuncture is regarded as "an insufficient but necessary part of a condition which is itself unnecessary but sufficient for the result" (Mackie 1965: 246). This is the hallmark of QCA, as discussed below.

then $P(Y|x) < 1$ while $P(Y|X)=1$. That is, the change from x to X raises the probability of Y from something less than 1 to precisely 1.

All of this presumes that the causal condition(s) is necessary or sufficient in a *nontrivial* fashion. A trivial necessary cause shows no difference (or no perceptible difference) across treatment and control groups. They are not the kind of causes that scholars and laypersons generally identify as necessary. When one says X is necessary for Y one presupposes that there is a systematic difference in the value of Y between units with x and units with X. Likewise for sufficiency.[23]

Sometimes, available evidence does not satisfy these assumptions. For example, a sample may lack variation in the causal factor of interest. Let us say that all cases are X and none are x. Assuming some variation in the outcome (Y/y), we might interpret this as evidence for a necessary condition argument: X could be necessary for Y. However, reaching this causal inference depends upon a counterfactual thought-experiment rather than on empirical evidence. We must presume, on the basis of our knowledge of a particular context, the value of an outcome when a case assumes the value of x. Specifically, we must assume that the combination x/Y is less likely than the combination X/Y. And this, in turn, fulfills the assumptions of a traditional causal effect.

That said, in measuring a difference of means – causal effects in the ATE sense – one has perhaps not arrived at the most *useful* statement of causal impact. For a necessary cause, the salient result is that in all cases with x, one will also find y. Cases exemplifying X are less useful, for the value of the outcome is inconsistent (sometimes Y, sometimes y). Likewise, for a sufficient cause, the salient result is that in all cases with X, one will also find Y. Cases with x are less useful, for the value of the outcome is inconsistent (sometimes Y, sometimes y).

Consider a pill that promises to prevent heart attacks among those with high cholesterol. A potential consumer of the anti-cholesterol pill will probably be less interested in the average treatment effect: that is, the decrease in likelihood that he or she will have a heart attack with the pill (X) as opposed to without the pill (x). Instead, he or she will probably want to know the effectiveness of the pill, *tout court*. That is, if he or she takes the pill (X) what are that person's chances of having a heart attack? How sufficient is the pill in preventing heart attacks?

This is a statement of probability based on a presumed causal relationship. It is not a causal effect (at least not in the usual counterfactual sense). But it

---

[23] Braumoeller and Goertz (2000: 854–856).

Table 12.1 Necessary-and-sufficient causal patterns

(a) *Necessity*

Y	0	[250]
y	500	[250]
	x	X

(b) *Sufficiency*

Y	[250]	500
y	[250]	0
	x	X

Values in cells indicate the number (N) of units that assume a particular value for the outcome under control (x) and treatment (X) conditions.

presumes a causal effect, and also (in set-theoretic language) nontriviality. (Nontriviality is where causal effects meet set-theoretic relationships.) If taking the pill is sufficient to prevent a heart attack but not taking the pill is also (for some other reason) sufficient for preventing a heart attack, the anti-cholesterol pill is trivially sufficient – and the causal effect is null. No one should bother taking the medication since it has no effect on the outcome; it is trivially sufficient.

The point is easiest to illustrate in an experiment with a binary treatment (X/x) and binary outcome (Y/y). Panel (a) in Table 12.1 shows results from a hypothetical study in which a treatment (such as an anti-cholesterol pill) is randomized across two groups, each consisting of 500 units. The first column illustrates the distribution of outcomes in the control condition (x). Here, all 500 cases cluster in the bottom cell. The second column illustrates the distribution of outcomes in the treatment condition (X). Here, cases are split evenly between both cells. The ATE can be calculated by comparing the probability of Y for the control group (0) with the probability of Y for the treatment group (0.5). A difference-of-means test reveals it to be a highly significant result. However, if the researcher is interested in necessity the relevant data is contained in column 1, the control condition. This contains the following finding: no units subject to the control condition achieve the outcome ($Y|x$ is a null set). By contrast, column 2 is irrelevant as long as it is not identical with column 1 (that is, there is *some* measurable ATE across the two groups).

The same pattern of relevance/irrelevance is found in the measurement of sufficiency, but in reverse, as illustrated in panel (b) in Table 12.1. Here, the treatment group (column 2) contains the finding, while the control group (column 1) is irrelevant – again, presuming that there is an average treatment effect across the two groups.

Conceptualizing necessary/sufficient arguments as statements of probability seems heterodox at first, especially since these relationships are commonly regarded as "deterministic." And yet the deterministic claim is, of course, a statement about probability. For a necessary cause, $P(Y|x)=0$. For a sufficient cause, $P(Y|X)=1$.

A helpful aspect of this interpretation is that it can incorporate exceptions, that is, *degrees* of necessity or sufficiency. Recall that in the context of many real-life settings – such as the pill that retards heart attacks – matters of degree are often crucial. We want to know *how necessary* or *how sufficient* an outcome is if a given treatment is administered, even if it is not a perfect causal law. What is the probability that I will have a heart attack if I take a cholesterol pill? This is, of course, quite different from ATE because it does not compare treatment and control conditions (the causal counterfactual). Instead, it looks only at outcome values in the control group (necessity) or the treatment group (sufficiency).

This suggests that claims of necessity and sufficiency may be evaluated in two steps. First, there is the question of causality: is there a causal effect? Second, there is the question of probability. If a causal relation exists, what is the probability of a certain outcome when the causal factor takes on a certain value (X/x)?

This suggests, finally, that ascertaining necessary and sufficient conditions is not so different from ascertaining other probabilistic relationships based on causal models (models presumed to be causal). For example, regression models are commonly employed to predict the likelihood of an outcome given chosen values for X (or some vector of Xs). This is directly analogous to calculating probabilities of $Y=0$ or $Y=1$ for a given value of X (0 or 1) in the example illustrated in Table 12.1. The caveat is that in order for the calculated probabilities to be interpreted as causal, the model upon which the probability calculations are based must represent a true causal model.

So conceptualized, relationships of necessity and sufficiency are not alien to mainstream causal analysis as understood through the potential-outcomes model (see below). This is a distinct advantage insofar as one might wish to create a single community of scholarship, rather than contending schools of causation.[24]

---

[24] For a contrary view, emphasizing differences across these traditions, see Goertz and Mahoney (2010).

Now, let us quickly take up the question of causal inference: how do we know when a necessary/sufficient covariational relationship is truly causal? I have suggested that the ideal approach proceeds in two stages: first, an experimental or quasi-experimental test for causal effects; next (if this test is passed), a measurement of necessity or sufficiency.

Unfortunately, many social science settings do not allow for the first stage. Instead, one is faced with observational data from which one must infer causality. Thus, in investigating the democratic peace hypothesis one finds a sample of cases (nation-states) that can be observed over time, but cannot be subjected to a randomized treatment. The observed cases exemplify patterns of regime type (democracy/autocracy) and dyadic outcomes (peace/war) that are consistent with causal necessity. But, of course, appearances may be deceptive; covariation (including set-relations) does not equal causation.[25]

One approach would be to interrogate the data for evidence of a causal effect with an appropriate nonrandomized research design (chosen from the menu of strategies outlined in Chapters 10 and 11). A panel analysis seems ideal, since it is capable of integrating both temporal and spatial evidence. If suitable instruments for regime type could be identified, an instrumental-variable analysis would be preferred – although in this instance it seems unlikely that any set of instruments would satisfy the exclusion restriction (Chapter 11). The resulting estimator might be logit regression or some version of matching.[26] In any case, robustness tests should be performed, given the considerable uncertainty about proper specification of the model. If a strong (robust) causal effect is confirmed, one has greater confidence that the relationship between regime type and war/peace is causal. Then, the estimation of probabilities for $Y|X$ and $Y|x$ are easier to justify. How necessary is autocracy for war (how sufficient is democracy for peace)?

Now, we must complicate things further. When analyzing observational data, questions of causality (causal effects) and probability (necessity/sufficiency) are not entirely segregated from each other. This is because patterns of necessity/sufficiency, if consistent across a large sample, also constitute evidence of causality. One is more inclined to believe there is a causal effect if X/x and Y/y co-vary in the perfect manner illustrated in Table 12.1. Thus, investigations of necessary/sufficient relationships are also, at the same time, investigations into causality.

---

[25] Yamamoto (2010) discusses the problem of confounding.

[26] Beware: statistical software using maximum likelihood models sometimes discards "perfect" predictors (Goertz forthcoming).

The point will seem obvious to those engaged in these studies, but it is perhaps not so obvious to those approaching causality from a traditional potential-outcomes perspective. Recall from our discussion in Chapter 4 that the believ-ability of a causal conjecture is enhanced whenever an especially severe test has been passed. Difficult hurdles, if cleared, inspire confidence. A set-theoretic hypothesis, if understood as exceptionless – $P(Y|x)=0$ (necessity) or $P(Y|X)=1$ (sufficiency) – is an extremely "risky" prediction. If this prediction holds up across a large number of cases and there is variation in the theoretical variable of interest (X/x), the causal conjecture is strongly corroborated. Note that the only plausible alternative explanation for perfect necessity or sufficiency across a large sample is a confounder or set of confounders that is perfectly correlated with X across the set of cases that exhibit y (for necessary causes) or Y (for sufficient causes). This helps to mollify concerns about spurious causal claims.[27]

Of course, if the posited necessary/sufficient relationship is less than perfect (there are exceptions), the prediction is less risky. And if the sample is small, or if there is little variation in X and Y, there is less supporting evidence. Still, the point remains that causal inference for necessary/sufficient relationships should ideally be considered at several levels – the search for a causal effect and for causal mechanisms (which is equally important for set-theoretic and non-set-theoretic causes), and tests for necessity/sufficiency.[28]

Qualitative comparative analysis (QCA)[29]

Resting on the idea of sufficient causal relations is the set-theoretic approach pioneered by Charles Ragin, known as qualitative comparative analysis (QCA).[30] This section thus builds directly on the previous.

The hallmark of QCA is to be found in the analysis of multiple configura-tions of factors, each of which (i.e., each configuration) is considered as a sufficient explanation for a particular outcome. More concisely, QCA is about

---

[27] Goertz (forthcoming).
[28] Braumoeller and Goertz (2000). See also the colloquy in *Political Analysis* (10:2) concerning what sort of cases are most useful for testing claims of necessity and sufficiency (Braumoeller and Goertz 2002; Clarke 2002; Seawright 2002).
[29] This section was written in close consultation with Carsten Schneider and with input from James Mahoney – though neither should be implicated in my conclusions.
[30] Ragin (1987, 2000, 2008); Rihoux and Ragin (2009); Schneider and Wagemann (2007, 2010). Reviews (sometimes critical) of the method can be found in Cat (2006); Lieberson (2001); Yamamoto (2010), and the symposia on QCA in *Qualitative Methods* 2(2) (2004): 2–25 (available on-line) and in *Studies in Comparative International Development* 40(1) (2005): 3–26.

causal conjunctions under conditions of equifinality. (Note that regression methods can also deal with causal conjunctures, but these are analyzed as causal effects rather than as relations of sufficiency, and usually as multiplicative terms rather than as set-theoretic relationships.) QCA also handles necessary conditions, though these are rarely the object of focus and may not require the advanced machinery of QCA. Thus, most of the following discussion focuses on configurations of causal factors understood as sufficient to produce an outcome.

Perhaps the easiest way of describing this technique is by exploring a particular example. Here, I rely on a discussion provided in a recent volume on QCA edited by Benoît Rihoux and Charles Ragin.[31] The substantive work under discussion, by Dirk Berg-Schlosser and Jeremy Mitchell, examines possible explanations for the breakdown/survival of democracy in interwar Europe.[32] My exposition will be brief and schematic, focusing on the most distinctive elements of the QCA technique and omitting elements of research design that are held in common with other methods.[33] For a more detailed introduction, with a guide to best-practices, the reader should look elsewhere.[34]

cs-QCA

The original, crisp-set (cs) version of QCA begins with a binary coding of key variables: the outcomes of theoretical interest and the factors that may have caused them. Drawing on the literature, the authors identify five key factors: development (per capita GNP); urbanization; literacy; an industrial labor force; and government stability. These are calibrated into set membership scores using cut-off points suggested by theoretical considerations. Development in 1930 is coded as 0 if per capita GNP is below US$600, and 1 if above. Urbanization (population in towns of greater than 20,000 inhabitants) is coded as 0 if below 50 percent, 1 if above. Literacy is coded as 0 if below 75 percent of the adult population, 1 if above. The industrial labor force is coded as 0 if below 30 percent of the active population, 1 if above. Government stability is coded as 0 if ten or more cabinets governed during the period under analysis, 1 otherwise. Democratic survival = 1, breakdown = 0.

---

[31] Rihoux and De Meur (2009) discuss the crisp-set (cs) version of the analysis and Ragin (2009) presents the fuzzy-set (fs) version of the analysis.

[32] Berg-Schlosser and De Meur (1994); Berg-Schlosser and Mitchell (2000, 2003).

[33] So, e.g., I will not dwell on the need for causal comparability in a chosen sample, a matter explored in Chapter 9. Likewise, I shall not discuss the viability of random versus purposive sampling techniques, a matter taken up in Chapter 4.

[34] Rihoux and Ragin (2009); Schneider and Wagemann (2007, 2010).

Table 12.2 cs-QCA truth-table

		Causal factors					Outcome
Configuration	Cases	Developed	Urban	Literacy	Industrial labor	Government stability	Survival
1.	FI, IR	1	0	1	0	1	1
2.	BE, CZ, NE, UK	1	1	1	1	1	1
3.	FR, SW	1	0	1	1	1	1
4.	ES	0	0	1	0	1	0
5.	AU	1	0	1	1	0	0
6.	GE	1	1	1	1	0	0
7.	GR, PL, SP	0	0	0	0	0	0
8.	HU, PO	0	0	1	0	0	0
9.	IT, RO	0	0	0	0	1	0

AU: Austria, BE: Belgium, CZ: Czechoslovakia, ES: Estonia, FI: Finland, FR: France, GE: Germany, GR: Greece, HU: Hungary, IR: Ireland, IT: Italy, NE: Netherlands, PL: Poland, PO: Portugal, RO: Romania, SP: Spain, SW: Sweden, UK: United Kingdom. (Logical remainders not included.) Coding explained in the text. Based on Rihoux and De Meur (2009: 55).

Based on this coding, a *truth-table* is constructed in which cases are grouped together in the same row if they share identical scores for all (potentially) causal factors. This truth-table reduces a plenitude of cases and variables to a parsimious grid. Eighteen cases become nine configurations (combinations of causal factors), as depicted in Table 12.2.

The next step is to look closely at the configurations that lead to positive outcomes. Survival might be understood as a product of three distinct causal paths:

1a.   *DEVELOPED*urban*LITERACY*indlab*GOVSTAB*   Cases: FI, IR
1b.   *DEVELOPED*URBAN*LITERACY*indlab*GOVSTAB*   Cases: BE, CZ, NE, UK
1c.   *DEVELOPED*urban*LITERACY*INDLAB*GOVSTAB*   Cases: FR, SW

Here, upper-case letters indicate a positive score on a factor (1) while lower-case letters indicate a negative score (0) – oftentimes understood as the presence/absence of a factor. Alternatively, democratic survival might be understood as a product of two causal paths:

2a.   *DEVELOPED*urban*LITERACY*GOVSTAB*   Cases: FI, IR
2b.   *DEVELOPED*LITERACY*indlab*GOVSTAB*   Cases: BE, CZ, FR, NE, UK, SW

Restated in prose: the survival of democracy is found in countries that combine high GNP, high literacy, an industrialized labor force, and governmental stability *OR* in countries that combine high GNP, low urbanization, high literacy, and governmental stability. A third interpretation, dropping several factors, views survival as the product of a single path among the remaining factors:

3. *DEVELOPED*LITERACY*GOVSTAB*   Cases: BE, CZ, FI, FR, IR, NE, UK, SW

These three conditions, in combination, are said to assure the outcome. A final interpretation of the truth-table, even more parsimonious, is that survival is the product of one path with only two conditions:

4. *DEVELOPED* GOVSTAB*   Cases: BE, CZ, FI, FR, IR, NE, UK, SW

A similar analysis might also be conducted on the negative outcome, where Survival=0 (breakdown) – though we will not follow the details here.

Each of the four solution terms reviewed above is consistent with the empirical information contained in the truth-table. Which to choose for further interpretation depends therefore on theoretical interests, on the usual demand for parsimony (Chapter 3), and – most importantly – on non-Boolean information about the cases (i.e., evidence that lies outside the realm of formal, deductive logic).

This includes assumptions about outcomes in so-called "logical remainder" rows. These are possible combinations of causal factors (configurations) *not* found in the empirical data, and may be viewed as counterfactual thought-experiments. Consider the most parsimonious interpretation offered above – that democratic survival in the interwar period was the product of high GNP combined with government stability (No. 4). These two factors, together, may constitute a sufficient condition of survival. However, making this argument presumes that no European democracy with this two-factor configuration would have broken down, even if its score along other parameters (urbanization, literacy, and industrial labor) were different. Only some of these potential cases (combinations of causal conditions) are actually observed. Indeed, the number of cases is modest relative to the number of possible combinations. Note that a QCA with five causal factors poses thirty-two possible configurations (2^5), only nine of which are actually observed in the historical data. (This is a common predicament in QCA, though it also affects other observational research.) Even so, if one can enlist in-depth case knowledge to make educated guesses about these counterfactuals they can be integrated into the QCA. Specifically, in order to assert that *GNP*GOVSTAB* comprise a sufficient condition for democracy survival, we must presume that all of the following configurations would also lead to democratic survival, even though they are not observed in the available data:

1. *DEVELOPED*urban*literacy*indlab*GOVSTAB*
2. *DEVELOPED*urban*literacy*INDLAB*GOVSTAB*
3. *DEVELOPED*URBAN*literacy*indlab*GOVSTAB*
4. *DEVELOPED*URBAN*literacy*INDLAB*GOVSTAB*
5. *DEVELOPED*URBAN*LITERACY*indlab*GOVSTAB*

Insofar as these seem like reasonable assumptions, based upon what we know about the cases and about the world, the argument is bolstered.

fs-QCA

The fuzzy-set (fs) version of QCA is more complicated than the crisp-set (cs) version, which is why it is introduced it here, rather than earlier (even though many QCA practitioners consider it to be a superior version of the method).

To begin with, cases do not need to be coded in a plainly categorical fashion. A case may occupy a position of *full* or *partial* membership in a set, coded from 0 to 1 – with 0.0 representing full nonmembership, 1.0 representing full membership, and 0.5 representing the cut-off point in between the two categories. Following our exemplar, the outcome – democratic survival – may be re-scored on the basis of the Polity2 variable drawn from the Polity IV index, a twenty-one-point index stretching from −10 to +10, where 0 is defined as the cut-off between democracy and nondemocracy. Thus, Austria, with a Polity2 score of −9, is coded as 0.05 on the outcome – representing 5 percent membership in the category "democracy." By contrast, Belgium, with a score of 10 on the Polity2 scale, is coded as 0.95 on survival – 95 percent membership in the category. Similar re-codings are constructed for other variables: developed; urbanization; literacy; industrial labor; and government stability. Three of these conditions are represented in Table 12.3 by way of illustration.

The process of reducing this information into (possibly causal) configurations occurs through the application of two rules. When combining multiple conditions into a single configuration (logical *AND*), the membership of each case is determined by the minimal score across all factors. Thus, Austria's membership in the configuration "Developed *AND* Urban" is 0.12 because this is the lowest score it receives across the two conditions, as can be seen in Table 12.3. Its membership in the configuration "Developed, Urban, *AND*

Table 12.3 Coding membership in causal factors and configurations with fs-QCA

	Conditions			*Configurations*				*Outcome*
				Logical *AND* (set intersection)		**Logical *OR*** (set union)		
Case	Developed	Urban	Unstable	Developed *AND* urban	Developed, urban, *AND* unstable	Developed *OR* urban	Developed, urban, *OR* unstable	Survival
AU	0.81	0.12	0.57	0.12	0.12	0.81	0.81	0.05
BE	0.99	0.89	0.02	0.89	0.02	0.99	0.99	0.95
CZ	0.58	0.98	0.09	0.58	0.09	0.98	0.98	0.89
ES	0.16	0.07	0.09	0.07	0.07	0.16	0.16	0.12
FI	0.58	0.03	0.42	0.03	0.03	0.58	0.58	0.77
FR	0.98	0.03	0.05	0.03	0.03	0.98	0.98	0.95
GE	0.89	0.79	0.69	0.79	0.69	0.89	0.89	0.05
GR	0.04	0.09	0.57	0.04	0.04	0.09	0.57	0.06
HU	0.07	0.16	0.87	0.07	0.07	0.16	0.87	0.42
IR	0.72	0.05	0.05	0.05	0.05	0.72	0.72	0.92
IT	0.34	0.10	0.42	0.10	0.10	0.34	0.42	0.05
NE	0.98	1.0	0.01	0.98	0.01	1.0	1.0	0.95
PL	0.02	0.17	1.0	0.02	0.02	0.17	1.0	0.12
PO	0.01	0.02	0.99	0.01	0.01	0.02	0.99	0.05
RO	0.01	0.03	0.16	0.01	0.01	0.03	0.16	0.21
SP	0.03	0.30	0.80	0.03	0.03	0.30	0.80	0.06
SW	0.95	0.13	0.09	0.13	0.09	0.95	0.95	0.95
UK	0.98	0.99	0.02	0.98	0.02	0.99	0.99	0.95

AU: Austria, BE: Belgium, CZ: Czechoslovakia, ES: Estonia, FI: Finland, FR: France, GE: Germany, GR: Greece, HU: Hungary, IR: Ireland, IT: Italy, NE: Netherlands, PL: Poland, PO: Portugal, RO: Romania, SP: Spain, SW: Sweden, UK: United Kingdom. Coding explained in the text. Based on Ragin (2009: 97–98).

Unstable" is also 0.12 because this is the lowest score it receives across the three conditions.

When coding alternative paths to an outcome (causal equifinality, implemented by the logical *OR*), the membership of each case is determined by the maximal score across all factors. Thus, Austria's membership in the configuration "Developed *OR* Urban" is 0.81 because this is the highest score it receives across the two conditions, as can be seen in Table 12.3. Its membership in the configuration "Developed, Urban, *AND* Unstable" is 0.89 because this is the highest score it receives across the three conditions.

Table 12.3 includes only three of the five causal factors in our example and only two of the possible configurations across those three conditions. But it is sufficient to illustrate the logic by which alternative configurations are formed with fuzzy-set coding.

Now we turn to the relationship between configurations and the outcome of interest. This relationship is deemed one of sufficiency when the score of a case for a particular configuration is *less* than its score on the outcome. Suppose we want to test the relationship of the configuration "Developed, Urban, *AND* Unstable" (column 6 in Table 12.3) with the outcome (the last column in Table 12.3). This data can be graphed in an *X/Y* scatter-plot to test relationships of sufficiency. If the configuration is a subset of the outcome (and therefore a possible sufficient condition) then the cases should lie above the diagonal; that is, the score for each case on the outcome should be higher than the score for each case on the configuration. As one can see from Figure 12.1, this is only partially so. There is one very deviant case: Germany.

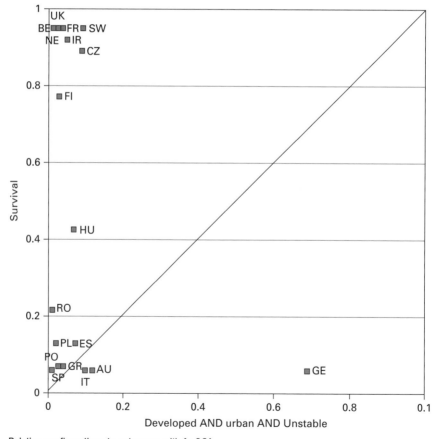

Figure 12.1   Relating configurations to outcomes with fs-QCA

Table 12.4 fs-QCA truth-table with consistency scores

Configuration	Cases with >0.5 membership	Developed	Urban	Literacy	Industrial labor	Government stability	Consistency as sufficient condition
1.	BE, CZ, NE, UK	1	1	1	1	1	0.90
2.	FI, IR	1	0	1	0	1	0.80
3.	FR, SW	1	0	1	1	1	0.71
4.	ES	0	0	1	0	1	0.53
5.	HU, PO	0	0	1	0	0	0.52
6.	GE	1	1	1	1	0	0.45
7.	AU	1	0	1	1	0	0.38
8.	IT, RO	0	0	0	0	1	0.28
9.	GR, PL, SP	0	0	0	0	0	0.22

AU: Austria, BE: Belgium, CZ: Czechoslovakia, ES: Estonia, FI: Finland, FR: France, GE: Germany, GR: Greece, HU: Hungary, IR: Ireland, IT: Italy, NE: Netherlands, PL: Poland, PO: Portugal, RO: Romania, SP: Spain, SW: Sweden, UK: United Kingdom.

In order to test all possible configurations one suggested technique reverts to the truth-table approach we explored earlier. Cases are re-coded in a binary fashion according to their degree of membership in the causal condition, using 0.5 as the threshold of membership. While each case has partial membership in all logically possible combinations of conditions (aka truth-table rows) it has a membership of higher than 0.5 in only one of them. This allows for the construction of a truth-table – represented in Table 12.4 – that is identical in causal conditions to the one presented in Table 12.2.

The additional feature associated with fuzzy-set analysis is the calculation of a *consistency* score – the degree to which each of the cases in the sample fit the proposition – as reported in the final column of Table 12.4. The outcome value for each of the truth-table rows is determined by running tests of their consistency (with the cases in the sample) as sufficient conditions for the outcome. If they pass this test, they receive the value of 1 in the outcome column; if they fail the test, the value is 0. The third possibility is that not enough cases have a membership higher than 0.5 in a particular row. Such rows are treated as logical remainders.

The general formula for measuring the consistency of a sufficient condition is:

$$\Sigma(\min(X_i, Y_i))/\Sigma(X_i) \tag{12.1}$$

This means that one chooses, for each case, the lower value of X (the membership score of a case in a configuration, as explained in Table 12.2) and Y (the membership score of a case on the outcome), divided by X. Positive deviance – when $Y > X$ – amounts to 0. Negative deviance – when $Y < X$ – is discounted by the value of X. This is then repeated for each case, and averaged across the sample, to achieve a consistency score for that particular proposition.

The resulting score ranges from 0 to 1, with higher values indicating more consistency. The decision where to put the threshold for conjunctions that are consistent enough to be considered as sufficient for the outcome depends on various specific features of the research such as the number of cases, one's trust in the data, and the specificity of existing theories

The final issue to resolve is the threshold of consistency that ought to be considered requisite for causal sufficiency. Note that if one chooses the relatively low threshold of 0.70 then the results reported in Table 12.4 mirror those reported in the earlier crisp-set analysis (Table 12.2). A higher threshold, of course, indicates a more restrictive configuration (fewer configurations meet the requirements).

Discussion

Any attempt to come to firm conclusions with respect to the viability of QCA is complicated by three features of the method. First, it has undergone continual evolution over the past few decades – most importantly from crisp-set (cs) QCA to fuzzy-set (fs) QCA, but in other respects as well. Because fs-QCA is relatively new, the QCA oeuvre is still tilted markedly toward cs-QCA. Thus, we know a lot about the achievements and limitations of the latter, and much less about the former – which remains an exciting, but as yet largely unproven, prospect. Beyond the fs/cs divide, QCA embraces a number of additional methodological options and interpretations. It is not a single method but rather a family of methods.[35]

Second, any discussion of strengths and weaknesses must distinguish between aspects of a method(s) that are intrinsic and aspects that are situational, that is, the product of what QCA researchers have chosen to do. The potential utility of a method should be differentiated from its actual employment. Unfortunately, the two are not always easy to tell apart. It is difficult to say what the potential achievements of a method might be – if employed in a manner different from its current employment. What *is* best-feasible practice QCA?[36]

[35] Rihoux and Ragin (2009: chs. 1–2).   [36] Rihoux and Ragin (2009); Schneider and Wagemann (2010).

Finally, the tradition against which QCA is to be evaluated – variously described as "statistical," "regression," or "linear/additive" – is also an ambient creature. Sometimes, it appears to embrace the entire field of methodology, as traditionally conceived. At other times, it appears to pertain only to regression analysis of observational data. Within the latter category, there is a world of difference between the naive employment of regression techniques and more sophisticated versions (e.g., with instrumental variables, combinatorial terms, and the like). Inevitably, the strengths and weaknesses of QCA – as well as its uniqueness – appear differently against these various backdrops.[37]

In sum, one's opinion of the QCA method depends partly upon one's view of the method – that is, which version of QCA one regards as best practice and which features of QCA one regards as intrinsic (defining) – as well as one's view of the alternatives. With these important caveats, the following strengths and weaknesses of the method may be highlighted.

(1) Whether or not one finds QCA an attractive method depends centrally on whether one views social phenomena as conforming to the template of causal conjunctions under conditions of equifinality and semi-determinism (no or few exceptions). This is, of course, an ontological assumption.[38]

We have seen how QCA authors Dirk Berg-Schlosser and Jeremy Mitchell approach the question of democratic survival in Europe during the interwar period – as one of discrete binary or fuzzy-set factors that combine in particular configurations to cause regimes to survive (or not). If, on the other hand, one believes that this question involves causes that are nonbinary, independent (rather than conjunctural), additive, and probabilistic, QCA does not present a plausible model of the data-generating process.

It is difficult to say, *a priori*, which set of assumptions about the world is more justified. Of course, I do not wish to imply that the choice between methods is entirely independent of empirical evidence. Even so, the same data may be regarded differently depending upon one's point of departure. And the choice between set-theoretic and independent/additive/probabilistic methods such as are traditional in most large-*N* analyses is highly consequential.

This is perhaps the most important point to be made about QCA, since it imposes a very specific shape on the data. Granted, all empirical tests impose *some* shape on the data. However, QCA presumes somewhat more about the

---

[37] Achen (2005) criticizes Ragin for constructing a straw-man opponent in the form of simple linear/additive regression models. Ragin counters that this is often how the technique is employed. In any case, it seems more germane to compare best practices in both fields, which is what I have endeavored to do in the following discussion.

[38] Hall (2003).

data-generating process than many alternative methods.[39] For example, regression methods can test both additive and interactive (multiplicative) relationships (though it assumes a causal-effects framework). QCA, however, is capable of handling only necessary-and-sufficient relationships, with an emphasis on relationships that take the special form of causal sufficiency achieved through combinations of factors (configurations). So the decision to employ QCA is also a decision about what sort of causal relationships are likely to be at work in a population.

(Readers may be curious why I provide extensive discussion of QCA but not of other techniques of data analysis such as regression. The main reason is that these other formats generally have little to say about research design, the focus of this section of the book. Another reason is that the link between principles of research design and standard techniques of data analysis such as regression or matching is fairly evident, while their link to QCA is less evident, justifying explicit discussion of the matter in this section.)

(2) Many assumptions are required for a complete QCA. Decisions must be made about how to define cases and the population of interest,[40] the conditions (causal factors) relevant for the analysis, coding of the cases (especially where thresholds must be assigned to concepts that are not naturally dichotomous), providing conditional coding for "logical remainder" cases, and identifying thresholds for sufficiency (how many exceptions to allow).

Properly employed, that is, with full transparency, QCA brings greater self-consciousness and honesty to the research process, hiding less "under the hood" relative to many traditional observational methods. It also calls attention to holes in the data – sometimes referred to as "extreme counterfactuals" – that remain hidden in many observational techniques and often affect regression results.[41] As we have seen, in QCA these "logical remainders" are identified and brought into the analysis as counterfactual thought-experiments. This degree of explicitness about what one does not know, and what one is assuming, may be considered an advantage of QCA relative to many other methods.

Nonetheless, the assumptions necessary for a complete QCA are probably greater in number than those required for a typical large-N data analysis. Certainly, they are much greater in number than the typical experiment (with randomized treatment). While researchers' decisions are presumably informed by theory and by in-depth knowledge of the cases under study, it remains the case that different choices about the same basic data are usually plausible, and

---

[39] Seawright (2005).   [40] For example, Berg-Schlosser and De Meur (2009: 23–24).
[41] King and Zheng (2006).

are likely to result in very different findings. This, in turn, suggests that QCA has stronger credentials as an exploratory form of research than as a confirmatory form of research.[42]

(3) Studies employing the QCA algorithm often study the entire population of an inference. Authors wish to understand why some outcome happened in one particular place/time or one circumscribed region/era, rather than why an outcome occurs generally (in a larger population). This means that there is no question of external validity because sample=population. Nonetheless, this approach to causal inference raises questions about internal validity insofar as the population of interest may be quite small, offering little evidence for the various propositions under investigation, out-of-sample testing is precluded, and the population itself may not be easy to delimit – raising issues of *boundedness*. Note that if the population cannot be easily defined, and if cases that appear to contradict the conclusions of a QCA lie outside the chosen population, the inference is problematic. Small- and medium-N analyses are especially prone to arbitrary domain restrictions, an issue discussed in Chapter 3.

Indeed, QCA is particularly sensitive to the composition of a chosen sample and its accompanying population. Adding or subtracting cases may fundamentally alter the pathways to Y, rendering a sufficient condition insufficient (or, in the probabilistic language of later versions, less sufficient).[43] Consider what happens if the population under consideration in our example is changed to include other countries (outside Europe) during the interwar period, or European countries in other historical periods. In this somewhat altered population the original arguments may not hold – GNP and government stability may no longer be sufficient for democratic survival (or may admit of many exceptions).

Of course, causal inferences based on other estimation techniques are also sensitive to the definition of a sample and population; this is a universal feature of causal argumentation. However, non-QCA approaches tend to be less sensitive because (a) the population is often defined in a more capacious fashion (so that small alterations have little effect on causal relationships), and (b) the relationships themselves are usually understood in a probabilistic fashion.

Note, finally, that there is nothing about the QCA algorithm that constricts the scope of inferences drawn from a chosen sample. Out-of-sample inferences

---

[42] Rihoux and De Meur (2009: 66) conclude that QCA techniques "allow the researcher to ask more focused 'causal' questions about ingredients and mechanisms producing (or not) an outcome of interest, with an eye on both within-case narratives and cross-case patterns." This seems a judicious description of the process.

[43] De Meur, Rihoux, and Yamasaki (2009: 157).

are still possible. Indeed, some QCA researchers embrace the search for general causal relationships.[44]

(4) QCA studies usually strive for a complete explanation of an outcome (in terms of sufficient causes), that is, *causes-of-effects*. Thus, Berg-Schlosser and Mitchell attempt to identify all the causes of democratic survival in interwar Europe. This means that QCA is much more ambitious than effects-of-causes studies (where only one or several related causes are examined), but also more challenging.

However, because each conjunction is evaluated separately (by the QCA algorithm and by case evidence) it is possible to disaggregate a single QCA into multiple effects-of-causes hypothesis. Here, we are likely to find that some conjunctures are more securely established than others. A conjuncture that describes a great number of cases with no exceptions is strongly supported by the evidence. By contrast, a conjuncture that describes no actual cases (a "logical remainders" case, constructed on the basis of a thought-experiment), or one for which there are many exceptions, is much less certain. These considerations are captured in the consistency score (see Table 12.4). Case-evidence not contained in the formal QCA may also provide differing levels of support for different conjunctures. Thus, while we tend to speak of a single QCA study as comprising a single analysis it may be more appropriately framed as multiple arguments nested within a single truth-table.

(5) QCA is not inherently a small- or large-N method. Although it is commonly described as qualitative (the "Q" in QCA), software developed by Ragin and his collaborators (now available for *Stata*, *R*, and *TOSMANA*) allows for the Boolean analysis of an infinite number of cases. That said, most QCA analyses to date have incorporated medium-sized samples ($10<N<50$) – presumably because relations of necessity/sufficiency are less likely to hold across larger populations.

Likewise, in principle QCA software allows for the analysis of an unlimited number of conditions. However, because each additional condition increases (by an order of magnitude) the number of possible combinatorial paths, the data is quickly exhausted.[45] Specifically, one finds increasing numbers of logical remainders (possible combinations of conditions that are void of empirical evidence). For this reason, most QCA work is conducted with a modest number of variables ($K<8$).

---

[44] For example, Schneider (2009).

[45] Berg-Schlosser and De Meur (2009: 27). The number of logical combinations is 2^K, where $K =$ the number of causal conditions.

This explains why, with respect to number of cases (N) and variables (K), QCA occupies a mid-station between traditional observational studies in the qualitative (small-N) and quantitative (large-N) traditions.

(6) There is an important difference in the level of *precision* offered by different versions of QCA. The crisp-set/deterministic version of QCA tells us the exact value of Y when X_1 (a configurational path to Y) is equal to 1. The crisp-set/not-quite-deterministic version of QCA (where there are exceptions to sufficiency) tells us the likely value of Y when X_1 is equal to 1. The fuzzy-set version of QCA tells us that, for a configuration with high consistency, $Y>X_1$ (probably) when $X_1=1$. Thus, with respect to the criterion of precision (Chapter 4), some versions of QCA are more informative than others.

(7) It is sometimes argued that the introduction of fuzzy sets (fs-QCA) solves problems associated with the original crisp-set version of QCA (cs-QCA). The obvious point here is that the coding of factors as fuzzy-sets is appropriate insofar as theory and data warrant it. That is, if there are strong reasons to suppose that a causal relationship between interval (or ratio) factors is discontinuous in nature, and one can intuit what those break-points are, then a fuzzy-set coding is warranted. If, on the other hand, one can neither intuit nor discover (empirically) plausible break-points in an interval scale then the use of fuzzy sets does not solve the problem of coding. Imposed set-relations are still arbitrary – though perhaps somewhat less arbitrary than crisp-set coding.

(8) Causal inferences based on QCA are vulnerable to specification errors – the inappropriate inclusion or exclusion of causal conditions/variables.[46] Suppose, for example, that democratic survival in the interwar era was affected not only by GNP and government stability but also by inequality. The inclusion of this new causal factor will introduce new pathways (configurations) to Y. Alternatively, suppose that one of the included factors turns out not to have a causal effect on democratic survival. If this factor is an element of an identified configuration – say, GNP – then naturally the whole argument is fallacious. If it is, instead, understood as a background factor – say, urbanization – then it has no effect on the results.

In this respect QCA is not fundamentally different from other analytic techniques. That said, one important contrast deserves to be flagged. In most analytic techniques the specification problem hinges on whether the included or omitted factor is correlated with the treatment (the causal factor of theoretical interest). If it is not – as in all experiments (if properly designed) and in

---

[46] Seawright (2005).

some natural experiments (if fortuitous) – then specification issues do not pose problems of confounding.

(9) QCA in its typical employment does not formally incorporate information about time, that is, the temporal ordering of variables. This has been attempted by a recent extension of QCA logic (tQCA),[47] as well as in a related technique known as sequence analysis.[48] However, when one adds the complexities of temporal ordering to the already challenging complexities of causal configurations the number of potential causal orderings is likely to overcome the data available to test them. Thus, relative to observational research designs with a significant temporal component (i.e., where there is observable variation within cases in causal variables of theoretical interest), QCA is a blunt instrument for causal assessment. We cannot directly observe the effect on Y of a change in X.

(10) QCA is usually understood as an observational technique for causal analysis. Granted, all the Boolean technique does is to clarify patterns in the data, patterns that are, of course, contingent upon the researcher's decisions about the inclusion and coding of variables (i.e., conditions and outcomes). A good deal of causal reasoning is required in order to infer causality from covariational (set-relational) patterns between X and Y, especially in situations where the treatment is not randomized, as the previous chapters have amply stressed. This aspect of QCA does not set it apart from other observational techniques.[49]

Naturally, one could also apply QCA to experimental data. Indeed, this might make sense if the experiment involves several treatments in various combinations (a *factorial* design, as explained in Chapter 10) and if one wishes to analyze causal sufficiency in addition to average treatment effects (ATE). To my knowledge, QCA has never been applied in this fashion; but this should be recognized as a choice, not an intrinsic limitation of the method. If experimental techniques were to be applied most of the concerns raised in this section would be obviated.

In other respects, the sort of obstacles and opportunities for reaching causal inference with QCA reiterates points we have already touched upon in the

---

[47] Caron and Panofsky (2005); Hino (2009). See also commentary in Ragin and Strand (2008).

[48] Abbott (1995, 2004); Abbott and Forrest (1986); Abbott and Tsay (2000); Everitt, Landau, and Leese (2001: ch. 4). See also Mahoney, Kimball, and Koivu (2009).

[49] QCA methodologists are generally cautious about inferring causality from QCA. "Technically speaking, such solutions express, more modestly, co-occurrences reflecting potential explicit connections. It is then up to researchers to decide (relying on their substantive and theoretical knowledge) how far they can go in the interpretation of the truth-table solution in terms of causality" (Ragin and Rihoux 2004: 6). "QCA minimization algorithms do not produce 'explanations' of a given outcome – they simply offer a reduced expression that *describes* a set of (observed) cases in a logically shorthand manner" (De Meur, Rihoux, and Yamasaki 2009: 155).

context of necessary/sufficient causes. Since causal sufficiency presumes a causal effect (as long as the sufficient condition is nontrivial), the investigation of causal effects may be employed to help prove causality. Thus, if one wishes to regard a particular configuration, X_1 (understood as a vector of causes), as causal it would be helpful if one could also provide evidence of a causal effect for X_1, using one of the strategies outlined in Chapter 11. Naturally, that may not always be possible, especially for conjunctures involving three or more causes and in samples of limited size. Even so, it is certainly desirable.

(11) By way of conclusion, one's willingness to accept a given conjuncture, X_1, as a sufficient cause of Y is bolstered if (a) the sample under investigation is large, (b) it is representative of the population of interest, (c) it is not arbitrarily bounded, (d) variables of interest (both conditions and the outcome) fall naturally into binary ("crisp") categories, (e) potential measurement errors appear to be minimal, (f) more than a few cases follow the designated path (so it cannot easily be dismissed as stochastic), and (g) there are no exceptions (the relationship is deterministic). It follows that one's willingness to accept a set of conjunctures as providing a complete (*causes-of-effects*) explanation for Y is contingent upon the foregoing factors for all such conjunctures, X_{1-N}. As has been pointed out, QCA is much more ambitious than the typical causal analysis insofar as it aims to provide a comprehensive explanation for an outcome.

This set of seven circumstances presents the most strenuous (severe, risky) test of a configurational hypothesis. If passed, strong evidence is provided for a proposition. Insofar as any one of these conditions is weakened, so is the evidence for causality.

Fortunately, other tools of causal inference may also be enlisted. (Indeed, some QCA-ers view these techniques as so integral to the method that they ought to be included within the rubric of "QCA." For our purposes, however, it is important to distinguish what is unique to QCA from what is not.) Typically, these include mechanisms, rival hypotheses, causal-process observations, and causal reasoning, as discussed in Chapter 11. Since these strategies often derive from a careful consideration of particular cases they are often described as case-based. Thus, Rihoux and De Meur inquire, "What is the 'narrative' behind the fact that ... high GNP per capita combined with governmental stability has led to survival ... of democracy in countries such as Belgium, Czechoslovakia, the Netherlands, and the UK?"[50]

A qualitative comparative analysis *by itself* is rarely definitive. Ragin affirms: "The interpretation of *sufficiency* must be grounded in the researcher's

---

[50] Rihoux and De Meur (2009: 65). See also Rihoux and Lobe (2009).

substantive and theoretical knowledge; it does not follow automatically from the demonstration of the subset relation."[51] Of course, the same could be said for most nonexperimental methods. Indeed, QCA was never intended to serve as a stand-alone method of causal inference. QCA methodologists generally recommend that this technique of data reduction be applied in conjunction with other methods.[52] If authors have not always heeded this advice, this is unfortunate.[53] But the point to focus on is that the QCA algorithm(s), if enlisted as one element of a broader, multimethod study, offers an insightful tool for causal inference wherever its configurational assumptions about causality seem plausible. It is a welcome addition to the toolkit of social science (and one worth exploring in a more detailed and nuanced fashion than we have been able to accomplish in this short discussion).[54]

---

[51] Ragin (2009: 99).

[52] For a list of studies that combine QCA with other methods see Ragin and Rihoux (2004: 5). See also Rihoux and Lobe (2009).

[53] Mahoney (2004).

[54] Interested readers are encouraged to explore the topic further through a rich, and ever-growing, literature (see sources cited above). There is, of course, much more to say about QCA than this short discussion can possibly touch upon.

Part IV

Conclusions

13

Unity and plurality

The sort of unity that is often thought to play a role in scientific theory choice ... involves both a unity and a plurality: "a *maximum number* of facts and regularities" are to be accommodated by "a *minimum* of theoretical conceptions and assumptions." Newton's theory is unified because it is able to bring a plurality of diverse phenomena under one theoretical treatment ... The situation we currently find in the literature on causation exhibits the opposite pattern. There is a plurality of theoretical perspectives on the nature of causation ... At the same time, there is a unity at the level of the phenomena to be comprehended.

Christopher Hitchcock[1]

Having laid out a framework of tasks, strategies, and criteria that define social science methodology, I now want to discuss how this framework maps onto the "paradigm wars" that have roiled the disciplines of social science over the past half-century.

For outsiders, as well as for many insiders, the distinctions evident across disciplines, methods, and schools are paramount. We sit at separate tables.[2] Yet there are also many things that we share. Moreover, there is little profit in emphasizing our differences, given that the presumed objective of scientific deliberation is, ultimately, to reach consensus. Incommensurability is not conducive to a productive interchange of ideas. If taken seriously, it prohibits knowledge cumulation. Consequently, this book has emphasized the methodological coherence of the social sciences.

In this chapter, I will address several controversies that have been left on the backburner until now: the debate between qualitative and quantitative methods; the debate between culturalist and rationalist models of behavior; and the debate among diverse schools of causality (positivist, potential outcomes, mechanismic, pluralist).

---

[1] Hitchcock (2003: 218).
[2] The term was applied by Almond (1990a) to political science, but it applies *a fortiori* to the social sciences at large.

At a high level of abstraction, these debates seem overwhelming. Scholars apparently adopt different theoretical constructs and methods and this prompts them to view the world in different ways. Cacophony rules – or a healthy pluralism, depending on one's point of view.

Yet the positions in these debates are less distinct than they first appear. It is difficult to say, precisely, what distinguishes qualitative and quantitative methods, culturalist and rationalist models of behavior, and various schools of causality. The terms that define these debates offer highly ambiguous formulations.

At a lower level of abstraction – that is, when talking about particular empirical questions – it is often difficult to distinguish cleanly among various theories and methodological perspectives. Thus, I will argue that at the level of *tasks*, *strategies*, and *criteria* there is greater consensus across the diverse disciplines of the social sciences than the high-order "philosophical" labels would suggest.

Qualitative versus quantitative

Perhaps no cleavage has been as persistent or as vociferous as the *qualitative versus quantitative* debate. For present purposes, I shall define "quantitative" as any inference based on large numbers of dataset observations, that is, statistical analysis. "Qualitative" will be understood as inferences based primarily on a few dataset observations (insufficient to form the basis for statistical analysis) and/or lots of causal-process observations (Chapter 12).[3]

Following this definition, one strategy of causal inference set forth in Chapter 10 – causal reasoning – is clearly qualitative (though it may build on quantitative findings). Likewise, several approaches – including regression-discontinuity, instrumental variables, and conditioning on confounders – are clearly quantitative.

Another set of approaches can be classified as commonly – but not intrinsically – qualitative. For example, the investigation of causal mechanisms is often carried out with causal-process observations, since the evidence available sometimes precludes the collection of a large sample of comparable

---

[3] The qualitative–quantitative distinction is discussed in Brady and Collier (2004); Bryman (1984); Caporaso (1995); Gerring and Thomas (2011); Glassner and Moreno (1989); Hammersley (1992); Mahoney and Goertz (2006); McLaughlin (1991); Munck (1998); Piore (1979); Shweder (1996); Snow ([1959] 1993); Tarrow (1995). See also entry for "Qualitative" in the Glossary.

observations. Even so, there are also plenty of quantitative investigations focused on causal mechanisms.[4]

Likewise, some approaches are generally – though, again, not intrinsically – practiced with large samples. In principle, an experiment could be conducted in a purely qualitative manner, for example, with a randomized treatment administered to one case (the treatment group), a second case serving as the control, and a few observations pre- and post-test. This small-N experiment would probably be superior in internal validity to a small-N observational analysis for all the reasons we have discussed. However, it would be subject to stochastic error. In any case, there are few examples of this sort of work in social science. The reason is that wherever randomization is possible it is usually possible to enlist multiple units. Indeed, it was pointed out that the virtue associated with randomization – that is, avoiding confounders – becomes plausible only as the number of units increases. From this perspective, the experimental method is implicitly a large-N method of analysis.

The same point might be made about nonrandomized approaches labeled *panel*, *cross-sectional*, and *longitudinal* in Chapter 10. A panel may be comprised of two cases, observed over a short period of time – hence, small-N. However, such an analysis will be open to threats to internal validity posed by stochastic error as well as systematic error, and – unlike large-N analyses – these threats cannot be effectively rectified by *ex post* statistical adjustments. There is, moreover, a serious problem of external validity. A small sample is less likely to be representative of a larger population since precision (reliability) co-varies with sample size. So, all things being equal, one would prefer that a panel (or cross-sectional or longitudinal) analysis enlist a large sample of observations.

Of course, all things are not always equal. Note that sample size is only one of many research design objectives (summarized in Table 9.3). It follows that sometimes it makes good sense to sacrifice N for the achievement of other virtues. Moreover, since qualitative evidence is often employed in tandem with other forms of evidence – a "multimethod" approach to causal inference – the relevant question is perhaps not whether or not to adopt a qualitative or quantitative method, but what *mixture* of methods is best (see below).

As an example, consider a classic question of political science: why parties?[5] And why, among parties, are some strong and highly centralized while others are weak and diffuse? This question may be approached at many levels and with a diverse array of methodological tools. A cross-national approach might

[4] Humphreys (2005); Imai *et al.* (2010).   [5] Aldrich (1995).

start with a measure of party strength such as legislative cohesion (how often do members of the same party vote together?), and then regress this indicator against various predictors.[6] Alternatively, if the hypothesis is narrowed to a single (binary) causal factor, such as parliamentarianism, a matching analysis could be applied. In either case, there are many threats to inference: for example, a relatively small and extremely heterogeneous sample, the possibility of many unmeasurable confounders, and the ubiquitous assignment problem. This does not mean that large-N cross-national analysis is fruitless. But it should engender skepticism and should spur additional modes of investigation.

One such mode is the case-study analysis in which a country experiences change on one of the causal factors of interest and the analyst can observe the outcome over time. Numerous studies, beginning with many of the pioneers of political science (e.g., Walter Bagehot, A. Lawrence Lowell, and Woodrow Wilson) have focused on the United States or Britain during the nineteenth century, the period in which mass parties appeared for the first time.[7] These cases offer certain advantages vis-à-vis most others insofar as the preconditions for parties appeared in a serial fashion rather than all at once, thus presenting some of the features of a natural experiment (where one feature is altered and everything else, or pretty much everything else, remains the same). Likewise, one might compare countries with similar background characteristics but dissimilar constitutions in order to discern the role of constitutional features in the development of party organization. Studies employing a most-similar comparison have often contrasted the United Kingdom, Canada, and the United States.[8]

Each of these single-case and small-N comparisons has the potential to enlist large-N analysis *within* the chosen case(s). Typically, authors focus on constituency and MP behavior. Thus, one might look to see if there is a connection between large constituencies (presumably less amenable to vote-buying and personalistic attachments) and party discipline within a country.[9] If so, this would support the contention that the expansion of suffrage paved the way for stronger parties.

There are many ways in which qualitative and quantitative evidence can be combined. Likewise, there are many purposes and styles of qualitative and quantitative analysis. Consequently, it is difficult to generalize about each

---

[6] Carey (2008).   [7] Cox (1987) reviews the literature and conducts his own analysis.
[8] For example, Epstein (1964).
[9] Cox (1987) addresses this issue, though it is not the main point of his argument.

genre's characteristic strengths and weaknesses. For example, some qualitative studies are undertaken with the objective of generating new hypotheses rather than testing extant hypotheses. In this context (explored in Chapter 2), problems of internal validity are somewhat less vexing, for the major contribution is theoretical rather than empirical. At some later date, one expects a follow-up study that adheres to high standards of appraisal. Its contribution is empirical rather than theoretical.

Returning to the main point, increasing the N of a research design is desirable if all things are equal. Size matters, for it means that more evidence is available to test a given hypothesis, providing insurance against errors caused by the presence of random variation, and allowing for statistical procedures to correct for the presence of confounders. A large sample usually means that sufficient variation is incorporated into the analysis along key parameters (X and Y). A large sample also means that the researcher may be able to apply random sampling techniques (selecting the sample randomly from the population of interest), enhancing a study's external validity. All this is to the good.

However, sometimes an increase in sample size causes more problems than it solves. It may enhance measurement error, for example. A larger sample may also involve the inclusion of observations that are not fully comparable (in ways that might affect the putative relationship between X and Y). This will create heterogeneities in the sample that may impair a valid, precise, and informative assessment of causal relationships. For this reason, it is often more sensible to work with a small, homogeneous sample than with a large, heterogeneous sample – especially if the latter requires complex modeling assumptions in order to render the analysis plausible.[10] Increasing sample size is also problematic if it does not enhance leverage on key factors of theoretical interest (X and Y). This is why rare events (revolutions, world wars, genocides) are often approached in a qualitative manner. Often, it makes more sense to look intensively at the few cases in which these phenomena occurred (relying on background knowledge of those cases in which these phenomena did not occur) rather than to diffuse our energies across the entire population, treating all observations equally within a large-N sample.

Note also that just because a sample is large does not mean that it has been selected randomly from the population of interest. Indeed, most large-N samples are not. So the size of a sample is not always an indication of its representativeness. (Sometimes, the addition of more observations renders a sample *less* representative.)

---

[10] These issues are discussed in greater length in Gerring (2007).

Finally, we must note the utility of causal-process observations (Chapter 12). Sometimes, a few causal-process observations are more important than many dataset observations. In this respect, the notion of judging a research design by sheer number of observations (N) is nonsensical.

Other contrasts between large- and small-N research designs can be imagined, and it is not my intention to offer a comprehensive review. However, I hope to have shown that many aspects of this venerable debate can be understood as a series of tradeoffs among specific tasks, strategies, and criteria. In this way, and to this extent, we may be able to reframe the debate in a more concrete, and less oppositional, fashion. One often finds that qualitative and quantitative research on the same general question prioritizes different methodological goals. Yet the goals themselves transcend the schism; they are universal, or nearly so. It is these goals that ought to guide our choice of research tools. Whether, or to what degree, the resulting study is classifiable as qualitative or quantitative – or some admixture – is a secondary concern.

Culturalism versus rationalism

Although this book is focused on formal issues of methodology, no methodological issue can be considered substantively neutral. Likewise, every theory has characteristic methodological affinities. In this respect, substantive arguments are also methodological arguments – arguments about how we ought to study a particular subject. As an example of this sort of theoretical/ methodological strife let us briefly consider the ongoing debate between cultural and rational models of human action.

The *cultural* model, broadly construed, derives from work by philosophers in the hermeneutic school (e.g., Dilthey, Schleiermacher, Heidegger, Gadamer, Habermas, Ricoeur, Taylor, von Wright, and Winch) and ethnographic work in the social-cultural wing of anthropology (e.g., Boas, Malinowski, Mead, Benedict, and Geertz). In recent years, this perspective has become identified with interpretivist and constructivist approaches to social science. Key points of synthesis include a focus on lived experience (as understood by the actors under study); the holistic quality of norms, values, and behavior; and the socially constructed (nonincentive-based) nature of the foregoing.[11]

---

[11] Almond and Verba ([1963] 1989); Anderson (1991); Banfield (1958); Barth (1969); Berger (1995); Cohen (1974); Eckstein (1988); Harrison and Huntington (2000); Hartz (1955); Hobsbawm and Ranger (1992); Inglehart (1977); Kertzer (1988); Kuper (1999); Laitin (1986); Munch and Smelser (1992);

The *rational* model of human action builds on the work of Enlightenment and post-Enlightenment writers like Hobbes, Bentham, Smith, and Mill, as well as more recent work emanating from the evolving field of economics (e.g., Jevons, Menger, Walras, Edgeworth, Marshall, and Pareto). Key analytic assumptions of the rational model of social action include utility maximization, perfect knowledge, and preferences that are complete, stable, and transitive. These assumptions (which may also be relaxed in various ways to allow for a more flexible model of human behavior) inform the social science genres of public choice, game theory, and political economy.[12]

Viewed methodologically, the ongoing debate between culturalism and rationalism may be reframed as a series of tradeoffs among specific tasks, strategies, and criteria. It might be argued, for example, that the culturalist camp prizes causal arguments that take the form of causes-of-effects rather than effects-of-causes (Chapter 12) and that their strategies of inference are focused on mechanisms rather than causal effects. More broadly, it might be argued that they privilege descriptive accounts over causal accounts. Indeed, it is often difficult to test a cultural theory because these factors can rarely be manipulated, even in principle (Chapter 8). One cannot assign individuals to a religion or a worldview (although the relative salience of a cultural factor can be manipulated in an experimental setting). Whether engaging in descriptive or causal accounts, culturalists are likely to privilege depth (i.e., fecundity or impact) over breadth and internal validity over external validity.

By contrast, those working within the rational-actor model have somewhat contrasting objectives – for causal accounts, for narrowly focused causes-of-effects hypotheses, for experimental or quasi-experimental research designs, and for models that are both parsimonious and general in scope.

So described, these schools are not so much hostile camps as varying – and potentially complementary – approaches to social science. Indeed, the lines drawn in the sand are less and less distinct as time goes on. Recent work has explored the causal impact of culture through experimental and quasi-experimental research designs, thus employing a set of methods associated with the rationalist tradition for a set of phenomena traditionally associated with the culturalist tradition.[13] Other scholars have constructed ethnographic and historical accounts of how markets and notions of self-interest and

Putnam (1993); Ross (1997); Scott (1985); Shweder and LeVine (1984); Thompson, Ellis, and Wildavsky (1990); Weber ([1904–5] 1958).
[12] Blaug (1978); Coleman and Fararo (1992); Friedman (1996); Levi (1997); Monroe (1991).
[13] Guiso, Sapienza, and Mingales (2006).

rationality evolve.[14] In this fashion, each school has transgressed the boundaries of the other.

The larger point of interest here is that these two schools – as well as others that might be identified – can be viewed as prioritizing different tasks, strategies, and criteria within the same overall methodological framework. What we gain from this portrayal is recognition of a common framework of understanding, which may help to heal the breach between these long-estranged approaches to social science.

Models of causality

Several causal frameworks vie for primacy in the contemporary social sciences. These may be summarized in a schematic fashion as (a) *covering law*, (b) *potential outcomes*, and (c) *pluralist* – of which the most important element is *mechanismic*. While no attempt will be made to systematically survey the voluminous literature on these venerable topics or to fully articulate arguments with various camps,[15] it is important that we advert to these debates, if only to signal how the current framework attempts to make sense of them.

The covering-law model

For many years, a unitary view of causal explanation held sway. Following Carl Hempel and others associated with the so-called "positivist" school in philosophy of science, it was assumed that there was (or ought to be) one meaning of causation and one method of constructing causal arguments – the *covering-law* (aka *deductive-nomological*) approach.[16]

According to this view, causality refers to a constant (deterministic) conjunction or a probabilistic association between X and Y. Causal explanation occurs by subsuming the particulars of an event or class of events under the rubric of a universal law, which can then be tested by reference to observable predictions derived from the theory. Hempel and colleagues were no doubt thinking of well-known natural laws such as Snell's law, Hooke's law, Ohm's law, Joule's law, Newton's law of gravitation, Newton's three laws of motion, Boyle's law, and the four laws of thermodynamics. They saw no reason to abandon the same approach that seemed so successful in natural science when

---

[14] Geertz (1968); Gudeman (2001); Hirschman (1977); Polanyi (1968); Smelser and Swedberg (1995).
[15] For a more extended version of the argument see Gerring (2005). [16] Hempel and Oppenheim (1948).

investigating social phenomena. Thus, in constructing a heuristic explanation for the French Revolution Hempel offered the following formulation: "A revolution will tend to occur if there is a growing discontent, on the part of a large part of the population, with certain prevailing conditions."[17]

Criticisms of the covering-law model are legion. Writers have focused on the narrowness of this view – its seeming neglect of causal mechanisms, its blasé attitude toward generalization (as if all subjects could be incorporated into precise, universal laws that completely account for a phenomenon), its neglect of additional criteria that would qualify a causal proposition as useful, and so forth. I will not bother to rehearse these arguments here.[18]

However, it is worth emphasizing that the approach to causality taken in this book regards generalizability, precision, and causal impact as legitimate goals of science (Chapters 3 and 8), and in this respect is in sync with the covering-law model. Of course, whether a given theory is properly regarded as a "law" depends on how successful it is in achieving these goals. How far does the theory stretch? (how universal?) How many exceptions are there? How precise are the predictions? If the theory is causal in nature, how many additional factors (outside the theory) also impact the outcome of interest? I think it is fair to say that all social science explanations *aspire* to law-like status, even though few come very close to the ideal established by physical laws such as those listed above.[19]

Thus, it might be said for the covering-law model of causality that it is true as an ideal-type. However, it implies an overly optimistic standard of generality, precision, and causal impact, one that is unlikely to be met very often in the social sciences. Moreover, it has little to say about many additional features of causal argumentation such as the generative component of causality – not to mention, the manifold features of causal analysis discussed in previous chapters – and as such does not offer a compelling overall framework. It is informative, but incomplete.

The potential-outcomes model

In recent decades, discussions of causality have shifted from the realm of causal explanation (what is a good causal theory?) to the realm of causal

---

[17] Quoted in Bohman (1991: 19). This interpretation of the French Revolution is offered hypothetically, as an illustration of the covering-law approach; it was not a subject that Hempel had studied.

[18] Virtually all of the studies cited under the pluralist model (below) might be cited here, as they tend to take the covering-law model as their point of departure. See also Hitchcock (2005).

[19] Kincaid (1990).

inference (what is a good test of causality?). In particular, discussion has focused on statistical work by Jerzy Neyman, Donald Rubin, Paul Holland, and their collaborators. This body of work has come to be known variously as the *counterfactual, experimental, interventionist, manipulation, potential-outcomes,* or *Neyman–Rubin–Holland* causal model.[20]

Strictly interpreted, the potential-outcomes model is about the measurement of causal effects, understood as average treatment effects (ATE) or some variant thereof (Chapter 9).[21] Subsequently, this model has been generalized so as to encompass graphical models (by James Heckman, Judea Pearl, James Robins, and others).[22] However, my discussion will focus on the earlier version promulgated by Rubin, Holland, and collaborators – potential outcomes, *tout court.*

My understanding of causality and of causal effects builds on the potential-outcomes model, but is not reducible to that model, or, rather, let us say, it is not reducible to a narrow view of that model.

First, ATE or one of its variants is not always achievable, even where desirable. Many social science studies focus instead on a much broader and more ambiguous question: namely, whether X causes Y, and if so what direction that causal effect might be (+ or –). Of course, the latter might be seen as a diffuse variant of the former (after all, one is still looking for changes in Y corresponding to changes in X). Yet it is not clear whether those in the potential-outcomes tradition would accept this more ambiguous objective as legitimate.

Second, ATE does not constitute the sum-total of causal inference or explanation. One might be interested, for example, in the distribution of Y given a particular value for X. This is the question of interest for *necessary* and *sufficient* causal arguments, as discussed above. One might also be interested in the *variance* of Y, given X.[23] Other practical and theoretical questions can be imagined, as sketched briefly in Chapter 9.

Third, the potential-outcomes model has little to say about problems of causal heterogeneity.[24] Note that wherever a treatment has heterogeneous effects across a sample of units the resulting analysis – even if it takes the form

---

[20] Neyman ([1923] 1990); Collingwood (1940); Fisher (1935); Gasking (1955); Holland (1986); Lewis (1973); Rosenbaum (1984); Rubin (2008); von Wright (1971). For accessible recent discussions, see Berk (2005); Brady (2008); Imbens and Wooldridge (2009); Morgan and Winship (2007: ch. 1); Woodward (2005). Accounts critical of various aspects of the potential outcomes model can be found in Dawid (2007); Heckman (2005); Morgan and Winship (2007: ch. 10); Pearl (2009a, 2009b, 2009c).
[21] This limited objective is recognized by Holland (1986: 945).
[22] Heckman (2005, 2008); Pearl (2005, 2009b).   [23] Braumoeller (2006).
[24] But see Rosenbaum (2010: ch. 15).

of a well-implemented experiment – will give a correct (unbiased) but potentially *misleading* estimate of causal effects. If, for example, a treatment has positive effects on some subjects and negative effects on others (because of complex interaction effects), the estimate will reveal only the ATE across all subjects. Depending upon the mix of subjects, this effect may be positive, negative, or nil. But it will not shed light on causal factors at work at the *unit* level, which may be the most theoretically and substantively relevant. There are, of course, ways of handling this sort of problem, for example, by choosing a more homogeneous sample at the outset, by comparing results across different sorts of units contained within a heterogeneous sample (making sure that the randomization procedure stratifies according to theoretically relevant parameters), or through interaction tests. To be sure, the potential-outcomes model can be adjusted so as to include a consideration of these matters, even though in the event they are often left aside.

Fourth, the potential outcomes model has little to say about many strategies of causal inference – including mechanisms, alternate outcomes, rival hypotheses, and causal reasoning. Again, these strategies could be integrated into the potential-outcomes model (via causal graphs), and some movement in this direction can be observed.[25]

A fifth problem is that the potential-outcomes model seems to exclude from consideration as causes any factors that cannot be directly manipulated – at least in principle – in a laboratory or field experiment.[26] This leaves many theoretical interests of social science, including race, sex, age, ethnicity, culture, and inequality in an ambiguous state of methodological purgatory. Of course, this is a matter of degree and of interpretation. Certain aspects of race, sex, age, ethnicity, culture, and inequality can be manipulated, and perhaps some day options for manipulation will expand (e.g., with the technology of genetics). It is unclear how to understand the notion of *manipulable in principle*, and it is unclear how strictly researchers in the potential-outcomes fold wish to adhere to this dictum.[27] The approach taken here recognizes manipulability as a *ceteris paribus* criterion of all causal models, but not one that can always be fully satisfied (Chapter 8).

A sixth problem is that the potential-outcomes model is focused on measuring the impact of a single causal factor on a specific outcome (effects-of-causes), leaving aside the more ambitious goal of ascertaining the wealth of

---

[25] For example, Glynn and Gerring (2011); Glynn and Quinn (2011).
[26] Holland (1986); Holland and Rubin (1988: 226).
[27] Morgan and Winship (2007: 278–280); Woodward (2005).

causal factors that may have contributed to an outcome (causes-of-effects), as discussed above. It seems possible – at least in principle – to expand the framework to include different types of causal investigations, including a relatively comprehensive accounting of all the causes of a particular effect. But it is not at all clear that members of the potential-outcomes tradition would approve of this more diffuse rendering of the framework, given that the solution of such a causal problem would in most circumstances be considerably more tentative than the usual effects-of-causes approach.

A seventh problem is that the technical vocabulary developed by Rubin and his collaborators in the context of statistics often obscures important issues in research design. Violations of SUTVA (the stable unit treatment assumption, or noninterference), for example, may arise from many sources.[28] As such, it is a rather unspecific designation and offers little assistance to scholars (whether working in an experimental or observational mode) who are seeking to establish a site of investigation and a method of analysis.[29]

A final problem is that the potential-outcomes model of causal analysis appears to have little to say to scholars whose work is qualitative, rather than quantitative. Again, the model may be capable of reformulation so that it would speak to nonstatistical research. But it is not clear whether this reformulation would appeal to those who currently identify with the label (most of whom are statisticians).

Where does this leave us? If strictly interpreted, the potential-outcomes model excludes many important issues pertaining to causal explanation and inference, as outlined above. If loosely interpreted it is more inclusive but also less concise, resembling the more diffuse framework presented in this book. Like many topics, one's opinion of the potential-outcomes model depends upon one's understanding of the model. And, like all active research agendas, it is a moving target. One is at pains to predict how the potential-outcomes model will be understood in 2020 or 2030. (Perhaps it will look like the framework presented here.)

---

[28] This is recognized implicitly in recent work by Rubin (2008) and some of his associates (e.g., Rosenbaum 1987). Insofar as the Rubin causal model comes to encompass these additional considerations, it becomes more satisfactory as a general framework for causal assessment. However, it also becomes less concise and less mathematical in nature. Indeed, it becomes more like the complex "criterial" approach presented in this text.

[29] Pearl (2009b).

Pluralism and monism

In contrast to the monist perspectives on causation presumed by the covering-law and potential-outcomes models, some scholars argue that causation is *plural* in nature. Accordingly, no single model can hope to encompass the multiple objectives of causal argumentation across the sciences (or the social sciences).

The pluralist perspective has a long lineage. Aristotle divided the subject into four types: *formal causes* (that into which an effect is made, thus contributing to its essence); *material causes* (the matter out of which an effect is fashioned); *efficient causes* (the motive force which made an effect); and *final causes* (the purpose for which an effect was produced).[30]

In recent times, it has become common to distinguish between *deterministic* and *probabilistic* causal arguments,[31] *correlational* arguments and arguments focused on causal *mechanisms*,[32] *top-down* and *bottom-up* explanations,[33] *dependence* and *production* causes,[34] *causes-of-effects* and *effects-of-causes*.[35]

Even more differentiated typologies have also been developed. Mario Bunge identifies four types of causal explanation: (1) *covering-law* models involve a "subsumption of particulars under universals"; (2) *interpretive* causation focuses on the sense, meaning, or intention of an action; (3) *functional* explanation focuses on the purpose (telos) of an action; and (4) *mechanismic* causation focuses on "the mechanism(s) likely to bring about the desired goal."[36] Henry Brady also discerns four types of causation: (1) a *regularity* theory associated with Hume, Mill, and Hempel; (2) a *counterfactual* theory associated with the work of David Lewis; (3) a *manipulation* theory associated with the experimental tradition (aka the potential-outcomes model), and (4) a *mechanisms/capacities* theory associated with the realist tradition in philosophy of science.[37] Charles Tilly claims to have discovered

---

[30] On the history of causality see Bunge (1959); Machamer and Wolters (2007).

[31] Goertz and Starr (2003); Spohn (1983); Waldner (2002).

[32] Bhaskar ([1975] 1978); Dessler (1991); Elster (1989); George and Bennett (2005); Harre (1970, 1972); Hedstrom and Swedberg (1998: 7); Mahoney (2001); McMullin (1984); Ragin (1987). Salmon (1990) distinguishes between statistical and aleatory causes, which to my mind is virtually identical to the distinction between correlational and mechanismic.

[33] Glennan (2002: 1) explains, "The top-down approach explains an event by showing it to be part of a larger nomological or explanatory pattern, while the bottom-up approach explains an event by describing the network of causes that are efficacious in bringing that event about" (see also Kitcher 1989 and Salmon 1989).

[34] The first understands causation in terms of "counterfactual dependence between wholly distinct events." The second understands as a cause any action that "helps to generate or bring about or produce another event" (Hall 2004).

[35] Holland (1986); Mahoney and Goertz (2006).   [36] Bunge (1997: 412–413).   [37] Brady (2002).

five views of causal explanation, which he labels *skepticism, covering-law, propensity, system,* and *mechanism.*[38]

Writers disagree on how, precisely, to divide up this complex subject. Indeed, causal pluralism can mean many different things.[39] But most self-identified pluralists probably agree on one general point: "Different types of causes require different approaches to empirical analysis."[40] That is, how we choose to understand causation has important – if often disguised – effects on what sort of causal arguments and empirical tests we are likely to pursue, as articulated by Charles Tilly in the epigraph to this chapter. And all of these models of causality have legitimate standing in the work of social science.[41]

Causal pluralism offers an important corrective to a naive monism such as that purveyed by the covering-law model. However, it also raises several potential difficulties.

First, causal typologies such as those sketched above may overstate the epistemological *different-ness* of causal explanations in the social sciences. Consider, for example, the distinction between causal arguments that are "correlational" (covariational) in nature and those that rely on the identification of causal mechanisms.[42] Stuart Glennan, in a widely cited article, argues explicitly that "there should be a dichotomy in our understanding of causation" – between mechanism causes and correlation causes.[43] Of course, much depends on how we choose to define the terms of this dichotomy. Let us suppose that correlations refer to covariational patterns between a cause and an effect, and that mechanisms refer to the connecting threads (pathways) between the purported cause and its effect. The question can then be posed as follows: are there causal explanations that feature only the associational patterns between an *X* and *Y*, without any consideration of what might link them together, or, alternatively, "mechanismic" accounts that ignore patterns of association between cause and effect?

My sense is that such constrained forms of inference are relatively rare in the social sciences. Granted, some correlational-style analyses slight the explicit discussion of causal mechanisms, but this is usually because the author considers the causal mechanism to be clear and hence not worthy of explicit

---

[38] Tilly (2001).   [39] De Vreese (2007); Hitchcock (2007).

[40] Marini and Singer (1988: 349). See also Tilly (2001: 22).

[41] Goertz and Starr (2003); Ragin (1987, 2000). Among philosophers, see Cartwright (2004, 2007); Hall (2003); Reiss (2009).

[42] Bhaskar ([1975] 1978); Dessler (1991); Elster (1989); George and Bennett (2005); Harre (1970, 1972); Hedstrom and Swedberg (1998: 7); Mahoney (2001); McMullin (1984); Ragin (1987).

[43] Glennan (1992: 50).

interrogation.[44] Moreover, a mechanismic argument without any appeal to covariational patterns between X and Y does not make any sense. The existence of a causal mechanism *presumes* a pattern of association between an exogenous X and an endogenous Y. Thus, to talk about mechanisms is also, necessarily, to talk about covariational patterns. Moreover, the suggested causal mechanism is itself covariational in nature since it presupposes a pattern of association among a set of intermediate variables (X with M, and M with Y). Granted, these patterns of intermediate association may not be directly observable; they may simply be assumed, based upon what we know about the world. They may be impossible to directly manipulate; even so, the causes of M must be manipulable and in this sense they achieve the general goal of manipulability (Chapter 8). In any case, it seems overly simplistic and perhaps misleading to separate out correlational and mechanismic patterns of explanation if these are understood as dichotomous (mutually exclusive) types.[45] Both are important. For the purpose of causal explanation (as opposed to causal effects), both are necessary.

Arguably, the apparent strife across schools of causality is a product of the fact that they are talking about different *aspects* of causation. The covering-law model draws attention to several of the ultimate goals of causal explanation: natural laws that are general in purview as well as precise. The potential-outcomes model focuses on how to define and estimate causal effects. The mechanismic model draws attention to the critical role of causal mechanisms in causal explanation and inference. Viewed in this fashion, debates between different schools are a bit like the fable of the blind men and the elephant. Each has something true to say about the subject, but the coherence of this truth is not apparent from the limited perspective adopted by each school.

A second point is that grand methodological and epistemological concepts are usually less contentious when disaggregated. For example, rather than speaking of covering laws I have spoken about the specific criteria that a covering law implies, for example, precision, generality, and causal impact. Rather than speaking of general approaches to causal inference (interpretive, covering law, mechanismic, regularity/covariational, manipulation, skepticism, propensity, system, bottom-up, bottom-down, etc.) I have attempted to delineate tasks, strategies, and criteria that persons identifying with these approaches might all recognize as legitimate (i.e., useful). Insofar as one

---

[44] This may or may not be a valid assumption; sometimes, writers are rather cavalier about the existence of causal mechanisms. My point is simply that in ignoring explicit discussion of causal mechanisms they are in no way challenging the significance of mechanisms in causal explanation.
[45] For further discussion see Gerring (2008, 2010).

wishes to overcome causal pluralism one is well advised to scope down – to smaller, more operational methodological issues.

Likewise, when debating specific causal questions – does economic development lead to democratization? do vouchers enhance educational attainment? – epistemological disagreements are rarely prominent.[46] It is not clear that covering-law, covariational, mechanismic, etc., answers to these questions would be so different. (And if they were, it is not clear that these different answers should have equal weight in our deliberations.) This suggests that epistemological debates may be more important at the level of theory than at the level of praxis. Some philosophical debates are merely philosophical.

Finally, as a practical matter, diversity at a foundational level is probably not helpful for the progress of social science. There is little *advantage* in a plural account of causation. If causation means different things to different people then causal arguments cannot meet. Ships are allowed to pass silently in the night, to invoke an old metaphor. Consider the correlational/mechanismic accounts of causation. What are we to make of a situation in which one writer supports an argument based on *X*/*Y* covariational patterns, while another supports a contrary argument based on the existence of causal mechanisms? Is this argument adjudicable if neither recognizes the relevance of the other's approach? Common sense suggests that both *X*/*Y* (correlations) and *M* (mechanisms) are important elements of any causal argument. Thus, although we can easily imagine situations in which these two sorts of evidence lead to different conclusions it does not follow that they are incommensurable.

Insofar as we value cumulation and consensus in the social sciences there is a strong *prima facie* case for a unified account of causation.[47] From a normative perspective, the pluralist vision of distinct causal types is unappealing. Unity, not plurality, should be the goal of any causal methodology. (This continues a refrain from Chapter 1, where I argued for the importance of methodological unity across the social sciences.)

A unified account

Now that pluralists have succeeded in taking causation apart, I believe that members of the social science community have strong incentives to put

---

[46] Of course, they may be prominent in the sort of questions we choose to pose.
[47] This expresses the spirit of Brady (2002) and Mahoney (2008).

Humpty Dumpty back together again. The crucial caveat is that this unified account of causation must be sufficiently encompassing to bring together all the styles of evidence that we find useful for identifying causal relationships in the social sciences. This includes the desiderata invoked by various schools of causation. Unity is useful, but not if achieved by arbitrary definitional fiat – unless, of course, it can be demonstrated that some approaches are manifestly wrong or unhelpful in achieving causal inference.

It is my hope that the account of causation offered in Part III of the book is sufficiently compelling, and sufficiently inclusive, to restore a degree of unity to this fragmented subject. My efforts lean heavily on the structure provided by causal graphs, as articulated by Judea Pearl and collaborators (Chapter 11).[48] Even so, important elements of causal inference are difficult to represent in graphical form. Here, too, there are limits to what a single set of tools can accomplish.

Thus, rather than a parsimonious model of causality this book presents a loose framework to describe the quest for causal knowledge. In my discussion of the definition of causality (Chapter 8), the goals of causal argumentation (Table 8.1), the goals of causal inference (Table 9.3), and the strategies that may be employed in reaching causal inferences (Table 10.1), the reader will find a wide variety of perspectives represented. Some of these perspectives on causal explanation and inference might be classified as mechanismic, others as covariational; other aspects might be associated with other schools of causation, as outlined above. And still others are not clearly aligned with any single school or tradition. In this respect, one might say that the pluralist's mission is fulfilled.

Yet the proposed framework also purports to be unified. There are not different tasks, strategies, and criteria for each school of causality. There is one set of tasks, strategies, and criteria that – I argue – applies to all schools. For example, while an author might decide to focus on the correlational aspect of a causal theory in a given study he or she can still be held accountable for ignoring the mechanismic aspect of that theory, and vice versa. In this respect, the monist's mission is fulfilled. Evidently, much hinges on how (at what level) one chooses to define pluralism and monism.[49]

---

[48] Halpern and Pearl (2005); Pearl (2009b).

[49] Hitchcock (2003). Perhaps all that needs to be said is that the author is defending a particular version of monism, as set forth in Chapter 1. If some writers (e.g., Reiss 2009) prefer to regard it as pluralist there is no harm in that, as long as it is recognized that this version of pluralism is a lot more monist than other versions.

By way of conclusion, perhaps it is fair to say that the present framework represents an account of social science that is at once plural (because there are many tasks, strategies, and criteria) and unitary (because each task, strategy, and criterion is ubiquitous). In any case, it is hoped that the framework can help to overcome the fragmentation of social science implicit in the proliferation of separate schools, without forcing us into a Procrustean bed that is too small to contain the diverse goals and subjects of contemporary social science.

14

Setting standards

Our problem as methodologists is to define our course between the extremes of inert skepticism and naive credulity . . .

Donald Campbell[1]

If you insist on strict proof (or strict disproof) in the empirical sciences, you will never benefit from experience, and never learn from it how wrong you are.

Karl Popper[2]

All the tasks, strategies, and criteria noted in the previous chapters are considered valid, *ceteris paribus*. And yet *ceteris* is not always *paribus*. A key theme of this book is that methodological choices frequently involve *tradeoffs*. Satisfying one dimension may involve sacrificing another. Tasks, strategies, and criteria often conflict. Accordingly, for every dimension listed in Table 1.1 and in subsequent tables throughout the book one can locate conflicting imperatives.[3]

The call for discovery is at odds with the call for accurate appraisal. Indeed, exploratory research is typically carried out in a different fashion than research whose primary goal is confirmatory (falsificationist), as emphasized in Chapter 2.

Truth and novelty (discovery) often collide. In the words of an old aphorism, What is new is not true, and what is true is not new.

In developing concepts, one often finds oneself torn between demands for resonance (i.e., accordance with established usage), on the one hand, and demands for fecundity, causal utility, and operationalization, on the other. Familiar definitions are not always useful. But entirely unfamiliar concepts – those that strain the limits of current usage – are also confusing (Chapter 5).

---

[1] Campbell (1988: 361).   [2] Popper ([1934] 1968: 50).

[3] The importance of methodological tradeoffs in the work of social science and natural science is featured in the work of David Collier, Daniel Haussman, Larry Laudan, Giovanni Sartori, and Rudra Sil.

Demands for good description (Part II) may conflict with demands for good causal explanation (Part III). *What* questions may call for a different approach than *why* questions. Likewise, the search for a fruitful causal theory (Chapter 8) may conflict with the search for a strong causal research design (Chapters 9, 10, and 11).

Among the criteria pertaining to a good causal theory the demand for theoretical breadth often conflicts with the demand for causal impact (Chapter 8). Researchers parse this conflict in different ways, leading to divergent aesthetics. Some would prefer to explain 10 percent of the variation across 1,000 cases (privileging breadth), while others would prefer to explain 90 percent of the variation across ten cases (privileging impact). This is sometimes viewed as a contrast between "lumping" and "splitting."[4]

Under the rubric of causal analysis there are additional tradeoffs (Table 9.3). One that we have commented on repeatedly is the tradeoff between internal and external validity. Sometimes, achieving one precludes achieving the other. This is especially marked in experimental research, which often makes strong claims to internal validity but may be unconvincing (or simply ambiguous) in generalizability.

Some inter-criteria relationships are nonmonotonic. For example, it is often observed that broadening a theory makes it easier to test, for in expanding the scope one clarifies the population of the inference and, more important, identifies a broader range of empirical opportunities to judge the theory's success or failure. Here, methodological criteria dovetail. However, beyond a certain point, as a theory's scope enlarges the empirical predictions emanating from the theory tend to multiply and become more diffuse. It is no longer so easy to identify clear "pass" and "fail" tests. This is what one finds with abstract macro-level social theories such as those based on the work of Smith, Marx, Weber, Durkheim, and Freud. At this point, the demand for theoretical breadth and the demand for accurate appraisal diverge. Thus, the relationship between theoretical breadth and falsifiability may be described as "Kuznets curve" (inverted U). A theory that applies to a single event is difficult to falsify, as is a theory that explains everything. Somewhere in between is the golden mean for which we strive.

These are just a few of the myriad tradeoffs involved in social science research. Many others can readily be identified. (Perhaps the reader has been keeping a running tally.)

---

[4] Hexter (1979).

Trade-ups

The "tradeoffs" perspective articulated above is pleasing from a pluralist perspective. One can choose to be a qualitativist or quantitativist, a culturalist or a rationalist, or anything else, by emphasizing different elements of the framework. All approaches seem to be validated, at least to some extent or in some degree. Social science methodology is a very large tent.

Yet if scholars are free to prioritize criteria as they see fit – perhaps in accordance with some *ex ante* theory of the way the world works – can we ever say that a researcher has made a wrong choice? Are all methodologies ultimately reducible to ontological (pre-empirical) commitments (sometimes referred to as *paradigms*)?[5] Does it all come down to a matter of taste?

There are several responses to this apparent dilemma. First, the dimensions of what might qualify as good taste are not limitless. Although scholars working within different traditions can, of course, choose which criteria to prioritize in a given study, they do not create their own (unique) criteria. I have argued that desiderata contained in Table 1.1 are universal in scope (across the disciplines of social science). Thus, when an author relinquishes his or her hold on one criterion for the more full possession of another, the value of the resulting work gains and loses accordingly.

In this spirit, many of the dichotomies that we habitually employ to categorize work in the social sciences – theoretical/empirical, small-*N*/large-*N*, experimental/nonexperimental, qualitative/quantitative, culturalist/rationalist, and so forth – might be better understood as choice-sets along various dimensions of tasks, strategies, and criteria. Each of these research traditions is an effort to maximize a particular set of virtues, while downplaying a corresponding set of vices. Indeed, arguments among schools, theories, and methods usually appeal to a shared set of norms. (How else can one convert the heathen?) It is these basic-level norms that I have tried to keep in view. From this perspective, there is somewhat less disagreement than is apparent from the constant to-and-fro among partisans of different methodological and theoretical camps. Each has chosen to maximize different goods, but the goods themselves are widely recognized.

Second, within the context of a given study some choices may be superior to others. That is, one set of concepts, arguments, and analyses may lead to a better reconciliation of methodological demands than another. We are thus led to a comparative approach that judges an argument or analysis against

[5] Walker (2010).

others that might be substituted in its place (i.e., others that would explain the same phenomenon). Wherever tradeoffs exist, the researcher must prioritize tasks, strategies, and criteria, deciding which combination provides the best overall fit. For example, it ought to be possible to decide whether a qualitative, quantitative, or mixed (qualitative/quantitative) approach to a particular problem is warranted. And, to the extent that this is possible, one may be able to bring intransigent debates to heel. The key is to transform abstract "philosophical" talk about broad schools and traditions into pragmatic discussions about specific tasks, strategies, and criteria.

The work of social science is a dynamic process of adjustment – not a rigid, rule-governed activity, as implied by many methods texts. Some adjustments are zero-sum (*tradeoffs*). Others are positive-sum (*trade-ups*). The methodological framework set forth in this book is quite different, therefore, from a methodological pluralism that considers all approaches equally fruitful, and worlds away from "relativism" and "incommensurability."[6] I would like to think of it as pluralism within limits, a happy median-point between the straitjacket of logical positivism and the anything-goes style of post-structuralism.

Of course, most methodologies also claim this fertile middle ground. (Neither logical positivism nor poststructuralism is very popular among social scientists today.) And there is so much room between these extremes that it scarcely clarifies things to declare one's fealty to the golden mean. And yet the point is not merely rhetorical. All areas of inquiry must reach an accommodation between freedom and constraint. It is hoped that an appropriate balance is achieved by the present framework.

Multimethod research

One potential solution to the problem of conflicting tasks, strategies, and criteria is to be found in *multimethod* research (aka triangulation). For each research problem, let a hundred – or at least several – research designs bloom.[7]

Given the large number of tasks, strategies, and criteria that vie for consideration in a work of social science it is not surprising that researchers often

---

[6] Laudan (1996: 19) provides a brief summary of relativist positions.

[7] Axinn and Pearce (2006); Leech and Onwuegbuzie (2009) offer a nice overview. See also Ahmed and Sil (2008); Bennett and Braumoeller (2006); Brewer and Hunter (2006); Campbell and Stanley (1963); Clark and Creswell (2007); Creswell (2008); Dunning (2008c); Greene (2007); Jick (1979); Lieberman (2005); Lutfey and Freese (2005); Paluck (2010); Rossi and Freeman (1993); Tashakkori and Teddie (1998); White (2002); Wong (2002), and the *Journal of Mixed Methods Research* (Sage).

find themselves in situations where several research designs offer plausible approaches to a given problem. For example, research into the causal effect of vouchers on school performance might be conducted with randomized designs, with large-N nonexperimental evidence (drawn from many school districts), or with in-depth case studies (of particular schools or classes). Although the experimental method is usually the superior research design from the perspective of internal validity (caveats are noted in Chapter 10), it would be folly to ignore other options. Often, there is much that can be gained from diversifying one's portfolio. In particular, observational research is generally essential at the initial stage of discovery. Note that the construction of an experiment presumes the identification of a fruitful hypothesis around which a treatment can be devised. However, the identification of a fruitful hypothesis usually grows out of *non*experimental encounters with the world. For this reason, experimental work feeds off observational research. Likewise, large-N observational research often feeds off research of an ethnographic or clinical nature – inductive studies in which conclusions grow out of deep knowledge of a particular context.

Thus, for a variety of reasons, multimethod research is increasingly popular in the social sciences today. At the same time, one must be wary of the ambiguities and limitations of this universal solvent.

First, there is the problem of defining the key term, *method* (or research design). As it happens, the boundaries of a method or research design are not always clear, and this means that it is often difficult to say where a single method leaves off and multimethod work begins. For example, many experiments involve some "thick description": for example, unstructured interviews with participants (usually at the conclusion of the experiment) or ethnographic observation of the experiment as it unfolds.[8] Sometimes, this is written up as a separate section of a book or report; sometimes, it is folded into the main discussion; sometimes, it serves merely as background, informing the conclusions of the experimenter (without formal comment). In which instance has triangulation occurred?

Similarly, in the analysis of large-N observational data there are many – indeed limitless – ways of setting up a research design, and of altering that analysis (*ex post facto*). One might, for example, change the sample, the population, the key inputs and outputs, or the technique of analysis. Any

---

[8] Kelman (1982) offers general reflections on research ethics in the social sciences. Mazur (2007) and Sales and Folkman (2000) discuss research on human subjects. Paluck (2009) and Wood (2006) investigate ethical dilemmas of field research, with special focus on areas of intense conflict.

one of these alterations might be referred to as a discrete method – or as robustness tests within the same overall research design. The distinction between "robustness tests" and "multimethod research" is thus a matter of taste.

None of this should dull our enthusiasm for multimethod research (or robustness tests). But it should engender some skepticism about our use of the term. If the concept of a "method" is ambiguous then the concept of "multimethod research" is doubly so.

We should also be aware of the costs associated with undertaking research across several sites or with multiple methods. At the very least, a given study will take longer to complete, and more space will be required to describe the results. That which is appropriate for a book or dissertation may be inappropriate for a journal article. Moreover, the employment of multiple methods often entails the deployment of multiple skill-sets, for example, a new language, knowledge of a different historical context, additional technical expertise, or entrée into a new site. This is not always possible or practical for an individual researcher to undertake. Needless to say, little is gained from a study that employs multiple methods in a naive or superficial fashion.

However, the same multimethod research project might be a practical undertaking for a *group* of researchers, who, collectively, possess the necessary skills, resources, access, and time to exploit the potential of different methods and/or research sites. This suggests that it may be helpful to conceptualize research as an iterative process in which multiple methods are brought to bear (by different scholars), each informing the other and over time contributing to the development of a field.[9]

One is reminded that the advancement of knowledge is not a solo activity. In designing research, therefore, one is compelled to consider how one's contribution might fit within the ongoing efforts of a community of scholars. What, specifically, is the value-added of pursuing a particular approach, relative to extant work on a subject? Multiple methods are usually worthwhile, but resolution of this question cannot be addressed in isolation from a field of study. This is the perspective of a research *cycle*, with multiple participants interacting over a long period of time, each bringing a different set of skills to bear on a problem.

Medical research provides a good example. Typically, research on a disease begins with the identification of a set of symptoms, which clinicians are able to classify as a particular disease type (new or old). This spurs the collection of

---

[9] Morrow (2003).

observational data, drawn initially from sources that are readily available. Clinicians work intensively with patients suffering from the disease, administering treatments and noting responses as best they can (the case-study method). They may also study subjects who are exposed to the disease but do not contract it (a deviant-case approach to case-study research). Epidemiologists collect data from populations, attempting to identify larger patterns from observational data (large-N cross-case analysis). Biologists work at the micro-level, seeking to identify disease patterns within the cell (a form of within-case analysis, focused on causal mechanisms). Eventually, from one of these research streams, a potential treatment is devised and researchers construct an experiment to test it – first with animal subjects and then, if the results are promising, with human subjects.

In this fashion, medical research benefits from diverse methodological approaches. Each is based on distinct technical and substantive expertise, often housed in different disciplines, for example, medicine, biology, chemistry, public health, and medical anthropology. Despite the diversity of methods, they take part in a single conversation about a topic – say, HIV/AIDS – which, over time, often leads to progress on that problem. Methodological diversity does not pose an obstacle (or at least, not an insuperable obstacle) to problem-solving.[10]

This brings us back to the ambiguity of multimethod research, which might be achieved (a) in a single study by one researcher who employs multiple methods, (b) in a single study conducted by a field of researchers, each of whom employs a different method, (c) in multiple studies by the same researcher, each of which employs a different method, or (d) in multiple studies by multiple researchers, each of which employs a different method. It is a practical question to decide which of these four "multimethod" approaches to a topic should be pursued.

It follows that a person who applies only one method to a given problem, or works within only one small research site, is not necessarily at odds with the ideal of multimethod work. The critical caveat is that the work produced by this researcher must be commensurable with research conducted by other researchers in other sites. (The reader will recall our discussions of commensurability (Chapter 3) and cumulation (Chapter 4).) In this manner, multimethod work produced by multiple researchers can be truly progressive (in the Lakatosian sense).

---

[10] The preceding paragraphs draw on suggestions from Evan Lieberman (personal communication, 2009).

Unfortunately, this sort of progress does not occur as regularly as one might hope in the social sciences. Because research programs are generally uncoordinated (leading to different choices across the various dimensions of research design), and because scholars are entrenched in different research communities (publishing work in different journals and often not citing members of a rival methodological camp), work conducted in different modes does not always cumulate. Instead, it simply accumulates.

From this perspective, it might be argued that it is incumbent upon the *individual* scholar or research team to conduct multimethod analyses – a much harder row to hoe, for that person must encompass all the requisite skills and knowledge-sets and must bring them together at one point in time.

In any case, the injunction to practice multiple methods is salutary, relative to the monomethod alternative. It also raises important strategic questions about which methods should be practiced when, and by whom. And it prompts us to consider the viability of a particular study within the context of a wider field of research. However, the multimethod approach does not entirely solve the problem of tradeoffs. It does not tell us which of myriad possible approaches ought to be pursued in a given instance. And it does not tell us how to reconcile divergent findings obtained when different methods are brought to bear on the same problem.

Setting standards

Methodology is a normative endeavor. It is about setting standards for a field or a set of fields. Thus, the tasks, strategies, and criteria listed in Table 1.1 may be regarded as constituting an overall standard for social science research.

What, then, is the appropriate standard for a work of social science? What is it that distinguishes a work of science (i.e., worthy of publication in an academic venue) from a work of journalism, or from informal coffee-house banter?

The traditional approach implicitly endorses a *threshold* standard of truth. Although there are some differences of opinion about where to establish the threshold, the general idea is that one can distinguish between scientific endeavors and those that are nonscientific by establishing a single threshold of methodological adequacy. I shall argue, in contrast, for a multidimensional, sliding-scale of truth, a *best-possible* standard of scientific adequacy.

Threshold tests

The traditional approach to causal theory appraisal in the social sciences focuses on questions of internal validity with respect to the main hypothesis (X's relationship to Y within the chosen sample), which is evaluated through a test of statistical significance. Truth (aka validity) is thereby understood in a binary fashion: theories are classified as either true or not proven, depending upon whether they surpass a chosen threshold of confidence (typically, 95 percent), allowing for the rejection of a null hypothesis. Thoroughgoing Popperians will regard these categories more skeptically: as "not yet disproven" and "false." In practice, this amounts to much the same thing. Truth is still dichotomous, and truth-value is evaluated with respect to a single null hypothesis.

This familiar approach has great appeal. After all, science should stand for something and should be differentiable from other domains, for example, cocktail conversation, political rhetoric, and journalism. The attraction of conventional social scientific practice is that it appears to demarcate science from nonscience in a clean, operational fashion. By contrast, a flexible standard might open the way for unscrupulous and unsophisticated practitioners, who propagate nonsense under the guise of science.

On closer inspection, however, the virtues of the traditional approach are more apparent than real. Statistical thresholds, while seeming precise, are often quite arbitrary. T statistics mean something very different when applied to experimental and nonexperimental studies, for example (Chapter 10). They have little relevance for the external validity of a study if the sample is not drawn randomly from a population (which it rarely is). They take no account of other potential threats to inference that cannot be neatly captured in a statistical measure (see Table 9.3). Relatedly, such thresholds are difficult to police. Scholars have strong incentives to beat the threshold, by hook or by crook, leading to methodological concealments that are not healthy for the discipline. We must also reckon with the fact that thresholds – whether experimental or nonexperimental – tend to write out of the discipline all work that is nonquantitative, since thresholds are virtually impossible to apply in the context of qualitative studies.

More broadly, it should be pointed out that thresholds presume a verificationist/falsificationist role for social science methodology: its job is to distinguish between true and false propositions. As we have seen, however, the role of science is broader, encompassing theory-generation as well as theory-testing (Chapter 2). It follows that social science methodology should honor the goal of discovery as well as that of appraisal. Finally, truth-thresholds have nothing to say about the real-world or theoretical significance of a finding.[11]

Yet even if we narrow the task of methodology to determining truth and falsehood with respect to internal validity (rather than larger questions of theoretical or practical significance), the significance test is still wanting. Note, that to say that a given correlation between X and Y is statistically significant at 95 percent is by no means equivalent to saying that one has 95 percent confidence that the null hypothesis can be rejected – not to mention the more specific claim that the nature of this relationship is captured by the estimated coefficient. The 95 percent statistical threshold is simply a line drawn in the sand; it has no intrinsic significance and does not reflect *overall* estimates of uncertainty in most settings.[12]

This is not the fault of statistics. The fault lies with practitioners who over-interpret statistical models, whose assigned role is quite modest if all accompanying caveats and assumptions are kept in view.

A fallback position, in keeping with the spirit of this text, is to regard research design (rather than the results of a statistical test) as establishing a *sine qua non* for science. Yet here, too, one is at pains to articulate a clear threshold distinguishing the good from the bad. While all would probably agree that a properly conducted experiment passes the bar of science (as long as it has some external validity and some theoretical relevance), few would argue that all nonexperimental designs should be banned from the toolkit of science.

A more permissive standard sets the bar at quasi-experimental: any study that can claim resemblance to a true experiment is acceptable, while those falling below this bar ought to be rejected. Unfortunately, it is difficult to establish and police this line, which rests largely on untestable assumptions about the degree to which the data-generating process conforms to a truly randomized treatment and the degree to which chosen modeling procedures correct the nonrandom elements of the research design. "Quasi-experiment," along with its close cousin, "natural experiment," are terms of art.[13]

Our problem, more generally considered, is that it is difficult to establish any single threshold of scientific adequacy that is meaningful and useful across the social sciences, or even within a single discipline. This is a function of the diversity of questions that social scientists pursue, the diversity of methods

---

[11] Ziliak and McCloskey (2008).   [12] Gerber, Green, and Nickerson (2001); Gill (1999).

[13] Dunning (2008b). Consider the judicious – but ultimately ambiguous – discussion of "ignorability" in Holland and Rubin (1988: 226–229).

employed to pursue those questions, and the fundamental complexity of descriptive and causal analysis, as adumbrated in preceding chapters. Consider briefly the various criteria summarized in Table 1.1. Few are liable to conventional statistical reasoning. Indeed, many of these factors are not easily assessed in a quantitative fashion, and it is virtually impossible to imagine aggregating all of them, with appropriate weightings, into a single statistic.

Best-possible, all things considered

Rather than attempting to specify a minimum threshold of truth – that which demarcates science from quackery – it may make more sense to inquire into the relative probability of a theory being true. In recent years, a shift can be seen in social science journals away from asterisks (measuring probability thresholds) and toward more flexible measures of probability, for example, t-statistics, p-values, and Bayesian probability distributions.[14] This is all to the good, as truth in social science is probably best considered a matter of degree. Nothing is certain, as Popperians emphasize, but degrees of certainty/uncertainty are nonetheless important (Chapter 4).

More provocatively, let us consider the notion that science is an ideal-type concept with multiple dimensions and no readily apparent aggregation rules. Consequently, it may not be possible to arrive at a unidimensional indicator of truth – an enhanced t-statistic, say.

The unified approach to social science methodology offered here does not provide a quick and easy test that might demarcate science from quackery. The hard task of vetting remains hard. And it remains hard precisely because there are so many divergent goals of social science, so many dimensions of methodological goodness to consider (as summarized in Table 1.1), and no necessary-and-sufficient conditions that apply universally across the fields of anthropology, archaeology, business, communications, demography, economics, education, environmental design, geography, law, political science, psychology, public administration, public health, public policy, social work, sociology, and urban planning.

Although a relative and multidimensional standard may seem rather open-ended, this does not imply that anything goes. It means that the investigator must search for the research design(s) that maximizes goodness along a set of

---

[14] Gill (1999). Gentle introductions to "Bayesian" inference are provided by Howson and Urbach (1989); Jackman (2004); Western (1999); Yudkowsky (2003).

(relatively fixed) dimensions, reconciling divergent demands wherever possible. The goodness of a research design is therefore assessable only by reference to all possible research designs that have been devised, or might be devised, to address the same research question. Best means *best-possible*.[15]

This allows for research flowing from methods lying far from the experimental ideal to enter the social science pantheon without shame or derogation – but only if no better expedient can be found. Just as society honors classicists, archaeologists, astronomers, and theoretical physicists – despite the speculative nature of their trades – it should also honor those who labor in the muddy fields of observational data in the social sciences.

Of course, this standard supposes that studies based on weak evidence answer a very difficult question: could an argument or research design be improved upon? What is achievable, *under the circumstances*? Here is a slippery notion if ever there was one. However, it is an indispensable one. If a research ideal is entirely out of reach – by virtue of lack of data, lack of funding sources, lack of cooperation on the part of relevant authorities, or ethical considerations – it is pointless to admonish an author for failing to achieve it. Perfection becomes the enemy of scientific advance. We must guard against the possibility that work adding value to what we know about a subject might be rejected even when no better approach is forthcoming. Standards must be realistic.

If, on the other hand, a better approach to a given subject can be envisioned and the costs of implementation are not too great, a work that chooses not to utilize that demonstrably better approach is rightly criticized and perhaps ultimately rejected as "unscientific." We must guard against the possibility that second-best approaches will drive out first-best approaches simply because the former adopt easier or more familiar methods. Mediocrity should not be the enemy of excellence.

Arguably, much of the angst behind the current *Methodenstreit* in the social sciences arises from the tacit belief that there exists (or ought to exist) one *single* standard of adequacy that can be applied across the board to all social science work, or at least to all work within a given discipline. This species of methodological monism serves to engender feelings of insufficiency on the part of many practitioners who do not measure up to the rigid strictures of this "Test of Truth." It also encourages methodological faddism, exemplified by the current raft of studies employing natural experiments (often not very experimental), instrumental variables (rarely with good instruments), or

---

[15] Lieberson and Horwich (2008).

matching estimators (often failing to solve the assignment problem). These are wonderful methodological tricks; but they are frequently applied inappropriately or given an overly optimistic interpretation.

We must acknowledge that work on the frontiers of social science, in common with work on the frontiers of natural science, is prone to a great deal of uncertainty. Moreover, some questions, such as the causes and effects of democratization, will *never* be understood with the degree of certitude possible with other questions, such as the effect of bed-nets on the transmission of malaria. Uncertainty cannot be vanquished from social science unless we restrict our activity to anodyne subjects. While there is no harm in proving the obvious, and much to be learned from experiments, I take it for granted that this style of research does not exhaust the ambitions of social science. There is much more to do.

The practical solution is to embrace the uncertainty of our enterprise, honestly and forthrightly. To this end, scholars have developed informal ways of introducing evidence whose status is dubious. Researchers may frame a statistical finding as "descriptive" rather than causal (even when the theoretical motivation of the analysis is causal). Evidence of questionable import may be framed as a "stylized fact" – consistent with a theory, but by no means conclusive. In this vein, after presenting a formal model of the development of state capacity, Tim Besley and Torsten Persson remark that "some correlations in cross-country data are *consistent with* the theory."[16]

These rhetorical devices serve a worthy purpose insofar as they overcome a perceived dichotomy between scientific evidence (evidence that meets accepted scientific standards and is therefore admissible) and nonscientific hunches (viewed as inadmissible). Sometimes, the best evidence available is nonetheless very weak. At other times, weak evidence serves a supporting role, in conjunction with a formal research design that provides the main evidence. In either case, "descriptive" correlations and "stylized facts" are often extremely useful in reaching causal inference. It should not be necessary to play games with words in order to introduce evidence relevant to solving a particular problem. Let us not hide behind rhetorical posturing.

Likewise, let us not apply a rigid, unbending code to our choice of analytic techniques. Sometimes, the best technique available is a simple ordinary least-squares regression. Sometimes, the best technique available is a two-stage instrumental-variable analysis that may violate one of the assumptions of IV analysis (we cannot tell for sure because it is not directly testable). Sometimes,

---

[16] Besley and Persson (2009: 1218), emphasis added.

the best available technique is a case study, leaning primarily on qualitative analysis of within-case evidence. All of these techniques lack the definitive quality of an experiment. In this respect, they will always be inferior tools of causal analysis.

However, the job of a research design is to add to knowledge on a subject, not necessarily to provide a definitive and incontrovertible analysis of that subject. An appropriate scientific standard is therefore defined by the research design that is best-possible, under the circumstances. "Circumstances" include all manner of practical constraints – time, money, access, cooperation, extant data, and so forth – as well as legal and ethical concerns.

It is to be hoped that a more realistic standard of truth will obviate some of the posing and prevarication that accompanies publication in top social science venues, where researchers are compelled to pretend they have attained the highest standards of truth, regardless of realities on the ground. Weaknesses in design and analysis should be openly acknowledged rather than hidden in footnotes or obscured in jargon and endless statistical tests. At the same time, these elements of uncertainty should not preclude publication in top journals, unless, of course, better methods are available.

This is important not just as a matter of intellectual honesty, but also for the long-term development of the social sciences. Note that the cumulation of knowledge in a field depends more critically on methodological transparency than on "statistically significant" results. We have a fighting chance of reaching consensus on the causal impact of a difficult question, such as school vouchers, if scholars are scrupulous in reporting the strengths and weaknesses of each piece of research, and if each result is accompanied by an overall estimate of uncertainty (taking all factors into consideration). By contrast, there is little prospect of attaining consensus if each study strives for some statistically significant finding, downplaying threats to inference and remaining silent on statistically insignificant results.

Standards of scholarship need to be adapted so as to structure the incentives of scholars in appropriate ways. It is to be hoped that a flexible and multi-dimensional standard, understandable in relation to other potential research designs that might be applied to the same problem, will serve this function.

Let me close with a sociology-of-science perspective on the current *Methodenstreit*.

The high ground in methodological debates is currently occupied by those who hold the most rigorous and discriminating view of science. These are the professional skeptics, whose self-proclaimed role is to preserve the realm of social science from messy, inconclusive (or too quickly concluding) studies.

All those who do not pass the bar are cast out – at least, from the most competitive journals. In this manner, a reign of terror has been erected against the previous reign of error.[17]

To be sure, it is vital that weaknesses in extant studies be identified. However, once this has been accomplished, the relevant question to be posed of any study is not whether it is good or bad in some abstract sense, but whether it could be improved upon, given extant constraints. If not, then criticism of the study is not moving the cause of science forward, it is merely a mechanism for display. Karl Popper notes:

Serious critical discussions are always difficult . . . Many participants in a rational, that is, a critical, discussion find it particularly difficult to unlearn what their instincts seem to teach them (and what they are taught, incidentally, by every debating society): that is, to win. For what they have to learn is that victory in debate is nothing, while even the slightest clarification of one's problem – even the smallest contribution made towards a clearer understanding of one's own position or that of one's opponent – is a great success. A discussion which you win but which fails to help you change or to clarify your mind at least a little should be regarded as a sheer loss.[18]

In order for social science to advance, a spirit of open debate must obtain and the nature of that debate must be deliberative. It cannot be simply about defending one's turf or defending some ideal vision of social science. This is possible to envision, but only if scholarly interactions focus on best-possible solutions rather than absolute thresholds of methodological adequacy, and only if scholars acknowledge the full range of methodological criteria that rightly inform a judgment of adequacy.

---

[17] One thinks, for example, of the career of David Freedman (2010).
[18] Popper (1994: 10), quoted in Rosenbaum (2002: 10).

Postscript
Justifications

I hope that my chosen approach to social science methodology strikes readers as commonsensical. Indeed, none of the tasks, strategies, and criteria were invented by the author (though I have chosen labels for things that do not have established names), and most have received extensive discussion. From this perspective, the present book qualifies as a compendium of truisms – a function shared, I might add, by any integrative work on methodology.[1] The first, and perhaps most important, justification for the proposed framework is that it represents a formalization of what we already know.

Nevertheless, readers are bound to have qualms about some elements of the argument. They might take issue with the criterion of generality, for example. They might like what I have to say about description, but not about causation. On what grounds might one adjudicate this sort of dispute?

It is not sufficient, even if it were possible, to resolve these disputes by counting heads. If four of five social scientists accept generality as a basic criterion of social science, this is not necessarily a good reason for the fifth to fall into line. There must be some reason, some underlying rationale, to which one can appeal in this sort of meta-methodological debate.

The question of justification is generally avoided by methodologists, who appeal to specific rules but often fail to clarify the reasons underlying their choices. Yet without addressing the grounding of a methodology one is unable to defend one approach against another, or, for that matter, to defend the enterprise of social science. Some recourse to broader "philosophical" questions is essential, therefore, even though we do not have the luxury of covering this complex terrain with the detail and nuance that it deserves.

---

[1] Mill's ([1853] 1872: iii) opening words, in a work that might be called the Old Testament of scientific methodology, deserve repeating: "This book makes no pretence of giving to the world a new theory of the intellectual operations. Its claim to attention, if it possess any, is grounded on the fact that it is an attempt not to supersede, but to embody and systematise, the best ideas which have been either promulgated on its subject by speculative writers, or conformed to by accurate thinkers in their scientific inquiries."

One line of defense may be found in the definitional attributes of our key term, *social science*. "Social" specifies the subject matter, and "science" the methodological goal. I stipulated in Chapter 1 that science has many defining attributes, including cumulation, evidence, falsifiability, generalization, non-subjectivity, rationality, replicability, rigor, skepticism, and transparency. If one is amenable to this definition of science one may be willing to accept the unified framework as an elaboration of these general goals. The latter follows from the former.

But what might one say to those who question the very idea of social science, or who have different ideas about how science ought to be defined? Here, I fall back on a pragmatic line of argument. Pragmatism suggests that in order to resolve issues of adequacy one must have some notion of what functions, purposes, or goals an institution is expected to achieve. If our purpose is normative – if one wishes, that is, to improve the state of affairs in a given area of human endeavor – it is logical to begin with a pragmatic interrogation. What does one expect social science to accomplish?[2]

This teleological question may be posed of any discipline, or of any human activity where the consequences of human action may reasonably be assessed. If, let us say, one is investigating the stock market to see how its operations could be improved one might begin by asking what improvement would

---

[2] My argument parallels pragmatic arguments within contemporary philosophy. In a landmark set of essays from several decades ago, Quine pointed out that since the universe impinges upon human consciousness only at the margins of human cognition we cannot reasonably use "objectivity" as the guide for reforming our language. Rather, Quine (1953: 79) counsels, "Our standard for appraising basic changes of conceptual scheme must be, not a realistic standard of correspondence to reality, but a pragmatic standard. Concepts are language, and the purpose of concepts and of language is efficacy in communication and in prediction. Such is the ultimate duty of language, science, and philosophy, and it is in the relation to that duty that a conceptual scheme has finally to be appraised." Laudan (1996: 140) writes, along similar lines: "Methodology, narrowly conceived, is in no position to make [teleological] judgments, since it is restricted to the study of means and ends. We thus need to supplement methodology with an investigation into the legitimate or permissible ends of inquiry." Yet my approach is not the same as that advocated in most of Quine's and Laudan's writings. It should also be distinguished from the "pragmaticism" of Peirce (see Kirkham 1992: 80–87) and – to some extent – from the pragmatism or "instrumentalism" of William James and John Dewey. James and Dewey tended to apply the pragmatic test to individual utterances. Thus, "the meaning of any proposition can always be brought down to some particular consequence in our future practical experience, whether passive or active" (quoted in Ogden and Richards [1923] 1989: 198), whereas I am applying pragmatism to the enterprise of social science, at large. Similarly, James and Dewey tended to look upon truth as an essentially undifferentiated realm, including quotidian truths, whereas I am marking out social science as a distinctive realm with its own (more or less) standards of appraisal. With "truth," and other topics of similar abstraction, it is rather problematic to specify a general goal, as James and Dewey suggest. It is all very well to define truth as that which accommodates our interests, but this begs a series of questions – whose interests? over what period of time (short term or long term)?, and so forth. In the end, we have not clarified very much at all when a pragmatic approach is applied at this very general level. When applied to a specific institution (e.g., social science), however, the pragmatic/consequentialist approach gains traction.

mean. What functions does one expect a stock market to perform? What would a "good" stock market look like? The pragmatist's line of inquiry can also be posed in the form of a counterfactual: where would we be without it? Implied in this question are the following additional questions: is there another institution that might perform these functions more effectively? Do its costs outweigh its benefits? In the case of the stock market I imagine an inquiry such as this leading fairly quickly to several conclusions: (a) its main purpose is to reduce transaction costs between investors and firms, that is, to raise capital; (b) no other institution that we are aware of does this as effectively; (c) its relative success in doing so can be judged, among other things, by the amount of money that it raises and the stability of stock prices over the long haul.

The purpose of social science, let us say, is to help citizens and policymakers better understand the world, with an eye to changing that world. Social science ought to provide useful answers to useful questions. Robert Lynd made this argument many decades ago, and the words still ring true. Social science, he writes:

is not a scholarly arcanum, but an organized part of the culture which exists to help man in continually understanding and rebuilding his culture. And it is the precise character of a culture and the problems it presents as an instrument for furthering men's purposes that should determine the problems and, to some extent, the balance of methods of social science research.[3]

Many others have echoed the same general sentiment, before and since.[4] Indeed, the presumed connection between social science and social progress has been present from the very beginning of the disciplines we now label social science. The Statistical Society of London, one of the first organized attempts to develop the method and employment of statistics, proposed in 1835 to direct their attention to the following question: "what has been the effect of the extension of education on the habits of the people? Have they become more orderly, abstemious, contented, or the reverse?"[5] Whatever one might think

---

[3] Lynd ([1939] 1964: ix).

[4] Adcock (2009); Bloch ([1941] 1953); Bok (1982); Gerring and Yesnowitz (2006); Haan *et al.* (1983); Lerner and Lasswell (1951); Lindblom and Cohen (1979); McCall and Weber (1984); Mills (1959); Myrdal (1970: 258); Popper ([1936] 1957: 56); Rule (1997); Simon (1982); Wilensky (1997); Zald (1990). Prior to the rise of the modern scientific ideal, the connection between the study of society and its reform (or preservation) was even stronger. Aristotle writes, "since politics . . . legislates as to what we are to do and what we are to abstain from, the end [of political science] must be the good for man" ("Nicomachean Ethics," in Aristotle 1941: 936). This "normative" sentiment did not die with the rise of social science, therefore; it merely went underground.

[5] Quoted in Turner (1997: 25–26), originally quoted in Porter (1986: 33). See also Collins (1985: 19).

about the perspectives embedded in this research question, it is clear that early statisticians were interested in the role that knowledge might play in social change. To paraphrase Marx (several decades later): the point of scholarly reflection is not merely to interpret the world, but also to reform it – perhaps even to revolutionize it.

Methodologists have not fully grasped the potential deliverance that this simple thesis presents. Bluntly put, whatever species of social science methodology seems most likely to produce useful knowledge ought to be embraced; whatever does not should be eschewed.[6]

Granted, "usefulness" is not always self-evident. Much depends upon one's time horizons (what is useful today may not be useful tomorrow, and vice versa). And utility functions vary. I do not suppose that everyone will agree on a precise metric by which the utility of social science can be measured. A vulgar version of pragmatism implies that a single telos, universally agreed upon, should guide all our actions. For Dewey, however, pragmatism meant "that it is good to reflect upon an act in terms of its consequences and to act upon the reflection. For the consequences disclosed will make possible a better judgment of good."[7] In this spirit, it is more important to ask the question of social science's purpose, in a serious and conscientious way, than to provide a very specific answer. The answers will surely vary from place to place, from time to time, and from person to person. What does seem certain is that if one ignores the question entirely – hunkering down in our insulated academic bunkers to perform our own (possibly quite idiosyncratic) genres of research – one is likely to fall far from the mark.

At the present point in historical time one might nominate prosperity, peace, democracy, individual freedom, human rights, and social justice as generally agreed-upon goals. To the extent that social science sheds light on these phenomena, one might argue that it is performing its appointed task. In this respect, the pragmatic exercise provides common ground. And one can go further.

The most obvious methodological conclusion to be drawn from pragmatism is that social science should be *relevant* to present-day problems and concerns. This is captured in the tenth criterion pertaining to all arguments (Chapter 10). Of course, any fool can be relevant simply by addressing issues of concern to the general public. Relevance, by itself, accomplishes little. In order to serve the commonweal a work must also add something of value to

---

[6] Rule (1997) argues along similar lines. See also Rescher (1977).
[7] Dewey (reprinted in Rorty 1966: 283–284).

our understanding of a topic. Opinionizing is not sufficient. The telos of social utility therefore presumes something broader than mere relevance.

Many of us would like very much to know why Hutus were killing Tutsis with such zeal in 1994. All work on Rwanda, or on genocide more generally, is therefore relevant. But obviously, not all work on these subjects is equal in value. Theories that are wrong, for example, are less helpful than theories that are true.[8]

It follows that any methodological task, strategy, or criterion that helps to provide useful knowledge should be honored. Any proposed task, strategy, or criterion that does not (or does so only fitfully) should be eschewed. This is the sort of argument that I would mount, if challenged, with respect to the various elements of Table 1.1. All tasks, strategies, and criteria should be justifiable as pragmatic expedients, helping us to understand the world in ways that are useful to citizens and policymakers. In this way, pragmatism provides philosophical ground for adjudicating methodological debates and allows us to move beyond sterile and essentially irresolvable debates between different philosophical camps ("culturalist," "interpretivist," "rationalist," "positivist," "poststructuralist," and so forth). Rather than choosing camps, let us ask what specific tasks, strategies, and criteria each camp entails. We can then ask the pragmatic question: would the social sciences, thus oriented, tell us about things that we want to know? Would this methodology allow us to reach societal consensus on important problems? Could it be integrated into a democratic politics? Which vision of social science is likely to prove, in the long run, most useful to society? These counterfactuals, while difficult, provide some bearing on meta-methodological debates.

The practice of social science

I do not wish to wage an argument for the primacy of social science in human history. It is important to remind ourselves that however mightily social science strives for social utility, solving problems such as racism, poverty, and the spread of AIDS requires much more than good social science. It requires, among other things, good polemic and compelling dramatizations. Surely, the cause of civil rights was advanced more by visual images – of peaceful protesters being sprayed with water cannons and beaten by police – than by social science. The sermons of Martin Luther King, Jr., resounded

---

[8] To this it should be added that if wrong theories are framed in such a way that they can be convincingly disproved they may help to elucidate the truth about a phenomenon.

with greater force than the lengthy and detailed analysis of Gunnar Myrdal's *An American Dilemma*.[9] Beyond rhetoric, social change requires political power, as the civil rights movement – and every other movement for social change – attests.

Yet whatever its relative impact on policy, politics, and public opinion, the work of social science is probably best carried forth by remaining true to standards proper to its domain.[10] It will not aid citizens and policymakers to have a field of anthropology that is undifferentiable from theology, or a field of political science indistinguishable from party ideology. If Christopher Jencks, a noted social policy expert, approached problems in the same manner as Edward Kennedy – or Ronald Reagan, for that matter – then we would have no need whatsoever to consult the views of Professor Jencks. What academics like Jencks have to add to the political debate is premised on their expertise. And what are the grounds for expertise, if not the practice of good social science? There is some utility to good social science, and none at all to bad social science.

Indeed, the willful avoidance of scientific methodology has doleful long-term consequences for social science, and for those who would see social science playing a role in the transformation of society. To the extent that social scientists forgo systematic analysis in favor of polemic, they compromise the legitimacy of the enterprise of which they are a part and from which they gain whatever prominence they currently enjoy. As judges walk a fine line between their assigned constitutional roles and their desire to affect public policy, so must social scientists walk a fine line between science and society. The day when this line disappears is the day when social science no longer has a calling.

Throughout this book the reader will discern a double-edged argument. I am opposed, on the one hand, to a post-positivist stance which says there is little except academic pretense separating social science from other modes of discourse and argumentation. I am equally opposed to a vision of social science modeled on the natural sciences – or perhaps, on an older view of the humanities – in which the conduct of social science is viewed as essentially autonomous from the concerns of ordinary people.

Let us explore this tension in greater detail.

The pulls and tugs – sometimes financial, sometimes personal, sometimes partisan – that social scientists experience from the "real world" are usually

---

[9] Myrdal (1944).

[10] Eckstein (1992: ch. 2) invokes Weber in support of this limited and differentiated role for social science vis-à-vis the public sphere.

looked upon as detriments to properly scientific work. "A social scientist has no place, qua scientist, as a party to power-politics," Lynd writes. "When he works within the constricting power curbs of a Republican or of a Communist 'party line,' or when he pulls his scientific punch by pocketing more important problems and accepting a retainer to work as an expert for the partisan ends of a bank or an advertising agency, he is something less than a scientist." However, Lynd adds perceptively, "when the social scientist hides behind the aloof 'spirit of science and scholarship' for fear of possible contamination, he is likewise something less than a scientist."[11]

Social scientists occupy positions of class and status in society, just like everybody else. They have personal and professional interests at stake in what they do, just like everybody else. It is folly to suppose that anyone could entirely dispense with these positional influences while conducting research on precisely these same questions. Indeed, investigations informed by personal experience may be more insightful than those that begin with a highly deductive, theoretically derived hypothesis. It is neither possible nor desirable for academics studying human behavior to strip themselves of all notion of self, isolating themselves in a cocoon of scienticity. As scholars in the hermeneutic tradition have pointed out, involvement with society is the stuff out of which any understanding of that society must evolve. No knowledge is possible in the abstract.

Worldly pressures, then, are both the bane and the boon of social science. Sometimes, it appears that one cannot live scientifically with the world. But it is equally true that one cannot live scientifically without the world. Thomas Bender puts it nicely: "To say that the university ought to be connected to society is not to say that it might properly be a synecdoche for the world. But neither should it claim a position of transcendence."[12] In my view, this issue has no general resolution; each researcher must strike his or her own bargain. The proper conclusion is therefore agnostic: a scholar's involvement with the state, with business, with university administration, or with other nonsocial science institutions is neither inherently good nor inherently bad.

This is about all one can say, as well, for the stance of social science vis-à-vis the status quo. To be sure, as Durkheim remarks, "if there is to be a social science, we shall expect it not merely to paraphrase the traditional prejudices of the common man but to give us a new and different view of them; for the aim of all science is to make discoveries, and every discovery more or less

---

[11] Lynd ([1939] 1964: 178).
[12] Bender *et al.* (1997: 47). For further observations on these matters see Karl (1982).

disturbs accepted ideas."[13] Lynd seconds the notion of a "disturbing" social science: "To the extent that social science accepts more or less uncritically the definition of its problems as set by tradition and current folk-assumptions, and views its role as the description and analysis of situations so defined, it forfeits thereby, if these problems are wrongly defined, its chief opportunity to contribute to the 'emancipation from error.'"[14]

At the same time, it would be folly to make rejection of the status quo the starting-point of social science research, as is seemingly advocated by writers in the critical theory mold. Brian Fay suggests that social science should lead the way for future transformations in society

by assuming a particular form, namely, one that isolates in the lives of a group of people those causal conditions that depend for their power on the ignorance of those people as to the nature of their collective existence, and that are frustrating them. The intention here is to enlighten this group of people about these causal conditions and the ways in which they are oppressive, so that, being enlightened, these people might change these conditions and so transform their lives (and, coincidentally, transcend the original theory).[15]

Are we to assume, as a point of departure, that existing consciousness is false, that existing knowledge reifies a structure of oppression? This seems about as senseless as its conservative counterpart, the glorification of the status quo.

The proper recourse, it seems to me, lies in maintaining the norms of social science – *methodology*, broadly speaking – rather than in cultivating a particular attitude toward society or the status quo. This should not prevent academics from acting in other capacities: as polemicists, politicians, activists, and bureaucrats. It should, however, dissuade us from labeling these activities in a misleading fashion. The line between activism and social science is a real one, and worth preserving. It is possible, I believe, to be a first-rate activist and a first-rate scholar, but probably not in the same breath or on the same page.

We ought to begin with a recognition that social science constitutes an independent – although never entirely autonomous – realm of endeavor. The trick is to make social science speak to problems that we care about without sacrificing the rigor that qualifies it as a science. This is not an easy trick, but it is the trick of the trade.

---

[13] Durkheim ([1895] 1964: xxvii).   [14] Lynd ([1939] 1964: 122).
[15] Fay ([1983] 1994: 108), emphasis in original. See also Fay (1976).

Appendix: A few words on style

Most people who bother with the matter at all would admit that the English language is in a bad way, but it is generally assumed that we cannot by conscious action do anything about it. Our civilization is decadent and our language – so the argument runs – must inevitably share in the general collapse. It follows that any struggle against the abuse of language is a sentimental archaism, like preferring candles to electric light or hansom cabs to airplanes. Underneath this lies the half-conscious belief that language is a natural growth and not an instrument which we shape for our own purposes.

Now, it is clear that the decline of a language must ultimately have political and economic causes: it is not due simply to the bad influence of this or that individual writer. But an effect can become a cause, reinforcing the original cause and producing the same effect in an intensified form, and so on indefinitely. A man may take to drink because he feels himself to be a failure, and then fail all the more completely because he drinks. It is rather the same thing that is happening to the English language. It becomes ugly and inaccurate because our thoughts are foolish, but the slovenliness of our language makes it easier for us to have foolish thoughts. The point is that the process is reversible. Modern English, especially written English, is full of bad habits which spread by imitation and which can be avoided if one is willing to take the necessary trouble. If one gets rid of these habits one can think more clearly, and to think clearly is a necessary first step toward political regeneration: so that the fight against bad English is not frivolous and is not the exclusive concern of professional writers.

George Orwell[1]

I cannot resist inserting a few words on the stylistic properties of social science. Although not methodological in the strict sense of the term, it is nonetheless difficult to separate the desiderata of good writing from the desiderata of good argumentation. Kristin Luker comments:

Writing engages a very different part of the brain than reading and talking do ... [It] is the door that opens out to the magic. Someone once asked Balzac, who supported

---

[1] Orwell (1970: 156).

himself by writing reviews of plays, how he liked a play he had just seen. "How should I know?" he is reported to have answered. "I haven't written the review yet!" Balzac was onto something: I find that when I write things down, I write and think things that I've never really thought before. Novelists sometimes say that their characters do things that surprise their authors, and I guess this is the sociological version of that phenomenon.[2]

In this respect, writing shares certain characteristics in all realms in which it is employed. Good writing is good thinking, to paraphrase Orwell.

However, the stylistic criteria that apply in the disciplines of the social sciences are, in some respects, distinct from those that properly apply in other realms. To my mind, the presentational goals appropriate to work in the social sciences are encapsulated in the criterion, *intelligibility*. It is difficult to imagine a useful work of social science that is not also, at least minimally, clear and understandable. Arguably, it is a principal feature distinguishing social science from the humanities (and perhaps the natural sciences as well). Let us consider this argument briefly.

Within the humanities some writers are fairly easy for the general reader to digest. One thinks, for example, of essayists like George Orwell (quoted in the epigraph), George Steiner, E. B. White, and Edmund Wilson – all masters of lucidity and enemies of pretense. Continuing an old and venerable tradition of arts and letters, these writers saw their work as an extension of critical thinking and cultivated living, not as a specialized product of academic endeavor. In the past half-century, however, the most influential figures in the humanities, writers such as Theodore Adorno, Paul De Man, Jacques Derrida, Michel Foucault, Jürgen Habermas, Fredric Jameson, and Jacques Lacan, have chosen to depart from the common tongue. In its place they have substituted their own idiomatic lexicons and locutions, which readers must master before a text becomes (at least minimally) comprehensible. (Even so, legions of critics and supporters argue over the meanings contained in writings produced by these masters of literary intrigue.) Under the spur of "theory," the fields of the humanities have moved with great verve and determination to sever lines of communication that once connected them to the broader culture. Consequently, humanities departments today exemplify neither high culture nor popular culture, but rather something that might be called academic culture.[3]

---

[2] Luker (2008: 21).

[3] See Jacoby (1987). The point is also made by Karl Popper in his debate with Adorno and colleagues, whom he accused of practicing a "cult of un-understandability" (quoted in Gellner 1985: 5). The irony is

Partisans of deconstruction may reasonably protest that it is not the goal of the humanities to achieve a readily digestible, television-ready format. In a world seemingly taken over by vulgar, commodified forms of art and entertainment, surely there is a place for more critical and challenging modes of discourse. From this perspective, denizens of the academy serve humanity better by maintaining a principled position outside the conventions of popular culture than by conforming slavishly to the common idiom.

I have presented this debate in rather stark terms precisely because it does not seem to me to be easily resolvable. It is a debate at the heart of the humanities, where the call of aesthetic excellence is often at war with the call for general acclaim. In short, there would seem to be no *a priori* demand for intelligibility in the fields comprising the arts and humanities.

In the social sciences, things are different. If social science is to have any effect at all other than achieving job tenure for its practitioners we must find ways of translating its wisdom into the vernacular.

The special need for intelligibility becomes clearer still if we contrast the social sciences with their cousins on the other end of the academic spectrum. Natural science may also influence a broader public, as, for example, in debates over evolution, global warming, and genetics. But it need not, and usually does not. One does not need to know much about climatology in order to make use of the weather report, of medical science in order to make use of radiation therapy, or of computer science in order to use a computer. Arguably, natural science has had its greatest impact on humanity in areas where ordinary men and women have been most ignorant of the science involved.

The subjects of social science are different in that they require decisions on the part of policymakers and the lay public, and these decisions are more complicated than the decision of whether to purchase a flat-screen television or a conventional television. It is no use discovering the benefits and drawbacks of an electoral system if one cannot influence public debate on electoral reform. Knowledge about the effects of public and private investment does not bring any benefits at all if economists are the only holders of that knowledge.[4] Whatever sociologists may learn about the sources of racism will not help anyone overcome this condition if sociologists are the sole repositories of this truth. A tree felled in the social science forest makes no sound.

greatest among those critics of bourgeois intellectual life, the presumed champions of a more open and democratic academy, who are themselves obscure to the point of hilarity.
[4] "The economist who wants to influence actual policy choices must in the final resort convince ordinary people, not only his confreres among the economic scientists," notes Gunnar Myrdal (1970: 450–451).

Of course, bureaucratic policymakers are often specialists and may be expected to understand a more technical level of discourse than the mass public. Even so, the top of the governmental pyramid is populated by decision makers who do not generally possess the requisite time and training to follow complex technical arguments. Politicians would like to know how to keep inflation under control without having to master the dismal science. Generally, they do not hold degrees in social science disciplines, nor are they in the habit of reading scholarly journals.

This does not mean that specialized journals should be shut down in preference for mass-circulation magazines and web sites. It does mean that whatever arguments are developed in those journals must, eventually, filter down to a broader audience. In order to make sure that this occurs, or at least has some chance of occurring, social science must be intelligible.

The problem of intelligibility, we might note, applies equally in democratic and nondemocratic settings. Kings, oligarchs, and generals, like the people they rule over, are disinclined to school themselves in the wiles of matching estimators. Bringing social science to the people is directly analogous to bringing social science to the prince. Machiavelli, like Mill, must speak in a language that can be generally understood.

What, then, makes a work intelligible? The paramount criterion is something that I shall call (albeit vaguely) *good writing*. A work should be coherently organized, so as not to endlessly repeat the same points. This is not an easy task, often requiring several drafts. Pascal once apologized to a correspondent: "The present letter is long, as I had no time to make it shorter" (*Je n'ai fait celle-ci plus longue que parce que je n'ai pas eu le loisir de la faire plus courte*). I have this reaction to a good many works of social science.[5]

Writing should employ standard English and a minimum of jargon.[6] In contrast to writing in other venues, good social science writing should privilege clarity and simplicity. Writers should state their arguments explicitly, rather than leaving matters hanging. Readers should not have to guess at an author's intended meaning. When reading works of certain writers (e.g., Bourdieu, Foucault, Parsons, Pocock, Unger) one feels that skills of interpretation worthy of a biblical exegete are required in order to decipher the passages. Subsequent debate over an author's argument is a sign that a writer has not paid sufficient attention to the criterion of intelligibility. Unclear

---

[5] Blaise Pascal, Letter No. XVI (December 4, 1656) to the Reverend Fathers, the Jesuits. Reprinted in Pascal (2004: 193).

[6] For further pointers, see general manuals of style (e.g., Strunk and White), or manuals focused on social science writing (e.g., Becker 1986).

writing, even if wonderfully elegant and entertaining at the level of the sentence or paragraph, is bad social science. Indeed, social science's failings may have as much to do with "methodology" as with the more mundane problem of effective communication.

Insofar as social science strives for intelligibility, we are well advised to stick as closely as we can to the terms of everyday discourse. "Fetishism of the Concept," as C. Wright Mills calls it, obscures what we already know by renaming it, and obscures genuinely new insights by cloaking them in a novel vocabulary.[7] When in doubt, do not neologize (Chapter 6). To construct social science in abstruse theoretical or mathematical languages subverts the goal of communicating the truths of social science to a broader audience.

Of course, communication failures are not always the fault of the social scientist. Social science methods are sometimes irreducibly complex. One cannot expect the average lay reader to understand all of our techniques of analysis. Yet we can expect the social scientist to summarize his or her findings in plain English, perhaps relegating technical discussion to footnotes, tables, methods chapters, or appendices. If the logic of an argument cannot be communicated in everyday language it is not likely to be very logical at all. Walt Rostow once noted, by way of excuse for a rather nontechnical essay in economic history (which began as a series of college lectures), "there are devices of obscurity and diversionary temptations that are denied the teacher of undergraduates."[8] I think we can take this justification more seriously than Rostow perhaps intended. Writing for a lay audience requires a clarity of exposition that we often overlook in specialized academic work, where the invocation of key buzzwords and citations to the literature often substitutes for clear argument. If some writers look upon the task of communicating with a lay audience as burdensome, perhaps it is just the sort of burden they should be required to carry.

To clarify: I am not arguing that all social science must be conducted in everyday language. Rather, I am pointing out that all propositions, in order to impact the lives of citizens, must at some point be translated into the vernacular. A theory that cannot be understood is, for that reason alone, less useful. A theory that has a wider range of comprehensibility, whose argument can be grasped by greater numbers of the general public, is (*ceteris paribus*) a better theory.

The motto of social science writing may be encapsulated in the following injunction: "the hell with beauty, let's try to communicate some truth."

---

[7] Mills (1959: 35).   [8] Rostow (1960: x).

Glossary

This glossary of key terms was constructed in consultation with other lexicons (e.g., Gerring 2007; Seawright and Collier 2004; Shadish, Cook, and Campbell 2002; Vogt 2005). It privileges specialized definitions, ones common to methodological contexts, or developed in this book. These definitions often draw on the language of statistics, though the far-reaching goals of this volume sometimes necessitate departures from the statistical lexicon. The reader should also bear in mind that most of these terms carry an ordinary-language meaning, one that should be clear from context.

Adjacent to each entry, I have tried to identify various synonyms or antonyms so that readers can make links across fields and subfields. Most of these associated terms are not exact synonyms or antonyms; however, their meaning is close enough to be confused with the term under definition and/or to aid in the clarification of meaning.

Where two or more definitions for a single term are quite disparate, each definition is given a separate number (indicated by Roman numerals).

Most terms are also defined in the text, where readers may go for further clarification. Where relevant, references to specific parts, chapters, tables, and figures are included.

A   See *Antecedent cause.*

Actual cause   See *Cause in fact.*

Alternate outcomes (aka *within-unit* or *nonequivalent dependent variables*)   A research design focused on variation across alternate outcomes, rather than (or in addition to) variation across groups or through time. One version, the *placebo test*, examines alternate outcomes that the potential confounder should have affected; if such an effect is noted then the relationship between X and Y is presumed to be spurious. Another version, often referred to as a *within-unit* design, examines a single group that is subject to two conditions, one of which may be understood as the treatment condition and the other as the control condition. Varying responses to these two conditions, if independent of each other, may then be regarded as evidence of a treatment effect. See Figure 11.7 and accompanying text in Chapter 11.

Antecedent cause (aka *Prior cause*)   A factor that affects the causal factor of primary theoretical interest (X) but has no direct effect on Y. See Figures 8.1 and 9.1 accompanying text in Chapters 8 and 9, where the antecedent cause is represented by A.

Antecedent confounder   A type of *confounder* encountered in small- to medium-N analyses in which a conditioned factor, C, affects Y only through X, thus introducing problems of collinearity between X and C. Contrast: *instrumental-variable* analysis, where an antecedent cause is employed as an instrument in a two-stage analysis. See Figure 11.2 and accompanying text in Chapter 11.

Appraisal   See *Discovery/Appraisal*.

Argument (aka *Explanation, Hypothesis, Inference, Model, Proposition, Theory*)   A complete argument consists of a set of key concepts, testable hypotheses (aka propositions), and perhaps a formal model or larger theoretical framework. A *causal* argument should also contain an explication of causal mechanisms, as discussed in Chapter 8. An argument is what we speculate might be true about the world; it engages the realm of theorizing. Often, it is important to distinguish among arguments lying at different levels of abstraction. The most abstract may be referred to as *macro-level theories, theoretical frameworks,* or *paradigms*. At a slightly less abstract level one finds *meso-level theories* or *models*. At the most specific level one speaks of *hypotheses, inferences, micro-level theories,* or *propositions*, which are assumed to be directly testable. (*Explanations* may apply to any level.) At the same time, it is important to bear in mind that different levels of abstraction are often hard to discern. Thus, the foregoing terms are often employed interchangeably in the text. See Chapter 3.

Assignment (aka *Exposure, Selection*)   The rule or process by which a treatment is assigned (or *selected*) to units in causal analysis. Determines whether units receive a treatment, and if so when and what level of treatment they receive. May be manipulated by the researcher or may occur naturally. *Randomization* is the assignment rule that defines an experimental research design (at least as understood in this text and in much of contemporary social science). When a treatment is assigned nonrandomly this creates an *assignment problem* (aka *selection effect* or *selection bias*). In causal graphs (see Figure 11.2), this is represented as a *common cause* confounder. Nonexperimental research designs and statistical adjustments are sometimes able to rectify confounders introduced by nonrandom assignment. Insofar as they are successful one may say that the assignment of a treatment is *ignorable*, that is, independent of, or "random" with respect to the outcome and potential confounders. *Conditional independence* has been achieved. (The latter terms were developed by Donald Rubin and collaborators and are used extensively in the statistics literature, though they do not play a central role in the text.) See Chapters 9, 10, and 11.

Association   *I*: See *Covariation*. *II*: In this text, association also carries a more specific meaning: a type of descriptive argument in which the focus is on relationships – comparisons or contrasts – across indicators or sets (cases). The key feature is that there are always at least two indicators or sets under examination and no typological relationship is presumed. Three types of associational argument are distinguished: (1) *trend*, (2) *network*, and (3) *correlation*. See Chapter 6.

ATE   Average treatment effect. See *Treatment effect*.

ATT   Average treatment effect on the treated. See *Treatment effect*.

Attrition   A type of *confounder*. Specifically, the loss of subjects during the course of a study (e.g., by mortality). See Table 9.3.

Average treatment effect (ATE)   See *Treatment effect*.

Average treatment effect on the treated (ATT)   See *Treatment effect*.

B   See *Covariate*.

Back door   If one is attempting to measure causal effects by looking at the covariation between X and Y there must be no back-door routes from X to Y. A back-door route is defined by Judea Pearl as any causally ordered sequence that leads from Y back to X (other than the direct route through M), such as the route through E/C in Figure 11.3. If a back-door route exists, as it assuredly does in almost all nonexperimental (and even in some experimental) settings, it must be blocked by one of several conditioning strategies. Note that the no-back-door rule is another way of phrasing the "no confounders" rule, although it states the problem in the general language of causal graphs rather than of individual factors. In the presence of back doors (confounders), variation in *Y* cannot be attributed to *X* alone; other factors are at work. See Chapter 10.

Behavioralism   *I*: The methodology associated with John Watson and B. F. Skinner according to which the meaningful elements of social action are manifested in behavior rather than ideas or attitudes. *II*: An implicit methodology according to which the appropriate goal of science is to investigate the world in a largely inductive fashion, that is, with small-bore hypotheses. Often associated with quantitative methods of analysis. (This second meaning is the one invoked in the text.)

Bias   (Antonym: *Validity*) Generally, any form of systematic (nonrandom) error. *I*: *Sample bias* refers to a sample that is unrepresentative of a larger population (Chapter 4). *II*: *Measurement* bias is introduced by a failure to operationalize a concept accurately (Chapter 7). *III*: Bias introduced by a *confounder* is a principal obstacle to causal inference (Chapters 9, 10, and 11).

Binary variable (aka *Dichotomous variable*)   A variable that has only two possible values, for example, $X=0$ and $X=1$. This may be represented as x/X. See *Measurement*.

Blocking (aka *Matching, Stratifying*)   A method of randomized assignment that attempts to minimize background noise by (a) stratifying a sample across a set of background characteristics thought to be relevant to the causal relationship, and then (b) randomizing the treatment within each stratified group (which may consist only of a pair of cases). Contrast: simple randomization, in which a treatment is randomized across units without prior stratification.

Boundedness (aka *Scope-conditions*)   A criterion pertaining to all arguments. An argument is properly bounded if the population includes cases that rightly fall within the realm of the argument, and excludes others. Since this cannot always be empirically verified, the criterion of boundedness rests on suppositions about how the world works. See Chapter 3.

C   See *Confounder*.

Case (aka *Unit*)   A spatially delimited phenomenon observed at a single point in time or over some period of time, for example, a political or social group, institution, or event. A case lies at the same level of analysis as the principal inference. Thus, if an inference pertains to the behavior of nation-states, cases in that study will comprise nation-states. An individual case may also be broken down into one or more observations, sometimes referred to as *within-case* observations. The term *unit* is synonymous in most circumstances, the only difference being that a case usually connotes an intensive focus on the case (and perhaps some sort of temporal boundaries), while a unit is simply the sort of thing one is looking at as evidence for a proposition.

Case-based analysis   Any analysis focused on a modest number of relatively bounded units (*cases*).

Case selection   The identification of cases for analysis, which then (collectively) compose the *sample* of that study. Methods of case selection may be *purposive* (where the researcher selects cases with desirable features) or *random* (drawn randomly from a population). *Stratified random sampling* (in which cases are purposefully placed into different strata and then drawn randomly from each strata) combines elements of both.

Case study   The intensive study of a single case for the purpose of understanding a larger class of similar units (a population). Note that while "case study" is singular – focusing on a single unit – a case-study research design may refer to a work that includes several case studies, for example, *comparative-historical analysis* or the *comparative method*. See Gerring (2007).

Causal chains (aka *Sequences*)   A type of causal relationship in which many intermediate causes lie between *X* and *Y*. See Chapter 8.

Causal comparability (aka *Equivalence, Exchangeability, Substitutability, Unit homogeneity*)   A criterion of causal analysis. Specifically, the expected value of *Y* for a given value of *X* should be the same for all units across a sample. If it is, we can say that a group of units is causally comparable, or equivalent, with respect to a given hypothesis. A minimal understanding of this criterion requires only that units be comparable to one another *on average*, which is to say that a large error rate across units is satisfactory as long as its distribution is centered on the true mean (i.e., as long as the error is random). A maximal understanding of causal comparability, sometimes expressed as *unit homogeneity*, is that units should evidence *identical* responses of *Y* to a given value of *X* across units – an ideal rarely, if ever, realized. However understood, the causal comparability of a sample must be maintained through the life of an analysis, that is, until the final post-test is administered.

Causal distance   A *distal* (aka remote, structural) cause lies far from the effect it is intended to explain. A *proximal* (or proximate) cause lies close to the effect it is intended to explain. *Causal mechanisms* are generally composed of proximal causes; they are, in any case, more proximal than the structural cause they explain – causal distance being a matter of degrees. See Figure 8.1 and accompanying discussion in Chapter 8.

Causal effect   See *Treatment effect*.

Causal factor (aka *Condition, Covariate, Exogenous variable, Explanans, Explanatory variable, Independent variable, Input, Intervention, Parent, Predictor, Right-side variable, Treatment, X*)   Variation in some factor (X) generates variation in an outcome (Y) if the relationship is causal. See Chapter 8.

Causal graph   A visual diagram of the data-generation process (DGP), including relevant assumptions pertaining to a set of causal relationships. In this text, the term is employed in a somewhat more open-ended manner than in work by Judea Pearl and others; for example, it is not limited to DAGs. See Chapters 9, 10, and especially 11.

Causal heterogeneity   *I*: Generally, the varying impact of a causal factor, X, on units within a sample. Usually regarded as noise. *II*: In certain situations it may also provide a strategy of causal inference. This is so in situations where causal heterogeneity is not stochastic (random), in which the relevant moderators (Z) can be measured, and in which the interaction effect of X^*Z on Y is not subject to confounding. See Figure 11.8 and accompanying text in Chapter 11.

Causal law   An exception-less relationship between X and Y. See Chapter 9.

Causal mechanism (aka *Intermediate variable, Mediator, Pathway, Process*)   The connecting thread between X and Y, which thereby serves to explain a covariational relationship. My usage of this key term encompasses any factor that may be considered part of the generative process by which X affects Y, whether it consists of a series of discrete steps (e.g., dominoes falling into one another on a table) or a continuous process (e.g., a billiard ball rolling across the table), and whether it is measurable or un-measurable. Denoted as M. The specification of a causal mechanism is a key component of causal arguments (usually embodied in a theory or model), and the investigation of causal mechanisms (aka *causal narrative, colligation, congruence, contiguity, discerning, intermediate processes, microfoundations, process analysis, process tracing*) is a key component of causal analysis. See Part III.

Causal pathway   See *Causal mechanism.*

Causal process observation   See *Observation.*

Causal reasoning   A strategy of causal inference that is not empirical in the usual sense. Involves judgments about assumptions undergirding a causal inference, including a consideration of the *data-generating process* (DGP) revealed by the data. See Chapter 11.

Causality   To say that X is a cause of Y is to say that a change in X generates a change in Y relative to what Y otherwise would be (the counterfactual condition), given certain background conditions and scope-conditions (*ceteris paribus* assumptions). Another way of saying this is that a cause, if it is indeed a cause, raises the prior probability of an outcome occurring. Causal relations may be of many sorts, as summarized in Table 9.2. See Chapters 8 and 9.

Cause in fact (aka *Actual cause, Singular cause, Single-event cause, Token-level cause*)   That which explains a particular outcome in a particular case. Contrast: *treatment effect*, a counterfactual understanding of causation. See Chapter 9.

Causes-of-effects   See *Effects-of-causes/Causes-of-effects.*

Ceteris paribus   All else being equal. *I*: The caveat that applies to every criterion in the unified framework of this book. See Chapters 1 and 13. *II*: The background conditions assumed by all causal arguments. To say that X causes Y is to say that X raises the probability of Y holding *ceteris paribus* conditions constant. See Chapters 8 and 9.

Circularity   See *Endogenous confounder.*

Clarity   In this text, a criterion of causal argumentation. Specifically, all causal arguments should clarify the operationalization of X and Y, envisioned variation on X and Y, assumed background conditions, and scope-conditions. See Chapter 8.

Coherence   A criterion of all arguments. Specifically, the degree of internal consistency. See Chapter 3.

Collider   A type of *confounder* in which a conditioned factor is affected by both X and Y. See Figure 11.2 and accompanying text in Chapter 11.

Collinearity   Where multiple causal factors in a sample are highly correlated, rendering the assessment of X's causal effect on Y imprecise.

Commensurability (aka *Consilience, Harmony, Logical economy, Theoretical utility*)   A criterion of all arguments. Specifically, an argument that fits comfortably within a larger theoretical framework, or which reorganizes that framework to create greater logical economy in a field. An argument that is idiosyncratic, that does not build upon other inferences, is incommensurable, that is, *ad hoc*. See Chapter 3.

Common cause   A *confounder* that affects both X and Y. See Figure 11.2 and accompanying text in Chapter 11.

Comparative-historical analysis   *Case-study* method focused on a small number of regions or states where spatial variation assumes a "most-similar" format and temporal variation includes the causal factor(s) of special interest.

Compliance (aka *Treatment adherence*)   In experimental research, the threat to inference that occurs when subjects do not comply with instructions. More generally, the idea that all units in the treatment group should receive the treatment. See Chapter 9.

Compound treatment confounder   A type of *confounder* encountered when neither X nor a factor, C, that is correlated with X (and may affect Y), are separately measurable. See Figure 11.2 and accompanying text in Chapter 11.

Concept   Four elements of an empirical concept are usefully distinguished: the *term* (a linguistic label comprising one or a few words); *attributes* that define those phenomena (the definition, intension, connotation, or properties of a concept); *indicators* that help to locate the concept in empirical space (the measurement or operationalization of a concept); and *phenomena* to be defined (the referents, extension, or denotation of a concept). See Chapter 5.

Conditional independence   See *Ignorability*.

Conditioning (aka *Stratification, Subclassification, Subgroup analysis, Tabular decomposition*)   To include a factor, Z, within a statistical model (e.g., regression or matching model) or to disaggregate that factor by its component parts (effectively the same thing). For example, if Z is "sex," conditioning on Z allows one to compare different values for that factor, that is, 0=Male, 1=Female. If Z is the factor of theoretical interest then the goal is to compare how the values of "sex" relate to some other factor(s). If Z is not of theoretical interest then the goal is probably to "control" this factor in an analysis focused on other factors. In the latter case, holding Z constant means evaluating the impact of some other factor, X, for men and for women (separately). See Chapter 11.

Conditioning confounders   A strategy of achieving causal comparability, that is, eliminating confounders, primarily used with nonexperimental data. Specifically, this approach depends upon conditioning factors that would otherwise confound the relationship between X and Y, and avoiding conditioning any factor that would create a confounder where none exists. See Chapter 11.

Configurational typology   See *Typology.*

Confirmation   See *Appraisal.*

Confounder (aka *Source of bias, Threat to inference*)   In this text, any factor that might interfere with an attribution of causality from covariational evidence, that is, anything that produces a spurious or biased association between X and Y. Specifically, a confounder is a factor (or a vector of factors) that impacts the outcome (Y) and is not independent of the treatment (X), given the chosen strategy of conditioning. Its association with X is what differentiates a confounder (C) from an orthogonal covariate (B) in Figure 9.1.

Most confounders take the form of "back-door" routes (causally ordered sequences) from Y to X. In the presence of back doors, variation in Y cannot be attributed to X alone; other factors are at work. Another way of thinking about confounders is that they introduce problems of *nonindependence* or *noncomparability* across units, as discussed in Chapter 9.

Three sorts of confounders are commonly distinguished. (1) Pre-treatment (aka *assignment* or *selection* bias) confounders include *self-selection* into treatment (where assignment to treatment is governed by the subjects under study). This is perhaps the most common and most obdurate of confounders.

(2) Post-treatment confounders include *attrition* (the loss of subjects during the course of a study, for example, by mortality), *noncompliance* (when subjects do not comply with instructions, that is, when members assigned to the treatment group remain untreated or members of the control group receive treatment), *contamination* (aka *spillover, interference*, where treatment and control groups are not effectively isolated from one another, creating the possibility that members of one group might affect members of the other group in ways relevant to the studied

outcome), *reputation effects* (where the reputation of the treatment in the minds of subjects, rather than the treatment condition itself (as defined by the researcher), affects an outcome), *researcher* (aka *experimenter, Hawthorne*) *effects* (where the condition of being tested or studied, rather than the treatment of theoretical interest, affects an outcome), and *testing effects* (where responses to a test are influenced by a previous test, or by expectations from previous testing experiences, rather than the treatment itself).

(3) Pre-/post-treatment confounders in longitudinal studies include *history* (aka *trends*, where the treatment is correlated with some other factor that affects the outcome of interest, which is to say, where the variation over time under observation is driven by some factor other than the treatment), *regression to the mean* (where some change observed over time is a product of stochastic variation rather than the treatment of interest), and *instrumentation effects* (a change in the measurement of an outcome – or, occasionally, a stimulus – over the course of a study in ways that might alter the estimate of X's effect on Y). These are summarized in Table 9.3.

Confounders can also be conceptualized through the use of causal graphs, as in Figure 11.2 and accompanying text in Chapter 11. Here, we distinguish among the *common cause* (aka classic confounder), which has a causal effect on both X and Y; the *incidental confounder*, which affects Y and is correlated with X but not by reason of any identifiable causal relationship; the *compound treatment confounder*, which fails to distinguish between a causal factor of theoretical interest and a confounder; the *mechanismic confounder*, in which a conditioned factor is endogenous to X; the *collider*, in which a conditioned factor is affected by both X and Y; the *antecedent confounder*, in which a conditioned factor affects Y only through X; and the *endogenous confounder*, in which Y affects X. Note that in discussing confounders one is usually presuming a simple strategy of causal inference resting on the covariation of X and Y.

Conjunctural causality   A type of causal relationship in which a particular combination of causes acting together produces an effect. See Chapter 8.

Consistency (Antonym: *Slippage*)   A criterion of concepts. Specifically, the consistency of meaning attached to a concept throughout a work. See Chapter 5.

Constant cause   A type of causal relationship in which a cause operates continually on an outcome. Contrast: discrete causal interventions. See Chapter 8.

Construct validity   See *Validity*.

Contamination   A type of *confounder*. Specifically, where treatment and control groups are not effectively isolated from one another, creating the possibility that members of one group might affect members of the other group in ways relevant to the studied outcome. See Table 9.3.

Control (aka *Comparison group*, *Placebo group*)   *I:* In research design: a group looked upon as exhibiting the counterfactual, that is, what the treatment group would have looked like had it not been exposed to the treatment. In order to perform this function, the control group must be causally comparable to the treatment group. *II:* In statistical models: a variable or vector of variables that are of peripheral concern but may help to achieve causal comparability or reduce background noise.

Correlation   See *Covariation*.

Counterfactual   A crucial aspect of any causal argument. Specifically, the state of affairs that would have obtained in the absence of an intervention, or with a different intervention. See Chapter 8.

Counterfactual thought-experiment   An attempt to re-play events in one's mind in order to determine what the result might have been under a different set of circumstances. An essential tool of causal analysis when the possibilities of real (observable) variation are meager.

Covariate   *I:* Any factor, other than the theoretical factor of interest, that affects an outcome of interest. *II:* Any right-side variable in a regression model. *III:* In this text, the term has a more specific meaning, as an *orthogonal* covariate. The orthogonal covariate is assumed to affect Y and at the same time to be orthogonal (independent) of the theoretical variable of interest, X. Represented as B in Figure 9.1 and subsequent figures. Factors of type B introduce noise (imprecision) but not bias into a covariational analysis. Contrast: *Confounder*.

Covariation   See *Association*.

Covariation (aka *Association*, *Concomitant variation*, *Constant conjunction*, *Correlation*)   *I:* Two factors co-vary (i.e., are associated, correlated) when the presence of one helps predict the presence of the other. Covariational patterns may be cross-sectional (synchronic) and/or temporal (diachronic, time-series). They may also be set-theoretic, that is, necessary or sufficient (although some authors prefer not to employ the term covariational for set-theoretic relationships). *II*: A covariational technique of causal analysis rests on the covariation of *X* and *Y*, as discussed in Chapter 10. This is sometimes contrasted to a *mechanismic* approach to causal inference; however, many approaches to causal inference depend upon more than conditioning on *X* and *Y*, as discussed in Chapter 11.

Covariational research design   A research design in which causal assessment rests primarily on the covariation between *X* and *Y* across a sample of observations. See Chapter 10.

Covering-law model (aka *Deductive-nomological model*)   A model or school of causality developed by Carl Hempel, Paul Oppenheim, and other so-called *positivists*. According to this view, causality refers to a constant (deterministic) conjunction or a probabilistic association between *X* and *Y*. Causal explanation occurs by subsuming the particulars of an event or class of events under the rubric of a universal law, which can then be tested by reference to observable predictions derived from the theory. See Chapter 13.

Critical juncture/path-dependence   A type of causal relationship in which a contingent moment determines a longer trajectory, that is, a period of path-dependence in which that trajectory is maintained and perhaps reinforced (through "increasing returns"). See Chapter 8.

Cross-over design   An experimental design with multiple treatments that are administered sequentially to all groups. That is, every group in a chosen sample receives the same treatments, but in a different order. See Table 10.2 and accompanying discussion in Chapter 10.

Cross-sectional   A nonrandomized research design with post-test only, that is, spatial (but not temporal) variation in *X* and *Y*. See Chapter 10.

Crucial case (aka *Critical case*)   A *case-study* method that offers particularly compelling evidence for, or against, a proposition. Assumes two varieties: least-likely and most-likely. A least-likely case is one that is very unlikely to validate the predictions of a model or a hypothesis. If found to be valid, this may be regarded as strong confirmatory evidence. A most-likely case is one that is very likely to validate the predictions of a model or a hypothesis. If found to be invalid, this may be regarded as strong disconfirming evidence.

Cultural model   A model of social behavior deriving from work by philosophers in the hermeneutic school (e.g., Dilthey, Schleiermacher, Heidegger, Gadamer, Habermas, Ricoeur, Taylor, von Wright, and

Winch) and ethnographic work in the social-cultural wing of anthropology (e.g., Boas, Malinowski, Mead, Benedict, and Geertz). Identified with interpretivist and constructivist approaches to social science. Key points of synthesis include a focus on lived experience (as viewed by the actors under study); the holistic quality of norms, values, and behavior; and the socially constructed (nonincentive based) nature of the foregoing. Contrast: *Rational model*. See Chapter 13.

Cumulative concept   A strategy of concept formation that attempts to reconcile *minimal* and *maximal* approaches by ranking the (binary) attributes commonly associated with a concept in a cumulative fashion, that is, as more or less essential to a concept, creating an *ordinal* scale. See Chapter 5.

Data collection   Methods for collecting evidence, for example, surveys, focus groups, interviews, ethnography, archival research, and other nonreactive measures. (Not a primary concern in this book.)

Data-generation process (DGP)   Factors presumed to account for observed patterns within a chosen sample. May be represented visually with a *causal graph*.

Dataset observation   See *Observation*.

Deductive-nomological explanation   See *Covering-law model*.

Dependent variable   See *Causal factor*.

Deterministic   An invariant relationship; there are no random (stochastic) components. May be interpreted as an ontological claim – about the true nature of some underlying reality – or an empirical claim about some available data. Usually, deterministic arguments take the shape of necessary, sufficient, or necessary-and-sufficient relationships. However, these set-theoretic relationships may also be interpreted in a probabilistic manner. See Chapter 12.

Deviant case   A *case-study* method in which the chosen case(s) exemplify deviant values according to some general model.

DGP   See *Data-generation process*.

Diachronic   See *Association*.

Dichotomous scale   See *Binary variable*.

Difference-in-difference (DD) design   A nonrandomized *panel* design in which one group receives a treatment while another does not, and the outcome of interest is measured pre- and post-test. Causal effects are estimated by comparing the difference in outcome within the treatment group before and after the intervention of theoretical interest (Y at T_2 minus Y at T_1 for group I) with the difference in that same outcome within the control group over the same period (Y at T_2 minus Y at T_1 for group II) – a difference-in-difference. Note that since the treatment is not randomized, the validity of this design hinges on an assumption: that ΔY within the control group represents the counterfactual that would have been realized for the treatment group. See Chapter 10.

Differentiation (aka *Context, Contrast-space, Perspective, Reference point, Semantic field*)   A criterion of concept formation. Specifically, the degree to which a concept is differentiable from neighboring concepts; the contrast-space against which a concept is defined. See Chapter 5.

Discrete-ness   A criterion of causal analysis. Specifically, an intervention (treatment) that is short in duration, with a clearly demarcated beginning and end. See Chapter 9.

Distal cause   See *Causal distance.*

Domain (aka *scope*)   A criterion of concepts. Specifically, the clarity and logic of a concept's linguistic and empirical scope. See Chapter 5. Compare: the *boundedness* of an argument (Chapter 3).

Dose   For causal treatments that are regular in quantity and discrete one may apply the medical terminology of *doses*. See Chapter 9.

Effect size   See *Impact.*

Effects-of-causes/Causes-of-effects   Commonly, arguments focus on a single X/Y hypothesis or a small set of related X/Y hypotheses, an *effects-of-causes* approach. Sometimes, however, causal arguments are more wide-ranging, encompassing all the systematic (i.e., nonstochastic) causal factors presumed to contribute to a particular outcome (Y) – a *causes-of-effects* approach. Here, X refers to a vector of causes rather than a single causal factor. Thus, instead of attempting to estimate the effect of vouchers on educational performance one might attempt to evaluate all the causes (and combinations of causes) of educational performance – socioeconomic, family, neighborhood, peer group, curriculum, classroom size, teacher, gender, age, personality, and so forth (including vouchers, if they are operative). See Chapter 12.

Endogeneity/Exogeneity   *I*: In a simple causal relationship, X is presumed to be unaffected by (exogenous to) Y and Y is assumed to be affected by (endogenous to) X. An *endogenous confounder* (aka bi-directionality, circularity, endogeneity, feedback, symmetry, tautology) is present when this is not the case, that is, when a causal model is subject to problems of circularity or reciprocal causation. See Figure 11.2 and accompanying discussion in Chapter 11. *II*: Exogeneity is sometimes (though not in this text) understood to describe a treatment that is randomized or as-if randomized (not correlated with potential confounders). Note that sense *II* implies sense *I*: if *X* is randomized, *Y* cannot affect *X*.

Endogenous confounder   See *Endogeneity/Exogeneity*.

Epistemology   The study of the nature and origins of knowledge.

Equifinality   A type of causal relationship in which multiple causal paths lead to the same outcome, that is, multiple causal factors are sufficient to cause *Y*. See Chapter 8.

Estimator   A statistical model employed in order to test a causal model. Should include relevant factors encoded in a *causal graph*, especially any potential confounders (*C*). See Chapter 10.

Ethnography (aka *Field research*, *Participant-observation*)   Work conducted "in the field," that is, in some *naturalistic* setting where the researcher observes his or her topic. Usually associated with nonexperimental research designs, but may also be combined with a randomized design.

Exclusion restriction   See *Instrumental-variable analysis*.

Exogeneity   See *Endogeneity/Exogeneity*.

Experiment   Maximally defined (as an ideal-type), an experiment implies (a) an *ex ante* research design, (b) researcher control (over relevant circumstances of the research setting), (c) manipulation of the treatment, (d) randomization of the treatment across treatment and control groups, (e) a large number of cases or observations (such that sufficient "power" is achieved), and (f) the preservation of causal comparability across treatment and control groups until the final post-test (preventing post-treatment confounders). In this text, we adopt a minimal definition with fewer attributes and relatively crisp boundaries: an experiment is a research design in which the treatment is randomized across treatment and control groups (d). This resonates with current usage in the social sciences – though less so in the natural sciences, where a control group is often unnecessary (Cook *et al.* 2010: 109). See Chapter 10.

Experimenter effects   A sort of *compound treatment* in which the treatment of theoretical interest, *X*, is indistinguishable from an additional treatment resulting from the experimental protocol. See Chapter 9.

Explanation   See *Argument*.

Exploration   See *Discovery/Appraisal*.

Exposure   See *Assignment*.

Extension   See *Concept*.

External validity   See *Internal/external validity*.

Factorial design   An experimental design which tests the interactive effects of several categorical treatment variables. See Table 10.2 and accompanying discussion in Chapter 10.

Falsifiability (aka *Testability*)   The likelihood that a theory or hypothesis can be proven wrong (understood in this book as a matter of degree). The key element in the philosophy of falsificationism, as developed by Karl Popper, and closely linked to the over-arching scientific goal of *appraisal*. See Chapter 2.

Family-resemblance concept   A concept that can be defined in a number of ways, but where no single attribute is shared across all definitions. Derived from work by Ludwig Wittgenstein. See Chapter 5.

Fecundity (aka *Coherence, Depth, Essence, Fruitfulness, Natural kinds, Power, Real, Richness, Thickness*)   A criterion of concepts. Specifically, the number of attributes that referents of a concept share. See Chapter 5.

Field research   See *Ethnography*.

Fuzzy sets   Sets that recognize degrees of membership, as well as boundaries between sets. See Chapters 7 (in the context of measurement) and 12 (in the context of QCA).

Generality (aka *Breadth, Domain, Generalizability, Population, Range, Scope*)   A presumed criterion of all scientific arguments. Specifically, the empirical breadth of an argument. See Chapter 3. See also *Internal/external validity*.

Hermeneutics   See *Interpretivism*.

History (aka *Trends*)   A type of *confounder*. Specifically, where the treatment is correlated with some other factor that affects the outcome of interest, which is to say, where the variation over time under observation is driven by some factor other than the treatment. See Table 9.3 and accompanying text in Chapter 9.

Hypothesis   See *Argument*.

I   In the context of measurement, *I* refers in this text to the indicator of a latent concept (*L*). See Figure 7.1 and accompanying text in Chapter 7.

Ideal-type   See *Maximal definition*.

Ignorable, Ignorability (aka *Conditional independence, Unconfoundedness*)   In causal analysis, when the assignment of a treatment to units is independent of the outcomes under study (as achieved by randomization) or when the assignment of a treatment to units is independent of the outcomes under study given certain background factors that can be conditioned on (in nonexperimental studies). Developed by Donald Rubin and associates. In this book, the issue of ignorability is encompassed within the rubric of *causal comparability* (Chapter 9).

Impact (aka *Effect size, Magnitude, Power, Significance, Strength*)   A criterion of causal arguments. Specifically, the more variation in Y an argument explains – the greater the impact of X on Y – the more significant that argument is likely to be. See Chapter 8.

Incidental confounder   A type of *confounder* that affects Y and is correlated with X but not by reason of any identifiable causal relationship. See Figure 11.2 and accompanying text in Chapter 11.

Independence   A criterion of causal analysis. Specifically, the assumption that each observation mustered in support of a causal hypothesis provides independent evidence of that proposition. This means that each observation must be independent of every other observation with respect to the effect of X on Y. When the assumption of independence is violated across units or observations we commonly refer to a process of *diffusion, contamination,* or *interference*. When the assumption of independence is violated in observations drawn from the same unit over time it is commonly referred to as a problem of *serial auto-correlation*. See Chapter 9.

Independent variable   See *Causal factor*.

Indicator (aka *Attribute, Dimension, Factor, Measure, Parameter, Property, Scale, Unidimensional description, Variable*)   The most basic type of descriptive generalization, aiming to describe one feature (i.e., one dimension) of a concept across a population. Underlies all other general propositions, descriptive or causal. See Chapter 6.

Individual treatment effect (ITE)   See *Treatment effect*.

Inference   Generally, the process of reaching conclusions as an extension of known facts or stated premises. In empirical contexts, this means inferring facts that are not immediately in evidence from facts that are. One infers from a sample to a population, for example. One may also infer missing data within a sample, or infer properties of a sample in order to correct for anticipated measurement error. Causal attribution is inferential since one cannot re-play the counterfactual (what Y would be if the value of X were different). All social science arguments are inferential in at least one of the foregoing senses. See *Argument*.

Inference to the best explanation Inference for a hypothesis stemming from its superiority vis-à-vis other possible explanations for a phenomenon. See *Rival hypotheses* strategy of causal inference.

Instrumental-variable (IV) analysis Nonrandomized research design used for correcting bias, especially that introduced by nonrandom assignment of the treatment. A good instrument is a variable or vector of variables that (a) is highly correlated with the treatment variable and (b) has no effect on the outcome except that which might occur through the treatment variable (the *exclusion restriction*). See Chapter 11.

Instrumentation effects A type of *confounder*. Specifically, a change in the measurement of an outcome (or, occasionally, a stimulus) over the course of a study in ways that might alter the estimate of X's effect on Y. See Chapter 9.

Intension See *Concept*.

Intent-to-treat/Intention-to-treat effect (ITT) See *Treatment effect*.

Interaction effect (aka *Moderator effect*) When X's relationship to Y is changed by the presence of a third variable. Contrast: *Causal mechanism* (aka *mediator*), which is understood in this text to serve as a medium of X's impact on Y. (Of course, some mechanisms may serve as both mediators and moderators.)

Intermediate cause See *Causal mechanism*.

Internal/external validity Internal validity refers to the truth of a proposition with respect to the chosen sample. External validity refers to the truth of a proposition with respect to the population of an inference – its *generalizability*. See Chapter 4.

Interpretivism (aka *Hermeneutics, Verstehen*) Broadly, the study of human meanings and intentions. More narrowly, the attempt to interpret human behavior in terms of the meanings assigned to it by the actors themselves.

Interrupted time-series design A nonrandomized research design in which a sequence of observations (multiple pre- and post-tests) is interrupted by a treatment. Here, one tests to see if the slope or intercept of the series changes as a result of the intervention. See Chapter 10.

Intervention See *Treatment*.

Irreversible causality   See *Reversible causality.*

ITE   Individual treatment effect. See *Treatment effect.*

ITT   Intent/Intention-to-treat effect. See *Treatment effect.*

K Number of variables in a model.

L In the context of measurement and in this text, L represents the latent concept for which an empirical indicator is sought. See Figure 7.1 and accompanying text in Chapter 7.

Ladder of abstraction   An inverse relationship is said to characterize (a) the number of attributes used to define a concept (its intension) and (b) the number of entities (phenomena) falling within the concept's extension. Accordingly, the problem of attaining a consistent meaning for a concept within a designated scope can be resolved by ascending (subtracting attributes, thus increasing the empirical scope of the concept) or descending (adding attributes, and thus decreasing the concept's scope) the ladder of abstraction. This inverse association is operative as long as defining attributes are not substitutable (sufficient conditions). See Figure 5.1 and accompanying discussion in Chapter 5, as well as Chapter 7.

Large-N   See *Observation.*

LATE   Local average treatment effect. See *Treatment effect.*

Level of analysis   The level of aggregation on which an analysis takes place. If a hypothesis is concerned primarily with the behavior of nation-states then lower levels of analysis would include individuals, institutions, and other actors at a substate level. Higher levels of analysis would include supranational entities such as regional groupings or international bodies. See Chapter 4.

Linear causality   A causal relationship in which the impact of X on Y is constant, that is, it does not change with the value of X (at least within a specified range). Contrast: nonlinear causality, in which the impact of X on Y varies. See Chapter 8.

Local average treatment effect (LATE)   See *Treatment effect.*

Longitudinal design (aka *Within-group design*)   *I*: Any design in which more than one observation through time is taken for studied units. *II*: In this book: a nonrandomized research design in which variation in key variables is longitudinal (temporal) but not cross-sectional, that is, all units are treated and the treatment effect is judged by comparing pre-treatment and post-treatment status. Subtypes include the *interrupted* *time-series* (where a single intervention affects a unit or a set of units, which are observed longitudinally, before and after) and *repeated observations* (aka *repeated measures*, where units are exposed multiple times to the same treatment). See Table 10.3 and accompanying text in Chapter 10.

M   See *Causal mechanism*.

Manipulability   A criterion of a causal argument: that the causal factor of theoretical interest should be manipulable by the researcher, at least in principle. See Chapter 8.

Matching methods   A technique for reaching causal inference in which units are "matched" after assignment to treatment so that comparisons can be drawn across units that closely resemble each other in background characteristics (covariates, including potential confounders). In principle, they ought to differ only in whether they receive the treatment. In more technical terms, matching ensures conditional independence of treatment assignment by balancing the treated and controlled groups across a host of potential confounders. Without strong balance, causal inference from matching methods is suspect. It should be noted that there are multiple techniques for matching units on background characteristics. *Exact matching* selects units that are matched on the precise values of the covariates. While desirable in principle, exact matching is rarely practicable. More common is *propensity-score matching*, where background characteristics are employed in order to determine an estimated probability for each unit being assigned to the treatment group (conditional on the covariates). This propensity score is then used to match the units within a sample. In other words, when looking for a match for a specific case in the treatment group the researcher looks for cases in the control group that would have been as likely to be in the treatment group as those cases actually chosen.

Matrix typology   See *Typology*.

Maximal definition (aka *Ideal-type*)   Aims for a collection of attributes that is maximal in that it includes all nonidiosyncratic characteristics that together define the concept in its purest, most ideal form. Ideal-types, as the term suggests, need not have a specific real-life empirical referent. However, in order to be of empirical use they must approximate real, existing entities. Contrast: *Minimal definition*. See Chapter 5.

Measurement (aka *Indicators*, *Operationalization*)   The task of locating a concept in empirical space. More specifically, the goal of achieving validity and precision from a set of indicators for a concept. See Chapter 7.

Mechanism   See *Causal mechanism.*

Mechanismic confounder   A type of *confounder* in which a conditioned factor, *C*, that affects *Y* is endogenous to *X*. See Figure 11.2 and accompanying text in Chapter 11.

Mediator   See *Causal mechanism.*

Method   May refer to a very specific protocol for gathering and/or analyzing data (e.g., the randomized field trial, deviant case study, interrupted time-series design) or for a more general approach to empirical analysis (e.g., case-study method, experimental method). Contrast: *Methodology.* See Chapter 1.

Method of difference   See *Most-similar method.*

Methodology   The tasks and criteria governing scientific inquiry, including all facets of the research enterprise. While *method* refers to the particular choices made in a given study, methodology refers to the larger, and presumably more uniform, features of the scientific enterprise. (Of course, the distinction is not hard and fast and these two terms are often used interchangeably.) See Chapter 1.

Minimal definition   Identifies the bare essentials of a concept, sufficient to bound it extensionally while maintaining all nonidiosyncratic meanings associated with the term. Attributes are understood as necessary and perhaps also sufficient. Contrast: *Ideal-type (maximal) definition.* See Chapter 5.

Missing variable   See *Omitted variable.*

Model   See *Argument.*

Moderator effect   See *Interaction effect.*

Monism   As employed in this text, the view that there is a single epistemology and/or methodological framework applying to social science research generally and to causal inference in particular. Contrast: *Pluralism.* See Chapters 1 and 13.

Monotonic causality   A type of causal relationship in which an increase (decrease) in the value of *X* causes an increase (decrease) or no change in *Y*. Contrast: *Nonmonotonic causality.* See Chapter 8.

Mortality   See *Attrition.*

Most-similar case analysis (aka *Method of difference* J. S. Mill)   *Case-study* method in which chosen cases are similar in all respects except the variables of theoretical interest (*X* and/or *Y*).

Multimethod research (aka *Triangulation*)   The use of multiple methods (e.g., qualitative and quantitative, randomized and nonrandomized, multiple levels of analysis) to address the same research question. See Chapter 13.

N   See *Observation*.

Natural experiment   See *Quasi-experiment*.

Naturalism   The view that *I*: all phenomena are subject to natural laws and/ or *II*: that the methods of natural science are applicable to other areas, that is, in social science.

Naturalistic   Research settings that are, or resemble, "real-life" settings, for example, *ethnography*. Unobtrusive methods of research. Contrast: *Laboratory setting*.

Necessary/sufficient (aka *Set-theoretic*)   *I*: In defining or operationalizing a concept, attributes may be regarded as necessary, sufficient, or necessary-and-sufficient. (Each of these may refer to a single attribute or to several attributes, jointly.) (a) If understood as a *necessary-and-sufficient* condition, attribute *X* is the only characteristic that matters. (b) If *X* is *necessary*, then a phenomenon must embody *X* though there may be other membership conditions as well. (*Minimal* definitions rely on necessary-condition attributes [Chapter 5].) (c) If *X* is *sufficient*, then it is sufficient by itself to define/operationalize a concept, though there may be other conditions that would also, independently, define/operationalize that concept – each sufficient condition is substitutable for the other. See Chapter 7.

II: The same relationships applied to causal arguments. (a) A factor is *necessary-and-sufficient* if its presence is both necessary-and-sufficient for an outcome: *X* always causes *Y* and is furthermore the only cause of *Y*. This means that *X* and *Y* go together invariably, as do *x* and *y*. In set-theoretic terms, the set of units containing *X* is coterminous with the set containing *Y*. (b) A factor is *necessary* if its presence is required for an outcome to occur: *X* is necessary for *Y*, but *X* does not always cause *Y* (at least not by itself). This means that one may find *X* without *Y*, but one does not find *Y* without *X*. In set-theoretic terms, the set of units containing *Y* is a subset of the set of units containing *X*. (c) A factor is *sufficient* if its presence guarantees the occurrence of an outcome: *X* always causes *Y*, though *Y* also has other causes. This means that one may find *Y* without *X*, but one never finds *X* without *Y*. In set-theoretic terms, the set of units containing *X* is a subset of the set of units containing *Y*. Sufficient causes – usually causal conjunctures – are the stock-in-trade of *qualitative comparative analysis* (QCA). See Chapter 12.

Neologism   An idiosyncratic concept, either by virtue of its unusual label or its unusual definition (or both). Contrast: *Resonance*. See Chapter 5.

Noise   Background features that may impede causal attribution. Usually understood as stochastic (random) rather than a source of bias (systematic error). Represented as *B* in Figure 9.1. See Chapter 9.

Nominal scale   See *Scales*.

Nominalism   The view that only individual objects exist, and that reference to abstract classes of objects is mistaken. More generally, a suspicion of concepts as arbitrary linguistic containers. See Chapter 5.

Noncompliance   A type of *confounder*. Specifically, when subjects do not comply with instructions, that is, when members assigned to the treatment group remain untreated or members of the control group receive treatment. See Chapter 9.

Noncovariational   See *Covariational research design*.

Nonequivalent dependent variable design   In causal analysis, a strategy for overcoming a common-cause confounder. Specifically, the identification of a secondary outcome, Y_2, that – although of no intrinsic theoretical interest – allows one to discern a true causal effect from a spurious causal effect. Two versions of the design are possible. In the first, the secondary outcome is a product of X that is not subject to confounding. In the second, the secondary outcome is a product of the confounder, C, and therefore regarded as a placebo test. See Figure 11.7 and accompanying text in Chapter 11.

Nonlinear causality   See *Linear causality*.

Nonmonotonic causality   See *Monotonic causality*.

Observation   The most basic element of any empirical endeavor. Any piece of evidence enlisted to support a proposition. *I*: In causal analysis, *dataset observations* are assumed to be causally comparable with one another, and therefore may be treated as rows in a matrix (a rectangular dataset). The total number of observations in a sample is conventionally referred to with the letter *N*. (Confusingly, *N* may also refer to the number of cases.) See Chapter 4. *II*: By contrast, a *causal-process observation* assists causal assessment, but is not comparable with other observations in a study, and therefore cannot be treated as part of a larger sample. Each observation is different from the next – apples and oranges. Each one is relevant to the central argument, but is drawn from different populations and therefore may be regarded as an *N*=1 sample. See Chapter 12.

Observational (aka *Ex post, Nonexperimental*)   A research design in which the data is generated naturally, rather than through the intervention of the researcher. Research occurs after the fact (*ex post*) rather than before the fact (*ex ante*), as in an experiment.

Omitted variable (aka *Missing variable*)   A *specification* problem caused by the omission of a key variable. See *Conditioning confounders.*

Ontology   *I*: A branch of metaphysics concerned with the nature of existence. *II*: A vision of reality – phenomena as they exist in the real world – with the implication that this vision cannot be easily proven or disproven. Ontological facts are real, but not necessarily amenable to empirical demonstration. (This is the connotation most often encountered in current methodological discussion.)

Operationalization   A criterion of concept formation. Specifically, the ease and validity with which a concept can be measured. See Chapter 5. See also *Measurement.*

Ordinal scale   See *Scales.*

Orthogonal covariate   See *Covariate.*

Outcome (aka *Dependent variable, Effect, Endogenous variable, Explanandum, Output, Response*)   The outcome is what a causal argument is about, what it purports to explain. Represented as *Y* in Figure 9.1 and subsequent figures. See Chapter 8.

Panel design   Nonrandomized research design in which several observations are taken from each unit (over time) and there is variation in *X* through time and across units. Includes *difference-in-difference* (DD) and *fixed-effect* designs.

Paradigm   See *Argument.*

Parsimony (aka *Occam's razor*)   An argument should be summarizable in a compact form (mathematical or verbal) and should require as few assumptions as possible. See Chapter 3.

Participant-observation   Ethnographic work in which the researcher is a participant in the activity under study.

Partition   The falsifiability of an analysis is enhanced insofar as an argument (theory) can be effectively isolated, or *partitioned*, from the subsequent empirical analysis. This reduces the possibility that a theory might be adjusted, *post hoc*, so as to accommodate negative findings. It also reduces the temptation to construct arguments closely modeled on a particular empirical setting ("curve-fitting"), and therefore of questionable internal and external validity, or research designs whose purpose is to prove (rather than test) a given argument. (Term coined by author.) See Chapter 4.

Path-dependence   See *Critical juncture/path-dependence.*

Periodization   See *Typology.*

Placebo effect   See *Experimenter effects.*

Placebo test   See *Alternate outcomes.*

Pluralism   As employed in this text, the view that there are multiple epistemologies and/or methodologies applying to social science research generally and to causal inference in particular. Contrast: *Monism.* See Chapters 1 and 13.

Population (aka *Breadth, Domain, Scope*)   The universe of cases and observations to which an argument refers. Generally larger than the sample under investigation. Note that the population of an inference has both spatial and temporal boundaries, though the latter often remain implicit. For example, the intended population of an inference about democracy and development might be all countries in the world in the modern era, stretching from 1800 to some undisclosed point in the future. See *Boundedness, Generality.*

Positivism   *I*: Belief that the only true knowledge is based on sensory experience – "positive facts" – thus avoiding metaphysical speculation concerning causes and normative purposes. *II*: Logical positivism (aka *Logical empiricism, Vienna Circle*): the philosophy of science developed by Rudolf Carnap, Hans Hahn, Otto Neurath, Hans Reichenbach, building on earlier work by Ludwig Wittgenstein. *III*: Loosely, a naturalist view of social science. Specifically, a strong faith in science as cumulative, falsifiable, objective, systematic, and logically unified endeavor. *IV*: A position that slights the importance of causality, or sees it only in a neo-Humean fashion, as constant conjunctions and *covering laws.*

Post-test only design   A design in which there is no pre-test, that is, the effect of a treatment is measured only after it is administered. Contrast: *Pre-test/post-test design.* See Table 10.2 and accompanying discussion in Chapter 10.

Potential outcomes model (aka *Counterfactual model, Experimental model, Interventionist model, Manipulation model, Neyman–Rubin–Holland model*)   Broadly, a view of causation developed by statisticians Neyman, Rubin, and Holland stressing the fundamental problem of causal inference: one cannot determine the cause of an individual outcome because the counterfactual cannot be directly observed. It is suggested therefore that we understand each unit (or group of units) as embodying two potential outcomes, an observed outcome (e.g., the treatment condition) and an unobserved "counterfactual" outcome (e.g., the control condition). The difference between these outcomes is the causal (treatment) effect. Given the unobservable nature of causal inference, establishing a plausible – observable – counterfactual condition is of crucial importance. Much of the work, as well as the specialized vocabulary associated with the potential outcomes model (e.g., *ignorability, SUTVA, conditional independence*), is directed at identifying the assumptions underlying this comparison. See Chapter 13.

Power   The probability of correctly rejecting a false null hypothesis (avoiding Type I error), that is, the probability of finding an effect when such an effect really exists.

Precision   *I*: A criterion pertaining to all arguments. See Chapter 3. *II*: A criterion pertaining to all analyses. Specifically, the consistency of a finding across repeated tests, a large-sample property. The *variance* across these results provides an empirical measure of the degree of precision attained. If there is no opportunity to compare multiple iterations of a single research design (if the research is qualitative in nature), then the variance remains a theoretical property. *Reliability* is one important aspect of precision. Note that precision is closely tied to the level of *uncertainty* or *probability* of an empirical test. Greater precision means greater certainty. Both may be indicated by the number of decimal points reported in a measurement or – in a statistical model – by the confidence interval and probability value associated with a coefficient. Contrast: *Validity*. See Chapter 4.

Prediction   *I*: A model that predicts future events, based on a rational, scientific set of assumptions (contrast, soothsaying). This model might be causal, noncausal, or may include elements of both. *II*: Point estimates for particular units (cases) as derived from a general model. *III*: The predictions emanating from a causal model. Thus, it is said that a causal model "predicts" certain outcomes, and forbids others. In this sense, predictions about past events ("post-dictions") are also relevant.

Pre-test/Post-test design   A research design in which units are observed before and after exposure to a treatment. Contrast: *Post-test only design*. See Table 10.2 and accompanying discussion in Chapter 10.

Probabilistic   A relationship with random (stochastic) properties. In a statistical model, these are captured by the error term.

Probabilistic causes   Causal factors that are imperfectly related to Y (there are exceptions, which may be represented with an error term) even though X is a cause of Y. Contrast: *Deterministic*. See Chapter 8.

Proposition   See *Argument*.

Proximal (proximate) cause   See *Causal distance*.

Pure description (aka *Reportage*)   Descriptive statements (including proximal causes) focused on single events. See Chapter 6.

Qualitative   *I*: An analysis with a small number of observations (small-N). See Chapter 13. *II*: In causal analysis, an analysis based on *causal-process observations*. See Chapter 12. *III*: A narrative-based analysis rather than one based on math (i.e., quantitative, statistical, formal modeling), for example, archival, ethnographic, field research, historical, open-ended interviewing. *IV*: Thick, case-based analysis. *V*: Variables formed from nominal or ordinal scales rather than continuous scales (in statistics). Contrast: *Quantitative*.

Qualitative comparative analysis (QCA)   A method of analyzing causal relationships developed by Charles Ragin that is sensitive to necessary-and-sufficient relationships, conjunctural causes, and causal equifinality, usually within the context of a medium to large sample. Later versions of QCA ("fs-QCA") incorporate elements of probabilism and fuzzy-set theory. See Chapter 12.

Quantitative (aka *Large-N*, *Statistical*)   Many comparable ("dataset") observations are analyzed statistically. Contrast: *Qualitative*. See Chapter 13.

Quasi-experiment (aka *Natural experiment*)   A nonrandomized research design that resembles a true experiment, that is, where the treatment is not perfectly randomized across groups, but where the assignment principle bears some resemblance to a randomized treatment. A fluid term covering a vast swath of observational research, all of which seeks to mimic the virtues of the experimental method. See Chapter 10.

Random sampling   A method of case selection in which each case from a broader population has an equal chance of being selected into the sample by virtue of some random case-selection procedure. If the chosen sample is not too small, random sampling should produce a sample that is representative of the population, that is, unbiased. Contrast: *Randomization*. See Chapter 4.

Randomization   The random assignment of cases to treatment and control groups. The hallmark of the *experimental* method. Contrast: *Random sampling*. See Chapter 10.

Rational model   A general model of social action building on the work of Enlightenment and post-Enlightenment writers like Hobbes, Bentham, Smith, and Mill, as well as more recent work emanating from the evolving field of economics (e.g., Jevons, Menger, Walras, Edgeworth, Marshall, and Pareto). Key analytic assumptions include utility maximization, perfect knowledge, and preferences that are complete, stable, and transitive. These assumptions (which may also be relaxed in various ways) inform the social science genres of public choice, game theory, and political economy. Contrast: *Cultural model*. See Chapter 13.

Realism   See *Scientific realism*.

Reciprocal causation   See *Endogeneity*.

Regression discontinuity (RD) design   A nonrandomized research design where worries about assignment bias are mitigated. Specifically, the assignment principle is known. It is measurable, prior to treatment, for all units in the sample. It consists of an interval variable in which a cut-off, or discontinuity, defines the assignment of subjects, producing a binary treatment variable. Many units fall on either side of this cut-off – ideally, situated at the middle of the distribution. Finally, this assignment principle is maintained (no exceptions). If units fall above (below) the cut-off they are treated; if they fall below (above) the cut-off they are not eligible for treatment. (Although these assumptions can be relaxed, doing so generally affects the precision and validity of estimates.) See Figure 10.1 and accompanying text in Chapter 10.

Regression to the mean   A type of *confounder*. Specifically, where some change observed over time is a product of stochastic variation rather than the treatment of interest. See Chapter 9.

Relevance (aka *Importance, Social significance*)   A criterion of all arguments. Specifically, the relevance of an argument to citizens and policymakers. See Chapter 3.

Reliability   See *Precision*.

Replicability   A criterion of all analyses. Specifically, the ability to reproduce extant findings in a setting that is similar to (though perhaps not identical to) a previous piece of research. It is ambiguous exactly how similar these circumstances must be in order to qualify as a replication (as opposed to an original piece of research). In any case, researchers should always strive for replicability. See Chapter 4.

Representativeness   A criterion of all analyses. A sample is representative when its cases are similar (i.e., causally comparable) to a broader population in all respects that might affect the hypothesis of interest. Contrast: *Bias*. See Chapter 4.

Reputation effects   A type of *confounder*. Specifically, where the reputation of the treatment in the minds of subjects, rather than the treatment condition itself (as defined by the researcher), affects an outcome. See Chapter 9.

Research design   Strictly defined, research design refers to the collection and arrangement of relevant evidence with an eye to setting up an appropriate empirical test, and may be contrasted with data analysis (the *ex post* analysis of evidence already gathered). The term derives from experimental techniques, where there is a clear separation between the experimental set-up (the research design) and the running of the experiment. Because many facets of an experiment are under the control of the researcher it is obviously essential to focus intently on elements of research design. In recent years, the notion of research design has been broadened so as to include observational analyses. Of course, an observational setting cannot be directly manipulated. Even so, the researcher is able to choose a context that may provide the most appropriate test for a given conjecture. Choice of settings thus becomes a functional substitute for the manipulated setting of an experiment. See Chapter 4.

Researcher effects (aka *experimenter* or *Hawthorne effects*)   A type of *confounder*. Specifically, where the condition of being tested or studied, rather than the treatment of theoretical interest, affects an outcome. See Chapter 9.

Resonance (aka *Familiarity, Normal usage*).   (Antonyms: *Idiosyncrasy, Neologism, Stipulation*) A criterion of concept formation. Specifically, the fit between a concept (as defined by an author) and its usual meaning. See Chapter 5.

Reversible causality   A type of causal relationship in which an increase in X leads to a positive (negative) effect on Y and a decrease in X leads to a negative (positive) effect. Contrast: *Irreversible causality*, in which X has "ratchet" effects on Y. See Chapter 8.

Rival hypotheses   A strategy of causal inference resting on the examination of rival hypotheses. Rather than looking at X, the factor of theoretical interest, one examines Z, a vector of alternative (possible) causes of Y. See Figure 11.9 and accompanying text in Chapter 11.

Robustness test (aka *Sensitivity test*)   A strategy of causal inference. Specifically, any alteration of a benchmark empirical test that serves to gauge the strength of a hypothesis according to varying (plausible) assumptions about the data-generating process. This includes the estimator, the specification, the operationalization of key variables, and so forth. May be quantitative or qualitative – though in the latter case it will probably take the form of counterfactual thought-experiments. See Chapter 11.

Roll-out design   An experimental design in which a treatment is "rolled out" across groups in a sequential fashion; all groups receive the treatment, but not at the same time. This serves to overcome potential confounders that may be coincident with the timing of the first intervention. It also provides a way to offer the treatment to all groups, which may be important for political or ethical reasons. See Table 10.2 and accompanying discussion in Chapter 10.

Sample   The set of units/cases or observations (drawn from those cases) upon which research efforts are focused, that is, the immediate focus of analysis. A sample of one or several may be referred to as a *case study* or a series of case studies, and may be analyzed qualitatively. A larger sample must be analyzed quantitatively. Of course, the two types of analysis may also be combined, as in *multimethod* studies. Indeed, most studies include more than one sample. Often these samples are nested within one another. Whatever the size of a sample or its level of analysis, a sample is assumed to be representative of some larger *population*. It is upon this assumption that claims to *external validity* rest. Very occasionally, an entire population is studied – in which case the sample equals the population, a *census*. See Chapter 4.

Scales   In order to operationalize a concept one must choose a scale, or set of scales (if the concept is multidimensional), to employ. Some scales are *categorical* (aka qualitative), by virtue of the fact that the distance between categories is undefined. Other scales are *numeric* (aka quantitative) by virtue of the fact that the distance between categories is defined and measured along a numerical scale. Other subtypes fall within this two-part classification. Among categorical scales, those that are *nominal* define members of the same class (they are examples of something) but are unranked. For example, apples, oranges, and grapes are not more or less of anything relative to each other, though they are all fruit. *Ordinal* scales are members of the same class and also ranked: very sweet is sweeter than sweet. Among numeric scales, those that are *interval* are characterized by a consistent measure of distance between categories. For example, the distance between 3 and 4 on a temperature scale (Celsius or Fahrenheit) is the same as the distance between 25 and 26, and is defined by a formal rule, consistently applied across the scale. *Ratio* scales are interval scales with a true 0, indicating the absence of whatever quantity is being measured (a null set). In the case of money, 0 signals no money. In the case of temperature on the Kelvin scale, 0 indicates the absence of all thermal energy. See Table 7.2 and accompanying discussion in Chapter 7.

Science   Understood in this text as an ideal-type. Specifically, the commitment to study phenomena in ways that are systematic, rigorous, evidence-based, falsifiable, replicable, generalizing, nonsubjective, transparent, skeptical, rational, cumulative, and open to both descriptive and causal inference. See Chapter 1.

Scientific realism   The view that (a) reality exists independently of our knowledge of it and (b) the goal of science is the description and explanation of observable and unobservable aspects of an (independently existing) world.

Scope-conditions   See *Boundedness*.

Selection   *I*: The process by which a treatment is *assigned* to units (e.g., by *randomization*). See *Assignment* and discussion in Chapter 10. (This is the meaning that is more common in social science circles nowadays.) *II*: The process of selecting case(s) from a population for inclusion in a sample (e.g., by *random sampling*). See discussion of *representativeness* in Chapter 4.

Selection bias   (aka *Selection effect* or *Assignment problem*) *I*: A form of *bias* often introduced to causal analysis when a treatment is not randomized across cases. In this situation, the assignment of the treatment is likely to be correlated with the outcome under investigation, thus violating the assumption causal *comparability*. See Chapter 10. *II*: Bias in a sample relative to a larger population that is introduced by a case-selection procedure (e.g., choosing cases based on their outcomes). Selection bias in large samples may be avoided by random sampling. See discussion of *representativeness* in Chapter 4. (Note: because of this double meaning, the text generally avoids this term.)

Self-selection   See *Confounder*.

Separation   A criterion of causal arguments. Specifically, a good causal argument features a causal factor that is separable from the outcome of interest. See Chapter 8.

Sequential typology   See *Typology*.

Set-theoretic (aka *Boolean, Logical, Mill-ean*)   Any descriptive or causal argument based on set-relations. In causal inference, factors (singular or plural) may be conceptualized as necessary, sufficient, or necessary-and-sufficient for an outcome (see Chapters 9 and 12). Qualitative comparative analysis (QCA) is a type of set-theoretic causal analysis (Chapter 12). Sometimes, this genre of argument is referred to as *deterministic*; however, since there may be exceptions to a set-theoretic pattern, and since there is always some uncertainty about the nature of the relationship, this is something of a misnomer.

Severity   A criterion of all analyses. The riskiness of a test relative to a particular hypothesis, that is, the chance of false positives (Type I error). See Chapter 4.

Singular cause   See *Cause in fact*.

Single-event cause   See *Cause in fact*.

Small-*N*   See *Observation*.

Social science   Focused on decisional aspects of human behavior (though not excluding the study of nondecisional influences on such behavior), to be studied in a scientific fashion. Situated methodologically between the humanities and the natural sciences. Includes the contemporary disciplines of anthropology, archaeology, business, communications, demography, economics, education, environmental design, geography, law, political science, public administration, public health, public policy, social work, sociology, urban planning, and that portion of psychology focused on outcomes where some decisional component is in evidence. See Chapter 1.

Solomon four-group   An experimental design whose purpose is to test the possible effects of a pre-test, which under certain circumstances may shape the behavior of subjects and thus confound the results of an experiment. See Table 10.2 and accompanying discussion in Chapter 10.

Specification   Usually refers to the problem of arriving at the correct set of explanatory variables in a statistical model. If an important variable is excluded, the model is said to suffer an *omitted variable* bias. Since all identification problems may be understood as specification problems, the term is rather open-ended.

Spurious   A covariational relationship between X and Y that is affected by *confounding*, and therefore represents a biased estimate of X's true relationship to Y.

Stable unit treatment value assumption (SUTVA) (aka *No-interference assumption*)   In causal analysis, the treatment status of any unit under examination should not affect the potential outcomes of other units. Otherwise stated, there should be no interference across units, each being isolated from the rest throughout the course of an analysis. This also implies that the treatment is uniformly administered to all units within the treatment group. An assumption associated with the *potential-outcomes model*. (Note: because SUTVA refers to a variety of research design issues, the term does not figure prominently in this text, where these issues are treated in a more disaggregated fashion.) See Chapter 10.

Standardization   A criterion pertaining to all analyses. Specifically, research designs should be standardized as much as possible with the industry standard (assuming there is one), at least initially, as a point of departure. The standardization of approaches provides a benchmark against which new findings may be judged, and eases the process of replication. See Chapter 4.

Statistical adjustments   In this text, a set of statistical modeling procedures that may serve to rectify biases in a causal analysis, especially those introduced by nonrandom assignment of the treatment. Two species of statistical adjustment are introduced, in a general vein: (a) conditioning on confounders; and (b) robustness tests. See Chapter 10.

Stochastic   *I*: Generally: having a random element (not entirely deterministic). *II*: More narrowly, and in the context of statistics: entirely random (having no systematic component).

Structural cause   See *Causal order*.

Sufficient cause   See *Deterministic*.

SUTVA   See *Stable unit treatment value assumption*.

Synchronic   See *Association*.

Synthesis   In this text, a descriptive argument that addresses a subject in a holistic, encompassing manner, emphasizing similarities rather than differences among a sample of cases with the aim of summarizing this set of features in a key concept or phrase. See Chapter 6.

Taxonomy   See *Typology*.

Temporal typology   See *Typology*.

Testing   See *Discovery/Appraisal*.

Testing effects   A type of *confounder*. Specifically, where responses to a test are influenced by a previous test, or by expectations from previous testing experiences, rather than the treatment itself. See Chapter 9.

Theoretical framework   See *Argument*.

Theory   See *Argument*.

Threats to inference   See *Confounder*.

Token-level cause   See *Cause in fact*.

Transparency   A criterion of all analyses. Specifically, all relevant features of an analysis should be easy to follow and hence to replicate. This may require keeping a laboratory notebook, posting original data, and so forth. See Chapter 4.

Treatment (aka *Intervention*)   The value of X that is of primary theoretical interest. By contrast, the *control* condition embodies the null hypothesis. Alternatively, a piece of research may feature several treatments, none of which is properly thought of as a pure control. In an experiment, the treatment is usually controlled by the experimenter. However, the term is used in a more general fashion in the text, to cover both experimental and nonexperimental contexts. See Chapters 9 and 10.

Treatment effect (aka *Causal effect*)   The change in Y corresponding to a given change in X. Within this rubric are a number of closely related concepts of importance to testing causal inferences. An *individual treatment effect* (ITE) is the impact of a treatment condition ($X=1$) on a single unit relative to the control condition ($X=0$). An *average treatment effect* (ATE; aka *average causal effect* or *expected treatment effect*) is the mean impact of a change in X on Y across a sample. An *intent-to-treat effect* (ITT) is another way of framing ATE in situations where it is suspected that some units assigned to the treatment group are not actually exposed to the treatment (a problem of *noncompliance*). It may be read as "ATE with probable noncompliance," that is, including units in the treatment group that are not actually treated. An *average treatment effect on the treated* (ATT) refers to the effect of X on Y for all units that are actually treated (assuming some are not). A *local average treatment effect* (LATE) is a more specialized term used in the context of *instrumental-variable* analysis. Specifically, it refers to the effect of X on Y for those units whose treatment status (treated/untreated) is affected by the chosen instrument. The foregoing treatment effects (except ITE) are usually assumed to apply to a larger population of units. If they apply only to the chosen sample the author should clarify that it is a sample average treatment effect (SATE), sample average treatment effect on the treated (SATT), and so forth. See Table 9.1 and accompanying text in Chapter 9.

Trend   Any consistent pattern through time, that is, where a variable is correlated with time (though not necessarily in a linear fashion). See Chapter 6.

Triangulation   See *Multimethod research.*

Type I error   Incorrectly rejecting a true null hypothesis (accepting a false argument).

Type II error   Failing to reject a false null hypothesis (rejecting a true argument).

Typology (aka *Classification*)   A descriptive argument resolving cases into discrete categories that are mutually exclusive and exhaustive on the basis of a uniform categorization principle(s). A *simple typology* follows only the general rules for a typology. *Temporal typologies*, or *periodizations*, are simple typologies that are temporally ordered. *Matrix typologies* are formed from the intersection of several (categorical) organizing principles (specialized definition). *Taxonomies* stretch in a hierarchical fashion across several levels of analysis, where each subordinate level of the taxonomy possesses all the attributes of the superordinate category, plus one (or several). *Configurational typologies*, like taxonomies, form subtypes out of a single superordinate category. However, subtypes are created from a superordinate category by subtracting, rather than adding, attributes. *Sequential* (or *processual*) *typologies*, like taxonomies, may be diagrammed in a tree fashion. However, a sequential typology presumes that the branches represent temporal sequences (which may or may not embody taxonomic features). See Table 6.1 and accompanying text in Chapter 6.

Unit   The type of phenomena – that is, subjects, participants, organizations, communities – that are the focus of study. In most situations, *unit* is equivalent to *case*, and these terms are used more or less equivalently, though the latter connotes a more intensive, case-centered style of analysis.

Unit homogeneity   See *Causal comparability*.

Unit of analysis   The species of observations to be analyzed in a particular research design. If the design is synchronic then the unit of analysis is spatial (e.g., nations or individuals). If the design is diachronic then the unit of analysis is temporal (e.g., decades, years, minutes). If the design is both synchronic and diachronic then the unit of analysis has both spatial and temporal components (e.g., country-years). Evidently, the unit of analysis may change in the course of a given study. Even so, within the context of a particular research design, it should remain constant. See Chapter 4.

Validity   *I*: *Conceptual validity* refers to the degree to which a concept, as defined, matches up with a set of empirical indicators (its operatio-nalization). See Chapter 6. *II*: A criterion of a research design and associated data analysis. Specifically, the absence of bias in an estimate. See *Internal/external validity*. Contrast: *Precision*. See Chapter 4. *III*: *Construct validity* refers to the match between a theory and a research design intended to test that theory. See Chapter 4.

Variable (aka *Attribute, Condition, Dimension, Factor*)   In this text, any uni-dimensional factor that has the potential to vary – whether measurable or unmeasurable, qualitative (small-*N*) or quantitative (large-*N*). In dataset format, a variable is depicted as a vertical column in a matrix. See Chapter 4.

Variance   A measure of dispersion around the mean of a distribution, calculated as the sum of squared deviations from the mean divided by *N* (the size of the sample) minus 1.

Variation   A criterion of causal analysis. Specifically, it is helpful if the causal factor of interest varies within a research design. In observational studies, it is also important that the outcome of interest vary (in experi-mental studies it is sufficient if the outcome is free to vary). See Chapter 9.

Verification   See *Discovery/Appraisal*.

Verstehen   See *Interpretivism*.

Vouchers   An example of social science work that is employed throughout the book. Vouchers are a system of government provision in which provision of a good is granted directly to the potential user of that good in the form of a non-cash voucher (redeemable for that good only), and producers of the good are thereby incentivized to produce the good to the user's satisfaction. A market-based method of social provision, especially common (and controversial) with schooling. See Chapter 1.

Within-case   Analysis of observations within a single case. May be small- or large-N. An important form of leverage in virtually all case studies.

Within-group design (aka *Longitudinal design*)   A research design that relies only on temporal variation before and after an intervention. The "control group" consists of the unit(s) prior to the intervention. May be implemented with one unit ($N=1$ research design), several units, or a large sample. See Chapter 10.

X   See *Causal factor*.

Y   *I*: In measurement, Y represents the indicator(s) that is employed to measure the concept of interest (M). See Chapter 7. *II*: In causal analysis, Y represents the outcome (aka dependent variable) of concern. See Figure 8.1 and elsewhere in Part III. When binary, $Y=0/1$ is sometimes represented as y/Y.

References

Abadie, Alberto 2005. "Semiparametric Difference-in-Differences Estimators," *Review of Economic Studies* 72(1): 1–19.

Abbott, Andrew 1990. "Conceptions of Time and Events in Social Science Methods: Causal and Narrative Approaches," *Historical Methods* 23(4): 140–150.

1992. "From Causes to Events: Notes on Narrative Positivism," *Sociological Methods and Research* 20(4): 428–455.

1995. "Sequence Analysis: New Methods for Old Ideas," *Annual Review of Sociology* 21: 93–113.

2004. *Methods of Discovery: Heuristics for the Social Sciences.* New York: W. W. Norton.

Abbott, Andrew and John Forrest 1986. "Optimal Matching Methods for Historical Sequences," *Journal of Interdisciplinary History* 16(3): 471–494.

Abbott, Andrew and Angela Tsay 2000. "Sequence Analysis and Optimal Matching Methods in Sociology," *Sociological Methods and Research* 29(1): 3–33.

Abdelal, Rawi, Yoshiko M. Herrera, and Alastair Iain Johnston (eds.) 2009. *Measuring Identity: A Guide for Social Scientists.* Cambridge University Press.

Abramo, Claudio Weber 2007. "How Much Do Perceptions of Corruption Really Tell Us?," Economics Discussion Papers, No. 2007-19, May 4.

Abrams, Philip 1982. *Historical Sociology.* Ithaca, NY: Cornell University Press.

Acemoglu, Daron and James A. Robinson 2005. *Economic Origins of Dictatorship and Democracy.* Cambridge University Press.

Acemoglu, Daron, Simon Johnson, and James A. Robinson 2001. "Colonial Origins of Comparative Development: An Empirical Investigation," *American Economic Review* 91 (5): 1369–1401.

2005. "Institutions as the Fundamental Cause of Long-run Growth," in Philippe Algion and S. Durlauf (eds.), *Handbook of Economic Growth.* Amsterdam: North-Holland.

Acharya, Arnab K., Giulia Greco, and Edoardo Masset 2010. "The Economics Approach to Evaluation of Health Intervention in Developing Countries Through Randomised Field Trial," *Journal of Development Effectiveness* 2: 4.

Achen, Christopher H. 1982. *Interpreting and Using Regression.* Beverley Hills, CA: Sage.

2005. "Two Cheers for Charles Ragin," *Studies in Comparative International Development* 40(1): 27–32.

Achen, Christopher H. and W. Philips Shively 1995. *Cross-Level Inference.* University of Chicago Press.

Achinstein, Peter 1983. *The Nature of Explanation.* Oxford University Press.

Adcock, Robert 2005. "What is a Concept?," *Political Concepts: A Working Paper Series of the Committee on Concepts and Methods*, Paper No. 1, April, available at: www.concepts-methods.org/papers.php.

2009. "Making Social Science Matter to Us," *Journal of Theoretical Politics* 21(1): 97–112.

Adcock, Robert and David Collier 2001. "Measurement Validity: A Shared Standard for Qualitative and Quantitative Research," *American Political Science Review* 95(3): 529–546.

Adler, Patricia A. and Peter Adler 2003. "The Promise and Pitfalls of Going into the Field," *Contexts* 2(2): 41–47.

Agodini, Roberto and Mark Dynarski 2004. "Are Experiments the Only Option? A Look at Dropout Prevention Programs," *Review of Economics and Statistics* 86(1): 180–194.

Ahmed, Amel F. and Rudra Sil 2008. "The Logic(s) of Inquiry: Reconsidering Multimethod Approaches," prepared for the Annual Meeting of the American Political Science Association, Boston, MA, August 31–September 2.

Aldrich, John H. 1995. *Why Parties? The Origin and Transformation of Party Politics in America*. University of Chicago Press.

Alford, John R. and John R. Hibbing 2008. "The New Empirical Biopolitics," *Annual Review of Political Science* 11: 183–203.

Algeo, John (ed.) 1991. *Fifty Years Among the New Words: A Dictionary of Neologisms, 1941–1991*. Cambridge University Press.

Allina-Pisano, Jessica 2004. "Sub Rosa Resistance and the Politics of Economic Reform: Land Redistribution in Ukraine," *World Politics* 56(4): 554–581.

Allison, Paul D. 2002. *Missing Data*. Thousand Oaks, CA: Sage.

Almond, Gabriel A. 1990a. *A Discipline Divided: Schools and Sects in Political Science*. Newbury Park, CA: Sage.

1990b. "The Study of Political Culture," in *A Discipline Divided: Schools and Sects in Political Science*. Newbury Park, CA: Sage, pp. 138–156.

Almond, Gabriel A. and Stephen J. Genco [1977] 1990. "Clouds, Clocks, and the Study of Politics," in *A Discipline Divided: Schools and Sects in Political Science*. Newbury Park, CA: Sage, pp. 32–65.

Almond, Gabriel A. and Sidney Verba [1963] 1989. *The Civic Culture: Political Attitudes and Democracy in Five Nations*. Newbury Park, CA: Sage.

Alvarez, Michael, Jose Antonio Cheibub, Fernando Limongi, and Adam Przeworski 1996. "Classifying Political Regimes," *Studies in Comparative International Development* 31 (2): 3–36.

Alvarez, Walter and Frank Assaro 1990. "An Extraterrestrial Impact," *Scientific American* (October): 78–84.

Aminzade, Ronald 1992. "Historical Sociology and Time," *Sociological Methods and Research* 20(4): 456–480.

Anderson, Benedict 1991. *Imagined Communities: Reflections on the Origin and Spread of Nationalism*, rev. edn. London: Verso.

Angeles, Peter A. 1981. *Dictionary of Philosophy*. New York, NY: Barnes & Noble.

Angrist, Joshua D. 1989. "Using the Draft Lottery to Measure the Effect of Military Service on Civilian Labor Market Outcomes," *Research in Labor Economics* 10: 265–310.

1990. "Lifetime Earnings and the Vietnam Era Draft Lottery: Evidence from Social Security Administrative Records," *American Economic Review* 80(3): 313–336.

Angrist, Joshua D. and Alan B. Krueger 1991. "Does Compulsory School Attendance Affect Schooling and Earnings?," *Quarterly Journal of Economics* 106(4): 979–1014.

2001. "Instrumental Variables and the Search for Identification: From Supply and Demand to Quasi-experiments," *Journal of Economic Perspectives* 15(4): 69–85.

Angrist, Joshua D. and Victor Lavy 1999. "Using Maimonides' Rule to Estimate the Effect of Class Size on Scholastic Achievement," *Quarterly Journal of Economics* 114(2): 533–575.

Angrist, Joshua D. and Jorn-Steffen Pischke 2009. *Mostly Harmless Econometrics: An Empiricist's Companion*. Princeton University Press.

2010. "The Credibility Revolution in Empirical Economics: How Better Research Design Is Taking the Con out of Econometrics," *Journal of Economic Perspectives* 24(2): 3–30.

Angrist, Joshua D., Guido W. Imbens, and Donald B. Rubin 1996. "Identification of Causal Effects Using Instrumental Variables," *Journal of the American Statistical Association* 91 (434): 444–455.

Ansolabehere, Stephen, James M. Snyder, Jr., and Charles Stewart III 2000. "Old Voters, New Voters, and the Personal Vote: Using Redistricting to Measure the Incumbency Advantage," *American Journal of Political Science* 44(1): 17–34.

Aristotle 1941. *The Basic Works of Aristotle*, ed. Richard McKeon. New York: Random House.

Austin, John L. 1961. *Philosophical Papers*. Oxford: Clarendon Press.

Axinn, William G. and Lisa D. Pearce 2006. *Mixed Method Data Collection Strategies*. Cambridge University Press.

Bailey, Kenneth D. 1972. "Polythetic Reduction of Monothetic Property Space," *Sociological Methodology* 4: 83–111.

Banerjee, Abhijit V. 2007. *Making Aid Work*. Cambridge, MA: MIT Press.

Banfield, Edward C. 1958. *The Moral Basis of a Backward Society*. Glencoe, IL: Free Press.

Barnes, Barry and David Bloor 1982. "Relativism, Rationalism and the Sociology of Knowledge," in Martin Hollis and Steven Lukes (eds.), *Rationality and Relativism*. Oxford: Basil Blackwell, pp. 21–47.

Barrett, Christopher and Jeffery Cason 1997. *Overseas Research*. Baltimore, MD: JHU Press.

Bartels, Larry M. 1991. "Instrumental and 'Quasi-Instrumental' Variables," *American Journal of Political Science* 35(3): 777–800.

1997. "Specification Uncertainty and Model Averaging," *American Journal of Political Science* 41: 641–674.

2006. "What's the Matter with *What's the Matter with Kansas*?," *Quarterly Journal of Political Science* 1: 201–226.

Barth, Fredrik 1969. *Ethnic Groups and Boundaries: The Social Organization of Cultural Differences*. Boston, MA: Little, Brown.

Bartholomew, David J. (ed.) 2007. *Measurement*, 4 vols. Thousand Oaks, CA: Sage.

Barton, Alan H. and Paul F. Lazarsfeld 1969. "Some Functions of Qualitative Analysis in Social Research," in George J. McCall and J. L. Simmons (eds.), *Issues in Participant Observation*. Reading, MA: Addison-Wesley.

Bates, Robert H., Avner Greif, Margaret Levi, Jean-Laurent Rosenthal, and Barry Weingast 1998. *Analytic Narratives*. Princeton University Press.

Battistin, Erich and Enrico Rettore 2002a. "Another Look at the Regression Discontinuity Design," available at: www.cepr.org/meets/wkcn/4/4528/papers/rettore.pdf.

2002b. "Testing for Programme Effects in a Regression Discontinuity Design with Imperfect Compliance," *Journal of the Royal Statistical Society A*, 165(1): 39–57.

Baumgartner, Frank R. and Bryan D. Jones 1993. *Agendas and Instability in American Politics.* University of Chicago Press.

Bayard de Volo, Lorraine and Edward Schatz 2004. "From the Inside Out: Ethnographic Methods in Political Research," *PS: Political Science and Politics* 37(2): 267–271.

Becker, Howard S. 1986. *Writing for Social Scientists: How to Start and Finish Your Thesis, Book, or Article.* University of Chicago Press.

Beckwith, Karen and Kimberly Cowell-Meyers 2007. "Sheer Numbers: Critical Representation Thresholds and Women's Political Representation," *Perspectives on Politics* 5(3): 553–565.

Beetham, David 1999. *Democracy and Human Rights.* Cambridge: Polity Press.

Beetham, David (ed.) 1994. *Defining and Measuring Democracy.* London: Sage.

Bender, Thomas, Carl E. Schorske, Stephen R. Graubard, and William J. Barber (eds.) 1997. *American Academic Culture in Transformation: Fifty Years, Four Disciplines.* Princeton University Press.

Bennett, Andrew 1999. "Causal Inference in Case Studies: From Mill's Methods to Causal Mechanisms," paper presented at the Annual Meeting of the American Political Science Association, Atlanta, GA, September.

2010. "Process Tracing and Causal Inference," in Henry E. Brady and David Collier (eds.), *Rethinking Social Inquiry: Diverse Tools, Shared Standards*, pp. 207–220.

Bennett, Andrew and Bear Braumoeller 2006. "Where the Model Frequently Meets the Road: Combining Formal, Statistical, and Case Study Methods," unpublished manuscript, Georgetown University, Washington, DC.

Benson, Kjell and Arthur Hartz, Jr. 2000. "A Comparison of Observational Studies and Randomized Controlled Trials," *New England Journal of Medicine* 342(25): 1878–1886.

Berelson, Bernard R. and Gary A. Steiner 1964. *Human Behavior: An Inventory of Scientific Findings.* New York: Harcourt.

Berger, Bennett M. 1995. *An Essay on Culture: Symbolic Structure and Social Structure.* Berkeley, CA: University of California Press.

Berg-Schlosser, Dirk (ed.) 2007. *Democratization: The State of the Art.* Farmington Hills, MI: Barbara Budrich Esser.

Berg-Schlosser, Dirk and Gisele De Meur 1994. "Conditions of Democracy in Interwar Europe: A Boolean Test of Major Hypotheses," *Comparative Politics* 26(3): 253–279.

2009. "Comparative Research Design," in Rihoux and Ragin (eds.), *Configurational Comparative Methods: Qualitative Comparative Analysis (QCA) and Related Techniques*, pp. 19–32.

Berg-Schlosser, Dirk and Jeremy Mitchell 2000. *Conditions of Democracy in Europe, 1919–39: Systematic Case Studies.* Basingstoke: Macmillan.

2003. *Authoritarianism and Democracy in Europe, 1919–39: Comparative Analyses.* Basingstoke: Macmillan.

Berk, Richard A. 1991. "Toward a Methodology for Mere Mortals," *Sociological Methodology* 21: 315–324.

1999. "Review of *Observational Studies* by Paul Rosenbaum," *Journal of Educational and Behavioral Statistics* 24(1): 95–100.

2004. *Regression Analysis: A Constructive Critique.* Thousand Oaks, CA: Sage.

2005. "Randomized Experiments as the Bronze Standard," unpublished manuscript. Department of Statistics, UCLA.

Berk, Richard A. and Jan de Leeuw 1999. "An Evaluation of California's Inmate Classification System Using a Generalized Regression Discontinuity Design," *Journal of the American Statistical Association* 94(448): 1045–1052.

Berk, Richard A. and David Rauma 1983. "Capitalizing on Nonrandom Assignment to Treatments: A Regression-Discontinuity Evaluation of a Crime-Control Program," *Journal of the American Statistical Association* 78(381): 21–27.

Berk, Richard A., Alec Campbell, Ruth Klapp, and Bruce Western 1992. "The Differential Deterrent Effects of an Arrest in Incidents of Domestic Violence: A Bayesian Analysis of Four Randomized Field Experiments," *American Sociological Review* 57(5): 698–708.

Bertrand, Marianne and Sendhil Mullainathan 2001. "Do People Mean What They Say? Implications for Subjective Survey Data," *American Economic Review* 91(2): 67–72.

2005. "Are Emily and Greg More Employable than Lakisha and Jamal?: A Field Experiment on Labor Market Discrimination," *American Economic Review* 94(4): 991–1013.

Bertrand, Marianne, Esther Duflo, and Sendhil Mullainathan 2004. "How Much Should We Trust Difference-in-Differences Estimates?," *Quarterly Journal of Economics* 119(1): 249–275.

Besley, Timothy and Torsten Persson 2009. "The Origins of State Capacity: Property Rights, Taxation, and Politics," *American Economic Review* 99(4): 1218–1244.

Bewley, Truman 1999. *Why Wages Don't Fall during a Recession*. Cambridge, MA: Harvard University Press.

Bhaskar, Roy [1975] 1978. *A Realist Theory of Science*. Hassocks: Harvester Press.

Bickman, Leonard and K. Peterson 1990. "Using Program Theory to Describe and Measure Program Quality," in Leonard Bickman (ed.), *Advances in Program Theory*. San Francisco, CA: Jossey-Bass, pp. 61–72.

Bierwisch, Manfred 1981. "Basic Issues in the Development of Word Meaning," in Werner Deutsch (ed.), *The Child's Construction of Language*. London: Academic Press, pp. 341–387.

Bierwisch, Manfred and Robert Schreuder 1992. "From Concepts to Lexical Items," *Cognition* 42: 23–60.

Bjorkman, Martina and Jakob Svensson 2009. "Power to the People: Evidence from a Randomized Experiment of a Citizen Report Card Project in Uganda," *Quarterly Journal of Economics* 124(2): 735–769.

Blalock, Hubert M., Jr. 1982. *Conceptualization and Measurement in the Social Sciences*. Beverly Hills, CA: Sage.

Blalock, Hubert M., Jr. 1984. "Contextual-Effects Models: Theoretical and Methodological Issues," *Annual Review of Sociology* 10: 977–1012.

Blaug, Mark 1978. *Economic Theory in Retrospect*. Cambridge University Press.

Bloch, Marc [1941] 1953. *The Historian's Craft*. New York: Vintage Books.

Bloom, Howard S. (ed.) 2005. *Learning More from Social Experiments: Evolving Analytic Approaches*. New York: Russell Sage Foundation.

Bloom, Howard S., Carolyn J. Hill, and James A. Riccio 2002. "Linking Program Implementation and Effectiveness: Lessons from a Pooled Sample of Welfare-to-Work Experiments," *Journal of Policy Analysis and Management* 22(4): 551–575.

Bohman, James 1991. *New Philosophy of Social Science: Problems of Indeterminacy.* Cambridge, MA: MIT Press.

Bok, Derek 1982. *Beyond the Ivory Tower: Social Responsibilities of the Modern University.* Cambridge, MA: Harvard University Press.

Bollen, Kenneth A. 1989. *Structural Equations with Latent Variables.* New York: John Wiley.

Bollen, Kenneth A. and Richard Lennox 1991. "Conventional Wisdom on Measurement: A Structural Equation Perspective," *Psychological Bulletin* 110: 305–314.

Borges, Jorge Luis [1942] 1999. *Selected Non-Fictions,* ed. Eliot Weinberger. New York: Penguin.

Boumans, Marcel (ed.) 2007. *Measurement in Economics: A Handbook.* Amsterdam: Elsevier.

Bourguignon, François and Christian Morrisson 2002. "Inequality among World Citizens: 1820–1992," *American Economic Review* 92(4): 727–744.

Bowers, Jake and Costas Panagopoulos 2009. "A Reasoned Basis for Inference: Randomization and Design Justifying Estimation and Testing," unpublished paper, Department of Political Science, University of Illinois at Urbana-Champaign.

Bowman, Kirk, Fabrice Lehoucq, and James Mahoney 2005. "Measuring Political Democracy: Case Expertise, Data Adequacy, and Central America," *Comparative Political Studies* 38 (8): 939–970.

Box-Steffensmeier, Janet, Henry Brady, and David Collier (eds.) 2008. *The Oxford Handbook of Political Methodology.* Oxford University Press.

Boyd, Richard, Philip Gasper, and J. D. Trout (eds.) 1991. *The Philosophy of Science.* Cambridge, MA: MIT Press.

Brady, Henry E. 2002. "Models of Causal Inference: Going Beyond the Neyman–Rubin–Holland Theory," paper presented at the Annual Meeting of the Political Methodology Group, University of Washington, Seattle, WA, July.

2004. "Data-Set Observations versus Causal-Process Observations: The 2000 U.S. Presidential Election," in Brady and Collier (eds.), *Rethinking Social Inquiry: Diverse Tools, Shared Standards,* pp. 267–272.

2008. "Causation and Explanation in Social Science," in Box-Steffensmeier, Brady, and Collier (eds.), *The Oxford Handbook of Political Methodology.* pp. 217–270.

Brady, Henry E. and David Collier (eds.) 2004. *Rethinking Social Inquiry: Diverse Tools, Shared Standards.* Lanham, MD: Rowman & Littlefield.

Brady, Henry E. and John E. McNulty 2004. "The Costs of Voting: Evidence from a Quasi-experiment," prepared for presentation at the Annual Meeting of the Society for Political Methodology, Stanford University, Palo Alto, CA, July.

Brady, Henry E., David Collier, and Jason Seawright 2006. "Toward a Pluralistic Vision of Methodology," *Political Analysis* 14(3): 353–368.

Braumoeller, Bear F. 2006. "Explaining Variance: Or, Stuck in a Moment We Can't Get Out Of," *Political Analysis* 14(3): 268–290.

Braumoeller, Bear F. and Gary Goertz 2000. "The Methodology of Necessary Conditions," *American Journal of Political Science* 44(3): 844–858.

2002. "Watching Your Posterior," *Political Analysis* 10(2): 198–203.

Breslow, N. E. 1996. "Statistics in Epidemiology: The Case-Control Study," *Journal of the American Statistical Association* 91(433): 14–28.

Brewer, John and Albert Hunter 2006. *Foundations of Multimethod Research: Synthesizing Styles*. Thousand Oaks, CA: Sage.

Briggs, Derek C. 2005. "Meta-Analysis: A Case Study," *Evaluation Review* 29(2): 87–127.

Brim, John A. and David H. Spain 1974. *Research Design in Anthropology: Paradigms and Pragmatics in the Testing of Hypotheses*. New York: Holt, Rinehart & Winston.

Brinks, Daniel and Michael Coppedge 2006. "Diffusion is no Illusion: Neighbor Emulation in the Third Wave of Democracy," *Comparative Political Studies* 39(4): 463–489.

Brown, Michael E., Sean M. Lynn-Jones, and Steven E. Miller (eds.) 1996. *Debating the Democratic Peace*. Cambridge, MA: MIT Press.

Brown, Robert 1984. *The Nature of Social Laws: Machiavelli to Mill*. Cambridge University Press.

Bryman, Alan 1984. "The Debate about Quantitative and Qualitative Research: A Question of Method or Epistemology?," *British Journal of Sociology* 35(1): 75–92.

Budge, Ian, David Robertson, and Derek Hearl 1987. *Ideology, Strategy and Party Change: Spatial Analyses of Post-War Election Programmes in 19 Democracies*. Cambridge University Press.

Buford, Bill 1991. *Among the Thugs*. New York: Vintage.

Bunge, Mario 1959. *Causality*. Cambridge, MA: Harvard University Press.

1963. *The Place of the Causal Principle in Modern Science*. Cleveland, OH: Meridian Books.

1979. *Causality and Modern Science*, 3rd edn. New York: Dover.

1997. "Mechanism and Explanation," *Philosophy of the Social Sciences* 27: 410–465.

Burawoy, Michael, Joshua Gamson, and Alice Burton 1991. *Ethnography Unbound: Power and Resistance in the Modern Metropolis*. Berkeley, CA: University of California Press.

Burger, Thomas 1976. *Max Weber's Theory of Concept Formation: History, Laws, and Ideal Types*. Durham, NC: Duke University.

Butler, Daniel M. 2006. "Are Voters in Primaries Biased against Female Candidates? A Regression Discontinuity Analysis," paper presented to the Annual Meeting of the American Political Science Association, Philadelphia, PA, August 30–September 3.

Butler, Daniel M. and Matthew J. Butler 2006. "Splitting the Difference? Causal Inference and Theories of Split-Party Delegations," *Political Analysis* 14: 439–455.

Cameron, Lisa A., Ananish Chaudhuri, Nisvan Erkal, and Lata Gangadharan 2009. "Do Attitudes toward Corruption Differ across Cultures? Experimental Evidence from Australia, India, Indonesia and Singapore," *Journal of Public Economics* 93: 843–851.

Campbell, Angus, Philip E. Converse, Warren P. Miller, and Donald E. Stokes 1960. *The American Voter*. New York: Wiley.

Campbell, Donald T. 1966. "Pattern Matching as an Essential in Distal Knowing," in K. R. Hammond (ed.), *The Psychology of Egon Brunswick*. New York: Holt, Rinehart & Winston, pp. 81–106.

[1968] 1988. "The Connecticut Crackdown on Speeding: Time-Series Data in Quasi-Experimental Analysis," in E. Samuel Overman (ed.), *Methodology and Epistemology for Social Science*. University of Chicago Press, pp. 222–238.

1975. "'Degrees of Freedom' and the Case Study," *Comparative Political Studies* 8(8): 178–193.

Campbell, Donald T. and Julian Stanley 1963. *Experimental and Quasi-Experimental Designs for Research*. Boston, MA: Houghton Mifflin.

Campbell, Norman Robert [1919] 1957. *Physics: The Elements*, reprinted as *Foundations of Science*. New York: Dover.

Capecchi, Vittorio 1968. "On the Definition of Typology and Classification in Sociology," *Quality and Quantity* 2(1–2): 9–30.

Caporaso, James A. 1995. "Research Design, Falsification, and the Qualitative–Quantitative Divide," *American Political Science Review* 89(2): 457–460.

Card, David and Alan B. Krueger 1994. "Minimum Wages and Employment: A Case Study of the Fast-Food Industry in New Jersey and Pennsylvania," *American Economic Review* 84 (4): 772–793.

Carey, Gregory 2002. *Human Genetics for the Social Sciences*. Thousand Oaks, CA: Sage.

Carey, John M. 2008. *Legislative Voting and Accountability*. Cambridge University Press.

Carmines, Edward G. and Richard A. Meller 1979. *Reliability and Validity Assessment*. Beverly Hills, CA: Sage.

Carnoy, Martin 1998. "National Voucher Plans in Chile and Sweden: Did Privatization Reforms Make for Better Education?," *Comparative Education Review* 42(3): 309–337.

Caron, Neal and Aaron Panofsky 2005. "TQCA: A Technique for Adding Temporality to Qualitative Comparative Analysis," *Sociological Methods and Research* 34(2): 147–172.

Carpenter, Jeffrey P., Glenn W. Harrison, and John A. List (eds.) 2005. *Field Experiments in Economics*. London: Elsevier.

Carr, Edward Hallett [1939] 1964. *The Twenty Years' Crisis, 1919–1939: An Introduction to the Study of International Relations*. New York: Harper.

Cartwright, Nancy 1983. *How the Laws of Physics Lie*. Oxford University Press.

2004. "Causation: One Word, Many Things," *Philosophy of Science* 71(5), Proceedings of the 2002 Biennial Meeting of the Philosophy of Science Association. Part II: Symposia Papers, December, pp. 805–819.

2007. *Hunting Causes and Using Them*. Cambridge University Press.

Cat, Jordi 2006. "Fuzzy Empiricism and Fuzzy-Set Causality: What Is All the Fuzz About?," *Philosophy of Science* 73: 26–41.

Caton, Charles E. (ed.) 1963. *Philosophy and Ordinary Language*. Urbana IL: University of Illinois Press.

Cavell, Stanley 1979. *The Claim of Reason: Wittgenstein, Skepticism, Morality, and Tragedy*. Oxford University Press.

Chakrabarti, Rajashri and Paul E. Peterson (eds.) 2008. *School Choice International: Exploring Public–Private Partnerships*. Cambridge, MA: MIT Press.

Chapin, F. Stuart 1939. "Definition of Definitions of Concepts," *Social Forces* 18(2): 153–160.

Chappell, V. C. (ed.) 1964. *Ordinary Language*. Englewood Cliffs, NJ: Prentice Hall.

Chattapadhyay, Raghabendra and Esther Duflo 2004. "Women as Policy Makers: Evidence from a Randomized Policy Experiment in India," *Econometrica* 72(5): 1409–1443.

Chaudhury, N. and J. S. Hammer 2003. "Ghost Doctors: Absenteeism in Bangladeshi Health Facilities," Policy Research Working Paper No. 3065, Washington, DC: World Bank.

Cheibub, Jose Antonio and Jennifer Gandhi 2004. "Classifying Political Regimes: A Six-Fold Measure of Democracies and Dictatorship," presented at the Annual Meeting of the American Political Science Association, Chicago, IL September 2–5.

Chen, H. T. and P. H. Rossi 1983. "Evaluating with Sense: The Theory-Driven Approach," *Evaluation Review* 7: 283–302.

Chong, Dennis 1993. "How People Think, Reason, and Feel about Rights and Liberties," *American Journal of Political Science* 37(3): 867–899.

Chubb, John E. and Terry M. Moe 1990. *Politics, Markets, and America's Schools.* Washington, DC: Brookings Institution.

Clark, Gordon L., Meric S. Gertler, and Maryann P. Feldman (eds.) 2000. *The Oxford Handbook of Economic Geography.* Oxford University Press.

Clark, Gregory 2008. *Farewell to Alms: A Brief Economic History of the World.* Princeton University Press.

Clark, John and Joseph Banks 1793. "Description of an Extraordinary Production of Human Generation, with Observations," *Philosophical Transactions of the Royal Society of London* 83: 154–163.

Clark, Vicki L. Plano and John W. Creswell (eds.) 2007. *The Mixed Methods Reader.* Thousand Oaks, CA: Sage.

Clarke, Kevin A. 2002. "The Reverend and the Ravens," *Political Analysis* 10(2): 194–197.

　　2005. "The Phantom Menace: Omitted Variable Bias in Econometric Research," *Conflict Management and Peace Science* 22: 341–52.

Clogg, Clifford C. and Adamantios Haritou 1997. "The Regression Method of Causal Inference and a Dilemma Confronting this Method," in McKim and Turner (eds.), *Causality in Crisis?: Statistical Methods and the Search for Causal Knowledge in the Social Sciences,* pp. 83–112.

Cochran, Thomas C. 1948. "The 'Presidential Synthesis' in American History," *American Historical Review* 53: 748–53.

Cohen, Abner 1974. *Two-Dimensional Man: An Essay on the Anthropology of Power and Symbolism in Complex Society.* Berkeley, CA: University of California Press.

Cohen, Jacob 1988. *Statistical Power Analysis for the Behavioral Sciences,* 2nd edn. Mahwah, NJ: Lawrence Erlbaum.

Cohen, Michael, James March, and Johan Olsen 1972. "A Garbage Can Model of Organizational Choice," *Administrative Science Quarterly* 17(1): 1–25.

Cohen, Morris R. and Ernest Nagel 1934. *An Introduction to Logic and Scientific Method.* New York: Harcourt.

Coleman, James S. and Thomas J. Fararo (eds.) 1992. *Rational Choice Theory: Advocacy and Critique.* Thousand Oaks, CA: Sage.

Coleman, Stephen 2007. "Testing Theories with Qualitative and Quantitative Predictions," *European Political Science* 6(2): 124–133.

Collier, David 1995. "Trajectory of a Concept: 'Corporatism' in the Study of Latin American Politics," in Peter Smith (ed.), *Latin America in Comparative Perspective.* Boulder, CO: Westview, pp. 135–162.

　　1998. "Putting Concepts to Work: Toward a Framework for Analyzing Conceptual Innovation in Comparative Research," paper presented at the Annual Meeting of the American Political Science Association, Boston, MA, September.

Collier, David and John Gerring (eds.) 2009. *Concepts and Method in Social Science: The Tradition of Giovanni Sartori.* London: Routledge.

Collier, David and Steven Levitsky 1997. "Democracy with Adjectives: Conceptual Innovation in Comparative Research," *World Politics* 49(3): 430–451.

Collier, David and James E. Mahon, Jr. 1993. "Conceptual 'Stretching' Revisited: Adapting Categories in Comparative Analysis," *American Political Science Review* 87(4): 845–855.

Collier, David and James Mahoney 1996. "Insights and Pitfalls: Selection Bias in Qualitative Research," *World Politics* 49(1): 56–91.

Collier, David, Henry Brady, and Jason Seawright 2010. "Sources of Leverage in Causal Inference: Toward an Alternative View of Methodology," in Henry E. Brady and David Collier (eds.), *Rethinking Social Inquiry: Diverse Tools, Shared Standards*, 2nd edn. Lanham: Rowman & Littlefield, pp. 161–200.

Collier, David, Jody LaPorte, and Jason Seawright 2008. "Typologies: Forming Concepts and Creating Categorical Variables," in Box-Steffensmeier, Brady, and Collier (eds.), *The Oxford Handbook of Political Methodology*, pp. 152–173.

Collier, Ruth Berins and David Collier 1991. *Shaping the Political Arena: Critical Junctures, the Labor Movement, and Regime Dynamics in Latin America*. Princeton University Press.

Collingwood, R. G. 1940. *An Essay on Metaphysics*. Oxford University Press.

Collins, Randall 1985. *Three Sociological Traditions*. New York: Oxford University Press.

Connolly, William E. [1974] 1983. *The Terms of Political Discourse*, 2nd edn. Princeton University Press.

Converse, Philip E. 1964. "The Nature of Belief Systems in Mass Publics," in David E. Apter (ed.), *Ideology and Discontent*. London: Free Press of Glencoe, pp. 206–261.

Cook, Thomas D. and Donald Campbell 1979. *Quasi-Experimentation: Design and Analysis Issues for Field Settings*. Boston, MA: Houghton Mifflin.

Cook, Thomas D. and Vivian C. Wong 2005. "Empirical Tests of the Validity of the Regression Discontinuity Design," unpublished manuscript, Institute for Policy Research, Northwestern University.

Cook, Thomas D., Michael Scriven, Chris L. S. Coryn, and Stephanie D. H. Evergreen 2010. "Contemporary Thinking about Causation in Evaluation: A Dialogue With Tom Cook and Michael Scriven," *American Journal of Evaluation* 31: 105–117.

Cook, Thomas D., William R. Shaddish, and Vivian C. Wong 2008. "Three Conditions under which Experiments and Observational Studies Produce Comparable Causal Estimates: New Findings from Within-Study Comparisons," *Journal of Policy Analysis and Management* 27: 724–750.

Coppedge, Michael forthcoming. *Approaching Democracy*. Cambridge University Press.

Coppedge, Michael and John Gerring 2011. "Conceptualizing and Measuring Democracy: A New Approach," *Perspectives on Politics* 9(2): 247–267.

Coppedge, Michael and Wolfgang H. Reinicke 1990. "Measuring Polyarchy," *Studies in Comparative International Development* 25(1): 51–72.

Coppedge, Michael, Angel Alvarez, and Claudia Maldonado 2008. "Two Persistent Dimensions of Democracy: Contestation and Inclusiveness," *Journal of Politics* 70(3): 335–350.

Corti, Louise, Andreas Witzel, and Libby Bishop 2005. Special Issue on Secondary Analysis of Qualitative Data, *Qualitative Sozialforschung/Forum for Qualitative Social Research* 6(1).

Cox, David R. 2007. "Applied Statistics: A Review," *Annals of Applied Statistics* 1: 1–16.

Cox, Gary W. 1987. *The Efficient Secret: The Cabinet and the Development of Political Parties in Victorian England*. Cambridge University Press.

Cox, Gary W., Frances M. Rosenbluth, and Michael F. Thies 2000. "Electoral Rules, Career Ambitions, and Party Structure: Comparing Factions in Japan's Upper and Lower Houses," *American Journal of Political Science* 44(1): 115–122.

Creswell, John W. 2008. *Research Design: Qualitative, Quantitative, and Mixed Methods Approaches*. Thousand Oaks, CA: Sage.

Crossman, Richard Howard Stafford 1976. *The Diaries of a Cabinet Minister*. New York: Henry Holt.

Crouse, Timothy 2003. *The Boys on the Bus*. New York: Random House.

D'Andrade, Roy G. 1995. *The Development of Cognitive Anthropology*. Cambridge University Press.

Dahl, Robert A. [1957] 1969. "The Concept of Power," reprinted in Roderick Bel, David V. Edwards, and R. Harrison Wagner (eds.), *Political Power: A Reader in Theory and Research*. New York: Free Press, pp. 79–93.

 1968. "Power," in David L. Sills (ed.), *International Encyclopedia of the Social Sciences, vol. XII*. New York: Macmillan, pp. 405–415.

 1971. *Polyarchy: Participation and Opposition*. New Haven, CT: Yale University Press.

Daniels, Ronald 2005. *Rethinking the Welfare State: Government by Voucher*. London: Routledge.

Darity, William A. and Patrick L. Mason 1998. "Evidence on Discrimination in Employment: Codes of Color, Codes of Gender," *Journal of Economic Perspectives* 12(2): 63–90.

Davis, David Brion 1988. *The Problem of Slavery in Western Culture*. Oxford University Press.

Dawid, A. Phillip 2007. "Fundamentals of Statistical Causality," unpublished manuscript, University of Sheffield.

Day, Timothy and Harold Kincaid 1994. "Putting Inference to the Best Explanation in its Place," *Synthese* 98: 271–295.

De Meur, Gisele, Benoît Rihoux, and Sakura Yamasaki 2009. "Addressing the Critiques of QCA," in Rihoux and Ragin (eds.), *Configurational Comparative Methods: Qualitative Comparative Analysis (QCA) and Related Techniques*, pp. 147–165.

de Saint-Exupéry, Antoine [1943] 1971. *The Little Prince*. Katherine Woods, trans. New York: Harcourt Brace Jovanovich.

De Vreese, Leen 2007. "Disentangling Causal Pluralism," unpublished manuscript, Centre for Logic and Philosophy of Science, Ghent University, Belgium.

Deaton, Angus 2010. "Instruments, Randomization, and Learning about Development," *Journal of Economic Literature* 48(2): 424–455.

Debnam, Geoffrey 1984. *The Analysis of Power: Core Elements and Structure*. New York: St. Martin's Press.

Dessler, David 1991. "Beyond Correlations: Toward a Causal Theory of War," *International Studies Quarterly* 35: 337–355.

Dewey, John 1938. *Logic: The Theory of Inquiry*. New York: Henry Holt.

Dexter, Lewis Anthony 2008. *Elite and Specialized Interviewing*. University of Essex, Colchester: ECPR Press.

Diamond, Jared 1992. *Guns, Germs, and Steel: The Fates of Human Societies*. New York: W. W. Norton.

DiNardo, John and David S. Lee 2004. "The Impacts of New Unionization on Private Sector Employers: 1984–2001," *Quarterly Journal of Economics* 119(4): 1383–1441.

Dion, Douglas 1998. "Evidence and Inference in the Comparative Case Study," *Comparative Politics* 30(2): 127–145.

DiRenzo, Gordon J. (ed.) 1966. *Concepts, Theory, and Explanation in the Behavioral Sciences.* New York: Random House.

Doherty, Daniel, Alan S. Gerber, and Donald P. Green 2006. "Personal Income and Attitudes toward Redistribution: A Study of Lottery Winners," *Political Psychology* 27(3): 441–458.

Dollar, David 2005. "Globalization, Poverty, and Inequality," in Michael M. Weinstein (ed.), *Globalization: What's New?* New York: Columbia University Press, pp. 96–128.

Dollar, David, Raymond Fisman, and Roberta Gatti 2001. "Are Women Really the 'Fairer' Sex? Corruption and Women in Government," *Journal of Economic Behavior and Organization* 46(4): 423–429.

Donaldson, S. I. 2003. "Theory-driven Program Evaluation," in S. I. Donaldson and Michael Scriven (eds.), *Evaluating Social Programs and Problems: Visions for the New Millennium.* Mahwah, NJ: Lawrence Erlbaum, pp. 109–141.

Doorenspleet, Renske 2000. "Reassessing the Three Waves of Democratization," *World Politics* 52(3): 384–406.

Dryzek, John S. 1988. "The Mismeasure of Political Man," *Journal of Politics* 50(3): 705–725.

Duflo, Esther 2004. "Scaling Up and Evaluation," Annual World Bank Conference on Development Economics, Paris, pp. 341–369.

Duflo, Esther, Rachel Glennerster, and Michael Kremer 2008. "Using Randomization in Development Economics Research: A Toolkit," in T. Paul Schultz and John A. Strauss (eds.), *Handbook of Development Economics, vol. 4.* London: Elsevier, pp. 3895–3962.

Dul, J., T. Hak, Gary Goertz, and C. Voss 2010. "Necessary Condition Hypotheses in Operations Management," *International Journal of Operations and Production Management* 30(11): 1170–1190.

Dumont, Richard G. and William J. Wilson 1967. "Aspects of Concept Formation, Explication, and Theory Construction in Sociology," *American Sociological Review* 32(6): 985–995.

Duncan, Nick 2006. "The Non-Perception Based Measurement of Corruption: A Review of Issues and Methods from a Policy Perspective," in Sampford, Shacklock, Connors, and Galtung (eds.), *Measuring Corruption*, pp. 131–161.

Duncan, Otis Dudley 1984. *Notes on Social Measurement: Historical and Critical.* New York: Russell Sage Foundation.

Dunning, Thad 2008a. *Crude Democracy: Natural Resource Wealth and Political Regimes.* Cambridge University Press.

2008b. "Improving Causal Inference: Strengths and Limitations of Quasi-experiments," *Political Research Quarterly* 61(2): 282–293.

2008c. "Natural and Field Experiments: The Role of Qualitative Methods," *Qualitative and Multimethod Research*, 17–23.

Dupre, John 1984. "Probabilistic Causality Emancipated," in French, Uehling, and Wettstein (eds.), *Midwest Studies in Philosophy, vol. IX: Causation and Causal Theories*, pp. 169–175.

Durkheim, Emile [1895] 1964. *The Rules of Sociological Method.* New York: Free Press.

Dyson, Tim 2001. "A Partial Theory of World Development: The Neglected Role of the Demographic Transition in the Shaping of Modern Society," *International Journal of Population Geography* 7: 67–90.

Easton, David 1953. *The Political System.* New York: Knopf.

Easton, David and Corinne Schelling (eds.) 1991. *Divided Knowledge: Across Disciplines, Across Cultures.* Newbury Park, CA: Sage.

Eckstein, Harry 1975. "Case Studies and Theory in Political Science," in Greenstein and Polsby (eds.), *Handbook of Political Science, vol. VII: Political Science: Scope and Theory,* pp. 79–138.
  1988. "A Culturalist Theory of Political Change," *American Political Science Review* 82.
  1992. *Regarding Politics: Essays on Political Theory, Stability, and Change.* Berkeley, CA: University of California Press.

Edin, Kathryn and Laura Lein 1997. *Making Ends Meet.* New York: Russell Sage.

Edin, Per-Anders, Peter Fredrikson, and Olof Åslund 2003. "Ethnic Enclaves and the Economic Success of Immigrants: Evidence from a Natural Experiment," *Quarterly Journal of Economics* 118(1): 329–357.

Eichengreen, Barry 1992. *Golden Fetters: The Gold Standard and the Great Depression, 1919–1939.* New York: Oxford University Press.

Einstein, Albert [1940] 1953. "The Fundaments of Theoretical Physics," in Herbert Feigl and May Brodbeck (eds.), *Readings in the Philosophy of Science.* New York: Appleton Century Crofts, pp. 253–262.

Eldridge, John E. T. 1983. *C. Wright Mills.* Chichester: Ellis Horwood.

Elman, Colin 2005. "Explanatory Typologies in Qualitative Studies of International Politics," *International Organization* 59(2): 293–326.

Elman, Miriam Fendius 1997. *Paths to Peace: Is Democracy the Answer?* Cambridge, MA: MIT Press.

Elster, Jon 1989. *Nuts and Bolts for the Social Sciences.* Cambridge University Press.

England, Paula, Barbara Stanek Kilbourne, George Farkas, and Thomas Dou 1988. "Explaining Occupational Sex Segregation and Wages: Findings from a Model with Fixed Effects," *American Sociological Review* 53(4): 544–558.

Epstein, Edward Jay 2000. *News from Nowhere: Television and the News.* Chicago, IL: Ivan R. Dee.

Epstein, Leon D. 1964. "A Comparative Study of Canadian Parties," *American Political Science Review* 58: 46–59.

Esping-Andersen, Gosta 1990. *The Three Worlds of Welfare Capitalism.* Princeton University Press.

Everitt, Brian S., Sabine Landau, and Morven Leese 2001. *Cluster Analysis,* 4th edn. London: Arnold.

Falk, Armin and James J. Heckman 2009. "Lab Experiments Are a Major Source of Knowledge in the Social Sciences," unpublished manuscript, Department of Economics, University of Chicago.

Falleti, Tulia G. 2010. *Subnational Politics after Decentralization in Latin America.* Cambridge University Press.

Fay, Brian 1976. *Social Theory and Political Practice.* London: Allen & Unwin.
  [1983] 1994. "General Laws and Explaining Human Behavior," in Martin and McIntyre (eds.), *Readings in the Philosophy of Social Science,* pp. 91–110.

Fearon, James D. 1991. "Counter Factuals and Hypothesis Testing in Political Science," *World Politics* 43: 169–195.

Fenno, Richard F., Jr. 1978. *Home Style: House Members in their Districts.* Boston, MA: Little, Brown.

1986. "Observation, Context, and Sequence in the Study of Politics," *American Political Science Review* 80(1): 3–15.

1990. *Watching Politicians: Essays on Participant Observation*. Berkeley, CA: IGS Press.

Feyerabend, Paul 1963. "How to be a Good Empiricist: A Plea for Tolerance in Matters Epistemological," *Philosophy of Science: The Delaware Seminar* 2: 3–39.

1975. *Against Method*. London: New Left Books.

Finan, Frederico and Claudio Ferraz 2005. "Exposing Corrupt Politicians: The Effect of Brazil's Publicly Released Audits on Electoral Outcomes," Working Paper No. 2005-53, Institute of Governmental Studies, University of California, Berkeley.

Finer, Samuel E. 1997. *The History of Government, vols. 1–3*. Cambridge University Press.

Finkel, Steve, Anibal Pérez-Liñán, and Mitchell A. Seligson 2007. "The Effects of US Foreign Assistance on Democracy Building, 1990–2003," *World Politics* 59: 404–439.

Finlay, Linda and Brendan Gough (eds.) 2003. *Reflexivity: A Practical Guide for Researchers in Health and Social Sciences*. Oxford: Blackwell.

Fiorina, Morris P. 2005. *Culture War?: The Myth of a Polarized America*. New York: Pearson Longman.

Firebaugh, Glenn 2003. *The New Geography of Global Income Inequality*. Cambridge, MA: Harvard University Press.

2008. *Seven Rules for Social Research*. Princeton University Press.

Fischer, David Hackett 1970. *Historians' Fallacies: Toward a Logic of Historical Thought*. New York: Harper.

1989. *Albion's Seed: Four British Folkways in America*. New York: Oxford University Press.

Fisher, Ronald Aylmer 1935. *The Design of Experiments*. Edinburgh: Oliver & Boyd.

Fisman, David, Raymond Fisman, Julia Galef, and Rakesh Khurana 2006. "Estimating the Value of Connections to Vice-President Cheney," working paper, Center for Health and Wellbeing, Princeton University.

Fisman, Raymond 2001. "Estimating the Value of Political Connections," *American Economic Review* 91(4): 1095–1102.

Fisman, Raymond and Edward Miguel 2007. "Corruption, Norms, and Legal Enforcement: Evidence from Diplomatic Parking Tickets," *Journal of Political Economy* 115(6): 1020–1048.

Fleck, Ludwik [1935] 1979. *The Genesis and Development of a Scientific Fact*. University of Chicago Press.

Forsyth, Donelson R. 1976. "Crucial Experiments and Social Psychological Inquiry," *Personality and Social Psychology Bulletin* 2(4): 454–459.

Fowler, Floyd J. 2008. *Survey Research Methods*, 8th edn. Thousand Oaks, CA: Sage.

Fowler, James H. and Darren Schreiber 2008. "Biology, Politics, and the Emerging Science of Nature," *Science* 322: 912–914.

Francis, Elizabeth 1991. "Qualitative Research: Collecting Life Histories," in Stephen Devereux and John Hoddinott (eds.), *Fieldwork in Developing Countries*. London: Harvester Wheatsheaf, pp. 86–101.

Frank, Thomas 2004. *What's the Matter with Kansas?: How Conservatives Won the Heart of America*. New York: Metropolitan Books.

Franklin, Ronald D., David B. Allison, and Bernard S. Gorman (eds.) 1997. *Design and Analysis of Single-Case Research*. Mahwah, NJ: Lawrence Erlbaum.

Freeden, Michael 1994. "Political Concepts and Ideological Morphology," *The Journal of Political Philosophy* 2(1): 140–164.

1996. *Ideologies and Political Theory: A Conceptual Approach.* Oxford University Press.

Freedman, David A. 1991. "Statistical Models and Shoe Leather," *Sociological Methodology* 21: 291–313.

1997. "From Association to Causation via Regression," in McKim and Turner (eds.), *Causality in Crisis?: Statistical Methods and the Search for Causal Knowledge in the Social Sciences,* pp. 113–162.

2008. "On Types of Scientific Inquiry: The Role of Qualitative Reasoning," in Box-Steffensmeier, Brady, and Collier (eds.), *The Oxford Handbook of Political Methodology,* pp. 300–318.

2010. David Collier, Jasjeet Sekhon, and Philip B. Stark (eds.), *Statistical Models and Causal Inference: A Dialogue with the Social Sciences.* Cambridge University Press.

Freedman, David A., Robert Pisani, Roger Purves, and Ani Adhikari 1991. *Statistics,* 2nd edn. New York: Norton.

Freese, Jeremy 2007. "Replication Standards for Quantitative Social Science: Why Not Sociology?," *Sociological Methods and Research* 36(2): 153–162.

Freese, Jeremy and Sara Shostak 2009. "Genetics and Social Inquiry," *Annual Review of Sociology* 35: 107–128.

French, Peter A., Theodore E. Uehling, Jr., and Howard K. Wettstein (eds.) 1984. *Midwest Studies in Philosophy.* Minneapolis, MN: University of Minnesota Press.

Frendreis, John P. 1983. "Explanation of Variation and Detection of Covariation: The Purpose and Logic of Comparative Analysis," *Comparative Political Studies* 16(2): 255–272.

Fried, Harold O., C. A. Knox Lovell, and Shelton S. Schmidt (eds.) 2008. *The Measurement of Productive Efficiency and Productivity Growth.* New York: Oxford University Press.

Friedlander, Daniel and Philip K. Robins 1995. "Evaluating Program Evaluations: New Evidence on Commonly Used Nonexperimental Methods," *American Economic Review* 85(4): 923–937.

Friedman, Jeffrey (ed.) 1996. *The Rational Choice Controversy: Economic Models of Politics Reconsidered.* New Haven, CT: Yale University Press.

Friedman, Kenneth S. 1972. "Empirical Simplicity as Testability," *British Journal for the Philosophy of Science* 23: 25–33.

Friedman, Michael 1974. "Explanation and Scientific Understanding," *Journal of Philosophy* 71: 5–19.

Friedman, Milton [1953] 1984. "The Methodology of Positive Economics," in Daniel M. Hausman (ed.), *The Philosophy of Economics: An Anthology.* Cambridge University Press, pp. 210–244.

1955. "The Role of Government in Education," in Robert A. Solo (ed.), *Economics and the Public Interest.* New Brunswick, NJ: Rutgers University Press, pp. 123–144.

Friedman, Milton and Anna Jacobson Schwartz 1963. *A Monetary History of the United States, 1867–1960.* Princeton University Press.

Fuller, Bruce and Richard F. Elmore 1996. *Who Chooses? Who Loses? Culture, Institutions, and the Unequal Effects of School Choice.* New York: Teachers College Press.

Gadamer, Hans-Georg 1975. *Truth and Method,* trans. Garrett Barden and John Cumming. New York: Seabury Press.

Gallie, W. B. 1956. "Essentially Contested Concepts," *Proceedings of the Aristotelian Society* 56: 167–198.

Galtung, Fredrik 2006. "Measuring the Immeasurable: Boundaries and Functions of (Macro) Corruption Indices," in Sampford, Shacklock, Connors, and Galtung (eds.), *Measuring Corruption*, pp. 101–130.

Gardiner, Patrick [1952] 1961. *The Nature of Historical Explanation*. Oxford University Press.

Garfinkel, Alan 1981. *Forms of Explanation: Rethinking the Questions of Social Theory*. New Haven, CT: Yale University Press.

Gasking, Douglas 1955. "Causation and Recipes," *Mind* 64: 479–487.

Gauri, Varun and Ayesha Vawda 2004. "Vouchers for Basic Education in Developing Economies: An Accountability Perspective," *World Bank Research Observer* 19(2): 159–180.

Gay, Peter 1984–98. *The Bourgeois Experience: Victoria to Freud*, 5 vols. New York: Oxford University Press and W. W. Norton.

Geddes, Barbara 1996. *Politician's Dilemma: Building State Capacity in Latin America*. Berkeley, CA: University of California Press.

2003. *Paradigms and Sand Castles: Theory Building and Research Design in Comparative Politics*. Ann Arbor, MI: University of Michigan Press.

2007. "What Causes Democratization?," in Carles Boix and Susan Stokes (eds.), *The Oxford Handbook of Comparative Politics*. Oxford University Press, pp. 317–339.

Geertz, Clifford 1968. *Peddlers and Princes: Social Development and Economic Change in Two Indonesian Towns*. University of Chicago Press.

1973. *The Interpretation of Cultures*. New York: Basic Books.

1980. *Negara: The Theatre State in Bali*. Princeton University Press.

Gellner, Ernest 1983. *Nations and Nationalism*. Ithaca, NY: Cornell University Press.

1985. *Relativism and the Social Sciences*. Cambridge University Press.

Gelman, Andrew 2011. Review of *Counterfactuals and Causal Inference*, by Stephen Morgan and Christopher Winship; *Causality: Models, Reasoning, and Inference*, 2nd edn., by Judea Pearl; and *Causal Models: How People Think About the World and Its Alternatives*, by Steven Sloman. *American Journal of Sociology* (forthcoming).

George, Alexander L. and Andrew Bennett 2005. *Case Studies and Theory Development*. Cambridge, MA: MIT Press.

George, Alexander L. and Timothy J. McKeown 1985. "Case Studies and Theories of Organizational Decision Making," *Advances in Information Processing in Organizations, vol. II*. Santa Barbara, CA: JAI Press.

Gerber, Alan S., Donald P. Green, and Edward H. Kaplan 2004. "The Illusion of Learning from Observational Research," in Ian Shapiro, Rogers M. Smith, and Tarek E. Masoud (eds.), *Problems and Methods in the Study of Politics*. Cambridge University Press, pp. 251–273.

Gerber, Alan S., Donald P. Green, and David Nickerson 2001. "Testing for Publication Bias in Political Science," *Political Analysis* 9(4) 385–392.

Gerring, John 1997. "Ideology: A Definitional Analysis," *Political Research Quarterly* 50(4): 957–994.

1999. "What Makes a Concept Good?: An Integrated Framework for Understanding Concept Formation in the Social Sciences," *Polity* 31(3): 357–393.

2001. *Social Science Methodology: A Criterial Framework*. Cambridge University Press.

2003. "Interpretations of Interpretivism." *Qualitative Methods: Newsletter of the American Political Science Association Organized Section on Qualitative Methods* 1(2): 2–6.

2005. "Causation: A Unified Framework for the Social Sciences," *Journal of Theoretical Politics* 17(2): 163–198.

2007. *Case Study Research: Principles and Practices*. Cambridge University Press.

2008. "The Mechanismic Worldview: Thinking Inside the Box," *British Journal of Political Science* 38(1): 161–179.

2009. "Mere description," unpublished manuscript, Department of Political Science, Boston University.

2010. "Causal Mechanisms: Yes, But . . .," *Comparative Political Studies* 43(11): 1499–1526.

Gerring, John and Paul A. Barresi 2003. "Putting Ordinary Language to Work: A Min-Max Strategy of Concept Formation in the Social Sciences," *Journal of Theoretical Politics* 15(2): 201–232.

Gerring, John and Rose McDermott 2007. "An Experimental Template for Case-Study Research," *American Journal of Political Science* 51(3): 688–701.

Gerring, John and Strom Thacker 2004. "Political Institutions and Corruption: The Role of Unitarism and Parliamentarism," *British Journal of Political Science* 34(2): 295–330.

2008. *A Centripetal Theory of Democratic Governance*. Cambridge University Press.

2011. "Democracy and Development: A Historical Perspective," unpublished manuscript, Boston University.

Gerring, John and Craig Thomas 2011. "Qualitative versus Quantitative Methods," in Bertrand Badie, Dirk Berg-Schlosser, and Leonardo Morlino (eds.), *International Encyclopedia of Political Science*. London: Sage.

Gerring, John and Joshua Yesnowitz 2006. "A Normative Turn in Political Science?," *Polity* 38 (1): 101–133.

Gerring, John, Daniel Ziblatt, Johan Van Gorp, and Julian Arevalo 2011. "An Institutional Theory of Direct and Indirect Rule," *World Politics* 63(3): 377–433.

Gerring, John, Strom Thacker, Ruben Enikolopov, and Julian Arevalo 2008. "Public Health Performance: A Model-Based Approach," unpublished manuscript, Boston University.

Gigerenzer, Gerd 2004. "Mindless Statistics," *Journal of Socio-Economics* 33: 587–606.

Gill, Christopher J., Lora Sabin, and Christopher H. Schmid 2005. "Why Clinicians are Natural Bayesians," *British Medical Journal* 330: 1080–1083.

Gill, Jeff 1999. "The Insignificance of Null Hypothesis Testing," *Political Research Quarterly* 52 (3): 647–674.

Gillespie, Richard 1991. *Manufacturing Knowledge: A History of the Hawthorne Experiments*. Cambridge University Press.

Glaser, James M. 1996. "The Challenge of Campaign-Watching: Seven Lessons of Participant-Observation Research," *PS: Political Science and Politics* 29(3): 533–537.

2003. "Social Context and Inter-Group Political Attitudes: Experiments in Group Conflict Theory," *British Journal of Political Science* 33: 607–620.

Glassner, Barry and Jonathan D. Moreno (eds.) 1989. *The Qualitative–Quantitative Distinction in the Social Sciences*. Boston Studies in the Philosophy of Science, p. 112.

Glazer, Amihai and Marc Robbins 1985. "Congressional Responsiveness to Constituency Change," *American Journal of Political Science* 29(2): 259–273.

Glazerman, Steven, Dan M. Levy, and David Myers 2003. "Nonexperimental versus Experimental Estimates of Earnings Impacts," *The Annals of the American Academy of Political and Social Science* 589(1): 63–93.

Gleditsch, Kristian and Michael D. Ward 2006. "Diffusion and the International Context of Democratization," *International Organization* 60(4): 911–933.

Glennan, Stuart S. 1992. "Mechanisms and the Nature of Causation," *Erkenntnis* 44: 49–71.
  2002. "Rethinking Mechanistic Explanation," *Philosophy of Science* 69: S342–S353.

Glymour, Clark 1980. *Theory and Evidence*. Princeton University Press.

Glynn, Adam N. and John Gerring 2011. "Strategies of Research Design with an Unmeasured Confounder: A Graphical Description," unpublished manuscript, Department of Government, Harvard University.

Glynn, Adam N. and Kevin M. Quinn 2011. "Why Process Matters for Causal Inference," *Political Analysis* 20: 1–19.

Goertz, Gary 2006. *Social Science Concepts: A User's Guide*. Princeton University Press.
  2008. "Concepts, Theories, and Numbers: A Checklist for Constructing, Evaluating, and Using Concepts or Quantitative Measures," in Box-Steffensmeier, Brady, and Collier (eds.), *The Oxford Handbook of Political Methodology*, pp. 97–118.
  Forthcoming. "Descriptive-Causal Generalizations: 'Empirical Laws' in the Social Sciences?," in Harold Kincaid (ed.), *Oxford Handbook of the Philosophy of the Social Sciences*. Oxford University Press.

Goertz, Gary and James Mahoney 2010. "Two Cultures: Hume's Two Definitions of Cause," *Qualitative and Multimethod Research* 8(1): 24–27.

Goertz, Gary and Harvey Starr (eds.) 2003. *Necessary Conditions: Theory, Methodology and Applications*. New York: Rowman & Littlefield.

Goesling, Brian and Glenn Firebaugh 2000. "The Trend in International Health Inequality," *Population and Development Review* 30(1): 131–146.

Golden, Miriam A. and Lucio Picci 2005. "Proposal for a New Measure of Corruption, Illustrated with Italian Data," *Economics and Politics* 17(1): 37–75.

Goldin, Claudia and Cecilia Rouse 2000. "Orchestrating Impartiality: The Impact of 'Blind' Auditions on Female Musicians," *American Economic Review* 90(4): 715–741.

Goldstone, Jack A. 1997. "Methodological Issues in Comparative Macrosociology," *Comparative Social Research* 16: 121–132.

Goldthorpe, John H. 1997. "Current Issues in Comparative Macrosociology: A Response to the Commentaries," *Comparative Social Research* 16: 121–132.

Goodin, Robert and Charles Tilly (eds.) 2006. *The Oxford Handbook of Contextual Analysis*. Oxford University Press.

Gorski, Philip S. 2004. "The Poverty of Deductivism: A Constructive Realist Model of Sociological Explanation," *Sociological Methodology* 34(1): 1–33.

Gough, Ian and J. Allister McGregor (eds.) 2007. *Wellbeing in Developing Countries: From Theory to Research*. Cambridge University Press.

Gould, Stephen Jay 1983. *Hen's Teeth and Horse's Toes: Further Reflections in Natural History*. New York: W. W. Norton.

Green, Donald P. and Alan S. Gerber 2001. "Reclaiming the Experimental Tradition in Political Science," in Helen Milner and Ira Katznelson, (eds.), *State of the Discipline, vol. III*. New York: W. W. Norton, pp. 805–832.

Green, Donald P. and Alan S. Gerber 2003. "The Underprovision of Experiments in Political Science," *Annals of the American Academy of Political and Social Science* 589(1): 94–112.

Green, Donald P. and Ian Shapiro 1994. *Pathologies of Rational Choice Theory: A Critique of Applications in Political Science*. New Haven, CT: Yale University Press.

Green, Donald P., Terence Y. Leong, Holger L. Kern, Alan S. Gerber, and Christopher W. Larimer 2009. "Testing the Accuracy of Regression Discontinuity Analysis Using Experimental Benchmarks," *Political Analysis* 17(4): 400–417.

Greene, Jennifer C. 2007. *Mixed Methods in Social Inquiry*. San Francisco, CA: Jossey-Bass.

Greene, William H. 2002. *Econometric Analysis*, 5th edn. Upper Saddle River, NJ: Prentice-Hall.

Greenstein, Fred I. and Nelson W. Polsby (eds.) 1975. *Handbook of Political Science*. Reading, MA: Addison-Wesley.

Gregory, Ian N. and Paul S. Ell 2007. *Historical GIS: Technologies, Methodologies and Scholarship*. Cambridge University Press.

Grier, Robin M. 1999. "Colonial Legacies and Economic Growth," *Public Choice* 98(3–4): 317–335.

Griffin, Larry J. 1992. "Temporality, Events, and Explanation in Historical Sociology: An Introduction," *Sociological Methods and Research* 20(4): 403–427.

  1993. "Narrative, Event-Structure Analysis, and Causal Interpretation in Historical Sociology," *American Journal of Sociology* 98: 1094–1133.

Grofman, Bernard 2007. "Toward a Science of Politics?," *European Political Science* 6: 143–155.

Grofman, Bernard, Thomas L. Brunell, and William Koetzle 1998. "Why Gain in the Senate but Midterm Loss in the House? Evidence from a Quasi-Experiment," *Legislative Studies Quarterly* 23: 79–89.

Groseclose, Tim and Jeffrey Milyo 2005. "A Measure of Media Bias," *Quarterly Journal of Economics* 120(4): 1191–1237.

Gruenbaum, Adolf 1976. "Can a Theory Answer More Questions than One of Its Rivals?," *British Journal for the Philosophy of Science* 27: 1–23.

Guala, Francesco 2005. *The Methodology of Experimental Economics*. Cambridge University Press.

Gudeman, Stephen 2001. *The Anthropology of Economy: Community, Market, and Culture*. Chichester: Wiley-Blackwell.

Guiso, Luigi, Paola Sapienza, and Luigi Mingales 2006. "Does Culture Affect Economic Outcomes?," *Journal of Economic Perspectives* 20(2): 23–48.

Gunther, Richard and Larry Diamond 2003. "Species of Political Parties: A New Typology," *Party Politics* 9: 167–199.

Haan, Norma, Robert Bellah, Paul Rabinow, and William M. Sullivan (eds.) 1983. *Social Science as Moral Inquiry*. New York: Columbia University Press.

Hadenius, Axel and Jan Teorell 2005. "Assessing Alternative Indices of Democracy," Committee on Concepts and Methods Working Paper Series, August.

Hahn, Jinyong, Petra Todd, and Wilbert van der Klaauw 2002. "Identification and Estimation of Treatment Effects with a Regression-Discontinuity Design," *Econometrica* 69(1): 201–209.

Hall, Ned 2004. "Two Concepts of Causation," in John Collins, Ned Hall, and L. A. Paul (eds.), *Causation and Counterfactuals*. Cambridge, MA: MIT Press, pp. 225–276.

Hall, Peter A. 2003. "Aligning Ontology and Methodology in Comparative Politics," in James Mahoney and Dietrich Rueschemeyer (eds.), *Comparative Historical Analysis in the Social Sciences*. Cambridge University Press, pp. 373–404.

Halpern, J. Y. and Judea Pearl 2005. "Causes and Explanations: A Structural-Model Approach. Part II: Explanations," *British Journal for the Philosophy of Science* 56: 4.

Hambleton, Ronald K., H. Swaminathan, and H. Jane Rogers 1991. *Fundamentals of Item Response Theory*. Newbury Park, CA: Sage.

Hamilton, James D. 1994. *Time Series Analysis*. Princeton University Press.

Hamilton, Malcolm B. 1987. "The Elements of the Concept of Ideology," *Political Studies* 35: 18–38.

Hammer, Dean and Aaron Wildavsky 1989. "The Open-Ended, Semi-Structured Interview: An (Almost) Operational Guide," in Aaron Wildavsky (ed.), *Craftways: On the Organization of Scholarly Work*. New Brunswick, NJ: Transaction, pp. 57–101.

Hammersley, Martyn 1992. "Deconstructing the Qualitative–Quantitative Divide," in Julie Brannen (ed.), *Mixing Methods: Qualitative and Quantitative Research*. Aldershot: Avebury, pp. 39–55.

1997. "Qualitative Data Archiving: Some Reflections on its Prospects and Problems," *Sociology: The Journal of the British Sociological Association* 31(1): 131–142.

Hanson, Norwood Russell 1958. *Patterns of Discovery*. Cambridge University Press.

1961. "Is There a Logic of Discovery?," in H. Feigle and G. Maxwell (eds.), *Current Issues in the Philosophy of Science*. New York: Holt, pp. 20–35.

Harding, Sandra 1986. *The Science Question in Feminism*, Ithaca, NY: Cornell University Press.

Harding, Sandra (ed.) 1987. *Feminism and Methodology: Social Science Issues*. Bloomington, IN: Indiana University Press.

Harman, Gilbert 1965. "The Inference to the Best Explanation," *Philosophical Review* 74: 88–95.

Harre, Rom 1970. *The Principles of Scientific Thinking*. University of Chicago Press.

1972. *The Philosophies of Science*. London: Oxford University Press.

Harre, Rom and E. H. Madden 1975. *Causal Powers: A Theory of Natural Necessity*. Oxford: Blackwell.

Harrington, David P. 2000. "The Randomized Clinical Trial," *Journal of the American Statistical Association* 95(449): 312–315.

Harrison, Lawrence E. and Samuel P. Huntington (eds.) 2000. *Culture Matters*. New York: Basic Books.

Hart, H. L. A. and A. M. Honore 1959. *Causality in the Law*. Oxford University Press.

Hartz, Louis 1955. *The Liberal Tradition in America*. New York: Harcourt, Brace, World.

1964. *The Founding of New Societies: Studies in the History of the United States, Latin America, South Africa, Canada, and Australia*. New York: Harcourt, Brace, World.

Hausman, Daniel M. (ed.) 1994. "Why Look under the Hood?," *The Philosophy of Economics: An Anthology*. Cambridge University Press, pp. 217–221.

Hayek, Friedrich A. von. 1956. "The Dilemma of Specialization," in L. D. White (ed.), *The State of the Social Sciences*. University of Chicago Press, pp. 462–473.

Heath, Anthony and Jean Martin 1997. "Why are there so Few Formal Measuring Instruments in Social and Political Research?," in Lars E. Fyberg, Paul Biemer, Martin Collins, Edith De

Leeuw, Cathryn Dippo, Norbert Schwarz, and Dennis Trewin (eds.), *Survey Measurement and Process Quality*. New York: Wiley, pp. 71–86.

Heckman, James J. 2000. "Causal Parameters and Policy Analysis in Economics: A Twentieth Century Retrospective," *Quarterly Journal of Economics* 115: 45–97.

2001. "Micro Data, Heterogeneity, and the Evaluation of Public Policy: The Nobel Lecture," *Journal of Political Economy* 109: 673–748.

2005. "The Scientific Model of Causality," *Sociological Methodology* 35: 1–97.

2008. "Econometric Causality," *International Statistical Review* 76(1): 1–27.

2010. "Building Bridges between Structural and Program Evaluation Approaches to Evaluating Policy," *Journal of Economic Literature* 48(2): 356–398.

Heckman, James J. and Peter Siegelman 1993. "The Urban Institute Audit Studies: Their Methods," in Michael Fix and Raymond Struyk (eds.), *Clear and Convincing Evidence: Measurement of Discrimination in America*. Washington, DC: The Urban Institute Press, pp. 187–258.

Heckman, James J. and Edward Vytlacil 2007a. "Econometric Evaluation of Social Programs. Part I: Causal Models, Structural Models and Econometric Policy Evaluations," in James Heckman and Edward Leamer (eds.), *Handbook of Econometrics, vol. 6B*. Amsterdam: North Holland Press.

2007b. "Econometric Evaluation of Social Programs. Part II: Using the Marginal Treatment Effect to Evaluate Social Programs, and to Forecast their Effects in New Environments," in James Heckman and Edward Leamer (eds.), *Handbook of Econometrics, vol. 6B*. Amsterdam: North Holland Press.

Hedstrom, Peter 2005. *Dissecting the Social: On the Principles of Analytical Sociology*. Cambridge University Press.

Hedstrom, Peter and Richard Swedberg (eds.) 1998. *Social Mechanisms: An Analytical Approach to Social Theory*. Cambridge University Press.

Heinz, John P., Edward O. Laumann, Robert L. Nelson, and Robert H. Salisbury 1993. *The Hollow Core: Private Interests in National Policymaking*. Cambridge. MA: Harvard University Press.

Held, David 2006. *Models of Democracy*, 3rd edn. Cambridge: Polity Press.

Helper, Susan 2000. "Economists and Field Research: 'You Can Observe a Lot Just by Watching,'" *American Economic Review* 90(2): 228–232.

Hempel, Carl G. 1942. "The Function of General Laws in History." *Journal of Philosophy* 39, 35–48.

1952. "Fundamentals of Concept Formation in Empirical Science," *Foundations of the Unity of Science* 2: 7.

1963. "Typological Methods in the Social Sciences," in Maurice Natanson (ed.), *Philosophy of the Social Sciences: A Reader*. New York: Random House, pp. 210–230.

1965. *Aspects of Scientific Explanation: And Other Essays in the Philosophy of Science*. New York: Free Press.

1966. *Philosophy of Natural Science*. Englewood Cliffs, NJ: Prentice Hall.

1991. "Empiricist Criteria of Cognitive Significance: Problems and Changes," in Boyd, Gasper, and Trout (eds.), *The Philosophy of Science*.

Hempel, Carl G. and Paul Oppenheim 1948. "Studies in the Logic of Explanation," *Philosophy of Science* 15(2): 135–175.

Henisz, Witold J., Bennet A. Melner, and Mauro F. Guillén 2005. "The Worldwide Diffusion of Market-Oriented Infrastructure Reform," *American Sociological Review* 70(6): 871–897.

Herrera, Yoshiko M. and Devesh Kapur 2007. "Improving Data Quality: Actors, Incentives, and Capabilities," *Political Analysis* 15(4): 365–386.

Hersen, Michel and David H. Barlow 1976. *Single-Case Experimental Designs: Strategies for Studying Behavior Change*. Oxford: Pergamon Press.

Hesse, Mary 1966. *Models and Analogies in Science*. Notre Dame, IN: University of Notre Dame Press.

1974. *The Structure of Scientific Inference*. London: Macmillan.

Hexter, J. H. 1979. *On Historians: Reappraisals of Some of the Masters of Modern History*. Cambridge, MA: Harvard University Press.

Highton, Ben 2004. "Voter Registration and Turnout in the United States," *Perspectives on Politics* 2(3): 507–515.

Hino, Airo 2009. "Time-Series QCA: Studying Temporal Change through Boolean Analysis," *Sociological Theory and Methods* 24: 219–246.

Hirsch, E. D. 1967. *Validity in Interpretation*. New Haven, CT: Yale University Press.

Hirschman, Albert O. 1970. *Exit, Voice, Loyalty: Responses to Decline in Firms, Organizations, and States*. Cambridge, MA: Harvard University Press.

1977. *The Passions and the Interests: Political Arguments for Capitalism before its Triumph*. Princeton University Press.

Hitchcock, Christopher Read 1995. "The Mishap of Reichenbach's Fall: Singular vs. General Causation," *Philosophical Studies* 78: 257–291.

1996. "The Role of Contrast in Causal and Explanatory Claims," *Synthese* 107: 395–419.

2003. "Unity and Plurality in the Concept of Causation," in Friedrich Stadler (ed.), *The Vienna Circle and Logical Empiricism: Re-Evaluation and Future Perspectives*. New York: Kluwer, pp. 217–224.

2005. ". . . And Away from a Theory of Explanation Itself," *Synthese* 143(1/2): 109–124.

2007. "How to be a Causal Pluralist," in Peter Machamer and Gereon Wolters (eds.), *Thinking about Causes: From Greek Philosophy to Modern Physics*. Pittsburgh, PA: University of Pittsburgh Press, pp. 200–221.

Hobsbawm, Eric and Terence Ranger (eds.) 1992. *The Invention of Tradition*. Cambridge University Press.

Holland, Paul W. 1986. "Statistics and Causal Inference," *Journal of the American Statistical Association* 81: 945–960.

Holland, Paul W. and Donald B. Rubin 1988. "Causal Inference in Retrospective Studies," *Evaluation Review* 12: 203–231.

Hollis, Martin 1994. *The Philosophy of Social Science: An Introduction*. Cambridge University Press.

Hollis, Martin and Steven Lukes (eds.) 1982. *Rationality and Relativism*. Oxford: Basil Blackwell.

Homans, George C. 1961. *Social Behavior: Its Elementary Forms*. New York: Harcourt.

1967. *The Nature of Social Science*. New York: Harcourt Brace Jovanovich.

Hoover, Kevin D. 2001. *Causality in Macroeconomics*. Cambridge University Press.

Howell, William G. and Paul E. Peterson 2002. *The Education Gap: Vouchers and Urban Schools*. Washington, DC: Brookings Institution.

Howson, Colin and Peter Urbach 1989. *Scientific Reasoning: The Bayesian Approach*. La Salle, IL: Open Court.

Hoxby, Caroline M. (ed.) 2003. *The Economics of School Choice*. University of Chicago Press.

Hoy, David Couzens 1982. *The Critical Circle: Literature, History, and Philosophical Hermeneutics*. Berkeley, CA: University of California Press.

Hsieh, Chang-Tai and Christina D. Romer 2001. "Was the Federal Reserve Fettered? Devaluation Expectations in the 1932 Monetary Expansion," NBER Working Paper No. W8113, February.

Huber, Gregory A. and John S. Lapinski 2006. "The 'Race Card' Revisited: Assessing Racial Priming in Policy Contests," *American Journal of Political Science* 50(2): 421–440.

2008. "Testing the Implicit–Explicit Model of Racialized Political Communication," *Perspectives on Politics* 6(1): 125–134.

Hume, David 1888. *Treatise of Human Nature*. Oxford University Press.

1960. "The Idea of Necessary Connexion [from *An Enquiry Concerning Human Understanding*, Section 7]," in Edward H. Madden (ed.), *The Structure of Scientific Thought: An Introduction to Philosophy of Science*. London: Routledge & Kegan Paul.

1985. *Essays: Moral, Political, and Literary*, ed. Eugene F. Miller. Indianapolis, IN: Liberty Classics.

2007. *An Enquiry concerning Human Understanding; And other Writings*, ed. Stephen Buckle. Cambridge University Press.

Humphreys, Macartan 2005. "Natural Resources, Conflict, and Conflict Resolution: Uncovering the Mechanisms," *Journal of Conflict Resolution* 49(4): 508–537.

Humphreys, Macartan and Jeremy Weinstein 2009. "Field Experiments and the Political Economy of Development," *Annual Review of Political Science* 12: 367–378.

Humphreys, Macartan, William A. Masters, and Martin E. Sandbu 2006. "The Role of Leaders in Democratic Deliberations: Results from a Field Experiment in Sao Tome and Principe," *World Politics* 58: 583–622.

Huntington, Samuel P. 1991. *The Third Wave: Democratization in the Late Twentieth Century*. Norman, OK: University of Oklahoma Press.

Hutchings, Vincent L. and Ashley E. Jardina 2009. "Experiments on Racial Priming in Political Campaigns," *Annual Review of Political Science* 12: 397–402.

Hyde, Susan 2007. "The Observer Effect in International Politics: Evidence from a Natural Experiment," *World Politics* 60(1): 37–63.

Imai, Kosuke, Luke Keele, and Dustin Tingley 2010. "A General Approach to Causal Mediation Analysis," *Psychological Methods* 15(4): 309–334.

Imai, Kosuke, Luke Keele, Dustin Tingley, and Teppei Yamamoto 2010. "Unpacking the Black Box: Learning about Causal Mechanisms from Experimental and Observational Studies," unpublished manuscript, Princeton University.

Imbens, Guido W. 2003. "Sensitivity to Exogeneity Assumptions in Program Evaluation," *American Economic Review* 93(2): 126–132.

Imbens, Guido W. and Thomas Lemieux 2007. "Regression Discontinuity Designs: A Guide to Practice," NBER Technical Working Paper No. 337.

Imbens, Guido W. and Jeffrey M. Wooldridge 2009. "Recent Developments in the Econometrics of Program Evaluation," *Journal of Economic Literature* 47(1): 5–86.

Inglehart, Ronald 1977. *The Silent Revolution in Europe: Changing Values and Political Styles among Western Publics.* Princeton University Press.

Institute of Medicine 2006. *Genes, Behavior, and the Social Environment: Moving beyond the Nature/Nurture Debate.* Washington, DC: National Academies Press.

Jackman, Simon 2004. "Bayesian Analysis for Political Research," *Annual Review of Political Science* 7: 483–505.

2008. "Measurement," in Box-Steffensmeier, Brady, and Collier (eds.), *The Oxford Handbook of Political Methodology*, pp. 119–151.

Jacoby, Russell 1987. *The Last Intellectuals: American Culture in the Age of Academe.* New York: Farrar, Straus & Giroux.

Jacoby, William G. 1999. "Levels of Measurement and Political Research: An Optimistic View," *American Journal of Political Science* 43(1): 271–301.

James, William 1981. *The Principles of Psychology.* Cambridge, MA: Harvard University Press.

Jamieson, Kathleen Hall 1996. *Packaging the Presidency: A History and Criticism of Presidential Campaign Advertising*, 3rd edn. Oxford University Press.

Jencks, Christopher and Meredith Phillips (eds.) 1998. *The Black–White Test Score Gap.* Washington, DC: Brookings Institution.

Jevons, W. Stanley [1877] 1958. *The Principles of Science.* New York: Dover.

Jick, Todd D. 1979. "Mixing Qualitative and Quantitative Methods: Triangulation in Action," *Administrative Science Quarterly* 24(4): 602–611.

Johnston, Michael and Arnold J. Heidenheimer (eds.) 2002. *Political Corruption: Concepts and Contexts.* New Brunswick, NJ: Transaction.

Judd, Charles M. and David A. Kenny 1981. *Estimating the Effects of Social Interventions.* Cambridge University Press.

Kagel, John H. and Alvin E. Roth (eds.) 1997. *Handbook of Experimental Economics.* Princeton University Press.

Kanbur, Ravi and Anthony J. Venables (eds.) 2005. *Spatial Inequality and Development.* Oxford University Press.

Kane, James G., Stephen C. Craig, and Kenneth D. Wald 2004. "Religion and Presidential Politics in Florida: A List Experiment," *Social Science Quarterly* 85(2): 281–293.

Kantorowicz, Ernst H. 1957. *The King's Two Bodies: A Study in Medieval Political Theology.* Princeton University Press.

Kaplan, Abraham 1964. *The Conduct of Inquiry: Methodology for Behavioral Science.* San Francisco, CA: Chandler Publishing.

Karl, Barry D. 1982. "The Citizen and the Scholar: Ships That Crash in the Night," in Kruskal (ed.), *The Social Sciences: Their Nature and Uses*, pp. 101–120.

Katznelson, Ira 1997. "Structure and Configuration in Comparative Politics," in Lichbach and Muckerman (eds.), *Comparative Politics: Rationality, Culture, and Structure*, pp. 81–112.

Kaufman, Herbert 1960. *The Forest Ranger: A Study in Administrative Behavior.* Baltimore, MD: Johns Hopkins University Press.

Kaufmann, Daniel, Aart Kraay, and Massimo Mastruzzi 2007. "Governance Matters IV: Governance Indicators for 1996–2006," Washington, DC: World Bank.

Keefer, Philip 2006. "Clientelism, Credibility and the Policy Choices of Young Democracies," *American Journal of Political Science* 51(4): 804–821.

Kelman, Herbert C. 1982. "Ethical Issues in Different Social Science Methods," in Tom L. Beauchamp, Ruth R. Faden, R. Jay Wallace, Jr., and LeRoy Walters (eds.), *Ethical Issues in Social Science Research*. Baltimore, MD: Johns Hopkins University Press, pp. 40–98.

Kempf-Leonard, Kimberly (ed.) 2004. *Encyclopedia of Social Measurement*, 3 vols. New York: Academic Press.

Kenney, Genevieve and Douglas A. Wissoker 1994. "An Analysis of the Correlates of Discrimination Facing Young Hispanic Job-Seekers," *American Economic Review* 84(3): 674–683.

Kenny, Charles 2006. "Measuring and Reducing the Impact of Corruption in Infrastructure," World Bank Working Paper No. 4099.

Kertzer, David I. 1988. *Ritual, Politics, and Power*. New Haven, CT: Yale University Press.

Key, V. O., Jr. 1958. "The State of the Discipline," *American Political Science Review* 52(4): 961–971.

Kim, Sangmoon and Eui-Hang Shin 2002. "A Longitudinal Analysis of Globalization and Regionalization in International Trade: A Social Network Approach," *Social Forces* 81 (2): 445–468.

Kincaid, Harold 1990. "Defending Laws in the Social Sciences," *Philosophy of the Social Sciences* 20(1): 56–83.

Kinder, Donald and Thomas R. Palfrey (eds.) 1993. *The Experimental Foundations of Political Science*. Ann Arbor, MI: University of Michigan Press.

King, Gary 1995. "Replication, Replication," *PS: Political Science and Politics* 28(3): 443–499.

King, Gary and Langche Zheng 2006. "The Dangers of Extreme Counterfactuals," *Political Analysis* 14(2): 131–159.

King, Gary, Robert O. Keohane, and Sidney Verba 1994. *Designing Social Inquiry: Scientific Inference in Qualitative Research*. Princeton University Press.

  1995. "The Importance of Research Design in Political Science," *American Political Science Review* 89(2): 475–481.

King, Gary, Christopher J. L. Murray, Joshua A. Salomon, and Ajay Tandon 2004. "Enhancing the Validity and Cross-Cultural Comparability of Measurement in Survey Research," *American Political Science Review* 98: 567–583.

Kingdon, John W. 1984. *Agendas, Alternatives, and Public Policies*. Boston, MA: Little, Brown.

Kirkham, Richard L. 1992. *Theories of Truth: A Critical Introduction*. Cambridge, MA: MIT Press.

Kirschenman, Kathryn M. and Joleen Neckerman 1991. "'We'd Love to Hire Them, but . . .': The Meaning of Race for Employers," in Christopher Jencks, and Paul E. Peterson (eds.), *The Urban Underclass*. Washington, DC: Brookings Institution, pp. 203–234.

Kiser, Edgar 1996. "The Revival of Narrative in Historical Sociology: What Rational Choice Can Contribute," *Politics and Society* 24: 249–271.

Kitcher, Philip 1981. "Explanatory Unification," *Philosophy of Science* 48: 507–531.

  1989. "Explanatory Unification and the Causal Structure of the World," in Kitcher and Salmon (eds.), *Scientific Explanation: Minnesota Studies in the Philosophy of Science, vol. XIII*, pp. 410–505.

Kitcher, Philip and Wesley Salmon (eds.) 1989. *Scientific Explanation: Minnesota Studies in the Philosophy of Science*. Minneapolis, MN: University of Minnesota Press.

Kittel, Bernhard 2006. "A Crazy Methodology?: On the Limits of Macroquantitative Social Science Research," *International Sociology* 21: 647–677.

Klimm, Lester E. 1959. "Mere Description," *Economic Geography* 35(1).

Knack, Stephen 2006. "Measuring Corruption in Eastern Europe and Central Asia: A Critique of the Cross-Country Indicators," World Bank Working Paper No. 3968.

Knoke, David and Song Yang 2008. *Social Network Analysis*, 2nd edn. Los Angeles, CA, Sage.

Knowles, Anne Kelly 2008. *Placing History: How Maps, Spatial Data, and GIS Are Changing Historical Scholarship*. New York: ESRI Press.

Koestler, Arthur 1964. *The Act of Creation*. New York: Macmillan.

Komarovsky, Mirra 1940. *The Unemployed Man and His Family: The Effect of Unemployment upon the Status of the Man in Fifty-nine Families*. New York: Dryden Press.

Krantz, David L., R. Duncan Luce, Patrick Suppes, and Amos Tversky 1971, 1989, 1990. *Foundations of Measurement, vols. 1–3*. New York: Academic Press.

Krasno, Jonathan S. and Donald P. Green 2008. "Do Televised Presidential Ads Increase Voter Turnout? Evidence from a Natural Experiment," *Journal of Politics* 70(1): 245–261.

Kremer, Michael 1993. "Population Growth and Technological Change: One Million B.C. to 1990," *Quarterly Journal of Economics* 108(3): 681–716.

Krieger, Susan 1991. *Social Science and the Self: Personal Essays on an Art Form*. New Brunswick, NJ: Rutgers University Press.

Kritzer, Herbert M. 1996. "The Data Puzzle: The Nature of Interpretation in Quantitative Research," *American Journal of Political Science* 40(1): 1–32.

Krueger, Alan B. and Pei Mhu 2004. "Another Look at the New York City School Voucher Experiment," *American Behavioral Scientist* 47: 658–698.

Kruskal, W. H. (ed.) 1982. *The Social Sciences: Their Nature and Uses*. University of Chicago Press.

Kuhn, Thomas S. [1962] 1970. *The Structure of Scientific Revolutions*. University of Chicago Press.

  1977. *The Essential Tension*. University of Chicago Press.

Kuper, Adam 1999. *Culture: The Anthropologists' Account*. Cambridge, MA: Harvard University Press.

Kurtz, Marcus J. and Andrew Schrank 2007. "Growth and Governance: Models, Measures, and Mechanisms," *Journal of Politics* 69(2): 538–554.

Ladd, Everett Carl, Jr. and Charles D. Hadley 1975. *Transformations of the American Party System: Political Coalitions from the New Deal to the 1970s*. New York: W. W. Norton.

Ladd, Helen F. 2002. "School Vouchers: A Critical View," *Journal of Economic Perspectives* 16: 3–24.

Laitin, David 1986. *Hegemony and Culture: Politics and Religious Change among the Yoruba*. University of Chicago Press.

Lakatos, Imre 1978. *The Methodology of Scientific Research Programmes*. Cambridge University Press.

  1981. "History of Science and its Rational Reconstructions," in Ian Hacking (ed.), *Scientific Revolutions*. New York: Oxford University Press, pp. 107–127.

Lakoff, George 1987. *Women, Fire, and Dangerous Things: What Categories Reveal about the Mind*. University of Chicago Press.

Lakoff, George and Herbert F. York 1989. *A Shield in Space: Technology, Politics, and the Strategic Defense Initiative*. Berkeley, CA: University of California Press.

LaLonde, Robert J. 1986. "Evaluating the Econometric Evaluations of Training Programs with Experimental Data," *American Economic Review* 76(4): 604–620.

Lambsdorff, Johann G. 2003. "Background Paper to the 2003 Corruption Perceptions Index," Mimeo, Transparency International, September.

Landau, Martin 1972. "Comment: On Objectivity," *American Political Science Review* 66(3): 847–856.

Landes, David S. 1999. *The Wealth and Poverty of Nations: Why Some Are So Rich and Some So Poor.* New York: W. W. Norton.

Landes, David S. and Charles Tilly (eds.) 1971. *History as Social Science.* Englewood Cliffs, NJ: Prentice Hall.

Lange, Peter and Hudson Meadwell 1991. "Typologies of Democratic Systems: From Political Inputs to Political Economy," in Howard J. Wiarda (ed.), *New Directions in Comparative Politics.* Boulder, CO: Westview Press, pp. 82–117.

Langley, Pat, Herbert A. Simon, Gary L. Bradshaw, and Jan M. Mytkow 1987. *Scientific Discovery: Computational Explorations of the Creative Process.* Cambridge, MA: MIT Press.

Lasswell, Harold and Abraham Kaplan 1950. *Power and Society: A Framework for Political Inquiry.* New Haven, CT: Yale University Press.

Latour, Bruno and Steve Woolgar 1979. *Laboratory Life: The Social Construction of Scientific Facts.* Beverly Hills, CA: Sage.

Laudan, Larry 1977. *Progress and its Problems: Toward a Theory of Scientific Growth.* Berkeley, CA: University of California Press.

1983. *Science and Values.* Berkeley, CA: University of California Press.

1996. *Beyond Positivism and Relativism: Theory, Method, and Evidence.* Boulder, CO: Westview Press.

Lauderdale, Diane S. 2006. "Birth Outcomes for Arabic-named Women in California before and after September 11," *Demography* 43(1): 185–201.

Lave, Charles and James March 1975. *An Introduction to Models in the Social Sciences.* New York: Harper.

Laver, Michael, Kenneth Benoit, and John Garry 2003. "Extracting Policy Positions from Political Text Using Words as Data," *American Political Science Review* 97(2): 311–331.

Lazarsfeld, Paul F. 1966. "Concept Formation and Measurement in the Behavioral Sciences: Some Historical Observations," in Gordon J. DiRenzo (ed.), *Concepts, Theory, and Explanation in the Behavioral Sciences.* New York: Random House, pp. 144–204.

Lazarsfeld, Paul F. and Morris Rosenberg (eds.) 1955. *The Language of Social Research.* Glencoe, IL: Free Press.

Leamer, Edward E. 1983. "Let's Take the Con out of Econometrics," *American Economic Review* 73(1): 31–44.

2010. "Tantalus on the Road to Asymptopia," *Journal of Economic Perspectives* 24(2): 31–46.

Lebow, Richard Ned 2007. "Counterfactual Thought Experiments: A Necessary Teaching Tool," *History Teacher* 40(2): 153–176.

Lee, Allen S. 1989. "Case Studies as Quasi-experiments," *Human Relations* 42(2): 117–137.

Lee, David S. 2008. "Randomized Experiments from Non-Random Selection in US House Elections," *Journal of Econometrics* 142(2): 675–697.

Lee, David S. and Thomas Lemieuxa 2010. "Regression Discontinuity Designs in Economics," *Journal of Economic Literature* 48(2): 281–355.

Lee, David S., Enrico Moretti, and Matthew J. Butler 2004. "Do Voters Affect or Elect Policies? Evidence from the US House," *Quarterly Journal of Economics* 119(3): 807–859.

Lee, Raymond M. 1993. *Doing Research on Sensitive Topics.* London: Sage.

Leech, Beth L. *et al.* 2002. "Symposium: Interview Methods in Political Science," *PS: Political Science and Politics* (December): 665–688.

Leech, Nancy L. and Anthony J. Onwuegbuzie 2009. "A Typology of Mixed Methods Research Designs," *Quality and Quantity* 43(2): 265–275.

Lehnert, Matthias 2007. "Typologies in Social Inquiry," in Thomas Gschwend and Frank Schimmelfennig (eds.), *Research Design in Political Science: How to Practice What They Preach.* London: Palgrave, pp. 62–82.

Lenski, Gerhard 1994. "Societal Taxonomies: Mapping the Social Universe," *Annual Review of Sociology* 20: 1–26.

Lerner, Daniel and Harold D. Lasswell (eds.) 1951. *The Policy Sciences.* Stanford University Press.

Levey, Geoffrey Brahm 1996. "Theory Choice and the Comparison of Rival Theoretical Perspectives in Political Sociology," *Philosophy of the Social Sciences* 26(1): 26–60.

Levi, Margaret 1997. "A Model, a Method, and a Map: Rational Choice in Comparative and Historical Analysis," in Lichbach and Zuckerman (eds.), *Comparative Politics: Rationality, Culture, and Structure,* pp. 19–41.

1999. "Producing an Analytic Narrative," in John R. Bowen and Roger Petersen (eds.), *Critical Comparisons in Politics and Culture.* Cambridge University Press, pp. 152–172.

Levine, Ross and David Renelt 1992. "A Sensitivity Analysis of Cross-Country Growth Regressions," *American Economic Review* 82(4): 942–963.

Levitsky, Steven and Lucan A. Way 2002. "The Rise of Competitive Authoritarianism," *Journal of Democracy* 13(2): 51–65.

Lewis, David K. 1973. *Counterfactuals.* Oxford: Basil Blackwell.

Lichbach, Mark Irving and Alan S. Zuckerman (eds.) 1997. *Comparative Politics: Rationality, Culture, and Structure.* New York: Cambridge University Press.

Lieberman, Evan S. 2005. "Nested Analysis as a Mixed-Method Strategy for Comparative Research," *American Political Science Review* 99(3): 435–452.

Lieberman, Evan S., Marc Howard, and Julia Lynch 2004. "Symposium: Field Research," *Qualitative Methods* 2(1): 2–15.

Lieberson, Stanley 1985. *Making It Count: The Improvement of Social Research and Theory.* Berkeley, CA: University of California Press.

1992. "Einstein, Renoir, and Greeley: Some Thoughts about Evidence in Sociology: 1991 Presidential Address," *American Sociological Review* 57(1): 1–15.

2001. "Review Essay: *Fuzzy Set Social Science,* by Charles Ragin," *Contemporary Sociology* 30: 331–334.

Lieberson, Stanley and Joel Horwich 2008. "Implication Analysis: A Pragmatic Proposal for Linking Theory and Data in the Social Sciences," *Sociological Methodology* 38(1): 1–50.

Liebow, Elliot 1967. *Tally's Corner: A Study of Negro Streetcorner Men.* Boston, MA: Little, Brown.

Lieshout, Robert H., Mathieu L. L. Segers, and Anna M. van der Vleuten 2004. "De Gaulle, Moravcsik, and *The Choice for Europe*: Soft Sources, Weak Evidence," *Journal of Cold War Studies* 6(4): 89–139.

Lijphart, Arend 1968. "Typologies of Democratic Systems," *Comparative Political Studies* 1: 3–44.

Lindblom, Charles E. 1979. "Still Muddling, Not Yet Through," *Public Administration Review* 39: 517–526.

   1997. "Political Science in the 1940s and 1950s," in Thomas Bender, Carl E. Schorske, Stephen R. Graubard, and William J. Barber (eds.), *American Academic Culture in Transformation: Fifty Years, Four Disciplines*. Princeton University Press.

Lindblom, Charles E. and David K. Cohen 1979. *Usable Knowledge: Social Science and Social Problem Solving*. New Haven, CT: Yale University Press.

Linsley, E. G. and R. L. Usinger 1959. "Linnaeus and the Development of the International Code of Moological Nomenclature," *Systematic Moology* 8: 39–47.

Little, Daniel 1991. *Varieties of Social Explanation: An Introduction to the Philosophy of Social Science*. Boulder, CO: Westview Press.

   1998. *Microfoundations, Method, and Causation*. New Brunswick, NJ: Transaction.

Lively, Jack 1975. *Democracy*. Oxford: Basil Blackwell.

Longford, Nicholas T. 2005. "Editorial: Model Selection and Efficiency – Is 'Which Model . . .?' the Right Question?," *Journal of the Royal Statistical Society, Series A* 168: 469–472.

Lowi, Theodore J. 1972. "Four Systems of Policy, Politics, and Choice," *Public Administration Review* 32(4): 298–310.

Ludwig, Jens and Douglas L. Miller 2007. "Does Head Start Improve Children's Life Chances? Evidence from a Regression Discontinuity Design," *Quarterly Journal of Economics* 122 (1): 159–208.

Luker, Kristin 1984. *Abortion and the Politics of Motherhood*. Berkeley, CA: University of California Press.

   2008. *Salsa Dancing into the Social Sciences: Research in an Age of Info-glut*. Cambridge, MA: Harvard University Press.

Lutfey, Karen and Jeremy Freese 2005. "Toward Some Fundamentals of Fundamental Causality: Socioeconomic Status and Health in the Routine Clinic Visit for Diabetes," *American Journal of Sociology* 110(4): 1326–1372.

Luy, Marc 2003. "Causes of Male Excess Mortality: Insights from Cloistered Populations," *Population and Development Review* 29(4): 647–676.

Lynd, Robert Staughton [1939] 1964. *Knowledge for What?: The Place of Social Science in American Culture*. New York: Grove Press.

Mach, Ernest [1902] 1953. "The Economy of Science," in Philip P. Wiener (ed.), *Readings in Philosophy of Science*. New York: Charles Scribner, pp. 446–452.

Machamer, Peter and Gereon Wolters (eds.) 2007. *Thinking about Causes: From Greek Philosophy to Modern Physics*. Pittsburgh, PA: University of Pittsburgh Press.

MacIntyre, Alasdair 1971. *Against the Self-Images of the Age: Essays on Ideology and Philosophy*. London: Duckworth.

MacIver, R. M. [1942] 1964. *Social Causation*. New York: Harper.

Mackie, John L. 1965. "Causes and Conditions," *American Philosophical Quarterly* 2: 245–264.

   1974. *The Cement of the Universe: A Study of Causation*. Oxford: Clarendon Press.

Mahon, James E., Jr. 1998. "Political Science and Ordinary Language: Why Don't We Have Conferences on 'The Transition to Polyarchy?,'" paper presented to the International Social Science Council Committee on Conceptual and Terminological Analysis, 14th World Congress of Sociology, Montreal, July.

Mahoney, James 2001. "Beyond Correlational Analysis: Recent Innovations in Theory and Method," *Sociological Forum* 16(3): 575–593.

2002. *The Legacies of Liberalism: Path Dependence and Political Regimes in Central America.* Baltimore, MD: Johns Hopkins University Press.

2004. "Reflections on Fuzzy-set/QCA," *Qualitative Methods* 2(2): 17–21.

2008. "Toward a Unified Theory of Causality," *Comparative Political Studies* 41(4–5): 412–436.

Mahoney, James and Gary Goertz 2006. "A Tale of Two Cultures: Contrasting Quantitative and Qualitative Research," *Political Analysis* 14(3): 227–249.

Mahoney, James and P. Larkin Terrie 2008. "Comparative-Historical Analysis in Contemporary Political Science," in Box-Steffensmeier, Brady, and Collier (eds.), *Oxford Handbook of Political Methodology*, pp. 737–755.

Mahoney, James and Dietrich Rueschemeyer (eds.) 2003. *Comparative Historical Analysis in the Social Sciences.* Cambridge University Press.

Mahoney, James, Erin Kimball, and Kendra L. Koivu 2009. "The Logic of Historical Explanation in the Social Sciences," *Comparative Political Studies* 42(1): 114–146.

Maki, Uskali (ed.) 2002. *Fact and Fiction in Economics: Models, Realism, and Social Construction.* Cambridge University Press.

Malinowski, Bronislaw [1922] 1984. *Argonauts of the Western Pacific.* Prospect Heights, IL: Waveland.

Mansbridge, Jane 1999. "Should Blacks Represent Blacks and Women Represent Women? A Contingent 'Yes,'" *Journal of Politics* 61(3): 628–657.

Manski, Charles F. 1995. *Identification Problems in the Social Sciences.* Cambridge, MA: Harvard University Press.

March, James G. and Johan P. Olsen 1995. *Democratic Governance.* New York: Free Press.

Mariani, Mack D. and Gordon J. Hewitt 2008. "Indoctrination U.? Faculty Ideology and Changes in Student Political Orientation," *PS: Political Science and Politics* 41(4): 773–783.

Marini, Margaret and Burton Singer 1988. "Causality in the Social Sciences," *Sociological Methodology* 18: 347–409.

Marquart, Jules M. 1989. "A Pattern Matching Approach to Assess the Construct Validity of an Evaluation Instrument," *Evaluation and Program Planning* 12: 37–43.

Marshall, Monty G. and Keith Jaggers 2007. "Polity IV Project: Political Regime Characteristics and Transitions, 1800–2006," available at: www.systemicpeace.org/inscr/p4manualv2006.pdf.

Marshall, T. H. 1964. *Class, Citizenship, and Social Development.* University of Chicago Press.

Martin, Michael and Lee C. McIntyre (eds.) 1994. *Readings in the Philosophy of Social Science.* Cambridge, MA: MIT Press.

Mauthner, Natasha S., Odette Parry, and Kathryn Backett-Milburn 1998. "The Data are Out There, or are They? Implications for Archiving and Revisiting Qualitative Data," *Sociology: The Journal of the British Sociological Association* 32(4): 733–745.

Mayo, Deborah G. 1996. *Error and the Growth of Experimental Knowledge.* University of Chicago Press.

Mayo, Deborah G. and Aris Spanos 2006. "Severe Testing as a Basic Concept in a Neyman–Pearson Philosophy of Induction," *British Journal for the Philosophy of Science* 57: 323–57.

Mazur, Dennis J. 2007. *Evaluating the Science and Ethics of Research on Humans: A Guide for IRB Members.* Baltimore, MD: Johns Hopkins University Press.

McArthur, John W. and Jeffrey D. Sachs 2001. "Institutions and Geography: Comment on Acemoglu, Johnson and Robinson," NBER Working Paper No. 8114.

McCall, George J. and George H. Weber (eds.) 1984. *Social Science and Public Policy: The Roles of Academic Disciplines in Policy Analysis.* New York: Associated Faculty Press.

McCarty, Nolan M., Keith T. Poole, and Howard Rosenthal 2008. *Polarized America: The Dance of Ideology and Unequal Riches.* Cambridge, MA: MIT Press.

McCloskey, Deirdre N. and Stephen T. Ziliak 1996. "The Standard Error of Regressions," *Journal of Economic Literature* 34(1): 97–114.

McClosky, Herbert, Paul J. Hoffmann, and Rosemary O'Hara 1960. "Issue Conflict and Consensus among Party Leaders and Followers," *American Political Science Review* 54: 406–427.

McDermott, Rose 2002. "Experimental Methods in Political Science," *Annual Review of Political Science* 5: 31–61.

McGinniss, Joe 1988. *The Selling of the President.* New York: Penguin.

McGuire, James W. 2010. *Wealth, Health, and Democracy in East Asia and Latin America.* Cambridge University Press.

McGuire, William J. 1997. "Creative Hypothesis Generating in Psychology: Some Useful Heuristics," *Annual Review of Psychology* 48: 1–30.

McIntyre, Lee C. 1996. *Laws and Explanation in the Social Sciences: Defending a Science of Human Behavior.* Boulder, CO: Westview.

McKeown, Timothy 1999. "Case Studies and the Statistical World View," *International Organization* 53(1): 161–190.

McKim, Vaughn R. and Stephen P. Turner (eds.) 1997. *Causality in Crisis?: Statistical Methods and the Search for Causal Knowledge in the Social Sciences.* Notre Dame, IN: Notre Dame University Press.

McKinney, John C. 1950. "The Role of Constructive Typology in Scientific Sociological Analysis," *Social Forces* 28(3): 235–240.

   1957. "Polar Variables of Type Construction," *Social Forces* 35(4): 300–306.

   1969. "Typification, Typologies, and Sociological Theory," *Social Forces* 48(1): 1–12.

McLaughlin, Eithne 1991. "Oppositional Poverty: The Quantitative/Qualitative Divide and Other Dichotomies," *The Sociological Review* 39: 292–308.

McLaughlin, Robert 1982. "Invention and Induction: Laudan, Simon and the Logic of Discovery," *Philosophy of Science* 49(2): 198–211.

McMullin, Ernan 1984. "Two Ideals of Explanation in Natural Science," in Peter A. French, Theodore E. Uehling, Jr., and Howard K. Wettstein (eds.), *Midwest Studies in Philosophy, vol. IX: Causation and Causal Theories.* Minneapolis, MI: University of Minnesota Press.

McSweeny, A. J. 1978. "The Effects of Response Cost on the Behavior of a Million Persons: Charging for Directory Assistance in Cincinnati," *Journal of Applied Behavioral Analysis* 11: 47–51.

Mead, Lawrence M. 2010. "Scholasticism in Political Science," *Perspectives on Politics* 8(2): 453–464.

Meehan, Eugene J. 1971. *The Foundations of Political Analysis: Empirical and Normative.* Homewood, IL: Dorsey Press.

Mendelberg, Tali 1997. "Executing Hortons: Racial Crime in the 1988 Presidential Campaign," *Public Opinion Quarterly* 61(1): 134–157.

   2001. *The Race Card: Campaign Strategy, Implicit Messages, and the Norm of Equality.* Princeton University Press.

   2008a. "Racial Priming Revived," *Perspectives on Politics* 6(1): 109–123.

   2008b. "Racial Priming: Issues in Research Design and Interpretation," *Perspectives on Politics* 6(1): 135–140.

Meyer, Bruce D. 1995. "Natural and Quasi-Experiments in Economics," *Journal of Business and Economic Statistics* 13: 151–161.

Miguel, Edward 2004. "Tribe or Nation: Nation-Building and Public Goods in Kenya versus Tanzania," *World Politics* 56(3): 327–362.

Miguel, Edward, Shanker Satyanath, and Ernest Sergenti 2004. "Economic Shocks and Civil Conflict: An Instrumental Variables Approach," *Journal of Political Economy* 112(4): 725–753.

Milanovic, Branko 2005. *Worlds Apart: Measuring International and Global Inequality.* Princeton University Press.

Miles, William F. S. 1994. *Hausaland Divided: Colonialism and Independence in Nigeria and Niger.* Ithaca, NY: Cornell University Press.

Mill, John Stuart [1843] 1872. *System of Logic*, 8th edn. London: Longmans, Green.

Miller, Richard W. [1983] 1991. "Fact and Method in the Social Sciences," in Boyd, Gasper, and Trout (eds.), *The Philosophy of Science.*

   1987. *Fact and Method: Explanation, Confirmation and Reality in the Natural and the Social Sciences.* Princeton University Press.

Mills, C. Wright 1959. *The Sociological Imagination.* New York: Oxford University Press.

Mink, Louis 1987. "History and Fiction as Modes of Comprehension," in Brian Fay, Eugene Golob, and Richard Van (eds.), *Historical Understanding.* Ithaca, NY: Cornell University Press.

Minton, Judith Huber 1975. "The Impact of 'Sesame Street' on Reading Readiness of Kindergarten Children," *Sociology of Education* 48: 141–151.

Miron, Jeffrey A. 1994. "Empirical Methodology in Macroeconomics: Explaining the Success of Friedman and Schwartz's 'A Monetary History of the United States, 1867–1960,'" *Journal of Monetary Economics* 34: 17–25.

Moffitt, R. A. 2004. "The Role of Randomized Field Trials in Social Science Research: A Perspective from Evaluations of Reforms of Social Welfare Programs," *American Behavioral Scientist* 47(5): 506–540.

Mokyr, Joel 1992. *The Lever of Riches: Technological Creativity and Economic Progress.* Oxford University Press.

Mondak, Jeffery J. 1995. "Newspapers and Political Awareness," *American Journal of Political Science* 39(2): 513–527.

Monroe, Kristen R. (ed.) 1991. *The Economic Approach to Politics.* New York: HarperCollins.

Montaner, Julio S. G., Viviane D. Lima, Rolando Barrios, Benita Yip, Evan Wood, Thomas Kerr, Kate Shannon, P. Richard Harrigan, Robert S. Hogg, Patricia Daly, and Perry Kendall

2010. "Association of Highly Active Antiretroviral Therapy Coverage, Population Viral Load, and Yearly New HIV Diagnoses in British Columbia, Canada: A Population-based Study," *The Lancet* pp. 1–8, July 18.

Montgomery, Jacob M. and Brendan Nyhan 2010. "Bayesian Model Averaging: Theoretical Developments and Practical Applications," *Political Analysis* 18(2): 245–270.

Montgomery, Robert L. 1996. *The Diffusion of Religions: A Sociological Perspective*. Lanham, MD: University Press of America.

Mooney, Christopher M. 1997. *Monte Carlo Simulation*. Thousand Oaks, CA: Sage.

Moore, Barrington, Jr. 1958. *Political Power and Social Theory*. Cambridge, MA: Harvard University Press.

Moravcsik, Andrew 1998. *The Choice for Europe: Social Purpose and State Power from Messina to Maastricht*. Ithaca, NY: Cornell University Press.

Morgan, Edmund S. 1975. *American Slavery/American Freedom: The Ordeal of Colonial Virginia*. New York: Norton.

Morgan, Mary S. 1997. "Searching for Causal Relations in Economic Statistics," in McKim and Turner (eds.), *Causality in Crisis?: Statistical Methods and the Search for Causal Knowledge in the Social Sciences*, pp. 47–80.

Morgan, Stephen L. and Christopher Winship 2007. *Counterfactuals and Causal Inference: Methods and Principles for Social Research*. Cambridge University Press.

Morgenthau, Hans J. 1955. "Reflections on the State of Political Science," *Review of Politics* 17: 431–460.

Morone, James 2004. *Hellfire Nation: The Politics of Sin in American History*. New Haven, CT: Yale University Press.

Morrow, James D. 2003. "Diversity through Specialization," *PS: Political Science and Politics* 36 (3): 391–393.

Moses, Jonathon and Torbjorn Knutsen 2007. *Ways of Knowing: Competing Methodologies in Social and Political Research*. Basingstoke: Palgrave Macmillan.

Most, Benjamin A. 1990. "Getting Started on Political Research," *PS: Political Science and Politics* 23(4): 592–596.

Mulligan, Casey, Ricard Gil, and Xavier Sala-i-Martin 2004. "Do Democracies Have Different Public Policies than Nondemocracies?," *Journal of Economic Perspectives* 18(1): 51–74.

Munch, Richard and Neil J. Smelser (eds.) 1992. *Theory of Culture*. Berkeley, CA: University of California Press.

Munck, Gerardo L. 1998. "Canons of Research Design in Qualitative Analysis," *Studies in Comparative International Development* 33(3): 18–45.

2009. *Measuring Democracy: A Bridge between Scholarship and Politics*. Baltimore, MD: Johns Hopkins University Press.

Munck, Gerardo L. and Jay Verkuilen 2002. "Conceptualizing and Measuring Democracy: Alternative Indices," *Comparative Political Studies* 35(1): 5–34.

Murphey, Murray G. 1994. *Philosophical Foundations of Historical Knowledge*. Albany, NY: State University of New York Press.

Murray, Charles A. 1984. *Losing Ground: American Social Policy, 1950–1980*. New York: Basic Books.

Murray, Michael P. 2006. "Avoiding Invalid Instruments and Coping with Weak Instruments," *Journal of Economic Perspectives* 20: 111–132.

Myrdal, Gunnar 1944. *An American Dilemma: The Negro Problem and Modern Democracy.* New York: Harper.

1970. *The Challenge of World Poverty: A World Anti-Poverty Program in Outline.* New York: Pantheon.

Nannestad, Peter 2008. "What Have We Learned about Generalized Trust, If Anything?," *Annual Review of Political Science* 11: 413–436.

Nathan, Richard P. and Robinson G. Hollister, Jr. 2008. "The Role of Random Assignment in Social Policy Research," *Journal of Policy Analysis and Management* 27(2): 401–415.

Neal, Derek 1997. "The Effects of Catholic Secondary Schooling on Educational Achievement," *Journal of Labor Economics* 15(1): 98–123.

2002. "How Vouchers Could Change the Market for Education," *Journal of Economic Perspectives* 16: 25–44.

Neuman, W. Lawrence 1997. *Social Research Methods: Qualitative and Quantitative Approaches,* 2nd edn. Boston, MA: Allyn & Bacon.

Neumark, David and William Wascher 2000. "Minimum Wages and Employment: A Case Study of the Fast-Food Industry in New Jersey and Pennsylvania: Comment," *American Economic Review* 90(5): 1362–1396.

Neumark, David, with Roy Bank and Kyle D. Van Nort 1996. "Sex Discrimination in Restaurant Hiring: An Audit Study," *Quarterly Journal of Economics* 111(3): 915–941.

Neurath, Otto 1971. "Foundations of the Social Sciences," in Neurath, Carnap, and Morris (eds.), *Foundations of the Unity of Science: Toward an International Encyclopedia of Unified Science,* pp. 1–52.

Neurath, Otto, Rudolph Carnap, and Charles Morris (eds.) 1971. *Foundations of the Unity of Science: Toward an International Encyclopedia of Unified Science, vol. II.* University of Chicago Press.

Neustadt, Richard E. 1960. *Presidential Power: The Politics of Leadership.* New York: John Wiley.

Neyman, Jerzy [1923] 1990. "On the Application of Probability Theory to Agricultural Experiments. Essay on Principles. Section 9," trans. and ed. D.M. Dabrowska and T.P. Speed, *Statistical Science* 5: 465–471.

Nickles, Thomas (ed.) 1980. *Scientific Discovery, Logic and Rationality.* Dordrecht: D. Reidel.

Nie, Norman H., Sidney Verba, and John R. Petrocik 1976. *The Changing American Voter.* Cambridge, MA: Harvard University Press.

Norris, Christopher 1997. *Against Relativism: Philosophy of Science, Deconstruction, and Critical Theory.* Oxford: Basil Blackwell.

Nowotny, Helga 1971. "The Uses of Typological Procedures in Qualitative Macrosociological Studies," *Quality and Quantity* 6(1): 3–37.

Ogden, C.K. and I.A. Richards [1923] 1989. *The Meaning of Meaning.* San Diego, CA: Harcourt.

Oliver, Jack E. 1991. *The Incomplete Guide to the Art of Discovery.* New York: Columbia University Press.

Olken, Benjamin A. 2006. "Corruption and the Costs of Redistribution: Micro Evidence from Indonesia," *Journal of Public Economics* 90: 853–870.

2007. "Monitoring Corruption: Evidence from a Field Experiment in Indonesia," *Journal of Political Economy* 115(2): 200–249.

2009. "Corruption Perceptions vs. Corruption Reality," *Journal of Public Economics* 93(7–8): 950–964.

Oppenheim, Felix E. 1961. *Dimensions of Freedom: An Analysis*. New York: St. Martin's Press.

1975. "The Language of Political Inquiry: Problems of Clarification," in Greenstein and Polsby (eds.), *Handbook of Political Science, vol. 1: Political Science Scope and Theory*.

1981. *Political Concepts: A Reconstruction*. University of Chicago Press.

Ortner, Sherry B. 2005. *New Jersey Dreaming: Capital, Culture, and the Class of '58*. Durham, NC: Duke University Press.

Orwell, George 1970. *A Collection of Essays*. New York: Harcourt.

Oxley, Douglas R., Kevin B. Smith, John R. Alford, Matthew V. Hibbing, Jennifer L. Miller, Mario Scalor, Peter K. Hatemi, and John Hibbing 2008. "Political Attitudes Vary with Physiological Traits," *Science* 321(5896): 1667–1670.

Pagden, Anthony 1998. "The Genesis of Governance and Enlightenment Conceptions of the Cosmopolitan World Order," *International Social Science Journal* 50(1): 7–15.

Pager, Devah 2007. "The Use of Field Experiments for Studies of Employment Discrimination: Contributions, Critiques, and Directions for the Future," *Annals of the American Academy of Political and Social Science* 609(1): 104–133.

Palmer, David Scott (ed.) 1992. *Shining Path of Peru*. New York: St. Martin's Press.

Paluck, Elizabeth Levy 2009. "Methods and Ethics with Research Teams and NGOs: Comparing Experiences across the Border of Rwanda and Democratic Republic of Congo," in Chandra Lekha Sriram, John C. King, Julie A. Mertus, Olga Martin-Ortega, and Johanna Herman (eds.), *Surviving Research: Working in Violent and Difficult Situations*. London: Routledge, pp. 38–56.

2010. "The Promising Integration of Qualitative Methods and Field Experiments," *Annals of the American Academy of Political and Social Science* 628(1): 59–71.

Parsons, Craig 2007. *How to Map Arguments in Political Science*. Oxford University Press.

Pascal, Blaise 2004. *The Provincial Letters*. Whitefish, MT: Kessinger Publishing.

Passmore, John [1961] 1967. "Arguments to Meaninglessness: Excluded Opposites and Paradigm Cases," in Richard Rorty (ed.), *The Linguistic Turn: Recent Essays in Philosophical Method*. University of Chicago Press, pp. 183–192.

Patterson, Orlando 1982. *Slavery and Social Death: A Comparative Study*. Cambridge, MA: Harvard University Press.

Paxton, Pamela 1999. "Is Social Capital Declining in the United States? A Multiple Indicator Assessment," *American Journal of Sociology* 105(1): 88–127.

Paxton, Pamela and Melanie Hughes 2007. *Women, Politics, and Power*. Thousand Oaks, CA: Pine Forge Press.

Peabody, Robert L. *et al.* 1990. "Interviewing Political Elites," *PS: Political Science and Politics* 23: 451–455.

Pearl, Judea 2000. *Causality: Models, Reasoning, and Inference*. Cambridge University Press.

2005. "Bayesianism and Causality, or, Why I am only a Half-Bayesian," unpublished manuscript, Department of Computer Science, University of California, Los Angeles.

2009a. "Causal Inference in Statistics: An Overview," *Statistics Surveys* 3: 96–146.

2009b. *Causality: Models, Reasoning, and Inference*, 2nd edn. Cambridge University Press.

2009c. "Myth, Confusion, and Science in Causal Analysis," unpublished manuscript, University of California, Los Angeles.

Peeters, Carel, F. W. Gerty, J. L. M. Lensvelt-Mulders, and Karin Lashuizen 2010. "A Note on a Simple and Practical Randomized Response Framework for Eliciting Sensitive Dichotomous and Quantitative Information," *Sociological Methods & Research* 39: 283–296.

Pemstein, Daniel, Stephen Meserve, and James Melton 2010. "Democratic Compromise: A Latent Variable Analysis of Ten Measures of Regime Type," *Political Analysis* 18(4): 426–449.

Petersen, Roger 2002. *Understanding Ethnic Violence: Fear, Hatred, and Resentment in Twentieth-Century Eastern Europe*. Cambridge University Press.

Petitti, D. E. 1993. *Meta-Analysis, Decision Analysis, Cost-Effectiveness*, 2nd edn. New York: Oxford University Press.

Pierre, Jon (ed.) 2000. *Debating Governance*. Oxford University Press.

Pierson, Paul 2004. *Politics in Time: History, Institutions, and Social Analysis*. Princeton University Press.

Piore, Michael J. 1979. "Qualitative Research Techniques in Economics," *Administrative Science Quarterly* 24(4): 560–569.

Pitkin, Hanna Fenichel 1967. *Representation*. Berkeley, CA: University of California Press.
    1972. *Wittgenstein and Justice: On the Significance of Ludwig Wittgenstein for Social and Political Thought*. Berkeley, CA: University of California Press.

Platt, John 1964. "Strong Inference," *Science* 146(3642): 347–353.

Pocock, J. G. A. 1975. *The Machiavellian Moment: Florentine Political Thought and the Atlantic Republican Tradition*. Princeton University Press.

Polanyi, Karl 1968. *Primitive, Archaic and Modern Economies*. Garden City, NY: Anchor.

Polanyi, Michael [1946] 1964. *Science, Faith and Society*. New York: Oxford University Press.

Poole, Keith T. and Howard Rosenthal 1985. "A Spatial Model for Legislative Roll Call Analysis," *American Journal of Political Science* 29(2): 357–384.
    1991. "Patterns in Congressional Voting," *American Journal of Political Science* 35(1): 228–278.

Popper, Karl [1934] 1968. *The Logic of Scientific Discovery*. New York: Harper & Row.
    [1936] 1957. *The Poverty of Historicism*. New York: Harper & Row.
    1965. *Conjectures and Refutations*. New York: Harper & Row.
    1976. *Unended Quest: An Intellectual Autobiography*. LaSalle, IL: Open Court.
    1994. *The Myth of the Framework*. New York: Routledge.

Porter, Jack 2003. "Estimation in the Regression Discontinuity Model," unpublished manuscript, Harvard University.

Porter, T. M. 1986. *The Rise of Statistical Thinking 1820–1900*. Princeton University Press.

Posner, Daniel N. 2004. "The Political Salience of Cultural Difference: Why Chewas and Tumbukas are Allies in Zambia and Adversaries in Malawi," *American Political Science Review* 98(4): 529–546.

Pressman, Jeffrey L. and Aaron Wildavsky 1973. *Implementation*. Berkeley, CA: University of California Press.

Przeworski, Adam and Henry Teune 1970. *The Logic of Comparative Social Inquiry*. New York: John Wiley.

Przeworski, Adam, Michael Alvarez, Jose Antonio Cheibub, and Fernando Limongi 2000. *Democracy and Development: Political Institutions and Material Well-Being in the World, 1950–1990*. Cambridge University Press.

Putnam, Hilary and Paul Oppenheim 1958. "Unity of Science as a Working Hypothesis," in Michael Scriven, Herbert Feigle, and Grover Maxwell (eds.), *Concepts, Theories, and the Mind–Body Problem*. Minneapolis, MN: University of Minneapolis Press, pp. 3–36.

Putnam, Robert D. 1993. *Making Democracy Work: Civic Traditions in Modern Italy*. Princeton University Press.

2001. *Bowling Alone: The Collapse and Revival of American Community*. New York: Touchstone.

Quadagno, Jill and Stan J. Knapp 1992. "Have Historical Sociologists Forsaken Theory?: Thoughts on the History/Theory Relationship," *Sociological Methods and Research* 20: 481–507.

Quine, Willard van Orman 1953. "Two Dogmas of Empiricism," in *From a Logical Point of View*. Cambridge, MA: Harvard University Press, pp. 20–46.

1966. "Simple Theories of a Complex World," *The Ways of Paradox and Other Essays*. New York: Random House.

Rabinow, Paul and William M. Sullivan (eds.) 1979. *Interpretive Social Science: A Reader*. Berkeley, CA: University of California Press.

Radcliffe-Brown, A. R. [1948] 1957. *A Natural Science of Society*. Glencoe, IL: Free Press.

1958. *Method in Social Anthropology*. University of Chicago Press.

Ragin, Charles C. 1987. *The Comparative Method: Moving beyond Qualitative and Quantitative Strategies*. Berkeley, CA: University of California.

1992. "'Casing' and the Process of Social Inquiry," in Charles C. Ragin and Howard S. Becker (eds.), *What is a Case? Exploring the Foundations of Social Inquiry*. Cambridge University Press, pp. 217–226.

2000. *Fuzzy-Set Social Science*. University of Chicago Press.

2008. *Redesigning Social Inquiry: Fuzzy Sets and Beyond*. University of Chicago Press.

2009. "Qualitative Comparative Analysis Using Fuzzy Sets (fsQCA)," in Rihoux and Ragin (eds.), *Configurational Comparative Methods: Qualitative Comparative Analysis (QCA) and Related Techniques*, pp. 87–122.

Ragin, Charles C. and Benoît Rihoux 2004. "Qualitative Comparative Analysis (QCA): State of the Art and Prospects," *Qualitative Methods* 2(2): 3–13.

Ragin, Charles C. and Ilene Strand 2008. "Using Qualitative Comparative Analysis to Study Causal Order. Comment on Caren and Panofsky (2005)," *Sociological Methods and Research* 36(4): 431–441.

Redman, Deborah A. 1991. *Economics and the Philosophy of Science*. New York: Oxford University Press.

Reedy, George E. 1970. *The Twilight of the Presidency*. New York: Mentor/New American Library.

Reichenbach, Hans 1938. *Experience and Prediction: An Analysis of the Foundations and the Structure of Knowledge*. University of Chicago Press.

1956. *The Direction of Time*. Berkeley, CA: University of California Press.

Reingold, Beth 2008. "Women as Officeholders: Linking Descriptive and Substantive Representation," in Christina Wolbrecht, Karen Beckwith, and Lisa Baldez (eds.), *Political Women and American Democracy*. Cambridge University Press, pp. 128–147.

Reinikka, Ritva and Jakob Svensson 2006. "Using Micro-Surveys to Measure and Explain Corruption," *World Development* 34(2): 359–370.

Reiss, Julian 2007. *Error in Economics: Towards a More Evidence-based Methodology*. London: Routledge.

2009. "Causation in the Social Sciences: Evidence, Inference, and Purpose," *Philosophy of the Social Sciences* 39(1): 20–40.

Rescher, Nicholas 1977. *Methodological Pragmatism*. New York University Press.

Reynolds, Andrew and Ben Reilly 2005. *New International Idea Handbook of Electoral System Design*. Stockholm: International Institute for Democracy.

Reynolds, K. D. and S. G. West 1987. "A Multiplist Strategy for Strengthening Nonequivalent Control Group Designs," *Evaluation Review* 11: 691–714.

Rhodes, William 2010. "Heterogeneous Treatment Effects: What Does a Regression Estimate?," *Evaluation Review* 34(4): 334–361.

Rihoux, Benoît and Gisele De Meur 2009. "Crisp-Set Qualitative Comparative Analysis (csQCA)," in Rihoux and Ragin (eds.), *Configurational Comparative Methods: Qualitative Comparative Analysis (QCA) and Related Techniques*, pp. 33–68.

Rihoux, Benoît and Bojana Lobe 2009. "The Case for Qualitative Comparative Analysis (QCA): Adding Leverage for Thick Cross-Case Comparison," in David Byrne and Charles C. Ragin (eds.), *Sage Handbook of Case-Based Methods*. Thousand Oaks, CA: Sage, pp. 222–242.

Rihoux, Benoît and Charles C. Ragin (eds.) 2009. *Configurational Comparative Methods: Qualitative Comparative Analysis (QCA) and Related Techniques*. Thousand Oaks, CA: Sage.

Riker, William H. 1982. "The Two-Party System and Duverger's Law: An Essay on the History of Political Science," *American Political Science Review* 76(4): 753–756.

1986. *The Art of Political Manipulation*. New Haven, CT: Yale University Press.

Rindskopf, David 2000. "Plausible Rival Hypotheses in Measurement, Design, and Scientific Theory," in Leonard Bickman (ed.), *Research Design: Donald Campbell's Legacy, vol. II*. Thousand Oaks, CA: Sage, pp. 1–12.

Roberts, Clayton 1996. *The Logic of Historical Explanation*. University Park, PA: Pennsylvania State University Press.

Robins, James M. and Larry Wasserman 1999. "On the Impossibility of Inferring Causation from Association without Background Knowledge," in Clark Glymour and G. Cooper (eds.), *Computation, Causation, and Discovery*. Menlo Park, CA, Cambridge, MA: AAAI Press/MIT Press, pp. 305–321.

Robinson, Gregory, John E. McNulty, and Jonathan S. Krasno 2009. "Observing the Counterfactual? The Search for Political Experiments in Nature," *Political Analysis* 17 (4): 341–357.

Robinson, Richard 1954. *Definition*. Oxford: Clarendon Press.

Rodrik, Dani 2005. "Why We Learn Nothing from Regressing Economic Growth on Policies," unpublished manuscript, Kennedy School of Government, Harvard University.

Rogin, Michael Paul 1987. *Ronald Reagan: The Movie, and Other Episodes in Political Demonology*. Berkeley, CA: University of California Press.

Rokkan, Stein with Angus Campbell, Per Torsvik, and Henry Valen 1970. *Citizens, Elections, Parties: Approaches to the Comparative Study of the Processes of Development*. New York: David McKay Co.

Root-Bernstein, Robert 1989. *Discovering: Inventing and Solving Problems at the Frontiers of Scientific Knowledge*. Cambridge, MA: Harvard University Press.

Root-Bernstein, Robert S. and Michele M. Root-Bernstein 1999. *Sparks of Genius: The Thirteen Thinking Tools of the World's Most Creative People*. Boston, MA: Houghton Mifflin.

Rorty, Amelia (ed.) 1966. *Pragmatic Philosophy: An Anthology*. Garden City, NY: Doubleday Anchor.

Rosenau, Pauline Marie 1992. *Post-Modernism and the Social Sciences: Insights, Inroads, and Intrusions*. Princeton University Press.

Rosenbaum, Paul R. 1984. "From Association to Causation in Observational Studies: The Role of Strongly Ignorable Treatment Assignment," *Journal of the American Statistical Association* 79(385): 41–48.

1987. "The Role of a Second Control Group in an Observational Study: Rejoinder," *Statistical Science* 2(3): 313–316.

1999. "Choice as an Alternative to Control in Observational Studies," *Statistical Science* 14 (3): 259–278.

2002. *Observational Studies*. New York: Springer.

2005. "Reasons for Effects," *Chance* 18: 5–10.

2007. "Interference between Units in Randomized Experiments," *Journal of the American Statistical Association* 102(477): 191–200.

2010. *Design of Observational Studies*. New York: Springer.

Rosenbaum, Paul and Donald Rubin 1983. "The Central Role of the Propensity Score in Observational Studies for Causal Effects," *Biometrika* 70(1): 41–55.

Rosenzweig, Mark R. and Kenneth I. Wolpin 2000. "Natural 'Quasi-experiments' in Economics," *Journal of Economic Literature* 38: 827–874.

Ross, H. L., Donald T. Campbell, and G. V. Glass 1970. "Determining the Social Effects of a Legal Reform: The British 'Breathalyser' Crackdown of 1967," *American Behavioral Scientist* 13: 493–509.

Ross, Marc Howard 1997. "Culture and Identity in Comparative Political Analysis," in Lichbach and Zuckerman (eds.), *Comparative Politics: Rationality, Culture, and Structure*, pp. 42–80.

Ross, Michael L. 2001. "Does Oil Hinder Democracy?," *World Politics* 53: 325–361.

Rossi, Peter H. and Howard E. Freeman 1993. *Evaluation: A Systematic Approach*, 5th edn. Newbury Park, CA: Sage.

Rostow, Walt W. 1960. *The Stages of Economic Growth: A Non-Communist Manifesto*. Cambridge University Press.

Roth, David 1987. *Meanings and Methods: A Case for Methodological Pluralism in the Social Sciences*. Ithaca, NY: Cornell University Press.

Roth, Paul A. 1994. "Narrative Explanations: The Case of History," in Martin and McIntyre (eds.), *Readings in the Philosophy of Social Science*, pp. 701–712.

Rubin, Donald B. 1975. "Bayesian Inference for Causality: The Importance of Randomization," *Proceedings of the Social Statistics Section of the American Statistical Association*, Alexandria, VA, pp. 233–239.

1977. "Assignment of Treatment Group on the Basis of a Covariate," *Journal of Educational Statistics* 2: 1–26.

1991. "Practical Implications of Modes of Statistical Inference for Causal Effects and the Critical Role of the Assignment Mechanism," *Biometrics* 47(4): 1213–1234.

2005. "Causal Inference Using Potential Outcomes: Design, Modeling, Decisions," *Journal of the American Statistical Association* 100(469): 322–331.

2008. "For Objective Causal Inference, Design Trumps Analysis," *Annals of Applied Statistics* 2(3): 808–840.

Rubin, Irene and Herbert J. Rubin 1995. *Qualitative Interviewing: The Art of Hearing Data.* Newbury Park, CA: Sage.

Rueschemeyer, Dietrich and John D. Stephens 1997. "Comparing Historical Sequences – A Powerful Tool for Causal Analysis," *Comparative Social Research* 16: 55–72.

Rueschemeyer, Dietrich, Evelyne Huber Stephens, and John D. Stephens 1992. *Capitalist Development and Democracy.* University of Chicago Press.

Rule, James B. 1997. *Theory and Progress in Social Science.* Cambridge University Press.

Russo, Federica 2009. *Causality and Causal Modelling in the Social Sciences: Measuring Variations.* New York: Springer.

Ryle, Gilbert 1949. *The Concept of Mind.* New York: Barnes & Noble.

Sala-I-Martin, Xavier X. 1997. "I Just Ran Two Million Regressions," *American Economic Review* 87(2): 178–183.

Sales, Bruce Dennis and Susan Folkman (eds.) 2000. *Ethics in Research with Human Participants.* Washington, DC: American Psychological Association Publishing.

Salmon, Wesley C. 1984. *Scientific Explanation and the Causal Structure of the World.* Princeton University Press.

1989. "Four Decades of Scientific Explanation," in Kitcher and Salmon (eds.), *Scientific Explanation: Minnesota Studies in the Philosophy of Science, vol. XIII*, pp. 3–219.

1990. "Causal Propensities: Statistical Causality vs. Aleatory Causality," *Topoi* 9: 95–100.

Sampford, Charles, Arthur Shacklock, Carmel Connors, and Fredrik Galtung (eds.) 2006. *Measuring Corruption.* Aldershot: Ashgate.

Samuels, David J. and Richard Snyder 2001. "The Value of a Vote: Malapportionment in Comparative Perspective," *British Journal of Political Science* 31: 651–671.

Samuelson, Paul A. 1959. "What Economists Know," in Daniel Lerner (ed.), *The Human Meaning of the Social Sciences.* New York: Meridian, pp. 183–213.

Sanchez Jankowski, Martin 1991. *Islands in the Street: Gangs and American Urban Society.* Berkeley, CA: University of California Press.

Sartori, Giovanni 1962. *Democratic Theory.* New York: Praeger.

1970. "Concept Misformation in Comparative Politics," *American Political Science Review* 64 (4): 1033–1046.

1975. "The Tower of Babble," in Giovanni Sartori, Fred W. Riggs, and Henry Teune (eds.), *Tower of Babel: On the Definition and Analysis of Concepts in the Social Sciences.* International Studies, Occasional Paper No. 6, pp. 7–38.

1976. *Parties and Party Systems.* Cambridge University Press.

1984. "Guidelines for Concept Analysis," in *Social Science Concepts: A Systematic Analysis.* Beverly Hills, CA: Sage, pp. 15–48.

Saward, Michael 2003. *Democracy.* Cambridge: Polity Press.

Schaeffer, Nora Cate and Stanley Presser 2003. "The Science of Asking Questions," *Annual Review of Sociology* 29: 65–88.

Schaffer, Frederic C. 1998. *Democracy in Translation: Understanding Politics in an Unfamiliar Culture.* Ithaca, NY: Cornell University Press.

Schaffer, Simon 1997. "What is Science?," in John Krige and Dominique Pestre (eds.), *Science in the Twentieth Century*. Amsterdam: Overseas Publishers Association, pp. 27–42.

Schattschneider, E. E. 1960. *The Semi-Sovereign People*. New York: Holt, Rinehart & Winston.

Schatz, Edward (ed.) 2009. *Political Ethnography: What Immersion Contributes to the Study of Power*. University of Chicago Press.

Schedler, Andreas forthcoming. "The Measurer's Dilemma: Coordination Failures in Cross-National Political Data Collection," *Comparative Political Studies* 45(2).

Scheper-Hughes, Nancy 1992. *Death without Weeping: The Violence of Everyday Life in Brazil*. Berkeley, CA: University of California Press.

Schiemann, Gregor 2003. "Criticizing a Difference of Contexts – On Reichenbach's Distinction between 'Context of Discovery' and 'Context of Justification,'" in Friedrich Stadler (ed.), *The Vienna Circle and Logical Empiricism: Re-Evaluation and Future Perspectives*. New York: Kluwer, pp. 237–252.

Schlesselman, James J. 1982. *Case-Control Studies: Design, Conduct, Analysis*. New York: Oxford University Press.

Schmitter, Philippe C. 1974. "Still the Century of Corporatism?," *Review of Politics* 36: 85–131.

Schneider, Carsten Q. 2009. *The Consolidation of Democracy: Comparing Europe and Latin America*. Abingdon: Routledge.

2011. "Issues in Measuring Political Regimes," DISC Working Paper, available at: disc.ceu.hu/working-papers.

Schneider, Carsten Q. and Claudius Wagemann 2007. *Qualitative Comparative Analysis (QCA) und Fuzzy Sets. Ein Lehrbuch für Anwender und alle, die es werden wollen*. Opladen and Farmington Hills: Verlag Barbara Budrich.

2010. "Standards of Good Practice in Qualitative Comparative Analysis (QCA) and Fuzzy-Sets," *Comparative Sociology* 9: 397–418.

Schwartz, Joel 1984. "Participation and Multisubjective Understanding: An Interpretivist Approach to the Study of Political Participation," *Journal of Politics* (November): 1117–1141.

Scott, James C. 1976. *The Moral Economy of the Peasant: Rebellion and Subsistence in Southeast Asia*. New Haven, CT: Yale University Press.

1985. *Weapons of the Weak: Everyday Forms of Peasant Resistance*. New Haven, CT: Yale University Press.

1998. *Seeing Like a State: How Certain Schemes to Improve the Human Condition Have Failed*. New Haven, CT: Yale University Press.

Scriven, Michael 1962. "Explanations, Predictions, and Laws," in Herbert Feigl and Grover Maxwell (eds.), *Minnesota Studies in the Philosophy of Science, vol. III: Scientific Explanation, Space, and Time*. Minneapolis, MN: University of Minnesota, pp. 170–230.

2008. "A Summative Evaluation of RCT Methodology: An Alternative Approach to Causal Research," *Journal of Multidisciplinary Evaluation* 5: 11–24.

Searle, John R. 1969. *Speech Acts: An Essay in the Philosophy of Language*. Cambridge University Press.

Seawright, Jason 2002. "Testing for Necessary and/or Sufficient Causation: Which Cases are Relevant?," *Political Analysis* 10: 178–193.

2005. "Qualitative Comparative Analysis vis-à-vis Regression," *Studies in Comparative International Development* 40(1): 3–26.

2010. "Regression-Based Inference: A Case Study in Failed Causal Assessment," in Henry E. Brady and David Collier (eds.), *Rethinking Social Inquiry: Diverse Tools, Shared Standards*, 2nd edn. Lanham, MD: Rowman & Littlefield, pp. 247–271.

Seawright, Jason and David Collier 2004. "Glossary," in Brady and Collier (eds.), *Rethinking Social Inquiry: Diverse Tools, Shared Standards*, pp. 273–313.

Sekhon, Jasjeet S. 2009. "Opiates for the Matches: Matching Methods for Causal Inference," *Annual Review of Political Science* 12: 487–508.

Seligson, Mitchell 2006. "The Measurement and Impact of Corruption Victimization: Survey Evidence from Latin America," *World Development* 34(2): 381–404.

Sen, Amartya 1980. "Description as Choice," *Oxford Economic Papers* 32: 353–369.

1990. "More than 100 Million Women Are Missing," *New York Review of Books* 37(20), December 20.

Sewell, William H., Jr. 1992. "Introduction: Narratives and Social Identities," *Social Science History* 16: 479–488.

1996. "Three Temporalities: Toward an Eventful Sociology," in Terrence J. McDonald (ed.), *The Historic Turn in the Human Sciences*. Ann Arbor, MI: University of Michigan Press, pp. 245–280.

Shadish, William R. and Thomas D. Cook 1999. "Design Rules: More Steps toward a Complete Theory of Quasi-Experimentation," *Statistical Science* 14(3): 294–300.

Shadish, William R., Thomas D. Cook, and Donald T. Campbell 2002. *Experimental and Quasi-experimental Designs for Generalized Causal Inference*. Boston, MA: Houghton Mifflin.

Shalhope, Robert E. 1972. "Toward a Republican Synthesis: The Emergence of an Understanding of Republicanism in American Historiography," *William and Mary Quarterly* 29: 49–80.

Shapiro, Ian 2005. *The Flight from Reality in the Human Sciences*. Princeton University Press.

Shefter, Martin 1994. *Political Parties and the State: The American Historical Experience*. Princeton University Press.

Shweder, Richard A. 1996. "*Quanta* and *Qualia*: What is the 'Object' of Ethnographic Method?," in Richard Jessor, Anne Colby and Richard A. Shweder (eds.), *Ethnography and Human Development: Context and Meaning in Social Inquiry*. University of Chicago Press, pp. 175–182.

Shweder, Richard A. and Robert A. LeVine (eds.) 1984. *Culture Theory: Essays on Mind, Self, and Emotion*. Cambridge University Press.

Sil, Rudra and Eileen Doherty (eds.) 2000. *Beyond Boundaries? Disciplines, Paradigms, and Theoretical Integration in International Studies*. Albany, NY: State University of New York Press.

Simon, Adam F. and Tracy Sulkin 2002. "Discussion's Impact on Political Allocations: An Experimental Approach," *Political Analysis* 10(4): 403–412.

Simon, Herbert A. 1982. "Are Social Problems Problems that Social Science Can Solve?," in Kruskal (ed.), *The Social Sciences: Their Nature and Uses*.

2001. "Science seeks Parsimony, not Simplicity: Searching for Pattern in Phenomena," in Arnold Mellner, Hugo A. Keuzenkamp, and Michael McAleer (eds.), *Simplicity, Inference, and Modeling: Keeping it Sophisticatedly Simple*. Cambridge University Press, pp. 32–72.

Simowitz, Roslyn and Barry L. Price 1990. "The Expected Utility Theory of Conflict: Measuring Theoretical Progress," *American Political Science Review* 84(2): 439–460.

Sims, Christopher A. 1988. "Uncertainty across Models," *American Economic Review* 78(2): 163–167.

Singer, J. David 1961. "The Level-of-Analysis Problem in International Relations," *World Politics* 14(1): 77–92.

Singer, J. David and Paul Diehl (eds.) 1990. *Measuring the Correlates of War.* Ann Arbor, MI: University of Michigan Press.

Skocpol, Theda 1979. *States and Social Revolutions: A Comparative Analysis of France, Russia, and China.* Cambridge University Press.

Skyrms, Brian 1980. *Causal Necessity: A Pragmatic Investigation of the Necessity of Laws.* New Haven, CT: Yale University Press.

Sloman, Steven 2005. *Causal Models: How People Think about the World and its Alternatives.* Oxford University Press.

Smelser, Neil J. and Richard Swedberg (eds.) 1995. *The Handbook of Economic Sociology.* Princeton University Press.

Smith, Daniel Jordan 2007. *A Culture of Corruption: Everyday Deception and Popular Discontent in Nigeria.* Princeton University Press.

Smith, Kevin B. 2002. "Typologies, Taxonomies, and the Benefits of Policy Classification," *Policy Studies Journal* 30(3): 379–395.

   2005. "Data Don't Matter? Academic Research and School Choice," *Perspectives on Politics* 3 (2): 285–299.

Smith, Rogers M. 1993. "Beyond Tocqueville, Myrdal, and Hartz: The Multiple Traditions in America," *American Political Science Review* 87(3): 549–566.

   2003. "Reconnecting Political Theory to Empirical Inquiry, or A Return to the Cave?," in Edward D. Mansfield and Richard Sisson (eds.), *The Evolution of Political Knowledge: Theory and Inquiry in American Politics.* Columbus, OH: Ohio State University Press, pp. 60–88.

Smithson, Michael J. 1987. *Fuzzy Set Analysis for Behavioral and Social Sciences.* New York: Springer.

Smithson, Michael J. and Jay Verkuilen 2006. *Fuzzy Set Theory: Applications in the Social Sciences.* Thousand Oaks, CA: Sage.

Sniderman, Paul M. and Edward G. Carmines 1997. *Reaching Beyond Race.* Cambridge, MA: Harvard University Press.

Sniderman, Paul M. and Douglas B. Grob 1996. "Innovations in Experimental Design in Attitude Surveys," *Annual Review of Sociology* 22: 377–399.

Sniderman, Paul M., Thomas Piazza, Philip E. Tetlock, and Anne Kendrick 1991. "The New Racism," *American Journal of Political Science* 35(2): 423–447.

Snow, C. P. [1959] 1993. *The Two Cultures.* Cambridge University Press.

Snyder, Richard 2007. "The Human Dimension of Comparative Research," in Gerardo L. Munck and Richard Snyder (eds.), *Passion, Craft and Method in Comparative Politics.* Baltimore, MD: Johns Hopkins University Press, pp. 1–32.

Sober, Elliot 1975. *Simplicity.* Oxford University Press.

   1988. *Reconstructing the Past: Parsimony, Evolution and Inference.* Cambridge, MA: MIT Press.

2001. "Venetian Sea Levels, British Bread Prices, and the Principle of the Common Cause," *British Journal for the Philosophy of Science* 52: 331–346.

Sokoloff, Kenneth L. and Stanley L. Engerman 2000. "Institutions, Factor Endowments, and Paths of Development in the New World," *Journal of Economic Perspectives* 14(3): 217–232.

Somers, Margaret R. 1992. "Narrativity, Narrative Identity, and Social Action: Rethinking English Working-Class Formation," *Social Science History* 16: 591–630.

Sparrow, Malcolm K. 2000. *License to Steal*. Boulder, CO: Westview Press.

Spiegler, Peter and William Milberg 2009. "The Taming of Institutions in Economics: The Rise and Methodology of the *New*, New Institutionalism," *Journal of Institutional Economics* 5 (3): 289–313.

Spohn, Wolfgang 1983. "Deterministic and Probabilistic Reasons and Causes," *Erkenntnis* 19: 371–396.

Stanley, T. D. 1991. "Regression-Discontinuity Design: By any Other Name Might be Less Problematic," *Evaluation Review* 15(5): 605–624.

Stasavage, David 2003. "Transparency, Democratic Accountability, and the Economic Consequences of Monetary Institutions," *American Journal of Political Science* 47(3): 389–402.

Steel, Daniel 2008. *Across the Boundaries: Extrapolation in Biology and Social Science*. Oxford University Press.

Stevens, S. S. 1946. "On the Theory of Scales of Measurement," *Science* 103: 677–680.

Stevens, S. S. (ed.) 1951. "Mathematics, Measurement and Psychophysics," in *Handbook of Experimental Psychology*. New York: John Wiley, pp. 1–49.

Stinchcombe, Arthur L. 1968. *Constructing Social Theories*. New York: Harcourt Brace.

1978. *Theoretical Methods in Social History*. New York: Academic Press.

Stoker, Laura 2003. "Is it Possible to do Quantitative Survey Research in an Interpretive Way?," *Qualitative Methods* 1(2): 13–16.

Stone, Lawrence 1979. "The Revival of Narrative: Reflections on a New Old History," *Past and Present* 85: 3–24.

Stratmann, Thomas and Martin Baur 2002. "Plurality Rule, Proportional Representation, and the German *Bundestag*: How Incentives to Pork-Barrel Differ across Electoral Systems," *American Journal of Political Science* 46(3): 506–514.

Strauss, Leo [1953] 1963. "Natural Right and the Distinction between Facts and Values," in Maurice Natanson (ed.), *Philosophy of the Social Sciences: A Reader*. New York: Random House.

Stryker, Robin 1996. "Beyond History versus Theory: Strategic Narrative and Sociological Explanation," *Sociological Methods and Research* 24(3): 304–352.

Summers, Lawrence H. 1991. "The Scientific Illusion in Empirical Macroeconomics," *The Scandinavian Journal of Economics* 93(2): 129–148.

Sundquist, James L. 1983. *Dynamics of the Party System: Alignment and Realignment of Political Parties in the United States*. Washington, DC: Brookings Institution Press.

Suppes, Patrick C. 1970. *A Probabilistic Theory of Causality*. Amsterdam: North-Holland.

Taagepera, Rein 2008. *Making Social Sciences More Scientific: The Need for Predictive Models*. Oxford University Press.

Tang, Shipeng 2010. "Foundational Paradigms of Social Sciences," *Philosophy of the Social Sciences* 20(10): 1–39.

Tarrow, Sidney 1995. "Bridging the Quantitative–Qualitative Divide in Political Science," *American Political Science Review* 89(2): 471–474.

Tashakkori, Abbas and Charles Teddie 1998. *Mixed Methodology: Combining Qualitative and Quantitative Approaches*. Thousand Oaks, CA: Sage.

Taylor, Charles [1967] 1994. "Neutrality in Political Science," in Michael Martin and Lee C. McIntyre (eds.), *Readings in the Philosophy of Social Science*. Cambridge, MA: MIT Press, reprinted in Peter Laslett and W. G. Runciman (eds.), *Philosophy, Politics and Society*, 3rd series. New York: Barnes & Noble, pp. 25–57.

1985. "Interpretation and the Sciences of Man," in *Philosophy and the Human Sciences: Philosophical Papers, vol. II*. Cambridge University Press, pp. 15–57.

Taylor, John R. 1995. *Linguistic Categorization: Prototypes in Linguistic Theory*, 2nd edn. Oxford: Clarendon Press.

Tetlock, Philip E. and Aaron Belkin (eds.) 1996. *Counterfactual Thought Experiments in World Politics*. Princeton University Press.

Thistlewaite, Donald L. and Donald Campbell 1960. "Regression-Discontinuity Analysis: An Alternative to the *Ex-Post Facto* Experiment," *Journal of Educational Psychology* 51: 309–317.

Thompson, Edward P. 1978. *The Poverty of Theory and Other Essays*. New York: Monthly Review Press.

Thompson, Michael, Richard Ellis, and Aaron Wildavsky 1990. *Cultural Theory*. San Francisco, CA: Westview Press.

Tilly, Charles 2001. "Mechanisms in Political Processes," *Annual Review of Political Science* 4: 21–41.

Tocqueville, Alexis de 1945. *Democracy in America*, 2 vols. New York: Alfred A. Knopf.

Tourangeau, Roger and Tom W. Smith 1996. "Asking Sensitive Questions: The Impact of Data Collection Mode, Question Format, and Question Context," *Public Opinion Quarterly* 60 (2): 275–304.

Treier, Shawn and Simon Jackman 2008. "Democracy as a Latent Variable," *American Journal of Political Science* 52(1): 201–217.

Trochim, William W. K. 1984. *Regression Design for Program Evaluation: The Regression-discontinuity Design*. Beverley Hills, CA: Sage.

1985. "Pattern Matching, Validity, and Conceptualization in Program Evaluation," *Evaluation Review* 9(5): 575–604.

1989. "Outcome Pattern Matching and Program Theory," *Evaluation and Program Planning* 12: 355–366.

Turner, Stephen P. 1997. "'Net Effects': A Short History," in McKim and Turner (eds.), *Causality in Crisis?: Statistical Methods and the Search for Causal Knowledge in the Social Science*, pp. 23–45.

Tversky, Amos and Itamar Gati 1978. "Studies of Similarity," in Eleanor Lloyd and B. B. Lloyd (eds.) *Cognition and Categorization*. Hillsdale, NJ: Lawrence Erlbaum, pp. 79–98.

UN Habitat 2004. *State of the World's Cities 2004–2005: Globalization and Urban Culture*. Nairobi: United Nations, Earthscan Publications.

USAID 1998. *Handbook of Democracy and Governance Program Indicators*. Technical Publication Series PN-ACC-390. Washington, DC: USAID Center for Democracy and Governance.

Useem, Bert 1997. "Choosing a Dissertation Topic," *PS: Political Science and Politics* 30: 213–216.

van der Klaauw, Wilbert 2002. "Estimating the Effect of Financial Aid Offers on College Enrollment: A Regression-Discontinuity Approach," *International Economic Review* 43 (4): 1249–1287.

van Evera, Stephen 1997. *Guide to Methods for Students of Political Science.* Ithaca, NY: Cornell University Press.

van Fraassen, Bas C. 1980. *The Scientific Image.* Oxford: Clarendon Press.

Verba, Sidney, Kay Lehman Schlozman, and Henry Brady 1995. *Voice and Equality: Civic Voluntarism in American Life.* Cambridge, MA: Harvard University Press.

Vidich, Arthur J. 1955. "Participant Observation and the Collection and Interpretation of Data," *American Journal of Sociology* 60(4): 354–360.

Vogt, W. Paul 2005. *Dictionary of Statistics and Methodology*, 3rd edn. Thousand Oaks, CA: Sage.

von Wright, Georg Henrik 1971. *Explanation and Understanding.* Ithaca, NY: Cornell University Press.

Wachter, K. W. 1988. "Disturbed about Meta-Analysis?," *Science* 241: 1407–1408.

Wade, Robert 1982. "The System of Administrative and Political Corruption: Canal Irrigation in South India," *Journal of Development Studies* 18: 3.

Waldner, David 2002. "Anti Anti-Determinism: Or What Happens When Schrodinger's Cat and Lorenz's Butterfly Meet Laplace's Demon in the Study of Political and Economic Development," presented to the Annual Meeting of the American Political Science Association, Boston, MA, August–September.

Walker, Thomas C. 2010. "The Perils of Paradigm Mentalities: Revisiting Kuhn, Lakatos, and Popper," *Perspectives on Politics* 8(2): 433–452.

Wallerstein, Immanuel 1974. *The Modern World-System. Capitalist Agriculture and the Origins of the European World Economy in the Sixteenth Century.* New York: Academic Press.

Wallerstein, Immanuel, *et al.* 1996. *Open the Social Sciences: Report of the Gulbenkian Commission on the Restructuring of the Social Sciences.* Stanford University Press.

Wantchekon, Leonard 2003. "Clientelism and Voting Behavior: Evidence from a Field Experiment in Benin," *World Politics* 55(3): 399–422.

Warner, Stanley L. 1965. "Randomized Response: A Survey Technique for Eliminating Evasive Answer Bias," *Journal of the American Statistical Association* 60: 63–9.

Wasserman, Stanley and Katherine Faust 1994. *Social Network Analysis: Methods and Applications.* Cambridge University Press.

Watkins, J. W. N. 1994. "Historical Explanation in the Social Sciences," in Martin and McIntyre (eds.), *Readings in the Philosophy of Social Science*, pp. 441–450.

Watson, James D. 1969. *The Double Helix: A Personal Account of the Discovery of the Structure of DNA.* New York: Mentor.

Weale, Albert 2007. *Democracy*, 2nd edn. Basingstoke: Palgrave Macmillan.

Weber, Max [1904–5] 1958. *The Protestant Ethic and the Spirit of Capitalism.* New York: Charles Scribner's.

[1905] 1949. *The Methodology of the Social Sciences.* New York: Free Press.

[1918] 1958. "Politics as a Vocation," in Hans Gerth and C. Wright Mills (eds. and trans.), *From Max Weber: Essays in Sociology.* New York: Oxford University Press, pp. 77–156.

Weisberg, Herbert F. 2005. *The Total Survey Error Approach: A Guide to the New Science of Survey Research*. University of Chicago Press.

Western, Bruce 1995. "Concepts and Suggestions for Robust Regression Analysis," *American Journal of Political Science* 39(3): 786–817.

1999. "Bayesian Analysis for Sociologists: An Introduction," *Sociological Methods and Research* 28(1): 7–34.

Weyland, Kurt Gerhard 1995. "Latin America's Four Political Models," *Journal of Democracy* 6(4): 125–139.

Whitbeck, C. 1977. "Causation in Medicine: The Disease Entity Model," *Philosophy of Science* 44: 619–637.

White, Howard 2002. "Combining Quantitative and Qualitative Approaches in Poverty Analysis," *World Development* 30(3): 511–522.

Whittaker, John C., Douglas Caulkins, and Kathryn A. Kamp 1998. "Evaluating Consistency in Typology and Classification," *Journal of Archaeological Method and Theory* 5(2): 129–164.

Wildavsky, Aaron B. 1995. *But Is it True? A Citizen's Guide to Environmental Health and Safety Issues*. Cambridge, MA: Harvard University Press.

Wilensky, Harold L. 1997. "Social Science and the Public Agenda: Reflections of Knowledge to Policy in the United States and Abroad," *Journal of Health Politics, Policy and Law* 22(5): 1241–1265.

Wilson, Edward O. 1998. *Consilience: The Unity of Knowledge*. New York: Alfred A. Knopf.

Winch, Peter 1958. *The Idea of a Social Science, and its Relation to Philosophy*. London: Routledge.

Winks, Robin W. (ed.) 1969. *The Historian as Detective: Essays on Evidence*. New York: Harper & Row.

Wiseman, H. V. 1966. *Political Systems: Some Sociological Approaches*. New York: Praeger.

Wittgenstein, Ludwig 1953. *Philosophical Investigations*. New York: Macmillan.

Wolin, Sheldon S. 1969. "Political Theory as a Vocation," *American Political Science Review* 63 (4): 1062–1082.

Wong, Wilson 2002. "Did How We Learn Affect What We Learn? Methodological Bias, Multimethod Research and the Case of Economic Development," *Social Science Journal* 39(2): 247–264.

Wood, Elisabeth 2006. "The Ethical Challenges of Field Research in Conflict Mones," *Qualitative Sociology* 29(3): 373–386.

Wood, Gordon S. 1969. *The Creation of the American Republic, 1776–1787*. Chapel Hill, NC: University of North Carolina Press.

Woodward, James 2005. *Making Things Happen: A Theory of Causal Explanation*. Oxford University Press.

Wooldridge, Jeffrey 2007. "What's New in Econometrics? Lecture 10: Difference-in-Differences Estimation," NBER Summer Institute, available at: www.nber.org/WNE/Slides7-31-07/slides_10_diffindiffs.pdf, accessed April 9, 2011.

Woolgar, Steve 1988. *Science: The Very Idea*. Chichester: Ellis Horwood.

Wu, Amery D. and Bruno D. Mumbo 2008. "Understanding and Using Mediators and Moderators," *Social Indicators Research* 87: 367–392.

Yamamoto, Tepei 2010. "Understanding the Past: Statistical Analysis of Causal Attribution," unpublished manuscript, Department of Politics, Princeton University.

Yanow, Dvora and Peregrine Schwartz-Shea (eds.) 2006. *Interpretation and Method: Empirical Research Methods and the Interpretive Turn*. New York: M. E. Sharpe.

Yin, Robert K. 2000. "Rival Explanations as an Alternative to Reforms as 'Experiments,'" in Leonard Bickman (ed.), *Validity and Social Experimentation: Donald Campbell's Legacy, vol. I*. Thousand Oaks, CA: Sage, pp. 239–266.

Yoon, Carol Kaesuk 2009. *Naming Nature: The Clash between Instinct and Science*. New York: W. W. Norton.

Young, Cristobal 2009. "Model Uncertainty in Sociological Research: An Application to Religion and Economic Growth," *American Sociological Review* 74(3): 380–397.

Yudkowsky, Eliezer S. 2003. "An Intuitive Explanation of Bayes' Theorem," available at: http://yudkowsky.net/rational/bayes.

Zahar, Elie 1983. "Logic of Discovery or Psychology of Invention?," *British Journal for the Philosophy of Science* 34(3): 243–261.

Zald, Mayer 1990. "Sociology as a Discipline: Quasi-Science and Quasi-Humanities," *The American Sociologist* 22(3–4): 165–187.

Zaller, John and Stanley Feldman 1992. "A Simple Theory of the Survey Response: Answering Questions versus Revealing Preferences," *American Journal of Political Science* 36(3): 579–616.

Zannoni, Paolo 1978. "The Concept of Elite," *European Journal of Political Research* 6: 1–30.

Zelizer, Julian E. 2002. "Beyond the Presidential Synthesis: Reordering Political Time," in Jean-Christophe Agnew and Roy Rosenzweig (eds.), *A Companion to Post-1945 America*. Oxford: Blackwell, pp. 345–370.

Zerubavel, Eviatar 1996. "Lumping and Splitting: Notes on Social Classification," *Sociological Forum* 11(3): 421–433.

Ziff, Paul 1960. *Semantic Analysis*. Ithaca, NY: Cornell University Press.

Ziliak, Stephen T. and Deirdre N. McCloskey 2008. *The Cult of Statistical Significance: How the Standard Error Costs Us Jobs, Justice, and Lives*. Ann Arbor, MI: University of Michigan Press.

Zuckerman, Ilene H., Euni Lee, Anthony K. Wutoh, Xheny Xue, and Bruce Stuart 2006. "Application of Regression-Discontinuity Analysis in Pharmaceutical Health Services Research," *Health Services Research* 41(2): 550–563.

Index

Note: For commonly used terms, page citations are limited to locations where a term is defined or where it forms the focus of the exposition.